Instructors
The Power of Connections

A complete course platform

Connect enables you to build deeper connections with your students through cohesive digital content and tools, creating engaging learning experiences. We are committed to providing you with the right resources and tools to support all your students along their personal learning journeys.

65%
Less Time
Grading

Laptop: Getty Images; Woman/dog: George Doyle/Getty Images

Every learner is unique

In Connect, instructors can assign an adaptive reading experience with SmartBook® 2.0. Rooted in advanced learning science principles, SmartBook 2.0 delivers each student a personalized experience, focusing students on their learning gaps, ensuring that the time they spend studying is time well-spent. **mheducation.com/highered/connect/ smartbook**

Affordable solutions, added value

Make technology work for you with LMS integration for single sign-on access, mobile access to the digital textbook, and reports to quickly show you how each of your students is doing. And with our Inclusive Access program, you can provide all these tools at the lowest available market price to your students. Ask your McGraw Hill representative for more information.

Solutions for your challenges

A product isn't a solution. Real solutions are affordable, reliable, and come with training and ongoing support when you need it and how you want it. Visit **supportateverystep.com** for videos and resources both you and your students can use throughout the term.

Students
Get Learning that Fits You

Effective tools for efficient studying

Connect is designed to help you be more productive with simple, flexible, intuitive tools that maximize your study time and meet your individual learning needs. Get learning that works for you with Connect.

Study anytime, anywhere

Download the free ReadAnywhere® app and access your online eBook, SmartBook® 2.0, or Adaptive Learning Assignments when it's convenient, even if you're offline. And since the app automatically syncs with your Connect account, all of your work is available every time you open it. Find out more at **mheducation.com/readanywhere**

"I really liked this app—it made it easy to study when you don't have your textbook in front of you."

- Jordan Cunningham, Eastern Washington University

iPhone: Getty Images

Everything you need in one place

Your Connect course has everything you need—whether reading your digital eBook or completing assignments for class—Connect makes it easy to get your work done.

Learning for everyone

McGraw Hill works directly with Accessibility Services Departments and faculty to meet the learning needs of all students. Please contact your Accessibility Services Office and ask them to email accessibility@mheducation.com, or visit **mheducation.com/about/accessibility** for more information.

WE THE PEOPLE

AN INTRODUCTION TO AMERICAN GOVERNMENT

FIFTEENTH EDITION

THOMAS E. PATTERSON

Bradlee Professor of Government and the Press
John F. Kennedy School of Government
Harvard University

WE THE PEOPLE: AN INTRODUCTION TO AMERICAN GOVERNMENT,
FIFTEENTH EDITION

Published by McGraw Hill LLC, 1325 Avenue of the Americas, New York, NY 10019.
Copyright ©2024 by McGraw Hill LLC. All rights reserved. Printed in the United States
of America. Previous editions ©2022, 2019 and 2017. No part of this publication may be
reproduced or distributed in any form or by any means, or stored in a database or retrieval
system, without the prior written consent of McGraw Hill LLC, including, but not limited to,
in any network or other electronic storage or transmission, or broadcast for distance learning.

Some ancillaries, including electronic and print components, may not be available to customers
outside the United States.

This book is printed on acid-free paper.

1 2 3 4 5 6 7 8 9 LCR 28 27 26 25 24 23

ISBN 978-1-265-02668-4 (bound edition)
MHID 1-265-02668-8 (bound edition)
ISBN 978-1-265-63300-4 (loose-leaf edition)
MHID 1-265-63300-2 (loose-leaf edition)

Executive Portfolio Manager: *Jason Seitz*
Senior Product Development Manager: *Dawn Groundwater*
Senior Product Developer: *Erin DeHeck*
Executive Marketing Manager: *Michael Gedatus*
Content Project Managers: *Rick Hecker, George Theofanopoulos*
Buyer: *Sandy Ludovissy*
Senior Design: *Beth Blech*
Content Licensing Specialist: *Carrie Burger*
Cover Image: *Pixtal/AGE Fotostock*
Compositor: *Aptara®, Inc.*

All credits appearing on page or at the end of the book are considered to be an extension
of the copyright page.

Library of Congress Cataloging-in-Publication Data

Names: Patterson, Thomas E., author.
Title: We the people : an introduction to American government / Thomas E.
    Patterson, Bradlee Professor of Government and the Press John F. Kennedy
    School of Government, Harvard University.
Description: Fifteenth edition. | Dubuque : McGraw Hill LLC, 2023. |
    Includes index.
Identifiers: LCCN 2022039478 (print) | LCCN 2022039479 (ebook) | ISBN
    9781265026684 (hardcover) | ISBN 9781265633004 (spiral bound) | ISBN
    9781265636609 (ebook) | ISBN 9781265632274 (ebook other)
Subjects: LCSH: United States—Politics and government—Textbooks.
Classification: LCC JK276 .P38 2023 (print) | LCC JK276 (ebook) | DDC
    320.473—dc23/eng/20220824
LC record available at https://lccn.loc.gov/2022039478
LC ebook record available at https://lccn.loc.gov/2022039479

mheducation.com/highered

To My Son and Daughter,
Alex and Leigh

ABOUT THE AUTHOR

Thomas E. Patterson is Bradlee Professor of Government and the Press in the John F. Kennedy School of Government at Harvard University. He was previously Distinguished Professor of Political Science in the Maxwell School of Citizenship at Syracuse University. Raised in a small Minnesota town near the Iowa and South Dakota borders, he attended South Dakota State University as an undergraduate and served in the U.S. Army Special Forces in Vietnam before enrolling at the University of Minnesota, where he received his PhD in 1971.

Since then, he has regularly taught introductory American government. In 2013, he was chosen as the teacher of the year and adviser of the year by Harvard University's Kennedy School of Government students, the first time a member of its faculty has received both awards in the same year.

He has authored numerous books and articles, which focus mainly on elections, the media, political parties, and citizenship. His recent book, *How America Lost Its Mind* (2019), charts the causes and consequences of the rapid rise in misinformation. Another book, *Informing the News* (2013), examines the need for news that is more trustworthy and relevant. An earlier book, *The Vanishing Voter* (2002), describes and explains the long-term decline in voter participation. His book *Out of Order* (1994) received national attention when President Clinton urged every politician and journalist to read it. In 2002, *Out of Order* received the American Political Science Association's Graber Award for the best book of the past decade in political communication. Another of Patterson's books, *The Mass Media Election* (1980), received a Choice award as Outstanding Academic Title, 1980–1981. Patterson's first book, *The Unseeing Eye* (1976), was selected by the American Association for Public Opinion Research as one of the 50 most influential books of the past half century in the field of public opinion. His current project is a pair of books, one on the problems facing the Republican Party, the other on the problems facing the Democratic Party.

His research has been funded by major grants from the National Science Foundation, the Markle Foundation, the Smith-Richardson Foundation, the Ford Foundation, the Knight Foundation, The Carnegie Corporation, and the Pew Charitable Trusts.

CONTENTS

CHAPTER TWO

CONSTITUTIONAL DEMOCRACY: PROMOTING
LIBERTY AND SELF-GOVERNMENT

CHAPTER FIVE

CHAPTER SIX

PUBLIC OPINION AND POLITICAL SOCIALIZATION: SHAPING THE PEOPLE'S VOICE

CHAPTER NINE

INTEREST GROUPS: ORGANIZING FOR INFLUENCE   233

CHAPTER ELEVEN

CHAPTER FOURTEEN

THE FEDERAL JUDICIAL SYSTEM: INTERPRETING THE LAW   390

CHAPTER FIFTEEN

ECONOMIC AND ENVIRONMENTAL POLICY: CONTRIBUTING TO PROSPERITY

CHAPTER SIXTEEN

CHAPTER SEVENTEEN

A LETTER FROM THE AUTHOR

Anyone who writes an introductory program on American government faces the challenge of explaining a wide range of subjects. One way is to pile fact upon fact and list upon list. It's a common approach to textbook writing, but it turns politics into a pretty dry subject. Politics doesn't have to be dry, and it certainly doesn't have to be dull. Politics has all the elements of drama plus the added feature of affecting the everyday lives of real people.

My goal has been to make this text the most readable one available. Rather than piling fact upon fact, it relies on narrative. A narrative text weaves together theory, information, and examples in order to bring out key facts and ideas. The response to this approach has been gratifying. As a previous edition was being prepared, I received the following note from a longtime instructor:

> I read this book in about three days, cover to cover. . . . I have never seen a better basic government/politics textbook. I think reading standard textbooks is "boring" (to use a favorite student word), but this one overcomes that. Dr. Patterson has managed to do something that I heretofore thought could not be done.

While writing, I regularly reminded myself that the readers are citizens as well as students. For this reason, the text encourages "critical thinking," by which I mean the process through which an individual determines what can reasonably be believed and then uses reason to reach a thoughtful conclusion. Each chapter has boxes that ask you to "think critically." Two of these—the "How the U.S. Differs" box and the "How the 50 States Differ" box—ask you to think critically about differences in governing systems. A third box—"Party Polarization"—asks you to critically analyze differences in the Republican and Democratic Parties. A fourth box—"Case Study"—discusses a political event and then asks you to analyze the outcome. The final box—"Fake or Fact?"—asks you to critically assess a factual claim. These various boxes are based on the idea that critical thinking is a skill that can be nurtured and, once acquired, can make you a more responsible citizen, whether in casting a vote, forming an opinion about a public policy, or contributing to a political cause.

Improving your ability to think critically is the primary goal of this text. If the only result of reading it was to increase your factual knowledge of American government, I would judge it a failure. As Albert Einstein once noted, "The value of a college education is not the learning of many facts but the training of the mind to think." Political science courses, like those in other social science and humanities disciplines, should help students hone their critical thinking skills. As I indicated, the critical thinking boxes in each chapter are designed for this purpose. So, too, is the "Critical Thinking Zone" at the end of each chapter. This feature asks you to make use of the chapter's information through the application of the three skills—conceptualizing, synthesizing, and analyzing—that are the foundation of critical thinking.

The well-being of a democracy rests on its citizens. Nevertheless, aside from voting, we seldom ask what citizenship requires of each of us. Each chapter includes suggestions on how you as a citizen can contribute. The suggestions are categorized by the founding principle they embody—liberty, equality, or self-government.

Finally, I have attempted to present American government through the analytical lens of political science but in a way that captures the vivid world of real-life politics. Only a tiny fraction of students in the introductory course are enrolled because they plan an academic career in political science. Most students take it because they have an interest in politics or because they are required to do so. I have sought to write a book that will deepen your political interest if you are the first type of student, and spark an interest in politics if you are the second type.

We the People has been in use in college classrooms for three decades. During this time, it has been adopted at more than 1,000 colleges and universities. I am extremely grateful to all who have used it and particularly indebted to the many instructors and students who have sent me suggestions on how to strengthen it. I particularly owe a deep thanks to Chris Worden of Sierra College who has provided thoughtful and constructive ideas on a regular basis. If you have ideas you would like to share, please contact me at thomas_patterson@harvard.edu.

Thomas E. Patterson

PREFACE

RELEVANCY AND READABILITY TO ENGAGE TODAY'S STUDENT

Tom Patterson's *We the People* is a **concise** approach to American government, emphasizing **critical thinking** through questions and examples **relevant** to today's students. This exceptionally **readable** text provides opportunities to **engage** with the political process through tools that help students **learn how to think about politics,** utilizing digital resources that connect students with the material in a **personalized** way.

Improve Student Performance with McGraw Hill Connect®

Connect improves student performance with a personalized reading experience, tools for sharpening writing skills, and activities for informative and engaging concepts.

Available within Connect American Government, SmartBook creates a personalized reading experience by highlighting the most impactful concepts a student needs to learn at that moment in time. This ensures that every minute spent with SmartBook is returned to the student as the most value-added minute possible.

SMARTBOOK®

The reading experience continuously adapts by highlighting content based on what the student knows and doesn't know. Real-time reports quickly identify the concepts that require more attention from individual students—or the entire class. SmartBook detects the content a student is most likely to forget and brings it back to improve long-term knowledge retention.

SmartBook is optimized for mobile and tablet and is accessible for students with disabilities. And as part of any American government course, SmartBook focuses on the broader context for and building blocks of the political system. Specifically, it has been enhanced with improved learning objectives to ensure that students gain foundational knowledge while they also learn to make connections for broader understanding of government institutions, events, and behavior. SmartBook personalizes learning to individual student needs, continually adapting to pinpoint knowledge gaps and focus learning on topics that need the most attention. Study time is more productive, and as a result, students are better prepared for class and coursework. For instructors, SmartBook tracks student progress and provides insights that can help guide teaching strategies.

Writing Assignment

McGraw Hill's Writing Assignment Plus tool delivers a learning experience that improves students' written communication skills and conceptual understanding with every assignment. Assign, monitor, and provide feedback on writing more efficiently and grade your assignments within McGraw Hill Connect®. Writing Assignment Plus gives you time-saving tools with a just-in-time basic writing and originality checker.

Features include

- Grammar/writing checking with McGraw Hill learning resources
- Originality checker with McGraw Hill learning resources
- Writing stats
- Rubric building and scoring
- Ability to assign draft and final deadline milestones
- Tablet ready and tools for all learners

Informing and Engaging Students on Political Concepts

New to this edition, **Civic Literacy** content appears within Connect and helps students prepare and become civically engaged on the principles reflected in the U.S. Constitution. The content is available for students to practice on their own or for instructors to assign and track as assessment.

Using Connect American Government, students can learn the course material more deeply and study more effectively than ever before.

At the *remember* and *understand* levels of Bloom's taxonomy, **Concept Clips** help students break down key concepts in American government. Using easy-to-understand audio narration, visual cues, and colorful animations, Concept Clips provide a step-by-step presentation that aids in student retention. Topics include Federalists and Anti-Federalists, What Is Devolution?, and Who Participates. In addition, several skills-based clips equip students for work within and outside the classroom, covering topics such as How to Read a Court Case, How to Understand Charts and Graphs, and How to Avoid Plagiarism.

Also at the *remember* and *understand* levels of Bloom's taxonomy, **Newsflash** ties current news stories to key American government concepts and learning

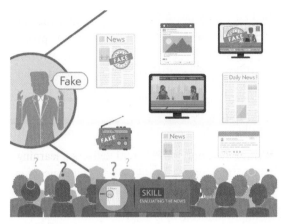

objectives. After evaluating a related news story, students are assessed on their ability to connect it to the course content. An example is the impact of the COVID-19 coronavirus on the U.S. economy.

Our **Podcast Assignments** also deepen students' understanding of real-life politics. These assignments allow you to bring discussion and debate to your courses through the storytelling power of actual podcasts.

At the *apply, analyze,* and *evaluate* levels of Bloom's taxonomy, **critical thinking activities** allow students to engage with the political process and learn by doing. For example:

- Quiz: What Is Your Political Ideology?
- Poll: Americans' Confidence in the Police
- Research: Find Your Senator
- Infographic: Compare the Courts

Practice Government, McGraw Hill's educational game focused on the American political system, is fully integrated inside Connect American Government! A set of focused introductory missions is paired with auto-grade and critical thinking.

Instructor Resources

We the People includes the following instructor resources.

Instructor's manual. The instructor's manual provides a wide variety of tools and resources for presenting the course, including learning objectives and ideas for lectures and discussions.

Test bank. By increasing the rigor of the test bank development process, McGraw Hill has raised the bar for student assessment. Each question has been tagged for level of difficulty, Bloom's taxonomy, and topic coverage. Organized by chapter, the questions are designed to test factual, conceptual, and higher-order thinking.

Test Builder. Available within Connect, Test Builder is a cloud-based tool that enables instructors to format tests that can be printed and administered within a Learning Management System. Test Builder offers a modern, streamlined interface for easy content configuration that matches course needs without requiring a download.

Test Builder enables instructors to

- Access all test bank content from a particular title
- Easily pinpoint the most relevant content through robust filtering options
- Manipulate the order of questions or scramble questions and/or answers
- Pin questions to a specific location within a test
- Determine their preferred treatment of algorithmic questions
- Choose the layout and spacing
- Add instructions and configure default settings

PowerPoint. The PowerPoint presentations highlight the key points of the chapter and include supporting visuals. All slides are WCAG compliant.

Remote proctoring. Remote proctoring and browser-locking capabilities are seamlessly integrated within Connect to offer more control over the integrity of online assessments. Instructors can enable security options that restrict browser activity, monitor student use, and verify the identity of each student.

Instant and detailed reporting gives instructors an at-a-glance view of potential concerns, thereby avoiding personal bias while fostering evidence-based claims.

CONTENT CHANGES

In addition to the 2022 midterm election results, there are thorough updates of the data and figures throughout the text, updated boxed features (*Fake or Fact?, Case Study, How the U.S. Differs, How the 50 States Differ*, and *Party Polarization*), and new photographs and other images. The revised *Citizen Action!* sidebars are now linked with three of America's founding principles—liberty, equality, and self-government—to encourage students to see themselves as active participants in the American democratic process.

Finally, *We the People*, 15th edition, includes the following specific chapter-by-chapter changes:

Chapter 1, Critical Thinking and Political Culture: Becoming a Responsible Citizen

- New "Citizen Action: Self-Government" sidebar encourages students to exercise their right to speak freely
- Updated "How the U.S. Differs" and "How the 50 States Differ" boxes with new Q&As (asking "What unites Americans?" in the former and "What do the states with the lowest percentage of college graduates have in common?" in the latter).
- New discussion of the Russian invasion of Ukraine as an example of the act of an authoritarian government.
- New "Citizen Action: Liberty" sidebar encourages students to use the classroom as an opportunity to develop public speaking skills.

Chapter 2, Constitutional Democracy: Promoting Liberty and Self-Government

- New chapter introduction highlights Joe Biden's use of the concepts of liberty and self-government in his first State of the Union Address where he stressed the right of people to govern themselves in the context of the then-recent Russian invasion of Ukraine.
- Additional historical context on the causes of the Revolutionary War, including discussion of the Stamp Act, Townshend Acts, and Tea Act by the British Parliament, as well as George Washington's strategy during the war.
- Additional historical context on the Articles of Confederation.
- Two new major restructured sections, "Creating a Constitution" and "Ratification of the Constitution" to help clarify what was at issue in each stage.

- New "Citizen Action: Liberty" sidebar highlights importance of exercising the right to speak freely.
- New "Case Study" box, "Assault on the Capitol."
- Two new key terms, *direct democracy* and *representative democracy*.
- New "Citizen Action: Self-Government" sidebar encourages students to participate in politics.

Chapter 3, Federalism: Forging a Nation

- New chapter introduction illustrates federal vs. state control through the dispute over Joe Biden's COVID-19 mandate directing companies with over 100 employees to meet specified safety standards.
- Thoroughly revised "How the U.S. Differs" box, "Federal versus Unitary Systems" compares the two systems and includes a new Q&A asking students to think about the advantages of each.
- New historical context on the factors that led to a larger role for the federal government in America's federal system.
- Additional discussion of Jim Crow laws.
- Thoroughly revised "Federalism Since the 1930s" section that now includes discussion of "New Federalism" and fuller explanation of the Republican-Democratic split on the role of federal government.
- New key term, *New Federalism.*
- New "Citizen Action: Self-Government" sidebar encourages students to take a part-time internship with a local, state, or national government unit.

Chapter 4, Civil Liberties: Protecting Individual Rights

- New "How the U.S. Differs" box, "Individual and Democratic Rights," examines how the U.S. compares with other countries in terms of free expression and fair trial rights.
- New "Citizen Action: Liberty" sidebar encourages students to speak out on controversial issues.
- Discussion of Sarah Palin's 2022 failed libel suit against *The New York Times* as a recent example of the imposing standard for libel of a public official.
- Discussion of *Carson v. Makin* (2022) in which Supreme Court ruled that a state cannot exclude religious schools from a tuition-assistant payment policy available to nonreligious private schools.
- Discussion of *Kennedy v. Bremerton School District* (2022) in which Supreme Court upheld a football coach's right to pray publicly at an athletic event.
- Discussion of *Oregon v. Smith* (1990) as an example of Supreme Court's limit on the free exercise of religion.

- Discussion of *United States v. Miller* (1939) as the first Supreme Court ruling on gun rights.
- Discussion of *New York State Rifle & Pistol Association Inc. v. Bruen* (2022) where the Supreme Court invalidated a state law limiting the carrying of handguns.
- Discussion of *Dobbs v. Jackson Women's Health Organization* (2022) in which the Supreme Court invalidated a woman's constitutional right to choose abortion.
- New "Citizen Action: Equality" sidebar encourages students to answer the call when summoned for jury duty.
- New "Fake or Fact" box, "Do You Have a Right to Refuse Vaccination?"

Chapter 5, Equal Rights: Struggling Toward Fairness

- New discussion in the chapter introduction includes the concepts of negative and positive rights.
- Additional discussion of the current status of the Voting Rights Act of 1965 in light of a 2020 Supreme Court decision weakening Section 2 of the Act.
- Discussion of the possible future of affirmative action in light of the current conservative majority on the Supreme Court and its pending review of key cases involving Harvard University and the University of North Carolina.
- Updates throughout "The Struggle for Equality" section, including new discussion of women (in terms of wages vs. men and status as top wage earners in families), Native Americans (in public office, particularly the record number elected to Congress in the 2020 election), Asian Americans (underrepresented in top management positions), and religious groups (discrimination against Muslim Americans).
- New "Citizen Action: Equality" sidebar encourages students to volunteer their time in college or community organizations seeking to help disadvantaged groups.

Chapter 6, Public Opinion and Political Socialization: Shaping the People's Voice

- New chapter introduction focuses on the 2022 school shooting in Uvalde, Texas, as illustration of the impact of public opinion on officials.
- Discussion of the faulty 1936 Literary Digest poll that predicted an easy win for Republican Alf Landon to emphasize the importance of random selection.
- Updated discussion of factors that contribute to the inaccuracy of telephone polls.
- New "Citizen Action: Self-Government" sidebar asks students to assess the nature of their political views.

- Discussion of the nationalization of political issues, which has reduced regional differences in how Republicans and Democrats respond to issues.
- Thoroughly updated "How the 50 States Differ" box with a revised map of the distribution of Democratic and Republican supporters with a new Q&A asking students to consider what might account for the distribution.
- New "Citizen Action: Self-Government" sidebar encourages students to stay informed in order to be able to make sound judgments about public matters.
- The "Fake or Fact" box, "Do You Have a Right to Speak Freely on Campus?" has been moved from Chapter 4 into this chapter.
- Discussion of how the public mood about leadership tends to shift as a presidency nears its end.

Chapter 7, Political Participation: Activating the Popular Will

- Discussion of post-2020 voting laws enacted in several states aimed at limiting absentee, early, and mail-in balloting.
- New "Citizen Action: Self-Government" sidebar encourages students to register to vote if they haven't already done so.
- Revised "Party Polarization" box compares Republications, Independents, and Democrats in terms of their vote in the 2020 Presidential election.
- New "Citizen Action: Self-Government" sidebar encourages students to volunteer for a community group dedicated to helping others.
- Revised "How the U.S. Differs" box, "A Nation of Joiners," has been moved into this chapter from its location in Chapter 9 of the previous edition.
- Discussion of the Make America Great Again (MAGA) movement as an atypical social movement.
- New discussion of how the Tea Party movement created a climate of opinion within the Republican party that gave rise to the MAGA movement, while the Occupy Wall Street movement contributed to Bernie Sanders' rise to prominence.
- Thoroughly revised and expanded discussion of the public's response to protest activity, including perceptions of the anti-Vietnam War and Black Lives Matter movements and the differing perceptions of Democrats and Republicans of the January 6, 2021 assault on the Capitol.

Chapter 8, Political Parties, Candidates, and Campaigns: Defining the Voters' Choice

- Expanded discussion of candidate-centered campaigns in the chapter introduction.
- Expanded discussion of how political parties foster collective action at leadership level

- Additional historical context about party realignments.
- Additional context about proportional representation systems.
- Discussion of how the Republican and Democratic parties have erected barriers to make it difficult for minor parties to compete in elections.
- Expanded discussion of different types of primaries employed by states.
- New "Citizen Action: Self-Government" sidebar encourages students to volunteer for a political party or campaign.
- Enhanced discussion of public financing of candidates.
- Expanded discussion of the disadvantages of candidate-centered campaigns.

Chapter 9, Interest Groups: Organizing for Influence

- New "Citizen Action: Self-Government" sidebar that asks students to consider joining a citizen's group that aligns with their views.
- Expanded discussion of ties between corporate interest groups and regulatory agencies by looking at Food and Drug Administration's approval of Pfizer's COVID-19 vaccine and earlier handling of Merck's arthritis drug Vioxx.
- New "How the U.S. Differs" box, "Lobbying," discusses why the United States has so many more lobbyists than other democracies.

Chapter 10, The News Media and the Internet: Communicating Politics

- New chapter introduction focuses on the news media's varying responses to Joe Biden's handling of the Russian invasion of Ukraine in 2022, plus a new list of chapter key points reflecting the substantial changes in this edition to the chapter's structure and content.
- New major section, "Creating the Information Commons" explains the nature and impact of the information commons of a half century ago.
- New subsection, "From a Partisan Press to Objective Journalism," explains how the partisan press yielded to objective journalism and the creation of the information commons.
- New subsection, "The Impact of the Information Commons," outlines how the information commons fostered a shared reality, a rising level of information, and a moderating (depolarization) of Americans' opinions.
- New "Citizen Action: Self-Government" sidebar encourages students to become daily consumers of the news.
- New major section, "The Making of Echo Chambers," introduces the concept of media echo chambers in which news consumers hear information that reinforces their biases.
- New subsection, "The Return of Partisan Media," charts the rise and dominance of partisan talk shows on media outlets such as Fox News and MSNBC.

- New subsection, in "The Rise of the Internet and Social Media," charts the origins of the Internet, the rise of partisan websites like Breitbart and HuffPost, the influence of bloggers, and the emergence of filter bubbles.
- New "How the 50 States Differ" box provides background, a comparative map, and a Q&A on America's digital divide.
- New subsection, "The Impact of Echo Chambers," discusses echo chambers as the antithesis of the information commons, distinguishes misinformation from disinformation, and discusses how echo chambers foster the spread of unfounded conspiracy theories.
- Expanded "Party Polarization" box contrasts the alternative realities to which Americans are exposed by comparing COVID-19 coverage on Fox News and CBS.
- Thoroughly revised "The Politics of Media Functions" section examines five functions of media: "The Signaling Function," "The Common-Carrier Function," "The Watchdog Function," "The Partisan Function," and "The Entertainment Function."
- "The Signaling Function" subsection discusses how issues uppermost in people's minds affect their political choices.
- "The Common-Carrier Function" subsection examines how controversial members of Congress like Marjorie Taylor Greene and Alexandria Ocasio-Cortez receive disproportionate media attention, how partisan media outlets frame events, and how traditional media contribute to misinformation.
- "The Watchdog Function" subsection includes discussion of how the Watergate scandal changed the watchdog function, how liberal and conservative media differ as watchdogs (the January 6, 2021 attack on the Capitol as an example), and the emergence of social media as watchdog, exemplified by a citizen video of the killing of George Floyd by a Minneapolis police officer.
- "The Partisan Function" subsection looks at how partisan media outlets bend their coverage to align it with audience preferences.
- "The Entertainment Function" subsection includes discussion of how audience competition drives media outlets to make their news more entertaining and how the tendency affects audience response to political developments.
- New "Citizen Action: Self-Government" sidebar encourages students to participate in online discussion forums such as those on Meetup.com.
- New section, "The Assault on Reason" focuses on how changes in the media have spawned misinformation and intense partisanship.
- New key terms, *disinformation, echo chambers, entertainment function, filter bubbles, hard news, the information commons, misinformation,* and *soft news.*
- Thoroughly revised chapter summary, reflecting the substantial changes to this edition's chapter.

Chapter 11, Congress: Balancing National Goals and Local Interests

- New "Citizen Action: Self-Government" sidebar encourages students to consider a congressional, state legislative, or city council internship.
- Discussion of how legislative deadlock in Congress is due in part to the fact that the parties are closely matched in electoral strength.
- Thoroughly revised and updated discussion of party leadership in the "Parties and Party Leadership" section.
- Discussion of why and how—as both Senate majority and minority leader—Mitch McConnell has maintained the support of the Republican caucus.
- Thoroughly revised "Congress's Policymaking Role" section, including discussion of the investigation of the January 6 assault on the U.S. Capitol.
- New "Citizen Action: Self-Government" sidebar encourages students to contact their congressional representative to express their opinion of a current issue.
- Discussion of how the framers of the Constitution did not recognize how its structure could be used to stymie the legislative process.

Chapter 12, The Presidency: Leading the Nation

- Thoroughly revised and streamlined "The Making of the Modern Presidency" section focuses on the gradual expansion of presidential power.
- Expanded discussion of the role of the Vice President.
- Thoroughly updated "Fake or Fact" box, "Is the President 'Above the Law?'" that focuses on Donald Trump's role in the January 6, 2021 assault on the Capitol.
- Thoroughly reorganized "Bridging the Power Gap" section, with a new introductory discussion of how powerful presidents like Franklin D. Roosevelt contribute to the public's belief that presidents have inherently great power.
- Expanded discussion of presidents' role as party leader and the importance of their power to set the policy agenda.
- A new "Case Study" box ("Presidential Character") examines the influence of presidents' personal traits on their performance.
- New "Citizen Action: Self-Government" sidebar encourages students to consider getting actively involved in a presidential campaign.
- New key term, *head of government*

Chapter 13, The Federal Bureaucracy: Administering the Government

- New "Citizen Action: Self-Government" sidebar encourages students to consider a career in public service.
- Additional discussion of how federal agencies acquire policy influence.
- New discussion of what scholars call "bureaucratic drift."

Chapter 14, The Federal Judicial System: Interpreting the Law

- Heavily revised "Judicial Power" section includes two new subsections ("Constitutional Authority" and "Judicial Review").
- Revised "How the U.S. Differs" box explores the advantages and disadvantages of lifetime tenure for judges.
- New "Judicial Review" subsection explains the importance of *Marbury v. Madison* (1803) in establishing the judiciary as a co-equal branch.
- New discussion of the political question doctrine, the shadow docket, and "cue theory" in the context of the courts.
- New "Citizen Action: Equality" sidebar encourages students to answer the call when called for jury duty.
- Discussion of Ketanji Brown Jackson's confirmation as the newest Supreme Court justice and the widening partisan divide in the Senate over Supreme Court appointments.
- Fully revised "Party Polarization" box, "Has Polarization Reached into the Supreme Court?," details the growing split between the Court's Republican and Democratic appointees.
- Discussion of Americans' changing perception of Supreme Court, now seeing it as more partisan than in the past.
- Thoroughly revised and expanded discussion of the judiciary's proper role in a democratic system of government.
- Two new key terms, *originalism theory* and *living constitution theory.*

Chapter 15, Economic and Environmental Policy: Contributing to Prosperity

- New "Citizen Action: Self-Government" sidebar asks students to do their part to protect the environment, such as drinking tap water rather than bottled water.
- Discussion of the Democrat-driven 2021 stimulus bill in response to the COVID-19 pandemic to illustrate demand-side policy and why the approach is favored by Democrats.
- Discussion of how Republicans overwhelmingly supported the Reagan, Bush, and Trump tax cuts to illustrate supply-side policy and why the approach is favored by Republicans.
- Discussion of how increased domestic spending by Democrats and increased military spending and tax cuts by Republics have contributed to the national debt, illustrating the downside of both demand-side and supply-side policies.
- Discussion of factors, including supply-chain disruptions due to the COVID-19 pandemic, that have contributed to the rapid increase in inflation rate.

Chapter 16, Income, Welfare, and Education Policy: Providing for Personal Security

- New "Citizen Action: Equality" sidebar encourages students to volunteer for a religious, civic, social, or economic program aimed at helping the poor.
- New "Citizen Action: Equality" sidebar encourages students to volunteer as tutors in a local school in a poorer neighborhood.

Chapter 17, Foreign Policy: Protecting the National Interest

- Thoroughly revised chapter, now reorganized around the main dimensions of foreign policy: diplomacy, military defense, intelligence, and economic exchange.
- New chapter title and chapter introduction focuses on America's foreign policy response to the Russian invasion of Ukraine in February 2022 in context of realism theory and liberalism theory.
- New section, "Diplomacy," discusses the functions of leading diplomatic agencies, such as Department of State; soft power as differentiated from hard power, and examples of diplomatic successes and failures.
- New "Citizen Action: Self-Government" sidebar encourages students to consider becoming part of diplomatic and public service organizations such as the Peace Corps, AmeriCorps, and Teach for America.
- Thoroughly revised "Military Power" section discusses the Department of Defense and United States military alliances and capabilities; a brief history of post-WWII ward, renewed conflict with Russia and China, and a discussion of the politics of national defense.
- New section, "Intelligence Gathering," discusses the nation's intelligence agencies, a brief history of their activities since World War II including the war on terrorism, and the use of intelligence prior to and since Russia's invasion of Ukraine.
- New "Economic Exchange" section discusses the many U.S. agencies that contribute to protecting and enhancing U.S. economic interests abroad, the trend in foreign trade, and growing threat of cybercrime to the national and global economies.
- New key terms, *bilateral, liberalism theory, multilateral,* and *realism theory.*
- Thoroughly updated chapter summary reflects the many changes in this edition's chapter.

Acknowledgments

Nearly three decades ago, when planning the first edition of *We the People,* my editor and I concluded that it would be enormously helpful if a way could be found to bring into each chapter the judgment of those political scientists who teach the introductory course year in and year out. Thus, in addition to soliciting general reviews from a select number of expert scholars, we sent each chapter to faculty members at U.S. colleges and universities of all types—public and private, large and small, two-year and four-year. These political scientists had years of experience teaching the introductory course, and they provided countless good ideas.

I decided to use that same review process for this edition. The response was gratifying and extraordinarily helpful. One set of reviewers was selected by McGraw Hill and concentrated on Chapters 2, 10, and 12. A second set, which I chose, had their pick of which chapter to review. All told, 144 reviewers contributed. It took a great deal of time to work their suggestions into the revisions, but it was worth every minute. I'm deeply grateful to each of them for giving so generously of their professional knowledge and time. They are:

Yishaiya Abosch, *California State University, Fresno*

Conner Alford, *Southeastern Oklahoma State University*

Stephanie N. Allen, *Alabama A&M University*

Bruce Anderson, *Western Wyoming Community College*

Alicia Andreatta, *Angelina College*

Milan Andrejevich, *Ivy Tech Community College of Indiana*

Nicholas Archer, *Middlesex County College*

Jimmy Arnold, *Cossatot Community College*

Mandi Bailey, *Valdosta State University*

Eric Baker, *University of Arkansas-Fort Smith*

Jodi Balma, *Fullerton College*

Richard Baranzini, *Liberty University*

Carl Beard, *Wayland Baptist University*

Annie Benifield, *Lone Star College-Tomball*

Paul Benson, *Tarrant County College-Northwest*

David Birch, *Lone Star College-Tomball*

Wesley Bishop, *Pitt Community College*

Leah Blumenfeld, *Barry University*

Madelyn Bowman, *Tarrant County College-South*

Travis Braidwood, *Texas A&M University-Kingsville*

Gary Bugh, *Texas A&M University-Texarkana*

Sarah Burgen, *Grantham University*

Paul Byrd, *Des Moines Area Community College*

Steven Campbell, *University of South Carolina-Lancaster*

Trisha Capansky, *University of Tennessee at Martin*

Michael Ceriello, *Clark College*

Jeffrey Christiansen, *Seminole State College*

Diana Cohen, *Central Connecticut State University*

Linda Collier, *Delaware County Community College*

Frank Colucci, *Purdue University Northwest*

Allan D. Cooper, *North Carolina Central University*

Charles Cooper, *North Central Texas College*

Jesse Cragwell, *Pellissippi State Community College*

Andrew Crocker, *Ozarks Technical Community College*

Martha Crone, *Columbus State Community College*

Caleb Curfman, *Northland Community & Technical College*

Anthony Dell'Aera, *Worcester State University*

Marco DeSena, *Baruch College-CUNY*

Elsa Dias, *Pikes Peak Community College*

Don Dugi, *Transylvania University*

Jerry Elix, *Langston University*

Leisha Estep, *Cameron University*

Charles Fagan, *Western Carolina University*

Mecheline Farhat, *Bergen Community College*

John FitzGerald, *Santa Fe College*

Brian Fletcher, *Truckee Meadows Community College*

Stacy Fox, *California State University-Fullerton*

Nathan Freeman, *Athens Technical College*

Flite Freimann, *Washington State Community College*

Jay Fulgencio, *Oklahoma State University-Oklahoma City*

Ray Fullard, *Grantham University*

Amy Funck, *Rutgers University*

Patrick Gilbert, *Lone Star College-Tomball*

Nicholas Giordano, *Suffolk Community College*

Colin Glennon, *East Tennessee State University*

Stephen Goggin, *San Diego State University*

Andrew Gooch, *Rowan University*

Jessica Gracey, *Northwest Missouri State University*

Gregory P. Granger, *Northwestern State University of Louisiana*

Sara Gubala, *Lamar University*

Robert C. Harding, *Valdosta State University*

Maureen Heffern Ponicki, *College of DuPage*

Julie Hershenberg, *Collin College*

Ronil Hira, *Howard University*

James Hite, *Clackamas Community College*

Matthew P. Hitt, *Colorado State University*

Floyd William Holder IV, *Western Texas College*

Jennifer Hopper, *Southern Connecticut State University*

Leigh Hornsby, *University of Texas, Dallas*

Joe Ialenti, *North Central Texas College*

Scott Johnson, *Frostburg State University*

Richard Johnson, *Oklahoma City University*

Natalie Johnson, *Francis Marion university*

Adam Kunz, *California State University-Monterey Bay*

Adam Kunz, *California State University-Sacramento*

Mary Frances Lebamoff, *University of Maryland-Global Campus*

Daewoo Lee, *Columbus State University*

Matthew Lees, *Southeastern Illinois College*

Eric Loepp, *University of Wisconsin-Whitewater*

Danielle Martin, *California State University-Sacramento*

Barry A. Maxwell, *Whatcom Community College*

Michael Mayo, *Florida SouthWestern State College*

Lauren McClain, *Tarrant County College-Northwest*

Elizabeth McNamara, *Alamance Community College*

James McQuiston, *Southern Arkansas University*

Nathan Melton, *Utah Valley University*

Stephen Michot, *Fletcher Technical Community College*

Eric Miller, *Blinn College-Bryan*

Justin Moeller, *West Texas A&M University*

Husam Mohamad, *University of Central Oklahoma*

Julie Mueller, *Southern Maine Community College*

Coyle Neal, *Southwest Baptist University*

Jacob Neiheisel, *University at Buffalo*

Jalal Nejad, *Northwest Vista College*

James Newman, *Southeast Missouri State University*

Adam J. Newmark, *Appalachian State University*

Eric Nystrom, *Merced College*
Jordan O'Connell, *Howard College*
Anthony O'Regan, *Los Angeles Valley College*
Karen Owen, *University of West Georgia*
Michael Parkin, *Oberlin College*
Jim Peitersen, *Walla Walla Community College*
Paul Pope, *Montana State University-Billings*
Robert Postic, *The University of Findlay*
Carol Pretlow, *Norfolk State University*
Nicholas Pyeatt, *Penn State University-Altoona*
Gregory Rabb, *Jamestown Community College*
Cherry Rain, *Redlands Community College*
Antonio Ramirez, *Elgin Community College*
Allexcia Rankin, *Carl Albert State College*
Sterling Recker, *North Central Missouri College*
Keith Reeves, *Swarthmore College*
Timothy Reynolds, *Alvin Community College*
Glenn Ricketts, *Raritan Valley Community College*
Sanne Rijkhoff, *Texas A&M University-Corpus Christi*
Ron Robinson, *Schoolcraft College*
Stephen Rockwell, *St. Joseph's University, New York*
Norman Julian Rodriguez, *John Wood Community College*
Trent Rose, *Brigham Young University-Idaho*
Jason Russell, *San Jacinto College*
Eric Schwartz, *Hagerstown Community College*

Ivy Shen, *Southeast Missouri State University*
Maurice Sheppard, *Madison Area Technical College*
Mark Shomaker, *Houston Community College-Central*
Daniel Smith, *Northwest Missouri State University*
Leniece Smith, *Jackson State University*
Clinton Smith, *Lane Community College*
Robert Speel, *Penn State University-Erie*
Kyle Stevenson, *Green River College*
Bryan Tellalian, *Reedley College*
Mark Tiller, *Houston Community College-Northwest*
Agostine Trevino, *Temple College*
Marc Turetzky, *Gavilan College and California State University, Monterey Bay*
Ewa Unoke, *Kansas City Kansas Community College*
Jeremy Walling, *Southeast Missouri State University*
Stephanie Mora Walls, *Bowling Green State University-Firelands*
Pamela West, *Jefferson Community College*
James White, *Concord University*
Robert Wilkes, Jr., *Atlanta Metro College*
Gregory Williams, *University of Northern Colorado*
Matthew Wilson, *Southern Methodist University*
Bruce Wilson, *University of Central Florida*
Christy Wright, *Wilmington University*
Adam Zucconi, *Richard Bland College of William & Mary*

I also want to thank those at McGraw Hill Education who contributed to the 15th edition: Jason Seitz, Dawn Groundwater, Rick Hecker, Carrie Burger, and Beth Blech, as well as product developer Bruce Cantley, marketing manager Michael Gedatus, copyeditor Debra DeBord, and photo researcher Bidit Siktar at Aptara. At Harvard, I had the dedicated support of Kevin Wren.

Thomas E. Patterson

CRITICAL THINKING AND POLITICAL CULTURE: BECOMING A RESPONSIBLE CITIZEN

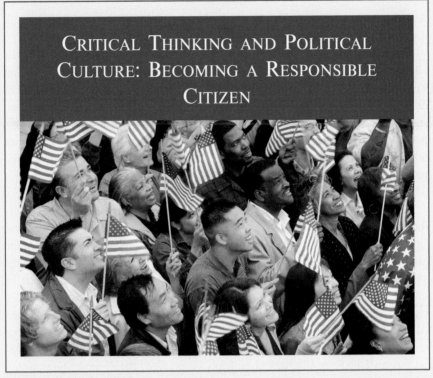

sirtravelalot/Shutterstock

❝ The worth of the state, in the long run, is the worth of the individuals composing it. ❞

JOHN STUART MILL[1]

In the span of a few months, the death toll from the COVID-19 pandemic had surpassed the number of Americans killed in the Korean war, the Vietnam War, the Afghan War, and the Iraq War combined. No part of the country was spared, although the toll was much higher in some areas than others.

Public officials and health experts warned Americans to protect themselves. Most people responded by limiting their social contact and covering their faces when going out. Yet lives were lost because some Americans didn't take the threat seriously. More than a third of Americans believed that COVID-19 was no more deadly than the seasonal flu.[2] They were badly mistaken. Over the next two years, COVID-19 would kill 1,000,000 Americans. In the same period, less than 50,000 would die from the flu.[3]

Years ago, journalist Walter Lippmann noted that people respond, not to the world as it actually is, but to what they think it is. Given that some

Americans believed that the coronavirus was no more dangerous than the flu, it's not surprising that they didn't take it seriously.

Some amount of misinformation is to be expected. The world of public affairs is large and complex, and most of what people believe about that world is a result of what they hear from others rather than what they experience directly. But there's an alarming aspect of misinformation. It's been rising steadily and is now at the highest level in the history of polling.[4] It's hard to name a leading issue on which large numbers of Americans are not misguided.[5] On everything from taxes to immigration to the nature of the terrorist threat, millions of Americans hold opinions that are wildly at odds with reality.[6]

Misinformation has its comic side. In one poll, 10 percent of respondents thought that Judith Sheindlin ("Judge Judy") holds a seat on the Supreme Court.[7] But the grim side is alarming. Democracy is at risk when large numbers of citizens believe what's not true. Theodore Sorensen, who was a policy aide to President John F. Kennedy, put his finger on the problem when he said, "To decide, you first have to know."[8] Most Americans believe, for example, that foreign aid accounts for 20 percent or more of the federal budget, which has led some of them to believe that eliminating foreign aid will balance the federal budget. In reality, less than 1 percent of the federal budget is spent on foreign aid. Even if it was completely eliminated, the United States would still have a large budget deficit.[9]

This chapter explains the role of critical thinking in responsible citizenship and then examines Americans' enduring political beliefs, the nature of politics,

A healthy democracy depends on citizen participation but also requires that this participation be informed and thoughtful. (Alexandros Michailidis/Shutterstock)

and key features of the U.S. political system. The main points of the chapter are these:

- *Critical thinking requires judgment and reliable information.* Although the obstacles to critical thinking in the realm of politics are many, political science provides analytical skills and knowledge that can foster critical thinking.

- *The American political culture centers on a set of core ideals—liberty, equality, self-government, and individualism—that serve as Americans' common bond.* The ideals affect what Americans see as reasonable and acceptable, and what they will try to achieve.

- *Politics is the process that determines whose values will prevail in society.* The play of politics in the United States takes place in the context of democratic processes, constitutionalism, and free markets, and involves elements of majority, pluralist, legal, corporate, and elite power.

LEARNING TO THINK CRITICALLY

A goal of this book is to help students to think critically about politics. Critical thinking is not the mere act of voicing an opinion about a current issue or development. **Critical thinking** is the process of forming an opinion after weighing relevant information. Opinions not reached in this way are incomplete at best, perhaps even wildly wrong.[10] Critical thinking also requires citizens to judge how their values relate to the choices they face. Citizens differ in their values and can reasonably hold different opinions even when they share the same information. But misinformation is a barrier to sound judgment. Many Americans believe, for example, that free trade is the main reason that America has lost millions of manufacturing jobs. Free trade has contributed to the job loss, but it's far from being the main source. Seven of every eight lost jobs are due to automation—the replacement of factory workers with machines.[11]

　　Unlike an authoritarian regime that requires people to think in a certain way or risk punishment, democracy lets people decide for themselves what to think and how much effort to put into it. Citizens can choose to engage in wild thinking, but they have only themselves to blame when things go wrong.[12] Many Americans, for example, supported the U.S. invasion of Iraq in 2003 on a belief that Iraq was no match for the American military and that the war would end within a few weeks.[13] Instead, it lasted for years. The notion that the conflict would end quickly was wishful thinking, not critical thinking.

Obstacles to Critical Thinking

The obstacles to critical thinking have increased in recent decades. Our media system has changed markedly, as first cable and then the Internet expanded our sources of information. Many of the newer sources are not to be trusted. Some talk-show hosts and bloggers care little about the accuracy of the claims they make. They routinely slant or invent information to suit their purpose while hiding contradictory facts.[14] Much of the misinformation about COVID-19 originated on partisan talk shows, including the claim that it was no more dangerous than the flu.[15]

Nor can the words of political leaders always be trusted. During the Vietnam conflict, President Lyndon Johnson told Americans that the conflict was going well when, in fact, it was going poorly. When the deception became known, Americans were outraged. That response is less common today. As our politics has become more heated and divisive, we've become more tolerant of leaders who twist the truth.[16]

CITIZEN ACTION!
SELF-GOVERNMENT

Citizens can exercise influence by speaking out on a political issue. To do that effectively, you need a reasonably accurate understanding of the issue. What sources do you rely on for your political information? How confident are you that the information they provide is reliable? How might you determine their reliability?

Our mental habits can also lead us to accept false claims. In *Thinking Fast and Slow,* Nobel laureate Daniel Kahneman notes that we often accept explanations based on what we'd like to believe rather than what the evidence shows.[17] We also engage in what behavioral scientists Gordon Pennycook and David Rand call "cognitive laziness." Faced with the choice between taking the time to find out whether something is true or sticking with what we already believe, we typically take the easy path.[18]

What Political Science Can Contribute to Critical Thinking

This text will not try to tell you *what* to think politically. There is no correct way of thinking when it comes to the "what" of politics. People differ in their political values and interests and thereby differ in their political views.

Instead, this text will help you learn *how* to think critically by providing you with analytical tools that can sharpen your understanding of American politics. The tools are derived from **political science**—the systematic study of government and politics. Political science has developed largely through the work of scholars, but political practitioners and writers have also contributed. One of

America's foremost political scientists was the chief architect of the U.S. Constitution and later a president. Even today, James Madison's *Federalist* essays on constitutional design are masterpieces of political science.

As a discipline, political science is descriptive and analytical–that is, it attempts to depict and explain politics. Political science provides a body of knowledge and analytical tools that can increase citizens' ability to think critically by providing them:

- Reliable information about how the U.S. political system operates
- Systematic generalizations about major tendencies in American politics
- Terms and concepts that define key aspects of politics

Like any skill, critical thinking is developed through practice. For this reason, each of the text's chapters includes boxes that ask you to think critically. Some boxes deal with perennial questions, such as the nature of the president's war powers. Other boxes ask you to think critically by having you compare politics in your state and the United States with politics in other states and nations. Some boxes present cases of actual events and ask you to analyze them. Other boxes ask you to judge whether a claim is fake or fact. Finally, some boxes deal with current controversies, including the rising level of party polarization in America.

Critical thinking is the process of forming an opinion after weighing the evidence. Failure to do so can lead citizens to form opinions that are detached from reality. (master_art/Shutterstock)

POLITICAL CULTURE: AMERICANS' ENDURING BELIEFS

An understanding of U.S. politics properly begins with an assessment of the nation's political culture. Every country has its **political culture**—the widely shared and deep-seated beliefs of its people about politics.[19] These beliefs derive from the country's traditions and help define the relationship of citizens to their government and to each other.

Although every country has a distinctive political culture, the United States, as the British writer James Bryce observed, is a special case.[20] Other people take their identity from the common ancestry that led them gradually to gather under one flag. Long before France, Germany, or Japan became nation-states, there were French, German, and Japanese people, each a kinship group united through ancestry. Not so for Americans. They are a multitude of people who have come together from different lands—England, Germany, Ireland, Africa, Italy, Poland, Mexico, and China, to name a few (see "How the U.S. Differs"). Americans are linked not by a shared ancestry but by allegiance to a common set of ideals. The French writer Alexis de Tocqueville was among the first to recognize that shared beliefs were Americans' common bond. "Habits of the heart" was how he described them.

America's core ideals are rooted in the European heritage of the first white settlers. They arrived during the Enlightenment period when people were awakening to the idea of individual progress, which could be pursued more fully in the open society of the New World. In the Old World, kings and nobles claimed special privileges and owned most of the land. Ultimately, the colonists overturned the European way of governing. The American Revolution was the first successful large-scale rebellion in human history, driven largely by the desire to create a radically different form of society.[21] In the words of the Declaration of Independence,

> We hold these truths to be self-evident, that all men are created equal; that they are endowed by their Creator with certain unalienable rights; that among these are life, liberty, and the pursuit of happiness. That, to secure these rights, governments are instituted among men, deriving their just powers from the consent of the governed; that, whenever any form of government becomes destructive of these ends, it is the right of the people to alter or to abolish it, and to institute a new government, laying its foundation on such principles, and organizing its powers in such form, as to them shall seem most likely to effect their safety and happiness.

Those words are now familiar, but they were revolutionary at that time. And a decade later, with the writing of the U.S. Constitution, the break with the old way of governing was complete. The highest authority would not be a king

HOW THE U.S. DIFFERS

CRITICAL THINKING THROUGH COMPARISONS

A Nation of Immigrants

Americans trace their roots to every country on earth, which has led the United States to be called a "nation of immigrants." Even today, one in every seven Americans is an immigrant. If the children of immigrants are included, the figure is one in four.

In other nations, as the accompanying chart illustrates, there is typically a single ethnic group that makes up a majority of the population. Ninety-eight percent of the residents of Japan are ethnically Japanese. In Italy, 92 percent are ethnically Italian. In Germany and Great Britain, roughly 80 percent have a shared ethnicity. Not so for Americans. The largest ethnic group in the United States is German Americans who constitute 14 percent of the population. Mexican Americans at 11 percent and Irish Americans at 10 percent are the second and third largest ethnic groups. America's great diversity is reflected in the Latin phrase *E Pluribus Unum* (one out of many) that appears on the official Seal of the United States.

Largest ethnic group, as a percentage of total population.

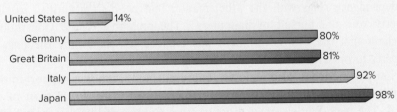

Source: Compiled by the author from various sources.

Q: Given Americans' diverse origins, what unites them?

A: Americans' attachment to their country and its way of life are among the reasons. Analysts have also identified the nation's cultural ideals—liberty, equality, individualism, and self-government—as a unifying force. Shared ideals tie people together.

but a written document that defined the lawful powers of government and the rights of citizens. A century later, British prime minister William Gladstone would call the U.S. Constitution "the most wonderful work ever struck off at a given time by the brain and purpose of man."[22]

Core Values: Liberty, Individualism, Equality, and Self-Government

An understanding of America's cultural ideals begins with recognition that the individual is paramount. Government is secondary. Government's role is to serve the people, as opposed to a system where people serve the government. No clearer statement of this principle exists than the Declaration of Independence's reference to "unalienable rights"—freedoms that belong to each and every citizen and that cannot lawfully be denied by government.

Liberty, individualism, equality, and self-government are widely regarded as America's core political ideals. **Liberty** is the principle that individuals should be free from arbitrary and oppressive government so that they can think and act as they choose.[23] Political liberty was nearly a birthright for early Americans. They did not have to accept the European system of absolute government when greater personal freedom was as close as the next area of unsettled land. Religious sentiments also entered into the thinking of the early Americans. Many of them had fled Europe to escape religious persecution and came to look upon religious freedom as part of a broader set of rights, including freedom of speech. Unsurprisingly, these early Americans were determined, when forming their own government, to protect their liberty. The Declaration of Independence rings with the proclamation that people are entitled to "life, liberty, and the pursuit of happiness." The preamble to the Constitution declares that the U.S. government was founded to secure "the Blessings of Liberty to ourselves and our Posterity."

Early Americans also enjoyed unprecedented economic opportunities. Unlike Europe, America had no hereditary nobility that owned most of the land. The New World's great distance from Europe and its vast stretches of open territory gave ordinary people the chance to own property, provided they were willing to work hard enough to make it a success. Out of this experience grew a sense of self-reliance and a culture of "rugged individualism." **Individualism** is a commitment to personal initiative and self-sufficiency. Observers from Tocqueville onward have seen fit to note that liberty in America, as in no other country, is tied to a desire for economic independence. Americans' chief aim, wrote Tocqueville, "is to remain their own masters."[24]

A third American political ideal is **equality**—the notion that all individuals are equal in their moral worth and thereby entitled to equal treatment under

Americans' cultural beliefs took root during the colonial period. The challenges and opportunities of settling the nation's vast space contributed to beliefs in individualism, liberty, equality, and self-government. These beliefs continue through today, reinforced by holidays like the Fourth of July and practices such as reciting the Pledge of Allegiance each day at the start of public school classes. (Jill Braaten/McGraw Hill)

the law. Europe's rigid system of aristocratic privilege was unenforceable in frontier America. It was this natural sense of personal equality that Thomas Jefferson expressed so forcefully in the Declaration of Independence: "We hold these truths to be self-evident, that all men are created equal." Nevertheless, equality has always been America's most elusive ideal. Even Jefferson professed not to know its precise meaning. A slave holder, Jefferson distinguished between free citizens, who were entitled to equal rights, and enslaved people, who were not. After slavery was abolished, Americans continued to argue over the meaning of equality, and the debate continues today. Does equality require that wealth and opportunity be widely shared? Or does it merely require that artificial barriers to advancement be removed? Despite differing opinions about such questions, an insistence on equality is a distinctive feature of the American experience. Americans, said Bryce, reject "the very notion" that some people might be "better" than others merely because of birth or position.[25]

America's fourth great political ideal is **self-government**—the principle that the people are the ultimate source of governing authority and should have a voice in their governing. Americans' belief in self-government formed in colonial America. The Old World was an ocean away, and European governments had no option but to give the American colonies a degree of self-determination. Out of this experience came the vision of a self-governing nation that led tens of thousands of ordinary farmers, merchants, and tradespeople to risk their lives fighting the British during the American Revolution. "Governments," the Declaration of Independence proclaims, "deriv[e] their just powers from the consent of the governed." The Constitution of the United States begins with the words "We the People." Etched in a corridor of the Capitol in Washington, D.C., are the words Alexander Hamilton spoke when asked about the foundation of the nation's government: "Here, sir, the people govern."

The Limits and Power of Americans' Ideals

America's cultural beliefs are idealistic. They hold out the promise of a government of high purpose, in which power is widely shared and used for the common good, and where individuals are free, self-governing, and equal under the law.

Yet high ideals do not guarantee that people will live up to them. The clearest proof of that in the American case is the human tragedy that began nearly four

The largest stain on America's founding principles is the nation's treatment of its Black citizens. For more than two centuries, they were bought and sold in public markets and, after being freed by the Civil War, were denied equal citizenship throughout the South. That tragic legacy continues today, as evidenced by high levels of poverty among African Americans who are also more likely to be victims of police misconduct. Shown here are demonstrators protesting the killing of an unarmed and hand-cuffed Black man, George Floyd, by Minneapolis police in 2020. (Tverdokhlib/Shutterstock)

centuries ago and continues today. In 1619, the first enslaved Black people were brought in chains to America. Slavery lasted 250 years. Enslaved people worked in the fields from dawn to dark (from "can see, 'til can't"), in both the heat of summer and the cold of winter. The Civil War brought an end to slavery but not to racial oppression. Slavery was followed by the Jim Crow era of legal segregation in the South. Black citizens were forbidden by law to use the same schools, hospitals, restaurants, and restrooms as white citizens. Those who spoke out against this system were subjected to beatings, fire bombings, rapes, and murder—hundreds of African Americans were lynched in the early 1900s by white vigilantes. Today, African Americans have equal rights under the law but are far from equal in their daily lives. Compared with white children, for example, Black children are twice as likely to live in poverty and to die in infancy.[26] There have always been two Americas, one for whites and one for Blacks.

Despite the lofty claim that "all men are created equal," equality has never been an American birthright. In 1882, Congress suspended Chinese immigration on the assumption that the Chinese were an inferior people. Calvin Coolidge in 1923 asked Congress for a permanent ban on Chinese immigration, saying they shouldn't be allowed "to settle in America."[27] Not to be outdone, California enacted legislation prohibiting individuals of Japanese descent from purchasing property in the state. Not until 1965 was discrimination against the Chinese, Japanese, and other Asians eliminated from U.S. immigration laws. (For more on America's conflicted relationship with immigrants, see "Fake or Fact? Do Immigrants Commit More Crimes?")

America's callous treatment of some groups is not among the stories that the American people like to tell about themselves. A University of Virginia survey found that American adults are far more likely to want children to be taught about the nation's achievements than about its shortcomings. For example, more than four out of five of those surveyed said children should be taught that "with hard work and perseverance anyone can succeed in America" while less than three in five said the same about teaching children about the nation's "cruel mistreatment of Blacks and American Indians." Selective memory can be found among all types of people, but the tendency to recast history is perhaps exaggerated in the American case because Americans' beliefs are so idealistic. How could a nation that proclaims "all men are created equal" have barred the Chinese, enslaved Blacks, killed Indians to steal their lands, and declared wives to be the "property" of their husbands?[30]

Although America's ideals obviously do not determine exactly what people will do, they are far from empty promises. If racial, gender, ethnic, and other forms of intolerance constitute the nation's sorriest chapter, the centuries-old struggle of Americans to build a more equal society is among its finest. Few

Detecting Misinformation

Do Immigrants Commit More Crimes?

At the base of the Statue of Liberty are the words of Emma Lazarus's oft-cited poem, "Give me your tired, your poor, your huddled masses yearning to breathe free."

Yet many Americans have opposed the entry of immigrants, particularly those of a different religious or ethnic background. In the mid-1800s, Catholic immigrants from Ireland and Germany were widely reviled by the Protestants already here. In the late 1800s and early 1900s, hos-

Everett Historical/Shutterstock

tility was directed at new arrivals from southern and eastern Europe—Italians, Greeks, Poles, Hungarians, Jews, Russians, and others. In 1924, Congress passed a law that largely halted immigration from southern and eastern Europe. Earlier, Congress had closed the door on immigrants from Asia.

An argument heard in those earlier periods and being heard again today is that immigrants pose a threat to public safety. A Pew Research Center poll found that Americans, by a ratio of seven to one, believe that immigrants are more likely than native-born Americans to commit crimes.[28]

Is that claim fact, or is it fake?

There has been substantial research on the issue, including recent studies by the National Academy of Sciences and the conservative Cato Institute. The studies found that immigrants are more law-abiding than native-born Americans. The 2017 Cato Institute study, for example, found that immigrants are 69 percent less likely to be incarcerated than are the native-born. That's true also of illegal immigrants. They are 44 percent less likely than the native-born to have been convicted of a crime and imprisoned.[29]

nations have battled so relentlessly against the insidious discrimination that stems from superficial human differences such as the color of one's skin. The abolition and suffrage movements of the 1800s and the more recent civil rights movements of Black Americans, women, Hispanics, and the LGBTQ community testify to Americans' persistent effort to build a more equal society. In 1848, at the first-ever national convention on women's rights, the delegates issued the Declaration of Sentiments, which read in part: "We hold these truths to be self-evident: that all men and women are created equal." A century later, speaking at the Lincoln Memorial at the peak of the Black civil rights movement, Martin Luther King Jr. invoked the words of the Declaration of Independence, saying "'We hold these truths to be self-evident, that all men are created equal.'"[31]

Americans' determination to build a more equal society can also be seen in its public education system. In the early 1800s, the United States pioneered the idea of free public education for children—this at a time when education in Europe was reserved for children of the wealthy. Even today, the United States spends more heavily on public education than European countries. Compared with Great Britain or France, for example, the United States spends about 30 percent more per pupil annually on its primary and secondary schools. The United States also has the world's most elaborate system of higher education, which includes roughly 4,000 two-year and four-year institutions. Although some of America's youth do not have a realistic chance of attending college, the nation's college system is a relatively open one. Roughly a third of Americans over the age of 25 have a college degree, which is one of the world's highest levels. Even the American states with the lowest proportion of college graduates have a higher percentage of residents with a bachelor's degree than most European countries (see "How the 50 States Differ").

The principle of self-government has also shaped American society. No country holds as many elections as does the United States or has anywhere near as many publicly elected officials. There are roughly a half-million American elected officials, everyone from the president of the United States to the local city council member. The principles of liberty and individualism have also shaped American society. Few people have pursued their individual rights—ranging from freedom of expression to fair-trial protections—as relentlessly as have Americans. And there are few countries where individualism is as deeply ingrained as in the United States. Political analysts William Watts and Lloyd Free described the United States as "the country of individualism *par excellence*."[32]

America's distinctive cultural beliefs are only one of the elements that affect the nation's politics, as subsequent chapters will show. The rest of this chapter introduces concepts and distinctions that are basic to a systematic understanding of politics.

HOW THE 50 STATES DIFFER

CRITICAL THINKING THROUGH COMPARISONS

A College Education

Reflecting their belief in individualism and equality, Americans have developed the world's largest college system—comprising roughly 4,000 institutions. According to U.S. Census Bureau figures, about one in three Americans over the age of 25 is a college graduate. Even the lowest-ranking state—West Virginia, with one in five—has a higher percentage of college graduates than do most European countries.

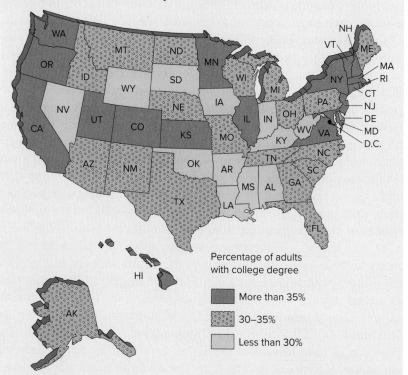

Percentage of adults with college degree

More than 35%

30–35%

Less than 30%

Q: What do states with the lowest percentage of college graduates have in common?

A: Most of them have relatively large rural populations and lower than average income levels. A college education is less often a job requirement in rural areas, and the expense of a college education is an obstacle to attending college for many low-income families.

POLITICS AND POWER IN AMERICA

Political scientist Harold Lasswell described politics as a conflict over "who gets what, when, and how."[33] Politics would be a simple matter if everyone thought alike and could have everything they pleased. But people do not think alike, and society's resources are limited. Conflict is the inevitable result. **Politics** is the means by which society settles its conflicts and determines who gets the benefits and who pays the costs.

Those who prevail in political conflicts are said to have **power**, a term that refers to the ability of persons, groups, or institutions to influence political decisions.[34] Power is basic to politics. The distribution of power in a society affects who wins and who loses when policy decisions are made. Those with enough power can raise or cut taxes, permit or prohibit abortions, impose or relax trade barriers, and make war or declare peace. With so much at stake, it is not surprising that Americans, like people elsewhere, seek political power.

French philosopher Michel Foucault called politics "war by other means,"[35] a phrase that literally describes politics in some countries. An **authoritarian government** is one that openly represses its political opponents, mostly through intimidation and prohibitions on free expression but sometimes through brute force. Such regimes are backed by the country's police and armed forces, forego free and fair elections, and exert tight control over the media. When Russia's authoritarian regime invaded Ukraine in 2022, it blocked social media platforms and foreign news outlets from communicating with the Russian people. Instead of hearing about their nation's military attack, the Russian people were told by state-controlled media that Russian troops were providing the Ukrainians with food and other assistance.[36]

The United States operates by a different standard. It has three basic "systems" designed to keep the government in check. These systems—democracy, constitutionalism, and a free market—determine which side will prevail when conflict occurs, as well as what is off-limits to the winning side (see Table 1-1).

table 1-1	GOVERNING SYSTEMS AND POLITICAL POWER
System	**Description and Implications**
Democratic system	A system of majority rule through elections; empowers majorities (majoritarianism), groups (pluralism), and officials (authority)
Constitutional system	A system based on rule of law, including legal protections for individuals
Free market system	An economic system that centers on the transactions between private parties; empowers business firms (corporate power) and the wealthy (elitism)

These systems will be examined in depth in later chapters, but a brief description of each system is helpful at this point.

A Democratic System

The word *democracy* comes from the Greek words *demos,* meaning "the people," and *kratis,* meaning "to rule." In simple terms, **democracy** is a form of government in which the people govern, either directly or through elected representatives. Democracy is thus different from *oligarchy* (in which control rests with a small group, such as top-ranking military officers or a few wealthy families) and from *autocracy* (in which control rests with a single individual, such as a king or dictator).

In practice, democracy has come to mean majority rule through the free and open election of representatives. More direct forms of democracy exist, such as town meetings in which citizens vote directly on issues affecting them, but the impracticality of such an arrangement in a large society has made majority rule through elections the operative form of democratic government, including that of the United States (see Chapter 2).

Majoritarianism is the term used to describe situations in which political leaders act on behalf of the majority.[37] In the American case, majoritarianism occurs primarily through the competition between the Republican and Democratic Parties (see "Party Polarization: Heightened Level of Party Conflict"). In the 2020 presidential campaign, for instance, Republican nominee Donald Trump and Democratic nominee Joe Biden differed sharply in their positions on immigration, health care, the environment, and other major policy issues, giving voters a choice about the direction of national policy.

Majoritarianism has its limits. The public as a whole takes an interest in only a few of the hundreds of policy decisions that officials make each year (see Chapter 6). Even if they wanted to, party leaders would have difficulty getting the majority to pay attention to most issues. Accordingly, most policies are formulated in response to the groups with a direct interest in the issue. Farmers, for example, have more influence over agricultural subsidies than do other Americans, even though these subsidies affect them, including the price that they pay for food. Some political scientists, like Yale's Robert Dahl, argue that democracies more often operate as pluralistic (multi-interest) systems than as majoritarian systems.[38] **Pluralism** holds that the government is chiefly responsive to interest groups (see Chapter 9).

A democratic system also bestows another form of power. Although officials are empowered by the majority, they also exercise power in their own right as a result of constitutional and legal grants of power. When President Biden decided in 2022 to impose severe economic sanctions on Russia in response

P A R T Y
POLARIZATION

Conflicting Ideas

Heightened Level of Party Conflict

Conflict between America's two major parties—the Republicans and the Democrats—has intensified in recent decades. Partisan divisions have surfaced on nearly every major issue, and the fights have been bitter and prolonged, so much so that the term **party (partisan) polarization** is used to describe today's politics. Subsequent chapters will examine various aspects of this polarization, but two things can be noted at the outset: The situation is different than it was a few decades ago but is not unprecedented.

A high level of bipartisanship—cooperation between the parties—marked the period from the end of World War II in 1945 until the late 1960s. Leaders and voters of both parties agreed on the need to contain Soviet communism. In addition, Republican leaders had largely abandoned their effort to turn back the New Deal policies of Democratic president Franklin Roosevelt, which had given the federal government a larger role in economic security (for example, the Social Security program) and economic regulation (for example, oversight of the stock market).

During much of the nation's earlier history, however, Americans disagreed strongly over policy and, in the case of the Civil War, took their fight to the battlefield. In fact, periods of bipartisanship have been the exception rather than the rule. President George Washington's first years in office, the so-called Era of Good Feeling in the early 1800s, and the World War I and World War II periods are among the few times when party conflict was relatively mild.

Q: Do you see any contradiction in the fact that Americans share a common set of ideals and yet often find themselves on opposite sides when it comes to party politics?

to its invasion of Ukraine, he was exercising his lawful power. **Authority** is the recognized right of officials to exercise power. Members of Congress, judges, and bureaucrats, as well as the president, routinely make authoritative decisions by virtue of the positions they hold.

A Constitutional System

In a democracy, the votes of the majority prevail over those of the minority. If the majority had absolute power, it could treat the minority in any manner of its choosing, including depriving it of liberty and property. As unrealistic as this possibility might seem today, it preoccupied the writers of the U.S.

Authority is the recognized right of officials to exercise power. The president of the United States exercises authority through the powers granted to the executive by the Constitution, just as do members of Congress and other public officials. Pictured here is President Joe Biden announcing that the United States was imposing economic sanctions on Russia in response to its invasion of Ukraine. (Bonnie Cash/UPI/Alamy Stock Photo)

CITIZEN ACTION!
LIBERTY

Americans have the right to speak freely on political issues. It is through words that we voice our opinions, try to persuade others, and negotiate our differences. Few situations provide greater opportunity to develop your ability to speak persuasively in a public setting than does the college classroom. Make use of the opportunities it offers.

Constitution. To guard against the possibility, they devised an elaborate system of checks and balances, dividing authority among the legislative, executive, and judicial branches so that each branch could check the power of the others (see Chapter 2). The Bill of Rights was subsequently added to the Constitution as a further check on government. It contains rights, such as freedom of speech, that government is obliged to protect. These limits reflect the principle of **constitutionalism**—the idea that there are lawful restrictions on the government's power. Officials are obliged to act within the limit of the law, which includes the protection of individual rights.

A Free-Market System

Politics is not confined to the halls of government. Many of society's costs and benefits are allocated through a country's economic system. Under *communism,* which characterized the former Soviet Union and is practiced most fully today in North Korea, the government owns most or all major industries and controls the economy, including production quotas, supply points, and pricing. Under *socialism,* as it is practiced today in Sweden and some other countries, the government does not attempt to manage the overall economy but owns a number of major industries and guarantees every individual a minimal standard of living. In contrast, a **free-market system** operates mainly on private transactions. Firms are largely free to make their own production, distribution, and pricing decisions, and individuals depend largely on themselves for economic security.

The U.S. economy is largely a free-market system. It has millions of small businesses, as well as a corporate sector that includes large firms such as Google, Ford, and Bank of America. **Corporate power**—the influence of business firms on public policy—has been a defining feature of American politics since the late 1800s. Corporate power can be seen today in the fact that roughly two-thirds of all lobbyists in the nation's capital represent business firms. Corporate power can also be seen in the workplace, where U.S. firms have greater control over wages and working conditions than do firms in other Western democracies. The annual income of a minimum-wage worker, for instance, is roughly $15,000 in the United States, compared with roughly $21,000 in Germany and $22,500 in France.[39]

As C. Wright Mills and other theorists have noted, corporate elites exercise substantial influence over public policy. The influence of the nation's major corporations goes beyond the halls of government. Through advertising and public relations efforts, they seek to build public support for the private enterprise system. (Library of Congress Prints & Photographs Division [LC-DIG-fsa-8a05460])

Economic power is also the foundation of **elitism**, which refers to the power exercised by well-positioned and highly influential individuals.[40] Sociologist C. Wright Mills concluded that corporate elites, operating behind the scenes, have greater control over economic policy than do elected officials.[41] Some scholars contend that Mills overstated the power of elites while downplaying the fact that some elites seek to serve society's interests as well as their own.[42] Few scholars, however, dispute the claim that corporate elites in America have more political power than they do in most Western democracies.

Who Governs?

This text's perspective is that a full explanation of American politics requires an accounting of all these forms of power—as exercised by the majority, interest groups, elites, corporations, individuals through legal action, and those in positions of governing authority. In fact, a defining characteristic of American politics is the widespread sharing of power. Few nations have as many competing interests and institutions as the United States.

THE TEXT'S ORGANIZATION

America's constitutional system defines how power is to be obtained and exercised. This system is the focus of the next few chapters, which examine how, in theory and practice, the Constitution defines the institutions of governments and the rights of individuals. The discussion then shifts to the political role of citizens and of the intermediaries like political parties and interest groups that enable citizens to act together and connect them to government. The functioning of governing officials is then addressed in chapters on the nation's elective institutions—the Congress and the presidency—and its appointive institutions—the federal bureaucracy and the federal courts. Throughout the text, but particularly in the concluding chapters, attention is given to the government's **public policies**. No aspect of a nation's politics is more revealing of how it is governed than are its public policies—everything from how it chooses to educate its children to how it chooses to use its military power.

Underlying the text's discussion of American politics and policy is the recognition of how hard it is to govern effectively and how important it is to try. It cannot be said too often that the issue of governing is the most difficult issue facing a democratic society. It also cannot be said too often that governing is a quest rather than a resolved issue. Political scientist E. E. Schattschneider said it clearly: "In the course of centuries, there has come a great deal of agreement about what democracy is, but nobody has a monopoly on it and the last word has not been spoken."[43]

SUMMARY

Critical thinking is the careful gathering and sifting of information in the process of forming knowledgeable views of political developments. Critical thinking is a key to responsible citizenship, but many citizens avoid it by virtue of paying scant attention to politics. The tools of political science can contribute to the critical thinking process.

The United States is a nation formed on a set of ideals. Liberty, individualism, equality, and self-government are the foremost among these ideals. These ideals became Americans' common bond and today are the basis of their political culture. Although imperfect in practice, these ideals have influenced what generations of Americans have sought to achieve politically.

Politics is the process by which it is determined whose values and interests will prevail in society. The basis of politics is conflict over scarce resources and competing values. Those who have power win out in this conflict and are able to control governing authority and policy choices. In the United States, no one faction controls all power and policy. Majorities govern on some issues, while other issues are dominated by interest groups, elites, corporations, or officials who hold public office.

Politics in the United States plays out through rules of the game that include democracy, constitutionalism, and free markets. Democracy is rule by the people, which in practice refers to a representative system of government in which the people rule through their elected officials. Constitutionalism refers to rules that limit the rightful power of government over citizens. A free-market system assigns private parties the dominant role in determining how economic costs and benefits are allocated.

CRITICAL THINKING ZONE

KEY TERMS

authoritarian government (*p. 15*)

authority (*p. 17*)

constitutionalism (*p. 18*)

corporate power (*p. 19*)

critical thinking (*p. 3*)

democracy (*p. 16*)

elitism (*p. 20*)

equality (*p. 8*)

free-market system (*p. 19*)

individualism (*p. 8*)

liberty (*p. 8*)

majoritarianism (*p. 16*)

party (partisan) polarization (*p. 17*)

pluralism (*p. 16*)

political culture (*p. 6*)

political science (*p. 4*)

politics (*p. 15*)

power (*p. 15*)

public policies (*p. 20*)

self-government (*p. 9*)

APPLYING THE ELEMENTS OF CRITICAL THINKING

Conceptualizing: Distinguish between political power (generally) and authority (as a special kind of political power).

Synthesizing: Contrast the American political culture with that of most Western democracies. What in the American experience has led its people to derive their national identity from a set of shared political ideals?

Analyzing: Explain the defining features of each of America's major systems of governing—democracy, constitutionalism, and a free market.

OF POSSIBLE INTEREST

A Book Worth Reading: Gordon S. Wood, *The Idea of America: Reflections on the Birth of the United States* (New York: Penguin Press, 2011). A perceptive book by a Pulitzer Prize–winning historian, it explores the ideals, such as liberty and equality, that powered the American Revolution.

A Website Worth Visiting: **https://americanhistory.si.edu/topics/american-culture** The National Museum of American History has a section that explores through culture "what it means to be American."

2

CHAPTER

CONSTITUTIONAL DEMOCRACY: PROMOTING LIBERTY AND SELF-GOVERNMENT

larry1235/Shutterstock

> ❝ Why has government been instituted at all? Because the passions of man will not conform to the dictates of reason and justice, without constraint. ❞
>
> ALEXANDER HAMILTON[1]

On March 1, 2022, Joe Biden stepped to the podium in the well of the U.S. House of Representatives to deliver his first State of the Union Address. Only days before, Russia had invaded Ukraine, adding urgency to a moment defined by the country's two-year struggle to contain the COVID-19 pandemic. Biden began his speech by praising the brave people of Ukraine, linking their fight to the age-old struggle for the right of people to govern themselves. He spoke of the "love of freedom" and the promise of "democracy." "In the battle between democracy and autocracies," he said, "democracies are rising to the moment." "We will meet the test," he exclaimed. "And we will save democracy."

Biden spoke of the sacrifices that Americans had made over the course of their history. "We fought for freedom, expanded liberty, defeated totalitarianism and terror." He concluded his State of the Union Address by urging today's

Pictured here is President Woodrow Wilson speaking to a joint session of Congress in 1918. In the speech, delivered near the end of World War I, Wilson outlined his "Fourteen Points" for world peace. They were rooted in America's governing experience and ideals. Like presidents before and since, Wilson drew inspiration from America's founding ideas about liberty, equality, and self-government. (Pictorial Press Ltd/Alamy Stock Photo)

Americans to meet the challenges of their time, saying: "Now is the hour. Our moment of responsibility. Our test of resolve and conscience, of history itself."

The ideas that guided Biden's speech would have been familiar to any generation of Americans. The ideas have been invoked when Americans have celebrated national holidays, gone to war, declared peace, and asserted their rights.[2] The ideas expressed in Biden's speech were the same ones that shaped the speeches of George Washington, Abraham Lincoln, Susan B. Anthony, Franklin D. Roosevelt, Martin Luther King Jr., and Ronald Reagan.

The ideas were there at the nation's beginning when Thomas Jefferson put them into words in the Declaration of Independence. They had been nurtured by the colonial experience in the New World, which offered the settlers a degree of liberty, equality, and self-government unimaginable in Europe. When the Revolutionary War secured Americans' independence, they faced the question of how to turn their ideals into a system of government. The Constitution of the United States became the instrument of that goal. The framers of the Constitution sought to create a **limited government**—one that is subject to strict legal limits on the uses of power so that it would not endanger the people's liberty. They also sought to establish a system of **representative government**—one in which the people would govern through the election of their representatives.

A challenge facing the framers was that limited government and representative government can conflict. Representative government requires that the majority, through its elected representatives, has the power to rule. However, limited government requires that the majority's power stop at the point where it infringes on the lawful rights and interests of the minority. This consideration led the framers to craft a constitution that provides for majority rule but with built-in restrictions on the power of the majority and its elected representatives.

This chapter describes how the principles of representative government and limited government are embodied in the Constitution and explains the tension between them. It also indicates how these principles have been modified in practice in the course of American history. This chapter presents the following main points:

- *America during the colonial period developed traditions of limited government and representative government.* These traditions were rooted in governing practices, political theory, and cultural values.

- *The Constitution provides for limited government mainly by defining lawful powers and by dividing those powers among competing institutions.* The Constitution, through the Bill of Rights, also prohibits the government from infringing on individual rights.

- *The Constitution in its original form provided for representative government mainly through indirect methods of electing representatives.* The framers' theory of representative government was based on the notion that political power must be separated from immediate popular influences if sound policies are to result.

- *The idea of popular government—in which the majority's desire have a more direct and immediate impact on governing officials—has gained strength since the nation's beginning.* Originally, the House of Representatives was the only institution subject to a direct vote of the people. This mechanism has been extended to other institutions and, through primary elections, even to the nomination of candidates for public office.

BEFORE THE CONSTITUTION: THE COLONIAL AND REVOLUTIONARY EXPERIENCES

Early Americans' admiration for limited government stemmed from their British heritage. Unlike other European governments of the time, Britain did not have an absolute monarchy. Parliament was an independent body with lawmaking power and local representation. Many of the colonial charters conferred upon Americans "the rights of Englishmen," which included, for example, the right to a trial by a jury. The colonies also had experience in self-government. Each colony had an elected representative assembly.

The American Revolution was partly a rebellion against Britain's failure to uphold the colonies' traditions. During the French and Indian War (1754–1763), the colonists fought alongside the British soldiers to drive the French out of the western territories. The British had borrowed heavily to finance the war, which contributed to a budget crisis in Britain. Claiming that the colonists had benefitted from eliminating the French, Britain looked to them to help pay the war debt and the cost of keeping a British army in North America. The British Parliament issued the Stamp Act, which taxed the colonies' newspapers and legal documents. Although Britain repealed the Stamp Act, it then enacted the Townshend Acts, which taxed imports to America, thereby raising the cost that colonists had to pay for British goods. That was followed by the Tea Act, which gave a British company sole authority to sell tea in the colonies, thereby cutting out American merchants. The colonies were not represented in Parliament, and they bitterly resented the new laws. "No taxation without representation" became the rallying cry.

In 1774, the colonists met in Philadelphia at the First Continental Congress to formulate their demands on Britain. They asked for their own councils for the imposition of taxes, an end to the British military occupation, and a guarantee of a trial by local juries. (British authorities had resorted to shipping "troublemakers" to London for trial.) King George III ignored their requests, and British troops and Massachusetts minutemen clashed at Lexington and Concord on April 19, 1775. Eight colonists died on the Lexington green in what became known as "the shot heard 'round the world." The American Revolution had begun.

Although the British had the world's strongest army and outnumbered the American army by more than two to one, George Washington's strategy of avoiding pitched battles kept the British from winning a decisive encounter. Americans' tactics eventually wore down the British, which in 1781 lost its southern army in the Battle of Yorktown, effectively ending any possibility of a British victory. The war ended in 1783 when Britain signed The Treaty of Paris, which formally granted America its independence.

The Declaration of Independence

Although British policies were the immediate cause of the American Revolution, ideas about the proper form of government also fueled the rebellion.[3] Building on the writings of Thomas Hobbes,[4] John Locke claimed that government is founded on a **social contract**. Locke asserted that people living in a state of nature enjoy certain **inalienable (natural) rights**, including those of life,

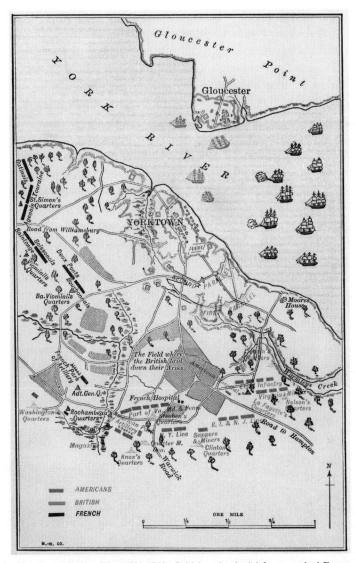

During the French and Indian War (1754–1763), British and colonial forces pushed France out of North America. After the war, the British imposed taxes on the colonies and kept a permanent army in the colonies—actions that were deeply resented by the colonists and contributed to the outbreak of the American Revolution. Ironically, France's resentment at the loss of its North American territory led it to side with the Americans in the Revolution, which proved decisive. In the Battle of Yorktown, which brought about the British surrender, French ships blockaded the harbor to Yorktown, preventing Britain from reinforcing its army. (North Wind Picture Archives/Alamy Stock Photo)

liberty, and property, which are threatened by individuals who steal, kill, and otherwise act without regard for others. To protect against such individuals, people agree among themselves to form a government (the social contract). They submit to the government's authority in return for the protection it can provide, but in doing so they retain their natural rights, which the government is obliged to respect. If it fails to do so, Locke contended, people can rightfully rebel against it.[5]

Thomas Jefferson declared that Locke "was one of the three greatest men that ever lived" and paraphrased Locke's ideas in passages of the Declaration of Independence, including those asserting that "all men are created equal," that they are entitled to "life, liberty, and the pursuit of happiness," that governments derive "their just powers from the consent of the governed," and that "it is the right of the people to alter or abolish" a tyrannical government. The Declaration was a call to revolution rather than a framework for a new form of government, but the ideas it contained—liberty, equality, individual rights, self-government, lawful powers—became the basis, 11 years later, for the Constitution of the United States. (The Declaration of Independence and the Constitution are reprinted in their entirety in this book's appendixes.)

John Adams, Roger Sherman, Robert Livingston, Thomas Jefferson, and Benjamin Franklin present their draft of the Declaration of Independence to the Continental Congress. Jefferson (tallest of the three men standing directly in front of the desk) was its principal author. Jefferson's bold declaration that "all men are created equal" was contradicted by the fact that he, like several of the signers, was a lifelong slave owner. (John Parrot/John Trumbull (American painter)/Stocktrek Images/Getty Images)

The Articles of Confederation

A **constitution** is a basic law that defines how a government will legitimately operate–the method for choosing its leaders, the institutions through which these leaders will work, the procedures they must follow in making policy, and the powers they can lawfully exercise. The U.S. Constitution is exactly such a law; it is the highest law of the land. Its provisions define how power is to be acquired and how it can be used.

The first government of the United States was based not on the Constitution but on the Articles of Confederation. Adopted during the Revolutionary War, the Articles reflected the governing systems that the colonists had experienced during the century and a half they were under British rule. Although Britain in theory could override their decisions, each colony had a representative assembly whose members were elected by property-owning males. Towns and cities also had self-governing bodies. From this experience, the colonists acquired a belief in *legislative supremacy*, the idea that a representative assembly rather than a strong executive is the proper means of governing. They also developed a commitment to local control, believing that a government close to the people was superior to a distant one.

Accordingly, the Articles created a very weak national government that was subordinate to the states. Each state retained its full "sovereignty, freedom, and independence." This feature of the Articles was also a natural extension of the colonial experience. The colonies had always been governed separately and had different histories and in some cases different religious traditions. Not surprisingly, people thought of themselves first as Virginians, New Yorkers, Pennsylvanians, and so on rather than as Americans.[6] Moreover, they were wary of centralized power. The American Revolution was a rebellion against the arbitrary policies of King George III, and Americans were in no mood to replace him with a powerful national government of their own making.

Legislative supremacy was also a defining feature of the government created by the Articles. It had no judiciary and no independent executive. All authority was vested in the Congress, which was beholden to the states. Each of the 13 states had one vote in Congress, and each state appointed its congressional representatives and paid their salaries. Legislation could be enacted only if 9 of the 13 state delegations agreed to it. The rule for constitutional amendments was even more imposing. The Articles of Confederation could be amended only if all states agreed.

The Articles prohibited Congress from levying taxes, so it had to ask the states for money. It was slow to arrive if it arrived at all. During one period, Congress requested $12 million from the states but received only $3 million.

By 1786, the national government was so desperate for funds that it sold the navy's ships and cut the army to less than 1,000 soldiers–this at a time when Britain had an army in Canada and Spain had one in Florida. Congress was also prohibited from regulating the states' trade policies, so it was powerless to forge a national economy. Free to do as they wanted, states enacted trade policies designed to protect their manufacturers from competitors in nearby states. Connecticut, for example, placed a higher tariff on goods produced in neighboring Massachusetts than on the same goods manufactured in England.

A Nation Dissolving

The American states had stayed together out of necessity during the Revolutionary War. They would have lost to the British if each state had tried to fend for itself. Once the war ended, however, the states felt free to go their separate ways. In a melancholy letter to Thomas Jefferson, George Washington wondered whether the United States deserved to be called "a nation."

A revolt in western Massachusetts put the weakness of the national government on full display. In 1786, a ragtag army of 2,000 farmers armed with pitchforks marched on county courthouses to prevent foreclosures on their land. Many of the farmers were veterans of the Revolutionary War; their leader, Daniel Shays, had been a captain in the American army. They had been given assurances during the Revolution that their land, which sat unused because they were away at war, would not be confiscated for unpaid debts and taxes. They were also promised the back pay owed to them for their military service. (Congress had run out of money during the Revolution.) Instead, they received no back pay, and heavy new taxes were levied on their farms. Many farmers faced not only losing their property but also being sent to prison for unpaid debts. The governor of Massachusetts asked Congress for help in putting down the revolt, but it had no army to send. He finally turned to the state's wealthy merchants who hired a private militia to quell the rebellion.

Even before the outbreak of Shays' Rebellion, Virginia and Maryland had invited the other 11 states to meet in Annapolis to propose amendments to the Articles of Confederation to strengthen the national government. Only 5 states sent delegates to the Annapolis Convention, which meant no formal action was taken. However, James Madison and Alexander Hamilton convinced the delegates to adopt a resolution calling for a constitutional convention. Congress agreed and called for it to be held in Philadelphia. Congress placed a restriction on the convention: It was to meet for "the sole and express purpose of revising the Articles of Confederation."

CREATING A CONSTITUTION

The delegates to the Philadelphia constitutional convention ignored the instructions of Congress, choosing instead to write an entirely new constitution. Prominent delegates (among them George Washington, Benjamin Franklin, and James Madison) were determined from the outset to create a strong central government. They had come to understand the foolishness of the idea that small government is always the best form of government. The lesson of the Articles of Confederation was that government must have the power necessary to carry out its responsibilities.

The Great Compromise: A Two-Chamber Congress

Debate at the constitutional convention of 1787 began over a plan put forward by the Virginia delegation, which was dominated by strong nationalists. The **Virginia Plan** (also called the *large-state plan*) included separate judicial and executive branches, as well as a two-chamber Congress that would have supreme authority in all areas "in which the separate states are incompetent," particularly defense and interstate trade. Members of the lower chamber would be chosen by the voters, while members of the upper chamber would be selected by members of the lower chamber from lists of nominees provided by their respective state legislatures. In both chambers, the heavily populated states would have more representatives than would the lightly populated ones. Small states such as Delaware and Rhode Island would be allowed only one representative in the lower chamber, while large states such as Massachusetts and Virginia would have more than a dozen.

The Virginia Plan was sharply attacked by delegates from the smaller states. They rallied around a proposal made by New Jersey's William Paterson. The **New Jersey Plan** (also called the *small-state plan*) called for a stronger national government than that provided for by the Articles of Confederation. It would have the power to tax and to regulate commerce among the states. In most other respects, however, the Articles would remain in effect. Congress would have a single chamber in which each state, large or small, would have a single vote.

The debate over the two plans dragged on for weeks before the delegates reached what is now known as the **Great Compromise**. It provided for a bicameral (two-chamber) Congress. One chamber, the House of Representatives, would be apportioned on the basis of population. States with larger populations would have more House members than states with smaller populations, although each state would have at least one representative. The other chamber, the Senate, would be apportioned on the basis of an equal number of senators

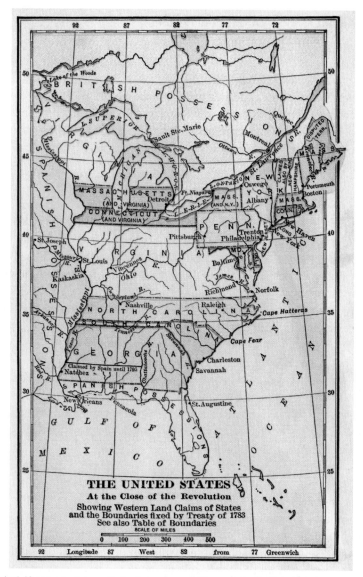

The original 13 states varied greatly in size and population and also in their histories, economies, and in some cases even their religious traditions. Such differences were a source of conflict at the constitutional convention held in Philadelphia in the summer of 1787. (North Wind Picture Archives/ Alamy Stock Photo)

(two) from each state. This compromise was critical. The small states would have refused to join a union in which their vote was always weaker than that of large states, a fact reflected in Article V of the Constitution: "No state, without its consent, shall be deprived of its equal suffrage in the Senate."

The Three-Fifths Compromise:
Issues of Trade and Slavery

Conflict between small-state and large-state delegates was not the only source of division at the Constitutional Convention. Delegates from the North and the South also clashed.

Southern delegates worried that the North, which included more states and had a larger population, would use its numerical majority in the House and Senate to enact tax policies harmful to the South. The North had most of the nation's manufacturing firms and if Congress sought to protect them by placing a heavy tax (tariff) on manufactured goods imported from Europe, the higher cost of these imports would be borne largely by the South, which depended more heavily on imported goods. If Congress also imposed a heavy tariff on the export of agricultural goods, which would make them more expensive and therefore less attractive to foreign buyers, the South would again bear most of the tax burden because it provided the bulk of the agricultural goods shipped abroad, primarily cotton and tobacco. That dispute was resolved when the delegates agreed to grant Congress the power to tax imports while denying it the power to tax exports.

Conflict between northern and southern delegates over the issue of enslaved people took longer to resolve. Southern delegates were concerned that northern representatives in Congress would tax or even bar the importation of enslaved people. A decade earlier, at the insistence of southern states, a statement critical of slavery had been deleted from Jefferson's initial draft of the Declaration of Independence, and southern delegates to the Philadelphia convention were determined to prevent northerners from using the new constitution as a way to end slavery.

After extended debate, a compromise was reached on the trade of enslaved people. Congress would be prohibited from ending it before 1808, which would give southern states two decades to increase the number of people held in involuntary bondage.

A second issue of slavery was the question of how enslaved people would be counted for the purposes of apportioning taxes and seats in the U.S. House of Representatives. Northern delegates had argued against the counting of enslaved people because they did not have legal rights. Southern delegates wanted to count them as full persons in apportioning House seats (which would have the effect of increasing the number of southern House members) and to count them as nonpersons in apportioning taxes (which would have the effect of decreasing federal taxes on the southern states). The delegates finally settled on the infamous **Three-Fifths Compromise**. For purposes of both apportionment and taxation, each enslaved person would be counted as three-fifths of a person, which was the ratio necessary to give the southern states nearly half of the House seats. If enslaved persons had not been counted at all, the southern states would have had only about a third of the seats.

These compromises have led critics to claim that the framers of the Constitution were proponents of institutionalized slavery. Some delegates were ardent slave holders, but many delegates were deeply troubled by slavery, recognizing the stark contrast between enslaved people and the nation's professed commitment to liberty and equality. "It is inconsistent with the principles of the Revolution," said Maryland's Luther Martin.[7] Benjamin Franklin and Alexander Hamilton were among the delegates who belonged to anti-slavery organizations.

Nevertheless, the southern states' dependence on enslaved Blacks was a reality that had to be confronted if there was to be a union of the states. The northern states had few enslaved Blacks, whereas the South's economy was based on slavery (see Figure 2-1). John Rutledge of South Carolina asked during

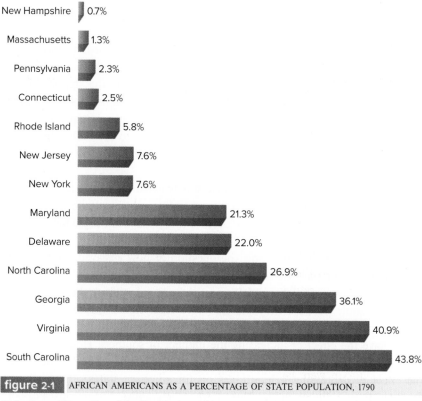

figure 2-1   AFRICAN AMERICANS AS A PERCENTAGE OF STATE POPULATION, 1790

At the time of the writing of the Constitution, African Americans (most of whom were slaves) were concentrated in the southern states. (*Source:* U.S. Census Bureau.)

the convention debate whether the North regarded southerners as "fools." Southern delegates declared that their states would form a separate union rather than join one that banned the institution of slavery.

Defining the Office of the President

The compromises over slavery and the structure of the Congress took up most of the four months that the convention was in session. Some of the other issues were subject to remarkably little debate. Decisions on the structure of the federal judiciary and bureaucracy, for example, were largely delegated to Congress.

The presidency was an exception. Although the delegates generally agreed on the powers of the presidency, they differed on its structure and method of selection. The delegates briefly considered but then abandoned the idea of multiple executives, concluding that executive power should be entrusted to a single individual to avoid the paralysis and in-fighting that could ensue if the presidency was divided. But it took more than 60 votes for the delegates to reach an agreement on how the president would be chosen, Along the way, proposals to have the president elected directly by the people, by a vote of Congress, or by the state legislatures were defeated. The delegates finally chose to have the president selected by the votes of electors (a process that came to be known as the *Electoral College*). Each state would have the same number of **electoral votes** as it had members in Congress and could pick its electors by a method of its choosing.

RATIFICATION OF THE CONSTITUTION

In authorizing the Philadelphia convention, Congress had stated that proposed changes in the Articles of Confederation would have to be "agreed to in Congress" and then "confirmed by [all] the states." Recognizing that one or more states would likely reject the Constitution, the delegates ignored Congress's instructions and established their own ratification process. The document was to be submitted to the states, where it would become law if approved by at least nine states in ratifying conventions of popularly elected delegates.

The Ratification Debate

The debate over ratification was heated. The **Anti-Federalists** (as opponents of the Constitution were labeled) raised objections that still echo in American politics. They claimed that the proposed national government would be too powerful and would threaten the liberty of the states and the people. Many Americans had an innate distrust of centralized power and worried that liberty could be eclipsed as easily by a distant American government as it had been by the British king. The Anti-Federalists acknowledged the need for more economic cooperation between the states and for a stronger common defense but argued these goals could be accomplished by revising the Articles of Confederation to give Congress more authority in these areas.

The Anti-Federalists also feared that the national government would be dominated by a political elite. They admired state governments for having legislatures whose members had local roots. New York's Melancton Smith argued that such representatives were "more competent" than "those of a superior class" who didn't understand the lives of ordinary people. Smith claimed that the new government would "fall into the hands of the few and the great. This will be a government of repression."[8]

The presidency was another source of contention. The office of chief executive did not exist under the Articles of Confederation, and some worried that it would degenerate into an American monarchy.

The **Federalists** (as the Constitution's supporters called themselves) responded with a strong case of their own. Their arguments were set forth primarily by James Madison and Alexander Hamilton, who along with John Jay, wrote a series of essays (*The Federalist Papers*) that were published in a New York City newspaper under the pen name Publius. Madison and Hamilton argued that the government of the Constitution would have the power required to forge a secure and prosperous union but not be so powerful as to endanger the states or personal liberty. In *Federalist* Nos. 47 through 51, for example, Madison explained how the separation of national institutions was designed to control the power of the federal government. (The Federalist and Anti-Federalist arguments are discussed further in Chapter 3.)

Demand for a Bill of Rights

One of the Anti-Federalist arguments against the Constitution resonated so strongly that it led to a change in the Constitution. The original Constitution did not contain a bill of rights. Did its absence indicate that the central government would be free to define for itself what the people's rights would be? Patrick Henry was outraged at the omission, saying, "The necessity of a Bill of Rights appears to be greater in this government than ever it was in any government before."

Although the delegates to the Philadelphia convention had discussed the possibility of placing a list of individual rights in the Constitution, they ultimately decided that such a list was unnecessary because the Constitution did not give the proposed federal government the power to deprive people of their rights. "Why declare things that shall not be done," Hamilton said, "when there is no power to do [them]?" The delegates also believed that a

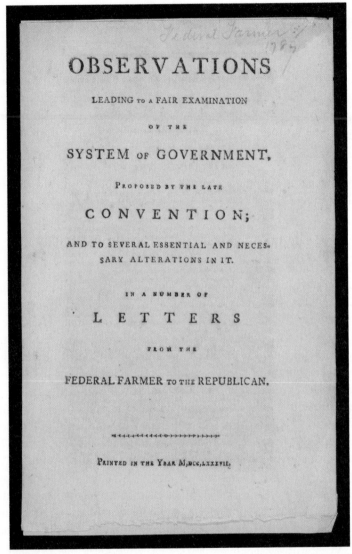

The power of ideas is often underestimated but was on full display during the debate over ratification of the Constitution. In a series of essays that came to be known as *The Federalist Papers*, James Madison, Alexander Hamilton, and John Jay argued in favor of the proposed Constitution. The Anti-Federalists also had their essayists. One of the most prominent wrote under the name "Federal Farmer." It is generally believed that the writer was Virginia's Richard Henry Lee. He attacked the Constitution as having "very little democracy in it." (Library of Congress, Rare Book and Special Collections Division)

bill of rights was undesirable because the government might disregard a right that was inadvertently left off the list or that might emerge in the future. These arguments failed to convince those who wanted a bill of rights. They worried that the Constitution, unlike the Articles of Confederation, granted

the federal government direct authority over individual citizens and yet did not contain a list of their rights.

The demand for a bill of rights led to its addition to the Constitution. Madison introduced a series of amendments during the First Congress, 10 of which were quickly ratified by the states. Called the **Bill of Rights**, the 10 amendments include free-expression rights such as freedom of speech and fair-trial protections such as the right to an attorney. (Individual rights are discussed in Chapter 4.)

The Vote on Ratification

Whether the ratification debate changed many minds is unclear. Historical evidence suggests that most Americans opposed the Constitution's ratification, preferring the state-centered government established by the Articles. But their voice in the state-ratifying conventions was smaller than that of wealthier interests, which favored the change. The pro-ratification forces were also strengthened by the assumption that George Washington, who had presided over the Philadelphia convention and was the country's most trusted leader, would become the first president. In the view of many historians, this assumption and the promise of a Bill of Rights tipped the balance in favor of ratification.

Delaware was the first state to ratify the Constitution, and Connecticut, Georgia, and New Jersey soon followed, an indication that the Great Compromise had satisfied some of the small states. In the early summer of 1788, New Hampshire became the ninth state to ratify. The Constitution was law. But neither Virginia nor New York had ratified it, and a stable union without these two states was almost unthinkable. As large in area as many European countries, Virginia and New York conceivably could have survived as independent nations. In fact, they nearly did choose separate paths. In both states, the Constitution passed only after the Federalists committed to amending it to include a bill of rights.

The ratifying vote revealed the wisdom of the framers' decision to ignore Congress's instructions in establishing the ratification process. If approval of all the states had been required, the Constitution would not have been ratified. North Carolina and Rhode Island were strongly opposed to the new arrangement and did not ratify the Constitution until the other 11 states had begun the process of forming the new government (see "Party Polarization: Fight over the Ratification of the Constitution").

PARTY POLARIZATION	Conflicting Ideas

Fight over the Ratification of the Constitution

The intense partisanship that typifies today's politics also marked the debate over the Constitution's ratification. Angry exchanges took place between proponents of a stronger national government and those arguing for a state-centered union. Although the pro-Constitution side won easily in most states, the balloting in New York and Virginia was so close that it took the promise of a bill of rights to secure the votes for ratification. North Carolina and Rhode Island (the latter had refused even to send delegates to the Philadelphia convention) initially rejected the Constitution, ratifying it only after the other states began to form a union without them. Here is the breakdown of the ratifying vote in each state:

State	Date of Ratification	Vote Totals
Delaware	December 7, 1787	30 for, 0 against
Pennsylvania	December 12, 1787	46 for, 23 against
New Jersey	December 18, 1787	38 for, 0 against
Georgia	January 2, 1788	26 for, 0 against
Connecticut	January 9, 1788	128 for, 40 against
Massachusetts	February 6, 1788	187 for, 168 against
Maryland	April 28, 1788	63 for, 11 against
South Carolina	May 23, 1788	149 for, 73 against
New Hampshire	June 21, 1788	57 for, 47 against
Virginia	June 25, 1788	89 for, 79 against
New York	July 26, 1788	30 for, 27 against
North Carolina	November 21, 1789	194 for, 77 against
Rhode Island	May 29, 1790	34 for, 32 against

Q: If historians are correct in concluding that the American public as a whole was evenly split over ratification of the Constitution, why might the pro-Constitution side have prevailed in so many states and so easily in some states?
A: State and local governments were in charge of selecting the delegates to the state ratifying conventions. For the most part, they chose prominent leaders to serve as delegates, with the result that wealthy merchants, large landholders, and top public officials dominated the conventions. They were more in favor of the Constitution than were small farmers, craftspeople, and shopkeepers.

PROTECTING LIBERTY: LIMITED GOVERNMENT

The writers of the Constitution had four major goals (see Table 2-1). One goal was to create a national government strong enough to meet the nation's needs, particularly in the areas of defense and commerce. A second was to preserve the states as governing entities through a system of government (federalism) that divided power between the national government and the states. These goals are discussed in Chapter 3.

The framers' other two goals were, first, to establish a national government that was restricted in its lawful uses of power (limited government) and, second, to create a national government that gave the people a voice in governing (representative government). These goals are the focus of the rest of this chapter.

Grants and Denials of Power

The framers of the Constitution sought to create a national government with the power to meet the nation's needs but not at the expense of liberty. History had taught them to mistrust an unrestrained majority rule. In times of stress or danger, popular majorities had often acted without regard for the law or the rights of others.

The preservation of **liberty**—the principle that people should be free from oppressive government—preoccupied the framers. Americans enjoyed an unparalleled level of personal freedom as a result of their open society, and the framers were determined that it not be sacrificed to either European-style monarchy or mob-driven democracy.

Government's threat to liberty was inherent in its coercive power. Government's unique feature is that it alone can legally arrest, imprison, or even kill people who violate its directives. Force is not the only basis by which

table 2-1	PRIMARY GOALS OF THE FRAMERS OF THE CONSTITUTION

1. *Strong government:* A government strong enough to meet the nation's needs—an objective sought through substantial grants of power to the federal government in areas such as defense and commerce
2. *Federal government:* A government that would not threaten the existence of the separate states—an objective sought through federalism and through a Congress tied to the states through elections
3. *Limited government:* A government that would not threaten liberty—an objective sought through an elaborate system of checks and balances
4. *Representative government:* A government based on popular consent—an objective sought through provisions for the direct and indirect elections of public officials

government maintains order but, without it, lawless individuals would prey on innocent people. The dilemma is that government itself can use force to intimidate or brutalize its opponents. "It is a melancholy reflection," James Madison wrote to Thomas Jefferson shortly after the Constitution's ratification, "that liberty should be equally exposed to danger whether the government has too much or too little power."[9]

The framers chose to limit the national government in part by confining its authority to constitutional **grants of power** (see Table 2-2). Congress's lawmaking powers are specifically listed in Article I, Section 8, of the Constitution. Seventeen in number, these listed powers include the powers to tax, establish an army and navy, declare war, regulate commerce among the states, create a national currency, and borrow money. Powers *not* granted to the government by the Constitution are in theory denied to it. In a period when other governments had unrestricted powers, this limitation was remarkable.

The framers also used **denials of power** (Table 2-2) as a means to limit government, prohibiting certain practices that European rulers used to oppress their political opponents. The French king, for example, could imprison a subject without charge for an indefinite period. The U.S. Constitution prohibits such action. Citizens have the right to be brought before a judge under a writ of habeas corpus for a determination of the legality of keeping them in jail. The Constitution also forbids Congress and the states from passing ex post facto laws, under which citizens can be prosecuted for acts that were legal at the time they were committed. When it was added to the Constitution, the Bill of Rights expanded the list of governmental restraints.

table 2-2	CONSTITUTIONAL PROVISIONS FOR LIMITED GOVERNMENT
Mechanism	**Purpose**
Grants of power	Powers granted to the national government; accordingly, powers not granted it are denied it
Denials of power	Powers expressly denied to the national and state governments by the Constitution
Separation of power	Division of national government's power among three power-sharing branches, each of which acts as a check on the powers of the other two
Bill of Rights	First 10 amendments to Constitution, which list individual rights that national government cannot abridge or deny
Elections	Power of voters to remove officials from office

Although not strictly a further denial of power, the framers made the Constitution difficult to amend, thereby making it hard for those in office to increase their power by changing the rules. An amendment could be proposed only by a two-thirds majority in both chambers of Congress or by a national constitutional convention called by two-thirds of the state legislatures. A proposed amendment would then become law only if ratified by three-fourths of state legislatures or state conventions.[10] The amending process has worked as the framers intended. Aside from the 10 amendments enacted as the Bill of Rights soon after the Constitution was ratified, only 17 amendments have been ratified during the nearly 240 years of the Constitution's existence.

Separated Institutions Sharing Power: Checks and Balances

Although the framers believed that grants and denials of power could act as controls on government, they had no illusion that written words alone were enough. As a consequence, they sought to limit government by dividing its powers among separate branches.[11]

Decades earlier, French theorist Montesquieu had argued that the power of government could be controlled by dividing it among separate branches rather than investing it entirely in a single individual or institution. His concept of a **separation of powers** (Table 2-2) was widely admired in America, and, when the states drafted new constitutions after the start of the Revolutionary War, they built their governments around the ideal. Pennsylvania was an exception, and its experience only seemed to prove the need for separated powers. Unrestrained by an independent judiciary or executive, Pennsylvania's all-powerful legislature ignored basic rights and freedoms: Quakers were disenfranchised for their religious beliefs, conscientious objectors to the Revolutionary War were prosecuted, and the right of trial by jury was eliminated.

In *Federalist* No. 10, Madison asked why governments often act according to the interests of overbearing majorities rather than according to principles of justice. He attributed the problem to "the mischiefs of faction." People, he argued, are divided into opposing religious, geographic, ethnic, economic, and other factions. These divisions are natural and desirable in that free people have a right to their personal opinions and interests. However, if a faction gains full power, it will seek to use the government to advance itself at the expense of all others. (*Federalist* No. 10 is widely regarded as the finest political essay ever written by an American.)

Out of their concern with unchecked power came the framers' special contribution to the doctrine of the separation of powers. Rather than dividing authority strictly between the three branches of government, as Montesquieu had proposed, they overlapped the branches' power so that each branch could

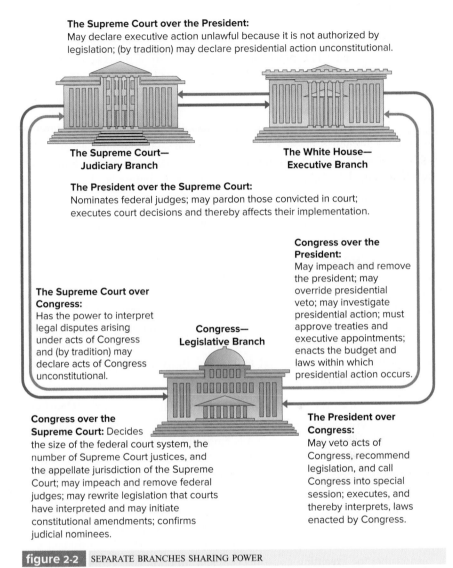

The Supreme Court over the President:
May declare executive action unlawful because it is not authorized by legislation; (by tradition) may declare presidential action unconstitutional.

The Supreme Court—
Judiciary Branch

The White House—
Executive Branch

The President over the Supreme Court:
Nominates federal judges; may pardon those convicted in court; executes court decisions and thereby affects their implementation.

Congress over the President:
May impeach and remove the president; may override presidential veto; may investigate presidential action; must approve treaties and executive appointments; enacts the budget and laws within which presidential action occurs.

The Supreme Court over Congress:
Has the power to interpret legal disputes arising under acts of Congress and (by tradition) may declare acts of Congress unconstitutional.

Congress—
Legislative Branch

Congress over the Supreme Court: Decides the size of the federal court system, the number of Supreme Court justices, and the appellate jurisdiction of the Supreme Court; may impeach and remove federal judges; may rewrite legislation that courts have interpreted and may initiate constitutional amendments; confirms judicial nominees.

The President over Congress:
May veto acts of Congress, recommend legislation, and call Congress into special session; executes, and thereby interprets, laws enacted by Congress.

figure 2-2   SEPARATE BRANCHES SHARING POWER

The U.S. Constitution separates power among the legislative, executive, and judicial branches but assigns each branch part of the power of the other two branches so that it can act as a check on their power. (*Source:* Richard Neustadt, *Presidential Power,* New York: Macmillan, 1986, 33.)

check the power of the others.[12] Political scientist Richard Neustadt described the framers' governing system as **separated institutions sharing power**.[13] The legislative, executive, and judicial branches share power in a way that creates a system of **checks and balances** (see Figure 2-2). Each branch checks the others' powers and balances their powers with powers of its own.

Shared Legislative Powers   Under the Constitution, Congress has legislative authority, but that power is partly shared with the other branches and thus is checked by them. The president can veto acts of Congress, recommend legislation, and call special sessions of Congress. The president also has the power to execute—and thereby interpret—the laws that Congress makes.

The Supreme Court has the power to interpret acts of Congress that are disputed in legal cases. The Court also has the power to declare laws of Congress void when it finds that they violate the Constitution.

Within Congress, there is a further check on legislative power: For legislation to be passed, a majority in each chamber of Congress is required. Thus, the Senate and the House of Representatives can block each other from acting.

Shared Executive Powers   Executive power is vested in the president but is constrained by legislative and judicial checks. The president's power to make treaties and appoint high-ranking officials, for example, is subject to Senate approval. Congress also has the power to impeach and remove the president from office. In practical terms, Congress's greatest checks on executive action are its lawmaking and appropriations powers. The executive branch cannot act without laws that authorize its activities or without the money that pays for them.

The judiciary's major check on the presidency is its power to declare an action unlawful because it is not authorized by the laws that the executive claims to be implementing.

Shared Judicial Powers   Judicial power rests with the Supreme Court and with lower federal courts, which are subject to checks by the other branches of the federal government. Congress is empowered to establish the size of the federal court system, restrict the Supreme Court's appellate jurisdiction in some circumstances, and impeach and remove federal judges from office. Congress also can rewrite legislation that the courts have misinterpreted and initiate amendments when it disagrees with court rulings on constitutional issues.

The president has the power to appoint federal judges with the consent of the Senate and to pardon persons convicted in the courts. The president also is responsible for executing court decisions, a function that provides opportunities to influence the way rulings are carried out.

PROVIDING FOR REPRESENTATIVE GOVERNMENT

The framers believed that citizens required a voice in their governing but worried that the majority could become inflamed by a passionate issue or fiery demagogue and trample on the rights of the minority. The framers' fear of **tyranny of the majority** was not unfounded. In 1786, debtors had gained control of Rhode Island's legislature and made paper money a legal means of paying

C A S E S T U D Y	Politics in Action

Assault on the Capitol

For the writers of the Constitution, the great danger of democracy was that it could degenerate into tyranny. They cited examples from Ancient Greece as well as a more recent development in Rhode Island where an uncontrolled mob had trampled on property rights.

Over the course of the nation's history, the framers' concern with mob rule faded in Americans' minds. There was a sense that irrational mobs were a thing of the past. That illusion was shattered on January 6, 2021, when protesters gathered at the U.S. Capitol and then began fighting with police, breaking through one barrier and then three more before reaching the Capitol steps. They fought their way up the steps and then proceeded to shatter windows and pry open doors to make their way into the building. Some employed clubs, poles, and pepper spray as they battled with police, gradually forcing their way into the House chamber, where they mounted the dais, chanting their demands. The mob in the Senate chamber rifled through senators' desks and destroyed their papers.

The House and Senate were scheduled to meet that day to formally certify the results of the 2020 presidential election. The rioters failed in

Sebastian Portillo/Shutterstock

Continued

their attempt to stop them from doing so. Five people died from the assault: a member of the Capitol police who was beaten to death, a protestor who was shot, another who was crushed by the mob, one from a heart attack, and one from a stroke. Dozens were injured. Not since a British army invaded Washington in 1814 and set fire to the Capitol and White House had America witnessed anything comparable.

Q: Who do you hold responsible for the assault on the Capitol? Do you think it was truly a rare event or, given the intensity of today's partisan politics, could something like it happen again in the near future?

ASK YOURSELF: What was on the minds of the rioters when they stormed the Capitol? Where were they getting their information? Given that others held the same opinion about the election as the rioters, but acted peacefully, do the rioters bear full responsibility for their actions? Do you think the criminal charges that were filed against some of them will deter others from copying what they did? Do you think violent protest is ever justified? Was it justified in this case?

debts, even though contracts called for payment in gold. Creditors were then hunted down and held captive in public places so that debtors could come and pay them in full with worthless paper money. A Boston newspaper wrote that Rhode Island ought to be renamed Rogue Island.

Democracy Versus Republic

No form of representative government can eliminate the possibility of majority tyranny, but the framers believed that the risk would be greatly reduced by creating a republican form of government.[14] Today, the terms *democracy* and *republic* are used interchangeably to refer to a system of government in which political power rests with the people through their ability to choose representatives in free and fair elections. To the writers of the Constitution, however, a democracy and a republic were different forms of government.

The framers distinguished between forms of democracy. A **direct democracy**, where the people meet to vote directly on policy issues, was impractical at the national level. A **representative democracy**, where the people's elected delegates decide policy issues, was feasible but risky if the representatives had full power. The danger was that they might choose to trample on the rights and interests of the minority. By the term **republic**, the framers meant a government where there are constitutional and institutional limits on the majority's power. The majority would have power through its representatives, but it would be exercised through institutions designed to check that power and be protected by laws guaranteeing the rights of the minority.[15]

Limited Popular Rule

The framers saw the separation of powers and other constitutional restraints on national power as hallmarks of a republican form of government. In addition, they devised a system of representation that placed most federal officials beyond the direct control of the voters (see Table 2-3).

The House of Representatives was the only institution that would be based on direct popular election—its members would be elected to serve for two years by a vote of the people. Frequent and direct election of House members was intended to make government responsive to the concerns of popular majorities.

U.S. senators would be appointed by the legislatures of the states they represented. Because state legislators were popularly elected, the people would be choosing their senators indirectly. Every two years, a third of the senators would be appointed to 6-year terms. The Senate, by virtue of the less frequent and indirect election of its members, was expected to be less responsive to popular pressure and thereby serve as a check on the House.

The president would also be chosen indirectly. Electors picked by the states and equal in number to each state's representatives in Congress would choose the president (the so-called **Electoral College**), who would serve for four years and be eligible for reelection.

The framers decided that federal judges and justices would be appointed rather than elected. They would be nominated by the president and confirmed if approved by a Senate majority. Once confirmed, they would "hold their offices during good behavior." In effect, they would be allowed to hold office for life unless they committed a crime or otherwise disgraced their office. The

table 2-3	METHODS OF CHOOSING FEDERAL OFFICIALS	
Office	**Method of Selection**	**Term of Service**
President	Electoral College	4 years
U.S. senator	State legislature, changed in 1913 to popular election	6 years (one-third of senators' terms expire every 2 years)
U.S. representative	Popular election	2 years
Federal judge	Nominated by president, approved by Senate	Indefinite (subject to "good behavior")

judiciary was an unelected institution that would uphold the rule of law and serve as a check on the elected branches of government.[16]

These different methods of selecting national officeholders would not prevent a determined majority from achieving unchecked power, but control could not be quickly acquired. Unlike the House of Representatives, institutions such as the Senate, presidency, and judiciary would not yield to an impassioned majority in a single election. The delay would reduce the chance that government would degenerate into mob rule driven by momentary passions.

Altering the Constitution: More Power to the People

The framers' conception of representative government was at odds with what many Americans in 1787 expected.[17] Self-government was the promise that had led tens of thousands of ordinary farmers, merchants, and tradesmen to risk their lives fighting the British in the American Revolution. The state governments had kept that promise. Every state but South Carolina held annual legislative elections, and several states also chose their governors through direct annual elections.

Not long after the ratification of the Constitution, Americans began to challenge the Constitution's restrictions on majority rule, an effort that would extend into the early 1900s.

Jeffersonian Democracy: A Revolution of the Spirit   Thomas Jefferson was among the prominent Americans who questioned the Constitution's limited provisions for self-government. In a letter to Madison, he objected to its system of representation, voicing the Anti-Federalists' fear that federal officials would lose touch with the people and ignore their interests. His concern intensified when John Adams became president after Washington's retirement. Under Adams, the national government increasingly favored the nation's wealthy interests. Adams publicly stated that the Constitution was designed for a governing elite and hinted that he might use force to suppress dissent.[18] Jefferson asked whether Adams, with the aid of the army, intended to deprive ordinary people of their rights. Jefferson challenged Adams in the next presidential election and, upon defeating him, hailed his victory as the "Revolution of 1800."

Although Jefferson was a champion of the common people, he had no clear vision of how a popular government might work in practice. He saw Congress, not the presidency, as the people's institution.[19] He also had no illusions about the ability of a largely uneducated population to play a substantial governing role and feared what would happen if the people were incited to rise up against the rich. Jeffersonian democracy was mostly a revolution of the spirit. Jefferson taught Americans to look at national institutions as belonging to all, not just to the privileged few.[20]

Jacksonian Democracy: Linking the People and the Presidency   Not until the election of Andrew Jackson in 1828 did the nation have a president who was willing to involve the public more fully in government. Jackson carried out the constitutional revolution that Jeffersonian democracy had foreshadowed.

Jackson believed that the president was the only official who could legitimately claim to represent the people as a whole. Unlike members of Congress, who were elected from separate states and districts, the president was chosen by the full country. Yet the president's claim to popular leadership was weakened by the fact that the president was chosen by electors rather than by a direct vote of the people. To tie the presidency more closely to the people, Jackson pressured Congress for a constitutional amendment that would authorize the president's election by popular vote. Failing in that effort, he urged the states to award their electoral votes to the candidate who won the state's popular vote. Soon thereafter, nearly all states adopted this method. This arrangement, still in effect, places the selection of the president in the voters' hands in most elections. The candidate who gets the most popular votes nationally is also likely to finish first in enough states to win a majority of the electoral votes. Since Jackson's time, all but four candidates—Rutherford B. Hayes in 1876, Benjamin Harrison in 1888, George W. Bush in 2000, and Donald Trump in 2016—have won the presidency after winning the popular vote (see "How the 50 States Differ").

HOW THE 50 STATES DIFFER

POLITICAL THINKING THROUGH COMPARISONS

Electing the President

The Constitution assigns the election of the president to electors chosen by the states, with each state having electors equal in number to its U.S. senators and representatives. Voters have an indirect voice in the selection. Every state, except for Maine and Nebraska, awards all of its electoral votes to the candidate who wins the state's popular vote—the so-called **unit rule**. This arrangement usually results in the election of the candidate who wins the national popular vote, but not always. In 2016, although Donald Trump lost the national popular vote to Hillary Clinton by almost 3 million votes, he prevailed in the Electoral College by winning in Pennsylvania, Michigan, and Wisconsin by a total of fewer than 100,000 votes, giving him a 304–227

Continued

edge in electoral votes. Trump nearly repeated the feat in the 2020 presidential election despite losing the national popular vote to Job Biden by 7 million votes. A switch of fewer than 100,000 votes in Georgia, Nebraska, Pennsylvania, and Wisconsin would have given Trump the victory.

The accompanying map shows whether a state was won by Biden or Trump in the 2020 election. The number of electoral votes each state will have in the 2024 election is also shown. As a result of the reapportionment that occurred after the 2020 census, a few states because of population change either gained (as with Texas) or lost (as with California) a House seat(s), which changed the number of electoral votes they will have in 2024 as compared with 2020.

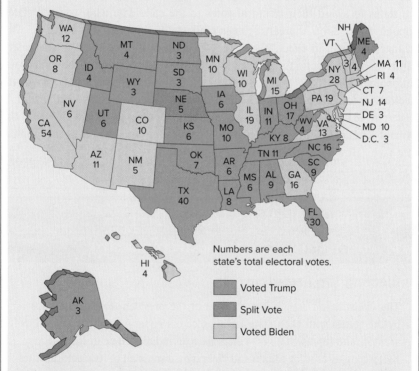

Numbers are each state's total electoral votes.

▨ Voted Trump

▨ Split Vote

▢ Voted Biden

Q: What might justify keeping the Electoral College system? Would you favor instead a system where the president is chosen by direct vote of the people?

Progressive Movement: Power to the People   The Progressive Era of the early 1900s brought another wave of democratic reforms. The Progressives sought to weaken the influence of large corporations and political party bosses by placing power more directly in the hands of voters.[21] Progressive reforms at the state and local levels included the *initiative*. In some states, if citizens gather enough signatures on a petition for a proposed change in the law, the proposal is placed on the ballot where it becomes law if a majority of voters support it.

A second change brought about by the Progressive movement was the **primary election** (also called the *direct primary*), which gives ordinary voters the power to select party nominees. By 1920, nearly all states had adopted the primary election as the means of choosing nominees for the Senate and House of Representatives. Some states also used the primary election method to elect their delegates to the national conventions that choose the parties' presidential nominees. Such a process is called an *indirect primary* because the voters are not choosing the nominees directly (as they do in House and Senate races) but rather are choosing delegates who in turn select the presidential nominees.

The Progressive movement also led to the direct election of U.S. senators who before the ratification of the Seventeenth Amendment in 1913 were chosen by state legislatures and were widely perceived as tools of big business (the Senate was nicknamed the "Millionaires' Club"). Senators who stood to lose their seats in a direct popular election had blocked earlier attempts to amend the Constitution. That opposition broke down largely because of two developments. One was the public outrage that resulted when it was revealed several senators owed their seats to corporate bribes. The other was the use in some states of primary elections to choose the Senate nominees, which the legislatures in these states then used to pick their senators. These senators had popular support and voted in favor of changing the Constitution to allow for direct Senate elections.

The Progressive Era spawned attacks on the framers. A prominent critic was historian Charles S. Beard. In *An Economic Interpretation of the Constitution*, Beard argued that the Constitution's elaborate system of institutions was designed to protect the wealthy.[22] Beard noted that the framers were nearly all men of wealth and that property interests were often discussed during the debate at the Philadelphia convention. Beard's thesis has some truth to it, but the framers were not opposed to representative government. Convinced that unchecked majority rule could devolve into tyranny, they wanted to balance the need for self-government with the need for limited government. They sought to create institutions that were responsive to majority opinion without being captive to it.

CONSTITUTIONAL DEMOCRACY TODAY

The type of government created in the United States in 1787 is accurately described as a **constitutional democratic republic**. It is constitutional in its requirement that power gained through elections be exercised in accordance with law and with due respect for individual rights; democratic in its provisions for majority influence through elections; and a republic in its multiple institutions (presidency, Congress, and the courts), each of which checks the power of the others.[23]

By some standards, the American system of today is a model of *representative government.*[24] The United States schedules the election of its larger legislative chamber (the House of Representatives) and its chief executive more frequently than does any other democracy. In addition, it is the only major democracy to rely extensively on primary elections rather than party organizations for the selection of party nominees. The principle of direct popular election to office, which the writers of the Constitution regarded as a method to be used sparingly, has been extended further in the United States than anywhere else.

CITIZEN ACTION!
SELF-GOVERNMENT

The United States holds more elections for more offices than does any other democracy, which gives citizens abundant opportunities to participate. Why not you? Consider volunteering for the campaign of a candidate who represents your values.

By other standards, however, the U.S. system is less democratic than that of some democracies. In the United States, popular majorities must work against the barriers to power devised by the framers—divided branches, staggered terms of office, and separate constituencies. In fact, the link between an electoral majority and a governing majority is less direct in the American system than in many democratic systems. In Europe's parliamentary democracies, for example, legislative and executive power is not divided, is not subject to close check by the judiciary, and is acquired through the winning of a legislative majority in a single national election. The framers' vision was a different one, dominated by a concern with liberty and therefore with placing controls on political power. It was a response to the experiences they brought with them to Philadelphia in the summer of 1787.

SUMMARY

The Constitution of the United States is a reflection of the colonial and revolutionary experiences of the early Americans. Freedom from abusive government was a reason for the colonies' revolt against British rule, but the English tradition also provided ideas about government, power, and freedom that were expressed in the Constitution and, earlier, in the Declaration of Independence.

The first American constitution was the Articles of Confederation, which created a weak national government dependent on the states. It proved to be too weak to meet the nation's governing needs, which led to the writing of the U.S. Constitution. Although the Constitution established a stronger national government, it also placed limits on that government to prevent it from threatening Americans' freedom. To this end, they confined the national government to expressly granted powers and denied it certain specific powers. Other prohibitions on government were later added to the Constitution in the form of the Bill of Rights. The most substantial constitutional provision for limited government, however, was a separation of powers among the three branches. The powers given to each branch enable it to act as a check on the exercise of power by the other two.

The framers of the Constitution, respecting the idea of self-government but distrusting popular majorities, devised a system of representative government that they felt would temper popular opinion and slow its momentum so that the public's "true interest" (which includes a regard for the rights and interests of the minority) would guide public policy. Different methods were advanced for selecting the president, the members of the House and the Senate, and federal judges as a means of protecting against the possibility of majority tyranny.

Since the adoption of the Constitution, the public has gradually assumed more direct control of its representatives, particularly through measures that affect the way officeholders are chosen. Presidential popular voting (linked to the Electoral College), direct election of senators, and primary elections are among the devices aimed at empowering the voters. These developments are rooted in the idea, deeply held by ordinary Americans, that the people must have substantial influence over their representatives if the government is to serve their interests.

CRITICAL THINKING ZONE

KEY TERMS

Anti-Federalists (*p. 35*)

Bill of Rights (*p. 38*)

checks and balances (*p. 43*)

constitution (*p. 29*)

constitutional democratic republic (*p. 51*)

denials of power (*p. 41*)

direct democracy (*p. 46*)

Electoral College (*p. 47*)

electoral votes (*p. 35*)

Federalists (*p. 36*)

grants of power (*p. 41*)

Great Compromise (*p. 31*)

inalienable (natural) rights (*p. 26*)

liberty (*p. 40*)

limited government (*p. 24*)

New Jersey Plan (*p. 31*)

primary election (direct primary) (*p. 51*)

representative democracy (*p. 46*)

representative government (*p. 24*)

republic (*p. 46*)

separated institutions sharing power (*p. 43*)

separation of powers (*p. 42*)

social contract (*p. 26*)

Three-Fifths Compromise (*p. 33*)

tyranny of the majority (*p. 44*)

unit rule (*p. 49*)

Virginia Plan (*p. 31*)

APPLYING THE ELEMENTS OF CRITICAL THINKING

Conceptualizing: Define the concept of judicial review. How does a court decision involving judicial review differ from an ordinary court decision, such as a ruling in a case involving robbery?

Synthesizing: Contrast the original system for electing federal officials with the system of today, noting in each case how voters acquired a more direct voice in the election process than was originally the case.

Analyzing: Why is it more accurate to say that the United States has a system of "separated institutions sharing power" rather than a system of "separated powers"? Provide examples of how shared power can act to check and balance the power of each institution.

OF POSSIBLE INTEREST

A Book Worth Reading: Danielle Allen, *Our Declaration* (New York: Liveright, 2014). An award-winning book that claims the Declaration of Independence is a powerful argument for political equality.

A Website Worth Visiting: www.archives.gov The National Archives is the repository of America's important documents. Its site includes an in-depth history of the writing of the Declaration of Independence.

3
CHAPTER

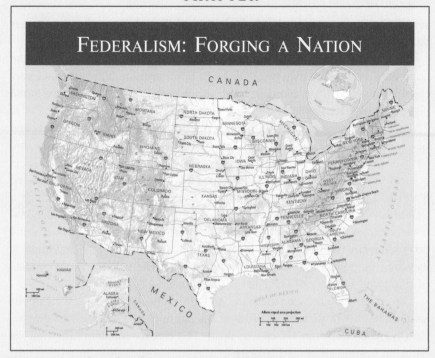

National Atlas of the United States/U.S. Geological Survey/U.S. Department of the Interior

66 The question of the relation of the states to the federal government is the cardinal question of our Constitutional system. It cannot be settled by the opinion of one generation, because it is a question of growth, and each successive stage of our political and economic development gives it a new aspect, makes it a new question. 99

WOODROW WILSON[1]

Ten months into his presidency, Joe Biden announced a policy aimed at curbing the spread of COVID-19. It would require companies with more than 100 employees to require each employee to be vaccinated or wear a mask and undergo weekly testing. Issued through the Occupational Safety and Health Administration (OSHA), the policy was proposed under rules for emergency measures, which allow for fast action. A spokesperson for the Biden administration said that "This is a real emergency. . . . Any delay would cause thousands of deaths."[2]

Within two days, more than two dozen Republican-controlled states had filed suit challenging the mandate, arguing that Biden had overstepped his lawful authority and was usurping state control over health policy. In announcing Missouri's intention to sue, its attorney general said, "This mandate is unconstitutional, unlawful, and unwise." Anticipating that OSHA would issue the mandate,

55

several Republican states already had in place laws or executive orders that prohibited employers from imposing COVID-19 restrictions on their workers.[3]

The dispute quickly made its way through the federal courts, reaching the Supreme Court in less than two months. In a 6–3 decision, the Supreme Court ruled against the Biden administration, saying that OSHA did not have broad power "to regulate public health."[4]

The conflict surrounding the Biden administration's vaccine mandate is one of the thousands of disagreements over the course of American history that have hinged on whether national or state authority will prevail. Americans possess what amounts to dual citizenship. They are citizens both of the United States and of the state where they reside. The American political system is a *federal system,* in which constitutional authority is divided between a national government and state governments. Each government is assumed to derive its powers directly from the people and therefore to have sovereignty (final authority) over the policy responsibilities assigned to it. The federal system consists of states and the nation, separate yet indivisible.[5]

The relationship between the states and the nation was the most contentious issue when the Constitution was written and has remained so. One such dispute, the Civil War, nearly tore the country apart. This chapter examines federalism—its

Public health is a policy area traditionally controlled by the states. Federal policy that would have mandated vaccination to stop the spread of COVID-19 spawned protests by some Americans and legal action by state officials who claimed it infringed on their constitutional authority.
(Artur Widak/NurPhoto/Getty Images)

creation through the Constitution, its evolution during the nation's history, and its current status. The chapter's main points are as follows:

- *The power of government must be equal to its responsibilities.* The Constitution was needed because the nation's preceding system (under the Articles of Confederation) was too weak to accomplish its expected goals, particularly those of a strong defense and an integrated economy.
- *Federalism—the Constitution's division of governing authority between two levels, nation and states—was the result of political bargaining.* Federalism was not a theoretical principle, but rather a compromise made necessary in 1787 by the prior existence of the states.
- *Federalism is not a fixed principle for allocating power between the national and state governments, but rather a principle that has changed over time in response to political needs and partisan ideology.* Federalism has passed through several distinct stages in the course of the nation's history that have shifted power from the states to the national government.
- *Federal grants to state and local governments are a defining feature of contemporary federalism and have enabled the federal government to exert influence in policy areas traditionally controlled by the states.* Although these grants have become a permanent feature of federalism, the scale of the spending and the purpose of the grants are sources of partisan conflict.

FEDERALISM: NATIONAL AND STATE SOVEREIGNTY

At the time of the writing of the Constitution, some of America's top leaders were dead set against the creation of a stronger national government. When rumors began to circulate that the Philadelphia convention was devising such a government, Virginia's Patrick Henry said that he "smelt a rat." His fears were confirmed when he obtained a copy of the draft constitution. "Who authorized them," he asked, "to speak the language of 'We, the People,' instead of 'We, the States'?"

The question of "people versus states" was precipitated by the failure of the Articles of Confederation. It had created a union of the states, and they alone had authority over citizens (see Chapter 2). The national government could not tax or conscript citizens, nor could it regulate their economic activities. Its directives applied only to the states, and they often ignored them. Georgia and North Carolina, for example, contributed no money at all to the national treasury between 1781 and 1786, and the federal government had no way to force them to pay. The only feasible solution to this problem was to give the federal government direct authority over the people. If individuals are ordered

"GIVE ME LIBERTY, OR GIVE ME DEATH !"

PATRICK HENRY delivering his great speech on the Rights of the Colonies, before the Virginia Assembly.

Patrick Henry was a leading figure in the American Revolution ("Give me liberty or give me death!"). He later opposed ratification of the Constitution on grounds that the national government should be subservient to the states. (Library of Congress Prints & Photographs Division [LC-USZC2-2452])

to pay taxes, most of them will do so rather than face imprisonment or confiscation of their property.

At the same time, the writers of the Constitution wanted to preserve the states. The states had their own constitutions and a governing history extending back to the colonial era. Although their residents thought of themselves as Americans, most of them identified more strongly with their state.[6] When Virginia's George Mason said that he would never agree to a constitution that abolished the states, he was speaking for nearly all of the delegates.

These two realities—the need to preserve the states and the need for a national government with direct authority over the people—led the framers to invent an entirely new system of government. Until this point in history, **sovereignty** (supreme and final governing authority) had been regarded as indivisible. By definition, a government cannot be sovereign if it can be overruled by another government. Nevertheless, the framers divided sovereignty between the national government and the states, a system now known as **federalism**. Each level—the national government and the state governments—directly governs the residents within its assigned territory. Each level has authority that is not subject to the other's approval.

And each level is constitutionally protected. The national government cannot abolish a state, and the states cannot abolish the national government.

In 1787, nations elsewhere in the world were governed by a **unitary system**, in which sovereignty is vested solely in the national government (see "How the U.S. Differs"). Regional governments in a unitary system do not have sovereignty. They have authority only to the degree that it is granted by the

HOW THE U.S. DIFFERS

CRITICAL THINKING THROUGH COMPARISONS

Federal Versus Unitary Systems

Federalism involves the division of sovereignty between a national government and subnational (state) governments. The United States established the first federal system, and 27 countries today have one. Nearly 170 countries have instead a unitary system, which vests sovereignty entirely in the national government.

Some unitary systems grant substantial authority to their subnational governments. The United Kingdom, for example, has granted Scotland, Wales, and Northern Ireland a degree of control in specific policy areas, including education and policing, and they have been allowed to form their own legislative bodies. Federal systems also vary in the authority granted to their subnational governments. Canada's provinces, for example, have more formal authority than the American states. Unlike the states, the provinces have constitutionally designated exclusive authority in some policy areas, including hospitals, natural resources, and civil rights.

Q: What are the relative advantages of a federal system? Of a unitary system?

A: Federalism allows regional differences to be represented in policies. Nevada and Utah are clear examples. Although they adjoin, Nevada allows gambling and recreational cannabis use whereas Utah outlaws both activities. Utah is only one of two states without a state lottery. Nevada has a city, Las Vegas, whose economy is based on gambling.

An advantage of a unitary system is that citizens are more likely to have access to equal services. In America's federal system, for example, there is wide variation in per-pupil spending on public schools, which depend on local and state governments for their funding. In Europe nations' unitary systems, per-pupil spending across school districts is far more equal than it is in the United States.

national government, which can also withdraw any such grant. (This situation applies to America's local governments. They are not sovereign, but instead derive their authority from their respective state governments, which can, though it rarely happens, even choose to abolish a local unit of government.)

Federalism is also different from a **confederacy**, which was the type of government that existed under the Articles of Confederation. In a confederacy, the states alone are sovereign. They decide the authority, even the continuing existence, of the central government. Confederacies have been rare in human history, and no nation today has a confederate form of government. (Despite its name, the Confederate States of America—the South's Civil War government—had a federal constitution rather than a confederate one. Sovereignty was divided between the central and state governments.)

The federal system established in 1787 divides the responsibilities of government between the nation and the states (see Figure 3-1). The system gives states the power to address local issues in ways of their choosing; for example, they have primary responsibility for public education and police protection. The national government, by contrast, is responsible for matters of national scope, such as military defense and the currency. The national and state governments also have some concurrent powers (that is, powers exercised over the same policy areas). Each of them has, for example, the power to raise taxes and borrow money.

The Argument for Federalism

The strongest argument for federalism in 1787 was that it would correct the defects in the Articles. Two of the defects were particularly troublesome. The national government had neither the power to tax nor the power to

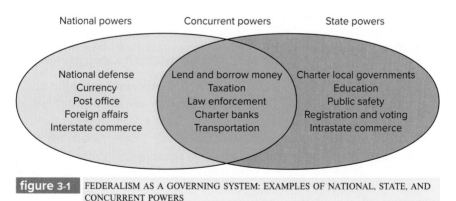

figure 3-1   FEDERALISM AS A GOVERNING SYSTEM: EXAMPLES OF NATIONAL, STATE, AND CONCURRENT POWERS

The American federal system divides sovereignty between a national government and the state governments. Each is constitutionally protected in its existence and authority, although their powers overlap somewhat, even in areas granted to one level (for example, the federal government has a role in education policy).

regulate commerce among the states. Without money from taxes, the national government lacked the financial means to maintain an army strong enough to prevent encroachment by European powers or to maintain a navy strong enough to protect America's merchant ships from harassment and attack by pirates and foreign navies. Also, without the ability to regulate commerce, the national government could neither promote the general economy nor prevent trade wars between the states. New York and New Jersey were among the states that imposed taxes on goods shipped into their state from other states.

Although it is sometimes claimed that "the government which governs least is the government that governs best," the Articles proved otherwise. Nevertheless, many Americans in 1787 feared that a strong central government would eventually swallow up the states. One of the Anti-Federalists (as opponents of the Constitution were called) worried that the states would eventually "have power over little else than yoking hogs."[7]

The challenge of providing a response to the Anti-Federalists fell to James Madison, Alexander Hamilton, and John Jay. During the ratification debate, they argued in a series of essays (*The Federalist Papers*) that a federal system would protect liberty and moderate the power of government.

Protecting Liberty   Although theorists such as John Locke and Montesquieu had not proposed a division of power between national and local authorities as a means of protecting liberty, the framers argued that federalism was a part of the system of checks and balances.[8] Alexander Hamilton wrote in *Federalist* No. 28 that the American people could shift their loyalties back and forth between the national and state governments in order to keep each under control. "If [the people's] rights are invaded by either," Hamilton wrote, "they can make use of the other as the instrument of redress."

Moderating the Power of Government   To the Anti-Federalists, the sacrifice of the states' power to the nation was unwise. They argued that a distant national government could never serve the people's interests as well as the states could. The Anti-Federalists claimed that the state governments would be more likely to protect liberty and self-government. To support their case, they turned to French theorist Montesquieu who had claimed that a small republic is more likely than a large one to serve people's interests because it is in closer touch with the people.

In *Federalist* No. 10, James Madison took issue with this claim. He argued that whether a government serves the common good is a function not of its size but of the range of interests that share political power. The problem with a small republic, Madison said, is that it can have a dominant faction—whether it be landholders, financiers, an impoverished majority, or some other group—that is strong enough to control government and use it to promote its interests at the expense of all others. Madison noted that a large republic is less likely to have an all-powerful faction. If financiers are strong in one area of a large republic, they are likely to be weaker elsewhere. The same will be true of farmers, merchants, laborers, and other groups. Madison argued that a large republic would make it more difficult for a single group to gain full control, which would force groups to share the exercise of power. In making this claim, Madison was arguing not for central authority but for limited government, which he believed would result if power was widely shared. "Extend the sphere," said Madison, "and you take in a greater variety of parties and interests; you make it less probable that a majority of the whole will have a common motive to invade the rights of other citizens."

The Powers of the Nation and the States

The U.S. Constitution addresses the lawful authority of the national government, which is provided through *enumerated* and *implied powers*. Authority that is not granted to the national government is left—or "reserved"—to the states.

Enumerated Powers and the Supremacy Clause   Article I of the Constitution grants to Congress **enumerated (expressed) powers**. Seventeen in number, these powers were intended to establish a government strong enough to forge a union that was secure in its defense and stable in its economy. Congress was granted the power, for example, to regulate commerce among the states, create a national currency, establish a postal service, and borrow money. These powers were intended as the basis for creating a sound national economy. Its power to tax, combined with its authority to establish an army and navy and to declare war, was intended to provide for the common defense.

In addition, the Constitution prohibits the states from actions that would encroach on national powers. Article I, Section 10, prohibits the states from making treaties with other nations, raising armies, waging war, printing money, or entering into commercial agreements with other states without the approval of Congress.

The writers of the Constitution recognized that the lawful exercise of national authority would at times conflict with the laws of the states (see "Fake or Fact? Do States Have Final Authority over Marijuana Laws?"). In such instances, national law would prevail. Article VI of the Constitution grants this dominance in the **supremacy clause**, which provides that "the laws of the United States . . . shall be the supreme law of the land."

Implied Powers: The Necessary and Proper Clause   The writers of the Constitution recognized that the national government to be effective would have to adjust to changing conditions. A weakness of the Articles was that the

F A K E	**Detecting Misinformation**
F A C T	**Do States Have Final Authority over Marijuana Laws?**

or

Roughly a fourth of the states have authorized the recreational use of marijuana, and other states have downgraded marijuana possession in limited amounts from a felony to a misdemeanor or citation. Additional states allow marijuana's use for medical purposes, although the medical conditions that qualify vary from one state to the next. From these examples, it would appear that states have final authority over the regulation of marijuana use.

Syda Productions/Shutterstock

Is that claim fact, or is it fake?

States have the final authority over marijuana use only in a limited respect. State courts have held that, if the state has decriminalized marijuana, an individual cannot be convicted in state court for possession or use of marijuana that complies with state law—for example, possession of an amount of marijuana that does not exceed the state limit. On the other hand, marijuana use and possession are prohibited by federal law. The U.S. government classifies marijuana as an illegal controlled substance, and the Supreme Court in Gonzales v. Raich *(2005) upheld the classification as a valid exercise of Congress's commerce power. Because of the Constitution's supremacy clause, federal law supersedes conflicting state law. Accordingly, residents of a state that has legalized marijuana could be charged with violating federal law. However, the federal government seldom pursues cases of marijuana possession when the individual is in compliance with state law. Law enforcement officers have leeway in deciding which criminal offenses will get their attention. Federal officials view personal marijuana use as a low priority relative to other types of federal crime.*

national government was prohibited from exercising powers not expressly granted to it, which limited its ability to meet the country's changing needs after the end of the Revolutionary War. To avoid this problem with the new government, the framers included in Article I of the Constitution the **"necessary and proper" clause** or, as it later came to be known, the *elastic clause.* It gives Congress the power "to make all laws which shall be necessary and proper for carrying into execution the foregoing [enumerated] powers." This clause gives the national government **implied powers**: powers that are not listed in the Constitution but that are related to the exercise of listed powers.

Reserved Powers: The States' Authority   The supremacy and "necessary and proper" clauses were worrisome to the Anti-Federalists. The two clauses stoked their fear of an overly powerful national government because they provided a constitutional basis for expanded federal authority. Such concerns led them to demand a constitutional amendment that would protect states' rights and interests. Ratified in 1791 as the Tenth Amendment to the Constitution, it reads "The powers not delegated to the United States by the Constitution, nor prohibited by it to the States, are reserved to the States." The states' powers under the U.S. Constitution are thus called **reserved powers**.

At the time of ratification, the Tenth Amendment was seen as strong protection of the states. It turned out to be something less. The logic of the Constitution is that the states control only those policies that are not within the lawful authority of the federal government. As a result, the constitutional issue in federal–state disputes is the limits on federal power. If an action is within the lawful power of the federal government, it's permissible. If it's outside the federal government's lawful power, it's not. This feature of the Constitution has enabled the national government to intrude on policy areas initially reserved for the states. Over time, there has been a **nationalization** of America's federal system—a gradual shift in power from the states to the national government.[9] During the course of the nation's history, the pendulum of power has sometimes swung toward the states and sometimes toward the national government but, overall, the national government has gained power relative to the states, as later sections of this chapter will show.

FEDERALISM IN HISTORICAL PERSPECTIVE

Since ratification of the Constitution over two centuries ago, no aspect of it has provoked more frequent or bitter conflict than federalism. By establishing two levels of sovereign authority, the Constitution created two centers of power and ambition, each of which was sure to claim disputed areas as belonging to it. Ambiguities in the Constitution have also contributed to conflict between the nation and the states. For example, the document does not specify the dividing line between *inter*state commerce (which the national government is empowered to regulate) and *intra*state commerce (which is reserved for regulation by the states).

Not surprisingly, federalism's development has been determined less by the words of the Constitution than by the strength of the contending interests and the country's changing needs. Federalism can be viewed as having progressed through three historical eras, each of which has involved a different relationship between the nation and the states. Each era ended with a national government that was stronger than at the beginning.

An Indestructible Union (1789–1865)

The issue during the first era—which lasted from the time the Constitution went into effect (1789) until the end of the Civil War (1865)—was the Union's survival. Given America's state-centered history before the Constitution, it was inevitable that the states would dispute national policies that threatened their interests.

The Nationalist View: **McCulloch v. Maryland**   An early dispute over federalism arose when President George Washington's secretary of the treasury, Alexander Hamilton, proposed that Congress establish a national bank. Hamilton and his supporters claimed that, because the federal government had the constitutional authority to regulate currency, it had the "implied power" to establish a national bank. Thomas Jefferson, Washington's secretary of state, opposed the bank on the grounds that it would enrich the wealthy at the expense of ordinary people. Jefferson claimed the bank was unlawful because the Constitution did not expressly authorize it. Jefferson said, "I consider the foundation of the Constitution as laid on this ground that 'all powers not delegated to the United States by the Constitution, nor prohibited by it to the states, are preserved to the states or to the people.'"

Hamilton's argument prevailed, and Congress in 1791 established the First Bank of the United States, granting it a 20-year charter. Although Congress did not renew the bank's charter when it expired in 1811, Congress decided in 1816 to establish the Second Bank of the United States. State and local banks did not want competition from a national bank and sought protection from their state legislatures. Several states, including Maryland, levied taxes on the national bank's operations within their borders, hoping to drive it out of existence by making it unprofitable. James McCulloch, who was in charge of the Maryland branch of the national bank, refused to pay the Maryland tax, and the resulting dispute was heard by the Supreme Court.

The chief justice of the Supreme Court was John Marshall who believed that the United States needed a strong national government. In *McCulloch v. Maryland* (1819) the Marshall-led Court ruled decisively in favor of national authority. Marshall argued that a government with powers to tax, borrow

Pictured here is Howard Chandler Christy's painting of the signing of the U.S. Constitution. George Washington is the tall figure on the platform. Benjamin Franklin is seated in the center. Leaning toward him is Alexander Hamilton. As secretary of the treasury in the Washington administration, Hamilton devised the nation's early economic policies, including a system of tariffs and a national bank, which were the foundation of America's economic prosperity. Even though Hamilton did not serve as president, a French diplomat called him the greatest leader of his era, ranking ahead even of Washington and Napoleon. (Architect of the Capitol)

money, and regulate commerce could reasonably establish a bank in order to exercise those powers effectively. Marshall's argument was a clear statement of *implied powers*—the idea that, through the "necessary and proper" clause, the national government's powers extend beyond its listed powers.

Marshall's ruling also addressed the meaning of the Constitution's supremacy clause. Maryland argued that, even if the national government had the authority to establish a bank, it had the authority to tax it. The Supreme Court rejected Maryland's position, concluding that valid national law supersedes conflicting state law. Because the national government had the power to create the bank, it also could protect the bank from state actions aimed at weakening it. Said Marshall, "The power to tax is the power to destroy."[10]

The *McCulloch* decision served as a precedent for later rulings in support of national power. In *Gibbons v. Ogden* (1824), for example, the Marshall-led Court rejected a New York law granting one of its residents a monopoly on a ferry that operated between New York and New Jersey, concluding that New York had encroached on Congress's power to regulate interstate commerce. The Court asserted that Congress's commerce power was not limited to trade between the states, but to all aspects of that trade, including the transportation of goods. The power over interstate commerce, the Court said, "is vested in Congress as absolutely as it would be in a single government."[11]

Marshall's opinions asserted that legitimate uses of national power took precedence over state authority and that the "necessary and proper" clause and the commerce clause were broad grants of power to the national government. As a nationalist, Marshall provided a legal basis for expanding federal power in ways that fostered the development of the United States as a nation rather than as a collection of states. As Justice Oliver Wendell Holmes Jr. noted a century later, the Union could not have survived if each state had been allowed to decide for itself which national laws it would obey.[12]

The States' Rights View: The Dred Scott *Decision*   Although John Marshall's rulings strengthened national authority, the issue of slavery posed a growing threat to the Union's survival. Westward expansion and immigration into the northern states were tilting power in Congress toward the free states, which increasingly signaled their determination to outlaw slavery. Fearing the possibility, southern leaders did what others have done throughout American history. They devised a constitutional interpretation that supported their position. John C. Calhoun declared that the United States was founded upon a "compact" between the states. The national government, he said, was "a government of states . . . not a government of individuals."[13] This line of reasoning led Calhoun to his famed "doctrine of nullification," which declared that a state has the constitutional right to nullify a national law.

In 1832, South Carolina invoked the doctrine, declaring "null and void" a national tariff law that favored northern interests. President Andrew Jackson called South Carolina's action "incompatible with the existence of the Union," a position that gained strength when Congress gave Jackson the authority to take military action against South Carolina. The state backed down after Congress agreed to changes in the tariff act. The dispute foreshadowed the Civil War, a confrontation of far greater consequence. Although the war would not break out for another three decades, the dispute over states' rights was intensifying.

The Supreme Court's infamous *Dred Scott* decision (1857), written by Chief Justice Roger Taney, an ardent states'-rights advocate, inflamed the dispute. Dred Scott, an enslaved person who had lived in the North for four years, applied for his freedom when his master died, citing a federal law—the Missouri Compromise of 1820—that made slavery illegal in a free state or territory. The Supreme Court ruled against Scott, claiming that enslaved people were not citizens and could never become citizens, and therefore had no right to have their case heard in federal court. The Court also invalidated the Missouri Compromise by holding that enslaved people were property, not people. Accordingly, since the Constitution prohibited Congress from interfering with owners' property rights, Congress lacked the power to outlaw slavery in any state.[14]

The Taney Court's decision provoked outrage in the North and contributed to a sectional split in the nation's majority party, the Democrats. In 1860, the Democratic Party's northern and southern wings nominated different candidates for the presidency, which split the Democratic vote, enabling the Republican candidate, Abraham Lincoln, to win the presidency with only 40 percent of the popular vote. Lincoln had campaigned on a platform that called not for an immediate end to slavery but for its gradual abolition through payments to slave holders. Nevertheless, southern states saw Lincoln's election as a threat to slavery. By the time Lincoln took office, seven southern states, led by South Carolina, had left the Union. Four more states followed. In justifying his decision to wage war on the South, Lincoln said, "The Union is older than the states." In 1865, the superior strength of the Union army settled by force the question of whether national authority is binding on the states.

The American Civil War was the deadliest conflict the world had yet known. Ten percent of fighting-age men died in the four-year war, and an additional 15 percent were wounded. The death toll was 618,000, which exceeds the combined total of American war dead in World War I, World War II, the Korean War, and the Vietnam War. Shown here is a portion of the Gettysburg National Cemetery. It was on this site that Abraham Lincoln gave his Gettysburg Address shortly after a three-day battle in which 50,000 Union and Confederate soldiers were killed or wounded. (Bob Pool/Shutterstock)

Dual Federalism and Laissez-Faire Capitalism (1865–1937)

Although the North's victory in the Civil War preserved the Union, new challenges to federalism were surfacing. Constitutional doctrine from the nation's beginning had held that certain policy areas, such as interstate commerce and defense, belonged exclusively to the national government, whereas other policy areas, such as public education and intrastate commerce, belonged exclusively to the states. This doctrine, known as **dual federalism**, was based on the idea that a precise separation of national and state authority was both possible and desirable. "The power which one possesses," said the Supreme Court, "the other does not."[15]

American society, however, was in the midst of changes that raised questions about the suitability of dual federalism as a governing concept. The freeing of enslaved Blacks, the rise of cities, and the increasing level of commerce among the states suggested that effective governing would require a larger role for the federal government, including intrusion into areas regarded as belonging exclusively to the states. Nevertheless, from the 1860s through the 1930s, the Supreme Court held firm to the idea that a sharp dividing line existed between national and state authority.

There was also the issue of government regulation of business. The Industrial Revolution had given rise to large business firms, which were using their economic power to dominate markets and exploit workers. The government was the logical counterforce to their economic power. Which level of government—state or national—would regulate big business? As it happened, the Supreme Court blocked both the federal government and the states from substantially regulating business activity.

The Fourteenth Amendment and State Discretion   Ratified after the Civil War, the Fourteenth Amendment was intended to protect former enslaved Blacks from discriminatory action by state governments. A state was prohibited from depriving "any person of life, liberty, or property without due process of law," from denying "any person within its jurisdiction the equal protection of the laws," and from abridging "the privileges or immunities of citizens of the United States."

Nevertheless, Supreme Court rulings in subsequent decades undermined the Fourteenth Amendment's promise of equal justice. In 1873, for example, the Court held that the Fourteenth Amendment did not significantly limit the power of the states to determine the rights to which their residents were entitled.[16] Then, in *Plessy v. Ferguson* (1896), the Court issued its infamous "separate but equal" ruling. A Black man, Homer Adolph Plessy, had been convicted of violating a Louisiana law that required white and Black citizens to ride in separate railroad cars. The Supreme Court upheld his conviction, concluding that state governments could force Blacks to use separate facilities as long as the facilities were "equal" in quality to those reserved for whites. "If one race be inferior to the other socially," the Court argued, "the Constitution of the United States cannot put them on the same plane." The lone dissenting justice in the case was John Marshall Harlan, a former slave owner who had become a staunch defender of equal rights. Said Harlan: "Our Constitution is color-blind and neither knows nor tolerates classes among citizens. . . . The thin disguise of 'equal' accommodations . . . will not mislead anyone nor atone for the wrong this day done."[17]

With its *Plessy* decision, the Supreme Court endorsed government-based racial segregation in the South. Black children were forced into separate public schools that had few teachers. Public hospitals for Blacks had few doctors and almost no medical supplies. The *Plessy* ruling had become a justification for the separate and *unequal* treatment of Black Americans.[18] Six decades would elapse before the Supreme Court in *Brown v. Board of Education* (1954) changed course. Invoking the Fourteenth Amendment, it held that separate public facilities were inherently

In *Plessy v. Ferguson* (1896), the Supreme Court ignored the equal protection clause of the Fourteenth Amendment and upheld the state-mandated policy of separate but equal, subjecting Black Americans throughout the South to second-class status in public schooling, access to public transportation, treatment at public hospitals, and use of public facilities such as zoos, restrooms, and water fountains. (Afro American Newspapers/Gado/Archive Photos/Getty Images)

unequal, thereby denying states the power to treat Black and white residents differently under the law (equal rights are addressed in Chapter 5).

Judicial Protection of Business   After the Civil War, the Supreme Court gave nearly free rein to business. A majority of the Court's justices favored laissez-faire capitalism (which holds that business should be "allowed to act" without interference) and interpreted the Constitution in ways that limited the government's ability to regulate business activity. In 1886, for example, the Court decided that corporations were "persons" within the meaning of the Fourteenth Amendment, and thereby were protected from substantial regulation by the states.[19] In other words, a constitutional amendment that had been enacted to protect former enslaved Blacks from being treated as second-class persons was ignored for that purpose but used instead to protect fictitious persons—business corporations.

The Court also weakened the national government's regulatory power by narrowly interpreting its commerce power. The Constitution's **commerce clause** says that Congress shall have the power "to regulate commerce" among the states. However, the clause does not spell out the economic activities included in the grant of power. When the federal government invoked the Sherman Antitrust Act (1890) in an attempt to break up the monopoly on the manufacture of sugar (a single company controlled 98 percent of it), the Supreme Court blocked the action, claiming that interstate commerce covered only the "transportation" of goods, not their "manufacture."[20] Manufacturing was deemed part of intrastate commerce and thus, according to the dual federalism doctrine, subject to state regulation only. However, because the Court had previously ruled that the states' regulatory powers were limited by the Fourteenth Amendment, the states were largely prohibited from regulating manufacturing.

Although some business regulation was subsequently allowed, the Court remained an obstacle to efforts to curb business practices. An example is the case of *Hammer v. Dagenhart* (1918), which arose from a 1916 federal law that prohibited the interstate shipment of goods produced by child labor. The law had broad public support in that factory owners were exploiting children, working them for long hours at low pay. Nevertheless, the Court invalidated the law, ruling that the Tenth Amendment gave the states, and not the federal government, the power to regulate factory practices.[21] However, in an earlier case, *Lochner v. New York* (1905), the Court had blocked states from regulating labor practices, concluding that such action violated factory owners' property rights.[22]

In effect, the Court had voided the principle of self-government. Neither the people's representatives in Congress nor those in the state legislatures were allowed to regulate business. The nation's economic policy was largely in the hands of America's corporations.[23]

National Authority Prevails   The Democratic Party, with its working-class base, attacked the Court's position, and its candidates increasingly called for greater regulation of business and more rights for labor. Progressive Republicans such as Theodore Roosevelt also fought against uncontrolled business power, but the Republican Party as a whole was ideologically committed to unregulated markets. Accordingly, when the Great Depression began in 1929, Republican president Herbert Hoover refused at first to use federal authority to put people back to work. Adhering to his party's free-market philosophy, Hoover argued that the economy would recover on its own and that government intervention would only delay it.

Unwilling to wait, voters in the 1932 election elected Democrat Franklin D. Roosevelt as president. Roosevelt understood that the economy was national in scope. Urban workers were dependent on farmers for their food and corporations for their jobs. Farmers were more independent, but they, too, were increasingly a part of a national economic network. Farmers' income depended

The Great Depression cost a fourth of workers their jobs. States lacked the resources to meet the needs of the unemployed and the national government stepped in, resulting in a permanent shift of power within the American federal system. Shown here is a soup kitchen in Chicago set up to feed the unemployed. This kitchen was opened and funded by Chicago mob boss Al Capone as a way to enhance his public image. (Everett Historical/Shutterstock)

on market prices and shipping and equipment costs.[24] Economic interdependence meant that when the Great Depression hit in 1929, its effects could not be contained. At the height of the Depression, a fourth of the nation's workers were jobless.

The states had responsibility for helping the poor, but they were nearly penniless because of declining tax revenues and the high demand for welfare assistance. Franklin Roosevelt's New Deal programs were designed to ease the hardship. The 1933 National Industrial Recovery Act (NIRA), for example, established a federal jobs program and authorized major industries to coordinate their production decisions. Economic conservatives opposed such programs, accusing Roosevelt of leading the country into socialism. They found an ally in the Supreme Court. In *Schechter Poultry Corp. v. United States* (1935), just as it had done in previous New Deal cases, the Supreme Court in a 5–4 ruling declared the NIRA to be unconstitutional.[25]

Frustrated by the Court's rulings, Roosevelt in 1937 sought to exploit the fact that the Constitution gives Congress the power to determine the number of Supreme Court justices. Although the number had stayed at nine justices for seven decades, there was no constitutional barrier to increasing the number, which had been altered several times in the nation's early years. Roosevelt asked Congress for legislation that would allow a president to nominate a new justice whenever a seated member passed the age of 70½. Since some of the justices had already reached that age, the legislation would enable Roosevelt to appoint enough new justices to swing the Court to his side. Congress refused to do so, but the attempt ended with the "switch in time that saved nine." For reasons that have never been fully clear, Justice Owen Roberts switched sides on New Deal cases, giving the president a 5–4 majority on the Court.

Within months, the Court upheld the 1935 National Labor Relations Act, which gave workers the right to organize and bargain collectively.[26] The Court reasoned that disputes between labor and management disrupted the nation's economy and therefore could be regulated through the commerce clause.[27] In a subsequent ruling, the Court declared that Congress's commerce power is "as broad as the needs of the nation."[28] Congress would be allowed to regulate *all* aspects of commerce.

The Supreme Court had finally acknowledged the obvious: that an industrial economy is not confined by state boundaries and must be subject to national regulation. It was a principle that business also increasingly accepted. The nation's banking industry, for example, was saved from almost complete collapse in the 1930s by the creation of a federal regulatory agency, the Federal Deposit Insurance Corporation (FDIC). By insuring depositors' savings against loss, the FDIC stopped the panic withdrawals that had already forced thousands of the nation's banks to close.

During the 1930s, the Supreme Court also loosened its restrictions on Congress's taxing and spending power. In *United States v. Butler* (1936), the Court held that the Constitution's taxing and spending clause confers a grant of power that is "limited only by the requirement that it shall be exercised to provide for the general welfare of the United States."[29] General welfare is a very broad category, so broad, in fact, that Congress has used its spending power to involve itself in policy areas traditionally controlled by the states, as will be explained later in the chapter.[30]

FEDERALISM SINCE THE 1930s

After the 1930s, relations between the nation and the states changed so fully that dual federalism was no longer an accurate description of the American system. The national government now operates in many policy areas that were once almost exclusively within the control of states and localities.

Few developments illustrate that more clearly than does President Lyndon Johnson's Great Society of the 1960s. A Democrat in the mold of Franklin Roosevelt, Johnson believed that federal power should be used to assist the economically disadvantaged. However, unlike Roosevelt's New Deal, which dealt mostly with the economy, Johnson's Great Society dealt mostly with social welfare issues, which have an indirect constitutional basis. The Constitution does not grant Congress the power to regulate "social welfare." However, Congress may tax and spend for that purpose, which was the basis of the Great Society. Johnson's presidency was marked by dozens of new federal assistance grants to states for programs in health care, public housing, nutrition, public assistance, urban development, education, and other policy areas traditionally reserved to states and localities.

Interdependency is a reason national authority has increased substantially. Modern systems of transportation, commerce, and communication transcend local and state boundaries. These systems are national—and even international—in scope, which means that problems affecting Americans living in one part of the country will affect Americans living elsewhere. National problems typically require a national policy response.

Interdependency has encouraged national, state, and local policymakers to work together to solve policy problems. This collaborative effort has been described as **cooperative federalism**.[31] The difference between the older dual federalism and cooperative federalism has been likened to the difference between a layer cake, whose levels are separate, and a marble cake, whose levels flow together.[32] An example is the Medicaid program, which was created in 1965 and provides health care for the poor. The Medicaid program is jointly funded by the national and state governments, operates within eligibility standards set by the national government, and gives states some latitude in determining recipient eligibility and benefits. States have the power, for example, to decide whether Medicaid will be limited to individuals whose income is below the federally designated poverty line or whether it will extend also to individuals with incomes somewhat above that line.

Hundreds of policy programs today are run jointly by the national and state governments. In many cases, local governments are also involved. These programs have the following characteristics:

- Jointly funded by the national and state governments (and sometimes by local governments)
- Jointly administered, with the states and localities providing most of the direct service to recipients and a national agency providing general administration
- Jointly determined, with both state and national governments (and sometimes local governments) having a say in eligibility and benefit levels and with federal regulations, such as those prohibiting discrimination, imposing a degree of uniformity on state and local efforts

Cooperative federalism should not be interpreted to mean that the states are powerless and dependent.[33] States have retained most of their traditional authority in areas such as education, health, public safety, and roadways. In the area of public schools, for example, states determine the length of the school year, teachers' qualifications, and graduation requirements.

The power of the states is also evident in their policy differences. For example, seven states do not tax personal income, whereas California is at the other extreme, with a tax rate that tops off at 13.3 percent for those with a net annual income in excess of $1 million. These differences translate into policy differences. States with high tax rates spend significantly more on a per capita basis on public education, welfare, roadways, and other services than do states with low tax rates. States have also been called "laboratories of democracy" in the sense that a successful policy innovation in one state may be copied by other states. California, for example, was the first state to legalize medical marijuana, and Colorado and Washington were the first to legalize recreational use of marijuana. Their experience has led other states to follow suit. Innovations at the state level have even contributed to changes in federal policy. Wisconsin's welfare reform effort helped inform the Welfare Reform Act that Congress passed in 1996, and Massachusetts' universal health care program provided a roadmap for the 2010 Affordable Care Act.

Nevertheless, the federal government's involvement in policy areas traditionally reserved for the states has reduced state-to-state policy differences. States and localities have received billions in federal assistance; in accepting federal money, they also have accepted both federal restrictions on its use and the national policy priorities that underlie the granting of the money.

Fiscal Federalism

The interdependency of American society—the fact that developments in one area affect what happens elsewhere—is one of the major reasons the federal government's policy role has expanded greatly since the early 20th century. The other is the federal government's superior taxing capacity. States and localities are in a competitive situation with regard to taxation. A state with high corporate and personal income taxes can lose firms and people to states with lower taxes. By contrast, firms and people are less likely to move to another country in search of lower taxes. The result is that the federal government raises more tax revenue than do all 50 states and the thousands of local governments combined (see Figure 3-2).

The federal government's revenue-raising advantage has enabled it to reach into areas traditionally controlled by the states. **Fiscal federalism** refers to the expenditure of federal funds on programs run, in part, through state and local governments.[34] The federal government provides some or all of the money through **grants-in-aid** (cash payments) to states and localities, which then administer the programs. The pattern of federal assistance to states and localities is shown in Figure 3-3. Federal grants-in-aid have increased dramatically since the mid-1950s. Roughly one in every five dollars spent by local and state governments in recent decades has been raised not by them but by the federal government (see "How the 50 States Differ").

Federal grants to states and localities have increased Washington's policy influence. State and local governments can reject a grant-in-aid but, if they accept it, must spend it in the way specified by Congress. Money designated for a school lunch program, for example, cannot be used for school construction

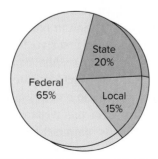

figure 3-2   FEDERAL, STATE, AND LOCAL SHARES OF GOVERNMENT TAX REVENUE

The federal government raises more tax revenues than do all state and local governments combined. (*Source:* Tax Policy Center, 2020)

Billions of dollars (in constant 2005 dollars)

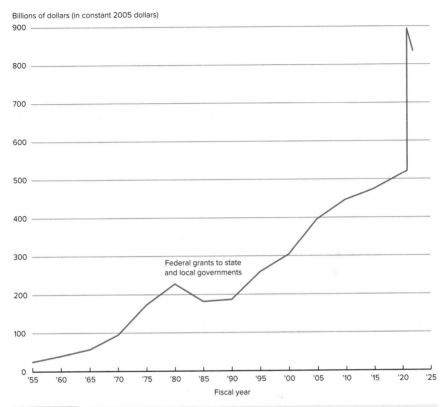

Federal grants to state
and local governments

Fiscal year

figure 3-3 FEDERAL GRANTS TO STATE AND LOCAL GOVERNMENTS

Federal aid to states and localities has increased dramatically since the 1950s. The large recent increase is attributable to grants to states and localities to fund their response to the COVID-19 pandemic. (*Source:* Office of Management and Budget (OMB), FY2021). Figures are based on constant (2005) dollars to control for effects of inflation. Figure for each year shown in graph is the average per year for previous five years.

or teachers' salaries. Also, because many grants require states to contribute matching funds, the federal programs, in effect, determine how states will allocate some of their tax dollars.

Nevertheless, federal grants-in-aid serve the policy interests of state and local officials. Although they complain that federal grants contain too many restrictions and infringe too much on their authority, most of them are eager to have the money because it allows them to offer services they could not otherwise afford and relieves them of having to raise taxes to provide the services. Said one observer, "it's free money—they get the benefits and they don't have to [raise] the revenues."[35] In 2021, for example, Congress passed an infrastructure bill that granted billions of dollars to states and localities to improve their roadways and mass transit systems.

HOW THE 50 STATES DIFFER

CRITICAL THINKING THROUGH COMPARISONS

Federal Grants-in-Aid to the States

Federal assistance accounts for roughly a fifth of state revenue, but the variation is considerable. Montana, which gets 29.2 percent of its revenue from the federal government, is at one extreme. Virginia, at 13.5 percent, is at the other extreme.

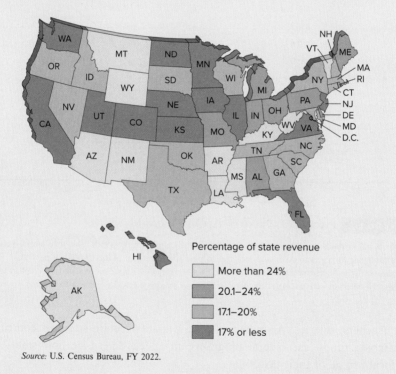

Percentage of state revenue

More than 24%

20.1–24%

17.1–20%

17% or less

Source: U.S. Census Bureau, FY 2022.

Q: What might explain why some states rely more heavily on federal grants than other states?

A: Many federal grants are designed to assist low-income people, and states with higher poverty rates tend to rely more heavily on federal grants. States with a small population relative to their geographical size also rely more heavily on grants as a result, for example, of their highway and rural development needs.

New Federalism and Devolution

The expansion of the federal government's domestic policy role from the 1930s onward was initiated by Democratic lawmakers. Although these policies had broad public support at the outset, it declined after the 1960s. Some of the programs, particularly those providing welfare benefits to the poor, were widely seen as too costly, too bureaucratic, and too lax—there was a widespread perception that many welfare recipients were getting benefits they neither needed nor deserved. Republican leaders increasingly questioned the effectiveness of the programs, a position that aligned with the party's ideology of lower taxes and local control.

In 1972, Republican president Richard Nixon persuaded the Democratic-controlled Congress to grant money to states and local governments that they could use nearly as they pleased. Nixon applied the term *revenue sharing* to the new grants, arguing that state and local officials understood their policy needs better than did federal officials.[36] The program continued over the next decade but was gradually phased out.

Upon becoming president in 1981, President Ronald Reagan, invoking a term first used by Nixon, proposed a **New Federalism** in which federal programs, regulations, and spending in policy areas traditionally reserved for the states would be reduced. "Federalism," Reagan said, "is rooted in the knowledge that our political liberties are best assured by limiting the size and scope of national government." Democrats controlled Congress during much of his presidency, and Reagan had only some success in reducing the federal government's role. Nevertheless, his presidency slowed the expansion of federal grants and saw some **categorical grants** converted to **block grants** to give states greater control over how the federal money was spent.

When Republicans scored a decisive victory in the 1994 midterm elections, gaining control of Congress for the first time since the early 1950s, they were finally positioned to act. Declaring that "1960s-style federalism is dead," Speaker of the House Newt Gingrich argued for **devolution**—a large shift in power from the federal government to state and local governments.[37]

The most significant policy change was the sweeping 1996 Welfare Reform Act. Opinion polls at the time indicated that a majority of Americans felt that the government was spending too much on welfare and that too many welfare recipients were abusing the system. The Welfare Reform Act tightened spending and eligibility. The legislation's key element, the Temporary Assistance for Needy Families (TANF) block grant, ended the decades-old federal program that granted cash assistance for an indefinite period to poor families with children. TANF restricts a family's eligibility for federal assistance to five years and gives states latitude in setting benefit levels. TANF also provides funds for states to develop training programs that have the goal of moving people off welfare and into jobs. (TANF and other social welfare policies are discussed more fully in later chapters.[38])

Pictured here is President Ronald Reagan who in the 1980s advocated a "New Federalism" that would return power to the states. Reagan's argument was picked up by other Republican leaders including Newt Gingrich who, as Speaker of the House in 1996, orchestrated the largest rollback in federal welfare spending in the nation's history. Reagan was a movie actor before turning to politics. The shirt he's holding refers to a role he played in a movie about Notre Dame's football team. (Vernon Lewis Gallery/Stocktrek Images, Inc./Alamy Stock Photo)

Federalism in Dispute

Republican efforts in the 1980s and 1990s shifted some power back to the states and slowed the growth of federal grants but did not reverse the long-term trend toward national power. A tipping point was the terrorist attacks on New York and Washington on September 11, 2001, which occurred when Republican George W. Bush was the president. The threat of future attacks led to the creation of the Department of Homeland Security (DHS), a cabinet-level federal agency with policing and emergency responsibilities traditionally belonging to states and localities.

Then, in 2010, Democratic president Barack Obama and the Democrat-controlled Congress established the Affordable Care Act (ACA), one of the largest expansions of federal authority since the 1960s. It requires business firms of a certain size to provide their employees with health insurance or pay a penalty. It also expanded eligibility for Medicaid by raising the income level at which Americans could receive government-paid health care, although. as a result of a Supreme Court decision,[39] Medicaid expansion is a state option and most Republican-controlled states have not adopted it.

Republicans sought to kill the ACA, believing they had done so during Donald Trump's presidency. The Republican-controlled Congress stripped from the ACA the requirement that individuals have health insurance or pay a penalty. The Supreme Court had earlier upheld the constitutionality of the ACA as a valid exercise of Congress's taxing power by concluding that the penalty provision was in effect a tax.[40] Republicans thought that, without the penalty provision, the ACA would be declared unconstitutional. A lower federal court did declare it unlawful, but the Supreme Court reversed the ruling.[41]

The 2020 election of Democrat Joe Biden continued the tug-of-war between Republicans and Democrats over the scope of federal policy. Shortly after

---

P A R T Y | **Conflicting Ideas**

POLARIZATION

The Power of the Federal Government

Although the Republican and Democratic Parties have had opposing views on the power of the federal government since the 1930s, the gap has widened in recent years. Republicans have sought to roll back federal power, resisted at nearly every turn by Democrats. A recent example is the health care reform act that the Democrat-controlled Congress enacted in 2010 and that Republican lawmakers then sought to overturn.

Differing opinions on federal power are not confined to lawmakers. As indicated by the accompanying graph, Americans who identify with the Republican Party are far more likely than Democratic identifiers to believe that the federal government "has too much power." The gap widened after the 2020 election, which shifted control of the presidency to the Democratic Party.

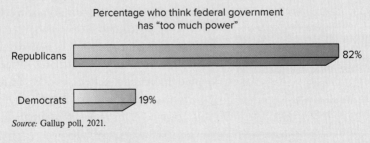

Percentage who think federal government has "too much power"

Republicans 82%

Democrats 19%

Source: Gallup poll, 2021.

Q: Can you think of a policy area in which Republicans are more likely than Democrats to support higher federal spending?

Biden took office, Congress enacted a $1.9 trillion COVID-19 economic relief bill. Most of the spending was in the form of grants to state and local governments. The vote in Congress divided sharply along party lines—Democrats in favor and Republicans opposed.

The partisan fight over the scope of federal power will continue, but one thing is certain. American federalism is a vastly different system than it was before the 1930s. The demands of contemporary life—a complex and integrated economy, a public that is insistent on its rights and reliant on government services, and a global environment filled with challenges and opportunities—have combined to give the federal government a bigger role in federal-state relations. The change can be seen in the structure of the federal government. Five cabinet departments—Health and Human Services, Housing and Urban Development, Transportation, Education, and Homeland Security—were created after the 1930s to administer federal programs in policy areas traditionally reserved to the states.

THE PUBLIC'S INFLUENCE: SETTING THE BOUNDARIES OF FEDERAL-STATE POWER

Public opinion has had a decisive influence on the ebb and flow of federal power during the past century. Every major change in federalism has been driven by a major shift in public support toward one level of government or the other.

During the Great Depression, when it became clear that the states were unable to help, Americans turned to Washington for relief. For people without jobs, the fine points of the Constitution were of little consequence. President Roosevelt's New Deal programs, which offered both jobs and income security, were a radical departure from the past but quickly gained public favor. A 1936 Gallup poll indicated, for example, that 61 percent of Americans supported Roosevelt's Social Security program, whereas only 27 percent opposed it.[42] The second great wave of federal social programs—Lyndon Johnson's Great Society—was also driven by public demands. Income and education levels had risen dramatically after World War II, and Americans wanted more and better services from the government.[43] When the states were slow to respond, Americans pressured federal officials to act. The Medicare and Medicaid programs, which provide health care for individuals who are elderly and poor,

CITIZEN ACTION!
SELF-GOVERNMENT

Under America's federal system, all levels of government have policy authority. Consider doing a part-time internship with your local government. You will gain an understanding of how your community is governed and contribute to its governing.

respectively, are examples of the Johnson administration's response. A 1965 Gallup poll indicated that two-thirds of Americans approved of federal involvement in the provision of medical care, despite the fact that health policy was traditionally the states' responsibility.

Public opinion was also behind the rollback of federal authority in the 1990s. Polls showed that a majority of Americans had come to believe that the federal government had become too large and intrusive. Americans' dissatisfaction with federal programs and spending provided the springboard for the Republican takeover of Congress in the 1994 midterm elections, which led to policies aimed at devolving power to the states, including the popular 1996 Welfare Reform Act.[44]

The public's role in determining the boundaries between federal and state power would come as no surprise to the framers of the Constitution. For them, federalism was a pragmatic issue, one to be decided by the nation's needs rather than by fixed rules. Alexander Hamilton and James Madison predicted as much when they said that Americans would look to whichever level of government was more responsive to their needs. Indeed, each succeeding generation of Americans has seen fit to devise a balance of federal and state power that met the demands of their era.

SUMMARY

A leading feature of the American political system is its division of authority between a national government and state governments. The first U.S. government, established by the Articles of Confederation, was essentially a union of the states.

In establishing the basis for a stronger national government, the U.S. Constitution also made provision for safeguarding state interests. The result was the creation of a federal system (federalism) in which sovereignty was vested in both national and state governments. The Constitution enumerates the general powers of the national government and grants it implied powers through the "necessary and proper" clause. Other powers are reserved to the states by the Tenth Amendment.

From 1789 to 1865, the nation's survival was at issue. The states found it convenient at times to argue that their sovereignty took precedence over national authority. In the end, it took the Civil War to cement the idea that the United States was a union of people, not of states. From 1865 to 1937, federalism reflected the doctrine that certain policy areas were the exclusive responsibility of the national government, whereas responsibility in other policy areas belonged exclusively to the states. This constitutional position validated the laissez-faire doctrine that big business was largely beyond governmental control. It also allowed the states to discriminate against African Americans in their public policies. Federalism in a form recognizable today began to emerge in the 1930s.

In the areas of commerce, taxation, spending, civil rights, and civil liberties, among others, the federal government now plays an important role, one that is the inevitable consequence of the increasing complexity of American society and the interdependence of its people. National, state, and local officials now work closely together to solve the nation's problems, a situation known as cooperative federalism. Grants-in-aid from Washington to the states and localities have been the chief instrument of national influence. In accepting federal grants, states and localities are adopting policy priorities established by federal officials.

Since the 1980s, Republicans and Democrats have been at odds over the scale of federal involvement in policy areas traditionally reserved for the states, with Democrats typically favoring a larger federal role and Republicans a smaller one. At times, as with the 2010 Affordable Care Act, Democrats have prevailed. At other times, as with the 1996 Welfare Reform Act, Republicans have had the upper hand.

Throughout the nation's history, the public, through its demands on government, has influenced the boundaries between federal and state power. The expansion of federal authority in the 1930s and the 1960s, for example, was driven by Americans' increased need for government assistance, whereas the devolutionary trend of the 1990s was sparked by Americans' belief that a rollback in federal power was needed.

CRITICAL THINKING ZONE

KEY TERMS

block grants (*p. 79*)
categorical grants (*p. 79*)
commerce clause (*p. 71*)
confederacy (*p. 60*)
cooperative federalism (*p. 74*)
devolution (*p. 79*)
dual federalism (*p. 69*)
enumerated (expressed) powers (*p. 62*)
federalism (*p. 58*)
fiscal federalism (*p. 76*)

grants-in-aid (*p. 76*)
implied powers (*p. 64*)
nationalization (*p. 64*)
"necessary and proper" clause (*p. 64*)
New Federalism (*p. 79*)
reserved powers (*p. 64*)
sovereignty (*p. 58*)
supremacy clause (*p. 62*)
unitary system (*p. 59*)

APPLYING THE ELEMENTS OF CRITICAL THINKING

Conceptualizing: Distinguish among a federal system, a unitary system, and a confederacy. What circumstances led the framers of the Constitution to create a federal system?

Synthesizing: Contrast dual federalism and cooperative federalism. Is the distinction between a layer cake and a marble cake helpful in understanding the difference between dual federalism and cooperative federalism?

Analyzing: How have the federal government's superior taxing policy and the economic interdependency of the American states contributed over time to a larger policy role for the national government? What role have federal grants-in-aid played in the expansion of federal authority?

OF POSSIBLE INTEREST

A Book Worth Reading: Ron Chernow, *Alexander Hamilton* (New York: Penguin, 2005). Written by a Pulitzer Prize–winning historian, this biography examines the life of Alexander Hamilton, including the role of his economic policies in America's development.

A Website Worth Visiting: **http://avalon.law.yale.edu/subject_menus/fed.asp**. This Yale Law School site includes a documentary record of the *Federalist Papers,* the Annapolis convention, the Articles of Confederation, the Madison debates, and the U.S. Constitution.

4
CHAPTER

CIVIL LIBERTIES: PROTECTING INDIVIDUAL RIGHTS

boyphare/Shutterstock

> **"** A bill of rights is what the people are entitled to against every government on earth, general or particular, and what no just government should refuse, or rest on inference. **"**
>
> THOMAS JEFFERSON[1]

Without a warrant from a judge, the police and the FBI had secretly attached a GPS tracking device to Antoine Jones's car and knew exactly where it was at any time of the day or night. For a month, they tracked the car's movements before arresting Jones on charges of conspiracy to sell drugs. The evidence obtained through the tracking device helped prosecutors gain a conviction. Jones was sentenced to life in prison.

Jones appealed his conviction and won a temporary victory when a federal appellate court—noting that individuals are protected by the Fourth Amendment from "unreasonable searches and seizures"—concluded that the officers should have sought a warrant from a judge, who would have decided whether they had sufficient cause to justify a search of Jones's possessions, much less the placing of a tracking device on his car.

In a unanimous 9-0 vote, the Supreme Court in *United States v. Jones* (2012) sided with Jones. The Court rejected the government's argument that attaching a small device to a car's undercarriage was too trivial an act to constitute an "unreasonable search." The government had also claimed that anyone driving a car on public streets can expect to be monitored, even continuously in some circumstances—after all, police had legally been "tailing" suspects for decades. The Court rejected those arguments, though the justices disagreed on exactly why the Constitution prohibits what the officers had done. Five justices said that the Fourth Amendment's protection of "persons, houses, papers, and effects" reasonably extends to private property such as an automobile. For them, the fact that the officers had placed a tracking device on the suspect's property without a warrant invalidated the evidence. Four justices went further, saying that the officers' actions intruded not only on the suspect's property rights but also on his "reasonable expectation of privacy." At its core, they said, the Fourth Amendment "protects people, not places."[2]

As the case illustrates, issues of individual rights have become increasingly complex. The framers of the Constitution could not possibly have envisioned a time when technology would have enabled authorities to track people's locations electronically. The framers understood that authorities would sometimes be tempted to snoop on people, which is why they wrote the Fourth Amendment. At the same time, the amendment protects Americans not from *all* searches but from *unreasonable* searches. The public would be unsafe if law enforcement officials could never track a suspect. The challenge for a civil society is to establish a level of police authority that meets the demands of public safety without infringing unduly on personal freedom. The balance point, however, is always subject to dispute. In this case, the Supreme Court sided with the accused. In other cases, it has sided with law enforcement officials.

This chapter examines issues of **civil liberties**—specific individual rights, such as the right to a fair trial, that are constitutionally protected against infringement by the government. Although the term *civil liberties* is sometimes used interchangeably with the term *civil rights,* they differ. Civil rights (which will be examined in Chapter 5) is a question of whether members of differing groups—racial, sexual, religious, and the like—are treated equally by the government and, in some cases, by private parties. By contrast, civil liberties are individual rights such as freedom of speech and the press. Civil liberties are the subject of this chapter, which focuses on the following points:

- *Freedom of expression is the most basic of democratic rights, but, like all rights, it is not unlimited.*

- *"Due process of law" refers to legal protections (primarily procedural safeguards) designed to ensure that individual rights are respected by the government.*

- *Over the course of the nation's history, Americans' civil liberties have been expanded in law and been more fully protected by the courts.* Of special significance has been the Supreme Court's use of the Fourteenth Amendment to protect individual rights from action by state and local governments.
- *Individual rights are constantly being weighed against the collective interests of society.* All political institutions are involved in this process, as is public opinion, but the judiciary plays a central role and is the institution most protective of civil liberties.

THE BILL OF RIGHTS, THE FOURTEENTH AMENDMENT, AND SELECTIVE INCORPORATION

As was explained in Chapter 2, the Constitution's failure to enumerate individual freedoms led to demands for the **Bill of Rights**. Ratified in 1791, these first 10 amendments to the Constitution provide a set of rights that the federal government is obliged to protect. The Bill of Rights initially applied only to the federal government and not also to the states, a position the Supreme Court affirmed a few decades later.[3]

Today, however, most of the rights contained in the Bill of Rights are also protected from action by the state governments, a development stemming from the ratification of the Fourteenth Amendment shortly after the Civil War. After the war, several southern states enacted laws that denied former enslaved Blacks their rights, including the right to own property and to travel freely. Congress responded by passing a constitutional amendment designed to protect their rights. The former Confederate states, with the exception of Tennessee, refused to ratify it. Congress then passed the Reconstruction Act, which placed the southern states under military rule until they did so. In 1868, the Fourteenth Amendment was ratified. It includes a **due process clause** that says "No State shall . . . deprive any person of life, liberty, or property, without due process of law."

Initially, the Supreme Court largely ignored the due process clause, allowing states to decide for themselves what rights their residents would have. In 1925, however, the Court invoked the Fourteenth Amendment in a case involving state government. Although the Court in *Gitlow v. New York* upheld a New York law that made it illegal to advocate the violent overthrow of the U.S. government, it ruled that states do not fully control what their residents can legally say. The Court said, "For present purposes we may and do assume that freedom of speech and of the press—which are protected by the First Amendment from abridgement by Congress—are among the fundamental personal rights and 'liberties' protected by the due process clause of the Fourteenth Amendment from impairment by the states."[4]

The ruling marked a fundamental shift in constitutional doctrine. The Court had concluded that a right protected by the Bill of Rights from action by the federal government was now also protected from action by state governments. Shortly thereafter, in a series of cases, the Court applied the new doctrine to other First Amendment rights. The Court invalidated state laws restricting expression in the areas of speech (*Fiske v. Kansas*), press (*Near v. Minnesota*), religion (*Hamilton v. Regents, University of California*), and assembly and petition (*DeJonge v. Oregon*).[5] The *Near* decision is the best known of the rulings. Jay Near was the publisher of a Minneapolis weekly newspaper that regularly made defamatory statements about Blacks, Jews, Catholics, and labor union leaders. His paper was closed down on the basis of a Minnesota law banning "malicious, scandalous, or defamatory" publications. Near appealed to the Supreme Court, which ruled in his favor, saying that the Minnesota law was "the essence of censorship."[6]

Three decades later, the Supreme Court began to require states to protect the fair-trial rights contained in the Bill of Rights. The breakthrough case was *Mapp v. Ohio* (1961). Police had forcibly entered the home of Dollree Mapp, saying they had a tip she was harboring a fugitive. They didn't find the suspect but handcuffed her and searched her possessions, where they found obscene photographs. Mapp was convicted under an Ohio law prohibiting the possession of such material. The Supreme Court overturned her conviction, ruling that police had acted unconstitutionally, citing the Fourth Amendment prohibition on unreasonable searches and seizures. The Court held that evidence acquired through an unconstitutional search cannot be used to obtain a conviction in state courts.[7] The Court had earlier applied that principle to federal courts.[8]

During the 1960s, the Court also ruled that defendants in state criminal proceedings must be provided a lawyer in felony cases if they cannot afford to hire one,[9] cannot be compelled to testify against themselves,[10] have the right to remain silent and to have legal counsel at the time of arrest,[11] have the right to confront witnesses who testify against them,[12] must be granted a speedy trial,[13] have the right to a jury trial in criminal proceedings,[14] and cannot be subjected to double jeopardy.[15]

In these various rulings, the Court was applying what is known as **selective incorporation**—the use of the Fourteenth Amendment to apply selected provisions of the Bill of Rights to the states. In its *Mapp* ruling, for example, the Court incorporated the Fourth Amendment protection against unreasonable search and seizure into the Fourteenth Amendment, thereby protecting it from infringement by states and localities. (The incorporation process is selective in that the Supreme Court has chosen to protect only some Bill of Rights guarantees from state action. Even today, for example, the Seventh Amendment right to a jury trial in civil cases is not required of the states.)

Selective incorporation has been of utmost importance. Because states and localities bear most of the responsibility for maintaining public order and safety, they are the authorities most likely to infringe on people's rights. If they were allowed to determine for themselves what these rights mean in practice—for example, how far local police can go in interrogating suspects—Americans' rights would be at risk and, in some locations, ignored. As it stands, nearly all freedoms in the Bill of Rights are now national rights and under the protection of the federal courts (see "How the U.S. Differs").

In the sections that follow, the law and practice of Americans' civil liberties will be examined, starting with rights protected by the First Amendment.

HOW THE U.S. DIFFERS

CRITICAL THINKING THROUGH COMPARISONS

Individual and Democratic Rights

Free expression and fair-trial rights are long-standing features of American government, as is the right to choose representatives in free and fair elections. How does the United States rank in comparison with other countries in the practice of these rights? According to Freedom House, an independent organization that tracks nations' respect for basic rights, the United States ranks above most countries in the world and far above countries like Russia and China, which greatly restrict the rights of their people.

Nevertheless, the United States falls below most Western democracies on Freedom House's ratings. The chart below shows, on a scale that runs from 0 (lowest) to 100 (highest), the most recent Freedom House ratings for selected countries for Individual Rights (free expression and fair-trial rights) and Democratic Rights (free and fair elections and voting). As you will note, the United States ranks below comparable Western democracies in its protection of individual rights and by a larger margin in its protection of democratic rights.

Q: Why might Freedom House rank the United States lower on individual rights and democratic rights than other leading democracies like France, Germany, and Great Britain?

A: Regarding individual rights, Freedom House cites things such as harsher policing and sentencing of minority-group members in comparison with

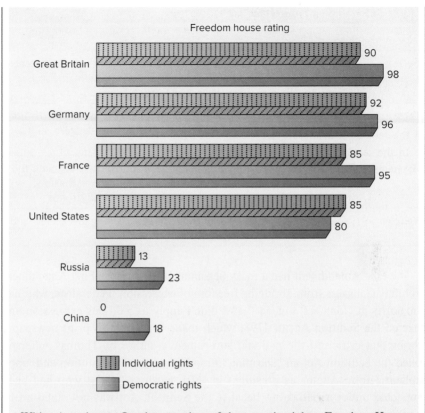

White Americans. On the question of democratic rights, Freedom House concludes that state-mandated voter ID laws and other impediments to registration and voting effectively deprive some U.S. citizens of their right to vote. It also notes that excessive partisan gerrymandering makes elections in the United States less fair than those in most democracies.

FREEDOM OF EXPRESSION

The First Amendment provides for **freedom of expression**–the right of individual Americans to express ideas of their choosing (see Table 4-1). Some forms of expression are not protected by the First Amendment because the courts have concluded that they fall outside the civic realm. Some forms of "commercial speech" are of this type. For example, pharmaceutical companies are required by law to disclose in their advertising the harmful side effects of drugs. Obscene forms of sexual expression–child pornography as an example– also do not have First Amendment protection.[16]

table 4-1	BILL OF RIGHTS: A SELECTED LIST OF FIRST AMENDMENT PROTECTIONS
First Amendment	
Speech	You are free to say almost anything except that which is obscene, slanders another person, or has a high probability of inciting others to take imminent lawless action.
Press	You are free to write or publish almost anything except that which is obscene, libels another person, or seriously endangers military action or national security.
Assembly	You are free to assemble, although government may regulate the time and place for reasons of public convenience and safety, provided such regulations are applied evenly to all groups.
Religion	You are protected from government-imposed religious beliefs and are free to believe what you like.

The First Amendment had a rocky beginning. Although the First Amendment prohibits Congress from abridging freedom of expression, Federalists, who had a majority in Congress, argued that it didn't apply to seditious expression and enacted the Sedition Act of 1798, which made it a crime to print newspaper stories that criticized the national government's authority. Thomas Jefferson called the Sedition Act an "alarming infraction" of the Constitution and, upon replacing John Adams as president in 1801, pardoned those who had been convicted under it. However, because the Sedition Act was not ruled on by the Supreme Court, the question of whether Congress had the power to restrict free expression was not settled.

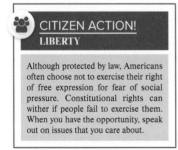

CITIZEN ACTION!
LIBERTY

Although protected by law, Americans often choose not to exercise their right of free expression for fear of social pressure. Constitutional rights can wither if people fail to exercise them. When you have the opportunity, speak out on issues that you care about.

Today, free expression is vigorously protected by the courts. Like other rights, it is not absolute in practice. Free expression does not entitle individuals to say whatever they want to whomever they want. Free expression can be denied, for example, if it seriously endangers national security or wrongly damages the reputation of others. Nevertheless, in nearly every situation Americans can freely express their political views without fear of government interference or retribution.

Free Speech

Until the 20th century, free expression was rarely at issue in the United States. However, as the country began to get enmeshed in world affairs, the government began to restrict expression that it believed was a danger to national security. One of the first restrictions was the 1917 Espionage Act, which prohibited forms of dissent that could harm the nation's effort in World War I.

This legislation became the object of the first-ever Supreme Court free-expression ruling. In *Schenck v. United States* (1919), the Supreme Court upheld the conviction of defendants who had distributed leaflets urging draft-age men to refuse induction into the military service. Writing for a unanimous Court, Justice Oliver Wendell Holmes said that Congress had the authority to restrict expression that posed "a clear and present danger" to the nation's security. In a famous passage, Holmes argued that not even the First Amendment would permit a person to falsely yell "Fire!" in a crowded theater and create a panic that could kill or injure innocent people.[17]

Although the *Schenck* decision upheld a law that limited free expression, it also established a constitutional standard—the **clear-and-present-danger test**—for determining when the government could legally do so. To meet the test, the government has to demonstrate that spoken or written expression presents a clear and present danger before it can prohibit the expression. (The use of a "test" to judge the limits of the government's authority is a common practice of the Supreme Court.)

In the early 1950s, the Court applied the clear-and-present-danger test in upholding the convictions of 11 members of the U.S. Communist Party who had been prosecuted under the Smith Act of 1940 which made it illegal to advocate the forceful overthrow of the U.S. government.[18]

By the late 1950s, Americans recognized that communist propaganda was not by itself a threat to the United States, and the Supreme Court abruptly switched its position, concluding that words alone do not endanger national security.[19] Ever since, Americans have been largely free to say what they want about politics. Over the past six decades, which includes the Vietnam and Iraq Wars, no individual has been convicted solely for criticizing the government's national security policies. (Some dissenters have been found guilty on other grounds, such as trespassing or assaulting a police officer.)

In addition to curbing the federal government's attempts to limit free speech, the Supreme Court has moved to protect speech from action by the states. A defining case was *Brandenburg v. Ohio* (1969). In a speech at a Ku Klux Klan rally, Clarence Brandenburg said that "revenge" might have to be taken if the national government "continues to suppress the white Caucasian race." He was convicted under an Ohio law, but the Supreme Court overturned the conviction, saying a state cannot prohibit speech that advocates the unlawful use of force unless it meets a two-part test: First, the speech must be "directed at inciting or producing imminent lawless action" and, second, it must be "likely to produce such action."[20] This test—the likelihood of **imminent lawless action**—is an imposing barrier to any government attempt to restrict speech. It is extremely rare for words alone to lead others to engage in rioting or other immediate forms of lawless action.

The imminent lawless action test gives Americans the freedom to express nearly any political opinion they want including "hate speech." In a unanimous 1992 opinion, the Court struck down a St. Paul, Minnesota, ordinance making it a crime to engage in speech likely to arouse "anger or alarm" on the basis of "race, color, creed, religion or gender." The Court said that the First Amendment prohibits the government from "silencing speech on the basis of its content."[21] (This protection of hate *speech* does not extend to hate *crimes,* such as assault, motivated by racial or other prejudice. A Wisconsin law that allowed lengthier sentences for hate crimes was challenged as a violation of the First Amendment. In a unanimous 1993 opinion, the Court said that the law was aimed not at free speech but at "conduct unprotected by the First Amendment."[22])

Few cases illustrate more clearly the extent to which Americans are free to speak their minds than does *Snyder v. Phelps* (2011). Pastor Fred Phelps of the Westboro Baptist Church (WBC) led a protest demonstration at the funeral

Despite the inflammatory nature of their signs and slogans, which members of the Westboro Baptist Church have displayed at military funerals, the Supreme Court has ruled that their actions are protected by the First Amendment. (Enigma/Alamy Stock Photo)

of Matthew Snyder, a U.S. Marine killed in Iraq. Like its protests at other military funerals, WBC's protest at Snyder's funeral service was directed at what the WBC believes is America's tolerance of gays and lesbians. Displaying signs such as "Fag troops" and "Thank God for dead soldiers," the protesters were otherwise orderly and stayed three blocks away from the memorial service. Snyder's father sued the WBC for "emotional distress" and was awarded $5 million in a federal trial. In an 8-1 decision, the Supreme Court overturned the award, holding that WBC's protest, although "hurtful," was protected by the First Amendment.[23]

Symbolic speech (action, not words) is also substantially protected by the First Amendment, although there are exceptions. In 1968, for example, the Supreme Court upheld the conviction of David O'Brien for burning his draft card in protest of the Vietnam War. The Court reasoned that Congress had a valid purpose in passing a law that prohibited the destruction or mutilation of draft cards.[24] In contrast, the Court in 1989 ruled that the symbolic burning of the American flag is a lawful form of expression. The ruling overturned the conviction of Gregory Lee Johnson who had set fire to the American flag outside the hall in Dallas where the 1984 Republican National Convention was being held. The Supreme Court rejected the state of Texas's argument that flag burning is, in every instance, an imminent danger to public safety. "If there is a bedrock principle underlying the First Amendment," the Court said, "it is that the Government may not prohibit the expression of an idea simply because society finds the idea itself offensive or disagreeable."[25]

In general, the Supreme Court has held that government regulation of the *content* of a message is unconstitutional. In the flag-burning case, for example, Texas was regulating the content of the message—contempt for the flag. Texas could not have been regulating the act itself in that the Texas government's own method of disposing of worn-out flags is to burn them.

Free Assembly

In a key case involving freedom of assembly, the U.S. Supreme Court in 1977 upheld a lower-court ruling against local ordinances of Skokie, Illinois, that had been invoked to prevent a parade there by the American Nazi Party.[26] Skokie had a large Jewish population, including survivors of Nazi Germany's concentration camps. The Supreme Court held that the right of free assembly takes precedence over the mere *possibility* that the exercise of that right might have undesirable consequences. Before the government can lawfully prevent a speech or rally, it must demonstrate that the event will likely cause harm and must show that it lacks an alternative way (such as assigning extra police officers to control the crowd) to prevent the harm from happening.

The Supreme Court has recognized that freedom of speech and assembly may conflict with the routines of daily life. Accordingly, individuals do not have the right to hold a public rally at a busy intersection during rush hour or the right to turn up the volume on loudspeakers to the point that they can be heard miles away. The Court allows public officials to regulate the time, place, and conditions of public assembly, provided the regulations are reasonable and are applied evenly to all groups, whatever their beliefs.[27]

Press Freedom and Libel Law

Freedom of the press also receives strong judicial protection. In *New York Times Co. v. United States* (1971), the Court ruled that the *Times*'s publication of the "Pentagon Papers" (secret government documents revealing that officials had deceived the public about aspects of the Vietnam War) could not be blocked by the government, which claimed that publication would harm the war effort. The documents had been obtained illegally by antiwar activists who gave them to the *Times.* The Court ruled that "any system of prior restraints" on the press is unconstitutional unless the government can provide a compelling reason the material should not be published.[28]

The unacceptability of **prior restraint**–government prohibition of speech or publication before it occurs–is basic to the current doctrine of press freedom. The Supreme Court has said that any attempt by the government to prevent expression carries "a 'heavy presumption' against its constitutionality."[29] One exception is wartime reporting; in some circumstances, the government can censor news reports that contain information that could compromise a military operation or risk the lives of American troops.

The constitutional right of free expression is not a legal license to avoid responsibility for the consequences of what is said or written. Although news outlets and individuals cannot ordinarily be stopped from speaking out, they can be held responsible for the impact of what they say. If false information harmful to a person's reputation is published (**libel**) or spoken (**slander**), the injured party can sue for damages. Nevertheless, slander and libel laws in the United States are based on the assumption that society has an interest in encouraging news organizations and citizens to express themselves freely. Accordingly, public officials can be criticized nearly at will without fear that the writer or speaker will have to pay them damages for slander or libel. (The courts are less protective of the writer or speaker when allegations are made about a private citizen. What is said about private individuals is considered to be less basic to the democratic process than what is said about public officials.)

The Supreme Court has held that factually accurate statements, no matter how damaging to a public official's reputation, are a protected form of expression.[30] Even false statements enjoy considerable legal protection. In *New York Times Co. v. Sullivan* (1964), the Supreme Court overruled an Alabama state court that had found the *New York Times* guilty of libel for publishing an advertisement that claimed Alabama officials had mistreated civil rights activists. Although only some of the allegations were true, the Supreme Court backed the *Times,* saying that libel of a public official requires proof of actual malice, which is defined as a knowing or reckless disregard for the truth.[31] It is hard to prove that a news outlet recklessly or knowingly published a false accusation. One of the most recent public figures to find that out is Sarah Palin who was the 2008 Republican vice-presidential nominee. She lost a libel suit against the *New York Times* in 2022 when it was ruled that she had failed to show that the newspaper had acted with malicious intent when making a false claim about her in an editorial. No federal official has won a libel judgment against a news outlet in the more than five decades since the *Sullivan* ruling.

FREEDOM OF RELIGION

Religious freedom was a reason why many Europeans chose to leave for the American colonies. In their home country, they had suffered discrimination because they held religious beliefs at odds with those established by the state. Not surprising, religious freedom made its way into the First Amendment, which reads "Congress shall make no law respecting an establishment of religion, or prohibiting the free exercise thereof."

Two clauses are contained in those words, one referring to the "establishment of religion" (the establishment clause) and the other referring to the "free exercise" of religion (the free-exercise clause).

The Establishment Clause

The **establishment clause** has been interpreted by the Supreme Court to mean that government may not favor one religion over another or support religion over no religion. (This position contrasts with that of a country such as England, where Anglicanism is the official, or "established," state religion, though no religion is prohibited.)

To this end, the Court has largely prohibited religious practices in public schools. A leading case was *Engel v. Vitale* (1962), which held that the establishment clause prohibits the reciting of prayers in public schools.[32] A year later, the Court struck down Bible readings in public schools.[33] Efforts to bring religion into the schools in less direct ways have also been invalidated. For example, the Supreme Court in 1985 invalidated an Alabama law that attempted to circumvent the prayer ruling by allowing public schools to set aside one minute each day for silent prayer or meditation.[34] On the other hand, the Supreme Court in 2022 held that a public-school football coach had a constitutional right to pray publicly on the field after a game even though players, to curry favor with the coach, might feel compelled to join him.[35]

Families have different beliefs about religion, which is a reason the Supreme Court has typically blocked schools from imposing particular religious beliefs on children. The Court has been less strict about the use of religious messages in other contexts. Congress, for example, opens its sessions with a prayer, which the Court accepts as a tradition that dates to the nation's founding.

The Court takes tradition into account in determining whether religious displays on public property will be allowed. Legal challenges to religious displays erected long ago have rarely succeeded.[36] In contrast, the Supreme Court in 2005 ordered the removal of displays of the Ten Commandments on the walls of two Kentucky courthouses. The displays were recent and had initially hung by themselves on the courtroom walls. Only after county officials were sued did they place a few historical displays alongside the religious ones. The Supreme Court concluded that the officials had a religious purpose in mind when they erected the displays and had to remove them.[37]

Although the Court can be said to have applied the *wall-of-separation doctrine* (separation of church and state) in these rulings, it has also relied upon what is called the *accommodation doctrine.* This doctrine allows the government to aid religious activity if no preference is shown toward a particular religion and if the assistance is of a nonreligious nature. In applying the doctrine, the Court at times has used a test articulated in *Lemon v. Kurtzman* (1971), a case involving state funding of the salaries of religious school instructors who teach secular subjects, such as math and English. In its ruling, the Court articulated a three-point test that has come to be known as the **Lemon test**. Government policy must meet all three conditions for it to be lawful: First, the policy must have a nonreligious purpose; second, its primary effect must be one that neither advances nor inhibits religion; third, the policy must not foster "an excessive government entanglement with religion."[38] In the *Lemon* case, the Court held that state funding of the salaries of religious school teachers failed the test because an instructor, even though teaching a subject such as math or science, could use class time for religious teaching. However, the Court has allowed states to pay for math, science, and other secular textbooks used in church-affiliated schools because the texts do not contain religious content.[39]

The Free-Exercise Clause

The First and Fourteenth Amendments also prohibit government interference with the free exercise of religion. The **free-exercise clause** has been interpreted to mean that Americans are free to hold religious beliefs of their choosing. However, Americans are not always free to act on their beliefs. The Supreme Court has allowed government interference when the exercise of religious beliefs conflicts with otherwise valid law. In *Oregon v. Smith* (1990), for example, the Court upheld Oregon's ban on the use of peyote even though the drug was part of a religious ritual, saying that the ban was not aimed at preventing the free exercise of religion but rather directed at anyone who would seek to use peyote. The Court noted that polygamy is also banned, even though some individuals accept it as a religious belief.[40]

In a more recent free-exercise decision (*Burwell v. Hobby Lobby Stores*), the Supreme Court in 2014 held that "closely held" companies (those with only a few owners) are not required to include contraceptives in employees' health insurance coverage if the owners object on religious grounds. The case stemmed from the 2010 Affordable Care Act, which required companies that provide employee health insurance to include contraceptives. The Court's majority said the requirement violates owners' free-exercise rights. In a 2020 case, the Court widened the range of companies and religious groups that can deny contraceptive coverage on religious grounds.[41]

In a 2022 ruling, the Court held that a State of Maine program that excluded religious schools from participating in a state tuition program violated the free exercise of religion. Maine had allowed non-religious private schools to receive tuition payments for their in-state secondary school students but had denied it to religious schools. The Court's 6–3 majority held that the policy discriminated "against religion."[42]

The free exercise of religion can clash with the prohibition on the establishment of religion, and the Supreme Court in these instances is forced to choose between them. In 1987, for example, the Court overturned a Louisiana law that required creationism (the Bible's account of how God created life in seven days about 10,000 years ago) to be taught along with the theory of evolution (the scientific account of how life evolved over millions of years) in public school science courses. The Court held that creationism is a religious doctrine rather than a scientific theory and that its inclusion in public school curricula violates the establishment clause by promoting a religious belief.[43] Some Christians see the Court's ruling as a violation of the free-exercise clause because it forces students to study a version of creation—evolution—that contradicts their religious beliefs.

A Pew Research Center survey found that about one in five Americans believes that life was created by God in its present form about 10,000 years ago. Some Americans believe that creationism should be taught in public school science classes where the theory of evolution is taught. The Supreme Court has rejected that argument, holding that creationism is a religious doctrine and that teaching it in public schools would violate the First Amendment ban on the establishment of religion. Shown here is artwork depicting Adam and Eve, who creationists believe were the first humans. The artwork is located at the Basilica of the Most Holy Annunciation in Florence, Italy. (Conde/Shutterstock)

THE RIGHT TO BEAR ARMS

The Second Amendment to the Constitution says, "A well regulated Militia, being necessary to the security of a free State, the right of the people to keep and bear Arms shall not be infringed." The meaning of those words was first addressed in *United States v. Miller* (1939), which challenged a federal law banning the interstate shipment of sawed-off shotguns. The Court upheld the ban, saying that such weapons did not have "any reasonable relation to the preservation or efficiency of a well-regulated militia."[44]

That interpretation of the Second Amendment governed until the Supreme Court changed it in *District of Columbia v. Heller* (2008). The ruling struck down a District of Columbia law that had banned the possession of handguns within the district's boundaries. The Court rejected the argument that the Second Amendment was intended to protect militias (roughly the equivalent to today's National Guard units), saying instead that "the Second Amendment protects an individual right to possess a firearm unconnected with service in a militia, and to use that arm for traditionally lawful purposes, such as self-defense within the home." Writing for the 5-4 majority, Justice Antonin Scalia said that the justices were "aware of the problem of handgun violence in this country."

The Supreme Court has ruled that gun ownership is protected by the Second Amendment but has not said how far that protection extends. (Ryan Rodrick Beiler/Shutterstock)

However, Scalia concluded, "The enshrinement of constitutional rights necessarily takes certain policy choices off the table. These include the absolute prohibition of handguns held and used for self-defense in the home."[45]

In a sharply worded dissent, Justice John Paul Stevens said the majority had devised a ruling that fit its partisan agenda rather than what the framers intended. Stevens declared, "When each word in the text is given full effect, the Amendment is most naturally read to secure to the people a right to use and possess arms in conjunction with service in a well-regulated militia. So far as it appears, no more than that was contemplated by its drafters."

The District of Columbia is federal territory, so the *Heller* ruling applied only to the federal government. In a 2010 decision, *McDonald v. Chicago,* the Supreme Court applied the same standard to state and local governments in striking down a Chicago ordinance that banned handgun possession.[46] In this and the *Heller* ruling, the Court did not prohibit all gun restrictions such as bans on gun ownership by former felons. However, the Court did not list all of the allowable restrictions, leaving the issue to be determined by future cases.

In *New York State Rifle & Pistol Association Inc. v. Bruen* (2022), the Supreme Court sharply curtailed the government's authority to place restrictions on guns. At issue was a century-old New York State law that limited carrying a concealed gun to individuals who had "proper cause," such as a threat on their life. In a 6–3 ruling, with all Republican-appointed justices in the majority and all Democratic-appointed justices in dissent, the Court struck down the New York law, holding that "A State may not prevent law-abiding citizens from publicly carrying handguns because they have not demonstrated a special need for self-defense." In a dissenting opinion, Justice Stephen Breyer wrote, "Many States have tried to address some of the dangers of gun violence . . . by passing laws that limit, in various ways, who may purchase, carry, or use firearms of different kinds. The Court today severely burdens States' efforts to do so."[47]

THE RIGHT OF PRIVACY

Until the 1960s, Americans' constitutional rights were confined largely to those listed in the Bill of Rights. This situation prevailed despite the Ninth Amendment, which reads "The enumeration of the Constitution, of certain rights, shall not be construed to deny or disparage others retained by the people." In 1965, however, the Supreme Court added to the list of individual rights, declaring that Americans have "a right of privacy." The Court's opinion came in the case of *Griswold v. Connecticut,* which challenged a state law prohibiting the use of condoms and other birth control devices even by married couples. The Supreme Court struck down the law, concluding that a state has no business dictating a married couple's method of birth control. Rather than invoking the Ninth Amendment, the Court's majority reasoned that constitutional protections, including the due process clauses of the 5th and 14th amendments, imply an underlying **right of privacy**. The Court held that individuals have a "zone of [personal] privacy" that government cannot lawfully invade.[48]

Although the Supreme Court's 1965 *Griswold* ruling on contraceptive use was widely said to have taken "government out of people's bedrooms," an exception remained. In a 1986 Georgia case, *Bowers v. Hardwick,* the Supreme Court held that the right of privacy did not extend to consensual sexual relations between adults of the same sex.[49] The Supreme Court reversed its position in 2003, ruling by 6–3 in *Lawrence v. Texas* that states' sodomy laws violate "the right of privacy" implied by the grant of liberty in the Fourteenth Amendment's due process clause.[50] The Court held that states cannot lawfully ban sexual relations between consenting same-sex adults. (In 2015, the Supreme Court legalized marriage for same-sex couples, a subject discussed in Chapter 5.)

In 2022, for the first time in its history, the Supreme Court took away a constitutional right. The ruling came in *Dobbs v. Jackson Women's Health Organization.* In a 5–4 ruling, the Court held that women do not have a constitutional right to abortion. That right had been established a half-century earlier in *Roe v. Wade* (1973), which declared that women have a right to privacy that gives them freedom to choose abortion during the first three months of pregnancy. In its *Roe* decision, the Court had held that the right of privacy is "broad enough to encompass a woman's decision whether or not to terminate her pregnancy."[51]

The *Roe* decision was a source of conflict from the day it was announced. Anti-abortion groups attacked the ruling and then tried but failed to get a constitutional amendment to ban abortion. However, they did persuade the Missouri and Pennsylvania legislatures to pass laws that placed restrictions on abortion, which the Supreme Court upheld in *Webster v. Reproductive Health Services*[52] and *Planned Parenthood v. Casey* (1992),[53] respectively. Although allowing restrictions, including parental notification requirements and limits on late-term abortions, the Court held to the core position that women have a right to abortion[54] and that states cannot impose an "undue burden" on women who might seek one.[55]

All of that changed with the Supreme Court's 2022 ruling. All five of the justices in the majority were Republican appointees to the Court who at one time or another had expressed their opposition to abortion. In the majority opinion, Justice Samuel Alito argued that the Roe decision "was egregiously wrong from the start," saying that there is no right to privacy in the Constitution. In dissent, the justices in the minority wrote, "one result of today's decision is certain: the curtailment of women's rights, and of their status as free and equal citizens."[56]

No decision in recent years has provoked more mass demonstrations than the Court's 2022 abortion ruling. Millions of women took the streets in support of or opposition to the decision. With the issue now to be decided in state legislatures rather than the courts, both sides vowed to make abortion a leading election issue. Said Democratic President Joe Biden, "Roe is on the ballot" (see "Party Polarization: Pro-Life Versus Pro-Choice").

RIGHTS OF PERSONS ACCUSED OF CRIMES

Due process refers to legal safeguards that have been established to protect the rights of individuals. The most significant of these protections is **procedural due process**; the term refers primarily to procedures that authorities must follow before a person can lawfully be punished for an offense.

No system of justice is foolproof. Even in the most careful systems, innocent people have been wrongly accused, convicted, and punished with imprisonment or death. But procedural safeguards, such as a defendant's right to legal counsel, greatly increase the likelihood of a fair trial. "The history of liberty

P A R T Y
POLARIZATION

Conflicting Ideas

Pro-Life Versus Pro-Choice

Since the Supreme Court ruled in *Roe v. Wade* (1973) that a woman has a constitutional right to choose abortion, every Republican Party national platform has expressed opposition to abortion. In the same period, every Democratic Party national platform has had a pro-choice plank. The sharp divide between the parties over the abortion issue has also split their followers, as can be seen in their response to the 2022 Supreme Court ruling that took away a woman's right to choose abortion. Overall, Americans by a 56-40 percent margin opposed the Court's ruling but Republicans and Democrats had sharply different views of the decision.

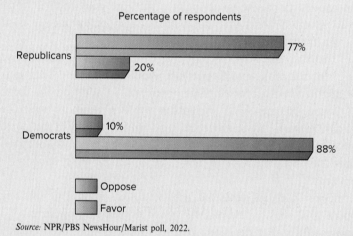

Percentage of respondents

Republicans — 77%, 20%

Democrats — 10%, 88%

☐ Oppose
☐ Favor

Source: NPR/PBS NewsHour/Marist poll, 2022.

Q: Do you think there is a "middle ground" that could bring Republicans and Democrats together on the abortion issue? Or is the moral and political divide over the issue so great that no compromise is possible?

has largely been the history of the observance of procedural guarantees," said Justice Felix Frankfurter in *McNabb v. United States* (1943).[57]

The U.S. Constitution offers procedural safeguards designed to protect a person from wrongful arrest, conviction, and punishment. The Fifth and Fourteenth Amendments provide generally that no person can be deprived of life, liberty, or property without due process of law. Specific procedural protections for the accused are listed in the Fourth, Fifth, Sixth, and Eighth Amendments.[58] (See Table 4-2.)

table 4-2	BILL OF RIGHTS: A SELECTED LIST OF DUE PROCESS PROTECTIONS
Fourth Amendment	**Sixth Amendment**
Search and seizure: You are protected from unreasonable searches and seizures, although you forfeit that right if you knowingly waive it. **Arrest:** You are protected from arrest unless authorities have probable cause to believe that you have committed a crime.	**Counsel:** You have a right to be represented by an attorney and can demand to speak first with an attorney before responding to questions from law enforcement officials. **Prompt and reasonable proceedings:** You have a right to be arraigned promptly, to be informed of the charges, to confront witnesses, and to have a speedy and open trial by an impartial jury.
Fifth Amendment	**Eighth Amendment**
Self-incrimination: You are protected against self-incrimination, which means that you have the right to remain silent and to be protected against coercion by law enforcement officials. **Double jeopardy:** You cannot be tried twice for the same crime if the first trial results in acquittal. **Due process:** You cannot be deprived of life, liberty, or property without proper legal proceedings.	**Bail:** You are protected against excessive bail or fines. **Cruel and unusual punishment:** You are protected from cruel and unusual punishment, although this provision does not protect you from the death penalty or from a long prison term for a minor offense.

Suspicion Phase: Unreasonable Search and Seizure

In 1766, Parliamentary leader William Pitt forcefully expressed a principle of English common law: "The poorest man may, in his cottage, bid defiance to all the forces of the Crown. It may be frail; its roof may shake; the wind may blow through it; the rain may enter; but the King of England may not enter; all his force dares not cross the threshold."[59] In the period immediately preceding the American Revolution, few acts provoked more anger among the colonists than British soldiers forcing their way into colonists' houses, looking for documents or other evidence of anti-British activity. The Fourth Amendment was included in the Bill of Rights to prohibit such actions by the U.S. government. The Fourth Amendment reads in part "The right of the people to be secure in their persons, houses, papers, and effects, against unreasonable searches and seizures, shall not be violated."

The Fourth Amendment protects individuals against arbitrary police action. Although a person caught in the act of a crime can be arrested (seized) and searched for weapons and incriminating evidence, the police ordinarily cannot search an individual merely on the basis of suspicion. In such instances, they have to convince a judge that they have "probable cause" (sufficient evidence) to believe that a suspect is engaged in criminal activity. If the judge concludes that the evidence is strong enough, the police will be granted a search warrant that allows them to legally search an individual's possessions.

In a unanimous 2014 decision, the Supreme Court delivered a landmark ruling on the Fourth Amendment's application to modern technology. At issue were two cases in which police without a warrant searched a suspect's cell phone after an arrest. In each case, they found information implicating the suspect. In *Riley v. California* and *United States v. Wurie,* the Court noted that, although police upon making an arrest can normally search a suspect and seize relevant physical items (such as weapons or drugs), cell phones and similar electronic devices are different in kind in that they contain large amounts of personal information (see "Case Study: *Riley v. California* (2014)"). The Court noted that "a cell phone search would typically expose to the government far

---

C A S E STUDY	Politics in Action

Riley v. California (2014)

The Fourth Amendment says "The right of the people to be secure in their persons, homes, papers, and effects, against unreasonable searches and seizures, shall not be violated." However, the Constitution does not distinguish between "unreasonable" search and seizure, which is prohibited, and "reasonable" search and seizure, which is permitted.

The Supreme Court addressed that issue in a key 2014 case, *Riley v. California*. David Riley had been pulled over by San Diego police in 2009 for having an expired vehicle registration tag. As it turned out, he also had a suspended driver's license, which, under California law, requires the vehicle to be towed. In such instances, officers must list the vehicle's contents to prevent the owner from later claiming that property had been stolen from it. In doing the inventory, police found two loaded handguns hidden under the vehicle's hood. Riley was a known gang member, and having a loaded handgun in a car is a criminal offense in California. Police arrested Riley, took his cell phone, and downloaded information from it that implicated him in a gang shooting. He was convicted of the shooting.

Riley appealed his conviction, arguing that police had violated his right to protection against unreasonable search and seizure. In a 9-0 ruling, the

Morakot Kawinchan/Shutterstock

Supreme Court ruled in Riley's favor. The Court noted that cell phones and similar electronic devices can contain a significant amount of personal information. The Court said that to equate such devices to physical objects such as weapons "is like saying a ride on horseback is materially indistinguishable from a flight to the moon." The Court likened a cell phone to a home, saying that both contain large amounts of personal information. Since police cannot normally search a person's home without getting a search warrant from a judge, a warrant is also required in *most* circumstances before a cell phone search. Police had failed to seek a warrant in Riley's case, and the Supreme Court held that the evidence gathered from his cell phone could not be used against him at a trial.

Q: Do you agree with the Court's reasoning in the *Riley* case? Can you think of circumstances in which police could lawfully search a suspect's cell phone without first getting a warrant?

ASK YOURSELF: Is a suspect's cell phone fundamentally different in kind from physical items, such as drugs, found on a suspect? What about a situation in which police have solid reason to believe the suspect's cell phone has information that could prevent an imminent criminal act by the suspect's accomplices, such as a terrorist attack or bank robbery? Would a warrantless search be legal in that type of situation?

more than the most exhaustive search of a house." The Court acknowledged that its ruling would make the work of police more difficult but said the protection of Americans' constitutional rights took priority. "We cannot deny that our decision today will have an impact on the ability of law enforcement to combat crime," said the Court. "Privacy comes at a cost."[60]

The Supreme Court allows warrantless searches in some circumstances. For example, the Court has generally given school administrators wide latitude to search students for drugs and weapons on the grounds that school administrators bear responsibility for the safety of other students.[61] The Court has also held, for example, that police roadblocks to check drivers for signs of intoxication are legal as long as the action is systematic and not arbitrary (for example, stopping only young drivers would be unconstitutional, whereas stopping all drivers is acceptable). The Court justified the decision by saying that roadblocks serve an important highway safety objective.[62] In contrast, the Court prohibits police roadblocks to check for drugs. The Court has held that narcotics roadblocks serve a general law enforcement purpose rather than one specific to highway safety and thereby violate the Fourth Amendment.[63]

Arrest Phase: Protection Against Self-Incrimination

The Fifth Amendment says, in part, that an individual cannot "be compelled in any criminal case to be a witness against himself." This provision is designed to protect individuals from the age-old practice of coerced confession. Trickery, torture, and the threat of an extra-long prison sentence can lead people to confess to crimes they did not commit.

At the time of arrest, police cannot legally begin their interrogation until the suspect has been warned that his or her words can be used as evidence.[64] This requirement emerged from *Miranda v. Arizona* (1966), which centered on Ernesto Miranda's confession to kidnapping and rape during police questioning. The Supreme Court overturned his conviction on the grounds that police had not informed him of his right to remain silent and to have legal assistance. The Court reasoned that suspects need to know their constitutional rights for these rights to be meaningful.[65] The Court's ruling led to the implementation of the "Miranda warning" that police are now required to read to suspects: "You have the right to remain silent. . . . Anything you say can and will be used against you in a court of law. . . . You have the right to an attorney." (Ernesto Miranda was subsequently retried and convicted on the basis of evidence other than his confession.)

Trial Phase: The Right to a Fair Trial

The right to a fair trial is basic to any reasonable notion of justice. Justice is denied if the trial process is arbitrary or biased against the defendant. It is sometimes said

MIRANDA WARNING

1. YOU HAVE THE RIGHT TO REMAIN SILENT.
2. ANYTHING YOU SAY CAN AND WILL BE USED AGAINST YOU IN A COURT OF LAW.
3. YOU HAVE THE RIGHT TO TALK TO A LAWYER AND HAVE HIM PRESENT WITH YOU WHILE YOU ARE BEING QUESTIONED.
4. IF YOU CANNOT AFFORD TO HIRE A LAWYER. ONE WILL BE APPOINTED TO REPRESENT YOU BEFORE ANY QUESTIONING IF YOU WISH.
5. YOU CAN DECIDE AT ANY TIME TO EXERCISE THESE RIGHTS AND NOT ANSWER ANY QUESTIONS OR MAKE ANY STATEMENTS.

WAIVER

DO YOU UNDERSTAND EACH OF THESE RIGHTS I HAVE EXPLAINED TO YOU? HAVING THESE RIGHTS IN MIND. DO YOU WISH TO TALK TO US NOW?

Shown here is a reproduction of the Miranda warning card that FBI agents carry. Agents are required in nearly all cases to read suspects their rights before interrogating them. The Miranda warning includes the Fifth Amendment right to remain silent and the Sixth Amendment right to have an attorney.

the American justice system is based on the principle that it is better to let one hundred guilty parties go free than to convict one innocent person. The system does not actually work that way. Once a person has been charged with a crime, prosecutors try to get a conviction. Defendants in such instances have fair-trial guarantees that are intended to protect them from wrongful conviction.

Legal Counsel and Impartial Jury   Under the Fifth Amendment, suspects charged with a *federal* crime cannot be tried unless indicted by a grand jury. The grand jury hears the prosecution's evidence and decides whether it is strong enough to allow the government to try the suspect. (This protection has not been incorporated into the Fourteenth Amendment. As a result, states are not required to use grand juries, although roughly half of them do so. In the rest of the states, the prosecutor usually decides whether to proceed with a trial.)

The Sixth Amendment provides a right to legal counsel before and during a trial. But what if a person cannot afford a lawyer? For most of the nation's history, the poor had no choice but to defend themselves. Then, in *Johnson v. Zerbst* (1938), the Supreme Court held that criminal defendants in federal cases must be provided a lawyer at government expense if they cannot afford one.[66] The Court extended this requirement to state cases with its ruling in *Gideon v. Wainwright* (1963). The case centered on Clarence Gideon who had been convicted in a Florida court of breaking into a pool hall. He had requested a lawyer, but the trial judge denied the request, forcing Gideon to act as his attorney. He appealed his conviction, and the Supreme Court overturned it on grounds that he did not have adequate legal counsel.[67] In his retrial, a Florida jury found Gideon not guilty. His lawyer was able to show that other men had committed the crime and blamed it on Gideon.

Criminal defendants also have the right to a speedy trial and to confront witnesses against them. At the federal level and sometimes at the state level, they have a right to a jury trial, which is to be heard by an "impartial jury." The Court has ruled that a jury's impartiality in capital cases can be compromised if the prosecution stacks a jury by using peremptory challenges to remove from the jury anyone who expresses doubt about the death penalty. To allow that practice, the Court ruled, is to virtually guarantee "a verdict of death" by a "hanging jury."[68] The jury's racial makeup can also be an issue, a concern that dates to a period in the South when Blacks accused of crimes against whites were tried by all-white juries, which invariably returned a guilty verdict. The Supreme Court in 1968 outlawed the stacking of juries by race, which, though rare, still happens. In 2019, the Supreme Court ordered the retrial of a Black defendant in a murder case where a Mississippi district attorney had used peremptory challenges to eliminate 41 of 42 potential Black jurors.[69]

The Supreme Court recently strengthened the right to a fair jury trial. The Sixth Amendment requires a unanimous jury verdict in federal cases but the Supreme Court had not applied the rule to state cases until *Ramos v. Louisiana* (2020), which held that the Fourteenth Amendment's equal-protection clause requires a unanimous jury for serious offenses. In a 6–3 ruling, the Court traced the practice of non-unanimous state juries ". . .to the rise of the Ku Klux Klan and efforts to dilute the influence of racial and ethnic and religious minorities [on jury decisions]."[70]

The Exclusionary Rule   An issue in some trials is the admissibility of evidence obtained in violation of the defendant's rights. The **exclusionary rule** bars the use of such evidence in some circumstances. The rule was formulated to deter police from violating people's rights. In *Weeks v. United States* (1914), the Supreme Court said, "The tendency of those who execute the criminal laws of the country to obtain convictions by means of unlawful searches and enforced confessions . . . should find no sanction in the judgment of the courts."[71]

The Supreme Court allows some exceptions to the exclusionary rule. One exception is called the *good faith exception*, which holds that otherwise inadmissible evidence can be used in a trial if police honestly believed they were following proper procedures, as when they obtain a search warrant that later turns out to have been faulty.[72] A second instance in which tainted evidence can be admitted is the *inevitable discovery exception*. It holds that, even if incriminating evidence is wrongly obtained, it can be used if it would have inevitably been discovered by lawful means.[73] A third instance is the *plain view exception*, which holds that evidence found in plain sight is admissible even when the evidence relates to an infraction other than the one for which the individual was stopped, as when a driver is pulled over for speeding and the officer spots illegal drugs on the back seat.[74]

Sentencing Phase: Cruel and Unusual Punishment

Most issues of criminal justice involve *procedural* due process. However, adherence to proper procedures does not necessarily produce reasonable outcomes. The Eighth Amendment was designed to address this issue. It prohibits the "cruel and unusual punishment" of those convicted of a crime. The Supreme Court has applied several tests in determining whether punishment is cruel and unusual, including whether it is "disproportionate to the offense," violates "fundamental standards of good conscience and fairness," and is "unnecessarily cruel."

Although the Supreme Court has recently employed the Eighth Amendment's "cruel and unusual punishment" clause to ban the death penalty for juveniles and the mentally ill and, in most cases, to ban life sentences without parole for juveniles,[75] it typically defers to Congress and the state legislatures on the appropriate penalties for crime (see "How the 50 States Differ"). For example, the Court upheld a conviction under California's "three strikes and you're out" law that sent a twice previously convicted felon to prison for life without parole for shoplifting items worth less than $500.[76]

Appeal: One Chance, Usually

The Constitution does not guarantee an appeal after conviction, but the federal government and all states permit at least one appeal. The Supreme Court has ruled that the appeal process cannot discriminate against poor defendants. At

HOW THE 50 STATES DIFFER
CRITICAL THINKING THROUGH COMPARISONS

Incarceration Rates

Most crimes in the United States are governed by state law rather than federal law, and states differ widely in their crime rates and sentencing practices. As a result, there is a wide variation in state prison populations. Massachusetts has the lowest rate: 108 inmates per 100,000 adults. Louisiana has the highest incarceration rate: 684 inmates for every 100,000 adults—six times the rate in Massachusetts. The figures include only those held in state prisons. The figures would be substantially higher if those held in local and county jails were included.

Continued

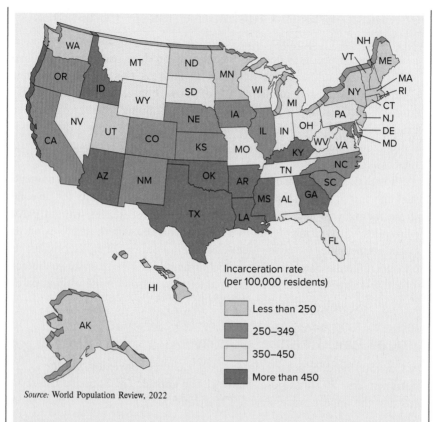

Incarceration rate
(per 100,000 residents)

Less than 250

250–349

350–450

More than 450

Source: World Population Review, 2022

Q: What do many of the low-incarceration states have in common?

A: Most of these states rank high on education and income levels. Studies indicate that individuals who are college-educated and those with higher incomes are less likely than others to engage in crime and, if convicted, less likely to receive a lengthy sentence. Most of these states also have relatively small minority-group populations. Studies have found that minority-group members, compared with White Americans, are somewhat more likely to be convicted and imprisoned for a longer period when accused of a crime.

a minimum, the government must provide indigent convicts with the legal resources to file a first appeal.[77]

Prisoners who believe their constitutional rights have been violated by state officials can appeal their conviction to a federal court. With a few exceptions, the Supreme Court has held that prisoners have the right to have their appeal heard in federal court unless they had "deliberately bypassed" the opportunity to first make their appeal in state courts.[78] Under a law enacted in 1996 to prevent inmates from filing frivolous and multiple appeals, they typically are allowed only a single appeal. The Supreme Court has ruled that, except in unusual cases, it is fair to ask inmates to first pursue their options in state courts and then limit themselves to a single federal appeal. In 2022, the Court further narrowed the options by ruling that the claim of new evidence of ineffective counsel in a state trial is an insufficient basis for a federal appeal.[79]

Crime, Punishment, and Police Practices

Supreme Court rulings have changed law enforcement practices. Most police departments, for example, require their officers to read suspects the Miranda warning before questioning them. Nevertheless, constitutional rights are applied unevenly. An example is the use of *racial profiling,* which is the targeting of individuals from minority groups, particularly Blacks, Hispanics, and Muslims. Research indicates that they are more likely than other Americans to be arbitrarily stopped, searched, and detained by police on everything from traffic infractions to public intoxication.[80] Such individuals are also more likely to become victims of police violence, an issue that sparked nationwide protests in 2020 when George Floyd, an unarmed black man, was killed by four Minneapolis police officers while handcuffed and lying face down in the street.

Sentencing policies are also an issue. Political candidates who are "tough on crime" are popular with some voters, which led state legislatures in the 1990s to enact stiffer penalties for crime while limiting the ability of judges to reduce sentences for nonviolent crimes committed by first-time offenders. It contributed to a doubling of the number of prison inmates after the 1990s. In fact, on a per-capita basis, the United States has the largest prison population in the world (see Figure 4-1). Cuba is the only country that's even close to the United States in terms of the percentage of its citizens who are behind bars.

The human and financial cost of keeping so many people in prison has prompted some states to change their sentencing laws and implement early-release programs, primarily for those convicted of nonviolent drug-related offenses. Some states have also set up treatment programs as an alternative to prison for some drug-related offenses, a policy in line with the practice in many Western democracies.

Incarceration rates (per 100,000 inhabitants)

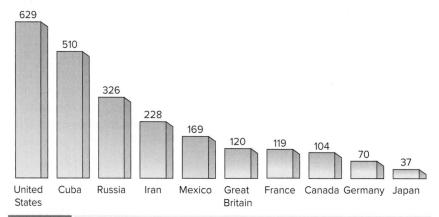

United States	Cuba	Russia	Iran	Mexico	Great Britain	France	Canada	Germany	Japan
629	510	326	228	169	120	119	104	70	37

figure 4-1   INCARCERATION RATE, BY COUNTRY

The United States is the world leader in terms of the number of people it places behind bars. More than half of the people in U.S. prisons were convicted of nonviolent offenses such as drug use or property theft. (*Source:* World Prison Brief, 2022)

F   A   K   E
or
F   A   C   T

Detecting Misinformation

Do You Have a Right to Refuse Vaccination?

As federal and state officials issued mandates requiring vaccination against COVID-19 as a condition of employment in public hospitals and schools, some of those affected claimed that it was a violation of their constitutional rights. A few even filed lawsuits, claiming that a vaccine mandate violates their due process right to life and liberty.

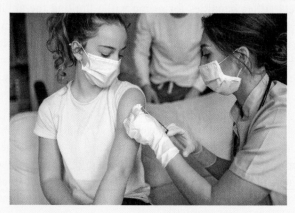

Sneksy/Getty Images

Is that claim fact or fake?

Supreme Court precedent on such claims goes back more than a century. In *Jacobson v. Massachusetts* (1905) which challenged a state law mandating that adults get vaccinated against smallpox or pay a fine, the Supreme Court ruled in the state's favor, saying that the issue was one of public health, an area in which states have constitutional authority.[81] That precedent, which was upheld in a later case,[82] governed federal courts' response to challenges relating to COVID-19 vaccine mandates. For example, in a case brought by eight Indiana University students, federal courts sided with the university rather than the students who had been denied registration because they had not complied with the university's vaccine mandate.

Unlike state governments, the federal government's authority to issue vaccine mandates is less clear-cut, given that the Constitution does not grant it direct authority over public health.[83] When the Biden administration issued such a mandate for firms with 100 or more employees, the Supreme Court invalidated the order on grounds that there was no legal authority for such a mandate. On the other hand, the Court upheld the Biden administration's vaccine mandate for workers at health care facilities that receive federal Medicare and Medicaid funding.[84] As explained in Chapter 3, the Supreme Court has held that recipients of federal grants are bound by the conditions required for getting such grants.

RIGHTS AND THE WAR ON TERRORISM

In time of war, the courts have upheld government policies that would not be permitted in peacetime.[85] After the Japanese attack on Pearl Harbor in 1941, for example, President Franklin D. Roosevelt ordered the forced relocation of tens of thousands of Japanese Americans living on the West Coast to detention camps in Arizona, Utah, and other inland locations. Congress endorsed the policy, and the Supreme Court upheld it in *Korematsu v. United States* (1944).[86] After the terrorist attacks of September 11, 2001, George W. Bush's administration invoked such precedents in declaring that customary legal protections would not be afforded to individuals it deemed to have engaged in terrorist activity.

Detention of Enemy Combatants

Soon after the terrorist attacks, the Bush administration announced its policy for handling captured "enemy combatants"—individuals judged to be engaged in, or in support of, hostile military actions against U.S. military forces. Some prisoners were subjected to abusive treatment, including torture, although the practice was denied by U.S. officials until photographic and other evidence surfaced.

In 2004, the Supreme Court issued its first ruling on these practices, holding that detainees held at the U.S. naval base, Guantánamo Bay on the tip of Cuba, had the right to challenge their detention in court. The Court reasoned that the naval base, although in Cuba, is on land leased to the United States and therefore under the jurisdiction of U.S. courts.[87] In a second 2004 case, the Court ruled that one of the Guantánamo Bay detainees, who was a U.S. citizen by virtue of having been born in the United States although raised in Saudi Arabia, had the right to be heard in U.S. courts. The Court said that the government has a legitimate interest in detaining individuals who pose a threat to the nation's security but argued that "an unchecked system of detention carries the potential to become a means of oppression and abuse of others who do not present that sort of threat."[88]

Two years later, the Supreme Court issued its sharpest rebuke of the Bush administration's detention policies. In a ruling nearly unprecedented in its challenge to a president's wartime authority, the Court held that the detainees were protected both by the U.S. Uniform Code of Military Justice and by the Geneva Conventions. At issue was the Bush administration's use of secret military tribunals to try detainees. In *Hamdan v. Rumsfeld* (2006), the Court ruled that

Shown here is the Guantánamo Bay detention camp where some of the enemy combatants detained after the U.S. invasion of Afghanistan in 2001 were imprisoned. Their treatment prompted three major Supreme Court rulings limiting Bush administration's policies. Roughly three dozen prisoners are still being held at Guantánamo Bay, and it's unclear whether some of them will ever be tried or released. (Roger L. Wollenberg/UPI/Alamy Stock Photo)

the tribunals were unlawful because they did not provide even minimal protections of detainees' rights, including the right to see the evidence against them. The Court said that the detainees were entitled to a trial by a court that upholds rights "which are recognized as indispensable by civilized peoples."[89]

Surveillance of Suspected Terrorists

After the September 11 terrorist attacks, Congress passed the USA Patriot Act, which gave the government additional tools for combating terrorism, including expanded surveillance power. The National Security Agency (NSA) launched a program that collected Americans' phone records as a means of detecting activity that might be terrorist-related. If a pattern of phone calls or e-mails suggested the possibility of terrorist activity, NSA had to obtain a warrant from a federal judge before it could eavesdrop on a person's actual conversations.

The NSA program became public in 2013 when Edward Snowden, an NSA contractor, leaked documents about the program to the press. The documents showed that NSA had collected data on nearly every call made by Americans and had actually listened in on the calls of some foreign leaders, including German chancellor Angela Merkel.

The NSA program was challenged in court and a federal appellate court ruled it unlawful, not on grounds that it violated the Fourth Amendment protection against unreasonable search and seizure but because it was not explicitly authorized by Congress. In 2015, after heated debate and a close vote in the Senate, Congress passed legislation authorizing the program while placing limits on it. For example, the legislation requires phone data to be stored with telecommunications companies rather than with NSA and to be available to NSA only if it obtains a warrant. In 2018, Congress reauthorized the program, extending it for a period of six years.

THE COURTS AND A FREE SOCIETY

The United States was founded on the idea that individuals have an innate right to liberty—to speak their minds, to worship freely, to be secure in their homes and persons, and to be assured of a fair trial. Americans embrace these freedoms in the abstract. In particular situations, however, many Americans think otherwise. A 2010 survey found, for example, that more than two in five Americans think police should not read the Miranda rights to individuals arrested by police on suspicion of terrorism.[90]

The judiciary is not isolated from the public mood. Judges inevitably must balance society's need for security and public order against the rights of the individual. Nevertheless, relative to elected officials, police officers, or the general public, judges are more protective of individual rights. How far the courts will go in protecting a person's rights depends on the facts of the case, the existing status of the law, prevailing social needs, and the personal views of the judges (see Chapter 14). Nevertheless, most judges and justices regard the protection of individual rights as their constitutional duty, which is the way the framers saw it. The Bill of Rights was created to transform the abstract idea that individuals have a right to life, liberty, and happiness into a set of specified constitutional rights, thereby bringing them under the protection of courts of law.[91]

SUMMARY

The Bill of Rights was added to the Constitution shortly after its ratification. These amendments guarantee certain political, procedural, and property rights against infringement by the national government.

The guarantees embodied in the Bill of Rights originally applied only to the national government. Under the principle of selective incorporation of these guarantees into the Fourteenth Amendment, the courts extended them to state governments, though the process was slow and uneven. In the 1920s and 1930s, the First Amendment guarantees of freedom of expression were given protection from infringement by the states. The states continued to have wide discretion in criminal proceedings until the early 1960s, when most of the fair-trial rights in the Bill of Rights were given federal protection.

Freedom of expression is the most basic of democratic rights. People are not free unless they can freely express their views. Nevertheless, free expression may conflict with the nation's security needs during times of war and insurrection. The courts at times have allowed government to limit expression substantially for purposes of national security. In recent decades, however, the courts have protected a wide range of free expression in the areas of speech, press, and religion. They have also established a right of privacy, which in some areas, such as abortion, remains a source of controversy and judicial action.

Due process of law refers to legal protections that have been established to preserve individual rights. The most significant form of these protections consists of procedures designed to ensure that an individual's rights are upheld (for example, the right of an accused person to have an attorney present during police interrogation). A major controversy in this area is the breadth of the exclusionary rule, which bars illegally obtained evidence from being used in trials.

The war on terrorism that began after the attacks on September 11, 2001, has raised new issues of civil liberties, including the detention of enemy combatants, the use of harsh interrogation techniques, and warrantless surveillance. The

Supreme Court has not ruled on all such issues but has generally held that the president's war-making power does not include the authority to disregard provisions of statutory law, treaties (the Geneva Conventions), and the Constitution.

Civil liberties are not absolute but must be judged in the context of other considerations (such as national security or public safety) and against one another when different rights conflict. The judicial branch of government, particularly the Supreme Court, has taken on much of the responsibility for protecting and interpreting individual rights. The Court's positions have changed with time and conditions, but the Court is typically more protective of civil liberties than are elected officials or popular majorities.

CRITICAL THINKING ZONE

KEY TERMS

Bill of Rights (*p. 88*)
civil liberties (*p. 87*)
clear-and-present-danger test (*p. 93*)
due process clause (*p. 88*)
establishment clause (*p. 97*)
exclusionary rule (*p. 110*)
freedom of expression (*p. 91*)
free-exercise clause (*p. 99*)
imminent lawless action (*p. 94*)

Lemon test (*p. 98*)
libel (*p. 96*)
prior restraint (*p. 96*)
procedural due process (*p. 103*)
right of privacy (*p. 102*)
selective incorporation (*p. 89*)
slander (*p. 96*)
symbolic speech (*p. 95*)

APPLYING THE ELEMENTS OF CRITICAL THINKING

Conceptualizing: Distinguish between the establishment clause and the free-exercise clause of the First Amendment. To which one does the *Lemon* test apply, and what are the components of that test?

Synthesizing: Assume that an individual has been arrested and is eventually brought to trial. Identify the procedural due process rights that the individual has at each step in the legal process. How might the exclusionary rule affect the outcome?

Analyzing: What is the process of selective incorporation, and why is it important to the rights Americans have today?

OF POSSIBLE INTEREST

A Book Worth Reading: Anthony Lewis, *Gideon's Trumpet: How One Man, a Poor Prisoner, Took His Case to the Supreme Court—and Changed the Law of the United States* (New York: Vintage, 1964). Written by a two-time Pulitzer Prize winner, this best-selling book recounts the story of how James Earl Gideon got the Supreme Court to accept his case, which led to a constitutional ruling requiring government to provide the poor with legal counsel.

A Website Worth Visiting: **www.sentencingproject.org/** The Sentencing Project works on issues and policies relating to criminal justice reform.

5
CHAPTER

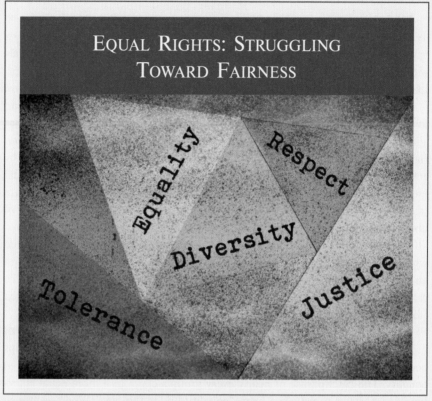

EQUAL RIGHTS: STRUGGLING TOWARD FAIRNESS

benjaminec/Shutterstock

> 66 The assertion that 'all men are created equal' was of no practical use in effecting our separation from Great Britain, and it was placed in the Declaration not for that, but for future use. 99
>
> ABRAHAM LINCOLN[1]

The Urban Institute paired up a large number of male college students. The students in each pair had similar majors, grades, work records, speech patterns, and physical builds. The students then responded to hundreds of classified job advertisements in Chicago and Washington, D.C. Within each pair, one type consistently got more interview invitations and job offers than the other type. What was the difference in the two types? In each pair, one of the students was white and the other was Black. The white students were far more likely than the Black students to get interviews and jobs. As the Urban Institute study concluded, "The level of reverse discrimination [favoring Blacks over whites] that we found was limited, was certainly far lower than many might have been led to fear, and was swamped by the extent of discrimination against black job applicants."[2]

The Urban Institute study suggests why some Americans still struggle for equality. Although Americans have equal rights in theory, they are not now equal, nor have they ever been. African Americans, women, Hispanic Americans, individuals with disabilities, Jews, Native Americans, Catholics, Mormons, Asian Americans, LGBTQ people, and others have been victims of discrimination in fact and in law.

This chapter focuses on **equal rights (civil rights)**—the right of every person to equal protection under the laws and equal access to society's opportunities and public facilities. As Chapter 4 explained, *civil liberties* are specific *individual* rights, such as freedom of speech, that are protected from infringement by government. Equal rights, or civil rights, are a question of whether individual members of particular *groups,* such as racial, gender, or ethnic groups, are treated equally by government and, in some instances, by private parties. Civil liberties and civil rights also differ in what's demanded of government. Civil liberties have been called *negative rights* in the sense that they are protected when government does not act (for instance, when it does not interfere with an individual's right to speak freely). In some instances, civil rights can be called *positive rights* in that they require government action if they are to realized (for example, when government intervenes to prevent racial discrimination).

Although the law refers to the rights of individuals first and to those of groups in a secondary and derivative way, this chapter concentrates on groups because the history of civil rights has been largely one of group claims to equality. The catchphrase of nearly every group's claim to a more equal standing in American society has been "equality under the law." When secure in their legal rights, people are positioned to pursue equality in other arenas, such as the economic sector. This chapter examines the major laws relating to equality and the conditions that led to their adoption. The chapter concludes with a brief look at some of the continuing challenges facing America's historically disadvantaged groups. The chapter emphasizes these points:

- *Americans have attained substantial equality under the law.* In purely legal terms, although not always in practice, they have equal protection under the laws, equal access to accommodations and housing, and an equal right to vote.

- *Legal equality for all Americans has not resulted in de facto equality.* African Americans, women, Hispanic Americans, and other traditionally disadvantaged groups have a disproportionately small share of America's opportunities and benefits. However, the issue of what, if anything, government should do to deal with this problem is a major source of contention.

- *Disadvantaged groups have had to struggle for equal rights.* African Americans, women, Native Americans, Hispanic Americans, Asian Americans, and a number of other groups have had to fight for their rights in order to achieve a fuller measure of equality.

EQUALITY THROUGH LAW

Equality has always been the least developed of America's founding concepts. Not even Thomas Jefferson, who wrote the words, believed that a precise meaning could be given to the claim of the Declaration of Independence that "all men are created equal."[3] Nevertheless, the promise of equality has placed history on the side of those denied it. Every civil rights movement, from suffrage for males without property in the 1830s to LGBTQ rights today, has derived moral strength from the nation's pledge of equality for all. Those efforts have led to policies that have made Americans more equal in law.

The Fourteenth Amendment: Equal Protection

Ratified in 1868 after the Civil War, the Fourteenth Amendment declares that no state shall "deny to any person within its jurisdiction the equal protection of the laws." The **equal-protection clause** was designed to require states to treat their residents equally, but the Supreme Court at first refused to interpret it that way. As discussed in Chapter 3, the Court in *Plessy v. Ferguson* (1896) ruled that "separate" public facilities for Black citizens did not violate the Constitution as long as the facilities were "equal."[4] The *Plessy* decision became a justification for the separate and *unequal* treatment of African Americans. Black children were forced to attend separate schools that rarely had libraries or enough teachers.

Decades passed before that policy began to change. In a first ruling, the Supreme Court held that Blacks must be allowed to use public facilities reserved for whites in cases where the states had not created separate facilities. When Oklahoma, which had no law school for Blacks, was ordered to admit Ada Sipuel in 1949, it did so but roped off her seat from the rest of the class and stenciled the word *colored* on it.[5]

Segregation in the Schools   Substantial judicial intervention on behalf of African Americans finally occurred in 1954 with *Brown v. Board of Education of Topeka* (see "Case Study: *Brown v. Board of Education* (1954)"). The case began when Linda Carol Brown, a Black child in Topeka, Kansas, was denied admission to an all-white elementary school that she passed every day on her way to her all-Black school, which was nearly a mile farther away. In a unanimous decision, the Court invoked the Fourteenth Amendment's equal-protection clause, declaring that racial segregation of public schools "generates [among Black children] a feeling of inferiority as to their status in the community that may affect their hearts and minds in a way unlikely ever to be undone. . . . Separate educational facilities are inherently unequal."[6]

The Jim Crow era of racial segregation in the South was marked not only by racially segregated schools and other public facilities but also by violence against Black citizens who spoke against racial injustice. More than 4,000 Black Americans were lynched by white mobs. The Equal Justice Initiative has recently sponsored the installation of markers to remind Americans of this horrific chapter of their history. Shown here is a sign marking the spot in Hahira, Georgia, where 21-year-old Mary Turner was brutally murdered in 1918 by a local mob after publicly denouncing her husband's lynching. The pockmarks on the sign are from bullets recently fired at it, presumably by individuals who harbor the racial hatred that led to the lynching of Black Americans. (Jen Wolf/Shutterstock)

CASE STUDY

Politics in Action

Brown v. Board of Education (1954)

The Fourteenth Amendment, ratified after the Civil War to protect formerly enslaved people, declared that no state shall "deny to any person within its jurisdiction the equal protection of the laws." Nevertheless, southern states soon established a two-race system. Black residents were prohibited from

Library of Congress, Prints and Photographs Division [LC-USF34-046235-D]

using the same public schools, hospitals, and other facilities as white residents. In 1896, the Supreme Court held that separate facilities for whites and Blacks were legal as long as they were "equal," ignoring both the intent of the Constitution and the fact that facilities reserved for Blacks were vastly inferior.

The South's two-race system began to crumble when the Supreme Court in 1954 voided the policy of separate public schools. In its unanimous decision in *Brown v. Board of Education*, the Court said, "Separate educational facilities are inherently unequal [and violate] the equal protection of the laws guaranteed by the Fourteenth Amendment."

A 1954 Gallup poll indicated that most southern whites opposed the *Brown* decision, and billboards were erected along southern roadways that called for the impeachment of Chief Justice Earl Warren. In the so-called Southern Manifesto, southern members of Congress urged their state governments to "resist forced integration by any lawful means." Rioting broke out in 1957 when Arkansas's governor called out the state's National Guard to prevent Black students from entering Little Rock's high school. They gained entry only after President Dwight D. Eisenhower used his power as the commander in chief to place the Arkansas National Guard under federal control.

The Supreme Court's *Brown v. Board of Education* decision became precedent for rulings that, over the years, have extended equal protection to other groups. Indeed, *Brown* is widely regarded as one of the Supreme Court's most important decisions, ranking alongside such rulings as *Marbury v. Madison* (1803), *McCulloch v. Maryland* (1819), and *Schenck v. United States* (1919).

Q: What is the major limit on the Fourteenth Amendment as a means of preventing discrimination?

ASK YOURSELF: Who is prohibited by the Fourteenth Amendment from discriminating against individuals on the basis of their race, creed, or ethnicity? Who is not? If an individual is denied service in a restaurant because of race, creed, or ethnicity, is that person entitled to sue the owner on grounds that his or her Fourteenth Amendment rights have been violated? Why or why not?

Although the *Brown* decision banned forced segregation in public schools, it did not require states to take steps to integrate their schools. Because most residential neighborhoods were racially segregated, so were the neighborhood schools. Even as late as 15 years after *Brown*, 95 percent of Black children were attending schools that were mostly or entirely Black.

In *Swann v. Charlotte-Mecklenburg County Board of Education* (1971), the Supreme Court upheld the busing of children out of their neighborhoods for the purpose of achieving racially integrated schools.[7] Forced busing produced angry demonstrations in Charlotte, Detroit, Boston, and dozens of other cities, and the policy had mixed results. Studies found that busing reduced school children's racial biases and improved minority children's academic performance without diminishing that of their white classmates.[8] On the other hand, the policy forced many children to spend long hours each day riding school buses and contributed to white flight to the suburbs, which were insulated by a 1974 Supreme Court decision that prohibited busing across school district lines except where district boundaries had been deliberately drawn to keep the races apart.[9] The declining number of white students in city schools made it harder through busing to create racially balanced classrooms. In a 2007 decision involving the Seattle and Louisville school systems, the Supreme Court effectively ended forced busing by ruling that it violated the equal-protection rights of students who were required to attend a distant school.[10]

As a result of white flight to private and suburban schools and the end of racial busing, America's schools have become less racially diverse. In fact, America's schools are now more racially segregated than they were when busing started.[11]

Court-ordered racial busing to integrate public schools was met with violence in many communities, including some in the North. Boston and surrounding towns witnessed some of the worst rioting, including the scene pictured here. (Spencer Grant/Archive Photos/Getty Images)

Judicial Tests of Equal Protection   The Fourteenth Amendment's equal-protection clause does not require the government to treat people equally in all circumstances. The judiciary allows inequalities that are "reasonably" related to a legitimate government interest. In applying this **reasonable-basis test**, the courts require government only to show that a particular law is reasonable. For example, 21-year-olds can legally drink alcohol but 20-year-olds cannot. The courts have held that the goal of reducing fatalities from alcohol-related accidents involving young drivers is a valid reason for imposing an age limit on the purchase and consumption of alcohol.

The reasonable-basis test does not apply to racial or ethnic classifications (see Table 5-1). The Supreme Court's position is that race and national origin are **suspect classifications**—in other words, laws that classify people differently on the basis of their race or ethnicity are assumed to have discrimination as their purpose. Any law that treats people differently because of race or ethnicity is subject to the **strict-scrutiny test**, which presumes that the law is unconstitutional unless the government can provide a compelling reason for it.

Although the notion of suspect classifications was implicit in earlier cases, including *Brown,* the Court did not use those words until *Loving v. Virginia* (1967). When Richard Loving, a white man, and Mildred Jeter, a woman of African American and Native American descent, got married in Washington, D.C., and then returned home to Virginia, police invaded their home and arrested them. The state of Virginia claimed that its ban on interracial marriage did not violate the equal-protection clause because the penalty for the offense—a prison sentence of one to five years—was the same for the white and the non-white spouse. The Supreme Court ruled otherwise, saying that the Virginia law was "subversive of the principle of equality at the heart of the Fourteenth Amendment."[12]

table 5-1	LEVELS OF COURT REVIEW FOR LAWS THAT TREAT AMERICANS DIFFERENTLY	
Test	**Application**	**Standard Used**
Strict scrutiny	Race, ethnicity	Suspect category—assumed unconstitutional in the absence of an overwhelming justification
Intermediate scrutiny	Gender	Almost suspect category—assumed unconstitutional unless the law serves a clearly compelling and justified purpose
Reasonable basis	Other categories (such as age and income)	Not suspect category—assumed constitutional unless no sound rationale for the law can be provided

The Supreme Court has not extended strict scrutiny to include women. Instead, the Court holds that women can be treated differently if the policy in question is "substantially related" to the achievement of "important governmental objectives."[13] The Court has placed women in an intermediate (or almost suspect) category, which has led it to strike down nearly every law it has reviewed that singled out women. A leading case is *United States v. Virginia* (1996), in which the Court invalidated the male-only admissions policy of Virginia Military Institute (VMI), a 157-year-old state-supported college. In its ruling, the Court said that Virginia had failed to provide an "exceedingly persuasive" argument for its policy.[14] However, in *Rostker v. Goldberg* (1980), the Court upheld a law that discriminates between men and women. The Court ruled that the male-only draft registration law serves the important objective of excluding women from *involuntary* combat duty.[15]

The Civil Rights Act of 1964

The Fourteenth Amendment prohibits discrimination by the government but not by private parties. As a result, for a long period in American history, private employers could freely discriminate in their hiring practices, and owners of restaurants, hotels, and other public accommodations could legally bar Black people from entering. That changed with the 1964 Civil Rights Act. Based on Congress's power to regulate commerce, the legislation entitles all persons to equal access to public accommodations. The legislation also bars discrimination on the basis of race, color, religion, sex, or national origin in the hiring, promotion, and wages of employees of medium-size and large firms. A few forms of job discrimination are still lawful under the Civil Rights Act. For example, a church-related school can take religion into account in hiring teachers.

The Civil Rights Act proved effective in reducing discrimination in access to public accommodations because it's relatively easy to prove discrimination when a person is denied service at a restaurant or hotel that has available space. The act proved less effective in the area of employment, where it's harder to prove discrimination. This situation led to the creation of affirmative action programs, discussed in a later section.

The Voting Rights Act of 1965

Although ratification of the Fifteenth Amendment in 1870 granted Black Americans the right to vote, southern whites invented an array of devices, such as whites-only primaries, poll taxes, and literacy tests, to keep Blacks from registering and voting. In the mid-1940s, for example, there were only 2,500 registered Black voters in the entire state of Mississippi, even though its Black population numbered half a million.[16]

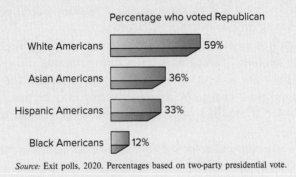

P A R T Y   POLARIZATION

Conflicting Ideas

The Politics of Civil Rights

When Democrats took the lead in enacting the 1964 Civil Rights Act and 1965 Voting Rights Act, President Lyndon Johnson predicted that the Democratic Party would lose support among white voters, particularly those in the South. Johnson's prediction was borne out. It has been decades since the Democratic Party received a majority of white votes in a presidential or congressional election. There is a wide gap today in the voting patterns of white and minority-group Americans, as this chart indicates.

Percentage who voted Republican

White Americans — 59%
Asian Americans — 36%
Hispanic Americans — 33%
Black Americans — 12%

Source: Exit polls, 2020. Percentages based on two-party presidential vote.

Q: Do you think the wide gap in the party loyalties of whites and minority-group members makes it easier or harder for Republicans and Democrats to bridge their other differences?

Racial barriers to voting began to crumble in the mid-1940s when the Supreme Court declared that whites-only primary elections were unconstitutional.[17] Ratification of the Twenty-Fourth Amendment in 1964 outlawed the poll tax, which was a fee that individuals had to pay before being allowed to register to vote. The Supreme Court subsequently banned the use of literacy tests as a condition for being allowed to register to vote.[18]

Nevertheless, the major policy change was the Voting Rights Act of 1965, which prohibited discrimination in voting and registration. The legislation empowered federal agents to register voters in states and localities with a history of voter discrimination. The Voting Rights Act had an immediate impact on Black participation. In the ensuing presidential election, Black turnout in the South jumped by 20 percentage points.

The Voting Rights Act is still in place but has been greatly weakened. In *Shelby County v. Holder* (2013), the Supreme Court invalidated the provision (Section 4) of the Voting Rights Act that included the formula for determining which states and counties were subject to federal oversight. The formula included factors such as an area's use of various devices to keep Black citizens from voting. Designated states and counties were required by the preclearance provision (Section 5) of the Voting Rights Act to obtain permission from federal officials before they made changes—such as altering registration requirements— that might adversely affect a minority group. In its *Shelby County* decision, the Court's majority held that the formula for identifying the states and counties subject to federal oversight was based on "obsolete statistics" and that Congress had to update it before it could be applied.[19] Congress has not updated the formula, with the result that no state or county requires federal permission to change their voting process.

In 2021, the Supreme Court further weakened the Voting Rights Act in a case involving Section 2, which bars states from imposing voting procedures that abridge the right to vote on account of race or color. The Court in a 6–3 decision upheld a change in Arizona's voting laws on grounds that the additional burden it imposed on voters was not large enough to invalidate the law.[20]

One area where race and color still restrict state lawmakers is the drawing of legislative district boundaries. In 2017, for example, the Supreme Court struck down the boundaries of two North Carolina congressional districts on grounds they had been deliberately drawn to reduce the power of Black Americans. But that protection, too, could be weakening. In 2022, the Supreme Court overturned a lower-court ruling that invalidated the congressional district plan of Alabama's Republican-controlled legislature because it eliminated a district that previously had a Black majority.[21]

These rulings have led to charges that the Supreme Court is pursuing a partisan agenda (see **Chapter 14**). In all of the decisions that have weakened the Voting Rights Act, the Court's majority has consisted solely of Republican-appointed justices.

The Civil Rights Act of 1968

In 1968, Congress passed civil rights legislation designed to prohibit discrimination in housing. A building owner cannot refuse to sell or rent housing because of a person's race, religion, ethnicity, or sex. An exception is allowed for owners of small, multifamily dwellings who reside on the premises.

Despite legal prohibitions on discrimination, housing in America remains highly segregated. Only a third of African Americans live in a neighborhood that is mostly white. One reason is that the annual income of most Black families is substantially below that of most white families. Another reason is banking practices. At one time, banks contributed to housing segregation by *redlining*—refusing to grant mortgage loans in certain neighborhoods, typically those with large Black populations. Since buyers could not get a mortgage, homeowners had to lower the selling price to sell their homes. As home values dropped, white families increasingly left these neighborhoods, which increased the percentage of Black families living there. The 1968 Civil Rights Act prohibits redlining, but many of the segregated neighborhoods it helped create still exist. Moreover, although discriminatory lending practices are now prohibited by law, studies indicate that Hispanics and African Americans still have more difficulty obtaining mortgages than do white applicants of the same income.[22] Nor does the problem end when they buy a home. When it comes to refinancing or selling their home, real estate appraisals of its value are often much less than an identical home being sold by a white owner.[23]

Affirmative Action

Changes in the law seldom have large or immediate effects on how people behave. Although the 1964 Civil Rights Act prohibited job discrimination on the basis of race, color, religion, sex, or national origin, many employers continued to favor white male employees. Membership in many union locals, for example, was handed down from father to son. Moreover, the Civil Rights Act did not require employers to prove that their employment practices were fair. Instead, the burden of proof was on the woman or minority-group member who was denied a job. It was costly and usually difficult for an individual to prove in court that gender or race was the reason for not being hired or promoted. Moreover, a victory in court applied only to the individual in question; it did not help other women and minorities faced with job discrimination.

Affirmative action programs were devised as a remedy for such problems. **Affirmative action** refers to deliberate efforts to provide full and equal opportunities in employment, education, and other areas for members of traditionally disadvantaged groups. Affirmative action applies only to organizations—such as universities, agencies, and construction firms—that receive federal funding or contracts. These organizations are required to establish programs designed to ensure that all applicants are treated fairly. They also bear a burden of proof. If an organization grants a disproportionate share of opportunities to white males, it must show that the pattern is the result of necessity (such as the nature of the job or the locally available labor pool) and not the result of systematic discrimination.

Equality of result, which was the aim of affirmative action, was a new concept. Other major civil rights policies had sought to eliminate **de jure discrimination**, which is discrimination based on law, as in the case of state laws requiring African American and white children to attend separate schools during the pre-*Brown* period. Affirmative action policy sought to alleviate **de facto discrimination**—the condition whereby historically disadvantaged groups have fewer opportunities because of prejudice and financial constraints.

Few issues have sparked more controversy than has affirmative action, and even today the public has a mixed response to it. Most Americans support programs designed to ensure that historically disadvantaged groups receive equal treatment but oppose programs that would give them preferential treatment. A Gallup poll found, for example, that only 4 percent of white Americans believe race and ethnicity should be a "major factor" in college admission decisions, while 67 percent say race and ethnicity should count "not at all" in such decisions.[24]

Policies that pit individuals against each other over jobs, college admissions, and the like typically end up in the Supreme Court, and affirmative action is no exception. In *Regents of the University of California v. Bakke* (1978), the Court issued its first affirmative action ruling, holding that a California medical school had violated the equal-protection rights of Alan Bakke, a white male applicant, by reserving a fixed number of admissions ("a quota") for minority applicants. In doing so, however, it did not invalidate affirmative action per se. The Court said that race can be among the factors that colleges take into consideration to create a diverse student body but that colleges cannot use quotas in determining admissions.[25]

The Court later narrowed the scope of affirmative action. In the key case of *Adarand v. Peña* (1995), for example, the Court invalidated a federal policy that had reserved 10 percent of federally funded construction projects for minority-owned firms. The Court held that such firms cannot benefit from the fact that minority-owned firms had been discriminated against in the past.[26]

Opponents of affirmative action thought that the *Adarand* decision might lead the Supreme Court to abolish it entirely. However, in *Grutter v. Bollinger* (2003), the Court upheld the University of Michigan law school's admissions policy, which took into account race (along with other factors such as work experience and extracurricular activities) in admissions decisions. The Court concluded that Michigan's program was being applied sensibly and that it fostered Michigan's "compelling interest in obtaining the educational benefits that flow from a diverse student body."[27] The Court reaffirmed that position in 2016 in *Fisher v. University of Texas*.[28]

In 2016, the Supreme Court ruled on an affirmative action case involving the University of Texas at Austin (pictured here). The Court ruled in favor of the university, holding that its affirmative action policy was constitutional. (Simon Leigh/Alamy Stock Photo)

The Michigan and Texas cases clarified the test that the Supreme Court applies in affirmative action cases. For affirmative action to be upheld, it must, first, serve a "compelling governmental interest." A diverse student body, for example, can be justified because it enhances understanding and fosters tolerance. Second, to be upheld, affirmative action must be "narrowly tailored" to achieve the desired goal. This test precludes overly broad action. That part of the test was what led the Supreme Court to strike down the 10 percent rule for government contracts. The awarding of contracts to minority firms merely because other such firms had been discriminated against in the past was not narrowly tailored to fit the current situation.

Affirmative action could conceivably go the way of racial busing. Several Supreme Court justices have indicated that it was not intended to be permanent, and the Court is currently reviewing cases involving Harvard University and the University of North Carolina that could lead it to end the policy.[29]

THE STRUGGLE FOR EQUALITY

American history indicates that disadvantaged groups have never achieved greater equality without a struggle.[30] The policies that protect these groups today are the result of sustained political action that forced entrenched interests to relinquish or share their privileged status. Progress has been made toward a more equal America, but civil rights problems involve deeply rooted conditions, habits, and prejudices.

The following discussion describes the struggles disadvantaged groups have faced historically and some of the struggles they face today.

Black Americans

The impetus behind the 1964 Civil Rights Act was the black civil rights movement. Without it, the legislation would have come later and possibly have been less sweeping.

During World War II, African American soldiers fought against Nazi racism, only to return to an America where racial discrimination was legal and oppressive.[31] Demands for change intensified after an incident in Montgomery, Alabama, on December 1, 1955. Upon leaving work that day, Rosa Parks boarded a bus for home, taking her seat as required by law in the section reserved for Blacks. When all the seats for white passengers were occupied, the bus driver ordered Parks to give her seat to a white passenger. She refused and was arrested. A young pastor at a local Baptist church, Dr. Martin Luther King Jr., led a boycott of Montgomery's bus system, which spread to other cities. The Black civil rights movement would continue for more than a decade. A peak moment occurred in 1963 with the March on Washington for Jobs and Freedom, which attracted 250,000 marchers, one of the largest gatherings in the capital's history. In a riveting speech to the massive crowd, King expressed his dream of a better America, one where people are judged by the quality of their personal character rather than by the color of their skin.[32]

The momentum of the March on Washington carried over into Congress, where major civil rights legislation was languishing in House committee. Although opponents employed every possible legislative maneuver in an effort to block it, it finally cleared the House the following February. Senate maneuvering and debate—including a 55-day filibuster—took another four months. Finally, in early July, President Lyndon Johnson signed into law the Civil Rights Act of 1964.

Nevertheless, Martin Luther King Jr.'s dream of an equal society for Black Americans remains elusive.[33] Poverty is a persistent problem in the Black community, affecting everyone from the very old to the very young. The median net worth of households headed by retired Black people is less than $20,000, compared with roughly $200,000 for retired white people. Among adults of employment age, the jobless rate of African Americans is twice that of white Americans. Black children are especially disadvantaged. Roughly

27 percent of them live below the government-defined poverty line, compared with about 14 percent of white children. In addition, more than half of Black children grow up in a single-parent family, and about 1 in 10 grow up in a home where neither parent is present. Children who grow up in a single-parent household are much more likely to have inadequate nutrition, not finish high school, not attend college, be unemployed as an adult, and spend time in prison.[34]

African Americans have made substantial progress in winning elective office. Although the percentage of Black elected officials is still far below the proportion of African Americans in the population, it has risen in recent decades.[35] There are now roughly 400 Black mayors and 60 Black members of Congress. Barack Obama's election to the presidency in 2008 marked the first time an African American was chosen to fill the nation's highest office. In 2022, Ketanji Brown Jackson became the first Black woman, and the third Black American, to serve on the Supreme Court.

F	A	K	E
		or	
F	A	C	T

Detecting Misinformation

Is Justice Color Blind?

Over the past half-century, the United States has made progress in upholding the ideal of "equal justice under the law." Supreme Court rulings based on the Fourteenth Amendment's due process and equal-protection clauses have boosted the legal standing of Black Americans and other historically disadvantaged groups. But does the reality of daily life match the legal gains? Most Black

Michael Matthews/Police Images/Alamy Stock Photo

Americans say no. An NBC poll found, for example, that only 12 percent of Blacks believe that their community's police officers treat white and Blacks equally.[36]

Continued

Is that claim fact, or is it fake?

Although there are communities where police treat white and Black residents equally, research indicates that Black Americans are more likely than white Americans to be ticketed or arrested for engaging in the same acts.[37] Black Americans are also more likely to be convicted and receive a stiffer sentence when charged with comparable crimes. A U.S. Department of Justice study found that, among persons convicted of drug crimes in state courts, half of the Black defendants received a prison sentence, compared with a third of the white defendants.[38] Moreover, as a study of 2013–2019 police killings revealed, unarmed Black persons are 30 percent more likely to be killed by police than unarmed white persons.[39] The unprovoked killing by Minneapolis police of George Floyd, an unarmed and handcuffed Black man, sparked nationwide protests in 2020. In response, more than half the states legislated policing reforms, including provisions relating to the use of force and the handling of cases of police misconduct.[40]

Women

The Black civil rights movement inspired other disadvantaged groups to demand their rights, of whom women were the most vocal and successful.

The United States carried over from English common law a political disregard for women, forbidding them to vote, hold public office, or serve on juries.[41] Upon marriage, a woman essentially lost her identity as an individual and could not own and dispose of property without her husband's consent. Even a wife's body was not fully hers. A wife's adultery was declared by the Supreme Court in 1904 to be a violation of the husband's property rights.[42]

The first highly organized attempt to promote women's rights came in 1848 in Seneca Falls, New York. Lucretia Mott and Elizabeth Cady Stanton had been barred from the main floor of an antislavery convention and decided to organize a women's rights convention. Thereafter, the struggle for women's rights became closely aligned with the abolitionist movement. However, when Congress wrote the Fifteenth Amendment after the Civil War, women were excluded. The amendment said only that the right to vote could not be abridged on account of race or color. Not until the ratification of the Nineteenth Amendment in 1920 did women acquire the right to vote.

In 1972, responding to the women's rights movement, Congress approved the Equal Rights Amendment (ERA), which would give equal rights to women.[43] The ERA came up three states short of the three-fourths majority required for ratification.[44] However, women did succeed in other efforts.

Among the congressional measures enacted were the Equal Pay Act of 1963, which prohibits sex discrimination in salary and wages by some categories of employers; Title IX of the Education Amendment of 1972, which prohibits sex discrimination in education; and the Equal Credit Act of 1974, which prohibits sex discrimination in the granting of financial credit. Two decades later, women gained another legislative victory when Congress passed the Family and Medical Leave Act. It provides for up to 12 weeks of unpaid leave and a secure job for employees to care for a new baby or a seriously ill family member. The law applies to men as well as women, but women were the driving force behind the legislation and are the primary beneficiaries because they usually bear most of the responsibility for newborn or sick family members.

In recent decades, women have entered the job market in increasing numbers. They are six times more likely today than a half-century ago to work outside the home and have made inroads in male-dominated fields. For example, roughly half of all graduating lawyers and physicians are women. The change in women's work status is also reflected in education trends. A few decades ago, more men than women were enrolled in college. Today, the reverse is true. A recent U.S. Education Department report showed that women are ahead of men in more than just college enrollment; they are also more likely on average to complete their degree, do so in a shorter period, and get better grades.[45]

Women have made inroads in male-dominated professions but still lag behind men in average pay and appointment to top positions. For example, although a slight majority of TV news reporters today are women, women make up less than a third of the top editors at major news outlets. (Alexander Podshivalov/Zoonar GmbH/Alamy Stock Photo)

Women are now the top earner in about a third of two-parent house-holds.[46] Women increasingly hold managerial positions, but, as they rise through the ranks, they can encounter the so-called glass ceiling, which is the invisible but nonetheless real barrier that some women face when firms pick their top execu-tives. Of the 500 largest U.S. corporations, less than 10 percent are headed by women. Women also get paid less than men. In 2020, full-time female employees' median annual income was 83 percent of that of full-time male employees ($50,982 versus $59,634). Many of the jobs traditionally held by women, such as office assistant, pay less than many of the jobs traditionally held by men, such as truck driver. Women's groups have had only limited success in persuading governments and firms to institute *comparable worth policies* that give women and men equal hourly pay for jobs that require a similar level of training and education.[47]

Most single-parent families are headed by women, and nearly one in four of these families live below the poverty line, which is five times the level of two-parent families (see Figure 5-1). The situation has been described as "the fem-inization of poverty." Especially vulnerable are single-parent families headed by women who work in a nonprofessional field. Women without a college educa-tion or special skills often cannot find jobs that pay significantly more than the child-care expenses they would incur if they worked outside the home.

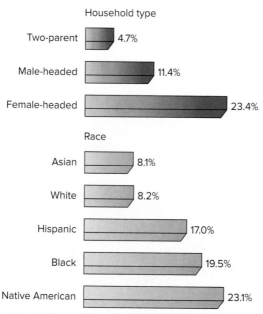

figure 5-1   PERCENTAGE OF FAMILIES LIVING IN POVERTY

Female-headed and minority-group households are most likely to have incomes below the poverty line. (*Source:* U.S. Census Bureau, 2022.)

Women have made major gains in the area of political office. In 1981, Sandra Day O'Connor became the first female Supreme Court justice. Four of the nine justices today are women. When the Democratic Party chose Geraldine Ferraro as its 1984 vice presidential nominee, she became the first woman to run on a major party's national ticket. In 2016, Hillary Clinton, as the Democratic presidential nominee, became the first woman to head the ticket. Kamala Harris in 2021 became the first woman (as well as the first Black and first Asian American) to hold the vice presidency. Nevertheless, women are still a long way from attaining political parity.[48] Women hold less than a third of congressional seats (see "How the U.S. Differs").

HOW THE U.S. DIFFERS

CRITICAL THINKING THROUGH COMPARISONS

Women's Representation in National Legislatures

Women today hold far more congressional seats than at earlier times in American history, but they are still far from achieving parity with men. Less than a third of congressional seats are held by women. As the chart indicates, the United States ranks below its neighboring countries, Mexico and Canada, as well as representative European democracies in terms of the percentage of women lawmakers.

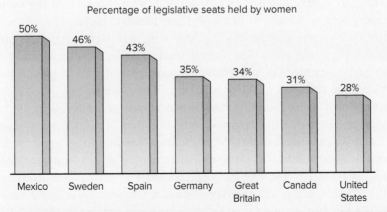

Percentage of legislative seats held by women

Mexico	Sweden	Spain	Germany	Great Britain	Canada	United States
50%	46%	43%	35%	34%	31%	28%

Source: Interparliamentary Union, 2022. Based on seats in the single or lower legislative chamber, which is the House of Representatives in the case of the United States.

Continued

Q: How might differences in the U.S. and European electoral systems contribute to differences in the number of women legislators? (Most European democracies rely on a proportional representation system, where the parties get seats in proportion to the number of votes they receive in the election. In contrast, U.S. candidates are elected singly in legislative districts.)

A: In a proportional representation system, each party lists its candidates in a priority order before the election. By placing women high on its list, a party can ensure that they will receive a certain proportion of the legislative seats that it wins in an election. In contrast, the U.S. system rests on the preferences of voters in individual contests, which makes it harder for a political party to control who gets its legislative seats. (The proportional and single-member district systems are explained more fully in Chapter 8.)

Hispanic Americans

Hispanic Americans—that is, people of Spanish-speaking background—are one of the nation's oldest ethnic groups. Hispanics helped colonize California, Texas, Florida, New Mexico, and Arizona before those areas were annexed by the United States. Nevertheless, most Hispanics are immigrants or the children or grandchildren of immigrants.

Hispanics are the nation's largest racial or ethnic minority group. More than 50 million Hispanics live in the United States—twice the number of three decades ago. They have emigrated to the United States primarily from Mexico and the Caribbean islands, mainly Cuba. About half of all Hispanics in the United States were born in Mexico or claim Mexican ancestry. Hispanics are concentrated in their states of entry. Florida, New York, and New Jersey have large numbers of Caribbean Hispanics, whereas California, Texas, Arizona, and New Mexico have many Mexican immigrants. Hispanics, mostly of Mexican descent, constitute more than half of the population of Los Angeles.

An early civil rights action by Hispanics occurred in California in the late 1960s, when Hispanic farm laborers, most of whom were migrant workers, went on strike over labor rights. Migrants were working long hours for low pay, were living in shacks without electricity or plumbing, and were unwelcome in many local schools and hospitals. Farm owners at first refused to bargain with the workers, but a well-organized national boycott of California grapes and lettuce forced the state to pass a law giving migrant workers the right to bargain collectively. The strikes were led by Cesar Chavez, who grew up in a Mexican American migrant family. Chavez's tactics were copied with less success in other states, including Texas.[49]

Recent Hispanic civil rights action has centered on undocumented immigrants, individuals who have entered the country illegally or stayed after their visa expired. Estimates of the number of undocumented immigrants run as high as 12 million people, most of whom are Hispanic. Although polls show that most Americans favor providing them a path to citizenship,[50] undocumented immigrants have periodically been the target of heightened legislative or law enforcement efforts aimed at their deportation. Such efforts have been resisted by the Hispanic community and, in some instances, have sparked mass demonstrations.

Hispanics make up the largest proportion of "Dreamers," who are undocumented immigrants brought into the country as young children. Several attempts in Congress to grant them legal status have been unsuccessful and, in 2012, the Obama administration established the Deferred Action for Childhood Arrivals program (DACA) to protect them from deportation. The Trump administration rescinded the program, but the Supreme Court in 2020 invalidated the action and the Biden administration extended the program upon taking office.[51]

Hispanics' average annual income is substantially below the national average, but the effect is buffered somewhat by Hispanics' family structure. Compared with Black Americans, Hispanics are nearly twice as likely to live in a two-parent family, often a two-income family.

President Donald Trump sought a border wall running the length of the U.S.-Mexico border to control illegal immigration and expanded efforts to detain and deport undocumented immigrants. Polls indicated that a large majority of Hispanic Americans opposed the policies. (a katz/Shutterstock)

More than 4,000 Hispanic Americans hold public office. Hispanics have been elected to statewide office in several states, including New Mexico and Arizona. Roughly 50 Hispanic Americans currently serve in Congress, six of whom are in the U.S. Senate. In 2009, Sonia Sotomayor was appointed to serve on the U.S. Supreme Court, becoming the first Hispanic to do so. In 2016, Senators Marco Rubio and Ted Cruz were leading contenders for the Republican presidential nomination—the first time any Hispanic had achieved that level of success. At present, only about half of all Hispanics are registered to vote, limiting the group's political power. Nevertheless, the sheer size of the Hispanic population in states such as Texas, Florida, and California will make the group a potent political force in the years to come (see Chapter 8).

Native Americans

When white settlers first arrived, an estimated 5–10 million Native Americans lived in what is now the United States. By 1900, they numbered less than a million. In the whole of recorded history, no people had suffered such a steep population decline in such a short period. Smallpox and other diseases brought by white settlers took the heaviest toll, but wars and massacres also contributed. Until Congress changed the policy in 1924, Native Americans by law were denied citizenship, which meant they lacked even the power to vote.

At first, Native Americans were not involved in the 1960s civil rights movement. That changed in 1972 when Native American leaders organized the "Trail of Broken Treaties," a caravan that journeyed from California to Washington, D.C., to protest federal policy. The next year, armed Native Americans took control of the village of Wounded Knee on a Sioux reservation in South Dakota. Over the next two months, they exchanged sporadic gunfire with U.S. marshals, leaving two Native Americans dead and one marshal paralyzed. Eight decades earlier at Wounded Knee, U.S. cavalry had shot to death 300 unarmed Sioux men, women, and children.

In 1974, Congress passed legislation that granted Native Americans living on reservations greater control over federal programs affecting them. Six years earlier, Congress had enacted the Indian Civil Rights Act, which gives Native Americans on reservations constitutional guarantees similar to those held by other Americans.

Full-blooded Native Americans, including Alaska Natives, currently number more than 2 million, about half of whom live on or close to reservations set aside for them by the federal government. State governments have no direct authority over federal reservations, and the federal government's authority is defined by the terms of its treaty with each tribe. U.S. policy toward the reservations has varied over time but is currently aimed at fostering self-government and economic self-sufficiency.[52]

By the late 1800s, Native Americans had been forcefully moved to reservations (shown here in red on this 1883 map) and their population was only a tenth of what it was when Europeans arrived in what is now the United States. Native Americans have never recovered from this early history. Among America's racial groups, they have today the lowest average annual income level, the highest average poverty rate, and the lowest life expectancy. (Library of Congress Geography and Map Division Washington [2009579467])

Preservation of Native American culture is another policy goal. At an earlier time, English was required of Native American children in schools run by the Bureau of Indian Affairs. They can now be taught in their native language. Nevertheless, the use of tribal languages has declined sharply. Of the larger tribes, the Navajo and Pueblo are the only ones in which a majority of the people still speak their native language at home. Ninety percent or more of the Cherokee, Chippewa, Creek, Iroquois, and Lumbee speak only English.

In recent years, a number of tribes have erected gaming casinos on reservation land. One of the world's largest casinos, Foxwoods, is operated in Connecticut by the Mashantucket Pequots. The employment level of Native Americans living on or near the reservations where casinos are located has increased by a fourth.[53] Nevertheless, the casinos have been a source of controversy among Native Americans–traditionalists argue that the casinos are creating a gaming culture that, whatever its economic benefit, is eroding tribal traditions.[54]

Although casino gambling has raised Native Americans' average income level, it is still far below the national average. Native Americans have the highest poverty rate and the lowest average income of any racial group. They are a disadvantaged group by other indicators as well. For example, they are less than half as likely as other Americans to have completed college, and their infant mortality rate is nearly twice that of white Americans.[55]

Native Americans are underrepresented in public office even by comparison with other minority groups but have made progress in recent years. In 2021, Deb Haaland became the first Native American cabinet secretary when appointed secretary of the interior. Six Native Americans—a record number—were elected to Congress in the 2020 election.

Asian Americans

Chinese and Japanese laborers were brought to the western states during the late 1800s to work in mines and to build railroads. When the need for their labor declined, Congress in 1892 suspended Asian immigration on grounds that Asians were inferior people. Over the next seven decades, laws and informal arrangements blocked the entry of people from most Asian countries, including China and Japan. In 1965, as part of its broader civil rights agenda, Congress lifted restrictions on Asian immigration. Strict limits on Hispanic immigration were also lifted at this time, and, since then, most immigrants have come from Latin America and Asia (see Figure 5-2).

Asian Americans were not active to any great extent in the civil rights movement, but their rights were expanded by the 1964 Civil Rights Act and other policies enacted in response to the efforts of other groups. However, in *Lau v. Nichols* (1974), a case initiated by a Chinese American family, the Supreme Court ruled unanimously that placing public school children for whom English is a second language in regular classrooms without special assistance violates

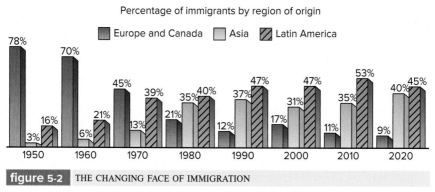

figure 5-2 THE CHANGING FACE OF IMMIGRATION

Until 1965, immigration laws were biased in favor of European immigrants. The laws enacted in 1965 increased the proportion of immigrants from Asia and Latin America. Percentages are totals for each decade; for example, the 2020 figures are for the 2011–2020 period. (*Source:* U.S. Immigration and Naturalization Service, 2022)

the Civil Rights Act because it denies them the opportunity to obtain a proper education.[56]

Asian Americans are the nation's fastest-growing ethnic group and now number nearly 20 million, or roughly 6 percent of the total U.S. population. Most Asian Americans live on the West Coast, particularly in California. China, Japan, Korea, India, Vietnam, and the Philippines are the ancestral homes of most Asian Americans.

Asian Americans have the highest percentage of two-parent families of any racial group and are upwardly mobile.[57] Most Asian cultures emphasize family-based self-reliance, which includes educational achievement. Asian Americans now make up a disproportionately large share of students at the nation's top universities.[58] In the past two decades, Asian Americans have become the group with the highest median family income. The median Asian American

Asian Americans have faced discrimination throughout their history. During World War II, for example, Japanese Americans living on the West Coast were relocated to inland detention camps on grounds they might assist America's enemy, Japan. Ironically, Japanese Americans were allowed to fight in Europe and made up the entirety of the U.S. Army's 442nd Regimental Combat Team. The 442nd became the most decorated unit of its size, not just in World War II but in the entire history of the U.S. Army. Twenty-one of its soldiers won the Congressional Medal of Honor—the nation's highest award for valor. (National Archives and Records Administration (26-G-3422))

family's income is roughly $85,000, which is about $10,000 more than that of the median non-Hispanic white family.[59]

Nevertheless, Asian Americans are underrepresented in certain areas of the workplace. According to U.S. government figures, Asian Americans account for about 5 percent of professionals and technicians but are substantially underrepresented in the top management jobs.[60] Asian Americans are also underrepresented politically, even by comparison with Hispanics and Blacks.[61] Less than 20 Asian Americans currently serve in Congress. Nevertheless, the election of Kamala Harris as vice president in 2020 was a breakthrough for Asian Americans. She is of Black and South Asian descent.

Other Disadvantaged Groups

The Civil Rights Act of 1964 classified women and minorities as legally protected groups, which has made it easier for them to pursue their claims in federal court. Other disadvantaged groups do not have the same degree of legal protection but do have some protections. For example, the 1967 Age Discrimination in Employment Act and the1975 Age Discrimination Act prohibit discrimination against older workers in hiring for jobs in which age is not a critical factor in job performance. More recently, mandatory retirement ages for most jobs have been eliminated by law. Nevertheless, the courts have given government and employers some leeway in establishing age-based policies.[62] Commercial airline pilots, for instance, are required by law to retire at 65 years of age and must pass a rigorous physical examination to continue flying after they reach the age of 60.

Individuals with disabilities also have legal protections. In 1990, Congress passed the Americans with Disabilities Act, which grants employment and other protections to this group. Government agencies are required, for instance, to take reasonable steps such as installing access ramps to make public buildings and services available to the disabled.[63] Earlier, through the Education for All Handicapped Children Act of 1975, Congress required that schools provide all children, however severe their disability, with free and appropriate education. Before the legislation, 4 million children with disabilities were getting either no education or an inappropriate one (for example, a blind child who is not taught braille).

No disadvantaged group has obtained more legal protection recently than has the LGBTQ community. In 2004, Massachusetts became the first state to permit same-sex marriage. The effort spread to other states, and in *Obergefell v. Hodges* (2015) the Supreme Court expanded the right to include all states, holding that bans on same-sex marriage violated the Fourteenth Amendment's guarantees of equal protection and due process.[64] Public opinion was a driving force behind the change. Rarely in the history of polling has public opinion

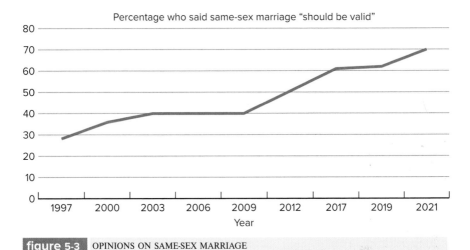

figure 5-3 OPINIONS ON SAME-SEX MARRIAGE

Twenty years ago, most Americans opposed same-sex marriage. Today, a large majority support it. (*Source:* Gallup poll, 2021)

on a major issue changed so dramatically and so quickly as in the case of same-sex marriage (see Figure 5-3). In the 1990s, less than 30 percent of Americans expressed support for same-sex marriage. Today, 70 percent do so.

Job discrimination against gay and transgender workers was legal in many states until recently. Then, in 2020, the Supreme Court ruled on the question of whether the ban on sexual discrimination in the 1964 Civil Rights Act includes a ban on sexual orientation. In a 6–3 decision, the Court concluded that it did. Speaking for the majority, Justice Neil Gorsuch wrote, "An individual's homosexuality or transgender status is not relevant to employment decisions."[65] A year later, however, the Supreme Court in a unanimous ruling held that a Catholic charity could exclude same-sex couples when screening potential foster parents.[66]

Other groups could have been discussed in this section. The United States has a long history of religious discrimination, targeted at various times against Catholics, Jews, Mormons, Muslims, various Protestant sects, and others. Religious discrimination is not a thing of the past, as Muslims exemplify. After the terrorist attacks on September 11, 2001, Muslims were singled out for surveillance and, when Donald Trump assumed the presidency in 2017, one of his first acts was to ban entry by people from seven predominantly Muslim countries on grounds they constituted a terrorist threat. Numerous ethnic groups, including the Irish, Italians, and Poles, have likewise faced severe discrimination. Space precludes a fuller discussion of discrimination in America, but there is no hiding the fact that equality has been America's most elusive ideal.

DISCRIMINATION: SUPERFICIAL DIFFERENCES, DEEP DIVISIONS

In 1944, Swedish sociologist Gunnar Myrdal gained fame for his book *An American Dilemma*, whose title referred to deep-rooted inequality in a country that idealizes equality.[67] Myrdal concluded that there were two Americas, one inhabited by its whites and one inhabited by its minorities. Few recent developments illustrate more clearly the two Americas than does the COVID-19 pandemic. Compared with white Americans, Black Americans were twice as likely to die from the disease, a reflection of their higher housing density, more limited access to quality medical care, and higher incidence of poverty-related comorbidity factors, including hypertension, obesity and diabetes.[68]

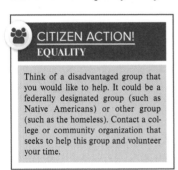

CITIZEN ACTION!
EQUALITY

Think of a disadvantaged group that you would like to help. It could be a federally designated group (such as Native Americans) or other group (such as the homeless). Contact a college or community organization that seeks to help this group and volunteer your time.

Myrdal called discrimination "America's curse." He could have broadened the generalization. Discrimination is civilization's curse, as is clear from the thousands of ethnic, national, and religious conflicts that have marred human history. But America carries a special responsibility because of its high ideals. In the words of Abraham Lincoln, the United States is a nation "dedicated to the proposition that all men are created equal."

SUMMARY

During the past half-century, the United States has undergone a revolution in the legal status of its traditionally disadvantaged groups, including African Americans, women, Native Americans, Hispanic Americans, and Asian Americans. Such groups are now provided equal protection under the law in areas such as education, employment, and voting. Discrimination by race, sex, and ethnicity has not been eliminated from American life, but it is no longer substantially backed by the force of law. This advance was achieved against strong resistance from established interests, which only begrudgingly and slowly responded to demands for equality in law.

Traditionally disadvantaged Americans have achieved fuller equality primarily as a result of their struggle for greater rights. The Supreme Court has been an instrument of change for disadvantaged groups. Its ruling in *Brown v. Board of Education* (1954), in which racial segregation in public schools was declared a violation of the Fourteenth Amendment's equal-protection clause, was a major breakthrough in equal rights. Through its affirmative action and other rulings, such as those providing equal access to the vote, the Court has also mandated the active promotion of social, political, and economic equality. However, because civil rights policy involves large issues concerned with social values and the distribution of society's opportunities and benefits, civil rights have also been advanced through legislative and administrative action. The history of civil rights includes landmark legislation, such as the 1964 Civil Rights Act and the 1965 Voting Rights Act.

In more recent decades, civil rights issues have receded from the prominence they had during the 1960s. The scope of affirmative action programs has narrowed, and the use of forced busing to achieve racial integration in America's public schools has been largely eliminated.

The legal gains of disadvantaged groups over the past half-century have not been fully matched by material gains. Although progress in areas such as education, income, and health care has been made, it has often been slow and incomplete. Tradition, prejudice, and the sheer difficulty of social, economic, and political progress stand as formidable obstacles to achieving a more equal America.

CRITICAL THINKING ZONE

KEY TERMS

affirmative action (*p. 131*)
de facto discrimination (*p. 132*)
de jure discrimination (*p. 132*)
equal-protection clause (*p. 123*)

equal rights (civil rights) (*p. 122*)
reasonable-basis test (*p. 127*)
strict-scrutiny test (*p. 127*)
suspect classifications (*p. 127*)

APPLYING THE ELEMENTS OF CRITICAL THINKING

Conceptualizing: Distinguish between de jure discrimination and de facto discrimination. Why is the latter form of discrimination more difficult to overcome?

Synthesizing: Using material in this chapter and the previous one, contrast the Fourteenth Amendment's due process clause with its equal-protection clause. What level of government in America's federal system is governed by the two clauses?

Analyzing: What role have political movements played in securing the legal rights of disadvantaged groups?

OF POSSIBLE INTEREST

A Book Worth Reading: Elizabeth Becker, *You Don't Belong Here* (New York: PublicAffairs, 2021). Winner of the 2022 Goldsmith Book Prize, it tells the story of three female war correspondents contending with antagonistic male journalists and military officers as they seek to cover the Vietnam War.

A Website Worth Visiting: www.cawp.rutgers.edu The Center for American Women and Politics at Rutgers University tracks women's political participation. Its website has state-by-state information on the subject.

Design credit: (People, Flag, U.S., Globe, Vote Icons): McGraw Hill; (Eagle): Feng Wei Photography/Moment/Getty Images; (Lincoln): Photographs in the Carol M. Highsmith Archive, Library of Congress, Prints and Photographs Division [LC-DIG-highsm-12542].

6
CHAPTER

PUBLIC OPINION AND POLITICAL SOCIALIZATION: SHAPING THE PEOPLE'S VOICE

Hisham Ibrahim/Getty Images

> 66 Towering over Presidents and [Congress] . . . public opinion stands out, in the United States, as the great source of power, the master of servants who tremble before it. 99
>
> JAMES BRYCE[1]

In the late morning of May 24, 2022, a gunman walked into Robb Elementary School in Uvalde, Texas, and opened fire, killing 19 grade-school students and 2 teachers, as well as wounding more than a dozen others. It was the twenty-seventh school shooting since the start of the year and the deadliest since the massacre of 14 students and 3 staff at Parkland, Florida's Marjory Stoneman Douglas High School in 2018.

The Uvalde shooting led to public demands for stricter controls on guns, and Congress responded. It passed a bill that included funding to help states establish crisis intervention and mental health programs aimed at reducing gun violence, expanded the ban on gun ownership of persons convicted of a domestic violence crime, and limited the ability of individuals under 21 years of age to purchase certain types of guns. It was the first time in three decades that Congress had acted to restrict gun ownership despite opinion polls throughout the period indicating that most Americans favored tighter controls. However, the 2022 legislation did not match what Americans said they wanted in the aftermath of the Uvalde massacre. A majority favored an outright ban on assault weapons of the type used in the shooting and strict background checks on anyone seeking to purchase a gun. Neither provision was in the bill that was passed by Congress.

Gun control is a telling example of the influence of public opinion on government. Public opinion is not something that public officials can completely ignore, but it is also not something that forces them to act. They have considerable freedom in deciding whether to act and what action to take when they do.

School shootings have become an all-too-frequent occurrence in the United States. Shown here are students from Marjory Stoneman Douglas High School in Parkland, Florida, speaking in support of gun control after 14 of their classmates and 3 staff members were shot to death by a former student in 2018. Only rarely have such shootings prompted lawmakers to take action to reduce gun violence. (Shawn Thew/EPA-EFE/Shutterstock)

This chapter discusses public opinion and its influence on U.S. politics. In this text, **public opinion** is defined as the politically relevant opinions held by ordinary citizens that they express openly. That expression can be verbal, as when citizens voice an opinion to a neighbor or respond to a question asked in an opinion poll. Public opinion can also take other forms—for example, participating in a protest demonstration or casting a vote in an election. The key point is that people's private thoughts become public opinion when revealed to others.

A major theme of the chapter is that public opinion is a powerful yet inexact force.[2] The policies of the U.S. government cannot be understood apart from public opinion; at the same time, public opinion is not a precise determinant of public policies. The chapter makes the following main points:

- *Public opinion consists of those views held by ordinary citizens that are openly expressed.* Public officials have various means of gauging public opinion but increasingly use public opinion polls for this purpose.

- *Public opinion is characterized by its direction (whether people hold a pro or con position on an issue), its intensity (how strongly people feel about their issue position), and its salience (how high a particular issue ranks in people's minds relative to other issues).*

- *The process by which individuals acquire their political opinions is called political socialization.* This process begins during childhood, when, through family and school, people acquire many of their basic political values and beliefs. Socialization continues into adulthood, during which time the news media, peers, and political leaders are important influences.

- *Americans' political opinions are shaped by several frames of reference, including partisanship, ideology, and group attachments.*

- *Public opinion has an important influence on government but ordinarily does not determine exactly what officials will do.*

THE MEASUREMENT OF PUBLIC OPINION

President Woodrow Wilson said that he had spent much of his adult life in government and yet had never seen "a government." What Wilson was saying, in effect, is that government is a system of relationships. A government is not tangible in the way that a building is. So it is with public opinion. No one has ever seen "a public opinion," and thus it cannot be measured directly. It must be assessed indirectly.

Election returns are a traditional method for assessing public opinion. Politicians routinely draw conclusions about what citizens are thinking by studying how they vote. Letters to the editor in newspapers and the size of crowds at mass demonstrations are among the other means of judging public opinion. All these indicators are useful guides for policymakers. Each of them, however, is a limited guide to what the public as a whole is thinking. Election results indicate how many votes each party or candidate received but do not indicate why voters acted as they did. As for letter writers and demonstrators, research indicates that their opinions are usually more intense and sometimes more extreme than those of other citizens.[3]

Public Opinion Polls

Opinion polls (also known as opinion surveys) have become the primary method for estimating public sentiment.[4] In a **public opinion poll**, a relatively few individuals—the **sample**—are interviewed in order to estimate the opinions of a whole **population**, such as the residents of a city or country.

How is it possible to measure the thinking of a large population on the basis of a relatively small sample of that population? How can interviews with, say, 1,000 Americans provide a reliable estimate of what millions of them are thinking? The answer is found in the laws of probability. Consider a hypothetical example of a huge jar filled with a million marbles, half of them red and half of them blue. If a blindfolded person reaches into the jar, the probability of selecting a marble of a given color is 50-50. And, if 1,000 marbles are chosen in this random way, it is likely that about half will be red and about half will be blue. Opinion sampling works in the same way. If respondents are chosen at random from a population, their opinions will approximate those of the population as a whole.

Random selection is the key to scientific polling. Individuals do not step forward to be interviewed; they are selected at random to be part of the sample. A scientific poll is thereby different from an Internet survey that invites visitors to a site to participate. Any such survey is biased because it includes only individuals who use the Internet, who happen for one reason or another to visit the particular site, and who have the time and inclination to complete the survey.

The classic case of a biased survey is the Literary Digest's poll of the 1936 presidential election which predicted an easy win for Republican nominee Alf Landon. He lost in a landslide to Franklin D. Roosevelt. The problem? Respondents to the Literary Digest's poll were chosen from telephone books and car registration lists. During the Great Depression, Republicans were more likely than Democrats to own a phone or car.[5]

The science of polling is such that the size of the sample, as opposed to the size of the population, is the key to a poll's accuracy. Although it might be assumed that a much larger sample would be required to poll accurately the people of the United States as opposed to, say, the residents of Georgia or San Antonio, the sample requirements are nearly the same. Consider again the example of a huge jar filled with marbles, half of them red and half blue. If 1,000 marbles were randomly selected, about half would be red and about half would be blue, regardless of whether the jar held 1 million, 10 million, or 100 million marbles. By contrast, the size of the sample—the number of marbles selected—would matter. If only 10 marbles were drawn, it could happen that 5 would be of each color but, then again, it would not be unusual for 6 or more of them to have the same color. In fact, the odds are higher of drawing 6 or more of the same color than getting a 5–5 split. However, if 1,000 marbles were drawn, it's highly unlikely that 600 or more of the marbles would be of the same color. In fact, the odds of drawing 600 of the same color would be about 1 in 100,000.

The accuracy of a poll is expressed in terms of **sampling error**—the error that results from using a sample to estimate the population. A sample provides an estimate of what the population is thinking, and sampling error is a measure of how accurate that estimate is likely to be. As would be expected, the larger the sample, the smaller the sampling error. A sample of 1,000 respondents would be expected to be more accurate than one of 200 respondents if the surveys were otherwise conducted in the same way.

Sampling error is usually expressed as a plus-or-minus percentage. For example, a properly drawn sample of 1,000 individuals has a sampling error of roughly plus or minus 3 percent. Thus, if 55 percent of a sample of 1,000 respondents say they intend to vote for the Republican presidential candidate, there is a high probability that between 52 and 58 percent (55 percent plus or minus 3 percent) of all voters actually plan to vote Republican.

Opinion Dimensions

In studying public opinion, scholars and pollsters focus on attributes of people's opinions. One attribute is **direction**—whether people have a pro or con position on a topic. A 2021 poll, for example, asked respondents whether marijuana use should be made legal. Sixty-eight percent of the respondents said it should be made legal and 29 percent said it should not.[6]

A second attribute of people's opinions is **intensity**—how strongly people feel about their opinion on a topic. Studies have regularly found, for example, a difference in intensity on the gun control issue.[7] Although a larger number of Americans favor tightening controls on guns, those opposed to such controls typically feel more strongly about the issue and are more likely to say they will only vote for candidates who share their view (see "Case Study: Gun Control").

Politics in Action

Gun Control

The United States has more gun-related deaths per capita than nearly any country, which has led to calls for increased gun control. Some federal laws have been enacted, such as those banning gun sales to felons and the mentally ill, but the United States has fewer controls on guns than other Western democracies. In fact, despite dozens of recent mass shootings, including ones that have taken place in schools, Congress has seldom acted to tighten controls on guns.

Chris Aschenbrener/Alamy Stock Photo

How might public opinion help to explain Congress's position? In terms of the *direction* of public opinion, most Americans favor stricter gun control laws, although a significant minority oppose such action. In terms of *intensity,* compared with gun control advocates, those who favor gun rights tend to be more committed to their position. They are much more likely to give money or contact a public official in an effort to influence gun policy.[8] Finally, in terms of *saliency,* gun control usually ranks low on the public's list of top issues. In most Gallup polls over the past two decades, 1 percent of respondents or fewer have named gun violence when asked what they see as the nation's "most important problem," although the percentage increases after a horrific mass shooting like happened in 2022 at the Robb Elementary School in Uvalde, Texas.

Q: How might the attributes of public opinion—its direction, intensity, and salience—help explain why Congress rarely takes action to curb gun violence?

ASK YOURSELF: What's the significance of the fact that those who oppose gun control have more intense opinions and are more likely to act on them? Does the relatively low salience of the issue give lawmakers leeway in deciding whether to take action?

A third opinion attribute is **salience**—how important people think an issue is relative to other issues. Salience is related to intensity; the more strongly people feel about an issue, the more likely they are to think that it's important. But the two attributes are not identical. An individual might, for example, have an intense opinion about genetically modified food but see it as less salient than an issue such as inflation or unemployment. In polls, salience is typically measured by asking respondents what they regard as the top issues.

People's opinions differ in important ways, one of which is intensity. On virtually every issue, some people feel more strongly about it than do others. Politicians are typically more attentive to intense opinions than to lightly held ones, knowing that those who hold intense views are more likely to act on them. (Andrius Repsys/Shutterstock)

Problems with Polls

Although polls are the most widely used method for assessing public opinion, they are not without flaws. One problem is that pollsters rarely have a list of all individuals in the population from which to draw a random sample. An expedient alternative is a sample based on telephone numbers. Pollsters use computers to randomly pick telephone numbers (now also including cell phone numbers), which are dialed by interviewers to reach households. Within each of these households, a respondent is then randomly selected. Because the computer is as likely to pick one telephone number as another, a sample selected in this way is assumed to be representative of the whole population. Nevertheless, some Americans do not have phones, and many of those who are called will not be home or refuse to participate. And refusals are not randomly distributed. People with higher education levels are somewhat more likely than those with lower levels to respond, and Democrats are somewhat more likely to agree to an interview than Republicans.[9] Pollsters adjust their findings to account for known tendencies, but the adjustments are not a fully reliable solution to the problem.

The accuracy of polling is also diminished when respondents are asked about issues with which they are not familiar. Although many respondents will answer the question anyway in order not to appear uninformed, their responses cannot be regarded as valid. Scholars label such responses "non-opinions." In other instances, respondents will have an opinion but choose to hide it. Respondents are not always truthful, for example, when it comes to expressing opinions that relate to race, gender, or ethnicity. A recent study that compared poll results and online behavior, for example, concluded that racism is far more prevalent in the United States than opinion polls would indicate.[10]

Finally, the way a poll question is framed affects responses. **Framing** refers to the process by which certain aspects of a situation are highlighted while other aspects are downplayed or ignored. For instance, responses to a poll question can vary by how the question is worded. A question about whether early parole for nonviolent offenders is a good idea will get a different set of responses if asked in the context of saving taxpayers' money than if asked in the context of a threat to public safety.

POLITICAL SOCIALIZATION: THE ORIGINS OF AMERICANS' OPINIONS

Although public opinion is a response to current issues, personalities, and events, it has deeper origins. People's opinions are affected by their prior attitudes, such as their preference for one political party rather than the other. Citizens' prior attitudes are acquired through a learning process called **political socialization**.

Just as language, a religion, or an athletic skill is acquired through a learning process, so are people's political orientations.

Broadly speaking, the process of political socialization has two distinguishing characteristics. First, although socialization continues throughout life, most people's political outlook is influenced by childhood learning. Basic ideas about whether the Democratic Party or the Republican Party is the better party, for example, are often formed uncritically in childhood, in much the same way that belief in the superiority of a particular religion—typically, the religion of one's parents—is acquired.

The second characteristic of political socialization is that it is a cumulative process. Early learning affects later learning because people's prior beliefs serve as a psychological screen through which new information is filtered. When watching a televised presidential debate, for example, Republicans and Democrats are looking at the same event but seeing different ones. When their party's candidate is speaking, they tend to see sincerity and strength. When the other party's candidate is talking, they tend to see evasion and weakness. There's rarely been a presidential debate where Republicans or Democrats concluded that their party's candidate had lost the debate.[11]

The political socialization process takes place through **agents of socialization**. They can be divided into primary and secondary agents. *Primary agents* interact closely and regularly with the individual, usually early in life, as in the case of the family. *Secondary agents* have a less intimate connection with the individual and are usually more important later in life, as in the case of work associates. It is helpful to consider briefly how key primary and secondary agents affect political learning.

Primary Socializing Agents: Family, School, and Religion

The family is a powerful primary agent because it has a near-monopoly on the attention of a young child, who trusts what a parent says. By the time children reach adulthood, many of the beliefs and values that will stay with them throughout life are firmly in place. Indeed, as sociologist Herbert Hyman concluded from his research, "Foremost among agencies of socialization into politics is the family."[12] Many adults are Republicans or Democrats today almost solely because their parents backed that party. They can give all sorts of reasons for preferring their party to the other, but the reasons came later in life.[13]

Like the family, schools have an influence on children's basic political beliefs. Teachers at the elementary level particularly praise the country's political institutions and mark the birthdays of national heroes such as George Washington, Abraham Lincoln, and Martin Luther King Jr.[14] U.S. schools are more instrumental in building support for the nation and its cultural beliefs than are the schools in most other democracies (see "How the U.S. Differs"). The Pledge

HOW THE U.S. DIFFERS

CRITICAL THINKING THROUGH COMPARISONS

National Pride

Political socialization in the United States is not the rigid program of indoctrination imposed by some countries on their people. Nevertheless, Americans are told of their country's greatness in many ways, everything from the Pledge of Allegiance that American children recite at the beginning of the school day to the flying of the flag on American homes and businesses. Such practices are uncommon in nearly all other democracies. At the same time, as the accompanying figure indicates, Americans' pride in their nation has declined because of increased partisan hostility, policy deadlock in Washington, wage stagnation, and other factors.

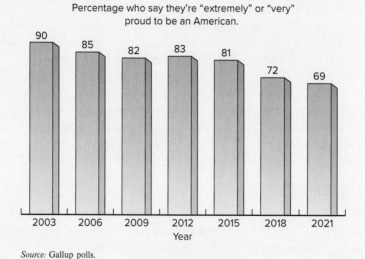

Percentage who say they're "extremely" or "very" proud to be an American.

Source: Gallup polls.

Q: Why might words and symbols of the nation's greatness be more important to Americans than to people of most countries? Why might the recent decline in Americans' pride in their political system be a worrying development?

A: The unifying bond in most countries is a common ancestral heritage. The French and Chinese, for example, have ancestral ties that go back centuries. In contrast, Americans come from many different countries and depend on national symbols and ceremonies as their unifying bond. When Americans' sense of being "one people" weakens, they can slip into scapegoating those who differ.

of Allegiance, which is recited daily at the start of classes in many American schools, has no equivalent in Europe. Schools there do not open the day by asking students to pledge loyalty to their nation.

Religious organizations are a powerful socializing agent for some children, especially those who regularly attend religious services. Although scholars have not studied the influence of religion on childhood political socialization as closely as they have studied the influence of families or schools, religion has been found to affect children's attitudes, including their beliefs about society's obligations to the poor and the unborn.[15]

Secondary Socializing Agents: Peers, Media, Leaders, and Events

With age, additional socializing agents come into play. An individual's peers—friends, neighbors, coworkers, and the like—become sources of opinion. Research indicates that many individuals are unwilling to deviate too far politically from what their peers think. In *The Spiral of Silence,* Elisabeth Noelle-Neumann showed that individuals tend to withhold opinions that conflict with those of the people around them. If nearly everyone in a group favors legalizing same-sex marriage, for example, a person who believes otherwise will often remain silent. The group's dominant opinion will then appear to be more widely held than it actually is, which can persuade those with lightly held opinions to accept the group's opinion as their own.[16]

The mass media are also a powerful socializing agent. Politics for the average citizen is a second-hand affair, observed mainly through the media rather than directly. In the words of journalist Walter Lippmann, "the pictures in our heads of the world outside" owe substantially to how that world is portrayed for us by the media.[17] The media's influence has become clearer in the past few decades as Americans have increasingly turned to alternative sources for their news. Viewers of Fox News, for example, are exposed to a different version of reality than are viewers of CNN, contributing to a difference of opinion on many issues.[18]

Trusted individuals in positions of authority are also sources of opinion. Few developments illustrate that more clearly than how state governors framed the threat posed by the COVID-19 pandemic. In states where the governor framed it largely as a threat to public health, residents were more likely to wear facemasks and engage in social distancing than in states where the governor framed the pandemic largely as a threat to the local economy.[19]

Finally, no accounting of the political socialization process would be complete without considering the impact of extraordinary events. The Great Depression, World War II, the Vietnam War, and the 2001 terrorist attacks are examples of events that had a lasting influence on Americans' opinions. Younger citizens

Pictured here is Florida governor Ron DeSantis, who clashed with federal, state, and local public health officials over the proper response to the COVID-19 pandemic. DeSantis stressed the importance of keeping restaurants and other businesses operating even if it raised the health risks, a stance that strengthened his standing with Republican voters to the point where he was talked about as a future GOP presidential nominee. (Paul Hennessy/SOPA Images/LightRocket/Getty Images)

were particularly affected in each case. Their opinions are generally not as deeply rooted, which heightens their response to disruptive events.[20]

FRAMES OF REFERENCE: HOW AMERICANS THINK POLITICALLY

Through the socialization process, citizens acquire frames of reference that can enable them to join together with others who share the same outlook. Briefly discussed here are three of the major frames of reference through which Americans evaluate political developments: party identification, political ideology, and group orientation. Subsequent chapters (particularly Chapters 7, 8, 11, and 12) will discuss them in greater detail.

Party Identification

Party identification refers to a person's sense of loyalty to a political party. Party identification is not formal membership in a party but rather an emotional attachment to it—the feeling that "I am a Democrat" or "I am a Republican." Most Americans think of themselves as either a Democrat or a Republican

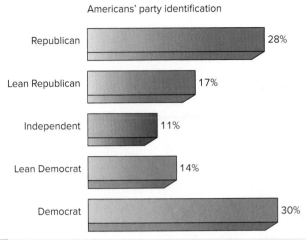

Americans' party identification

Republican   28%

Lean Republican   17%

Independent   11%

Lean Democrat   14%

Democrat   30%

figure 6-1   PARTY IDENTIFICATION

Most Americans say they identify with the Republican or Democratic Party. Among those who call themselves independents, most say they "lean" toward a party and typically vote for that party's candidates. (*Source:* Gallup poll, 2022)

(see Figure 6-1). Even most of those who call themselves independents are not truly independent. When independents are asked if they lean toward the Republican or Democratic Party, about two in every three say they lean toward one of the parties. In fact, "leaners" are nearly as likely to support their preferred party's candidates as are voters who call themselves Republicans or Democrats.

Many Americans grow up thinking of themselves as Republicans or Democrats and remain that way throughout their adult lives, even when changes in their personal lives might reasonably lead them to switch to the other party.[21] That's not true of everyone, but massive shifts in Americans' party identification are relatively rare and typically occur in response to disruptive events.[22] During the Great Depression, for example, Franklin Roosevelt's New Deal prompted large numbers of Republicans to switch their loyalty to the Democratic Party. Younger adults accounted for most of those who switched. Older adults tend to have firmer party loyalties and to be less responsive than younger adults to the issues and candidates of the moment.

In the everyday world of politics, nothing shapes Americans' opinions more fully than does their partisanship. After the 2020 presidential election, for example, Republican Donald Trump claimed the election was stolen from him as a result of millions of illegal votes being cast for his opponent. Although dozens of state and federal judges ruled that there was no evidence of widespread voter fraud, Trump persisted in his claim. Polls indicated that two-thirds of Republican voters believed his claim.[23]

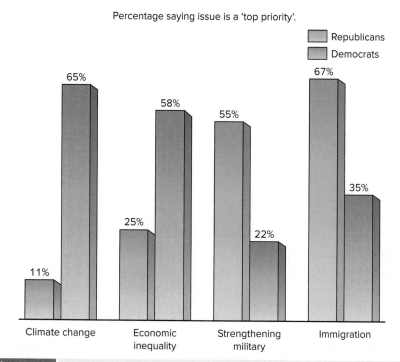

figure 6-2   PARTISANSHIP AND POLICY PROBLEMS

Republicans and Democrats differ in their opinions on the nation's top policy problems. (*Source:* Pew Research Center poll, 2022)

On nearly every major issue, Republicans and Democrats have conflicting opinions (see Figure 6-2). A recent Pew Research Center poll found, for example, that Democrats are more likely than Republicans to see climate change and income inequality as top policy priorities, whereas Republicans are more likely than Democrats to think that strengthening the military and immigration are top priorities.

Political Ideology

During the 20th century, the broad ideologies—communism, fascism, and socialism—that captured the loyalty of many Europeans proved to be of little interest to most Americans. But political ideology doesn't have to take an extreme form, as it did in the case of Soviet communism or German fascism. Conceptually, **ideology** refers to a general belief about the role and purpose of government.[24] Some Americans believe, for instance, that government should use its power to help people who are economically disadvantaged. Such individuals can be labeled **economic liberals**. Other Americans believe that the government should leave the distribution of economic benefits largely to the workings of the free market. They can be described as **economic conservatives**. Americans differ also in their views on the government's role on social and cultural issues, such as abortion and the legalization of marijuana. **Cultural (social) liberals** would leave lifestyle choices to the individual. In contrast, **cultural (social) conservatives** would use government to promote traditional values—for example, through laws banning abortion.

CITIZEN ACTION!
SELF-GOVERNMENT

"Know thyself" was a basic tenet of Socrates' notion of citizenship. If you think of yourself as a liberal or conservative, what do you mean by that label? How do you feel about the proper role of government in helping people meet their economic needs? About the proper role of government in upholding traditional values? As defined by political scientists, conservatives think that the government should not play a large role in helping people meet their economic needs but believe government should act to uphold traditional values, such as those stemming from traditional religious beliefs. Liberals are those who hold the opposite views.

Although it is sometimes said that liberals believe in big government while conservatives believe in small government, the claim is inaccurate, as the foregoing discussion would indicate. Conservatives prefer a smaller role for government on economic issues but want to use the power of government to uphold cultural traditions. The reverse is true of liberals. Each group wants the government to be active or inactive, depending on which approach serves its policy goals.[25]

Group Orientations

Many Americans see politics through group attachments. Their identity or self-interest is tied to a group, and they respond accordingly when a policy issue arises that affects it. Issues surrounding social security, for example, usually evoke a stronger response from senior citizens than from younger adults. Later chapters examine group tendencies more fully, but it is useful here to describe briefly a few groupings—religion, economic class, region, race and ethnicity, gender, and age.

Religion   Religious beliefs have long been a source of solidarity among group members and a source of conflict with outsiders. As Catholics came to America in large numbers in the 19th and early 20th centuries, they faced hostility from the Protestant majority. Religious hatred sparked the rebirth of the Ku Klux Klan, which resurrected itself in the early 1900s as anti-Catholic, as well as anti-Jewish, anti-Mormon, and anti-Black. At the Klan's peak in the 1920s, one in every six Protestant adult males was a Klan member.[26] It took the nation's all-out effort in World War II to convince the Protestant majority that Catholics weren't their enemy.

Today, Catholics, Protestants, and Jews hold similar opinions on many policy issues. Nevertheless, important religious differences remain, although the alignment differs across issues.[27] Fundamentalist Protestants and Roman

Catholics are more likely than mainline Protestants and Jews to oppose legalized abortion, a split that partly reflects differing religious beliefs about whether human life begins at conception or later in the development of the fetus. On the other hand, support for poverty programs is higher among Catholics and Jews than among Protestants. An obligation to help the poor is a basic tenet of Catholic and Jewish teachings, whereas self-reliance is a basic tenet of the teachings of many Protestant denominations.

A major divide today is between the religiously devout, who are disproportionately Republicans, and those who rarely practice their religion or profess no religious attachment, who are disproportionately Democrats (see "Party Polarization: Religion and Politics"). Older adults make up the bulk of the religiously devout. More than a third of adults under 30 say they have no religious affiliation and a larger number of them say they rarely attend religious services.[28]

Economic Class   Economic class has always been a weaker force in the United States than in Europe. Friedrich Engles, who was Karl Marx's closest associate, said that socialism, which was sweeping through Europe at the time, would fail to take hold in America. Engels said that American workers lacked class consciousness because of a belief they could succeed individually.

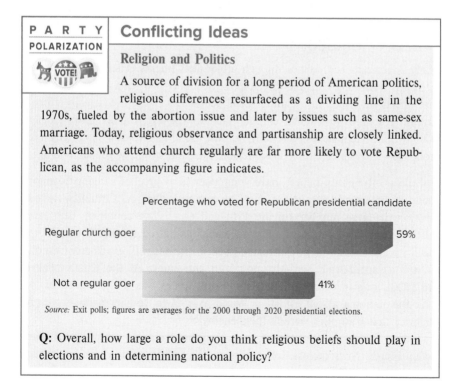

PARTY POLARIZATION

Conflicting Ideas

Religion and Politics

A source of division for a long period of American politics, religious differences resurfaced as a dividing line in the 1970s, fueled by the abortion issue and later by issues such as same-sex marriage. Today, religious observance and partisanship are closely linked. Americans who attend church regularly are far more likely to vote Republican, as the accompanying figure indicates.

Percentage who voted for Republican presidential candidate

Regular church goer   59%

Not a regular goer   41%

Source: Exit polls; figures are averages for the 2000 through 2020 presidential elections.

Q: Overall, how large a role do you think religious beliefs should play in elections and in determining national policy?

Nevertheless, economic class influences Americans' opinions on some issues. For example, lower-income Americans are more likely to support government-provided health care, while higher-income Americans are more likely to favor business deregulation.

An obstacle to class-based politics in the United States, particularly among those of low or modest income, is that they have different ideas about how to get ahead economically. Support for collective bargaining, for example, is higher among factory workers than among small farmers, white-collar workers, and workers in the skilled crafts, even though the average income of these groups is similar. Class-based action is also blunted by racial and ethnic differences. In *Strangers in Their Own Land*, Arlie Russell Hochschild describes how working-class whites see themselves as having waited patiently in line for a piece of the American Dream, only to see working-class minorities and immigrants cut the line, ushered there by affirmative action and other policy initiatives.[29] Working-class whites are better off economically than minorities, but many of them feel that they're being held back so that minorities can get ahead.[30] The interplay of class and opinion is examined more closely in Chapter 9, which discusses interest groups.

Region   For a lengthy period in U.S. history, region was the chief dividing line in American politics. The North and South were deeply split over questions of race and states' rights, which persisted for a century after their bitter civil war.

Racial progress has shrunk the regional divide, as has the relocation to the South of millions of Americans from less conservative parts of the country. Then, too, political issues have been "nationalized" by the political parties, reducing regional differences in how Republicans or Democrats respond to issues. Nevertheless, regional differences have persisted on some issues. Midwestern Republicans, for example, typically hold conservative opinions on issues like race, ethnicity, immigration, and union organizing but their opinions are not as conservative on average as those of southern Republicans.[31]

HOW THE 50 STATES DIFFER
CRITICAL THINKING THROUGH COMPARISONS

Party Support in the States

The states differ widely in their support of the Republican and Democratic Parties. The map below classifies states by how they voted in the 2020 presidential election. States that supported the Republican nominee with

Continued

55 percent or more of the two-party vote are classified as Republican states, whereas those that gave 55 percent or more of the two-party vote to the Democratic nominee are classified as Democratic states. States that gave the victor less than 55 percent of the two-party vote are classified as competitive states. By this indicator, Republican strength is concentrated in the South and the Great Plains, and Democratic strength is concentrated in the Northeast and the West Coast. The five most heavily Republican states are, in order, Wyoming, West Virginia, North Dakota, Oklahoma, and Idaho, whereas Vermont, Massachusetts, Maryland, Hawaii, and California (in that order) are the five most heavily Democratic states.

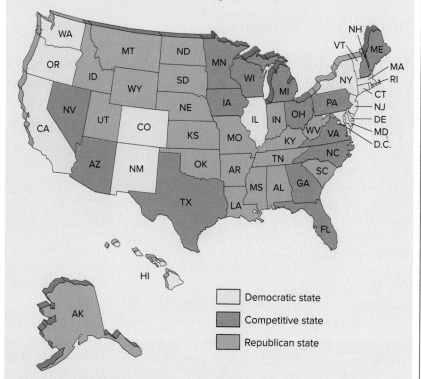

Q: What might account for the regional differences in the strength of the Republican and Democratic Parties?

A: The South and Great Plains are relatively rural and are traditionally more conservative on economic and social issues than most of the country. The Northeast and West Coast are more urbanized and more diverse, including a disproportionate number of more recent immigrants, which, along with other factors, make them more liberal than most of the country.

Race and Ethnicity   As was discussed in Chapters 4 and 5, race and ethnicity affect opinions on civil rights and civil liberties issues. Blacks and Hispanics, for example, are generally more supportive of affirmative action and less trusting of police and the judicial system than are non-Hispanic whites. Blacks and Hispanics also tend to differ from non-Hispanic whites on social welfare spending, although this difference largely reflects differences in their income levels.

Gender   Although men and women think alike on many issues, they diverge on others.[32] Polls have found, for example, that women have more liberal opinions than men on education and social welfare issues, reflecting their greater economic vulnerability and greater role in child care. Women also differ from men on issues of national defense. Polls indicate, for example, that women were less supportive than men of America's use of military force in Afghanistan and Iraq.[33]

Generations and Age   As a generation comes of age, it encounters a different political environment than its predecessors, with the result that its political views will differ somewhat from those of previous generations. Those Americans who came of age during World War II, for example, acquired a sense of civic duty unmatched by the preceding generation or by any generation since. By contrast, those who came of age during the Vietnam War era were more distrustful of government than the generation before them or the one that followed. Today's young adults are no exception to the pattern. Their political views are, to some extent, a reflection of their generation's experiences. A recent Kaiser Family Foundation poll found, for example, that climate change is of far greater concern to young adults than to older ones.[34]

Crosscutting Groups and Identity Politics

Although group loyalties have an impact on people's opinions, the influence is diminished when identification with one group is offset by identification with other groups. In a pluralistic society such as the United States, groups tend to be "crosscutting"—that is, each group includes individuals who also belong to other groups, where they can encounter different opinions. Exposure to such opinions fosters political moderation. By comparison, in societies such as Northern Ireland, where group loyalties are reinforcing rather than crosscutting, opinions are intensified by personal interactions. Northern Ireland's Catholics and Protestants live largely apart from one another, differing not only in their religious beliefs but also in their income levels, residential neighborhoods, ethnic backgrounds, and loyalties to the government. The result has been widespread mistrust between Northern Ireland's Catholics and Protestants and a willingness on the part of some on each side to resort to violence.

Americans' crosscutting group attachments have long been a unifying force in the nation's politics, but this influence is weakening, Americans are increasingly divided by how they look and where they live, contributing to the rise of identity politics, which pits groups against each other politically. (dotshock/Shutterstock)

The moderating influence of crosscutting group attachments in the United States is weakening. Although the situation is still far different than in a place like Northern Ireland, Americans today interact less with those of different backgrounds. Residential neighborhoods have become less diverse in recent decades. That's true also of the workplace. Many office workers and professionals, for example, spend their workday interacting with others of similar backgrounds. Americans' "virtual" interaction has also narrowed. Before the 1980s, Americans were exposed through television to a version of news coverage that gave Republican and Democratic arguments roughly equal time. Today, many Americans get their news from a cable outlet or Internet site that plays up one side of the partisan debate while playing down the other side (see Chapter 10).

In addition, three of America's deepest divides—race, religion, and geography—are now closely linked to partisanship.[35] White Americans, the religious-minded, and rural residents now lean strongly toward the Republican Party, while minorities, the secular-minded, and urban residents lean heavily toward the Democratic party. The party polarization that defines today's politics thus goes beyond conflict over issues. Republicans and Democrats are increasingly separated by how they look and where they live, making partisan conflict a question of identity as well as a question of issues.[36] **Identity politics** is the term used to describe the situation where people base their outlook on group identity (such as race or religion) and align themselves politically with those who share that identity and against those who don't.[37]

THE INFLUENCE OF PUBLIC OPINION ON POLICY

The impact that public opinion *should* have on policy has been the subject of long-standing debate. One view has held that a representative should act as his or her constituents' **delegate** by responding to what constituents say they want. That view was embraced by George Gallup, a pioneer in the field of polling. Said Gallup, "The task of the leader is to decide how best to achieve the goals set by the people."[38] An opposing view was put forth by 18th-century English theorist Edmund Burke, who argued that representatives should act as their constituents' **trustees**. Burke argued that they should be responsive to constituents' interests but use their own judgment in deciding which policies would best serve that interest. That view was embraced by journalist and writer Walter Lippmann. "Effective government," Lippmann wrote, "cannot be conducted by legislators and officials who, when a question is presented, ask themselves first and last not what is . . . the right and necessary course, but 'What does the Gallup Poll say?'"[39]

Limits on the Public's Influence

Even if officials were intent on governing by public opinion, they would face obstacles, including contradictions in what citizens say they want. In the entire history of polling, there has never been a national survey in which a majority of respondents said their taxes should be raised significantly.[40] In a recent Gallup poll, for example, 45 percent of respondents claimed that taxes were too high, and only 7 percent said taxes were too low. At the same time, when respondents are asked in polls whether they would support steep cuts in Social Security, defense, and other costly spending programs in order to pay for a large tax cut, a majority says no.

People's opinions are often inconsistent, contradictory, or poorly informed. Polls have repeatedly found that most citizens are not well informed about politics and some are badly misinformed.[41] Early in the COVID-19 coronavirus pandemic, for example, roughly a third of American adults were convinced that the virus was no more dangerous than the seasonal flu despite countless news reports and official announcements to the contrary.[42]

To become an American citizen, immigrants must pass a citizenship test that asks basic questions about the U.S. political system. Ironically, when the test was given to a cross section of Americans who were already citizens, many of them failed it. Citizens' lack of information limits the impact of public opinion on policy. (John Moore/Getty Images)

Of course, citizens do not have to be well informed to have appropriate opinions on some issues.[43] Knowing only that the economy is performing poorly, a citizen could reasonably expect the government to take action to fix it and judge officials by what happens.[44] It's also the case that information is not a prerequisite for judgment on some policy issues. Opinions on the abortion issue, for example, are largely a question of people's values and beliefs.

Nevertheless, the public's inadequate understanding of issues can make it difficult for policymakers to respond to public opinion, even when they're inclined to do so. The problem has become more acute with the recent rise in misinformation and unfounded conspiracy theories. When citizens lose touch with reality, lawmakers face an impossible task. Even if they wanted to respond to public opinion, it would make no sense for them to do so when citizens' opinions bear no relationship to reality.

Another obstacle to using public opinion as a guide is that there are many issues on which most citizens have no awareness or opinion.[45]

CITIZEN ACTION!
SELF-GOVERNMENT

Studies indicate that most Americans are largely uninformed about politics. Self-government entails responsibility, including taking time to inform yourself. As an informed citizen, you will be better able to make judgments about policy issues and choose wisely when voting in elections.

Agricultural conservation programs, for example, are of keen interest to some farmers, hunters, and environmentalists but of little or no concern to most people.[46] In deciding such issues, policymakers tend to respond to those who are the most interested (see Chapter 9). A study by political scientists Martin Gilens and Benjamin Page examined nearly 1,800 policy issues and concluded that "economic elites and organized groups representing business interests" have far more influence on most policies than do "average citizens."[47]

The influence of public opinion is also limited by what's been called "manufactured consent."[48] Political scientists James Druckman and Lawrence Jacobs have shown, for example, that presidents typically pursue their own goals, using the power of their office to frame issues in a way that will get the public to back their agenda.[49] When they succeed, policy and opinion will coincide, but it speaks more to the power of leaders than to the power of public opinion. A case in point is the period leading up to the U.S. invasion of Iraq in 2003. Although Americans had been hearing about Iraqi leader Saddam Hussein for years and had concluded that he was a tyrant, they were unsure whether an attack on Iraq made sense. Polls indicate that many Americans preferred to have UN inspectors investigate Iraq's weapons program before an invasion decision was made. Other Americans expressed support for an invasion only if the United States had the backing of its European allies. Still others thought that, if a war were launched, it should be conducted entirely through the air. However, over the course of a roughly six-month period, the Bush administration framed Iraq's weapons program as a dire threat to Americans' safety, which led to a gradual increase in public support for a ground invasion.[50] When the war began, polls showed that President Bush's decision to invade Iraq had the backing of 70 percent of Americans.

The way in which citizens often form their opinions also limits the influence of public opinion. Most citizens are far too busy to take the time to carefully assess every policy issue, relying instead on what scholars call heuristics, or shortcuts, as when they take their cue from what a trusted political leader or their political party is saying.[51] In 2015, for example, Republicans had a more favorable view of free-trade agreements than did Democrats. Nearly 60 percent of Republicans said that free trade was good for the country. Two years later, however, Republicans had switched sides on the issue. More than 60 percent now said that these agreements were bad for the country.[52] Free trade itself hadn't changed in any significant way during this period. What, then, would explain the shift? It was the rise of Donald Trump to leadership in the Republican Party. Before then, top Republican leaders had been proponents of free trade. Trump opposed it, arguing that it resulted in a loss of American jobs and the closing of American factories. Taking their cue from Trump, many Republicans lined up behind him on the issue.[53]

FAKE or FACT

Detecting Misinformation

Do You Have a Right to Speak Freely on Campus?

The Supreme Court has placed substantial limits on the ability of the government to limit free speech. Officials are prohibited from banning speech that they find offensive or contrary to their own beliefs. Some college students believe that the same rule applies on their campus.

Is that claim fact, or is it fake?

Eric Crama/Shutterstock

Students have substantial free-speech rights, but they're not as broad as those that apply in public settings. The Supreme Court has ruled that speech in a school setting can be limited if it is disruptive of "the educational mission."[54] *At many colleges, both public and private, there have been instances where speakers have been disinvited or shouted down because some students oppose what the speaker represents or is saying. "Political correctness"–speech that is lawful but deemed to violate social norms–has diminished the range of free speech on many campuses.*

In addition, students are governed by their college's code of conduct, which, on many campuses, prohibits expression that might offend other students. Although students who violate their college's code of conduct can be subject to disciplinary action by their college, they have due process rights, including the right to be informed of the charge and the basis for it, as well as an opportunity to contest it. Finally, even free-speech rights that are protected in a campus setting do not extend to hostile actions. It is permissible for you to voice your disagreement with the opinions of others but not to physically threaten them, which on virtually every campus violates the code of conduct and, in some states, is a criminal offense.

Public Opinion and the Boundaries of Action

Although there are limits to the influence of public opinion, it nevertheless influences the choices that officials make. For one thing, it limits their options. As political scientist V. O. Key noted, officials typically must operate within the boundary of what the public will accept.[55] Social Security is a prime example. During his second presidential term, George W. Bush attempted to privatize a part of Social Security, only to back down in the face of determined opposition from senior citizens. The founder of Social Security, Franklin D. Roosevelt, understood that public opinion would protect the program. Because Social Security benefits are funded by payroll taxes, workers feel that they have earned their retirement benefits and will fight to keep them. "No damn politician," Roosevelt said, "can ever scrap my social security program."[56]

Public opinion also places boundaries on officials' actions in a second way. Sweeping changes in public opinion invariably led to lasting and substantial changes in the direction of national policy. During the Great Depression of the 1930s, for example, a massive shift in popular support from the Republican Party to the Democratic Party ushered in a three-decade period of Democratic dominance of American politics, as well as a host of major policies, including Social Security, the minimum wage, and Medicare. Then, in the 1970s, the American public began to question the scope of federal power and spending, which led to a range of policy changes, including major tax cuts and a tightening of the eligibility rules for welfare assistance. Public opinion was also behind the tougher crime and sentencing laws enacted in the 1990s, which led to a sharp increase in the nation's prison population. As a congressman said at the time, "Voters were afraid of criminals, and politicians were afraid of voters."[57]

Even smaller changes can bring policy more in line with public opinion. Political scientist Christopher Wlezien found that, as a presidency is nearing its end, voters tend to want the government to do less of what the president has been doing, which changes the "mood" or "temperature" of the policy environment and can lead the government to actually do less or reverse some of what's been done.[58]

The influence of public opinion is also felt through political parties. Republican and Democratic leaders cannot stray too far from what their party's voters want without risking a loss of support. Nowhere is that more clearly seen than in Congress. Members of Congress are career politicians who want to keep their jobs, which requires them to maintain the support of the voters who hold the key to their reelection.[59] "Running scared" is how political scientist Anthony King described the strategy.[60] In 2014, Eric Cantor, the House majority leader and next in line to become Speaker, lost in his district's Republican primary to a right-wing

Public opinion places boundaries on what public officials will do. Republican lawmakers backed away from their support of free trade after Republican voters turned against it in response to Donald Trump's vow to "make America great again." (George Sheldon/Shutterstock)

political unknown. Cantor had said that Republicans should give legal status to "dreamers"–those who had come to the country illegally as children. For anti-immigration voters in his district, Cantor's stand amounted to treachery. The lesson of Cantor's defeat was not lost on House Republicans. "Immigration reform, any hope of it, just basically died," said a Republican insider.[61]

The immigration issue illustrates what is broadly true about the power of public opinion. When an issue is highly salient and people feel intensely about it, elected officials tend to follow public opinion. Numerous studies show that the power of public opinion is greatest on issues of high salience that people care deeply about.[62]

SUMMARY

Public opinion can be defined as the opinions held by ordinary citizens that they openly express. Public officials have many ways of assessing public opinion, such as the outcomes of elections, but they have increasingly come to rely on public opinion polls. There are many possible sources of error in polls, and surveys sometimes present a misleading portrayal of the public's views. However, a properly conducted poll can be an accurate indication of what the public is thinking. Polls are typically used to measure three attributes of people's policy opinions: direction (whether they favor or oppose a particularly policy), intensity (how strongly they feel about their position on a policy), and salience (how important they think a policy issue is relative to other issues).

The process by which individuals acquire their political opinions is called political socialization. During childhood, the family, schools, and religious institutions are important sources of basic political attitudes, such as beliefs about the parties and the nature of the U.S. political and economic systems. Many of the basic orientations that Americans acquire during childhood remain with them in adulthood, but socialization is a continuing process. Adults' opinions are affected mostly by peers, the news media, and political leaders. Events themselves also have a significant short-term influence on opinions.

The frames of reference that guide Americans' opinions include political ideology and group orientations—notably, religion, economic class, region, race and ethnicity, gender, and generation and age. Partisanship is the main political frame of reference for most people. Republicans and Democrats differ in their voting behavior and views on a wide range of policy issues.

Public opinion has a significant influence on government but seldom determines exactly what government will do in a particular instance. Public opinion constrains the policy choices of officials but also is subject to their efforts to influence what the public is thinking. Evidence indicates that officials are particularly attentive to public opinion on highly visible issues of public policy that are of great concern to a large number of people.

CRITICAL THINKING ZONE

KEY TERMS

agents of socialization (*p. 159*)
cultural (social) conservatives (*p. 165*)
cultural (social) liberals (*p. 165*)
delegate (*p. 171*)
direction (*p. 155*)
economic conservatives (*p. 165*)
economic liberals (*p. 165*)
framing (*p. 158*)
identity politics (*p. 171*)
ideology (*p. 164*)

intensity (*p. 155*)
party identification (*p. 162*)
political socialization (*p. 158*)
population (*p. 154*)
public opinion (*p. 153*)
public opinion poll (*p. 154*)
salience (*p. 157*)
sample (*p. 154*)
sampling error (*p. 155*)
trustee (*p. 171*)

APPLYING THE ELEMENTS OF CRITICAL THINKING

Conceptualizing: *Population, sample,* and *sampling error* are terms associated with public opinion polling. Explain each term and how it relates to the others.

Synthesizing: Contrast the views of conservatives and liberals on how far government should go to help individuals who are economically disadvantaged, and then contrast their views on how far government should go to promote traditional social (cultural) values. Note that each group wants government to be active or inactive, depending on which approach serves its policy goals.

Analyzing: What factors limit the influence of public opinion on the policy choices of public officials?

OF POSSIBLE INTEREST

A Book Worth Reading: Amy Chua, *Political Tribes: Group Instinct and the Fate of Nations* (New York: Penguin Books, 2019). Written by a best-selling author and Yale Law School professor, this book argues that political identity has come to define both the American left and the right and threatens national unity.

A Website Worth Visiting: **www.people-press.org** The Pew Research Center for the People and the Press is an independent, nonprofit institute. Its website includes recent and past poll results, including cross-national comparisons.

7
CHAPTER

POLITICAL PARTICIPATION:
ACTIVATING THE POPULAR WILL

Leigh Prather/Shutterstock

❝ We are concerned in public affairs, but immersed in our private ones. ❞

WALTER LIPPMANN[1]

At stake in the 2022 midterm elections was control of the House and Senate. Which political party would end up with the larger say on legislation dealing with health care, immigration, wage stagnation, foreign trade, and other national issues? With so much at stake, it might be thought that Americans would have raced to the polls to vote for the party of their choice. Many did vote, but many did not. Tens of millions of vote-eligible Americans did not bother to cast a ballot on Election Day.

Political participation refers to involvement in activities intended to influence public policy and leadership. Besides voting, political participation includes activities such as joining political groups, writing to elected officials, demonstrating for political causes, and giving money to political candidates.

Self-government would be an empty promise if citizens did not participate in public affairs. It would also be an empty promise without *meaningful* opportunities

179

to participate—ones that will make a difference in how the country is governed. It would also be empty if those opportunities were provided only to a select few. For self-government to be meaningful, the opportunities must be available to all. As this chapter shows, the U.S. political system offers citizens abundant opportunities to participate while presenting barriers that work against full participation, particularly by citizens of low income and education. The chapter also shows that the pattern of participation in the United States differs from that of most Western democracies. The United States has a relatively low level of voter participation while having a relatively high level of other types of political and civic participation. The chapter's main points are the following:

- *Voter turnout in U.S. elections is low in comparison with that of other Western democracies.* The reasons include U.S. election laws, particularly those pertaining to registration requirements and the scheduling of elections.

- *Most citizens do not participate actively in politics in ways other than voting.* Only a minority of Americans can be classified as political activists. Nevertheless, Americans are more likely than citizens of other democracies to contribute time and money to political and community organizations.

- *Political movements are a way for citizens to express opposition to government policy through protest rallies, marches, and the like.* Most political movements do not succeed, but a few of them, including the Black civil rights movements, have had a large and lasting impact on the nation's politics.

- *Most Americans distinguish between their personal lives and public lives.* This outlook reduces their incentive to participate and contributes to a pattern of participation that benefits citizens of higher income and education.

VOTER PARTICIPATION

In its original form, the Constitution gave states control over **suffrage**—the right to vote. State legislatures were granted the power to decide the "Times, Place, and Manner of holding elections" for federal office. The states at first chose to restrict voting to property-owning males, a practice that Benjamin Franklin ridiculed. Observing that a man whose only item of property was a jackass would lose his right to vote if the jackass died, Franklin asked, "Now tell me, which was the voter, the man or the jackass?" Fifty years elapsed before the property qualification for voting was eliminated in all states.

African Americans appeared to have gained suffrage after the Civil War through the Fifteenth Amendment, which says that a state cannot abridge the

Alabama Literacy Test Questions (1940s)

- A United States Senator elected at the general election in November takes office the following year on what date?
- How many states were required to approve the original Constitution in order for it to be in effect?
- After the presidential electors have voted, to whom do they send the count of their votes?
- Of the original 13 states, the one with the largest representation in the first Congress was _____.
- Does enumeration affect the income tax levied on citizens in various states?
- On the impeachment of the Chief Justice of the Supreme Court, who tries the case?

Until literacy tests were banned in the 1960s, they were used in some states to keep Black citizens (and, in some cases, poor white citizens) from registering to vote. The tests often contained questions on obscure topics and were selectively graded to allow most whites to pass and to disqualify most Blacks. The questions shown here were taken from Alabama literacy tests of the 1940s, a time when less than 20 percent of the state's eligible Black voters were registered to vote. (The answers to the above questions are, from top to bottom, January 3, nine, Archivist of the United States at the Office of the Federal Register, Virginia, no, Senate.)

right to vote "on account of race, color, or previous condition of servitude." Nevertheless, African Americans were disenfranchised throughout the South by intimidation and electoral trickery. One such trick was to require a literacy test as a precondition for eligibility to vote. The tests were selectively administered to exclude Black voters and contained questions so difficult that often the examiner had to look up the answers. If that was not obstacle enough, the names of those who took the test were sometimes published in the local newspaper so that employers, the local police, and even the Ku Klux Klan (KKK) would know the names of the "troublemakers." The state of Mississippi was the extreme case. Even as late as the 1950s, less than 5 percent of its Black citizens were registered to vote,[2] Not until the 1960s did Congress and the courts sweep away the last legal barriers to equal suffrage for African Americans (see Chapter 5).

Women did not secure the vote until the Nineteenth Amendment was ratified in 1920. Decades earlier, Susan B. Anthony, a leader in the effort to give women the right to vote, was arrested when she tried to cast a ballot in her hometown of Rochester, New York. By 1920, men had run out of excuses for denying the vote to women. Said social activist Wendell Phillips, "One of two things is true: either woman is like man—and if she is, then a ballot based on brains belongs to her as well as to him. Or she is different, and then man does not know how to vote for her as she herself does."[3]

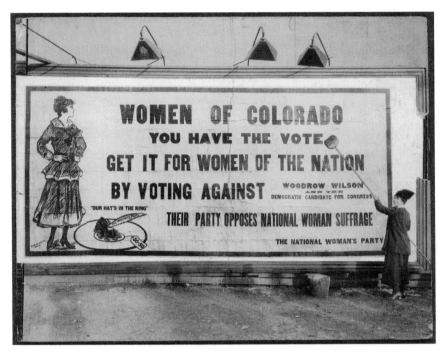

After a hard-fought, decades-long campaign, women across the nation finally won the right to vote in 1920. Fifteen states, most of them west of the Mississippi River, had earlier granted suffrage to women. Wyoming in 1869 was the first to do so. Colorado in 1893 was the second. (Library of Congress Manuscripts Division [mnwp000345])

The nation's youngest adults are the most recent group to gain access to the ballot. The Twenty-Sixth Amendment, which was ratified during the Vietnam War, lowered the voting age to 18 years. "If you're old enough to die, you're old enough to vote" was the rallying cry behind the amendment.

Factors in Voter Turnout: The United States in Comparative Perspective

Although nearly all Americans say they have a duty to vote, many of them shirk their duty. Voter turnout in the U.S. presidential elections is lower than turnout in the national elections of most Western democracies (see Figure 7-1). And turnout in U.S. midterm elections, which are the congressional elections that occur midway between the presidential elections, is lower still.

Registration and Voting Requirements   America's relatively low turnout rate owes partly to its demanding registration requirement. Before Americans are allowed to vote, they must make the effort to register—that is, they need to get their names on the official list of eligible voters.

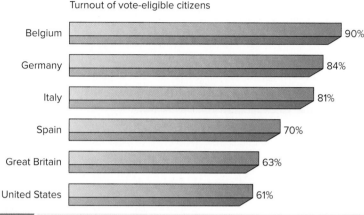

Turnout of vote-eligible citizens

Belgium	90%
Germany	84%
Italy	81%
Spain	70%
Great Britain	63%
United States	61%

figure 7-1   VOTER TURNOUT

Voter turnout is lower in the United States than in most Western democracies. The tendency owes in part to the nation's voter registration system, which places the burden of registration on the individual. In addition, states have leeway in defining registration and voting requirements, and some states have used their power to erect barriers to participation. (*Source:* Compiled by author from multiple sources. Percentages are average for the five most recent elections.)

Although other democracies also require **registration**, most of them place the responsibility on government officials. When someone moves to a new address, for example, the postal service will notify registration officials of the change. In keeping with its culture of individualism, the United States is one of the few democracies in which registration is the individual's responsibility. Scholars estimate that turnout would be roughly 10 percentage points higher in the United States if it had European-style registration.[4]

Moreover, registration is largely controlled by the state governments, which vary in how easy or hard they make it for citizens to register and vote. Nineteen states, including Idaho, Maine, and Minnesota, allow people to register at their polling places on Election Day. Studies indicate that same-day registration increases voter turn by roughly 5 percentage points on average.[5]

States with more restrictive registration laws—for example, those that make it difficult to cast an absentee ballot and require a government-issued ID such as a driver's license or passport to register—have turnout rates below the national average. Indiana, Georgia, and Wisconsin are among the seven states in this category. The first such law was passed in 2005 by Indiana's Republican-controlled legislature, which said it was intended to prevent voter fraud. Each of the six states that followed suit also had Republican-controlled legislatures. Young adults, minorities, and low-income individuals, all of whom tend to vote Democratic, are the Americans who are least likely to have a driver's license or passport.[6] In a 2008 case involving Indiana's law, the Supreme Court upheld such laws by a 6–3 vote, saying that states have a "valid interest" in deterring fraud. All six of the justices in the majority were appointed by a Republican president. They acknowledged that Indiana's Republican legislators were seeking a partisan advantage in enacting the law but argued that the law "should not be disregarded simply because partisan interests may have provided one motivation for the votes of individual legislators."[7]

| F A K E | **Detecting Misinformation** |

| *or* |
| F A C T |

Is Illegal Voting Widespread?

A poll conducted by researchers at Stanford University found that most Americans believe that a "meaningful amount" of illegal voting takes place in U.S. elections. The poll revealed that large numbers of Americans believe that many noncitizens vote illegally and that a significant number of people vote using the names of registered voters who have died.[8]

Guy J. Sagi/Shutterstock

Is that claim fact, or is it fake?

Studies indicate that illegal voting is extremely rare.[9] One study, for example, obtained the election fraud records of every state and found an "infinitesimal" amount of documented fraud, concluding that the odds of an individual being hit by lightning is 40 times greater than the likelihood that the individual will commit voter fraud.[10] In an attempt to show that voter fraud was widespread, Texas's attorney general launched an exhaustive investigation and found only two prosecutable instances of it—this in a state where 9 million voters go to the polls.[11] Kansas's secretary of state sought to prosecute illegal voters, searching the state's nearly 2 million registered voters, looking for violations. He ended up with only a few, which a judge concluded were "explained by administrative error, confusion or mistake."[12] There are reasons that voter fraud is rare. It's difficult enough to get eligible voters to the polls, much less to get those who are ineligible to knowingly take the risk. The penalty for illegal voting can be high—as much as a $10,000 fine and five years in prison in some states—and the incentive is low—the probability that a single vote will change the outcome of a national or state election is virtually zero.

After Democrats won the 2020 presidential election, relying heavily on a get-out-the-vote drive aimed at absentee, early, and mail-in balloting, a number of Republican-controlled states, including Texas, Arizona, Florida, Georgia, and Iowa, enacted laws to limit these forms of voting, arguing that they were a large source of illegal voting. Democrats argued that the new laws selectively targeted Democratic voters, particularly minorities and those of low income. The Georgia law, for example, restricted the number of Sundays on which early voting and registration could occur. Sunday was traditionally a time when Black congregations after church services would collectively register and vote. Democrats' legal challenges to the changes in election law were largely unsuccessful.

Frequency of Elections   Just as America's registration system places a burden on voters, so does its election schedule. The United States holds elections more often than other nations. No other democracy has elections for the lower chamber of its national legislature (the equivalent of the U.S. House of Representatives) as often as every two years, and no democracy schedules the election of its chief executive more frequently than every four years.[13] In addition, most local elections in the United States are held in odd-numbered years, unlike the even-year schedule of federal elections and most state elections. Finally, the United States uses primary elections to select the party nominees. In other democracies, party leaders choose them. Americans are asked to vote two to three times as often as Europeans, which increases the likelihood that they will not vote every time.[14]

In an earlier period, most state-wide elections coincided with the presidential election, when turnout is highest. This scheduling usually worked to the advantage of the party that won the presidential race—its candidates got a boost from the strong showing of its presidential nominee. In an effort to eliminate "presidential coattails" that could help a state's weaker party, states began in the 1930s to hold gubernatorial elections in nonpresidential years. Over three-fourths of the states have adopted this schedule, and two states—Virginia and New Jersey—elect their governors in odd-numbered years, insulating them even further from the turnout effects of federal elections.

Why Some Americans Vote and Others Do Not

Even though turnout is lower in the United States than in other major Western democracies, some Americans vote regularly, while others seldom or never vote. Among the explanations for these individual differences are education and income, age, civic attitudes, and political interest.

Education and Income   College-educated and upper-income Americans have above-average voting rates. They have the financial resources and communication skills that encourage participation and make it personally rewarding. Nevertheless, the United States is unusual in the degree to which education and income are related to voter participation. Europeans with less education and income vote at only slightly lower rates than other citizens. By comparison, Americans with a high income or college degree turn out to vote at a much higher rate in elections than do those of lower income or educational achievement.

Why do income and education make a greater difference in the United States than they do in Europe? Part of the explanation rests with America's more imposing voter registration requirements. Americans with less income and education are the individuals most adversely affected by the country's registration system. Many of them do not own cars or homes and are thus less likely to be registered in advance of an election or have the type of personal identification that some states require as a condition for registration. They are also less familiar with registration locations and times.[15]

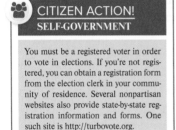

CITIZEN ACTION!
SELF-GOVERNMENT

You must be a registered voter in order to vote in elections. If you're not registered, you can obtain a registration form from the election clerk in your community of residence. Several nonpartisan websites also provide state-by-state registration information and forms. One such site is http://turbovote.org.

Age   Young adults are substantially less likely than middle-aged and older citizens to vote. For one thing, younger adults are more likely to change residence from one election to the next, which requires them to reregister to retain their voting eligibility. Even senior citizens, despite the infirmities of old age, have a much higher turnout rate than do voters under the age of 30.

Civic Attitudes and Political Interest   People differ in their attitudes toward politics, which affects the likelihood they will exercise their right to vote.

Some Americans have a keen sense of **civic duty**—a belief that they ought to participate in public affairs. Citizens who hold this belief tend to vote more regularly. A sense of civic duty is typically acquired from one's parents. When parents vote regularly and take an active interest in politics, their children usually grow up thinking they have an obligation to participate. When parents never vote and show no interest in public affairs, their children are less likely to see voting as a personal duty.

Interest in politics also affects the likelihood that a citizen will vote. **Political interest** is like people's other interests. People with an interest in computer games are more likely than other people to participate in these games. So it is with political interest and the likelihood of voting.[16] Political interest tends to be higher among partisans than independents. Although independents are often idealized in high school civics classes, they have lower voting rates than citizens who identify with a political party. Party loyalty deepens people's political commitment, including their determination to vote (see "Party Polarization: Party Identification and Voter Turnout").

P A R T Y	
POLARIZATION	

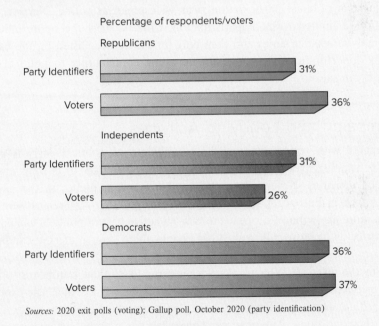

Conflicting Ideas

Party Identification and Voter Turnout

American politics in recent decades has been marked by party polarization—a widening divide between Republicans and Democrats. The divide is exaggerated in elections because party identifiers are more likely than those who call themselves independents to turn out to vote. The chart below compares the percentage of adults who voted in the 2020 presidential elections by whether they identified as Republican, Democratic, or Independent with a pre-election Gallup poll that asked respondents about their party identification. As can be seen, self-defined Republicans and Democrats are more likely than self-defined Independents to show up at the polls on Election Day.

Percentage of respondents/voters

Republicans

Party Identifiers — 31%
Voters — 36%

Independents

Party Identifiers — 31%
Voters — 26%

Democrats

Party Identifiers — 36%
Voters — 37%

Sources: 2020 exit polls (voting); Gallup poll, October 2020 (party identification)

Q: How might higher voter turnout among Republican and Democratic identifiers contribute to polarization?

A: Higher turnout among party identifiers increases the likelihood that candidates with more strongly held partisan views will get elected to office, which can result in a heightened partisan conflict on legislative issues.

Other attitudes are associated with low turnout. **Apathy**—a lack of interest in politics—typifies some citizens. They rarely, if ever, vote. Just as some people would not attend the Super Bowl even if it were free and being played across the street, some Americans care so little about politics that they would not bother to vote even if a ballot was delivered to their door. Other Americans refrain from voting because of a sense of **alienation**—a feeling of powerlessness rooted in the belief that government doesn't care what they think. This belief is more prevalent among low-income citizens and is a reason for their relatively low turnout rate.[17]

CONVENTIONAL FORMS OF PARTICIPATION OTHER THAN VOTING

No form of political participation is as widespread as voting. Nevertheless, voting is a limited form of participation. Citizens have the opportunity to vote only at specific times and then only for the choices listed on the ballot. Fuller opportunities exist, however, including contributing to political and civic organizations.

Campaign and Lobbying Activities

Compared with voting, working for a candidate or political party is more time-consuming. Not surprisingly, only a small percentage of citizens engage in such activities. Nevertheless, the number is much higher in the United States than in Europe. A study found, for example, that Americans were five times more likely than Europeans to take an active part in political campaigns and twice as likely to talk with other people about their preferred candidate or party.[18]

Why the reversal? Why are Americans more likely than Europeans to take part in election activity even though they are less likely to vote? The explanation rests in part on differences in the American and European election systems. For one thing, American campaigns last for months, whereas those in Europe start and end within a few weeks, offering citizens plenty of chances to join in. Then, too, the United States has a federal system. Each state elects its legislative and executive officials. Most European democracies are unitary systems (see Chapter 3) and thus do not have elected state officers.

Americans are also more likely than Europeans to contribute to groups that seek to influence public policy. This support typically takes the form of monetary contributions but can also take more active forms, such as contacting lawmakers or attending public rallies. Among the hundreds of groups that rely

Although Americans are less likely than Europeans to vote, they are more likely than Europeans to participate actively in political campaigns. Most Americans are not active participants, but many do get involved by working for a candidate or party, contributing to a favorite candidate, or, as in the case of those pictured here, encouraging people to register and vote. (Ariel Skelley/Blend Images)

on citizens' contributions are Greenpeace, Common Cause, AARP (American Association of Retired Persons), the Christian Coalition of America, and the NRA (National Rifle Association). (Interest groups are discussed further in Chapter 9.)

Virtual Participation

The advent of the World Wide Web in the 1990s opened up an entirely new venue for political participation—the Internet. Although this participation is "virtual" rather than face-to-face, much of it involves contact with friends, acquaintances, and activists through Facebook, Twitter, Instagram, e-mail, and other social media. Internet participation peaks during presidential campaigns and now easily outstrips conventional participation.

Internet fundraising is also flourishing. In the 2020 presidential race, for example, Donald Trump and Joe Biden each raised tens of millions of dollars for their campaigns through small, online donations. Many lobbying groups also rely on online contributions. MoveOn.org, for example, has a network of roughly 3 million "online liberal activists." In 2022, MoveOn spent more than $30 million in support of Democratic House and Senate candidates.[19]

Americans for Prosperity is another example. It has roughly 3 million members and has chapters in 35 states, each of which is dedicated to electing conservative candidates. (The Internet is discussed further in Chapter 10.)

Community Activities

Political participation extends beyond campaigns and elections to involvement in the community. Citizens can join community groups, work to accomplish community goals, and contact local officials. Such efforts generate what Harvard University's Robert Putnam has labeled **social capital**—face-to-face interactions between people. Research indicates that such contacts contribute to a sense of community and help foster civic cooperation.[20]

CITIZEN ACTION!
SELF-GOVERNMENT

There are many local and college groups dedicated to helping others through everything from operating food banks to beautifying public parks. Consider contacting such a group to volunteer your time. You'll have a chance to work with individuals who share your values while also working to improve the life of your community.

A lack of motivation is an obstacle to civic participation. Most people choose not to get involved, particularly when it requires a major commitment. Then, too, America's culture of individualism relieves pressure that people might feel about not contributing. Nevertheless, many Americans are involved in community affairs through local organizations, such as parent-teacher associations, neighborhood groups, business clubs, and church-affiliated groups (see "How the 50 States Differ"). Studies have found that participation in such organizations is twice as high in the United States as it is in Europe.[21] Religious practice is a reason. Americans are more than twice as likely as Europeans to attend church regularly, and many of them engage in church-related community work. In addition, U.S. cities and

HOW THE 50 STATES DIFFER
CRITICAL THINKING THROUGH COMPARISONS

Volunteer Activity

Although community volunteering is a tradition in every state, the rate varies greatly, as indicated by a recent study by the Corporation for National and Community Service. Utah, at 51 percent, and Minnesota, at 45 percent, have the highest volunteer rate in terms of the percentage of residents 16 years of age or older who are engaged yearly in community volunteer work. Mississippi, at 23 percent, and Florida, at 22 percent, rank lowest.

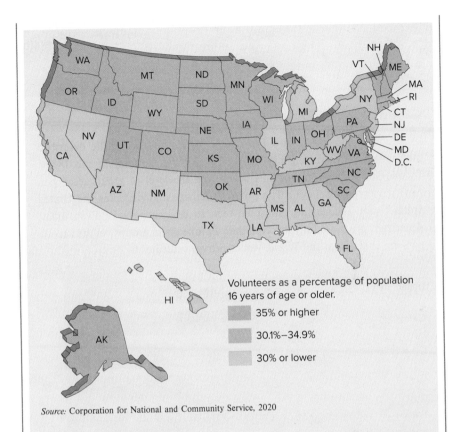

Volunteers as a percentage of population 16 years of age or older.

- 35% or higher
- 30.1%–34.9%
- 30% or lower

Source: Corporation for National and Community Service, 2020

Q: Why might the more northern states that lie west of the Mississippi River have higher-than-average volunteer rates?

A: Many residents of these states live in smaller communities with relatively stable populations. People in such communities are more likely to know each other and work together on community activities. In addition, these states were identified by political scientist Daniel Elazar as having participatory cultures as a result of their settlement by immigrants who came from European countries, such as Sweden and Norway, with a tradition of civic participation.

towns have more control over local and public school policy than do European cities and towns. Americans' volunteer activity takes many forms, but more than 70 percent of this participation takes place through church-related groups, school-related groups, and local civic organizations[22] (see "How the U.S. Differs").

HOW THE U.S. DIFFERS

CRITICAL THINKING THROUGH COMPARISONS

Groups: "A Nation of Joiners"

"A nation of joiners" is how Frenchman Alexis de Tocqueville described the United States during his writing tour of this country in the 1830s. Tocqueville said that Europeans would find the level of group activity in America hard to believe. "The political activity that pervades the United States," said Tocqueville, "must be seen to be understood." Even today, Americans are more fully involved than Europeans in groups, as the accompanying chart from the World Values Survey indicates.

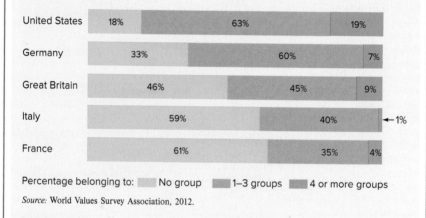

	No group	1–3 groups	4 or more groups
United States	18%	63%	19%
Germany	33%	60%	7%
Great Britain	46%	45%	9%
Italy	59%	40%	←1%
France	61%	35%	4%

Percentage belonging to: No group 1–3 groups 4 or more groups

Source: World Values Survey Association, 2012.

Q: What might account for the relatively high level of group activity in the United States?

A: Compared with Europeans, Americans have a stronger tradition of citizen involvement in local affairs centering on public schools, churches, and small businesses. Each of these is a prime source of group activity as, for example, in the case of school-based groups like Parent-Teacher Associations (PTAs), church-based groups like the Knights of Columbus, and business-based groups like Rotary Clubs. Americans are also more likely than Europeans to donate time and money to charitable and other causes, which analysts trace to a tradition of greater emphasis on citizen action as a way of addressing social problems and issues.

UNCONVENTIONAL ACTIVISM: POLITICAL MOVEMENTS AND PROTESTS

During the pre-democratic era, people resorted to protests and rioting to express displeasure with government. When democratic governments came into existence, elections gave citizens a regular and less disruptive way to express themselves. Nevertheless, voting is double-edged. It gives citizens power over government while giving government power over citizens.[23] Election by the people grants legitimacy to those in power, which can be used to justify self-serving policies.

Political movements, or *social movements* as they are also called, are a way for citizens to openly express their opposition to government policy.[24] As political scientist Sidney Tarrow notes, political movements take place largely outside established institutions in the form of protest rallies, marches, and the like. Thus, participation in political movements differs from participation through a political party, which takes place through scheduled elections.[25] Hundreds of political movements have arisen during the nation's history, including a number of highly successful ones, including the 1960s Black civil rights movement (see Chapter 5).

Recent Protest Movements

Recent years have witnessed a rise in protest activity. As Republicans and Democrats have moved apart, the issues that divide them have intensified and, in some cases, spilled over into protest activity. As well, because of partisan deadlock in Washington, many policy problems have been neglected, compounding the anxiety and frustration that result when problems worsen. In any case, Americans have increasingly looked outside established political channels to make their voices heard. The following discussion highlights several recent protest movements and their success in achieving their goals.

Tea Party Movement The Tea Party came to the public's attention on April 15, 2009–the date that federal income taxes were due. The timing was not a coincidence, nor was the movement's name. Like the participants in the legendary Boston Tea Party, those who took to the streets in hundreds of cities and towns on that April day were expressing their opposition to taxes.

Occupy Wall Street When the Occupy Wall Street (OWS) movement emerged in 2011, it began small–a single encampment in New York City's Zuccotti Park, adjacent to Wall Street. Within a few weeks, however, it had spread to dozens of American cities. OWS was sparked by anger at the government's bailout of the financial industry and its failure to hold bankers accountable for their role in the financial crisis of 2008. Unlike the Tea Party, OWS's target was the widening income gap between the wealthiest 1 percent of Americans and the rest of society. "We are the 99%" was the movement's rallying cry.

Black Lives Matter   Sparked by the killing of unarmed young Black men by police officers in several cities, including Baltimore, Chicago, and Ferguson, Missouri, the Black Lives Matter movement sought to change not just local law enforcement but local governments generally, many of which provide inferior services in Black neighborhoods. Through public demonstrations, marches, and the reenactment of police killings, the movement has sought to highlight disparities in how white and Black citizens are treated by local officials. The movement gained strength in 2020 after George Floyd, who was handcuffed and face down in the street, was killed by Minneapolis police officers. His death led to the largest protests yet of police violence directed at Black Americans.

The #MeToo Movement   In 2017, #MeToo spread virally as a social media hashtag to show the extent to which women are subjected to sexual assault and harassment. Popularized by actress Alyssa Milano, the hashtag was used

The #MeToo movement emerged rapidly in 2017 as thousands of women used social media to say that they, too, had been the victims of sexual assault or harassment. Within a relatively few weeks, powerful men in media, politics, and business who were credibly accused of sexual misconduct had been fired or resigned. The movement sought to raise public awareness of sexual misconduct and to get firms and organizations to take steps to prevent such abuses. (Tassii/E+/Getty Images)

200,000 times on the first day she proposed it and was subsequently posted millions of times, often accompanied by the sender's personal story. The movement has contributed to the firing or resignation of a large number of powerful men, including Hollywood producer Harvey Weinstein, television host Charlie Rose, casino magnate Steve Wynn, and U.S. Representative John Conyers. The movement's larger goal is to raise awareness of the level of sexual misconduct, show its devastating effect on victims, and pressure firms and organizations to take steps to stop it.

Movement Against Gun Violence   The movement against gun violence had a relatively low profile until the 2018 mass killing at Marjory Stoneman Douglas High School in Parkland, Florida. The school's students responded with impassioned pleas for an end to school shootings. Their pleas captured the nation's attention. It led to National School Walkout Day and March for Our Lives demonstrations in hundreds of cities and towns. The movement sought to pressure lawmakers at the national, state, and local levels to enact tougher gun control measures, including rigorous background checks on gun buyers and a ban on military-style assault rifles, which had been used in several recent mass killings, including the Parkland shooting.

Make America Great Again (MAGA)   Protest movements normally arise outside of formal political institutions. Make America Great Again (MAGA), which began with Donald Trump's 2016 presidential campaign, is an exception.

Political movements typically arise outside of established political institutions as a protest against what government officials are doing. Make America Great Again (MAGA) is an exception. It began with Donald Trump's 2016 presidential campaign and then gained momentum when Trump won the election and carried the message into the White House. (Jeff Malet Photography/Newscom)

MAGA's influence works through the Republican Party but is also felt outside of it, making it a political movement although an atypical one.[26] MAGA supporters promote ideas and policies based on their version of what America once stood for and which they feel is being destroyed by social and political change. Political scientists Christopher Sebastian Parker and Rachel surveyed MAGA supporters, concluding that they "feel like they're losing their country and their identity," believing that their "way of life" is being displaced by immigrants, career women, and communities of color.[27]

Factors in the Success of Social Movements

Most political movements fail to achieve their goals. Some of the earlier movements, including anarchist and communist movements, had goals that were so at odds with American values that they failed to attract sizable followings. Others failed because they lacked the resources to sustain the effort. Typically, a lengthy period of intense and sustained action is required for a movement to succeed. Finally, movements can fail if they are unable to find ways to institutionalize their goals. If, for example, the Black civil rights movement had not succeeded in getting some of its goals institutionalized through the 1964 Civil Rights Act and the 1965 Voting Rights Act, its impact would have been far less substantial.

Recent political movements have had varying levels of success. Each has drawn attention to its core issue, but they otherwise differ. The Tea Party has had substantial influence. It was able to transform itself from a movement to a permanent force within the Republican Party, which provided it with an institutional base from which to pursue cuts in taxes and government spending. In their book, *Reactionary Republicanism*, political scientists Bryan Gervais and Irwin Morris show that the Tea Party created a climate of opinion within the Republican Party that enabled Donald Trump to win its 2016 presidential nomination.[28] From that perspective, the Tea Party gave rise to MAGA, although it was Trump who named the movement, personified it, and made cultural conflict its signature issue.[29]

In contrast, Occupy Wall Street protesters rejected the idea of creating institutional links, which meant that when their encampments were disbanded they didn't have an organization through which to pursue their goals. Nevertheless, analysts trace Senator Bernie Sander's rise to national prominence to the Occupy movement. Its message about corporate power and wealth inequality mirrored what Sanders had been saying for years.[30]

It is too early to say with certainty whether Black Lives Matter, the #MeToo movement, and the movement against gun violence will achieve lasting institutional and policy gains. Each movement has had an impact. Black Lives Matter has led to changes in police practices, a process that accelerated after widespread protests erupted in the wake of George Floyd's killing by Minneapolis police. The #MeToo movement has led some firms and organizations to establish policies aimed at curbing sexual misconduct. The movement against gun violence has led some states and localities to curb the sale and possession of particular types of firearms and accessories. But none of these movements, as of yet, has succeeded in bringing about large-scale policy change. The history of the Black civil rights movement suggests that any judgment on the success of these movements could come years from now. It took several decades before the Black civil rights movement was able to get lawmakers to enact the landmark laws that are now its lasting legacy.

The Public's Response to Protest Activity

Protest politics has a long history in America. Indeed, the United States was founded on a protest movement that sparked a revolution against Britain. Despite this tradition, protest activity is less common today in the United States than in many Western democracies. Spain, France, Germany, Sweden, and Mexico are among the countries that have higher rates of protest participation.[31]

America's protest tradition is no guarantee that the public will back a protest movement. The Vietnam War prompted the largest sustained protest movement in the nation's history, but the protesters failed to win broad public support in part because some of the protests resulted in violent clashes with police and were accompanied by the burning of the American flag. A 1968 Gallup poll found that 75 percent of respondents had an unfavorable opinion of Vietnam War protestors, compared with 21 percent with a favorable opinion. When unarmed student protesters at Kent State University were shot to death in May 1970 by members of the National Guard, a *Newsweek* poll found that 58 percent of respondents blamed the Kent State killings on the student demonstrators while only 11 percent said the Guard was at fault.

When protesters' grievance is widely seen as legitimate, the public is supportive. A Reuters poll found, for example, that Americans by a ratio of three to one believed that protests over the death of George Floyd by police in 2020 were justified. However, as the protests progressed, some of the protesters called for defunding the police. Less than one in five Americans supported the idea and approval of the Black Lives Matter movement declined.[32] A year after Floyd's killing, support for the movement had dropped to the point where the number of Americans with an unfavorable view of Black Lives Matter equaled the number with a favorable view.

The decline in support for Black Lives Matter was concentrated among white Americans, which reveals another tendency in political movements. People without a direct stake in a movement's goal are typically far less supportive of the movement. That tendency characterized the anti-Vietnam War protests,

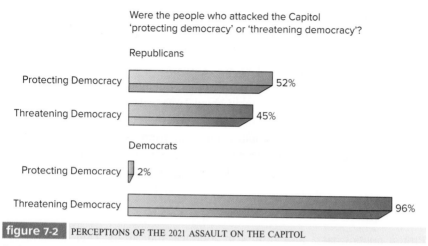

figure 7-2   PERCEPTIONS OF THE 2021 ASSAULT ON THE CAPITOL

On January 6, 2021, protestors stormed the Capitol seeking to prevent Congress from certifying Democrat Joe Biden's election as president and giving the victory instead to Republican Donald Trump. Windows were shattered, doors broken, and lives lost when the protest turned violent. Consistent with other protests, Americans' reaction to the assault depended on how they felt about the protestors' goal. A slight majority of Republicans believed their actions were justified while an overwhelming majority of Democrats saw the protestors as a threat to democracy. (*Source:* ABC/Ipsos poll, January 2022.)

which had much greater support among draft-age men than it did among older Americans. The January 6, 2021, assault on the nation's Capitol, which aimed at giving Republican presidential nominee Donald Trump a second term, also fit the typical pattern. A poll found that 52 percent of Republicans, but only 2 percent of Democrats, believed that the protestors were "protecting democracy" as opposed to "threatening democracy" (see Figure 7-2).[33]

In short, although most Americans recognize that protests are part of America's tradition of free expression, they do not embrace them as fully as they do voting. Many Americans would prefer that people voice their discontent at the ballot box rather than by taking to the streets. In this sense, most Americans see protest as something to be accepted, but not always something to be embraced.

PARTICIPATION AND THE POTENTIAL FOR INFLUENCE

Most Americans are not highly active in politics. One reason is the emphasis that the American culture places on individualism. Most Americans under most conditions expect to solve their problems on their own rather than through political action. "In the United States, the country of individualism *par excellence,*" William Watts and Lloyd Free write, "there is a sharp distinction in people's minds between their own personal lives and national life."[34]

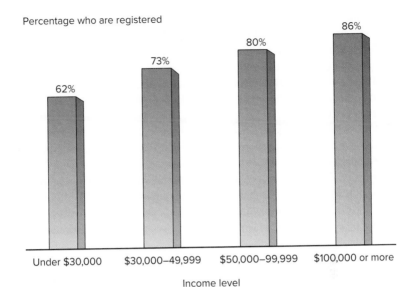

Percentage who are registered

figure 7-3   VOTER REGISTRATION AND INCOME LEVEL

Low-income Americans are much less likely to be registered to vote than those of higher income. (*Source:* U.S. Census Bureau, 2022)

Paradoxically, although they have more need for government help, lower-income Americans are the least likely to engage in collective action. Lower-income individuals tend to have less education, less access to transportation, less access to permanent housing, and less understanding of how to get involved in politics—all of which work to reduce their level of political participation.[35] Indeed, Americans at the low end of the income ladder are a third less likely to be registered to vote than those at the high end (see Figure 7-3). Research indicates that one of the largest differences between voters and nonvoters is support for assistance programs that would benefit low-income Americans.[36] It is no surprise that studies have found that elected officials are far more responsive to the concerns of wealthier constituents than to the concerns of poorer ones.[37]

Without question, Americans who have the least economic power also have the least political power. However, the issue of individual participation is only one piece of the larger puzzle of how power is distributed in America. Subsequent chapters will provide additional pieces.

SUMMARY

Political participation is involvement in activities designed to influence public policy and leadership. A main issue of democratic government is the question of who participates in politics and how fully they participate.

Voting is the most widespread form of active political participation among Americans, yet voter turnout is significantly lower in the United States than in other democratic nations. The requirement that Americans personally register in order to become eligible to vote is one reason for lower turnout among Americans; other democracies place the burden of registration on government officials rather than on the individual citizens. The fact that the United States holds frequent elections also discourages some citizens from voting regularly.

Only a minority of citizens engage in the more demanding forms of political activity, such as work on community affairs or on behalf of a candidate during a political campaign. Nevertheless, the proportion of Americans who engage in these more demanding forms of activity exceeds the proportion of Europeans who do so. Most political activists are individuals of higher income and education; they have the skills and material resources to participate effectively and tend to take a greater interest in politics. More than in any other Western democracy, political participation in the United States is related to economic status.

Social movements are broad efforts to achieve change by citizens who feel that government is not properly responsive to their interests. These efforts typically take place outside established channels; demonstrations, picket lines, and marches are common means of protest. Despite America's tradition of free expression, protest activities do not always have a high level of public support.

Overall, Americans are only moderately involved in politics. Although they are concerned with political affairs, they are mostly immersed in their private pursuits—a reflection, in part, of a cultural belief in individualism. The lower level of participation among low-income citizens has particular significance in that it works to reduce their influence on public policy and leadership.

CRITICAL THINKING ZONE

KEY TERMS

Alienation (*p. 188*)
apathy (*p. 188*)
civic duty (*p. 186*)
political interest (*p. 186*)
political movements (*p. 193*)

political participation (*p. 179*)
registration (*p. 183*)
social capital (*p. 190*)
suffrage (*p. 180*)

APPLYING THE ELEMENTS OF CRITICAL THINKING

Conceptualizing: How do alienation, apathy, and civic duty differ?

Synthesizing: Why is voter turnout relatively low in the United States? Why are community participation rates relatively high in the United States?

Analyzing: Why does economic status—differences in Americans' education and income levels—make such a large difference in their level of political participation? Why does it make a larger difference in the United States than in Europe?

OF POSSIBLE INTEREST

A Book Worth Reading: Thomas Paine, *The American Crisis* (Scotts Valley, Calif.: CreateSpace, 2017). A compilation of Thomas Paine's pamphlets written between 1776 and 1783, including his famed *Common Sense*. The pamphlets have a message for citizens: Get involved in politics; there's a lot at stake.

A Website Worth Visiting: **www.votesmart.org** Project Vote Smart is a nonpartisan, nonprofit organization. Its website includes helpful information for voters on the backgrounds and policy positions of Republican and Democratic candidates for office.

CHAPTER 8

POLITICAL PARTIES, CANDIDATES, AND CAMPAIGNS: DEFINING THE VOTERS' CHOICE

Hill Street Studios/Blend Images/Getty Images

66 Political parties created democracy and . . . modern democracy is unthinkable save in terms of the parties. 99

E. E. SCHATTSCHNEIDER[1]

Toe-to-toe, they slugged it out in states and districts across the breadth of America, each side claiming it had the answers to America's problems. One side promised to raise the minimum wage, reduce student loan obligations, enhance the status of women, widen access to health care, promote racial progress, protect immigrants, and tighten controls on guns. The other side pointed to its support of tax cuts, tough stance on illegal immigration, support of the military, and commitment to deregulating business. The scene of the showdown was the 2022 midterm elections. The opposing sides were the Democratic Party and the Republican Party, each with a slate of candidates that carried its message to voters across America.

Political parties are in the business of offering voters a choice. A **political party** is an ongoing coalition of interests joined together under a common label in an effort to get its candidates elected to public office.[2] By offering a choice between policies and leaders, parties give voters a chance to influence the direction of government. "It is the competition of [parties] that provides the people with an opportunity to make a choice," political scientist E. E. Schattschneider wrote. "Without this opportunity popular sovereignty amounts to nothing."[3]

This chapter examines political parties and the candidates who run under their banners. U.S. campaigns are **party-centered campaigns** in the sense that the Republican and Democratic compete across the country, election after election. However, they are also **candidate-centered campaigns** in the sense that individual candidates devise their own strategies, choose their own issues, and form their own campaign organizations. They, more than their party, are in charge of their campaigns. Parties are a vital component, but they act primarily in a service function, providing funding, volunteers, and other forms of support aimed at ensuring their candidates' success. The following points are emphasized in this chapter:

- *Political competition in the United States has centered on two parties, a pattern that is explained primarily by America's single-member district system of elections.* Minor parties exist in the United States but have been unable to attract enough votes to win legislative seats.

- *To win an electoral majority, candidates of the two major parties must appeal to a large number of voters.* This can lead them to advocate moderate policies, although in recent years they've increasingly positioned themselves away from the political center because of party polarization and a decline in the number of competitive states and districts.

- *U.S. party organizations play an important role in campaigns, although one that is less substantial than in their heyday.* The introduction of primary elections and the emergence of televised campaigning gradually shifted control of elections toward candidates and away from parties. Nevertheless, party organizations at the local, state, and national levels make significant contributions to candidates' election campaigns.

- *Presidential and congressional campaigns are largely candidate centered.* These campaigns are based on money and media and utilize the skills of professional consultants.

PARTY COMPETITION AND MAJORITY RULE

Citizens have influence but only when they act together. Parties give them that ability. Parties are **linkage institutions**; they connect citizens with political leaders. When Americans go to the polls, they have a choice between candidates representing the Republican and Democratic Parties. This **party competition** narrows voters' options to two and, in the process, enables people with different opinions to act together. In casting a majority of its votes for one party, the electorate chooses that party's candidates, philosophy, and policies over those of the opposing party.

Parties also enable elected leaders to act collectively. Shared partisanship connects House and Senate members and ties them to the president when their party controls the White House. Parties bring together the institutions that the Constitution has divided.

The history of democratic government is inseparable from the history of parties. When the people of Eastern Europe gained their freedom from the Soviet Union in the early 1990s, one of their first steps toward democracy was the formation of political parties. When the United States was founded over two centuries ago, the formation of parties was also a first step toward ensuring its democracy. The reason is simple: It is the competition among parties that gives popular majorities a choice over how they will be governed.[4]

The First Parties

Many of America's early leaders mistrusted parties. George Washington, in his farewell address, warned the nation of the "baneful effects" of parties, and James Madison likened parties to special interests. However, Madison's misgivings about parties slowly gave way to grudging admiration. He came to realize that parties were the best way for like-minded leaders and citizens to act together to achieve common goals.

America's first parties originated in the rivalry between Alexander Hamilton and Thomas Jefferson. Hamilton envisioned a nation connected by commerce and a strong central government and organized his followers into the Federalist

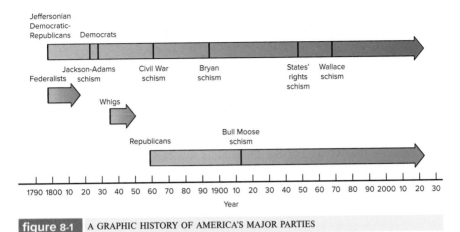

figure 8-1   A GRAPHIC HISTORY OF AMERICA'S MAJOR PARTIES

The U.S. party system has been remarkable for its continuity. Competition between two major parties has been a persistent feature of the system.

Party, taking the name from the faction that had championed ratification of the Constitution (see Figure 8-1). Siding with small farmers and states' rights advocates, Jefferson responded by creating the Democratic-Republican Party, a name that evoked the spirit of the Declaration of Independence. The Federalists' efforts to promote wealthy interests fueled Jefferson's claim that they were determined to create a government that favored the rich and wellborn. In the election of 1800, Jefferson defeated John Adams, who had succeeded Washington as the president. Adams's presidency marked the end of the Federalist Party's reign. It would never again hold power and gradually disappeared.

During the so-called Era of Good Feeling, when James Monroe ran unopposed in 1820 for a second presidential term, it appeared as if the political system might operate without competing parties. However, by the end of Monroe's second term, policy differences had split the Democratic-Republicans. The larger faction, under the leadership of Andrew Jackson, embraced Jefferson's commitment to the common people and shortened the party' name to the Democratic Party. Thus, the Democratic-Republican Party of Jefferson is the forerunner of today's Democratic Party rather than of today's Republican Party.

Andrew Jackson and Grassroots Parties

Jackson's goal was to take political power from entrenched elites. Each of the previous presidents had come from a prominent family, as had many of those in Congress and top executive positions. Jackson saw a reorganized Democratic Party as the vehicle for change. Whereas Jefferson's party had operated largely at the leadership level, Jackson sought a **grassroots party**. As such, it was organized chiefly at the local level and was open to all voters. During campaigns, the Democratic Party held parades, rallies, and barbecues in order to engage voters. Such efforts, along with the extension of voting rights to citizens without property, contributed to a nearly fourfold rise in voter turnout during the 1830s.[5]

During this period, a new opposition party—the Whig Party—emerged to challenge the Democrats. The Whigs were united less by a governing philosophy than by their opposition to Jackson and his followers. However, competition between the Whigs and the Democrats was relatively short-lived. During the 1850s, the slavery issue began to tear both parties apart. The Whig Party

Although largely forgotten, the Whig Party was once one of America's two major parties. Four Whigs served as the president—William Henry Harrison, John Tyler, Zachary Taylor, and Millard Fillmore. The party came into being in the early 1830s and lasted into the 1850s before being replaced by the newly created Republican Party. (Library of Congress, Prints and Photographs Division [LC-DIG-pga-09004])

disintegrated, and a new, northern-based party, calling itself Republican, emerged as the Democrats' main challenger. In the 1860 presidential election, the Democratic Party's northern and southern factions nominated different candidates and the Democratic vote split along regional lines between the two nominees, enabling the Republican nominee, Abraham Lincoln, who had called for the gradual elimination of slavery, to win the presidency with only 40 percent of the popular vote. Lincoln's election prompted southern states to secede from the Union.

The Civil War was the first and only time in the nation's history that the party system failed to peacefully settle Americans' political differences. The issue of slavery was simply too explosive to be settled through elections.[6]

Republicans Versus Democrats: Realignments and the Enduring Party System

After the Civil War, the nation settled into the pattern of competition between the Republican and Democratic Parties that has lasted through today. The durability of the two parties is due not to their ideological consistency but to their ability to change during periods of crisis. By abandoning their old ways of doing things at these crucial times, the Republican and Democratic Parties have reorganized themselves—with new bases of support, new policies, and new public philosophies.

These periods of extraordinary party change are known as **party realignments**. A realignment typically involves three basic elements:

1. The emergence of unusually powerful and divisive issues
2. Election contests in which the voters shift their partisan support
3. An enduring change in the parties' policies and coalitions

Realignments are rare. They do not occur simply because one party takes control of the government from the other party in a single election. Realignments result in deep and lasting changes in the party system, which affect multiple elections. By this standard, there have been four realignments since the 1850s.

The first was a result of the nation's Civil War and worked to the advantage of the Republicans. Called the "Union Party" by many, the Republicans dominated elections in the larger and more populous North, while the Democrats had a stronghold in what became known as "the Solid South." The Republicans championed federal power and business growth, while the Democrats promoted states' rights and the interests of small farmers, immigrants, and low-wage workers. During the next three decades, the Republicans held the presidency, except for Grover Cleveland's two terms in office, and had a majority in Congress for all but four years.

The 1896 election also resulted in realignment. Three years earlier, a banking crisis had precipitated a severe depression. Democrat Grover Cleveland was the president when the crash happened, and people blamed him and his party. Before then, Democrats had slowly been gaining strength, threatening Republicans' control of national politics. Although the 1890s realignment did not fundamentally alter the parties' platforms, it reversed the Democratic Party's momentum. Republicans picked up additional support in the Northeast and Midwest, solidifying their position as the nation's dominant party. During the four decades between the 1890s realignment and the next one in the 1930s, the Republicans held the presidency except during Woodrow Wilson's two terms and had a majority in Congress for all but six years.

The Great Depression of the 1930s triggered a third realignment. The Republican Herbert Hoover was the president when the stock market crashed in 1929, and many Americans blamed Hoover, his party, and its business allies for the crisis. When the Democratic Party won the presidency in 1932 and gained the confidence of the American people through its economic recovery programs, it set itself up to be the nation's dominant party. Franklin D. Roosevelt's election as the president began a 36-year period of Democratic presidencies that was interrupted only by Dwight D. Eisenhower's two terms in the 1950s. In this period, the Democrats also dominated Congress, losing control only in 1947–1948 and 1953–1954. The 1930s realignment produced a fundamental change in the Democratic Party's positioning. It had been a states' rights party but was now using federal power to regulate business and assist the economically disadvantaged. It was during this period that the term "liberal" came into popular use as a way to describe the Democratic Party.[7]

Party realignments have a lasting effect because they are powered by changes in people's long-term party loyalties. Young voters, in particular, embrace the newly ascendant party, giving it a solid base of support for years to come. First-time voters in the 1930s came to identify with the Democratic Party by a two-to-one margin (see Figure 8-2). They retained their loyalty to the Democratic Party, enabling it to dominate national politics into the 1960s.[8]

The Democratic Party built during the New Deal era was made up largely of low- and moderate-income groups, including blue-collar workers, inner-city dwellers, minority-group members, and small farmers. Democrats prided themselves on being "the party of the little man," helping lower-income Americans by enacting, for example, the minimum wage and social security. In contrast, the Republican Party in this period was dominated by middle- and upper-income groups, including businesspeople, merchants, well-to-do farmers, and professionals.

Party identification of first-time voters

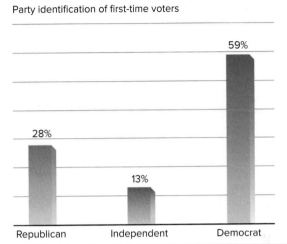

figure 8-2   THE MAKING OF A DEMOCRATIC MAJORITY

During the Great Depression period, first-time voters strongly backed the Democratic Party, positioning it to dominate national politics for the next three decades. (*Source:* Kristi Andersen, *The Creation of a Democratic Majority, 1928-1936* [Chicago: University of Chicago Press, 1979], 63. Based on first-time eligible voters in 1932, 1936, and 1940.)

The Nature and Origins of Today's Party Alignment

The fourth and most recent party realignment began with the decline of the Democrats' New Deal coalition. Party realignments don't last forever. They gradually lose strength as issues change. By the late 1960s, with the Democratic Party divided over the Vietnam War and civil rights, it was apparent that the era of New Deal politics was coming to an end.[9]

The change was most dramatic in the South. The region had been solidly Democratic since the Civil War, but the Democratic Party's leadership on civil rights alienated the region's white conservatives. In the 1964 presidential election, five southern states voted Republican and other southern states followed in quick succession. The change in congressional elections occurred more slowly, but Republicans would eventually come to dominate those elections as well (see Figure 8-3). Meanwhile, as white southerners became a larger voice in the Republican Party, the Northeast and West Coast shifted toward the Democrats, most dramatically in the New England states (Connecticut, Maine, Massachusetts, New Hampshire, Rhode Island, and Vermont).[10] The Northeast and West Coast were once the stronghold of the Republicans' moderate wing, which had dominated the party in the century after the Civil War. Many moderate Republican voters felt less at home in the Republican Party

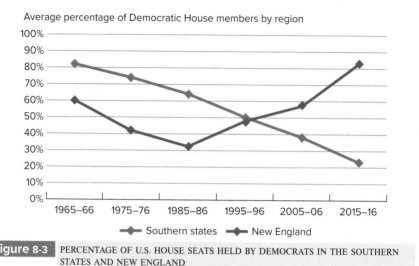

Average percentage of Democratic House members by region

figure 8-3 PERCENTAGE OF U.S. HOUSE SEATS HELD BY DEMOCRATS IN THE SOUTHERN
STATES AND NEW ENGLAND

In elections to the U.S. House of Representatives in recent decades, the southern states have
increasingly elected Republicans, while the New England states have increasingly elected Democrats.

when, in response to its growing strength in the South, it shifted to the right
on issues like race and social welfare.

The net result of these and other regional changes has been a party realignment. Rather than occurring abruptly in response to a disruptive issue, as
happened with the earlier realignments, the change took place gradually and
is the product of several issues rather than an overriding one. Civil rights
triggered the change, but it was soon followed by what analysts Richard
Scammon and Ben Wattenberg called the "social issue"—a loose set of controversies including crime, abortion, drugs, school prayer, and changing sexual and
family norms.[11] Conservative Christians were the ones most alarmed by social
change, solidifying Republican gains in the southern and border states, particularly among white evangelicals.[12] President Lyndon Johnson's Great Society
programs, which included programs such as Medicare and Medicaid, had
expanded the federal government's social welfare role and increased federal
spending. Conservatives felt the government was spending too much and doing
too many things that were better left to the states. Elected in 1980, President
Ronald Reagan gave voice to their concerns, vowing to cut taxes, reduce the
welfare rolls, trim the federal budget, and devolve power to the states.

Although America's parties had realigned themselves without going through
the sudden shock of a single realigning election, the change has been dramatic,
especially for the Republican Party.[13] Although it began under Lincoln as the

White evangelical Christians began to vote heavily Republican during Ronald Reagan's presidency and have been a large and reliable Republican voting bloc ever since. (Jim West/Alamy Stock Photo)

party of national power, it is now more clearly a states' rights party that seeks to shift power from Washington to the states (see Chapter 3).

The realignment of America's parties has been accompanied by a widening gap in the opinions of Republicans and Democrats.[14] On the question of federal assistance for the economically disadvantaged, for example, the gap in Republican and Democratic opinions has more than doubled since the 1980s and is now nearly 40 percentage points.[15] Many of the issues that divide the parties defy compromise. The "social issue" of the 1970s evolved into "culture wars"—conflict over which party's values will define what America is and will be.[16] The fight over abortion policy is a long-standing example. More recent examples are fights over same-sex marriage and the teaching of racial history in public schools.

Parties and the Vote

The enduring power of partisanship is clearest when, election after election, Republican and Democratic candidates reap the vote of their party's identifiers. It is relatively rare—in congressional races as well as the presidential race—for a party nominee to get less than 80 percent of the partisan vote.

The power of partisanship can be seen in the tendency of most voters to cast a *straight ticket*—meaning that they uniformly support their party's candidates. Most voters who cast a ballot for the Republican or Democratic presidential candidate also vote for that party's congressional candidate. Only about 10 percent of today's voters cast a *split-ticket*—meaning that they vote for one party's presidential candidate and the other party's congressional candidate.

ELECTORAL AND PARTY SYSTEMS

Throughout nearly all of its history, the United States has had a **two-party system**: Federalists versus Jeffersonian Democratic-Republicans, Whigs versus Democrats, Republicans versus Democrats. A two-party system, however, is the exception rather than the rule (see "How the U.S. Differs"). Most democracies have a **multiparty system**, in which three or more parties have the capacity to gain control of government, separately or in coalition. Why the difference? Why are there three or more major parties in most democracies but only two major parties in the United States?

The Single-Member System of Election

America's two-party system is largely the result of the nation's method of choosing its officials. They are elected by winning a plurality of the votes in **single-member districts**. Each constituency elects a single member to a particular office, such as U.S. senator or state representative; the candidate with the most votes (*the plurality*) in a district wins the office. The **single-member system** (sometimes called the *winner-take-all or plurality* system) discourages minor parties by reducing their chances of winning anything, even if they perform well by minor-party standards. Assume, for example, that a minor party receives exactly 20 percent of the vote in each of America's 435 congressional races. Even though one in five voters nationwide backed the minor party, it does not win a single seat in Congress because none of its candidates placed first in any of the 435 single-member-district races. The winning candidate in each race is the major-party candidate, with the larger share of the remaining 80 percent of the vote.

By comparison, most European democracies use a **proportional representation system** in which seats in the legislature are allocated according to a party's percentage of the popular vote. In most such systems, campaigns are party centered in that, when casting a ballot, voters are choosing from a list of parties rather than, as in the American case, choosing from a list of candidates. Proportional representation systems enable smaller parties to compete for power. In Germany's 2021 election, for example, the Green Party won 15 percent of the national vote and thereby received roughly 15 percent of the seats in the German parliament. If the Greens had been competing under America's electoral rules, they would not have received any seats.

Politics and Coalitions in the Two-Party System

The overriding goal of a major American party is to gain power by getting its candidates elected to office. Because there are only two major parties, the Republicans and Democrats need to attract more votes than the other party in order to win. If either party confines its support to too narrow a slice of voters, it forfeits its chance of victory.

Seeking the Center Without Losing the Support of the Party Faithful
A two-party system typically requires the major parties to avoid positions that will position them too far from the political center. The **median voter theorem** holds that, if there are two parties, the parties can maximize their vote only if they position themselves at the location of the median voter—the voter whose preferences are exactly in the middle.[17]

Although hypothetical, the median voter theorem helps explain the risk a party faces when moving too far from the center, leaving it open to the other party. In 1964, the Republican nominee, Barry Goldwater, proposed the elimination of mandatory Social Security and suggested he might be open to the use of small nuclear weapons in the Vietnam conflict—extreme positions that cost him many votes. Eight years later, the Democratic nominee, George McGovern, took positions on Vietnam and income security that alarmed many voters. Like Goldwater, he was buried in one of the biggest landslides in presidential history.

Although voters in the political center can hold the balance of power in an election, they are now less important to the parties' strategies. Because of party polarization, most voters today are positioned to the right or left of center.[18] If candidates move too close to the center, they risk alienating their party's core voters, some of whom may stay home on Election Day.

In addition, there are fewer competitive states and districts than in the past. As a result of unrestricted partisan gerrymandering (see Chapter 11) and the fact that the party realignment of recent decades occurred along geographic lines, most states and congressional districts are now so lopsidedly Republican or Democratic that the stronger party is virtually certain to win the general election.[19] In these elections, the key race is the stronger party's primary election. Primaries have relatively low turnout, and the voters who show up are disproportionately the party's more hardcore voters. Thus, rather than positioning themselves toward the political center, candidates take positions away from the center in order to appeal to these voters. It's a reason that Congress has far fewer moderate members today than in the past.

Party Coalitions   The groups and interests that support a party are collectively referred to as the **party coalition**. The Republican and Democratic coalitions differ substantially in their composition (see Figure 8-4).

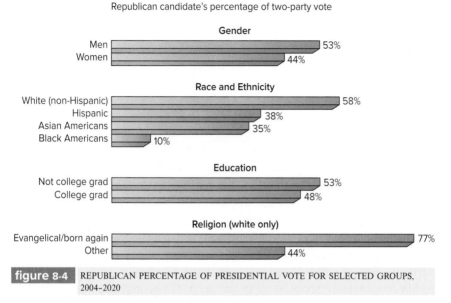

Republican candidate's percentage of two-party vote

Gender
Men — 53%
Women — 44%

Race and Ethnicity
White (non-Hispanic) — 58%
Hispanic — 38%
Asian Americans — 35%
Black Americans — 10%

Education
Not college grad — 53%
College grad — 48%

Religion (white only)
Evangelical/born again — 77%
Other — 44%

figure 8-4 REPUBLICAN PERCENTAGE OF PRESIDENTIAL VOTE FOR SELECTED GROUPS, 2004–2020

The Republican and Democratic parties differ in their coalitions, as can be seen from the average percentage of the two-party vote received by the Republican presidential candidate in the five most recent elections. (*Source:* Exit polls, 2008–2020)

The Republican Party gets its votes largely from non-Hispanic white Americans. In the 2020 election, they cast roughly 9 of every 10 votes that Republicans received.[20] Not since Lyndon Johnson's landslide victory in the 1964 election has the Democratic presidential nominee won a majority of the white vote.[21] Working-class whites, defined here as white voters who do not have a college degree, were the backbone of the Democratic Party during the New Deal era. They now vote heavily Republican. By a narrower margin, most older adults and higher-income Americans vote Republican.[22]

The Democratic Party coalition is more diverse. White voters account for most of the Democratic vote, but roughly two-fifths of the party's vote recently has come from minority-group members. Black Americans have voted roughly nine-to-one Democratic. Hispanics and Asian Americans have voted more than three-to-two Democratic. Younger voters and lower-income Americans also have voted disproportionately Democratic. Since the 1980s, women have voted more heavily Democratic than have men, a tendency known as the **gender gap**.[23] College graduates were once solidly Republican. In recent elections, they have tilted slightly Democratic.

The parties' future prospects might depend on whether recent trends persist.[24] The Democratic Party has had a significant edge with three groups—Hispanics,

Asian Americans, and younger adults—who are becoming a larger part of the electorate. Meanwhile, the Republican Party's edge is with older white Americans who are declining in number. The Hispanic vote is a key to the long-term prospects of both parties. With the exception of Cuban Americans, who are concentrated in southern Florida, Hispanics have disproportionately backed Democratic candidates in recent elections.[25] Nevertheless, many Hispanics have conservative views on issues such as abortion and same-sex marriage, and recent polls indicate that their support for Democratic candidates is weakening.[26]

Few developments have more implications for the parties' future chances than the voting pattern of young adults. Over the past five presidential elections, voters under 30 years of age have preferred the Democratic nominee by an average of roughly 20 percentage points (see Figure 8-5). It's the first time since the New Deal era that young voters have heavily backed the same party in a sequence of the presidential elections. These voters now include everyone between the ages of 18 and 45, which is more than a third of the electorate. And they have remained loyal to the Democratic Party as they have aged, drawn to it by its positions on issues like climate change and racial and ethnic equality. If they continue to support it, the Democratic Party at some point will come to dominate U.S. elections. No greater challenge faces the Republican Party than finding ways to make inroads among the nation's younger voters.[27]

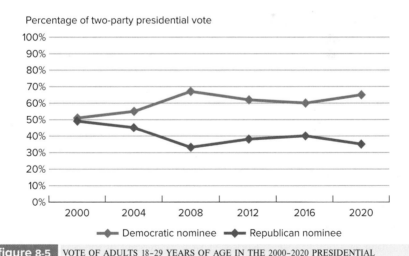

Percentage of two-party presidential vote

Democratic nominee   Republican nominee

figure 8-5 VOTE OF ADULTS 18-29 YEARS OF AGE IN THE 2000-2020 PRESIDENTIAL ELECTIONS

Since the presidential election of 2004, young adults have voted heavily Democratic each time, marking the first time since the Great Depression era that they have voted overwhelmingly for the same party in a lengthy series of elections. (*Source:* Exit polls, 2000–2020. Votes for third-party candidates not included in percentages.)

Minor (Third) Parties

Although the U.S. electoral system discourages the formation of minor parties (or third parties, as they are sometimes called), the nation has always had minor parties—more than 1,000 over its history.[28] Even the more successful ones have usually been short-lived. If a minor party starts to gain a following, one of the major parties is likely to pick up its issue, at which time it will begin to take support away from the minor party. Another problem for minor parties is that their candidates rarely win office. Most voters don't want to waste their ballot on a losing cause. Only one minor party, the Republican Party, has achieved majority status. Yet another obstacle is the barriers that the Republican and Democratic parties have erected that make it hard for minor parties to compete. In some states, for example, minor parties have to get petitions signed by thousands of registered voters to get a candidate's name placed on the election ballot, whereas the Republican and Democratic parties' candidates are automatically included.

Minor parties peaked in the 19th century, a time when the party system was still in flux.[29] Many of these parties were *single-issue parties* formed around an issue of overriding interest to their followers. Examples are the Free Soil Party, which fought the extension of slavery into new territories, and the Greenback Party, which sought a currency system based on paper money rather than gold and silver. The role that single-issue parties played in the 19th century is now played by single-issue interest groups (see Chapter 9).

The most important minor parties of the 20th century were *factional parties* that resulted from a split within one of the major parties. Although the Republican and Democratic Parties are usually successful at managing internal conflict, it has sometimes prompted a dissident faction to break away and form its own party. The States' Rights Party in 1948 and George Wallace's American Independent Party in 1968 were factional parties formed by white southern Democrats angered by northern Democrats' support of Black civil rights. The most electorally successful factional party was the Bull Moose Party in 1912.[30] Four years earlier, Theodore Roosevelt had declined to seek another presidential term, but he became disenchanted with the conservative policies of his hand-picked successor, William Howard Taft, and challenged him for the 1912 Republican nomination. After losing out in the nominating race, Roosevelt formed the progressive Bull Moose Party (a reference to Roosevelt's claim that he was "as strong as a bull moose"). Roosevelt won 27 percent of the presidential vote to Taft's 25 percent, which enabled the Democratic nominee, Woodrow Wilson, to win the 1912 presidential election with 42 percent of the vote.

Large-scale political reform has been the goal of some minor parties. The most successful of the *reform parties* is the Progressive Party, which in the early 1900s persuaded a number of states and localities into adopting primary elections,

PUCK

THE CROWD AS IT LOOKS TO THEODORE

Although the United States has long had a two-party system, numerous minor parties have surfaced. The most electorally successful was the Bull Moose Party, a factional party that split from the Republican Party. Headed by former President Theodore Roosevelt, it garnered 27 percent of the popular vote. The Republican nominee, incumbent William Howard Taft, came in third with 25 percent of vote. The Democratic nominee, Woodrow Wilson, won the presidency with 42 percent of the vote. (Library of Congress Prints and Photographs Division [LC-DIG-ppmsca-38463])

recall elections, nonpartisan elections, initiatives, and popular referendums (see Chapter 2). A more recent reform party was titled just that—the Reform Party. Created by Texas business executive Ross Perot after he garnered an astonishing 19 percent of the vote in 1992 as an independent presidential candidate (second only to Roosevelt's 27 percent in 1912), its platform called for fiscally responsible government. The Reform Party virtually disappeared after a divisive internal fight over its 2000 presidential nomination.

Other minor parties have been characterized by an ideological commitment such as redistribution of wealth. The strongest *ideological party* was the Populists, whose 1892 presidential nominee, James B. Weaver, won 9 percent of the national vote and carried six western states on a radical platform that included a call for a government takeover of the railroads.[31] The strongest ideological parties today are the Libertarian Party, which calls for less government intervention in the marketplace and people's lives, and the Green Party, which promotes social equality and environmentalism.

Americans have increasingly expressed dissatisfaction with how their government is working, which has led to calls for a third party. In 2022, Andrew Yang, a former Democratic presidential candidate, and Christine Todd Whitman, a former Republican governor, announced the formation of a third party, Forward. There is also speculation that a factional party or independent candidacy formed by anti-Trump Republicans could surface in the 2024 election. Some of that speculation has centered on former Republican congresswoman Liz Cheney, who voted to impeach Trump in 2021 and was vice chairman of the House committee investigating the January 6, 2021 attack on the U.S. Capitol. Recent history suggests that, even if such possibilities take full form, they will not result in victory but could alter an election's outcome. In the 2016 presidential election, for example, the Libertarian Party's Gary Johnson and the Green Party's Jill Stein received a combined 4 percent of the popular vote. Polls indicated that, if they had not been in the race, most of their votes would have gone to Hillary Clinton, perhaps by a margin large enough to tip the election in her favor.[32]

PARTIES AND CANDIDATES IN THE CAMPAIGN

The Democratic and Republican Parties have organizational units at the national, state, and local levels. These **party organizations** concentrate on electing candidates to office. A century ago, party organizations enjoyed nearly complete control of elections. Two developments—the introduction of primary elections and changes in the media system—gradually shifted control to the candidates. Today, they rather than the parties have the lead role in the presidential and congressional elections.[33]

Primary Elections and Candidate Control

Nomination is the selection of the individual who will run as the party's candidate in the general election. Until the early 20th century, the party organizations picked the nominees, who, if elected, were expected to share with it the spoils of office—government jobs and contracts. The party built its organization by giving jobs to loyalists and granting contracts to donors. Bribes and kickbacks were not unknown. New York City's legendary Boss Tweed once charged the city 20 times what a building had actually cost, amassing a personal fortune before winding up in prison. Reform-minded Progressives invented primary elections as a way to deprive party bosses of their power over nominations (see Chapter 2).

A **primary election** (or *direct primary*) gives control of nominations to the voters (see Chapters 2 and 12). The candidate with the most votes in a party's primary gets its nomination for the general election. In some states, the nominees are chosen in *closed primaries*, where participation is limited to voters registered with the party. Registered voters of the other party are not allowed to "cross over" to vote in the primary. The logic of a closed primary is that a party's voters should have the power to choose its general election candidate. In contrast, some states use *open primaries*, which allow independents and sometimes voters of the other party to vote in the party's primary (although they cannot vote simultaneously in both parties' primaries). The logic of the open primary is that it gives all voters a say in the choices they will have in the general election. Five states have yet different types of primaries. California and Washington conduct *top-two primaries*. Candidates are listed on the primary ballot without regard to party; the top two finishers become the general election candidates. Nebraska uses that system only for its state legislature, whereas in Louisiana if the top candidate receives over 50 percent of the vote that candidate is automatically elected to the office being contested. Alaska has a top-four primary system where the top four candidates advance to the general election, where voters then cast *ranked-choice ballots*. If no candidate gets a simple majority, the votes of those who backed the fourth-place finisher are redistributed to the second choice on their ballot. If there is still no candidate with a majority, the votes of those who backed the third-place finisher are redistributed to their preferred choice of the remaining two candidates, which will give one of them the victory (see "How the 50 States Differ").

HOW THE 50 STATES DIFFER

CRITICAL THINKING THROUGH COMPARISONS

Primary Elections

All states hold primary elections, but they differ in the types of primaries they hold. Roughly a third of them have *open primaries*, which allow any registered voter to vote in the primary. Other states have *partially open primaries*, which allow independents but not registered voters of the other party to participate. A third have *closed primaries*, which are limited to voters registered as members of the party holding the primary, or *partially closed primaries*, which give the parties the option of conducting a closed primary. Finally, five states—Alaska, California, Louisiana, Nebraska, and Washington—have varying forms of primaries in which candidates of both parties are on the same ballot and the top finishers, regardless of party, compete in the general election.

Continued

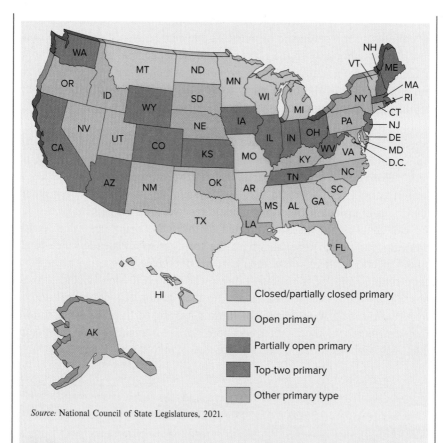

Source: National Council of State Legislatures, 2021.

Q: The top-two primary (California and Washington) and top-four primary (Alaska) are relatively new. What do you think are the chief arguments for and against these types of primary elections?

A: Proponents argue that these types of primaries give independent voters a larger say in the selection of nominees and may result in the selection of more moderate nominees. Opponents say that these types hurt the state's weaker party and can limit voters' choice in the general election to candidates of the same party.

Primaries shift the control of campaigns from the parties to the candidates. In Europe, where there are no primary elections, the parties are stronger. They control their nominations, and their candidates are expected to support the party's platform. A candidate or an officeholder who fails to do so can be denied renomination by the party in the next election. In the United States, however, candidates can try to win nomination by entering the party's primary and running on a platform of their own choosing. If elected, they are largely free to act as they please as long as they retain the support of the voters in their home district.

The Parties' Role in Campaigns

Although the parties have less control over campaigns than in their heyday, they retain a key role.[34] They provide a permanent organizational base for party activists and candidates. Moreover, certain activities, such as get-out-the-vote efforts on Election Day, affect all of a party's candidates and are done most efficiently through party organizations.

Local Political Parties   Of the roughly 500,000 elective offices in the United States, fewer than 500 are contested state-wide and only 2—the presidency and vice presidency—are contested nationally. The rest are local offices; not surprisingly, at least 95 percent of party activists work within local organizations.

Local parties vary greatly in their activities. Only a few local parties, including the Democratic organizations in Philadelphia and Chicago, bear even a faint resemblance to the fabled old-time party machines like New York City's Tammany Hall that could deliver victory after victory on Election Day. In many urban areas, and in most suburbs and towns, the party organizations today do not have enough volunteers to play an active role except during the campaign period, at which time—to the extent their resources allow—they conduct registration drives, hand out leaflets, and help get out the vote.

State Party Organizations   At the state level, each party is headed by a central committee made up of members of local party organizations and local and state officeholders. State central committees do not meet regularly and provide only general guidance to the state party organization, which is directed by a chairperson who is a full-time, paid employee. Most of the state party organizations are relatively small, having fewer than 20 full-time employees. The state party organizations engage in activities, such as fundraising and voter registration, that can improve their candidates' chances of success.[35]

National Party Organizations   The parties also have organizational units at the national level, although there is no chain of command that connects the local, state, and national organizations. The national party organization cannot tell the state organizations what to do, and, in turn, the state organizations cannot tell the local organizations what to do. The Texas state Democratic Party, for example, does not take orders from the national Democratic Party and does not give orders to the state's local Democratic Party organizations,

"WHAT ARE YOU LAUGHING AT? TO THE VICTOR BELONG THE SPOILS."

Pictured here is cartoonist Thomas Nash's depiction of the legendary William ("Boss") Tweed, head of New York City's Tammany Hall famed political machine in the late 1800s. Tweed controlled New York's Democratic Party nominations, and his machine was able to deliver the votes needed to get the nominees elected. Tweed used his power to extract bribes from those doing business with the city, and he became one of New York's richest men, although his corrupt practices eventually landed him in prison. Reform-minded Progressives invented primary elections as a way to take nominations out of the hands of party bosses. (North Wind Picture Archives/Alamy Stock Photo)

whether in a large city such as Dallas or Houston or in a smaller one such as McAllen or Amarillo. Each party organization is free to act as it wants. Nevertheless, party organizations at all levels have a shared interest in their party's success and thus have an incentive to work together to get the party's candidates elected to office.[36]

The national Republican and Democratic Party organizations, which are located in Washington, D.C., are structured much like those at the state level: They have a national committee and a national party chairperson. Neither the

Democratic National Committee (DNC) nor the Republican National Committee (RNC) has great power. The RNC (with more than 150 members) and the DNC (with more than 300 members) are too large and meet too infrequently to run the national party. Their power is largely confined to establishing organizational policy, such as determining the location of the party's presidential nominating convention and deciding the rules governing the selection of convention delegates. They also choose the party chair who directs the national party's day-to-day operations.

The national parties run training programs for candidates and their staff, raise money, seek media coverage of party positions and activities, conduct issue and group research, and send field representatives to help state and local parties with their operations. Their major role is fundraising. Although they spend most of it to fund their own operations, they provide some help to the party's House and Senate candidates, who also get funding from campaign committees that the parties have formed in the House and Senate. In any case, the amount of money that party committees can give directly to a candidate is limited by law—$5,000 for House candidates and $46,800 for Senate candidates.

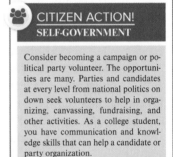

CITIZEN ACTION!
SELF-GOVERNMENT

Consider becoming a campaign or political party volunteer. The opportunities are many. Parties and candidates at every level from national politics on down seek volunteers to help in organizing, canvassing, fundraising, and other activities. As a college student, you have communication and knowledge skills that can help a candidate or party organization.

Media Changes and Candidate Control

Primaries are not the only reason for the shift in control of election campaigns from parties to candidates. Changes in the media also contributed. When primaries were introduced in the early 1900s, the party organizations remained strong enough to pick most of the nominees. Although it was possible for candidates to run and win on their own in primaries, it was difficult. They could buy newspaper ads to promote their candidacy, but newspaper advertising was not a solid foundation for an effective campaign.[37]

Rise of Television   The introduction of television in the 1950s provided candidates with the tool they needed to take greater control of their campaigns. Televised ads proved to be an effective way to promote their candidacies, and television quickly became the principal medium of election campaigning. Televised ads enable candidates to communicate directly—and on their own terms—with voters.[38] The production and airing of such ads account for roughly half of all campaign spending.[39] Modern production techniques enable well-funded candidates to air new ads within a few hours' time, which allows them to rebut attacks and exploit fast-breaking developments, a tactic known as *rapid response.*

Candidates also rely on the news media to get their message across, although the coverage they get varies widely. Many candidates for the House of Representatives are almost completely ignored by local news media. The New York City media market, for example, includes more than 20 House districts in New York, New Jersey, Pennsylvania, and Connecticut, and House candidates in these districts get little or no coverage from the New York media. They also make little use of televised ads because it is too expensive to buy ads in a metropolitan area where the voters in any one congressional district are only a small fraction of the audience. Such candidates conduct their campaigns the old-fashioned way, through leafleting, door-to-door canvassing, and the like. In contrast, presidential candidates get daily coverage from both national and local media. Between these extremes are Senate campaigns, which always get some news coverage and get heavy coverage if closely contested.[40]

The media campaign includes televised candidate debates, which are the centerpiece of presidential and many Senate general election campaigns, although they are seldom decisive.[41] By the time of the debates, most voters

Televised debates are a key moment in the presidential general election campaign, although they seldom influence enough voters to tip the balance in the election. Pictured here are Donald Trump and Joe Biden during the first general election debate of the 2020 presidential campaign. (Kevin Dietsch/ UPI/Bloomberg/Getty Images)

have decided on their candidate and stay with it even if their preferred candidate doesn't perform all that well.

Rise of the Internet and Social Media   New communication technology usually makes its way into campaign politics, and the Internet and social media are no exception. Nearly all of the congressional candidates in the 2022 midterm elections had websites dedicated to providing information, generating public support, attracting volunteers, and raising money. and most had staff dedicated to spreading the candidate's message through social media platforms like Twitter, Facebook, and Instagram.

Although television is still the principal medium of election politics, some analysts believe that digital media will eventually overtake it. Internet and social media messaging is much less expensive than television advertising and can more easily be targeted at particular types of voters. However, this messaging has some disadvantages relative to television, especially in the greater control that individual users have over the message. On television, when a brief political ad appears during a favorite program, many viewers will sit through it. An unsolicited message on the Internet or through social media is more easily skipped. So far, the Internet and social media have shown themselves to be better mechanisms for fundraising and mobilizing supporters, whereas television has proven to be the better mechanism for building name recognition and reaching less interested voters.[42]

Rise of Campaign Money   The "election game" is how political consultant Joe Napolitan characterized television-based campaigning.[43] The game requires money—lots of it. Campaigns for high office are expensive, and the costs keep rising. In 1980, about $250 million was spent by Senate and House candidates in the general election. By 1990, the figure had jumped to more than $400 million. In 2020, the figure exceeded $2 billion—eight times the 1980 level.[44] As might be expected, incumbents have a distinct advantage in fundraising. They have contributor lists from past campaigns and, because they already hold office, have the policy influence that donors are seeking. House and Senate incumbents outraise their challengers by more than two to one.[45]

Because of the high cost of campaigns, candidates spend much of their time raising funds, which come primarily from individual contributors, political parties, and interest groups (discussed in Chapter 9). The **money chase** is relentless.[46] A U.S. senator must raise an average of $30,000 a week throughout the entire six-year term in order to raise the minimum of $10 million that it takes to compete in a close race, even in a small state. A Senate campaign in a larger state can easily cost far more than that amount. In the 2022 Florida Senate race, for example, incumbent Marco Rubio and his Democratic challenger Val

Demings spent more than $50 million. House campaigns are less costly, but expenditures of $2 million or more are commonplace.

The most expensive campaign by far is the presidential race. Nearly $6 billion was spent on the 2020 presidential campaign, including what was spent by candidates, party organizations, and independent groups.[47] There was a time when leading presidential candidates availed themselves of the option to fund their campaigns through public financing but that time has passed. If they accept public financing in the general election, the amount is relatively small (less than $125 million for a major party candidate) and the candidate is prohibited from raising other funds. John McCain, the 2008 Republican presidential nominee, was the last major-party nominee to run on public financing.

The money that candidates raise from political parties, individuals, and interest groups is subject to legal limits (for example, $2,900 from an individual contributor and $5,000 from a group per election). These contributions are termed **hard money**—the money is given directly to the candidate and can be spent as he or she chooses. This money is hardly the only source of campaign spending. Super PACs, for example, are organizations that can raise and spend money freely on campaigns as long as they do not coordinate their efforts with those of the candidates they support. Super PACs spent $3.3 billion on the 2020 elections. (Super PACs are discussed at greater length in Chapter 9.)

American political campaigns last longer than campaigns in other democracies and are far more costly, running into the billions of dollars. (Valentyn Semenov/Alamy Stock Photo)

Rise of Political Consultants   The key operatives in today's campaigns—congressional as well as presidential—are highly paid *political consultants*, including campaign strategists who help the candidate plot and execute a game plan. Over the years, some of these strategists, including James Carville and Roger Ailes, developed legendary reputations. Fundraising specialists are also part of the new politics. They are adept at tapping donors and interest groups that regularly contribute to election campaigns. Campaign consultants also include pollsters, whose surveys are used to identify issues and messages that will resonate with voters. Media consultants are another staple of the modern campaign. They are adept at producing televised political advertising, generating news coverage, and developing Internet-based strategies.

Campaign consultants are skilled at **packaging** a candidate—highlighting those aspects of the candidate's policy positions and personality that are thought to be most attractive to voters. Even so, consultants now spend less time building up their candidate than tearing down the opponent.[48] Negative televised ads were once the exception, but, as evidence mounted of their effectiveness ("mud sticks," as one consultant put it), they came to dominate.[49] Studies indicate that many of them are based on false or deceptive claims.[50]

Do Campaigns Make a Difference?   Given the amount of money and attention they consume, it might be thought that campaigns determine who wins and who loses. That's not the case in most races. Less than half the states and an even smaller number of congressional districts are considered competitive in the sense that both parties have a reasonable chance of winning a state-wide race. The other states and districts are so heavily Republican or Democratic that only in unusual circumstances does the weaker party win. It can happen, but it's rare.

Moreover, when parties do lose seats, it's often because of national conditions rather than what happens during the campaign. Nothing so tips the balance in close races as voters' satisfaction with the party that holds power. Although some voters are swayed by what candidates promise to do if elected (a form of voting known as *prospective voting*), a greater number respond to past performance (*retrospective voting*). National economic conditions are particularly important in voters' judgments. An analysis by political scientists John Sides and Lynn Vavreck found that, typically, the in-party loses votes when the economy is weak and gains votes when it's strong.[51] A high rate of inflation, for example, contributed to voter dissatisfaction with Democratic President Biden's job performance, which helped Republicans to gain seats in Congress in the 2022 midterm elections.

Although the candidates' campaigns do not determine the outcome of most races, each political party has a stake in conducting a strong campaign. If a party can win enough votes to control the presidency, House, or Senate, it gains political power. That's incentive enough for the parties and their candidates to mount large-scale campaign efforts.[52]

PARTIES, CANDIDATES, AND THE PUBLIC'S INFLUENCE

Candidate-centered campaigns have advantages. First, they can bring new blood into electoral politics. Candidate recruitment is typically a slow process in party-centered systems. Would-be officeholders pay their dues by working in the party and, in the process, tend to adopt the outlook of those already there. By comparison, a candidate-centered system is more open and provides opportunities for newcomers to gain office quickly. Donald Trump is a case in point. He had never held, or even run for, political office before entering the race for the 2016 Republican presidential nomination. His public profile was based almost entirely on his real estate dealings and his role as host of a reality-TV show. Nevertheless, in a field of more than a dozen Republican candidates, most of whom had held high office, Trump easily prevailed. Trump's quick rise to political prominence would be almost unthinkable in a party-centered system.

Candidate-centered campaigns also encourage national officeholders to be responsive to local interests. In building personal followings among their state or district constituents, members of Congress respond to local needs. Nearly every significant domestic program enacted by Congress is adjusted to accommodate the interests of states and localities that otherwise would be hurt by the policy. Where strong national parties exist, national interests take precedence over local concerns. In France, for example, the pleas of legislators from underdeveloped regions have often gone unheeded by their party's majority.

Yet, candidate-centered campaigns also have disadvantages. They can yield candidates who prevail on the basis of money, visibility, or deception and who have little or no understanding of how government works, and perhaps not even an interest in making it work better. Their motivation is self-promotion rather than responsible representation and governing.

Then, too, candidate-centered campaigns provide opportunities for powerful interest groups to shower money on the candidates in an effort to acquire influence over public policy. The role of campaign money, and the influence it buys, has long been an issue in American politics and has achieved new heights as a result of the Supreme Court's *Citizens United* decision (see Chapter 9). In no other Western democracy does money play as large a role as it does in American elections.

Candidate-centered campaigns also weaken accountability by making it easier for officeholders to deny personal responsibility for the government's failings.

F	A	K	E		**Detecting Misinformation**

or

F A C T

Do Republicans and Democrats Understand Each Other?

A YouGov/More in Common poll asked Americans what they personally believed and what they thought most people in the opposing party believed.[53] A substantial majority of the Republicans said, for example, that most Democrats would prefer an open border policy on immigration. As another example, most of the Democrats said that most Republicans believe that those of the Muslim religion cannot be good Americans. And Democrats and Republicans alike said that most people in the other party hold extreme views on political issues.

Lightwise/123RF

Is that claim fact, or is it fake?

These claims are untrue. The poll found that Americans' understanding of opposing partisans is highly distorted. Americans believe that nearly twice as many in the opposing party hold extreme views as the number who actually hold such views. As for open borders, only one in four Democrats prefers that policy to a policy of secure borders. For their part, most Republicans believe that Muslims are good citizens. The pollsters attribute the perception gap to a number of factors, including the partisan polarization that leads many Americans to think that most of those in the opposing party hold extreme views.

An incumbent can always say that he or she represents only one vote out of many and that the real problem resides with "others" in Congress. The problem of accountability is apparent from surveys that ask Americans about their confidence in Congress. Most citizens have a low opinion of Congress as a whole but say they have confidence in their local congressional representative. This paradoxical attitude is so prevalent that it contributes to the high reelection rate of incumbents.

Nevertheless, because of party polarization, America's parties are subject to greater voter accountability than previously. The parties are sharply divided on many issues, which has made it easier for voters to see the difference between the parties and to support or oppose candidates on the basis of what each party represents. (Congressional and presidential campaigns are discussed further in Chapters 11 and 12, respectively.)

SUMMARY

Political parties link the public with its elected leaders. In the United States, this linkage is provided by the two-party system. Only the Republican and Democratic Parties have a realistic chance of winning control of government. The fact that the United States has only two major parties is explained in large part by an electoral system (single-member districts) that favors large parties and makes it difficult for smaller parties (minor, or third, parties) to win legislative seats in an election.

For more than 150 years, competition in America's two-party system has centered on the Republican and Democratic Parties. The remarkable endurance of these two parties is due to their ability to adapt to change. They have undergone several realignments, emerging each time with somewhat different coalitions and philosophies. The most recent realignment began in the 1960s over the issue of civil rights and progressed further in response to social issues, such as abortion and the issue of the size of the federal government. The realignment led to party polarization—a widening divide between Republicans and Democrats, at the level of both elected officials and voters.

Because the United States has only two major parties, each of which seeks to gain majority support, their candidates traditionally have taken moderate positions in order to attract support from voters in the political center. However, as a result of party polarization and an increase in the number of states and districts that strongly favor the Republic or Democratic Party, candidates have increasingly appealed to their party's more ideologically extreme voters who turn out more heavily than do moderate voters in primary elections.

At one time, America's party organizations largely controlled campaigns—picking the nominees, choosing the issues, and conducting the campaign. Candidates gradually came to the forefront in campaigns, largely because of primary elections, which allow them to gain nomination directly from the voters rather than going through the party organization, and changes in the media, which allow them to pitch their appeals directly to the voters. Nevertheless, party organizations continue to play a key role in elections. Local party organizations build support for the party's candidates and conduct get-out-the-vote efforts on Election Day. The state and national party organizations help the party's candidates through fundraising, issue research, media training, and other activities.

American political campaigns, particularly those for higher office, are candidate centered. Presidential and congressional candidates spend much of their time fundraising and creating personal campaign organizations built around pollsters, media producers, fundraisers, and campaign managers. Strategy and image making are key components of the modern campaign, as is televised political advertising, which accounts for half or more of all spending in the presidential and congressional races.

The advantages of candidate-centered politics include heightened responsiveness to new leadership and local concerns. Yet this form of politics can result in campaigns that are personality driven, depend on powerful interest groups, and blur responsibility for what government has done.

CRITICAL THINKING ZONE

KEY TERMS

candidate-centered campaigns (*p. 203*)
gender gap (*p. 214*)
grassroots party (*p. 206*)
hard money (*p. 226*)
linkage institutions (*p. 204*)
median voter theorem (*p. 213*)
money chase (*p. 225*)
multiparty system (*p. 212*)
nomination (*p. 218*)
packaging (*p. 227*)
party-centered campaigns (*p. 203*)

party coalition (*p. 213*)
party competition (*p. 204*)
party organizations (*p. 218*)
party realignments (*p. 207*)
political party (*p. 203*)
primary election (*p. 218*)
proportional representation
 system (*p. 212*)
single-member districts (*p. 212*)
single-member system (*p. 212*)
two-party system (*p. 212*)

APPLYING THE ELEMENTS OF CRITICAL THINKING

Conceptualizing: Explain the difference between proportional representation and single-member districts as methods of electing candidates to office. Why is the first method more likely than the second to foster a multiparty system?

Synthesizing: Contrast the pattern of earlier political party realignments (such as the realignment brought about by the Great Depression) with the pattern of the most recent party realignment.

Analyzing: Why are elections conducted so differently in the United States than in European democracies? Why are American campaigns more expensive and more candidate centered?

OF POSSIBLE INTEREST

A Book Worth Reading: Ezra Klein, *Why We're Polarized* (New York: Simon & Schuster, 2020). Written by one of America's most insightful journalists, this sophisticated but highly readable book examines the roots of party polarization.

A Website Worth Visiting: www.gop.org or **www.democrats.org** These are the websites of the Republican Party and the Democratic Party, respectively. Each site has information on the party's issue positions, as well as information on how to become a party volunteer.

9
CHAPTER

INTEREST GROUPS: ORGANIZING
FOR INFLUENCE

James Crisp/AP Images

66 The flaw in the pluralist heaven is that the heavenly chorus sings with a strong upper-class bias. **99**

E. E. SCHATTSCHNEIDER[1]

As the 2017 Tax Cuts and Jobs Act was making its way through Congress, lobbyists were working feverishly. Public Citizen, a government watchdog group, found that 6,000 lobbyists were trying to influence the legislation—11 lobbyists for every member of Congress. Most of the lobbyists represented corporations and trade associations, which were seeking a steep cut in the corporate tax rate. The Chamber of Commerce alone had 100 lobbyists working on the tax issue while 20 corporations and trade associations each had at least 50 lobbyists dedicated to the issue. "The mind-boggling number of lobbyists that corporate America has hired to reshape the tax code is of almost biblical proportions," said Lisa Gilbert, Public Citizen's vice president for legislative affairs.[2] When the bill passed, the corporate tax rate had indeed been slashed, reduced from 35 percent to 21 percent.

Corporate lobbyists' efforts to shape the 2017 tax cut bill suggest why interest groups are both necessary and unloved. Business firms have legitimate policy interests. It is perfectly appropriate for them to lobby on issues affecting them. The same can be said of farmers, consumers, minorities, college students— indeed, of virtually every interest in society. In fact, the *pluralist* theory of American politics (see Chapter 1) holds that society's interests are best represented through interest groups.

Yet groups can wield too much power. Was the 2017 tax bill necessary to protect American workers' jobs and make U.S. firms more competitive? Or was it a tax giveaway to corporations? Opinions differ on such questions, but there is no doubt that groups have a large influence on policy decisions.

Interest groups—also called "factions," "pressure groups," "special interests," "organized interests," or "lobbying groups"—are organizations that actively seek to influence public policy.[3] Like political parties, groups are a linkage mechanism.

The 2017 Tax Cuts and Jobs Act lowered the corporate tax rate from 35 percent to 21 percent. As the bill was making its way through Congress, hundreds of corporate lobbyists urged the members to pass the bill, arguing that it would protect American jobs and make U.S. firms more competitive in global trade. (Z_wei/iStock/Getty Images)

They connect citizens with governing officials. However, unlike political parties, which address a range of issues in order to attract a coalition broad enough to win elections, groups focus narrowly on issues of direct concern. A group may get involved in elections, but its chief goal is to influence policies affecting it.[4]

This chapter examines the degree to which various interests in American society are represented by organized groups, the process by which interest groups exert influence, and the costs and benefits of group politics. The chapter makes the following main points:

- *Although nearly all interests in American society are organized to some degree, those associated with economic activity, particularly business activity, are by far the most thoroughly organized.* Their advantage rests on their superior financial resources and on the private goods (such as wages and jobs) they provide to those in the organization.

- *Groups that do not have economic activity as their primary function often have organizational difficulties.* These groups pursue public or collective goods (such as a safer environment) that are available even to individuals who are not group members, so individuals may free ride by choosing not to pay the costs of membership.

- *Lobbying and electioneering are the traditional means by which groups communicate with and influence political leaders.* Recent developments, including grassroots lobbying and political action committees, have heightened interest groups' influence.

- *The interest-group system overrepresents business interests and fosters policies that serve groups' interest more than society's broad interest.* Thus, although groups are an essential part of the policy process, they also distort that process.

THE INTEREST-GROUP SYSTEM

In the 1830s, Frenchman Alexis de Tocqueville wrote that the "principle of association" was nowhere clearer than in America. His description still holds. No other nation has as many organized interest groups as does the United States. The country's tradition of free association makes it natural for Americans to join together for political purposes, and their diverse interests give them a reason to pursue influence through group action. The nation's political structure also contributes to group action. Because of federalism and the separation of powers, groups have multiple points of entry through which to influence policy. At the federal level, lobbying groups can target the House, the Senate, the executive branch, and even the courts. State governments are also the target of lobbying, which, as political scientist James Strickland has shown, has intensified in recent decades.[5] Few political systems offer as many paths for group influence as does the American system.

The extraordinary number of interest groups in the United States does not mean that the nation's various interests are equally well organized. Groups develop when people with a shared interest have the opportunity and incentive to join together. Some individuals or organizations have the skills, money, contacts, or time to participate in group politics; others do not. In addition, some groups are inherently more attractive to potential members than are others and thus find it easier to organize. Groups also differ in their financial resources and thus in their capacity for political action.

Accordingly, a first consideration about group politics is the issue of how thoroughly various interests are organized. Interests that are highly organized stand a good chance of having their views heard by policymakers. Those that are poorly organized run the risk of being ignored.

Economic Groups

No interests are more fully or effectively organized than those that have economic activity as their primary purpose. Corporations, labor unions, farm groups, and professional associations, among others, exist primarily for economic purposes—to make profits, provide jobs, improve pay, or protect an occupation. For the sake of discussion, we will call such organizations **economic groups**. Almost all such organizations engage in political activity as a means of promoting and protecting their economic interests. An indicator of this is the fact that Washington lobbyists who represent economic groups outnumber those of all other groups by two to one.

Among economic groups, the most numerous are business groups. Writing in 1929, political scientist E. Pendleton Herring noted, "Of the many organized groups maintaining offices in [Washington], there are no interests more fully, more comprehensively, and more efficiently represented than those of American industry."[6] Although corporations do not dominate lobbying as thoroughly as they once did, Herring's conclusion still holds (see Figure 9-1). More than half of all groups formally registered to lobby Congress are business organizations. Virtually all large corporations and many smaller ones are politically active. Business firms are also represented through trade associations. Some of these "organizations of organizations" seek to advance the broad interests of business. One of the oldest associations is the National Association of Manufacturers, which was formed in 1894 and today represents 14,000 manufacturers. Another large business association is the U.S. Chamber of Commerce, which represents

Lobbying groups in Washington, D.C.

Other types
of groups
35%

Business firms &
trade associations
65%

figure 9-1   TYPES OF LOBBYING GROUPS

Roughly two-thirds of the lobbying groups in Washington, D.C., are associated with business. Every large corporation has its lobbyists, as do business-related trade associations such as the National Association of Manufacturers. (*Source:* Compiled by author from multiple sources.)

3 million businesses of all sizes. Other business associations, such as the American Petroleum Institute and the National Association of Home Builders, are confined to a single trade or industry.

Economic groups also include those associated with organized labor. Labor groups seek to promote policies that benefit workers in general and union members in particular. Although there are some major independent unions, such as the United Mine Workers of America and the Teamsters, the dominant labor group is the AFL-CIO, which has its national headquarters in Washington, D.C. The AFL-CIO has 12.5 million members in its 57 affiliated unions, which include the International Brotherhood of Electrical Workers and the American Federation of Teachers.

At an earlier time, about a third of the U.S. workforce was unionized. Today, only about 1 in 10 workers is a union member. Blue-collar workers once made up the bulk of organized labor, but their number has decreased with the shrinking of the nation's manufacturing sector. Professionals, technicians, and service workers have increased in number but are less inclined to join a labor union. Professionals identify with management and a mere 2 percent of them are union members. Service workers and technicians can also be difficult for unions to organize because they work closely with managers and, often, in small offices.

However, unions have made inroads in their efforts to organize government employees. Most union members today work in the public sector, despite the fact that it has only a fifth as many workers as does the private sector. The most heavily unionized employees are those who work for local government, such as teachers, police officers, and firefighters; roughly 40 percent of them are union members. State and federal employees are also heavily unionized. All told, 34 percent of public-sector workers are union members, compared with only 6 percent of private-industry workers. Even the construction industry, which ranks high by comparison with most private-sector industries, has a unionization rate of less than 15 percent.[7]

Farm groups represent another large economic lobby. The American Farm Bureau Federation is the largest of the farm groups, with more than 4 million members. The National Farmers Union, the National Grange, and the National Farmers Organization are smaller farm lobbies. Agricultural groups do not always agree on policy issues. For instance, the Farm Bureau typically sides

This 1873 lithograph illustrates the benefits of membership in the National Grange, an agricultural interest group. Throughout their history, Americans have organized to influence government policy. (Library of Congress Prints and Photographs Division [LC-DIG-ppmsca-02956])

with agribusiness and owners of large farms, while the Farmers Union typically promotes the interests of smaller "family" farms. There are also numerous specialty farm associations, including the National Association of Wheat Growers, the American Soybean Association, and the Associated Milk Producers. Each association acts as a separate lobby, seeking policies that will serve its members' particular interests.

Most professions also have lobbying associations. Among the most powerful of these *professional groups* is the American Medical Association (AMA), which includes 250,000 physicians. Other professional groups include the American Bar Association (ABA) and the American Association of University Professors (AAUP).

Citizens' Groups

Economic groups do not have a monopoly on lobbying. There is another category of interest groups—**citizens' groups** (or *noneconomic groups*). Members of citizen groups are joined together not by a *material incentive*—such as jobs, higher wages, or profits—but by a *purposive incentive,* the desire to contribute to what they regard as a worthy cause.[8] Whether a group's purpose is to protect the environment, return prayer to the public schools, or feed the poor at home or abroad, there are citizens who are willing to participate simply because they believe the cause is a worthy one.

A simple but precise way to describe citizens' groups is that they are "groups anyone can join." This does not mean that everyone would want to join a particular group. A conservative would not choose to join a liberal group, just as a liberal would not join a conservative group. But there is no barrier to joining a citizens' group if one is willing to contribute the required time or money. In this way, citizens' groups are distinct from business firms, which are closed to all but their employees, as well as distinct from labor groups, farm groups, and professional associations, whose members have a particular type of training or occupation.[9]

Nearly every conceivable issue or problem has its citizens' group, often several of them. Some citizens' groups work to advance the interests of a particular social grouping; examples are the National Association for the Advancement of Colored People (NAACP), the National Organization for Women (NOW), and La Raza, which is the largest Hispanic American lobbying group. College campuses are the locus of some groups, including state-level Public Interest Research Groups (PIRGs),

CITIZEN ACTION!
SELF-GOVERNMENT

Citizens' groups cover the political spectrum from right to left and depend on small donations to fund their activities. Consider contributing to such a group. You can easily locate a group that shares your values by searching the Internet. If you want to contribute time instead, some citizens' groups have college or local chapters.

such as NYPIRG (New York), CALPIRG (California), and TexPIRG (Texas). Drawing on their network of researchers and students, they tackle pressing social issues like climate change and poverty. Other citizens' groups have an ideological agenda. The American Conservative Union (ACU) is the largest conservative organization, and it lobbies on issues such as taxation and national defense. Americans for Democratic Action (ADA) is a liberal counterpart to the ACU. Another example is the Christian Coalition of America, which describes itself as "America's leading grassroots organization defending our godly heritage" (see "Party Polarization: Ideological Interest Groups").

Most citizens' groups focus on a specific issue. *Single-issue groups* have risen sharply in number in the past half-century and now pressure government officials

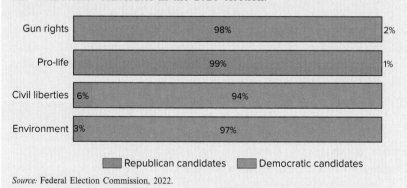

PARTY POLARIZATION

Conflicting Ideas

Ideological Interest Groups

Although citizen groups include many nonpartisan groups, many citizen groups take sides in partisan politics. They have contributed to party polarization by their tendency to favor candidates who hold strongly conservative or liberal views. Examples of such groups are Emily's List, which promotes liberal Democratic candidates, and the Family Research Council, which supports conservative Republican candidates. The tendency of ideological groups to support one side of the partisan divide can also be seen in the figures shown here, which indicate how ideological groups in a few areas divided their money between Republican and Democratic candidates in the 2020 election.

	Republican	Democratic
Gun rights	98%	2%
Pro-life	99%	1%
Civil liberties	6%	94%
Environment	3%	97%

■ Republican candidates   ■ Democratic candidates

Source: Federal Election Commission, 2022.

Q: Why do you think politically active citizens' groups are generally more ideological—whether conservative or liberal—than is the society as a whole? Are citizens with strong views more inclined to get involved in organized political activity than those with moderate opinions?

on almost every conceivable policy, from nuclear arms to drug abuse. Notable current examples are the National Rifle Association and the various right-to-life and pro-choice groups. Most environmental groups can also be seen as single-issue organizations in that they seek to influence public policy in a specific area, such as pollution reduction, wilderness preservation, or wildlife protection. The Sierra Club, one of the oldest environmental groups, was formed in the 1890s to promote the preservation of scenic areas. The Environmental Defense Fund, established in 1967, concentrates on environmental problems such as air and water pollution. Since 1960, membership in environmental groups has more than tripled in response to increased public concern about the environment.[10]

The Organizational Edge: Economic Groups Versus Citizens' Groups

Although the number of citizens' groups has mushroomed in recent decades, they are outnumbered by economic groups. The predominance of economic interests was predicted in *Federalist* No. 10, in which James Madison declared that property is "the most common and durable source of factions." Stated differently, nothing seems to matter more to most people than their economic well-being. Several factors (summarized in Table 9-1) give economic groups an organizational advantage, including their resources and size.

table 9-1	ADVANTAGES AND DISADVANTAGES HELD BY ECONOMIC AND CITIZENS' GROUPS
Economic Groups	**Citizens' Groups**
Advantages	*Advantages*
Economic activity provides the organization with the resources necessary for political action.	Members are likely to support leaders' political efforts because they joined the group in order to influence policy.
Individuals are encouraged to join the group because of economic benefits they individually receive (such as wages).	*Disadvantages*
In the case of firms within an industry, their small number encourages organization because the contribution of each firm can make a difference.	The group has to raise funds, especially for its political activities.
	Potential members may choose not to join the group because they get collective benefits even if they do not join.
Disadvantages	Potential members may choose not to join the group because their
Members may not support the group's political efforts because they didn't join for political reasons.	individual contribution may be too small to affect the group's success one way or the other.

Unequal Access to Resources   One reason for the abundance of economic groups is their ready access to financial resources. Political lobbying is not cheap. If a group is to make its views known, it typically must have a headquarters, an expert staff, and communication facilities. Economic groups pay for these things with money generated by their economic activity. Corporations have the greatest built-in advantage. They do not have to charge membership dues or conduct fundraisers to support their lobbying. Their funds come from business profits.

Other economic groups rely on dues rather than profits to support their lobbying, but they have something of economic value to offer in exchange. Labor unions, for example, provide their members access to higher-paying jobs in return for the dues they pay. Such groups offer what are called **private (individual) goods**, which are benefits, such as jobs, that are given directly to particular individuals. An important feature of private goods is that they can be held back. If an individual is unwilling to pay organizational dues, the group can withhold the benefit.

Citizens' groups do not have these inherent advantages. They do not generate profits or fees as a result of economic activity. Moreover, the incentives they offer to members are available to others as well. As opposed to the private or individual goods provided by many economic groups, most noneconomic groups offer **collective (public) goods** as an incentive for membership. By definition, collective goods are goods that belong to all; they cannot be granted or withheld on an individual basis. The air that people breathe and the national forests they visit are examples of collective goods. These goods are available to one and all, those who do not pay dues to a clean-air group or a wilderness preservation group as well as those who do.

The shared characteristic of collective goods creates what is called the **free-rider problem**: Individuals can obtain the goods even if they do not contribute to the group's effort. National Public Radio (NPR) is an example. Although NPR's programs are funded primarily through listeners' donations, those who do not contribute are free to listen to its programs. They are free riders, getting the benefit of NPR's programs without helping to pay for them. A mere 1 in 10 listeners donate to NPR.[11]

As economist Mancur Olson noted, it's not rational for an individual to contribute to a group when its benefit can be obtained for free.[12] Moreover, the dues paid by any single member are too small to affect the group's success one way or another. Why pay dues to an environmental group when any improvements in the air, water, or wildlife from its lobbying efforts are available to everyone and when one's individual contribution is too small to make a difference? Although many people do join such groups, the free-rider problem is one reason citizens' groups are organized less fully than economic groups.

Business interests dominate the lobbying sector. Their advantage stems largely from the fact that they can use their profits to fund their lobbying activities. Citizens' groups are in a weaker financial position. They depend on voluntary contributions to fund their lobbying efforts. (S-F/Shutterstock)

In recent decades, the free-rider problem has been lessened by changes in technology. Computer-assisted direct mail, e-mail, and social networks have made it easier and less costly for citizens' groups to reach out to prospective donors. For some individuals, a contribution of $25 to $50 annually represents no great sacrifice and offers the satisfaction of supporting a cause in which they believe. "Checkbook members" is how political scientist Theda Skocpol describes such contributors.[13]

The Advantages and Disadvantages of Size   Although the number of citizens' groups has multiplied in recent decades, the organizational muscle in American politics rests primarily with economic groups. Business interests, in particular, have an advantage that economist Mancur Olson calls "the size factor."[14] Although it might be thought that groups with large memberships typically prevail over smaller groups, the reverse is often true. Olson notes that small groups are ordinarily more united on policy issues and often have more resources, enabling them to win out against large groups. Business groups in a specific industry are usually few in number and have an incentive to work together to influence government on issues of joint interest. The U.S. automobile industry, for example, has its "Big Three"—General Motors, Ford, and Chrysler. Although they compete for car sales, they usually work together on policy issues. They have succeeded, for example, in persuading government to delay or reduce higher fuel efficiency and safety standards, which has meant billions in additional profits for them at an incalculable cost to car owners, who are many in number but are not an organized group.

The 2017 Tax Cut and Jobs Act revealed the power of business groups. At issue was the largest overhaul of the tax code since the 1980s. When the legislation was passed, individual taxpayers clearly benefited, receiving an average annual tax cut of nearly $1,300, increasing their after-tax income by 1.7 percent. Corporations got a significantly larger cut, having their income tax rate reduced from 35 percent to 21 percent. Moreover, whereas the corporate tax cut has no time limit, the individual tax cut will end in 10 years, at which time, unless the cut is extended, a fourth of taxpayers will be paying a higher rate than they would have under the previous tax law.[15] Getting millions of taxpayers to join together to influence policy is infinitely more difficult than getting top corporations to work together. "[T]he larger the group," Olson wrote, "the less it will further its common interests."[16]

Nevertheless, there can be strength in numbers. No group illustrates this better than AARP (formerly known as the American Association of Retired Persons). Although not every retired person belongs to AARP, its dues are so low ($16 a year) that it has nearly 40 million members. AARP has a staff of more than 1,000 and is a formidable lobby on Social Security, Medicare, and other issues affecting retirees. Congress receives more mail from members of AARP than from members of any other group. A *Fortune* magazine survey of 2,200 Washington insiders, including members of Congress and their staffs, ranked AARP as the nation's most powerful lobbying group.[17]

INSIDE LOBBYING: SEEKING INFLUENCE THROUGH OFFICIAL CONTACTS

Modern government is involved in so many issues—business regulation, income maintenance, urban renewal, cancer research, and energy development, to name only a few—that nearly every interest in society could benefit from influence over federal policy. Moreover, federal officials are inclined to assist with problems that in earlier times would have been seen as strictly local or state in nature. When wildfires swept through West Texas in 2022, for example, the federal government stepped in to provide the affected communities with disaster relief funding.

Groups seek government support through **lobbying**—efforts by groups to influence public policy through contact with public officials.[18] Groups pursue two lobbying strategies, which have been called *inside lobbying* and *outside lobbying*.[19] This section discusses **inside lobbying**, which is based on group efforts to develop and maintain direct ("inside") contact with policymakers. (Outside lobbying is described in the next section.)

Gaining Access to Officials

Lobbying once depended significantly on tangible payoffs, including bribes. Such incidents are rare today. Bribery is illegal, and lobbying behavior is regulated more closely than in the past. Lobbyists are required by law to register and to file detailed reports on their lobbying expenditures.

Modern lobbying rests in part on the skillful use of information. Lobbyists concentrate on providing lawmakers with arguments and evidence that support their position. The goal is to persuade officials that what the group seeks is the best course of action.[20] "If I don't explain what we do . . . Congress will make uninformed decisions without understanding the consequences to the industry," said one lobbyist.[21] The power of information is a reason for the "revolving door" between lobbying firms and government officials. Many lobbyists worked previously in government, and some top officials were once lobbyists. Upon retirement, many members of Congress join lobbying firms. Although prohibited by law from lobbying Congress for a set period of time after leaving office, they are free to do so thereafter and usually lobby in the policy areas that they worked on while in Congress.[22]

Inside lobbying is typically directed at policymakers who are inclined to support the group rather than at those who have opposed it in the past. This tendency reflects both the difficulty of persuading opponents to change long-held views and the advantage of working through sympathetic officials. Thus, union lobbyists work mainly with pro-labor officeholders, just as corporate lobbyists work mainly with pro-business policymakers.

Money is a key ingredient of inside lobbying. Many groups have a Washington office and a professional staff of lobbyists and public relations specialists. Roughly 12,000 registered lobbyists work in Washington, along with a greater number who lobby informally or assist those who are registered.[23] Given the costs of maintaining a Washington lobby, the domination by corporations and trade associations is understandable. They have the money to retain high-priced lobbyists, while many other interests do not. The amount of money spent on lobbying is staggering. In a 2010 study, the Center for Responsive Politics divided the amount of money spent on lobbying by the number of hours Congress was in session to dramatize the extent of lobbying. The figure turned out to be more than $1 million per hour.[24] Currently, the biggest spender on lobbying is the U.S. Chamber of Commerce (see Figure 9-2). All of the top 10 spenders represent business interests. No citizen group is in the top 10 with the AARP, which ranks 15th, being the leading spender in that category.

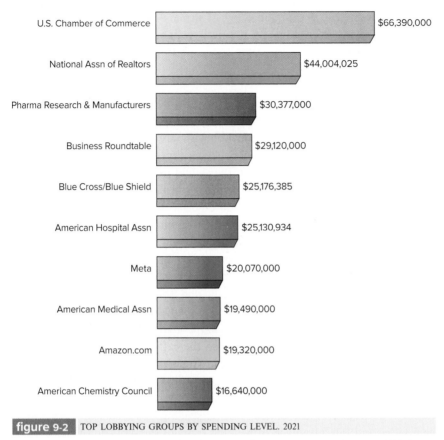

figure 9-2 TOP LOBBYING GROUPS BY SPENDING LEVEL. 2021

Lobbying is big business in two ways. First, huge sums of money are spent each year on lobbying. Second, most of the money is spent by business lobbies. (*Source:* Open Secrets, 2022.)

Lobbying Congress Officials of all three government branches are the targets of lobbying, but the benefit of a close relationship with members of Congress is the most obvious. Every member of the House and Senate has the authority to introduce legislative bills, which makes each of them a pathway to favorable legislation (see "How the U.S. Differs"). By the same token, members of Congress benefit from ties to lobbyists. The volume of legislation facing Congress is heavy, and members rely on trusted lobbyists to identify bills that deserve their attention. When Republican lawmakers took control of the House of Representatives in 2023, they consulted closely with business lobbyists on legislative issues affecting business. Congressional Democrats complained, but Republicans said they were merely getting advice from those who best understood business's needs and noted that Democrats had worked closely with labor lobbyists when they controlled the House.

HOW THE U.S. DIFFERS

CRITICAL THINKING THROUGH COMPARISONS

Lobbying

Lobbying occurs in every democratic country. Constitutional guarantees of free assembly and speech are one reason, as is the natural tendency of interest groups to try to influence government policy in ways favorable to them. Yet, there is wide variation among democracies in the number of individuals who lobby government officials. The United States, as the accompanying chart indicates, is at the high end with roughly 12,000 registered lobbyists, and the U.S. figure greatly underestimates the number of people involved in lobbying the federal government. Lobbyists are only required to register if they spend at least 20 percent of their time on Capitol Hill meeting with congressional members and staff. Political scientist James Thurber estimates that as many as 100,000 people are engaged in lobbying the federal government, including the researchers that support lobbying efforts. And that figure doesn't include lobbying in the form of campaign contributions.[28]

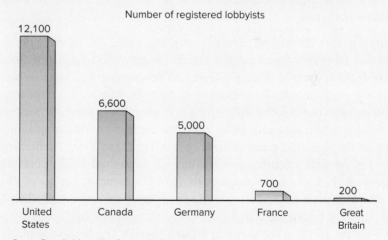

Number of registered lobbyists

Source: Compiled by author from multiple sources.

Q: Why does the United States have so many more lobbyists than do other democracies?

A: Washington, D.C., is a lobbyist's dream. The U.S. system of separated powers gives lobbyists abundant opportunities to contact and influence

Continued

policymakers. Every member of the House and Senate (535 members in all) has the authority to submit bills and therefore is a point of influence for lobbyists. Top executives in the roughly 400 federal agencies are also lobbying targets, as are key members of the White House staff. By comparison, there is no separation of legislative and executive power in the Canadian and European parliamentary systems and, in most of them, only top leaders of the majority party can introduce legislation. There are fewer points of access in these systems for lobbyists to try to exert influence.

Lobbyists' effectiveness depends in part on their reputation for playing it straight. Said one member of Congress, "If any [lobbyist] gives me false or misleading information, that's it—I'll never see him again."[25] Bullying is also frowned upon. During the debate over the North American Free Trade Agreement in 1993, the AFL-CIO threatened to campaign against congressional Democrats who supported the legislation. The backlash from Democrats on both sides of the issue was so intense that the union withdrew its threat. The safe lobbying strategy is the aboveboard approach: Provide information, rely on trusted allies in Congress, and push steadily but not aggressively for favorable legislation.

Lobbying the Executive Branch   As the range of federal policy has expanded, lobbying of the executive branch has grown in importance. Some of this lobbying is directed at the president and presidential staff, but they are less accessible than top officials in the federal agencies, who are the chief targets.

Group influence is particularly strong in the regulatory agencies that oversee the nation's business sectors. Pharmaceutical companies, for example, provide much of the scientific evidence used by the Food and Drug Administration (FDA) in deciding whether a new product is safe to market. The potential for influence is high, as are the stakes. After the FDA approved the use of Pfizer's vaccine as protection against COVID-19, Pfizer's revenues skyrocketed. In 2019, the year before the start of the Covid pandemic, Pfizer's revenues were $49.5 billion. In 2021, the year that Pfizer's vaccine first became available, its revenues were $81.5 billion.[26]

Regulatory agencies' dependence on groups for information creates a risk known as *agency capture*—the situation where a regulatory agency sides with the industry it is supposed to regulate rather than with the public that it is supposed to protect. It's not the norm but happens from time to time. The FDA was lax, for example, in accepting the pharmaceutical company Merck's claim that its arthritis drug Vioxx was safe. After the FDA approved it for sale, Vioxx generated

$2.5 billion a year in sales for Merck. As it turned out, Vioxx was unsafe. Its users suffered an abnormally high number of heart attacks and strokes. When that became known, Merck was forced to take the drug off the market, and Congress responded by passing legislation that required the FDA to tighten its safety tests.[27]

Lobbying the Courts   Interest groups can sometimes achieve their policy goals through the courts.[29] Groups have several judicial lobbying options, including efforts to influence the selection of federal judges. Right-to-life groups have pressured Republican administrations to make opposition to abortion a prerequisite for nomination to the federal bench. Democratic administrations have, in turn, faced pressure from pro-choice groups in their judicial nominations.[30] Judicial lobbying also includes lawsuits. For some organizations, such as the American Civil Liberties Union (ACLU), legal action is the primary means of influencing policy. The ACLU often takes on unpopular causes such as the free-speech rights of fringe groups. Such causes have little chance of success in legislative bodies but may prevail in a courtroom. Even when groups are not a direct party to a lawsuit, they sometimes get involved through amicus curiae ("friend of the court") briefs. An amicus brief is a written document in which an interested party explains to a court its position on a case under review.

As interest groups have increasingly resorted to legal action, they have often found themselves facing one another in court. Environmental litigation groups, such as the Environmental Defense Fund, have fought numerous court battles with oil, timber, and mining interests in recent decades.

Webs of Influence: Groups in the Policy Process

To get a fuller picture of how inside lobbying works, it is helpful to consider two policy processes—iron triangles and issue networks—of which many groups are a part.

Iron Triangles   An **iron triangle** consists of a small and informal but relatively stable set of bureaucrats, legislators, and lobbyists who seek to develop policies beneficial to a particular interest. The three "corners" of one such triangle are the Department of Defense (bureaucrats), the armed services committees of Congress (legislators), and weapons manufacturers such as Lockheed Martin and Northrop Grumman (lobbyists). Together, they determine many of the policies affecting national security. Although new laws require the support of the president and a congressional majority, they often defer to the judgment of the defense sector triangle, whose members are intimately familiar with security needs.

Groups embedded in iron triangles have an inside track to well-positioned legislators and bureaucrats. They can count on getting a full hearing on issues affecting them. Moreover, because they have something to offer in return, the triangular relationship tends to be solid and enduring, which is why they're called "iron" triangles. The groups provide lobbying support for agency programs and campaign contributions to members of Congress. Defense contractors, for instance, donate millions of dollars to congressional campaigns during each election cycle. In the 2022 elections, as is typically the case, defense contractors' donations went primarily to the campaigns of House and Senate incumbents on the armed services committees.[31] Figure 9-3 summarizes the benefits that flow to each member of an iron triangle.

Issue Networks   Iron triangles represent the pattern of influence in only some policy areas. Another influence pattern is the **issue network**—an informal grouping of officials, lobbyists, and policy specialists (the "network") who come together *temporarily* around a policy problem (the "issue").

Issue networks are a result of the increasing complexity of policy problems. An issue network is built around specialized knowledge. Participants must understand the issue in question in order to engage it in a meaningful way. On any given issue, the participants might come from a variety of executive agencies, congressional committees, interest groups, and institutions such as universities or think tanks. Issue networks are less stable than iron triangles. As the issue develops, new participants may join the debate and old ones may drop out. Once the issue is resolved, the network disbands.[32]

An example of an issue network is the set of participants who would come together over the issue of whether a large tract of old forest should be opened to logging. A few decades ago, this issue would have been settled in an iron triangle consisting of the timber companies, the U.S. Forest Service, and relevant

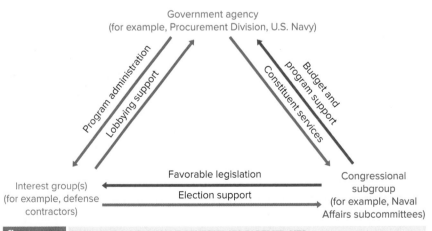

figure 9-3   HOW AN IRON TRIANGLE BENEFITS ITS PARTICIPANTS

An iron triangle works to the advantage of each of its participants—an interest group, a congressional subgroup, and a government agency.

members of the House and Senate agriculture committees. However, as forest lands have diminished and environmental concerns have grown, such issues can no longer be controlled by those who are linked through an iron triangle. Today, an issue network would form that included logging interests, the U.S. Forest Service, House and Senate agriculture committee members, research scientists, and representatives of environmental groups, the housing industry, and animal-rights groups. Unlike the old iron triangle, which was confined to like-minded interests, this issue network would include opposing interests (for example, the loggers and the environmentalists). And, unlike an iron triangle, the issue network would dissolve once the issue that brought the parties together was resolved.

In sum, issue networks differ substantially from iron triangles. In an iron triangle, a common interest brings the participants together in a long-lasting and mutually beneficial relationship. In an issue network, an immediate issue brings together the participants in a temporary network based on their ability to knowledgeably address the issue and where they voice their separate interests before disbanding once the issue is settled.

Despite these differences, iron triangles and issue networks have one thing in common: They are arenas in which organized groups exercise influence. The interests of the general public may be taken into account in these webs of power, but the interests of the participating groups are the primary focus.

K Street in Washington, D.C., has no significance to most Americans but it's a powerful symbol for Washington insiders. K Street was the location of most of the top lobbying firms, and is still where many of them have their offices. Washington's K Street is to lobbying what New York City's Wall Street is to the buying and selling of stocks. (Bob Korn/Shutterstock)

OUTSIDE LOBBYING: SEEKING INFLUENCE THROUGH PUBLIC PRESSURE

Although an interest group may rely solely on inside lobbying, this approach is more likely to be successful when the group can demonstrate that it represents an important constituency. Accordingly, groups also engage in **outside lobbying**, which involves bringing public ("outside") pressure to bear on policymakers (see Table 9-2).[33]

Constituency Advocacy: Grassroots Lobbying

Outside lobbying includes efforts, such as letter-writing campaigns or public demonstrations, aimed at convincing lawmakers that a group's policy position has popular support. Few groups have been better at outside lobbying than the National Rifle Association (NRA). Opposition from the NRA is a reason that the United States has lagged behind other Western societies in its gun control laws, despite opinion polls indicating that most Americans would like to see stricter controls on guns.[34] Influential groups usually have one of two resources: either a lot of money or a committed membership. The NRA has had both, although its campaign funding has declined somewhat in recent elections due to shrinking financial resources. Its chief resource, however, is its 5 million members, many of whom can be counted on to support pro-gun candidates and oppose those who seek stricter gun laws.[35]

Electoral Action: Votes and Money

"Reward your friends and punish your enemies" is a political adage that loosely describes how interest groups approach elections. One lobbyist said it directly: "Talking to politicians is fine, but with a little money they hear you better."[36] The possibility of campaign opposition from a powerful group can restrain an officeholder. In 2017, for example, the AARP lobbied hard,

table 9-2	TACTICS USED IN INSIDE AND OUTSIDE LOBBYING EFFORTS
Inside Lobbying	**Outside Lobbying**
Developing contacts with legislators and executives	Encouraging group members to contact their representatives
Providing information to key officials	Promoting their message through advertising and public relations
Forming coalitions with other groups	Supporting political candidates through money and endorsements

and did so successfully, against a bill that would have imposed additional health care costs on older Americans.[37]

Political Action Committees (PACs)   A group's contributions to candidates are funneled through its **political action committee (PAC)**. A group cannot give organizational funds (such as corporate profits or union dues) directly to candidates, but through its PAC a group can solicit voluntary contributions from members or employees and then donate this money to candidates. A PAC can back as many candidates as it wants but is legally limited in the amount it can contribute to a single candidate. The ceiling is $10,000 per candidate–$5,000 in the primary campaign and $5,000 in the general election campaign. (These financial limits apply only to candidates for federal office. State and local campaigns are regulated by state laws, and some states allow PACs to make unlimited contributions to individual candidates.)

There are roughly 4,000 PACs, and more than 60 percent of them are associated with business.[38] Most of these are corporate PACs, such as the Ford Motor Company Civic Action Fund, the Sun Oil Company Political Action Committee, and the Coca-Cola PAC. The others are tied to trade associations, such as the National Association of Realtors (RPAC). The next largest set of PACs consists of those linked to citizens' groups (that is, public-interest, single-issue, and ideological groups), such as the liberal People for the American Way and the conservative National Conservative Political Action Committee. Labor unions, once the major source of group contributions, constitute less than 10 percent of PACs.

PACs contribute roughly seven times as much money to incumbents as to their challengers (see Figure 9-4). PACs recognize that incumbents are likely to win and thus to remain in a position of power. Business PACs are more pragmatic than issue-based PACs and bestow roughly 95 percent of their contributions on incumbents.[39] "Anytime you go against an incumbent, you take a minute and think long and hard about what your rationale is," said Desiree Anderson, director of Realtors PAC.[40]

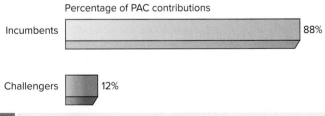

Percentage of PAC contributions

Incumbents ▬▬▬▬▬▬▬▬▬▬▬▬▬ 88%

Challengers ▬▬ 12%

figure 9-4   PAC CONTRIBUTIONS FAVOR INCUMBENTS

In allocating campaign contributions, PACs favor incumbent members of Congress over their challengers by a large margin. (*Source:* Center for Responsive Politics, 2022. Based on average PAC contribution in past five election cycles to incumbents and their challengers only.)

Super PACs   A decade ago, the term *super PAC* was not part of the political lexicon. That changed with the Supreme Court's *Citizens United v. Federal Election Commission* (2010) ruling, which held that federal laws outlawing campaign spending by corporations and unions violated their First Amendment right of free expression. The Court ruled that corporations and unions can spend an unlimited amount of their funds on elections, as long as the spending is not directly coordinated with that of the candidate or party they're supporting (see Chapter 8).[41]

In a follow-up case, a lower federal court applied the free expression principle of *Citizens United* to rule that political activists can form **super PACs**, or, as they are officially known as *independent-expenditure-only committees* (*IEOCs*). Super PACs are not allowed to give money directly to candidates or parties but are otherwise free to raise and spend unlimited amounts. They have become major players in U.S. election campaigns, spending hundreds of millions, for instance, to influence the 2022 midterm elections.

Critics have assailed the fact that super PACs can spend unlimited amounts of money and, unlike regular PACs, can take advantage of loopholes in the law to delay or not disclose the sources of their money.[42] Senator Bernie Sanders (D-VT) is a critic of super PACs, saying that election outcomes should reflect the will of "all of the people and not that of wealthy individuals and corporations who can pour millions into political campaigns."[43] Advocates of super PACs say that they communicate messages that voters have a right to hear. Bradley Smith, a Republican who served as chair of the Federal Election Commission, said, "While people like to complain about political spending, research shows that increased spending improves voter knowledge of candidates and issues."[44]

THE GROUP SYSTEM: INDISPENSABLE BUT BIASED IN FAVOR OF ECONOMIC GROUPS

As was noted in the chapter's introduction, pluralism theory holds that Americans' interests are best represented through group activity. On one level, this claim makes sense. Groups are a way to get government officials to pay attention to people's particular needs and interests. The fact that most people are not retirees, union members, farmers, or college students does not mean that the interests of such "minorities" are unworthy of government attention. What better instrument exists for promoting their interests than interest groups working on their behalf? Pluralists argue, in fact, that society is best seen as a collection of separate interests and is best served by a process that accommodates a wide array of interests. Thus, if manufacturing interests prevail on one issue, environmentalists on another, farmers on a third, minorities on a fourth, and so on until a great many interests are served, the "public interest" is served.

Pluralists also note that interest groups expand the range of issues that get lawmakers' attention. Political parties sometimes avoid controversial issues and, in any case, concentrate on the most prominent ones, which leaves hundreds of issues unaddressed through the party system. Interest groups advocate for and against many of these issues.[45]

Although much of what pluralists say is valid, it's not the full story of group influence. Political scientist Theodore Lowi points out that there is no concept of the public interest in a system that gives special interests the ability to decide the policies affecting them.[46] Nor can it be assumed that what a lobbying group receives is what the majority would also want. Consider the case of the federal law that required auto dealers to list the known defects of used cars on window stickers. The law was repealed after the National Association of Automobile Dealers contributed more than $1 million to the reelection campaigns of members of Congress. Auto dealers won another victory when their loans to car buyers were exempted from regulation by the new consumer protection agency that was created as part of the Dodd-Frank Act of 2010 (see "Case Study: Dodd-Frank Act and the Auto Lobby").

Another weakness in the pluralist argument resides in its claim that the group system is broadly representative. Although pluralists acknowledge that well-funded interests have more clout, they say that the group process is relatively open and few interests are entirely left out. This claim contains an element of truth, but it is not the full story. As this chapter has shown, economic

---

C A S E S T U D Y

Politics in Action

Dodd-Frank Act and the Auto Lobby

In 2008, the U.S. economy went into a deep recession as a result of reckless lending by the financial industry. Banks had given out huge numbers of mortgages to unqualified home buyers. When home prices then dropped sharply, many of the mortgages were "underwater," meaning that the houses were worth less than their mortgages. At that point, many homeowners stopped making their monthly payments. Banks were left with vacant houses and mortgage defaults. It put many of them in the red, sparking the financial crisis. Many banks survived only because they received bailout money from the federal government.

RainerPlendl/iStock/Getty Images

Continued

In 2010, Congress passed the Dodd-Frank Act in order to protect borrowers and end risky lending on everything from mortgages to credit cards to consumer loans. The legislation was named for its chief sponsors, Senator Christopher Dodd of Connecticut and Representative Barney Frank of Massachusetts.

As the Dodd-Frank bill was being drafted, more than 500 lobbyists from the auto industry—nearly one per member of Congress—went to Capitol Hill in an effort to get auto loans removed from the new regulations. They argued that auto loans do not pose the same risk as home mortgages. Failed mortgages, the lobbyists claimed, can bring down the economy but repossessed cars cannot. The auto industry succeeded in its effort. Members of Congress removed auto loans from the legislation. It was not the automobile lobby's first such victory. A few years earlier, it had persuaded Congress to repeal a law that required auto dealers to list on window stickers the known defects of the used cars they were selling.

Q: Why do you think the auto industry has so much influence in Congress?

ASK YOURSELF: How many jobs, directly and indirectly, does the auto industry generate? How prominent are auto dealers in their local communities? Are automobiles a commodity important to both labor and business and thus important to both Democratic and Republican lawmakers? What type of financial resources does the auto industry have to invest in lobbying and election campaigns?

interests, particularly corporations, are the most highly organized and the most advantaged when it comes to exerting influence on policy.[47] Of course, economic groups do not dominate everything, nor do they operate unchecked. Most environmental groups, for example, work to shield the environment from threats posed by business activity. Activist government has also brought the group system into closer balance; the government's poverty programs have spawned groups that act to protect the programs. Nevertheless, the power of poverty-related groups is tiny compared with the power of wealthy interests. Nearly two-thirds of all lobbying groups in Washington are business-related, and their political clout is enormous.

At the time of the writing of the Constitution, James Madison grappled with the dilemma posed by group activity. In his famous essay *Federalist* No. 10., Madison warned against "the dangers of faction"—a situation where factions (groups) become so powerful that their interests trump those of society as a whole. Yet, he noted that a free society must allow the pursuit of self-interest. Unless people can promote the separate opinions that stem from differences in their needs, values, and possessions, they are not free. The constitutional solution, Madison concluded, was a system of checks and balances that would prevent a *majority faction* from trampling on the interests of smaller groups.

Ironically, Madison's constitutional solution is now part of the problem. America's system of checks and balances makes it relatively easy for *minority factions*—or, as they are called today, special-interest groups—to gain government support. Because of the system's division of power, they have numerous points at which to gain access and exert influence. Often, they need only to

---

F A K E
  or
F A C T

Detecting Misinformation

Do "the People" Govern?

Democracy is a system of government by the people, although in practice the people govern through their elected representatives. By implication, the major influence on representatives' decisions should be the voters' policy preferences.

Steve Allen/Brand X Pictures/Getty Images

Is that claim fact, or is it fake?

Political scientists Martin Gilens and Benjamin Page conducted a massive study to address the question of policy influence. They examined nearly 1,800 policy decisions between 1981 and 2002 on which there were polling data that indicated Americans' preferences on these policies. They then tested lawmakers' policy decisions against four possible explanations: whether their decisions aligned with the preferences of the majority of citizens ("majoritarian electoral democracy"), with the preferences of wealthier citizens ("economic-elite domination), with the preferences of mass-based interest groups ("majoritarian pluralism"), or with the preferences of business/professional interest groups ("biased pluralism").

Their analysis found that the preferences of wealthy citizens and business/ professional interest groups had far more influence on policy than did those of the majority of citizens and those of mass-based interest groups. Gilens and Page concluded that "policymaking is dominated by powerful business organizations and a small number of affluent Americans."[48]

Other studies have found stronger evidence of majority influence,[49] but nearly all studies of policy influence have concluded that interest groups, particularly those associated with business, exert a powerful influence on public policy.

find a single ally, whether it is a congressional committee, an executive agency, or a federal court, to get at least some of what they seek. Once they obtain a government benefit, it is likely to last. Benefits are hard to eliminate because the executive branch and both houses of Congress have to agree to abolish them. If a group has strong support in even a single institution, it can usually fend off attempts to eliminate a policy or program that serves its interest. Such support can be easy to acquire if the group has resources—information, money, and votes—that officeholders want. (Chapters 11 and 13 discuss further the issue of interest-group power.)

SUMMARY

A political interest group is composed of a set of individuals organized to promote a shared concern. Most interest groups owe their existence to factors other than politics. These groups form for economic reasons, such as the pursuit of profit, and they maintain themselves by making profits (in the case of corporations) or by providing their members with private goods, such as jobs and wages. Economic groups include corporations, trade associations, labor unions, farm organizations, and professional associations. Collectively, economic groups are by far the largest set of organized interests. The group system tends to favor interests that are already economically and socially advantaged.

Citizens' groups do not have the same organizational advantages as economic groups. They depend on voluntary contributions from potential members, who may lack interest and resources or who recognize that they will get the collective good from a group's activity even if they do not participate (the free-rider problem). Citizens' groups include public-interest, single-issue, and ideological groups. Their numbers have increased dramatically since the 1960s despite their organizational problems.

Organized interests seek influence largely by lobbying public officials and contributing to election campaigns. Using an inside strategy, lobbyists develop direct contacts with legislators, government bureaucrats, and members of the judiciary in order to persuade them to accept the group's perspective on policy. Groups also use an outside strategy, seeking to mobilize public support for their goals. This strategy relies in part on grassroots lobbying—encouraging group members and the public to communicate their policy views to officials. Outside lobbying also includes efforts to elect officeholders who will support group aims. Through political action committees (PACs), organized groups now provide nearly a fourth of all contributions received by congressional candidates. A more recent development is the emergence of super PACs. They are independent campaign committees that can raise and spend nearly unrestricted amounts of money on elections as long as they do not coordinate their efforts with those of the candidate they are supporting.

The policies that emerge from the group system bring benefits to many of society's interests and often serve the collective interest as well. However, when groups can essentially dictate policy, the common good is rarely served. The majority's interest is subordinated to group (minority) interests. In most instances, the minority consists of business firms and individuals who already enjoy a substantial share of society's benefits.

CRITICAL THINKING ZONE

KEY TERMS

citizens' groups (*p. 239*)
collective (public) goods (*p. 242*)
economic groups (*p. 236*)
free-rider problem (*p. 242*)
inside lobbying (*p. 244*)
interest groups (*p. 234*)
iron triangle (*p. 249*)

issue network (*p. 250*)
lobbying (*p. 244*)
outside lobbying (*p. 252*)
political action committee
  (PAC) (*p. 253*)
private (individual) goods (*p. 242*)
super PACs (*p. 254*)

APPLYING THE ELEMENTS OF CRITICAL THINKING

Conceptualizing: How do iron triangles and issue networks differ? How do they contribute to group influence?

Synthesizing: Contrast the methods of inside lobbying with those of outside lobbying.

Analyzing: Why are there so many more organized interest groups in the United States than in other Western democracies? Why are so many of these groups organized around economic interests, particularly business?

OF POSSIBLE INTEREST

A Book Worth Reading: Lee Drutman, *The Business of America Is Lobbying: How Corporations Became Politicized and Politics Became More Corporate* (New York: Oxford University Press, 2015). Written by an astute political analyst, this book details corporate lobbying and its influence on national policy.

A Website Worth Visiting: **www.opensecrets.org** The Center for Responsive Politics is a nonpartisan, nonprofit organization. Its website includes up-to-date analysis and data on lobbying, PAC spending, and other interest-group activity.

Design credit: (People, Flag, U.S., Globe, Vote Icons): McGraw Hill; (Eagle): Feng Wei Photography/Moment/Getty Images; (Lincoln): Photographs in the Carol M. Highsmith Archive, Library of Congress, Prints and Photographs Division [LC-DIG-highsm-12542].

10
CHAPTER

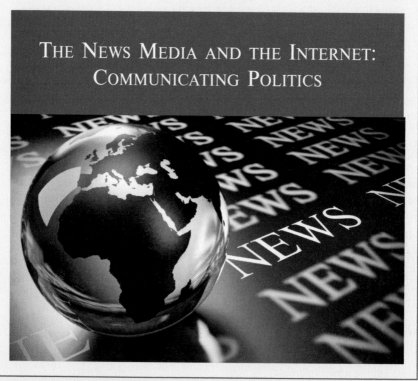

THE NEWS MEDIA AND THE INTERNET: COMMUNICATING POLITICS

Le Moal Olivier/123RF

66 The press in America . . . determines what people will think and talk about, an authority
that in other nations is reserved for tyrants, priests, parties, and mandarins. **99**

THEODORE H. WHITE[1]

As Russian troops streamed into Ukraine, President Joe Biden took credit
for uniting the NATO alliance in defense of Ukraine. "NATO has never, never
been more united than it is today," Biden said. The *Washington Times* told a
different story, quoting Senator Lindsay Graham (R-SC) as saying, "At every
turn it seems [the] Biden Administration is being caught flat-footed." The *New
York Times* Michael Crowley and Edward Wong sided with Biden, saying he
had infused "the United States with a new sense of mission." Fox News host
Maria Bartiromo slammed Biden's policy, asking whether he wanted Ukraine
"taken down." MSNBC backed Biden, quoting an analyst who called Biden's
Ukraine policy the "best showing in foreign policy in a generation."

The **news** is mainly an account of obtruding events, particularly those that are *timely* (new or unfolding developments rather than old or static ones), *dramatic* (striking developments rather than commonplace ones), and *compelling* (developments that arouse people's emotions).[2] Yet, the news is a construct, shaped by those who report and comment on events. Biden's response to the war in Ukraine was big news in every media outlet but portrayed differently from one outlet to the next.

Americans depend on the media for information about public affairs. The world of politics is largely a second-hand experience, something people hear about through media outlets rather than directly observing. The media outlets dedicated to covering and reporting on events are called the **news media (press)**. Other media outlets engage Americans largely through commentary. They include political talk-show hosts, bloggers, opinion magazines, and social media users.

This chapter describes the media's political role and influence. The main points presented in the chapter are the following:

- *Until a few decades ago, the United States had "an information commons."* Americans were exposed through the media to a relatively standard version of national politics, which had a unifying and depolarizing effect.

Shown here is President Joe Biden speaking on the U.S. response to Russia's invasion of Ukraine. His pronouncements were covered by every leading news outlet but, whereas some of them heaped praise on his policy, others were sharply critical. (Drew Angerer/Getty Images)

- *Today's media system is fragmented with options that range from traditional news outlets to highly partisan ones.* The system has contributed to party polarization and a rising level of misinformation.

- *The media have several functions, each of which has an impact on the nation's politics.* An example is the watchdog function, whereby the media take responsibility for exposing incompetent, hypocritical, or corrupt officials.

CREATING THE INFORMATION COMMONS

No institution has changed more in recent decades than has the media system. The change is so dramatic that a modern-day Rip Van Winkle, awakening from a decades-long sleep, would be bewildered by what he was hearing, and by where people are getting their information.

A half-century ago, Americans were immersed in what scholars call the **information commons**.[3] They were all hearing much the same thing about national politics. The national stories in local newspapers were provided by national wire services like the Associated Press. It didn't matter if you were reading the *Sacramento Bee* or the *Fort Worth Telegram* or the *Charlotte Observer*, the stories about national politics were nearly the same. And they were the same

Broadcast news dominated television until the advent of cable. Today, the ABC, CBS, and NBC broadcast newscasts compete with cable-based Fox News, CNN, and MSNBC for viewers. Cable news includes partisan outlets. Fox News pursues a politically conservative news agenda, while MSNBC pursues a liberal one. (Scott J. Ferrell/Congressional Quarterly/Alamy Stock Photo)

stories being told on the newscasts of America's three broadcast networks, ABC, CBS, and NBC. It was a *low-choice media system.* If citizens were looking for a different option for their daily news, they couldn't find it in most locations.

Today's information system is much different. It is a *high-choice media system.*[4] Americans still have access to broadcast news and the local newspaper. But they can now also get their information from cable television, social media, and Internet outlets, many of which portray politics in a markedly different way than the traditional media, and from each other. The shared version of national politics—the information commons—has given way to alternative realities.

The remainder of this section will explain the developments that gave rise to the information commons and the subsequent developments that gave rise to today's high-choice media system.

From a Partisan Press to Objective Journalism

The nation's first media system developed in support of the nation's emerging political parties. One of the first newspapers, the *Gazette of the United States,* was started at the urging of Alexander Hamilton to promote the Federalist Party. Hamilton's political rival, Thomas Jefferson convinced Philip Freneau to start the *National Gazette* as the Democratic-Republican Party's alternative paper. The papers were a model for those that followed, nearly all of which were financed through government printing contracts. Hamilton, as secretary of the Treasury, steered the Treasury Department's contracts to the *Gazette of the United States,* whereas Jefferson, as secretary of State, made sure that the *National Gazette* got the State Department's contracts.

Early newspapers were hand-printed a page at a time on a flat press, a process that limited production and kept the cost of the newspaper copy beyond the reach of most citizens. Even the leading papers had fewer than 1,500 paid subscribers and needed government contracts to survive. Most "news" stories were little more than partisan diatribes with facts twisted to favor the publisher's party.[5]

New technology gradually weakened the partisan press. When the telegraph came into use in the mid-1800s, newspapers had ready access to developments outside the local area, which led them to replace partisan commentary with news reports. The subsequent invention of the power-driven rotary printing press enabled publishers to print their newspapers more cheaply and rapidly. As circulations rose, so did advertising and subscriber revenues, reducing newspapers' need for government patronage.

By 1900, some American newspapers were selling 100,000 copies a day, luring readers with loud headlines and sensational claims—a style of reporting that came to be called "yellow journalism."[6] Influential publishers used their papers to advance personal agendas. William Randolph Hearst's *New York Journal* may have contributed to the outbreak of the Spanish-American War through sensational (and largely inaccurate) reports on the cruelty of Spanish rule in Cuba. Frederic Remington (who later became a noted painter and sculptor) was working in Cuba as a news artist for Hearst and planned to return to New York because Cuba appeared calm. Hearst allegedly cabled back "Please remain. You furnish the pictures and I'll furnish the war."[7]

Yellow journalism's unrestrained reporting led to demands for more responsible reporting, which contributed to the development of **objective journalism**, which emphasized the reporting of "facts" rather than opinions and called for the evenhanded treatment of the Republican and Democratic Parties. The *New York Times'* Adolph Ochs was a leading proponent of the new model. Ochs told his reporters that he "wanted as little partisanship as possible . . . as few judgments as possible."[8] The *Times* gradually acquired a reputation as the country's best newspaper. Objective reporting was also the model taught in the newly created journalism programs at Columbia University and the University of Missouri—the nation's first such programs.

Although it took several decades for objective journalism to become the model for nearly every American newspaper, it helped create an information commons. Readers were exposed equally to Republican and Democratic leaders and were reading stories that were largely factual accounts of major events. As radio and then television entered Americans' lives, they, too, applied the objective model. Broadcasters were licensed by the Federal Communications Commission (FCC), and the licensees were prohibited, because broadcasting frequencies are limited in number, from promoting a political viewpoint or party.

The information commons reached deep into American lives. Until the end of the 1970s, the news was the only broadcast television programming available in the early evening, and most viewers tuned in. More than 50 million viewers watched the network news each evening.[9] Newspaper circulation was also high—the combined daily circulation of morning and evening papers exceeded 60 million.[10] Even young adults, who typically had pay less attention to the news than older adults, were engaged. "There was little variation in news viewing habits by age," political scientist Martin Wattenberg wrote. "TV news producers could hardly write off young adults, given that two out of three said they had watched such broadcasts every night."[11]

Impact of the Information Commons

The emergence of the information commons changed how Americans thought about politics. For one thing, it fostered a shared reality. Wherever Americans lived, they were exposed to a common version of national politics. Not every American derived the same meaning from the news they were getting, and the reporting had its blind spots, including downplaying stories about ordinary Americans in favor of stories about the rich and powerful.[12] But it was a balanced rendition of the news that treated Republican and Democratic leaders by the same standards.

Studies found that Americans' information about politics was on the rise. Citizens have never been highly informed about politics. Those who pay close attention to the news are more informed than those who don't, but even they have large knowledge gaps. A reason is that citizens don't "study" the news. They "follow" it, and much of what they see and hear is quickly forgotten. But, in the era of the information commons, Americans were slowly acquiring a better understanding of political issues and their elected representatives.[13]

The information commons had a depolarizing effect. Exposed equally to the Democratic and Republican Parties, Americans' opinions were becoming more moderate. Studies found that differences in the opinions of Republicans and Democrats had narrowed and that citizens had come to believe that they had more in common with those in the other party than they had previously thought.[14]

All of that has changed. Americans today are less likely to have a shared view of reality, less likely to have accurate perceptions of political developments, and less likely to believe they have a lot in common with those in the other party. The reasons are several, but a dramatic change in the media system is one of them.

CITIZEN ACTION!
SELF-GOVERNMENT

Although more passive than other forms of involvement, attention to daily news allows citizens to keep up with events and informs their judgment about current issues. If you're not now a daily consumer of news, consider becoming one. Seek out several sources so that you're exposed to different points of view.

THE MAKING OF ECHO CHAMBERS

Technological change contributed to the rise of the information commons. Ironically, technological change has also contributed to its decline and the emergence of **echo chambers**, which are media outlets where people hear what they like to believe and where contrary voices are excluded or debunked.[15] "We're increasingly able to choose our information sources based on their tendency to back up what we already believe," notes *Vox*'s Ezra Klein. "We don't even have to hear the arguments from the other side."[16]

The Return of Partisan Media

In the era of the information commons, a handful of newspapers like New Hampshire's *Manchester Union Leader* were outwardly partisan in their news reporting, and there were a few influential opinion weeklies like *The Nation* and *The National Review.* But, aside from the editorial page of their local paper, most Americans were rarely exposed to overtly partisan commentary.

That began to change in 1987 when the FCC rescinded the Fairness Doctrine, which had required broadcasters to "afford reasonable opportunity for the discussion of conflicting views of public importance." The FCC concluded that the development of cable television and the expansion of FM radio had alleviated the problem of scarce frequencies and that broadcasters were now free to air political programming of their choosing.

Radio station owners quickly responded. Under the Fairness Doctrine, if they carried a conservative talk show in prime time, they also had to carry a liberal one. Unlike journalists, who lean Democratic,[17] most station owners are Republicans,[18] and they weren't interested in giving equal time to liberal ideas. With the Fairness Doctrine eliminated, many of them shifted from music and other formats to a talk-show format, most of which had a conservative slant.[19] Partisan talk shows offered a version of politics radically different—more opinionated and less devoted to factual accuracy—than that of traditional news outlets. Talk shows quickly found an audience. In less than a decade, the weekly audience for partisan talk shows jumped ten-fold to almost 20 million listeners. It would grow to more than 40 million listeners.[20]

In this same period, cable television came into American homes, made possible by the wide availability of coaxial cable. The first of the cable networks, CNN, was formed in 1980 by media entrepreneur Ted Turner who instructed his reporters to follow the objective reporting model. Then, in 1996, billionaire media owner Robert Murdoch started Fox News, hiring Republican consultant Roger Ailes to run it and instructing him to promote conservative views. Within a few years, propelled by a largely Republican audience, Fox News had become the nation's most heavily watched cable news network. Fox's success prompted the third-ranking cable news network, MSNBC, to recast itself in 2004 as the liberal alternative to Fox. Partisanship also seeped into cable's comedy talk shows, which unlike partisan talk shows, where the top draws were conservative hosts like Rush Limbaugh and Glenn Beck, the top-rated partisan comedy talk shows had liberal hosts like Jon Stewart and Bill Maher.

Whatever their form, partisan talk shows are echo chambers. They heap praise on their side of the partisan divide while slamming the other. Not surprisingly, they attract people who share their political outlook. Republicans are 13 times more likely than Democrats to say that Fox is their main source of news. Democrats are 19 times more likely than Republicans to cite MSNBC as their main source.[21] The audience for *Breitbart News*'s website is 10-to-1 Republican over Democratic, while the audience for *HuffPost*'s website is lopsided in Democrats' favor.[22] The same pattern holds for talk shows. The audience of every conservative talk show is heavily Republican, while Democrats make up the bulk of the audience of every liberal talk show.[23]

In the era of the information commons, the highest-paid individuals in media were the anchors of the broadcast evening news programs. Today, the highest earners are partisan talk-show hosts with large audiences. Pictured here is Fox's Sean Hannity, who is the highest-paid talk-show host. (Jason Kempin/Getty Images)

The Rise of the Internet and Social Media

The Internet was invented in the early 1980s to enable the U.S. military's computer networks to communicate with each other. A decade later, it was opened to commercial and personal use (see "How the 50 States Differ").

Because of the relatively low start-up cost, the Internet was expected to allow ordinary citizens to start an online news and information outlet. Many did so, but most didn't last. As it turned out, news on the Internet is characterized by what analysts call "the long tail."[24] When news-based websites are arrayed by the number of visitors to each site, there are a few heavily visited sites on one end and thousands of lightly visited sites on the other end—the long tail.[25] Economies of scale define success on the Internet. Only the most heavily trafficked sites generate the revenue needed to attract and hold a large audience over the long term.

Many of the most heavily visited sites are those of the traditional media, including nytimes.com and nbcnews.com. Of the prominent sites that came into existence with the Internet, most have a partisan slant, including HuffPost.com on the left and Breitbart.com on the right. *HuffPost* was started and funded by the wealthy

HOW THE 50 STATES DIFFER

CRITICAL THINKING THROUGH COMPARISONS

Broadband Internet Access

Although the Internet has expanded access to news and information, high-speed broadband is not available to every American. The number of individuals without broadband access varies by state, as the accompanying map indicates. One in every four homes in Mississippi and New Mexico—the states with the lowest levels of penetration—do not have broadband access. On the other end are Washington, Utah, and Colorado, where only one in every ten homes lacks broadband access. In 2021, Congress passed the American Rescue Plan Act, which includes tens of billions of dollars to expand broadband access to nearly all Americans.

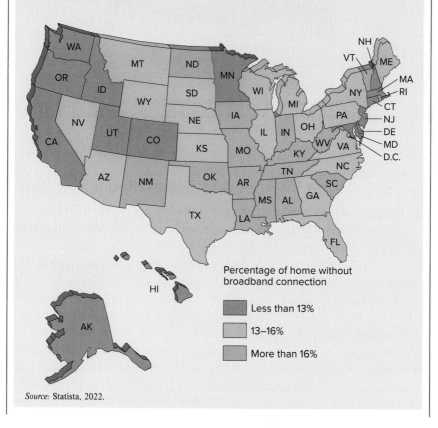

Percentage of home without broadband connection

▮ Less than 13%

▮ 13–16%

▮ More than 16%

Source: Statista, 2022.

> **Q:** What might account for state-to-state differences in access to high-speed broadband?
>
> **A:** States that have more rural residents tend to have lower rates of high-speed broadband access. Cable companies have been less likely to offer it in rural areas because of the high installation costs relative to the number of subscribers.

liberal activist Arianna Huffington. *Breitbart News* was started with the financial backing of conservative donor Robert Mercer[26] and was once headed by Steve Bannon, who served for a time as President Donald Trump's chief political advisor.

The Internet has spawned thousands of bloggers, many of whom rely on YouTube to carry their message.[27] Of the top 25 bloggers, about half are on the right and half on the left. And over 90 percent of the time when they link to another site, it's to a site with the same partisan slant, reinforcing the echo chamber. Of the top 25 blog sites, only one caters to both liberals and conservatives, an indication that most blog users aren't interested in hearing what the other side has to say.[28]

The Internet has also spawned social media. Two-thirds of adults say they use Facebook while a smaller but still huge number use Instagram, Snapchat, TikTok, WhatsApp, and Twitter.[29] The political messages that people encounter on social media tend to be one-sided in that Republicans and Democrats are more likely to connect with individuals from their political party.[30] Moreover, social media create echo chambers of their users' own making, a phenomenon known as **filter bubbles**. Platforms like Facebook monitor users' behavior and then apply algorithms to selectively filter for content consistent with each user's preferred content. The algorithmic "filtering" is ongoing and gradually encases the user in a "bubble" of one-sided content.[31]

The Impact of Echo Chambers

In their impact on people's political opinions and perceptions, echo chambers are the antithesis of the information commons. Rather than a shared reality, echo chambers create alternative realities that align with what people already believe or would like to believe, rather than what the facts would indicate. Such realities are not entirely divorced from reality but they're constructed from selected facts. Information that supports what people already believe is brought to the fore while information that contradicts what's believed is downplayed or omitted.

Rather than bringing people together, echo chambers drive them apart. Exposure to echo chambers heightens people's belief in the superiority of their side of the partisan divide while increasing their sense that the opposing side's views are inferior, perhaps even dangerous. Exposure to partisan outlets is also associated with more extreme views, although scholars differ on whether the correlation is a result of exposure or a result of individuals seeking messages that reinforce their already intense opinions (see "Party Polarization: Living in Alternative Worlds").[32]

P A R T Y
POLARIZATION

Conflicting Ideas

Living in Alternative Worlds

In the 1970s, Americans' choice of TV news programs was limited to the three broadcast networks—ABC, CBS, and NBC. Each headlined the same stories and interpreted them in much the same way while giving more or less equal coverage to the two major parties. The situation changed with the emergence of cable TV. Today's Americans have a range of choices, including outlets that heap praise on one party while attacking the other.

Americans who prefer partisan news rely on news outlets aligned with their beliefs. For example, Republicans are far more likely than Democrats to say they get "most" of their news from conservative-leaning Fox News, whereas Democrats are far more likely than Republicans to say they get "most" of their news from liberal-leaning MSNBC.

The choice of a news outlet can make a world of difference. "Reality" as portrayed in partisan outlets can bear little resemblance to how traditional news outlets present it. During the peak of the COVID-19 pandemic, as the chart below indicates, viewers of CBS evening news heard mostly about its impact on public health, which was less favorable to Republican President Donald Trump, while viewers of Fox News heard mostly about its impact on the economy, which was more favorable to Trump.

Percentage of COVID-related coverage

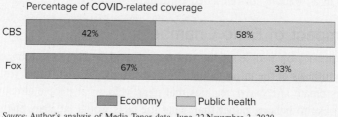

Source: Author's analysis of Media Tenor data, June 22-November 3, 2020

Q: Do you find it troubling that Americans are regularly exposed to different versions of reality? In what way might it have an undesirable effect? A desirable one?

Finally, rather than making people better informed, echo chambers foster **misinformation**, which is false information that is held or spread without regard for intent (misinformation is different from **disinformation**, which is false information that is spread with the intent to deceive). People enmeshed in echo chambers are selectively misinformed. They are not always misled about what their party represents,[33] but they are grossly misinformed about what the opposing party represents.[34]

Echo chambers are fertile ground for the spread of unfounded conspiracy theories. Without opposing voices to contest such claims, they can take on a life of their own and become widely believed even when there's not a shred of evidence behind them. An unsupported claim circulating on the right holds that prominent Democratic Party leaders for years have been operating a massive child sex trafficking ring. Left-wing conspiracy theorists have claimed that several Republican leaders are secret Russian agents and that Russian President Vladimir Putin murdered Andrew Breitbart, founder of Breitbart News, to install a pro-Russia publisher in his place.[35]

Echo chambers can have a motivating effect.[36] They can mobilize citizens by persuading them that there's a lot at stake in which party wins the next election, increasing the likelihood that they will vote, contribute money, or work on a campaign. Moreover, the impact of echo chambers is reduced by the fact that many citizens who rely on partisan outlets also get news from traditional outlets, which can act as a check on extreme claims. Yet, the power of this check is diminishing. Americans are slowly gravitating toward partisan media as their main or only source of news.[37] Such individuals are still outnumbered by those who rely on traditional news outlets, but the gap is shrinking.[38] One reason for the trend is heightened polarization. A second is that partisan outlets undermine faith in traditional outlets by claiming their information is not to be trusted.[39]

THE POLITICS OF MEDIA FUNCTIONS

Recognizing that the free flow of information was a key to self-government,[40] the framers gave the media special protection. The First Amendment provides for freedom of the press, a guarantee that the Supreme Court has strongly defended (see Chapter 4).

Yet, the media are unlike other political institutions in that they are not solely a public entity. They are also a private entity that seeks to make a profit, which requires them to find ways to attract and hold an audience.[41] Without advertising or other revenue sources, a media outlet would go out of business. Each of the media's functions—their signaling, common-carrier, watchdog, partisan, and entertainment functions—derives from one or both of the media's two imperatives: their constitutional responsibility to inform the public and their need to make money.

The Signaling Function

The media provide a **signaling (signaler) function**—alerting the public to important developments. Occasionally, an event enters the media stream through social media, usually when someone captures a newsworthy scene on his or her cell phone camera. Nevertheless, consequential messages typically originate with media outlets.

In their role as signalers, media outlets have the power to focus the public's attention. **Agenda setting** refers to the media's ability to influence what is on people's minds.[42] By reporting the same events, problems, issues, and leaders—simply by giving them space or time—the media place them on the public agenda. The media, as Bernard Cohen noted, "may not be successful much of the time in telling people what to think, but it is stunningly successful in telling them what to think about."[43] A striking example was news coverage of the spread of the COVID-19 coronavirus. For months, it dominated the headlines. Americans were told of its spread, how to protect themselves, what governments

The news media act as signalers, bringing important developments to the public's attention. When inflation swept the United States in 2022, it dominated news coverage. (Michael Vi/Alamy Stock Photo)

and health care workers were doing to save lives, and the damage it was inflict-ing on the economy. Not since the terrorist attacks of September 11, 2001, had a single story so dominated the news. In its monthly poll in February 2020, the Gallup organization found that fewer than 1 percent of adult Americans thought the coronavirus was the nation's most important problem. By April, it was at the top of the list.

The issues that are uppermost in people's minds can affect their political choices. Much of the coverage of the COVID-19 pandemic, for example, told of the shortcomings in the Trump administration's response to the crisis. Exit polls of the 2020 presidential election found that, among the third of voters for whom the pandemic was the top issue, Democratic nominee Joe Biden easily outpolled Republican nominee Donald Trump, whereas Trump had the edge among other voters, though more narrowly. Two years into Biden's presidency, Democrats felt the sting of an issue that was at the top of the news—inflation. Exit polls of the 2022 midterm elections indicated that Republican candidates had the edge among voters for whom inflation was the leading issue.

The Common-Carrier Function

The media also exercise a **common-carrier function**, serving as a conduit through which political leaders communicate with the public. Leaders need exposure to get the public's support while citizens need to know what their political leaders are doing. The media serve these needs.

Among public officials, the president benefits the most from the media's common-carrier role (see Chapter 12).[44] More than 200 reporters are assigned to cover the White House, and the president gets roughly as much coverage in the national press as do all 535 members of Congress combined (see Chapter 12). And among those in Congress, a few get disproportionate attention. They include, not surprisingly, the Speaker of the House and the House and Senator majority and minority leaders. But they also include members who get coverage because they're controversial, stir up conflict, or have large personalities, and are thereby seen as "newsworthy" by journalists. Two such members are Democrat Alexandria Ocasio-Cortez and Republican Marjorie Taylor Greene. Their policy views are out of step with most of their colleagues, which limits their legislative influence, but they're sought out by journalists for their outspoken opinions.[45]

During the era of the information commons, newsmakers could take a stand with the assurance they would get a somewhat full and balanced hearing. That's less true today.[46] Partisan media outlets act as a common carrier only for news-makers who share their partisan views. Those who don't are ignored or disparaged. Even the traditional media are less accommodating than in the past. On network newscasts, for example, the average length of a newsmaker's sound bite (the length of time within a television story that a newsmaker speaks without interruption) was once 40 seconds but is now about 10 seconds, roughly enough time for the newsmaker to utter a long sentence.[47] Reporters do most of the talking and, more often than not, seek to deflate much of what the newsmaker is saying.[48]

The fact that journalists, talk-show hosts, bloggers, and other communicators shape their messages is a source of power. **Framing** is the process by which a communicator selects a particular aspect of a situation and builds the message around it.[49] The way that communicators frame their stories has what scholars call a priming effect.[50] **Priming** is how the framing of a message affects how people will respond to it.[51] Framing and priming can affect how an audience interprets what it sees and hears. As inflation rose sharply in 2022, for example, conservative media framed the inflationary rise in the context of the Biden administration's spending policies, thus priming their audience to blame it on Biden. Meanwhile, liberal media framed it in the context of supply chain problems and other factors related to the economic disruption of the COVID-19 pandemic, thus priming their audience to see it as a problem outside Biden's control.[52]

Social media function as a common carrier. They provide political leaders, as well as ordinary citizens, a way to communicate directly with others. No politician has done so more actively than Donald Trump. He sent nearly 25,000 tweets during his time as president. Even then, however, Trump wasn't in full control of the framing of his message. A study found that more than 95 percent of Americans' exposure to Trump's tweets occurred, not from seeing them directly, but from hearing about them in the news, where they were accompanied by journalists' reactions to what he had tweeted.[53]

It is largely through their common-carrier function that traditional media contribute to America's misinformation problem. One way that traditional media refrain from taking sides in partisan disputes is by reporting what newsmakers say without commenting on the accuracy of the claim being made.[54] As long as journalists quote the newsmaker correctly, they are adhering to their standard of factual reporting. But what if the newsmaker is making a deceptive claim? In that case, the news story is a conduit for disinformation. It happens often enough for a Columbia University study to conclude that traditional news outlets "play a major role in propagating hoaxes, false claims, questionable rumors, and dubious viral content."[55]

The Watchdog Function

Through their **watchdog function**, the media take responsibility for exposing incompetent, hypocritical, or corrupt officials. It's a reason the news media are sometimes called the fourth branch of government—part of the political system's checks on abuses by those in power.

Although the watchdog function dates to the earliest newspapers, the Watergate scandal elevated its significance in journalists' minds. Led by investigative reporters at *The Washington Post,* the press uncovered evidence that high-ranking officials in the Nixon administration had lied about their role in the 1972 burglary of the Democratic National Committee's headquarters at the Watergate complex in Washington, D.C. President Richard Nixon was forced to resign, as was his attorney general, John Mitchell. Ever since then, journalists have aggressively pursued even the slightest hint of wrongdoing by public officials.

The fallout from the Watergate scandal spilled over to daily reporting. Before Watergate, journalists seldom questioned politicians' motives or challenged what they said. Ever since Watergate, journalists have been less deferential to political leaders.[56] Every president since Nixon, whether a Democrat or a Republican, has received more negative than positive news coverage.[57] Congressional coverage has also been steadily negative, regardless of which party has controlled Congress or how much or little was accomplished.[58] Scholars attribute part of the decline in Americans' trust in government over the past half-century to the media's negative tendency.[59] The tendency is also claimed to work to the disadvantage of the Democratic Party, given that it relies more heavily on the government as a policy instrument than does the Republican Party. To initiate a new program, Democrats must not only convince voters that it's needed but also that the government can be trusted to carry it out effectively.[60]

The emergence of partisan media has had the paradoxical effect of both heightening and depressing the media's watchdog function. Partisan outlets, even more so than traditional news outlets, play up official wrongdoing, but they do so selectively, highlighting even the smallest transgression when it involves the other party and doing their best to downplay it when their party is involved. Few developments illustrate that more clearly than how partisan media responded to the January 6, 2021 assault on the U.S. Capitol. Liberal media were relentless in tying top Republicans, including Trump, to the assault and gave heavy coverage to the House investigative committee's examination of the assault and the criminal proceedings of those charged in the assault. For their part, the conservative media attacked the legitimacy of the House investigative committee and the criminal charges while framing many of their comments in the context of the claim that the 2020 election was stolen from Trump.[61]

Although the watchdog role is played mostly by media outlets, social media have played it in situations where wrongdoing is captured on tape or video. No recent example illustrates that more clearly than the videos taken by onlookers of a white Minneapolis police officer as he pressed his knee against the throat of George Floyd, an African American, for 9 minutes and 29 seconds. After the videos went viral, massive protests against police violence took place across the country. The videos also played a pivotal role in the trial and conviction of the police officer who killed George Floyd.

F A K E	
or	**Detecting Misinformation**
F A C T	

Is a Picture Worth a Thousand Words?

The introduction of television and more recently smart-phones have made images a larger part of politics. At any earlier time, photographs in newspapers and in magazines like *Time*, *Life*, and *Look* provided Americans with visual images beyond what they could see for themselves. Images can be powerful, which has led to the popular saying, "a picture is worth a thousand words."

TonyPrato/Shutterstock

Is that claim fact, or is it fake?

There are times when a picture is more powerful than the written or spoken word, as exemplified by the video that captured George Floyd's killing in 2020 by a Minneapolis policeman. The video sparked massive "Black Lives Matter" demonstrations throughout the country.

In the ordinary course of politics, however, words matter more than images. Politics includes a clash of interests and ideas, which are expressed largely through words. And America's founding ideals were conveyed with words, as in the Declaration of Independence's proclamation "that all men are created equal, that they are endowed by their Creator with certain unalienable Rights, that among these are Life, Liberty and the pursuit of Happiness."

Words are also the foundation of an informed public. Citizens can learn from images but words give context and meaning to issues of policy and leadership. It is perhaps not surprising, then, that studies have found that citizens who regularly read a daily newspaper tend to be the most informed. They are more informed than citizens who invest an equivalent amount of time watching television news and far more informed than citizens who largely avoid the news.[62]

Newspaper reading has declined sharply in recent decades, which has contributed to a decline in Americans' understanding of politics and a rise in the level of misinformation. The drop-off in newspaper readership is particularly pronounced among young people.[63] A few decades ago, they were nearly as likely to read a newspaper as older adults and nearly as well informed about politics. In writing about the sharp decline in young adults' political knowledge, political scientist Martin Wattenberg used the title, "Don't Ask Anyone Under 30."[64]

The Partisan Function

As was discussed earlier, the media's **partisan function**—serving as an advocate for a particular viewpoint or interest—defined America's early newspapers, but then gave way to the objective reporting model, which required journalists to be neutral in covering the Republican and Democratic Parties. That's still the practice in most papers, but overt partisanship is a defining feature of many of today's media outlets.

The political talk shows on radio and television epitomize partisan media. When they launched after the elimination of the Fairness Doctrine in the late 1980s, their hosts discovered through trial and error what listeners wanted to hear. Most listeners were bored when hearing careful analysis. What listeners liked best were rants about the opposing party, a discovery that turned partisan "outrage" into the defining feature of political talk shows.[65]

Outrage is the selling card of conservative and liberal talk-show hosts alike. Although they differ in their ideology, they are similar in how they talk, the images they invoke, and the devices they use. Name-calling, misrepresentation, mockery, character assassination, and fabricated horrors are but a few of their tools. The goal is to make the opposing side look stupid, inept, or dangerous. Democratic senator Charles Schumer is "Up-Chuck," and

Donald Trump is "a clown." As for the ordinary citizens who side with the other party, they're "fools" or "morons."[66] The partisan divide is the main point of attack for talk-show hosts, but the cultural divide is a close second. Issues are played less as policy questions than as questions of cultural identity or naked self-interest. On conservative talk shows, gun control isn't about trigger locks or background checks but instead about guns as a cultural identity. Attempts to control guns are portrayed as a liberal plot to destroy a way of life that's been around since frontier days.[67] On liberal talk shows, tax cuts for business are not about making firms more competitive or productive but about corporate greed.[68]

Outrage is also the format of most partisan Internet sites. They seek to inflame the partisan divide by nearly every conceivable means, including, in some cases, outright lies and distortions. One device is *fake news*—entirely fictional stories that originate on the Internet and aim to undermine the opposing party. Early in the coronavirus outbreak in 2020, stories circulated that the disease was "a hoax" devised by Democrats to damage President Trump's chances of winning the 2020 election.

Partisan outlets are the leading source of disinformation. Harvard University's Jochai Benkler, Robert Faris, and Hal Roberts examined four million media messages, concluding that partisan media are distinctive for their "disinformation, lies, and half-truths."[69] Unlike traditional news outlets, which primarily impart information, partisan outlets are "bias confirming." They invent realities that align with the partisan bias of audience members who relish being told things that support what they already believe. And it sets them up for manipulation by other purveyors of disinformation, as in the case of the Russian hackers who flooded social media with false claims during the 2016 and 2020 U.S. presidential elections (see "How the U.S. Differs").

A long-standing issue is whether traditional news outlets, although professing to treat the Republican and Democratic Parties by the same standards, are politically biased. The claim of bias has been made by followers of both parties but most often by Republicans.[70] Trump is among them, having attacked the traditional press as the "liberal media," "Democratic media," "lying media," and "left-wing media." Scholars have studied media bias extensively and have found little evidence to support the claim that the traditional media are a covert instrument of the Democratic Party.[71] Overall there's a slight liberal tilt to their coverage but it's contingent on the nature of the audiences. Traditional outlets with more liberal audiences tend to slant their coverage in a liberal direction whereas those with more conservative audiences tilt somewhat conservative in their coverage, suggesting that marketing more than partisanship is driving the coverage.[72]

The situation may be changing, however. Trump's attacks on the media and disregard for presidential norms turned many traditional news outlets against him. His news coverage while in office was the most negative ever recorded. A study of news reporting during the 2020 presidential campaign found that Trump's coverage in a traditional news outlet was more negative even than Biden's coverage on Fox News, leading the study's author to conclude that the "coverage was a clear departure from that expected of a mainstream news outlet, fitting instead the pattern expected of a partisan outlet."[73] Since the 2020 election, traditional news outlets have been harshly critical of Trump for repeating his claim that the election was stolen and of Republican lawmakers who have used the claim to pass dozens of state laws restricting ballot access. The traditional media may be entering a phase where their negative coverage is aimed mainly at Republicans. Earlier, both parties had to equally confront media criticism. Before Trump took office, the president with the most negative press was Democrat Bill Clinton. During his eight years in office, there was not a single quarter in which his favorable coverage outpaced his unfavorable coverage.[74]

HOW THE U.S. DIFFERS

CRITICAL THINKING THROUGH COMPARISONS

Russian Interference in Western Elections

After the 2016 presidential campaign, Americans became aware of Russia's attempts to influence the outcome of the election through social media messaging. They learned about it a second time in 2020 when Russia again tried to sway the outcome. What many Americans might not know is that Russia has used social media messaging to disrupt elections in a dozen Western countries, including Germany, France, Great Britain, Norway, the Netherlands, and Austria.

Q: Is there a pattern to Russia's efforts?

A: Russia's disinformation efforts seek to pit citizens against each other.[75] A widely circulated fake story during the 2016 U.S. election, for instance, tried to stir up anger against Muslims by falsely claiming that Muslim men in Michigan with multiple wives were collecting welfare checks for each of them.[76] Russia has also tried to stir up resentment to weaken Western alliances. In referendums in Britain and the Netherlands, for example, Russia's

Continued

disinformation efforts were aimed at undermining support for the European Union. Russia has also tried to tilt popular support toward right-wing parties on the assumption that such parties undermine national unity. Russia used that strategy during the French, Austrian, and Bulgarian elections.

Russia's disinformation efforts are not confined to citizens of Western democracies. In the leadup to Russia's invasion of Ukraine, the Russian people were falsely told that Ukraine had a neo-Nazi government and was part of Russia rather than a country in its own right. The false claims heightened Russians' support for the invasion of Ukraine.[77]

Russia's disinformation apparatus includes a "troll factory" located in St. Petersburg. Each of the 1,000 "trolls" at the "factory" operates at least 10 accounts and is expected to send 50 fake, inflammatory, or misleading messages a day from each account.[78]

The Entertainment Function

If asked, most Americans would distinguish between news and entertainment. Yet, news outlets have never fully made the distinction. The **entertainment function**—making the news pleasurable to attract an audience—is nearly as old as the media themselves. Legendary publisher William Randolph Hearst, who helped pioneer yellow journalism, said that an "editor has no objection to facts if they are also novel. But he would prefer a novelty that is not a fact to a fact that is not a novelty."[79]

Audience competition is what drives news outlets to find ways to make their news more entertaining. It prompted Hearst in the early 1900s to use nearly every device imaginable to lure readers. And it was competition in the 1980s that produced what has come to be known as soft news. The introduction of cable programming in that decade had suddenly given viewers a wide range of choices. During the period when the three broadcast networks—ABC, CBS, and NBC—had a monopoly on the television audience, the news was the only programming available at the dinner hour. But cable expanded viewers' options, everything from HBO's movies to ESPN's sporting events, and the news audience began to shrink. Soon thereafter, a theatrical style of news emerged that was designed to compete with cable entertainment. It was aimed at marginal news consumers—those who might stay tuned in if the news was made more sensational and entertaining. Celebrity gossip, hard-luck stories, good-luck tales, lurid crimes, scandals in high places, and other human interest stories became a larger part of the news mix. Such stories were labeled **soft news** to distinguish them from traditional **hard news** stories (breaking events involving public figures, major issues, or significant disruptions to daily routines).[80] A few news outlets, including *The New York Times*, *The Wall Street Journal*, and

Although politics has long been a source of comic material, cable television bred a new form—an entire show built around politics. One of the first such programs was Jon Stewart's *The Daily Show*. Pictured here is Trevor Noah who succeeded Stewart in 2015 and hosted the show for seven years before stepping down in 2022. (Brian Cahn/ZUMA Wire/ZUMA Press,Inc./Alamy Stock Photo)

The Washington Post, largely stuck to the old way of doing things, but most outlets softened their news to attract followers.[81]

Many of the newer digital publishers have embraced an entertainment strategy, doing little in the way of serious original reporting while letting readers' tastes drive what they distribute.[82] In posting its stories, Upworthy puts out a large sampling using a dozen or more versions of the headline. Whichever headline attracts the most attention—usually a sensationalized version of "You Won't Believe What Just Happened"—is then slapped onto the rest of the feed.[83] Hundreds of news outlets use a service called CrowdTangle, which alerts them to topics that are trending on social media, a signal to begin producing stories on that topic until the traffic slows down.[84]

The blurring of the line between news and entertainment is clearest in political humor shows. One of the first was *The Daily Show*, hosted by Jon Stewart. Its format had the look of a conventional newscast, but its content aimed to entertain—its headlines were sensationalized and slanted, its news reports poked fun at those in power, and its editorials blended satire with serious commentary. It was a rating hit and helped spawn similar programs, many of which are carried on Comedy Central and other nontraditional news channels.

CITIZEN ACTION!
SELF-GOVERNMENT

Before the Internet, freedom of the press was enjoyed only by the very few who owned or worked in the news media. With the Internet, the opportunity for citizen communication, though not unlimited, is greater than at any previous time. Take advantage of the opportunity. Meetup.com is one of many social media sites where you can participate in public affairs forums.

Although sensationalism can draw an audience, it can also distract it, and sometimes mislead it. When newscasts play up crime (the "if it bleeds, it leads" formula), viewers have a fear of crime that exceeds the actual risk.[85] CNN's coverage of the Ebola epidemic in 2014 provides another example. When the first Ebola patient in the United States was diagnosed, CNN reporters speculated on what would happen if Ebola, which is transmitted by direct contact with bodily fluids, went airborne and could be caught in the same way as the common cold. "Ebola in the Air? A Nightmare That Could Happen" is how CNN headlined an online story that also warned that most people who get Ebola die. In fact, according to the World Health Organization, there is *no* recorded case in human history in which a fluid-transmitted disease, like Ebola, has transformed itself into an airborne-transmitted disease. Although no one who contracted Ebola while in the United States died from it, the sensationalized coverage frightened millions of Americans, even those hundreds of miles from the nearest Ebola patient. A Pew Research Center poll found that a third of Americans worried that they or a family member would catch the disease.[86]

THE ASSAULT ON REASON

Writing in the 1980s, when the marketing strategy of blending soft news with hard news was gaining strength, New York University's Neal Postman warned of the consequences of treating news as a form of entertainment. "I am saying something far more serious than that we are being deprived of authentic information," Postman wrote. "I am saying we are losing our sense of what it means to be well informed. Ignorance is always correctable. But what shall we do if we take ignorance to be knowledge?"[87]

Postman wrote those words before the emergence of partisan networks, talk shows, and blogs. They have turned news into an instrument of partisan warfare, promoting alternative realities to promote their partisan goals. The danger is as serious as the one of which Postman warned. When citizens embrace opposing realities, they lose their ability to work and talk with each other.[88]

There's yet another assault on our ability to reason. It's the distraction that comes with the accelerated pace of messaging. As the media have become a larger part of Americans' lives—the typical citizen now devotes about 10 hours a day to media—the number of messages to which people are exposed has multiplied.[89] The typical American is now exposed to hundreds of discrete messages

Studies have found that multitasking and the rapid pace of digital messaging are contributing to declining attention spans and rising levels of misinformation. (JKstock/Shutterstock)

every day, everything from the ads they see on television to the social media messages they receive to the images and statements they encounter in news stories. Message abundance might be thought to be a good thing. However, as Nobel Laureate Herbert Simon noted, message abundance creates information overload, reducing people's ability to concentrate and think clearly.[90] A 2015 Microsoft study used surveys and electroencephalograms (EEGs) to study the length of people's attention spans, finding that individuals on average lose their concentration after 8 seconds. When the same study was conducted 15 years earlier, the average was 12 seconds. And just how short is an 8-second attention span? Before the 2015 study was conducted, the baseline for comparisons was the attention span of a goldfish, which is 9 seconds.[91]

Digital tools magnify the problem. Cell phones, TV remotes, and other devices offer instant gratification, conditioning us to seek ever more of it. The typical American adult sends and receives more than 50 texts a day. Young adults send and receive more than 100 on average.[92] Even the act of reading a newspaper has accelerated. In the 1970s, the average reader spent more than 30 minutes reading the printed newspaper. It's now less than half that amount of time.[93] When people read the online version of the paper, the time is even shorter.[94]

During the era of the information commons, citizens had a degree of protection from information overload by the fact that the messages were fewer and mutually reinforcing. That protection has been lost. News sources today offer conflicting messages delivered at a fast clip, thereby increasing the likelihood that confusion and misinformation will result.

The founders of the United States believed that an informed public was the best guarantee that the U.S. governing system would last. A year after the Constitution was ratified, Thomas Jefferson wrote, "wherever the people are well informed they can be trusted with their own government; that whenever things get so far wrong as to attract their notice, they may be relied on to set them to rights."[95] Today's media system works against the creation of the well-informed public that Jefferson envisioned, fostering instead a distracted and misinformed public.[96]

SUMMARY

In the nation's first century, the media were closely allied with the political parties but gradually freed themselves from this dependence and developed a form of reporting known as objective journalism, which emphasized fair and accurate accounts of newsworthy developments. It contributed to the emergence of the information commons, which was characterized by a shared understanding of reality that had a moderating and depolarizing effect on American politics.

The objective reporting model still largely governs the news reporting of traditional media outlets—daily newspapers and broadcasters—but does not hold for many of the newer media outlets—partisan networks, political talk shows, political bloggers, and the like. They convey information through a partisan lens, creating echo chambers where their audiences are largely told what they'd like to believe. Media echo chambers have contributed to America's heightened level of party polarization and misinformation.

Media outlets perform five functions. Through their signaling function, media outlets communicate information to the public about important developments affecting their lives, which affects what they think and talk about (agenda setting). Through their common-carrier function, media outlets provide political leaders a channel through which to address the public about what they're doing and advocating. Traditional media outlets act as a common carrier for both parties, whereas partisan media serve that function only for the party with whom they align. Through a third function, that of watchdog, the media act to protect the public by exposing deceitful, careless, or corrupt officials although, here again, partisan media concentrate only on wrongdoing by those in the opposing party. The fourth function, that of partisanship, has grown in significance with the rise of partisan media outlets. Some media outlets are, in effect, auxiliaries of the party they favor. The fifth function, that of entertainment, derives mainly from media outlets' need to attract and hold an audience if they are to stay in business. Though driven by the profit motive, the function has political consequences by affecting what citizens know and believe.

Trends in the media over the past few decades constitute an "assault on reason." Misinformation is at a dangerously high level, as is party polarization. Rather than working to deflate these developments, media outlets have been contributing to them.

CRITICAL THINKING ZONE

KEY TERMS

agenda setting (*p. 272*)
common-carrier function (*p. 273*)
disinformation (*p. 271*)
echo chambers (*p. 265*)
entertainment function (*p. 280*)
filter bubbles (*p. 269*)
framing (*p. 274*)
hard news (*p. 280*)
information commons (*p. 262*)

misinformation (*p. 271*)
news (*p. 261*)
news media (press) (*p. 261*)
objective journalism (*p. 264*)
partisan function (*p. 277*)
priming (*p. 274*)
signaling (signaler) function (*p. 272*)
soft news (*p. 280*)
watchdog function (*p. 274*)

APPLYING THE ELEMENTS OF CRITICAL THINKING

Conceptualizing: Define *high-choice media system*. How does it contribute to a less informed public? To a more partisan public?

Synthesizing: Contrast the media's watchdog role with their common-carrier role. Is there a tension between these roles—does carrying out one of them work against carrying out the other?

Analyzing: What are the consequences of the fact that the press is charged with informing the public but at the same time needs to attract an audience in order to make a profit and fund its news-gathering operations?

OF POSSIBLE INTEREST

A Book Worth Reading: Yochai Benkler, Robert Faris, and Hal Roberts, *Network Propaganda: Manipulation, Disinformation, and Radicalization in American Politics* (New York: Oxford University Press, 2018). This pathbreaking book explores the media networks that spread disinformation.

A Website Worth Visiting: www.mediatenor.com Media Tenor is a nonpartisan organization that analyzes U.S. and overseas news coverage on a daily basis. The site has information of interest to anyone curious about tendencies in news coverage, such as how various news outlets portray the president.

CONGRESS: BALANCING NATIONAL GOALS AND LOCAL INTERESTS

❝ There are two Congresses. . . . The tight-knit complex world of Capitol Hill is a long way from [the member's district], in perspective and outlook as well as in miles. ❞

ROGER DAVIDSON AND WALTER OLESZEK[1]

It was a bill the likes of which Washington had rarely seen in recent years. A bipartisan group of senators had worked out the framework for what would become the 2021 Infrastructure and Jobs Act, a $550 billion spending bill that constituted the largest infrastructure investment in the nation's history. Included was money for highways, bridges, and mass transit, as well as money to expand broadband access. Every state would share in the funding.

The infrastructure spending bill illustrates the dual nature of Congress. It is both a lawmaking institution for the country and a representative assembly for states and districts.[2] Members of Congress have a duty to serve both the interests of the nation as a whole and the interests of their individual constituencies. The spending bill addressed the nation's need for critical infrastructure while simultaneously targeting particular local needs. The nation's needs are of concern to lawmakers, but so, too, are local needs because members' reelection depends on the support of the voters back home.[3]

The framers of the Constitution regarded Congress as the leading branch of the federal government and granted it the highest power of a democratic government, which is the power to make laws. Congress was even granted the authority to decide the form and function of the executive departments and the lower courts. No executive agency or lower court can exist unless authorized by Congress.

The positioning of Congress as the first among equals in a system of divided powers reflected the framers' faith in representative institutions. Nevertheless, the framers' vision of a preeminent Congress has not fully stood the test of time. Power has gradually shifted from Congress to the presidency, and today both institutions have a central role in lawmaking. This chapter emphasizes the following points:

- *Congressional incumbents get reelected at a very high rate.* Holding congressional office provides incumbents with substantial resources (free publicity, staff, and legislative influence) that give them (particularly House members) a major advantage in election campaigns.

- *Leadership in Congress is provided by party leaders, including the Speaker of the House and the Senate majority leader.* In recent decades, congressional Republicans have become more uniformly conservative and congressional Democrats have become more uniformly liberal, which has made it easier for party leaders to take policy positions that will be supported by their party's members.

- *Much of the work of Congress is done through its committees, each of which has its leadership and its designated policy jurisdiction.*

- *Because of its fragmented structure, Congress is not well suited to take the lead on major national policies, which has allowed the president to assume this role. At the same time, Congress is well organized to handle policies of narrower scope.*

- *Congress's policymaking role is based on three major functions: lawmaking, representation, and oversight.*

CONGRESS AS A CAREER: ELECTION TO CONGRESS

"Single-minded seekers of reelection" is how political scientist David Mayhew described members of Congress.[4] They are professional politicians, and a seat in the House or Senate is about as high on the political ladder as they can expect to rise. The pay is attractive (about $175,000 a year), as is the prestige of their office. It's not surprising that members of Congress seek to stay in office, a goal

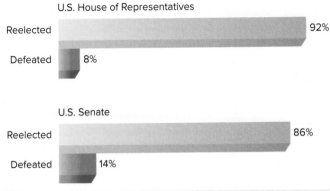

figure 11-1   REELECTION RATES OF HOUSE AND SENATE INCUMBENTS

Congressional incumbents have a very good chance of winning another term, as indicated by the reelection rates of U.S. representatives and senators who sought reelection during the last six congressional elections. The actual chances of reelection are somewhat less than the rates indicate. Faced with a reelection campaign that they might lose, some incumbents chose not to seek reelection.

that most of them achieve (see Figure 11-1). **Incumbents** (as officeholders are called) have about a 90 percent probability of winning reelection.

Although Congress is an institution that operates by established rules and norms, members' preoccupation with reelection is a key to understanding Congress. Members seldom act in ways that will put their reelection at risk.

Using Incumbency to Stay in Congress

Incumbents have high reelection rates in part because most states and congressional districts are so strongly Republican or Democratic that candidates of the stronger party seldom lose. No more than 60 of the 435 House seats—about 1 in 7—are competitive enough that each party has a realistic chance of victory. In any case, whether their constituency is lopsided or competitive, incumbents have built-in advantages over their challengers, as will now be explained.

The Service Strategy: Taking Care of Constituents   Incumbents promote their reelection prospects by catering to their **constituency,** a term that refers to the people residing in their state or district. Members of Congress pay attention to constituency opinions when taking positions on legislation, and they work hard to get their share of federal spending projects. Such projects are often derided as **pork** (or *pork-barrel spending*) by outsiders but are welcomed by those who live in the state or district that gets a federally funded project, such as a new hospital, research center, or highway. Incumbents also respond to their constituents' requests, a practice known as the **service strategy**. Whether a

CITIZEN ACTION!
SELF-GOVERNMENT

Each year, thousands of college students serve as summer interns in Congress, state legislatures, and city councils, an experience that can make them more effective citizens and lead a career in public service. The student support office or political science department at some colleges has information about legislative internships, or you can apply directly to a state legislator, city councilor, or member of Congress. Make the request early because some offices get more applicants than they can accommodate.

constituent is seeking information about a government program or looking for help in obtaining a federal benefit, the representative's staff is ready to assist.

It might be assumed that congressional staffs spend most of their time on legislative matters but constituency service and public relations—efforts that can pay off in votes on Election Day—take up most of their time.[5] Each House member receives an annual office allowance of roughly $1 million with which to hire up to 18 permanent staff members.[6] Senators receive annual office allowances that range between $3 million and $5 million, depending on their state's population. Smaller-state senators have staffs of about 30 people, whereas larger-state senators have staffs closer in number to 50 people.[7] Although subject to limits, each member of Congress is also provided free trips back to their home state and free mailings to constituent households (a privilege known as the "frank"). These trips and mailings, along with press releases and other public relations efforts, help incumbents build name recognition and constituent support—major advantages in their reelection campaigns. Legislators in other Western democracies do not have the large personal staff or the travel and publicity budget of a member of Congress. A member of the British parliament, for example, has a staff of three people.[8]

Campaign Fundraising: Raking in the Money   Running for Congress is costly and has gotten increasingly expensive decade by decade (see Figure 11-2). Rarely do incumbents have trouble raising the money it takes to run a robust campaign, whereas their challengers often fall far short of their funding needs.[9] In recent House elections, for example, incumbents have outspent their challengers by roughly five to one on average.[10] Senate races are more expensive than House races, typically costing more than $20 million. Senate incumbents also have a fundraising advantage, although less so than House incumbents. Senate races often attract high-profile challengers who are adept at fundraising or wealthy enough to personally underwrite most of their campaign.

Incumbents' past campaigns and constituent service give them a list of potential contributors, which gives them an edge over their challengers. Individual contributions, most of which are $200 or less, account for the single largest share of all funds received by congressional candidates and are obtained mainly through fundraising events, websites, and direct-mail solicitation.[11] Incumbents also have an edge with political action committees (PACs), which are the fundraising units

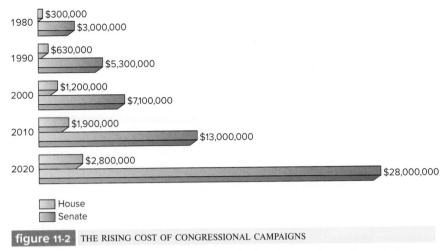

1980
$300,000
$3,000,000

1990
$630,000
$5,300,000

2000
$1,200,000
$7,100,000

2010
$1,900,000
$13,000,000

2020
$2,800,000
$28,000,000

House
Senate

figure 11-2   THE RISING COST OF CONGRESSIONAL CAMPAIGNS

Each decade, the cost of running for congressional office has risen sharply as campaign techniques—TV advertising, opinion polling, and so on—have become more elaborate and sophisticated. The increase in spending can be seen from a comparison of the approximate median spending by both candidates per House or Senate seat at 10-year intervals, beginning in 1980. (*Source:* Federal Election Commission.)

of interest groups (see Chapter 9). Most PACs are reluctant to oppose an incumbent unless the candidate appears beatable. More than 85 percent of PAC contributions in recent elections have gone to incumbents.[12,13]

Redistricting: Favorable Boundaries for House Incumbents   House members, but not senators, have a final electoral advantage. Because House incumbents are hard to unseat, they are always a force to be reckoned with, a fact that is apparent during redistricting. Every 10 years, after each population census, the 435 seats in the House of Representatives are reallocated among the states in proportion to their population. This process is called **reapportionment**. States that have gained population since the last census may acquire additional House seats, while those that have lost population may lose seats. After the 2020 census, for example, Texas and Florida were among the states that gained House seats, and California and New York were among those that lost seats.

States are required by law to have House districts that are as nearly equal in population as possible. As a result, they must redraw their district boundaries after each census to account for population shifts within the state during the previous 10 years. (The Senate is not affected by population change because each state has two senators regardless of its size.) In most states, the responsibility for redrawing House election districts—a process called **redistricting—** rests with the respective state legislatures. The party that controls the legislature typically redraws the boundaries in a way that favors candidates of its party—a process called **gerrymandering**. (Among the few exceptions to this practice are Arizona, California, and Iowa, which entrust redistricting to an independent commission.)

Incumbents typically benefit from gerrymandering. When redistricting, the majority party in the state legislature places enough of its party's voters in its incumbents' districts to ensure their reelection. Many of the minority party's incumbents are also awarded a safe district. If opposing incumbents have a strong base of support and would be difficult to defeat, the optimal strategy is to pack their district with as many voters of their party as possible so that, in effect, the party "wastes" votes, reducing its competitiveness elsewhere in the state. Partisan gerrymandering can have the effect of giving the state legislature rather than the voters the power to choose representatives, but the Supreme Court has declined to limit the practice.[14]

Although gerrymandering is widely thought to be the reason so many House seats are not competitive, a more important reason is the increased geographic concentration of Republican and Democratic voters, a development that writer

Gerrymandering in most states is controlled by the state legislature, and the party in control of the legislature draws the boundaries of congressional districts in a way that enables its candidates to win as many seats as possible. Although the choice of House members in these districts rests in reality with the party that drew the boundaries and not the voters, the Supreme Court has refused to limit the practice. (Evelyn Hockstein/The Washington Post/Getty Images)

Bill Bishop calls "The Big Sort."[15] In recent decades, most states have become more heavily Republican or Democratic. And, within states, urban areas have become more heavily Democratic, while rural areas have become more heavily Republican, which has made the House districts in these areas less competitive.[16]

Pitfalls of Incumbency

Incumbency is not without its risks. Senate and House incumbents can fall victim to disruptive issues, personal misconduct, turnout swings, strong challengers, and campaign money.

Disruptive Issues   Most elections are not waged in the context of disruptive issues, but, when they are, incumbents are at greater risk. When voters are angry about existing political conditions, they are more likely to believe that those in power should be tossed from office. The 2018 congressional election, which was waged in the context of contentious issues such as immigration, gun control, and income inequality, saw the retirement or defeat of an unusually large number of incumbents. The majority of them were Republicans, which was the party in power at the time of the election.

Personal Misconduct   Life in Washington can be fast-paced, glamorous, and expensive, and some members of Congress get caught up in influence peddling, sex scandals, and other forms of misconduct. "The first thing to being reelected is to stay away from scandal, even minor scandal," says political scientist John Hibbing.[17] More than a few members of Congress have lost their reelection bids or resigned as a result of personal scandals. California representative Duncan Hunter, for example, resigned his seat in 2020 after pleading guilty to diverting campaign funds for personal use, including shipping his pet rabbit across the country by plane.

Turnout Variation: The Midterm Election Problem   In 22 of the last 25 **midterm elections**—those that occur midway through a president's term—the president's party has lost House seats. The 2022 midterm elections, when the Democratic Party lost seats, fit that pattern. The tendency is explained in part by what political scientists call *surge and decline theory*.[18] There is a "surge" in the number of voters in a presidential election, followed by a substantial "decline" in the number who turn out for the midterm election. People who vote only in the presidential election tend to have weaker party ties and are more responsive to the issues of the moment. These issues typically favor one party, which contributes to the success not only of its presidential candidate but also of its congressional candidates. Two years later in the midterm elections, many of these voters stay home, and those who do go to the polls vote largely along party lines. Accordingly, congressional candidates of the president's party do not get the boost of extra votes that they enjoyed in the previous election, and House seats are lost as a result.[19] Moreover, some voters treat the midterm elections as a referendum on the president's performance. Presidents usually lose popularity during their term of office as a result of the policy decisions they make. As the president's support declines, so does voters' support of congressional candidates of the president's party.[20] When the 2022 midterm elections were held, President Biden's approval rating was well below 50 percent, which helped Republicans pick up enough seats to take control of the House of Representatives.[21]

Primary Election Challengers   Primary elections can also be a time of risk for incumbents, especially those who hold politically moderate views. If they are confronted with a strong challenger from the extreme wing of their party, they stand a chance of losing because hardcore partisans are more likely than party moderates to vote in primary elections.[22] Some moderate incumbents have responded by shifting their position on legislation toward the extreme wing of their party.[23] Others have risked the possibility of a primary challenger and have not always survived, as happened to House majority leader Eric Cantor who lost in a 2014 Republican primary to a conservative political unknown after saying that Republicans should grant legal status to "Dreamers" (undocumented aliens brought to the United States as children).[24]

Never has the risk of a primary election challenger been more evident than in the case of the 10 House Republican members who voted to impeach Donald Trump for his role in the assault on the U.S. Capitol on January 6, 2001. Each of them faced the prospect of a Trump-backed right-wing challenger in the 2022 Republican primaries. Four of them chose not to seek reelection, and four of them lost in the primary election.

General Election Challengers: A Problem for Senators   Incumbents can also be vulnerable to strong challengers. Senators particularly often find themselves running against a high-ranking politician, such as their state's governor or attorney general. Such opponents have an established political base and can be expected to mount a strong challenge. Republicans might have captured the Senate in the 2022 midterm elections except for nominating several weak contenders, helping otherwise vulnerable Democratic incumbents to win reelection.

House incumbents are less likely to face a prominent challenger. A House seat is often not attractive enough to induce a leading politician to risk losing to the incumbent.[25]

A New Threat: Super PACs   Although incumbents ordinarily have a funding advantage over their challengers, the situation can change if they appear vulnerable. Although this threat has existed for years, it has increased with the emergence of super PACs, which can pour millions of dollars into a race (see Chapters 8 and 9). This scenario played itself out in the 2018 Senate race in Missouri, which pitted the Democratic incumbent Claire McCaskill against Republican Josh Hawley. Their race turned out to be one of the most expensive campaigns in Senate history, with much of the money coming from outside donors. McCaskill lost her reelection bid, running against not only Hawley but also the $40 million that outside groups spent to defeat her.[26]

Who Are the Winners in Congressional Elections?

The Constitution places only a few restrictions on who can be elected to Congress. House members must be at least 25 years of age and have been a citizen for at least 7 years. For senators, the age and citizenship requirements are 30 years and 9 years, respectively. Senators and representatives alike must be residents of the state from which they are elected.

However, if the formal restrictions are minimal, the informal limits are substantial. Although lawyers constitute less than 1 percent of the population, they make up a fourth of the House and more than half of the Senate. Attorneys enter politics in large numbers in part because knowledge of the law is an asset in Congress and because campaign publicity—even if a candidate loses—is a good way to boost a law practice. Along with lawyers, professionals such as business executives, educators, bankers, and journalists account for roughly 90 percent of congressional membership.[27] Blue-collar workers,

HOW THE 50 STATES DIFFER

CRITICAL THINKING THROUGH COMPARISONS

Women in the State Legislatures

Women have had more success in gaining election to state legislatures than to Congress, partly because there is more turnover and less of an incumbency advantage at the state level, which creates more opportunities for newcomers to run and win. Three in 10 state legislators are women, a sixfold increase since 1970. Nevada (59 percent) is the only state where a majority are women. Colorado (45 percent) has the second-highest percentage. West Virginia (13 percent) and Tennessee (15 percent) have the lowest.

Continued

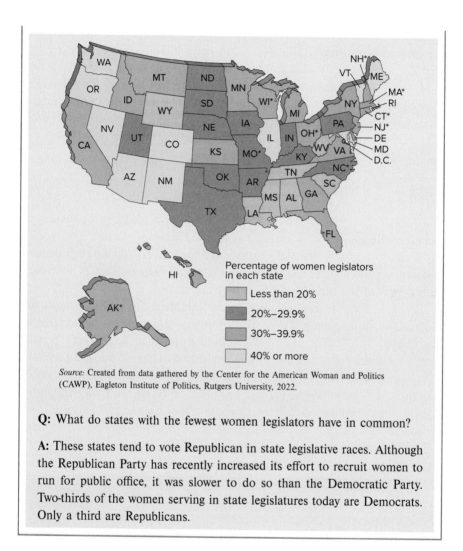

Source: Created from data gathered by the Center for the American Woman and Politics (CAWP), Eagleton Institute of Politics, Rutgers University, 2022.

Q: What do states with the fewest women legislators have in common?

A: These states tend to vote Republican in state legislative races. Although the Republican Party has recently increased its effort to recruit women to run for public office, it was slower to do so than the Democratic Party. Two-thirds of the women serving in state legislatures today are Democrats. Only a third are Republicans.

clerical employees, and homemakers are seldom elected to Congress. Farmers and ranchers fare better; several House members from rural districts have an agricultural background. Although the demographic imbalance does not mean that the interests of other groups are ignored by Congress, the imbalance does favor the interests of groups that are heavily represented.[28]

Women and minorities are also underrepresented in Congress. Although the number of women in Congress is 10 times that of a half-century ago, they account for only slightly more than a fourth of the membership (see Chapter 5). Minorities account for slightly less than a fourth.

PARTIES AND PARTY LEADERSHIP

The U.S. Congress is a **bicameral legislature**, meaning it has two chambers, the House and the Senate. Both chambers are organized largely along party lines. At the start of each two-year congressional term, party members in each chamber meet to elect their **party leaders**, the individuals who will lead their party's efforts in the chamber. Party members also meet periodically in a closed session, which is called a **party caucus**, to plan strategy, develop issues, and resolve policy differences. (Table 11-1 shows the party composition in Congress during the past decade.)

Party Unity in Congress

Political parties are the strongest force within Congress. Parties are the primary source of unity among members of Congress, as well as the primary source of division.

The partisan divide in Congress is wider than in the past. Earlier, Republicans had both a conservative wing and a progressive wing, while Democrats had a liberal northern wing and a conservative southern wing. Since then, the Republican progressive wing and the Democratic southern wing have withered. In a recent study, political scientists Keith Poole and Howard Rosenthal found in both the House and the Senate that the least conservative Republican was more conservative than the most conservative Democrat.[29]

table 11-1	THE NUMBER OF DEMOCRATS AND REPUBLICANS IN THE HOUSE OF REPRESENTATIVES AND THE SENATE, 2015–2024				
	2015–2016	2017–2018	2019–2020	2021–2022	2023–2024
House					
Democrats	184	194	236*	222	214
Republicans	251*	241*	199	213	221*
Senate					
Democrats	46	48	47	50	50
Republicans	54*	52	53	50	49

*Chamber not controlled by the president's party. Independents are included in the total for the party with which they caucused. Figures based on election results. Subsequent changes due to resignation or death are not included. Senate total for 2023–2024 excludes a Georgia seat that was scheduled for a run-off election at time of text's publication.

As a result, each congressional party has attained a high level of **party unity**—the situation where members of a party band together on legislation and stand against the opposite party.[30] The tendency can be seen by looking at *roll-call votes*, which are votes on which each member's vote is officially recorded, as opposed to voice votes where the members simply call out an unrecorded "aye" or "nay" on a bill. Since the mid-1980s, party-line voting on roll calls has risen sharply (see "Party Polarization: Partisan Conflict in Congress"). A case in point is The American Rescue Plan of 2021, which provided economic relief to counter the impact of the COVID-19 pandemic. Whereas 100 percent of Senate Democrats and 99 percent of House Democrats voted for it, no Republican senator or House member backed it.

As the partisan divide in Congress has widened, the number of lawmakers in the political center has declined. Congressional moderates were once numerous enough to force other lawmakers to join them in the middle if they wanted a say in shaping legislation. Today, there are too few moderates in Congress to force other members to engage in compromise.[31] Legislative deadlock has frequently resulted. Neither Republicans nor Democrats have been willing to make the compromises necessary to enact legislation.

The fact that the parties are so closely matched has intensified the conflict between them. Congressional majorities in the past two decades are the smallest in the nation's history. Each party has recognized that it could win, or lose, control of the House or Senate in the next election, which gives it an incentive to deny the opposing party any claim to legislative success. The minority party in Congress has tried to block the policy initiatives of the party in power, whereas the majority party has done everything possible to marginalize the weaker party to undermine its credibility. Each party portrays the other in stark terms—too extreme and too beholden to special interests to govern in the interests of ordinary Americans. As Frances Lee notes in *Insecure Majorities*, members of Congress are engaged in "messaging" rather than "governing."[32] In positioning themselves on bills, they are sometimes less concerned with whether their position will prevail in Congress than whether it will attract votes in the next election. Reflecting on the partisan fights and policy deadlock, a longtime congressional veteran said that Congress has become a "campaign stage" rather than a place to debate legislation.[33] (The impact of heightened partisanship on Congress is discussed further in a later section of the chapter.)

As congressional partisanship has intensified, the public's image of Congress has plummeted (see Figure 11-3). In the period before partisan deadlock gripped Congress, it had a somewhat respectable approval rating. Today, only one in five Americans approve of the job that Congress is doing.

| P A R T Y | Conflicting Ideas |
| POLARIZATION | |

Partisan Conflict in Congress

Until the 1990s, most roll-call votes in Congress did not pit a majority of Republicans on one side of the bill against a majority of Democrats on the other side. Since then, as the graph indicates, roll-call votes have usually split along party lines. Underlying these developments is the eclipse of the Democratic Party's conservative southern wing and the Republican Party's progressive northern wing. As congressional Democrats have become more uniformly liberal and congressional Republicans more uniformly conservative, the overlap between the congressional parties has diminished, resulting in increased party-line voting on legislation.

Percentage of roll-call votes in the House and Senate in which a majority of Democrats voted against a majority of Republicans

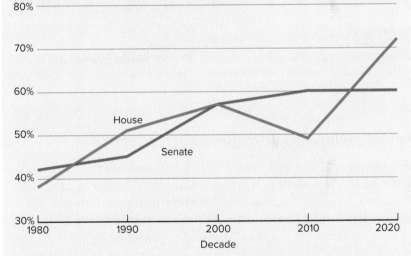

Source: Brookings Institution's Vital Statistics on Congress. The numbers are the average for the previous decade. The 2020 numbers, for example, are the House and Senate averages for the 2011–2020 period.

Q: Some observers claim that heightened partisanship in Congress is crippling the institution as a legislative body. Party disputes on everything from health care to immigration policy have produced legislative deadlock and delay. Do you share the view that excessive partisanship is undermining the legislative process, or do you think members of Congress should stick to their partisan principles, whatever the consequences?

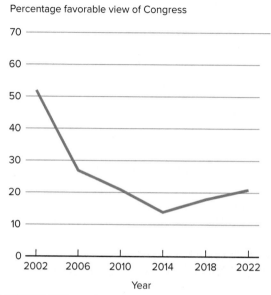

Percentage favorable view of Congress

figure 11-3 PUBLIC APPROVAL OF CONGRESS

As Congress has become more polarized, animosity and policy deadlock have increased. One result has been a decline in Americans' approval of how Congress is doing its work. (*Source:* Gallup polls)

Party Leadership in Congress

Each party has House and Senate leaders who are expected to advance the party's legislative positions. However, unlike party leaders in most national legislatures, those in Congress cannot assume that party members will automatically follow their lead. In other legislatures, members who fail to support the party's position on a bill can be denied renomination by the party organization in the next election. In the United States, however, nomination occurs through primary elections, which gives incumbents the freedom to decide for themselves how they will vote on a bill.

Indeed, the fact that Democratic and Republican lawmakers tend to vote in line with other members of their party on most bills is due less to the influence of party leaders than to the fact their views are more closely aligned with those of lawmakers from their party.[34] Nevertheless, party leaders do wield influence, particularly if they're adept at crafting legislation that matches the desires of their party's members.

House Leaders The Constitution specifies that the House of Representatives will be presided over by a Speaker elected by the vote of its members. Since the majority party has the largest number of members, it also has the most votes, and the Speaker has always been a member of the majority party.

The Speaker of the House has been called the nation's most powerful elected national official aside from the president. The Speaker's power owes primarily to the large size of the House. With 435 members, it requires strict rules to operate effectively, and the Speaker is in charge of many of the rules. The Speaker's formal powers include the right to speak first during House debate on legislation and the power to recognize members—that is, to permit them to speak from the floor. Because the House places a time limit on floor debate, only a relatively few members have a chance to speak on a given bill, and the Speaker can sometimes influence legislation simply by exercising the power to decide who will speak. The Speaker also chooses the chairperson and the majority-party members of the powerful House Rules Committee, which controls the scheduling of bills. Bills that the Speaker supports are likely to reach the floor under favorable conditions. The Speaker might, for example, ask the Rules Committee to delay sending a bill to the floor until there are enough votes to pass it.

Although the Speaker holds a powerful office, the Speaker is ultimately beholden to the party's members. Party members look to the Speaker for leadership on legislative issues, but the Speaker cannot force them to vote for or against a particular bill. As a result, the Speaker must take party members' views into account when developing the party's legislative positions. Rarely will a Speaker, Republican or Democratic, bring a bill to the floor that doesn't have the support of most of the party's members. Republicans even have an informal arrangement known as the *Hastert Rule,* which says that the Speaker should bring a bill to the floor only if it's backed by a majority of House Republicans. A Republican Speaker is not bound by the rule—it's an informal directive—but Republican speakers rarely violate it, knowing that they could lose their position if they do so. In 2015, House Speaker John Boehner (R-Ohio) resigned his position after he ignored the rule on a few key bills and lost the support of his party's most conservative members.[35]

The Speaker is assisted by the House majority leader and the House majority whip, who are chosen by the majority party's members. The majority leader acts as the party's floor leader, organizing the debate on bills and lining up legislative support. The whip has the job of informing party members when key votes are scheduled. When voting takes place, the whip will sometimes stand at a location that is easily seen by party members and let them know where the leadership stands on the bill by giving them a thumbs-up or thumbs-down signal.

The minority party also has its House leaders. The House minority leader heads the party's caucus and plays the leading role in developing the party's legislative positions. The minority leader is assisted by a minority whip.

Senate Leaders   In the Senate, the most important party leadership position is that of the majority leader. This role resembles that of the Speaker of the House in that the Senate majority leader develops the majority party's legislative agenda. Like the Speaker, the Senate majority leader chairs the party's policy committee and acts as the party's voice in the chamber. The majority leader is assisted by the majority whip, who sees to it that members know when important votes are scheduled. The minority party in the Senate also has its leaders. The minority leader and minority whip have roles comparable to those of their House counterparts.

The Senate majority leader's position is less powerful than that of the House Speaker. Unlike the House, where the Speaker directs the floor debate, the Senate has a tradition of unlimited debate. Ordinarily, any senator who wishes to speak on a bill can do so and for any length of time.[36] Also, unlike the Speaker, the Senate majority leader is not the chamber's presiding officer. The Constitution assigns this position to the vice president of the United States. But because the vice president is allowed to vote only in case of a tie, the vice

The House of Representatives, with its 435 members, is a very large legislative body that could not operate effectively without strict rules, such as a limit on the number of House members who are allowed to speak on a bill and for how long. Control over many of these rules rests with the Speaker of the House. (Office of Photography, U.S. House of Representatives.)

president rarely attends Senate sessions. In the absence of the vice president, the right to preside over the Senate resides with the president pro tempore (temporary president), who by tradition is the majority party's most senior member. The position is largely honorary in that the Senate's presiding officer has no power over who's allowed to speak. Any senator who wants to speak on a bill has the right to do so.

Moreover, unlike the Speaker, the Senate majority leader does not strictly control the rules of debate on a bill. Through the House Rules Committee, the Speaker can introduce a bill under what's called a *closed rule*. This rule prohibits amendments to the bill. In contrast, the Senate allows its members to propose amendments to any bill. Such amendments do not have to relate to the bill's content—for example, a senator could propose a climate-change amendment to a bill dealing with defense expenditures. Such amendments are called *riders*. The House does not permit riders. Only amendments that relate directly to a bill's content are allowed in the House, and, as noted, some House bills are debated under a closed rule, which prohibits amendments of any kind.

Because the Senate has only 100 members, it operates differently than the much larger House. Senators are allowed to speak on any bill, which increases their power individually while diminishing the power of party leaders. The Senate majority leader has less control over Senate business than the House Speaker does over House business. (Photograph courtesy of United States Senate)

Finally, the Senate majority leader's power is limited by the fact that senators have greater stature than House members. The Senate is smaller in size—100 members versus 435 House members—which leads senators to act as coequals in a way that House members do not. As well, senators serve six-year terms and do not face the unrelenting reelection pressures faced by House members, who serve two-year terms. Bob Dole of Kansas, who served as Republican Senate leader, said: "There's a lot of free spirits in the Senate. About 100 of them."[37]

Despite these limitations, a Senate majority leader can exert influence by having been entrusted by the majority party's members to develop legislative positions that will keep them united. Mitch McConnell (R-KY) has been both Senate majority and Senate minority leader and has adeptly held his caucus together while thwarting Democratic members' initiatives.[38]

COMMITTEES AND COMMITTEE LEADERSHIP

Most of the work in Congress is conducted through **standing committees**, which are permanent committees with responsibility for particular areas of public policy. At present, there are 20 standing committees in the House and 16 in the Senate (see Table 11-2). Each chamber has, for example, a standing committee that handles foreign policy issues. Other important standing committees are those that deal with agriculture, commerce, the interior (natural resources and public lands), defense, government spending, labor, the judiciary, and taxation. House committees, which average about 35 to 40 members each, are about twice the size of Senate committees.

Each standing committee has legislative authority in that it can draft and rewrite proposed legislation and can recommend to the full chamber the passage or defeat of the bills it handles. Legislative committees in many democracies don't have this power. They simply act as advisory bodies to party leaders.

Except for the Budget Committees, each standing committee has subcommittees with defined jurisdictions. The Senate Committee on Health, Education, Labor, and Pensions, for instance, has three subcommittees: Primary Health and Retirement Security, Children and Families, and Employment and Workplace Safety. Each House and Senate subcommittee has about a dozen members. These few individuals do most of the work and have a leading voice in the fate of most bills in their policy area.

Congress could not manage its workload without the help of its committee system. About 10,000 bills are introduced during each two-year session of Congress. Even though a large majority of these bills do not get serious consideration, Congress would grind to a halt if its work were not divided among its standing committees, each of which has its staff. Unlike the members' personal staff, which concentrate on constituency relations, the committee staffs

| table 11-2 | THE STANDING COMMITTEES OF CONGRESS |

House of Representatives	Senate
Agriculture	Agriculture, Nutrition, and Forestry
Appropriations	Appropriations
Armed Services	Armed Services
Budget	Banking, Housing, and Urban Affairs
Education and Labor	Budget
Energy and Commerce	Commerce, Science, and Transportation
Ethics	Energy and Natural Resources
Financial Services	Environment and Public Works
Foreign Affairs	Finance
Homeland Security	Foreign Relations
House Administration	Health, Education, Labor, and Pensions
Judiciary	Homeland Security and Governmental Affairs
Natural Resources	Judiciary
Oversight and Reform	Rules and Administration
Rules	Small Business and Entrepreneurship
Science, Space, and Technology	Veterans' Affairs
Small Business	
Transportation and Infrastructure	
Veterans' Affairs	
Ways and Means	

focus on legislative issues. They help draft legislation, gather relevant information, and organize hearings.

In addition to its permanent standing committees, Congress also has a few *select committees* that have a designated responsibility but, unlike the standing committees, do not create legislation. An example is the Senate Select Committee on Intelligence, which receives periodic classified briefings from intelligence agencies. Congress also has *joint committees,* composed of members of both houses, which perform advisory functions. The Joint Committee on the Library, for example, oversees the Library of Congress, the largest library in the world. Finally, Congress has *conference committees*–joint committees formed temporarily to work out differences in House and Senate versions of a particular bill.

Committee Jurisdiction

The 1946 Legislative Reorganization Act requires that each bill introduced in Congress be referred to the proper committee. An agricultural bill introduced in the Senate must be assigned to the Senate Agriculture Committee, a bill dealing with foreign affairs must be sent to the Senate Foreign Relations Committee, and so on. This requirement is a source of each committee's power. Even if a committee's members are known to oppose certain types of legislation, bills clearly within its **jurisdiction**—the policy area in which it is authorized to act—must be assigned to it.

Jurisdiction is not always clear-cut, however. Which House committee, for example, should handle a bill addressing the role of financial institutions in global commerce? The Financial Services Committee? The Energy and Commerce Committee? The Foreign Affairs Committee? All committees seek legislative influence, and each is jealous of its jurisdiction, so a bill that overlaps committee boundaries can provoke a "turf war" over which committee will control it.[39] Party leaders can take advantage of these situations by assigning the bill to the committee that is most likely to handle it in the way they would like. However, because party leaders depend on the committees for support, they cannot regularly ignore a committee that has a strong claim to a bill. At times, party leaders have responded by dividing up a bill, handing over some of its provisions to one committee and other provisions to a second committee.

Committee Membership

Each committee has a fixed number of seats, with the majority party holding most of the seats. The ratio of Democrats to Republicans on each committee is approximately the same as the ratio in the full House or Senate, but there is no fixed rule on this matter, and the majority party determines the ratio (mindful that at the next election it could become the chamber's minority party). Members of the House typically serve on only two committees. Senators often serve on four, although they can sit on only two major committees, such as the Finance Committee or the Foreign Relations Committee. Once appointed to a committee, a member can usually choose to stay on it indefinitely. Subcommittee assignments are decided by the committee's members who take into account the members' preferences and the nature of their constituencies.

Because each committee has a fixed number of seats, a committee must have a vacancy before a new member can be appointed. Most vacancies occur after an election as a result of the retirement or defeat of committee members. Each party has a special committee in each chamber that decides who will fill the vacancies. A variety of factors influence these decisions, including members' preferences. Most newly elected members of Congress ask for and receive a

Most of the work in Congress is done through its standing committees, each of which has a policy jurisdiction and the authority to rewrite legislation and hold hearings. Typically, bills reach the floor of the House or Senate after first being shaped and voted on in committee. Pictured here is a Senate committee hearing. (Graeme Sloan/Sipa USA/Alamy Stock Photo)

committee assignment that will allow them to serve their constituents' interests and at the same time improve their reelection chances. For example, when Roger Marshall was elected to the Senate from the agricultural state of Kansas in 2018, he was appointed to the Committee on Agriculture, Nutrition, and Forestry.

Some members of Congress prefer a seat on the most prestigious committees, such as the Senate Foreign Relations Committee or the House Ways and Means (taxation) Committee.[40] Although these committees do not align closely with constituency interests, they handle key policy issues. Factors such as party loyalty, level of knowledge, work ethic, and length of congressional service determine whether a member is granted a seat on a prestigious committee.

Committee Chairs

Each committee (as well as each subcommittee) is headed by a chairperson, who has a degree of control over the committee's work. The chair schedules committee meetings, determines the order in which committee bills are considered, presides over committee discussions, directs the committee's majority staff, and can choose to lead the debate when a committee bill goes to the floor of the chamber for a vote.

HOW THE U.S. DIFFERS

CRITICAL THINKING THROUGH COMPARISONS

Structure, Rules, and Legislative Power

The U.S. House and Senate are equal in their legislative powers; without their joint agreement, no law can be enacted. This arrangement is unusual. Although most democracies have a bicameral (two-chamber) legislature, one chamber is usually more powerful than the other. In the Canadian parliament, for example, nearly all bills originate in the House of Commons, with the Senate functioning more as a check on its actions than as a co-equal body. Moreover, some democracies, including Sweden and Israel, have unicameral (one-chamber) legislatures. If the United States had an equivalent legislature, it would consist only of the House of Representatives.

Power in the U.S. Congress is divided in other ways as well: Congress has elected leaders with limited formal powers, a network of committees, and members who are free to follow or ignore other members of their party. It is not uncommon for a legislator to vote against the party's position on legislative issues. In contrast, European legislatures have a centralized power structure. Top leaders have substantial authority, the committees are weak, and the parties are unified. European legislators are expected to support their party unless granted permission to vote otherwise on a particular bill. If they defy the party leadership, they might be denied renomination by the party in the next election.

Q: In terms of enacting legislation, what is the relative advantage and disadvantage of how Congress is structured and operates, compared with a national legislature with a dominant chamber in which the majority party can count on its members to support its policy agenda?

A: A relative advantage of Congress is that it is structured in a way that slows the passage of legislation, which can be a safeguard against ill-conceived or weakly supported bills. A relative disadvantage of Congress's structure is that it can result in legislative deadlock even on pressing national issues. A Senate filibuster can enable a determined minority to block legislation even if it has majority support within and outside Congress. And, if one party controls the House and the other party controls the Senate, each party has the power to block the other from acting.

Committee chairs are always members of the majority party and usually are the party member with the most **seniority** (consecutive years of service) on the committee. Seniority is based strictly on time served on a committee, not on time spent in Congress. Thus, if a member switches committees, the years spent on the first committee do not count toward seniority on the new one. The seniority system has advantages: It reduces the number of power struggles that would occur if the chairs were decided each time by open competition, it places committee leadership in the hands of experienced members, and it enables members to look forward to the reward of a position as chair after years of service on the same committee. The seniority system is not absolute, however, and is applied less uniformly than in the past, as the next section will explain.

Committee or Party: Which Is in Control?

In a sense, committees are an instrument of the majority party in that it controls a majority of each committee's seats and appoints the chair. In another sense, each committee is powerful in its own right. Committees have been described as "little legislatures," each secure in its jurisdiction and membership, and each wielding influence over the legislation it handles.

Committees decentralize power in Congress and serve individual members' power and reelection needs. Less than a dozen members hold a party leadership position, but several hundred serve as committee or subcommittee chairs or are *ranking members,* the term for the minority party's committee and subcommittee leaders. In these positions, they can pursue local or personal policy agendas that may or may not coincide with the party leadership's goals.

Nevertheless, committees are less powerful today than in the past. An effect of polarization has been to increase the number of issues on which Republicans and Democrats compete nationally. This development has led party leaders in Congress to seek greater control over the legislative agenda, including the bills in committee. The consolidation of control has been more pronounced among Republicans, who, for example, have placed a six-year limit on how long a member can chair a particular committee, which limits the chair's ability to accumulate power.

Although committees have less influence than previously, the balance between party power and committee power is an ongoing issue. Congress is at once a place where the parties pursue their national policy agendas and where the members pursue the policy interests of their local constituencies through their committee work. The balance of power has at times tipped toward the committees and at other times toward the party leaders. At all times, there has been an effort to strike a workable balance between the two. The distinguishing feature of congressional power is its division among the membership, with provision for added power—sometimes more and sometimes less—in the hands of the top party leaders.

How a Bill Becomes Law

A **bill** is a proposed law that must be passed by the House and Senate before it can become law. The formal process by which bills become law is shown in Figure 11-4. Many bills are drafted by executive agencies, interest groups, or other outside parties, but members of Congress also draft bills, and they alone can submit a bill for consideration by their chamber.

Committee Hearings and Decisions

When a bill is introduced in the House or the Senate, it receives a bill number and is sent to the relevant committee, which assigns it to one of its subcommittees. Less than 10 percent of such bills get to the floor for a vote. Most bills are "killed" when committees decide they lack sufficient merit or support. The full House or Senate can overrule such decisions but seldom does. Some bills are not even supported by the members who introduce them. A member may submit a bill to appease a powerful constituent group and then quietly tell the committee to ignore it.

The fact that committees kill more than 90 percent of the bills submitted to Congress does not mean that they exercise 90 percent of Congress's power. Committees rarely decide the fate of major bills that are of keen interest to many members. Committees must also consider that their decisions can be reversed by the full chamber, just as subcommittees must recognize that the full committee can override their decisions.[41]

If a bill appears to have merit, the subcommittee will schedule hearings on it. After the hearings, if the subcommittee still feels that the legislation is worthwhile, members will recommend the bill to the full committee, which might hold additional hearings. In the House, both the full committee and a subcommittee can *mark up* a bill—that is, they have the authority to change its content. In the Senate, markup usually is reserved for the full committee.

From Committee to the Floor

If the majority on a committee recommends a bill's passage, it is referred to the full chamber for action. In the House, the Rules Committee has the power to determine when the bill will be voted on and how long the debate on it will last. The Rules Committee also decides whether a bill will receive a "closed rule" (no amendments will be permitted), an "open rule" (members

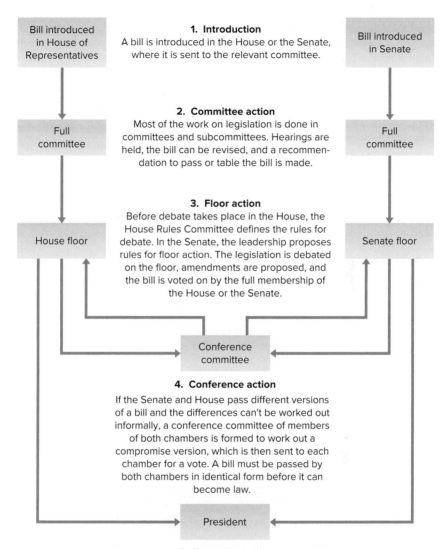

figure 11-4 HOW A BILL BECOMES LAW

Although the legislative process can be short-circuited in many ways, this simplified diagram shows the major steps through which a bill becomes law. A key difference between the House and Senate that's not shown in the diagram is the role of the House Rules Committee, which has no equivalent in the Senate. The House Rules Committee controls the scheduling of House bills and the conditions under which they will be debated, including whether amendments will be allowed.

can propose amendments relevant to any of the bill's sections), or something in between (for example, only certain sections of the bill will be subject to amendment). The rules are a means by which the majority party tries to control legislation. When Democrats had a majority in the House in the period before 1995, they used closed rules to prevent Republicans from proposing amendments to major bills, a tactic House Republicans said they would forgo when they took control in 1995. Once in control, however, the Republicans applied closed rules to several major bills. The tactic was simply too effective to be abandoned.

Detecting Misinformation

Are Policy Problems Easy to Fix?

A recent poll found that most people think "ordinary Americans" would do a better job than "elected officials" of "solving the country's problems."[42] That finding coincides with what political scientists John Hibbing and Elizabeth Theiss-Morse discovered in *Stealth Democracy*: Millions of Americans believe that the nation's elaborate legislative process is a waste of time.[43] If, as these Americans think, policy problems are simple and easy to fix, there is no reason for extended debate and deliberation. All that's required is for politicians to get out of the way and turn the job of lawmaking over to no-nonsense leaders.

thesomeday123/Shutterstock

Is that claim fact, or is it fake?

It's understandable that Americans would be frustrated by the failure of elected leaders to resolve pressing national problems. Petty partisan feuds have frequently blocked congressional action in recent years. At the same time, although policy issues may look simple, they seldom are. Foreign trade, for example, affects thousands of American businesses, some of which benefit from free trade and some of which don't. Moreover, foreign trade is not simply an economic issue. It's also a means of strengthening ties between nations, which has implications for national security. As a result, the notion that America's trade problem, or other major problems, has an easy fix is mistaken. Legislating requires weighing a range of factors, some of which are complex and interrelated. Moreover, policymaking in a democratic system includes a wide range of competing interests; accommodating them requires time-consuming negotiation and compromise.

In the Senate, the majority leader schedules bills, usually in consultation with the minority leader. Although the Senate like the House has a rules committee, it lacks the power to determine the rules of debate. All Senate bills are subject to unlimited debate unless a three-fifths majority (60 of the 100 senators) vote for **cloture**, which limits debate to 30 hours. Cloture is a way of defeating a Senate **filibuster**, which is a procedural tactic whereby a minority of senators can block a bill by talking about it until other senators give in and the bill is withdrawn from consideration or changed to meet opponents' demands. (In 2013, the filibuster was eliminated for Senate votes on presidential nominees, although it was retained for legislation and the confirmation of Supreme Court justices. In 2017, it was eliminated for Supreme Court justices as well.)

Leadership and Floor Action

A bill that passes in committee with the members' strong support is usually passed by an overwhelming majority of the full chamber. However, when the committee vote is closely divided, other members may conclude that they need to give the bill a close look before deciding whether to support it. Members are also less deferential to committee action on major bills and those that affect their constituents.

On major bills, the majority party's leaders often take the lead.[44] They shape the bill's broad content and work closely with the relevant committee during the committee phase. Once the bill clears the committee, they often direct the floor debate. (The role of parties in Congress is discussed further in a later section of the chapter.)

Conference Committees and the President

For a bill to pass, it must get the support of a simple majority (50 percent plus one) of the House or Senate members voting on it. However, for a bill to become law, it must be passed in an identical form by both the House and the Senate. About 10 percent of the bills that pass both chambers differ in their House and Senate versions. Unless the differences are worked out informally, these bills are referred to conference committees to resolve the differences. Each **conference committee** is formed temporarily for the sole purpose of nego-tiating a particular bill. Its members are usually appointed from the House and Senate standing committees that drafted the bill. The conference committee's job is to develop a compromise version, which then goes back to the House and Senate floors for a final vote.

A bill passed in an identical form by the House and the Senate is not yet law. The president also has a say. If the president signs the bill, it becomes a **law**. The president also has the option of the **veto**, either by rejecting it outright or by letting it sit unsigned for 10 days, which is called a *pocket veto*. For a vetoed bill to become law, a two-thirds vote in both the House and Senate is required. That's a large barrier, and only rarely does a bill have enough support to override a veto.

CONGRESS'S POLICYMAKING ROLE

Congress is a lawmaking institution but that's not its only important function. It also functions as a representative institution—a place where Americans through their Senate and House members have a voice in governing. Congress also has an oversight function—ensuring that the executive branch is carrying out the law in the proper way. These three functions—*lawmaking*, *representation*, and *oversight*—overlap in practice but are conceptually distinct (see Table 11-3), as the following sections will explain.

The Lawmaking Function of Congress

Under the Constitution, Congress is granted the **lawmaking function**: the authority to make the laws necessary to carry out the powers granted to the national government. Congress's lawmaking authority includes the power to tax, spend, regulate commerce, and declare war. However, whether Congress takes the lead in lawmaking usually depends on the type of policy at issue.

table 11-3	THE MAJOR FUNCTIONS OF CONGRESS
Function	**Basis and Activity**
Lawmaking	Through its constitutional grant to enact law, Congress makes the laws authorizing federal programs and appropriating the funds necessary to carry them out.
Representation	Through its elected constitutional officers—U.S. senators and representatives—Congress represents the interests of constituents and the nation in its deliberations and its lawmaking.
Oversight	Through its constitutional responsibility to see that the executive branch carries out the laws faithfully and spends appropriations properly, Congress oversees and sometimes investigates executive action.

Broad Issues: Fragmentation as a Limit on Congress's Role   Although Congress sometimes takes the lead on major national policy issues,[45] it often looks to the president to play that role. Congress is not well suited to tackling large, complex issues. Congress is not one house but two, each with its own authority and constituency base. Neither the House nor the Senate can enact legislation without the other's approval, and the two chambers are hardly identical. California and South Dakota have the same representation in the Senate (two senators each), but, in the House, which is apportioned by population, California has 52 seats compared to South Dakota's 1. And when one party controls the House and the other the Senate, the likelihood that Congress will take the lead diminishes sharply.

Congress also includes a lot of lawmakers: 100 members of the Senate and 435 members of the House. They come from different constituencies and represent different and sometimes opposing interests, which can lead to disagreement even among members of the same party. Most members of Congress, for example, say they favor global free trade but are likely to withdraw their support if provisions of a free trade bill will weaken key businesses in their state or district.

The presidency is institutionally better suited to the task of providing leadership on major national issues. Whereas Congress's authority is divided, executive power is vested constitutionally in the hands of a single individual—the president. Unlike congressional leaders, the president doesn't have to bargain with others in deciding what policy to pursue. Moreover, whereas members of Congress often see issues from the perspective of their state or constituency, presidents have a national constituency and tend to look at policy from a national perspective. Finally, the president has access to far more policy expertise and advice than members of Congress.* As will be explained in Chapter 12, the president is assisted by hundreds of policy specialists, both directly and through executive agencies, such as the Departments of Treasury and Defense. They have the knowledge required to draft complex legislation.

Presidential leadership on major policy issues means that Congress will listen to White House proposals, not that Congress will back them. Even if a presidential proposal has congressional support, it is rarely adopted in that form. It is usually taken as a starting point for negotiation, saving Congress the time and trouble of developing the legislation from scratch. It may reject a presidential proposal outright, particularly when the president is from the opposing party. After Republicans took control of the House in 2023, some of President Biden's legislative proposals were essentially "dead on arrival" when they reached the House. (The legislative roles of Congress and the president are discussed further in Chapter 12.)

Congress in the Lead: Fragmentation as a Policymaking Strength

Congress's strength as a legislative body is its ability to handle scores of small issues simultaneously. The great majority of the hundreds of bills that Congress considers each session deal with narrow issues, such as authorizing a new weapons system for the navy. Such bills are handled largely through standing committees, each of which has policy expertise resulting from the fact that it concentrates on a particular policy area, such as taxation, agriculture, or military affairs. And, because the standing committees operate separately, the committee system as a whole can work simultaneously on a large number of bills. As political scientist James Sundquist noted, "Congress [is] organized to deal with narrow problems but not with broad ones."[46]

Narrow policy issues can serve the reelection interests of members of Congress. The resulting legislation tends to be "distributive"—that is, it confers

---

*Members of Congress do have some access to policy experts. Each congressional committee has staff members, some of whom are hired for their expertise in the committee's policy area. Congress also has three agencies of its own, although they function as nonpartisan bodies rather than as policy bodies. One of these agencies is the Congressional Budget Office (CBO), which has a staff of 250 employees and provides Congress with estimates of government expenditures and revenues, which Congress uses in determining fiscal policy. A second congressional agency is the Government Accountability Office (GAO), with 3,000 employees. Its job is to determine whether executive agencies are complying with laws passed by Congress. The third agency is the Congressional Research Service (CRS) with 1,000 employees. The CRS functions as a research and information service for congressional members and committees. By law, it is prohibited from making policy recommendations.

a benefit on a particular group while spreading the cost across the taxpaying public. The 2011 Veterans Jobs Act, for example, provided funding for job training for veterans. Distributive policies have a clear political advantage. The benefit is large enough that members of the recipient group will recognize and appreciate getting it, while the cost to each taxpayer is barely noticeable. Such policies are also the type that Congress, through its committee system, is organizationally best suited to handle. Most committees parallel a major constituent interest, such as agriculture, commerce, labor, or veterans.

C A S E S T U D Y

Politics in Action

Leadership Style of Women in Congress

Recent elections have marked the first time that more than 100 women have been elected to the House of Representatives. On the Senate side, a fourth of the members are women, the highest number ever. Although women are still greatly underrepresented, their growing presence in Congress is thought by some analysts to foreshadow a change in how Congress operates. They see female legislators as being more collaborative, more interested in problem-solving, and more responsive to the policy needs of families and children than their male counterparts.

Eric Lee/Bloomberg/Getty Images

Continued

Evidence supports the claim. A 2017 study by Rutgers's Center for Women and Politics found that women bring new issues and perspectives to congressional deliberations and have distinctive work styles that can foster bipartisanship.[47] Another study found that women sponsor and co-sponsor more bills than men while introducing more bills relating to education, health, and poverty.[48] That study's findings coincide with those of another that examined more than 150,000 bills introduced in the House over a 40-year period. It identified health, education, and civil rights bills as ones that female members disproportionately sponsored.[49]

At the same time, the distinctive contribution of women may be declining as a result of the polarization that has reshaped Congress in recent years. A study of House roll-call votes found that the votes of male and female members of the same party have been converging to the point that they are nearly indistinguishable, a pattern that analysts have attributed to the election of fewer female moderates.[50] Increasingly, female members of Congress—Republican Senator Cindy Hyde-Smith and Democratic Representative Alexandria Ocasio-Cortez being examples—have taken positions that reflect their party's ideology more than their gender. Jennifer Lawless, who directs American University's Women & Politics Institute, notes that polarization has reduced the "incentive for anyone, male or female, to reach across the aisle."[51]

Q: Like women, Blacks, Hispanics, and Asian Americans have been under-represented in Congress relative to their population percentage. What issues might get more attention in Congress if they were more fully represented?

ASK YOURSELF: What problems do most Black Americans face that are more severe or different from those faced by most white Americans? What distinctive problems do Hispanics face? Asian Americans?

The Representation Function of Congress

In the process of making laws, the members of Congress represent various interests within American society, giving them a voice in the national legislature. How lawmakers should carry out their **representation function** has been debated since the nation's founding. Should they be guided by the interests of the nation as a whole? Or should they be guided by the narrower interests of their constituents? These interests do not always coincide. Free trade in steel is an example. Although U.S. manufacturers as a whole benefit from access to low-priced steel from abroad, domestic steel producers and the communities where they're located are hurt by it.

Representation of States and Districts   The choice between national and local interests is not a simple one even for legislators who are inclined toward one or the other orientation. To be fully effective, members of Congress must be reelected time and again, which forces them to pay attention to local demands, yet they serve in the nation's legislative body and cannot ignore national needs. In making the choice, most members of Congress, on narrow issues at least, vote in a way that will not antagonize local interests.[52] Opposition to gun control legislation, for example, is stronger among members of Congress representing rural areas where hunting is prevalent than it is among those from urban areas where guns tend to be seen as a threat to public safety.

Local representation occurs in part through the committee system. Although studies indicate that the policy positions of most committees are not radically different from those of the full House or Senate,[53] committee memberships roughly coincide with constituency interests. For example, farm-state legislators dominate the membership of the House and Senate Agriculture Committees. Committees are also the site of most *logrolling*— the practice of trading one's vote with another member's so that both get what they want, as in the case of agricultural committee members from corn-producing northern states trading votes with members from cotton-producing southern states.

Local representation also shapes how Congress distributes funds for federal programs. Members of Congress typically withhold their support unless their locality gets a share of the money, even if it makes the program less efficient and effective. The bill that Congress passed in 2020 to help states deal with the COVID-19 pandemic is an example. Even though the threat was worse in more populous states, the legislation automatically granted each state a minimum of $1.25 billion in aid.

Representation of constituency interests has its limits. Constituents have little awareness of most issues that come before Congress. Whether Congress appropriates a few million dollars in foreign aid to Bolivia is not the sort of issue that local residents will hear or care about. Moreover, members of Congress often have no choice but to go against the wishes of some constituents. In such cases, members of Congress typically side with the interest that aligns with their party. When local business and labor groups take opposing sides on issues before Congress, for example, Republican members tend to back business's position, whereas Democratic members tend to line up with labor.

CITIZEN ACTION!
SELF-GOVERNMENT

Consider e-mailing or writing to your congressional representative to express your opinion on a current issue. You can inform yourself about the member's position on the issue through his or her website, which will also have the contact information you need.

Representation of the Nation Through Parties   When a vital national interest is at stake, members of Congress, although agreeing on a need for national action, usually disagree on the best course of action. Most lawmakers believe, for example, that the nation's immigration system needs to be overhauled. But what action is necessary and desirable? Should the millions of undocumented immigrants already here be given a path to citizenship? What should be done to stop additional individuals from unlawfully entering the United States? Should immigrants with high skill levels be given priority over those with family members in the United States? Republican and Democratic lawmakers disagree on such questions because their parties differ philosophically and politically.

Party polarization has made it harder for Democratic and Republican members to bridge their differences. The great majority of Republicans are on the conservative side of issues, whereas the great majority of Democrats are on the liberal side. Party polarization has also been accompanied by the *nationalization* of issues, whereby voters within the same party hold similar opinions regardless of where they reside in the United States, which has made it riskier for members of Congress to cross party lines on pending legislation even if the legislation would benefit the member's constituency.

As a result of these developments, representation in Congress on prominent issues now occurs largely through the parties, with Republican members seeking what Republican voters want and Democratic members catering to the opinions of Democratic voters. Local differences have correspondingly had less influence on the actions of congressional members. Some political scientists see this as a positive development, arguing that voters deserve a choice between candidates who take clear-cut, consistent, and opposing positions, as opposed to an earlier situation where candidates of the same party sometimes took starkly different positions, making it harder for voters to know what they were getting in voting for a party's candidates.[54]

The Oversight Function of Congress

In addition to enacting the laws, Congress monitors the executive branch to ensure that the laws are being carried out properly, a responsibility known as Congress's **oversight function**.[55]

Oversight is carried out largely through the committee system of Congress, with each standing committee overseeing its corresponding agencies of the executive branch. The House and Senate Agriculture Committees, for example, monitor the Department of Agriculture. The Legislative Reorganization Act of 1970 spells out each committee's responsibility for overseeing its parallel agency: "Each standing committee shall review and study, on a continuing basis, the application, administration, and execution of those laws, or parts of laws, the subject matter of which is within the jurisdiction of that committee."

Oversight is a demanding task. The bureaucracy has hundreds of agencies and thousands of programs. Congress gets some leverage from the fact that federal agencies have their funding renewed each year, which provides an opportunity for congressional committees to review agency activity.[56] Nevertheless because the task is so large, oversight is not pursued vigorously unless members of Congress are annoyed with an agency, have discovered that a legislative authorization is being abused, or intend to modify an agency program.

When an agency is alleged to have acted improperly, committee hearings into the allegations can occur. Congress's investigative power is not listed in the Constitution, but the Supreme Court has upheld this power as a reasonable extension of Congress's power to make the laws. Except in cases involving *executive privilege* (the right of the executive branch to withhold confidential information), executive branch officials are ordinarily required to testify when

Through its oversight function, Congress seeks to hold the executive branch accountable for its actions. A dramatic example is the 2022 hearings of the House Select Committee to Investigate the January 6th Attack on the United States Capitol. Televised to the nation, the hearings exposed efforts to overturn the results of the 2020 presidential election. Pictured here during one of the hearings is Liz Cheney, the committee's vice chairperson. (Tom Williams/CQ-Roll Call Inc/Getty Images)

called by Congress to do so. If they refuse, they can be cited for contempt of Congress, which is a criminal offense if a court upholds the contempt charge. On the other hand, an executive officer's refusal to testify requires Congress to go to court to compel the testimony, which would delay the inquiry. In such cases, Congress will sometimes forego the testimony, as House committees did during their impeachment inquiry of President Trump (see Chapter 12).

Congress's interest in oversight declines when the president is from the same party as the congressional majority. During the House Intelligence Committee's initial investigation of Russian meddling on behalf of Donald Trump in the 2016 presidential election, for example, the committee's Republican majority refused to call key witnesses or subpoena those who refused to answer questions. It then issued a report claiming that Russian meddling was inconsequential—a claim at odds with the conclusion of the CIA, FBI, National Security Agency, and director of national intelligence.[57]

The dynamic shifts when the majority party sees an advantage in oversight. After Republican members refused to support the creation of a bipartisan special committee to investigate the January 6, 2021 assault on the U.S. Capitol, House Democrats created one. They had a majority in the House and thus had the votes needed to establish it. Over months, the investigative committee called witnesses and gathered documents relating to the assault, which led to televised public hearings and a final report that was critical of the role in the assault played by former Republican president Trump, several of his assistants, and even some Republican members of Congress.

CONGRESS: AN INSTITUTION DIVIDED

Congress is not an institution in which majorities rule easily. Agreement within each chamber, and between the two chambers, is required to pass legislation. That can typically be achieved only if lawmakers are willing to act in a spirit of compromise. Such was the intention of the framers of the Constitution. They designed the institution to foster compromise for the purpose of legislating in the interests of the many rather than that of a powerful faction.

What the writers of the Constitution did not fully anticipate was the degree to which intense partisanship could disrupt the workings of Congress. Party unity is the clearest way for the majority to overcome the obstacles to action inherent in Congress's fragmented structure. At the same time, party unity is the surest way for the minority to block action. And because Congress's structure makes it easier to block legislation than to enact it, a determined minority party—if it has nearly as many members as the majority party—can act in ways that deadlock the institution even in the face of urgent national problems.

SUMMARY

Members of Congress, once elected, are likely to be reelected. Members of Congress can use their office to publicize themselves, to pursue a service strategy of responding to the needs of individual constituents, and to secure pork-barrel projects for their states or districts. The fact that they hold a position in Congress also helps them attract campaign contributions from individual donors and PACs. Incumbency carries some risks. Members of Congress must take positions on controversial issues, may blunder into political scandal or indiscretion, must deal with changes in the electorate, or may face strong challengers. By and large, however, the advantages of incumbency far outweigh the disadvantages.

Congress is a fragmented institution. It has no single leader; rather, the House and the Senate have separate leaders, neither of whom can presume to speak for the other chamber. The chief party leaders in Congress are the Speaker of the House and the Senate majority leader. They share leadership power with committee and subcommittee chairpersons, who have influence on the policy decisions of their respective committees or subcommittees.

Congress's fragmentation is offset partially by partisanship, which serves as a common bond between members of the same party. In the past few decades, that bond has strengthened to the point that congressional Republicans and Democrats have regularly found themselves on the opposite sides of legislative issues. In some cases, the partisan gap has been so wide that compromise has failed, resulting in legislative delay and deadlock.

Committees are the locus of most of the day-to-day work of Congress. Each House and Senate standing committee has jurisdiction over bills in a particular area (such as agriculture or foreign relations), as does each of its subcommittees. In most cases, the full House and Senate accept committee recommendations about the passage of bills, although amendments to bills are not uncommon and committees are careful to take other members of Congress into account when making legislative decisions. On major bills, committees work closely with the party leaders, knowing that a bill will not win the necessary support if it is at odds with what party leaders and the party caucus are expecting.

The major function of Congress is to enact legislation, yet the role it plays in developing legislation depends on the type of policy involved. Because of its divided chambers and committee structure, as well as the concern of its members with state and district interests, Congress only occasionally takes the lead on broad national issues. Congress instead typically looks to the president for this leadership. Nevertheless, presidential initiatives are passed by Congress only if they meet members' expectations and usually only after a lengthy process of compromise and negotiation. Congress is more adept at handling legislation that deals with problems of narrow interest. Legislation of this sort is decided mainly in congressional committees, where interested legislators, bureaucrats, and groups concentrate their efforts on issues of mutual concern.

A second function of Congress is the representation of various interests. Members of Congress are highly sensitive to the state or district on which they depend for reelection. They do respond to overriding national interests, but local concerns usually take priority. National or local representation often operates through party representation, particularly on issues that divide the Democratic and Republican Parties and their constituent groups, which is increasingly the case.

Congress's third function is oversight—the supervision and investigation of the way the bureaucracy is implementing legislatively mandated programs. Although oversight is a difficult and time-consuming process, it is one of the major ways that Congress exercises control over the executive branch.

CRITICAL THINKING ZONE

KEY TERMS

bicameral legislature (*p. 297*)
bill (*p. 310*)
cloture (*p. 313*)
conference committee (*p. 314*)
constituency (*p. 289*)
filibuster (*p. 313*)
gerrymandering (*p. 292*)
incumbent (*p. 289*)
jurisdiction (*p. 306*)
law (*p. 314*)
lawmaking function (*p. 314*)
midterm election (*p. 293*)

oversight function (*p. 320*)
party caucus (*p. 297*)
party leaders (*p. 297*)
party unity (*p. 298*)
pork (*p. 289*)
reapportionment (*p. 291*)
redistricting (*p. 291*)
representation function (*p. 318*)
seniority (*p. 309*)
service strategy (*p. 289*)
standing committees (*p. 304*)
veto (*p. 314*)

APPLYING THE ELEMENTS OF CRITICAL THINKING

Conceptualizing: Explain the lawmaking, representation, and oversight functions of Congress.

Synthesizing: Contrast the advantages that incumbents have in seeking reelection with the disadvantages they have. Which of these advantages and disadvantages apply only to House members? Which apply only to senators?

Analyzing:

1. How does the structure of Congress—for example, its two chambers and its committee system—affect its role in the making of policy on broad national issues, as compared with its role on narrower, group-centered issues?

2. Compared with past times, there are now fewer conservative Democrats and fewer progressive Republicans in Congress. How has this development increased the importance of party and party leaders in Congress? How has it increased the chances of partisan deadlock on key legislative issues?

OF POSSIBLE INTEREST

A Book Worth Reading: Frances E. Lee, *Insecure Majorities: Congress and the Perpetual Campaign* (Chicago: University of Chicago Press, 2016). An insightful book by a leading political scientist that examines the destructive interplay of election pressures and the work of Congress.

A Website Worth Visiting: **www.house.gov** and **www.senate.gov** The websites of the U.S. House of Representatives and the U.S. Senate, respectively. Each site has information on the chamber's party leaders, pending legislation, and committee hearings, as well as links to each member's office and website.

12
CHAPTER

THE PRESIDENCY:
LEADING THE NATION

Steve Allen/Brand X Pictures/Getty Images

❝ The presidency has made every man who occupied it, no matter how small, bigger than
he was; and no matter how big, not big enough for its demands. ❞

LYNDON JOHNSON

Donald Trump's presidency was expected to be different, but few predicted
just how different it would be. Presidents traditionally have sought to unite the
country. Trump relished conflict. Asked about it, he said, "I like conflict. . . . I
like watching it, I like seeing it, and I think it's the best way to go." When
nationwide protests erupted after George Floyd, an unarmed and handcuffed
Black man, was killed in the custody of Minneapolis police in 2020, Trump said

326

that the states should use force to quell the demonstrators. Claiming that many of the governors and mayors were "weak," Trump sent federal officers into several cities to disrupt the demonstrations. After losing the 2020 presidential election to Democrat Joe Biden, Trump refused to concede, saying "We will never give up, we will never concede." He urged his followers "to fight" and then "to fight harder" to overturn the election. Former Marine General James Mattis, who served as secretary of Defense in the Trump administration, said: "Donald Trump is the first president in my lifetime who does not try to unite the American people—does not even pretend to try. Instead, he tries to divide us."[1]

The presidency is America's least predictable institution. Lyndon Johnson's and Richard Nixon's pursuit of the Vietnam War led to talk of "the imperial presidency," an office so powerful that constitutional checks and balances were no longer an effective constraint. Within a few years, because of the Watergate scandal and disruptive events during the Ford and Carter presidencies, the watchword became "the imperiled presidency," an office too weak to meet the nation's needs. The foreign policy successes of Ronald Reagan and George H. W. Bush hearkened to earlier claims of "a heroic presidency" that disappeared as the economy weakened. Bill Clinton overcame a fitful start to his presidency to win

Shown here is President Donald Trump speaking at a rally outside the White House on January 6, 2021. Claiming the 2020 election had been "stolen," he urged his supporters to march on the U.S. Capitol to contest the pending House and Senate vote certifying Joe Biden's election as the president. An hour later, the peaceful protest turned violent when hundreds of his loyalists attacked police and stormed the Capitol. (Eric Lee/Bloomberg/Getty Images)

a second term but then got mired in a scandal that led to his impeachment and weakened his claim to national leadership. After the terrorist attacks of September 11, 2001, George W. Bush's job approval rating soared to a record high. By the time he left office, Americans had turned against his economic and war policies and only a third of the public had a positive view of his leadership. Barack Obama, in his first two years of office, had a level of legislative success higher than any president since Johnson. In his last six years, his legislative success rate was the lowest of any president in six decades.

No other political institution has been subject to such varying characterization as the modern presidency. One reason is that the presidency, unlike Congress or the courts, is in the hands of a single individual, whose personal style and ambitions shape its direction. Moreover, the formal powers of the office are relatively modest, so presidential power changes with political conditions and the personal capacity of the office's occupant. The American presidency is always a central office in that its occupant is a focus of national attention, yet the presidency operates in a system of divided powers, which means that presidential power is conditional. It depends on the president's abilities but even more on circumstances—on whether the situation demands strong leadership and whether there is public and congressional support for that leadership. When circumstances are favorable, the president exercises considerable power. When circumstances are unfavorable, the president struggles to exercise power effectively.

This chapter examines the roots of presidential power, the presidential selection process, the staffing of the presidency, and the factors associated with the success and failure of presidential leadership. The chapter covers the following main ideas:

- *Over time, the presidency has become a more powerful office.* This development owes largely to the legacy of strong presidents and to domestic and international developments that have increased the need for executive leadership.

- *The president could not control the executive branch without a large number of presidential appointees—advisers, experts, and skilled managers—but the sheer number of these appointees is itself a challenge to presidential control.*

- *The president's election by national vote and position as sole chief executive make the presidency the focal point of national politics, but the formal authority of the president is not substantial enough to meet the demands on the office.* Presidents can seek to bridge the power gap through their party leadership and use of the bully pulpit, as well as what they can do under their authority. Ultimately, their success depends largely on their ability to gain the backing of other Washington officials, the members of Congress particularly.

THE MAKING OF THE MODERN PRESIDENCY

The Constitution states that the president must be at least 35 years old and must have been a U.S. resident for at least 14 years. It also requires the president to be a natural-born U.S. citizen, a provision that was added to the Constitution in the final draft and reflected the belief of some of the framers that an individual born elsewhere might have divided loyalties. Ratification of the Twenty-second Amendment placed another limitation on the occupant. It limits a president to two terms of office.

The informal barriers to becoming president are more substantial (see Table 12-1). Until Donald Trump won the presidency in 2016, no one had been

table 12-1	THE PATH TO THE WHITE HOUSE (SINCE 1901)	
President	**Years in Office**	**Highest Previous Office**
Theodore Roosevelt	1901–1908	Vice president*
William Howard Taft	1909–1912	Secretary of war
Woodrow Wilson	1913–1920	Governor
Warren G. Harding	1921–1924	U.S. senator
Calvin Coolidge	1925–1928	Vice president*
Herbert Hoover	1929–1932	Secretary of commerce
Franklin D. Roosevelt	1933–1945	Governor
Harry S Truman	1945–1952	Vice president*
Dwight D. Eisenhower	1953–1960	U.S. Army general
John F. Kennedy	1961–1963	U.S. senator
Lyndon Johnson	1963–1968	Vice president*
Richard Nixon	1969–1974	Vice president
Gerald Ford	1974–1976	Vice president*
Jimmy Carter	1977–1980	Governor
Ronald Reagan	1981–1988	Governor
George H. W. Bush	1989–1992	Vice president
Bill Clinton	1993–2000	Governor
George W. Bush	2001–2008	Governor
Barack Obama	2009–2016	U.S. senator
Donald Trump	2017–2020	None
Joe Biden	2021–	Vice president

*Became president on death or resignation of incumbent.

elected without having first served in high public office or been a military general. Until Barack Obama's election in 2008, all presidents had been white. In 2016, Hillary Clinton came the closest that a woman has come to becoming president, winning the popular vote but losing the decisive electoral vote. Historians have devised rankings of the presidents, and their rankings reveal that there is no ironclad training ground for a successful presidency. Of the four army generals, for example, two of them (George Washington and Dwight D. Eisenhower) are ranked high, while the other two (Ulysses S. Grant and Zachary Taylor) are ranked low.

Expansion of Presidential Power

The framers expected the president to provide leadership in national affairs, take command in war, provide direction in foreign affairs, and properly execute the laws, but they didn't have a full idea of how the office would work in practice. They sought what Alexander Hamilton in *Federalist* No. 70 called an "energetic" presidency, knowing that a government headed by a "feeble" president would itself be feeble and unable to meet the nation's needs. But they didn't have a clear vision of what an "energetic" presidency would involve.

Accordingly, they defined the powers of the president in general terms. By comparison with the precise listing of Congress's powers in Article I of the Constitution, the provisions in Article II that contain the president's authority are briefly stated.[2] The clause that establishes the president's role as **commander in chief** says simply, "The President shall be commander in chief. . . ." The role of **chief diplomat** rests largely on provisions granting the president the power to "appoint" and "receive" ambassadors. The president's role as **chief legislator** is found largely in the provision that says the president can "recommend" measures to Congress and inform it of the "state of the Union." The clause that establishes the president as **chief executive** says simply, "He shall take care that the laws be faithfully executed, and shall commission all the officers of the United States." The president's responsibilities as the highest-ranking executive also establish the president as **head of government**, a role that's distinct from the president's role as **head of state**, which refers to the president's ceremonial role as the government's representative. (In some countries, the head of government and the head of state are held by different individuals, as in Great Britain where the prime minister, as the chief executive, is the head of government and the queen or king is the ceremonial head of state.)

Throughout American history, each of the president's constitutional roles has been expanded in practice beyond the framers' intent. For example, the Constitution grants the president command of the nation's military, but only Congress can declare war. In *Federalist* No. 69, Alexander Hamilton wrote that insurrections and surprise attacks on the United States were the only situations that would justify a president's use of military force without congressional authorization. Nevertheless, more than 80 percent of U.S. military engagements since World War II have been waged solely on presidential authority.

The Constitution also authorizes the president to act as a diplomatic leader with the power to appoint ambassadors, and also to negotiate treaties with other countries, subject to approval by a two-thirds vote of the Senate. The framers anticipated that Congress would define the nation's foreign policy objectives, while the president would oversee their implementation. However, presidents increasingly took charge of U.S. foreign policy, and today nearly every foreign policy initiative originates with the president. For example, it was President Joe Biden, and not Congress, who took the lead in rallying the nation and European countries to assist Ukraine in its war with Russia.

The Constitution also vests "executive power" in the president. This power includes the responsibility to execute the laws faithfully and to appoint the heads of federal agencies. In *Federalist* No. 76, Hamilton indicated that the president's real authority as chief executive was to be found in this appointive capacity. Presidents have, indeed, exercised power through their appointments, but they have also found their administrative authority—the power to execute the laws—to be significant because it enables them to influence how laws will be implemented. President Trump used his executive power to *prohibit* the use of federal funds by family-planning clinics that offered abortion counseling. President Biden exerted the same power to *allow* the use of federal funds for this purpose. The same act of Congress was the basis for each of these decisions. The act authorizes the use of federal funds for family-planning services, but it neither requires nor prohibits their use for abortion counseling, enabling the president to decide the issue.

Finally, the Constitution provides the president with legislative authority, including the veto and the option of proposing legislation to Congress. The framers expected this authority to be used in a limited way, largely as a check on laws that the president believed were unconstitutional. George Washington acted as the framers anticipated. He proposed relatively few legislative measures and vetoed only two acts of Congress.[3] Modern presidents have assumed a more active legislative role. They regularly submit proposals to Congress and do not hesitate to veto legislation that conflicts with their policy goals.

Changing Conception of the Presidency

For many reasons, the presidency is a more powerful office than the framers envisioned. But two features of the office in particular—*national election* and *singular authority*—have enabled presidents to make use of changing demands on government to claim national policy leadership. It is a claim that no other elected official can routinely make. Unlike the president, who is elected by nationwide vote and is the sole chief executive, members of Congress are elected from separate states or districts and operate in an institution where they share power with the other members.

The first president to forcefully assert a broad claim to national policy leadership was Andrew Jackson, who was elected in 1828 on a tide of popular support that broke the upper class's hold on the presidency. Jackson used his popularity to challenge Congress's claim to national policy leadership, contending that he represented "the people's voice." To tie the presidency closer to the people, Jackson sought a constitutional amendment that would allow for the election of the president by popular vote rather than through electors chosen by the states. The effort failed, but Jackson succeeded in persuading states to allocate their electoral votes to the winner of the state's popular vote, as is still the case (see Chapter 2). Voters gained additional control over the choice of a president in the early 1900s when some states adopted primary elections to choose their delegates to the national conventions where the presidential nominees are chosen. In the 1970s, a reform of the nominating process required all states to choose their delegates through popular voting (see "Case Study: Presidential Nominating Campaigns"). These changes in the presidential selection process have strengthened the presidency by providing the office with the added authority that the vote of the people confers upon the president's claim to national leadership.[4]

C A S E S T U D Y — Politics in Action

Presidential Nominating Campaigns

To win their party's presidential nomination, candidates enter state primaries and open caucuses. The goal is to run strongly enough to accumulate a majority of the delegates to the party's national party convention where the nominee is formally chosen. The competition can be stiff. A dozen and a half candidates entered the 2016 Republican nominating race, which was won by Donald Trump. The 2020 Democratic race, won by Joe Biden, also attracted a large field of contenders.

Candidates for nomination have no choice but to start early and run

Matt Smith/Shutterstock

hard. The year before the first contest is a critical period, one that has been called the *invisible primary*. It is the time when candidates demonstrate through their fundraising ability, poll standing, and debate performance that they are serious contenders. A candidate who falls short in these areas is quickly dismissed as an also-ran. Once the state caucuses and primaries get underway, a key to success is *momentum*—a strong showing in the early contests that contributes to voter support in subsequent ones. Nobody—not the press, not donors, not the voters—has an interest in candidates who are far back in the pack.

The race starts with stand-alone single contests in several states but then broadens to include days on which multiple states hold their contests. Money is a key factor at this point. Candidates need money to buy televised ads and hire staff to run in several states at once. In 2020, Biden and his main Democratic rival, Senator Bernie Sanders, each spent more than $200 million on their nominating campaigns. But money is not everything, as the billionaire and former New York mayor Michael Bloomberg discovered in his quest for the 2020 Democratic nomination. Bloomberg spent nearly $500 million of his own money and ended up with little to show for it. Biden and Sanders had a huge edge over Bloomberg in the amount of news coverage (the so-called free media) that they received, and it gave their campaigns a level of credibility that paid advertising alone cannot buy.[5]

In theory, a presidential nominating race could unfold in a way in which no candidate can secure a majority of delegates by the time of the national convention. In that case, bargaining and negotiation at the convention would determine which contender received the party's nomination. In practice, nominating races have had a winnowing effect whereby the strongest candidate gradually accumulated a majority of the delegates before the convention began. The last time that a nominee wasn't picked in advance was 1952, when, as it happened, both the Republican nominee (Dwight D. Eisenhower) and the Democratic nominee (Adlai Stevenson) were chosen in brokered conventions.

Q: Every election process has features that favor certain types of candidates over others. Which types of candidates benefit from the way presidential nominees are chosen?

ASK YOURSELF: How much does name recognition in advance of the race affect a candidate's chances? How about the ability to raise campaign funds? Support from party leaders? A candidate's qualifications to hold the nation's highest office? Whether a candidate has the backing of a particular group of voters, such as Hispanics, white evangelical Christians, or young adults?

Jackson's view of the presidency was not shared by his successors. The nation's major issues were sectional (especially the North-South divide over the institution of slavery) and were suited to action by Congress, which represented state interests. In fact, throughout most of the 19th century (the Civil War presidency of Abraham Lincoln was an exception), Congress jealously guarded its constitutional authority over national policy. James Bryce wrote in the 1880s that Congress paid as much or more attention to the policy positions of leading newspaper publishers as it did to those of the president.[6]

The 19th-century conception of the presidency was expressed in the **limited presidency theory** (also called the *Whig theory*), which held that the presidency is a constrained office. According to this theory, the president's chief duty was overseeing the administration of government. The president would sometimes act as a policy leader but would typically defer to Congress. President James Buchanan, who held this view of the office, said, "My duty is to execute the laws . . . and not my individual opinions."[7]

On taking office in 1901, Theodore Roosevelt tossed aside the limited presidency tradition.[8] He embraced what he called the **stewardship theory**, which calls for a "strong presidency"— one limited, not by what the Constitution allows, but by what it prohibits. The stewardship theory holds that presidents are free to act as they choose, as long as they do not violate the law. In his autobiography, Roosevelt wrote, "My belief was that it was not only [the president's] right but his duty to do anything that the needs of the nation demanded unless such action was forbidden by the Constitution or by the laws."[9] Acting on his belief, Roosevelt took on the job of breaking up the business monopolies that had emerged during the nation's Industrial Revolution (see Chapter 3). He also opened world markets to American goods, using the navy and marines to project U.S. influence southward into the Caribbean and Latin America and westward toward Hawaii, the Philippines, and China (the "Open Door" policy). When congressional leaders objected, he forced a showdown, knowing that the American people would support the troops. Roosevelt said, "I have the money to send [the navy's ships] halfway around the world—let Congress bring them back."

Theodore Roosevelt's notion of a strong presidency was not embraced by his successor, William Howard Taft. Taft said, "The President can exercise no power which cannot be fairly and reasonably traced to some specific grant of power."[10] Herbert Hoover, who was the president when the Great Depression hit in 1929, was also reluctant to aggressively apply the power of his office and was slow in advocating policies that could put Americans back to work. His successor, Franklin D. Roosevelt (a distant cousin of Theodore Roosevelt), acted differently. His New Deal policies included social welfare programs, economic regulatory action, and massive public jobs projects (see Chapter 3). The New Deal effectively marked the end of the notion of a limited presidency. FDR's successor,

Theodore Roosevelt (shown here with running mate Charles Fairbanks in a 1904 campaign poster) is widely seen as the first of the "modern" presidents. Roosevelt aggressively advanced America's influence in Latin America and the Pacific. On the domestic front, he battled the business trusts, believing that unregulated capitalism was incompatible with social justice. Roosevelt held the presidency as a Republican from 1901 to 1908 and was defeated when trying to recapture it as a third-party candidate in 1912. (Library of Congress, Prints and Photographs Division [LC-DIG-pga-08163])

Harry S Truman, wrote in his memoirs "The power of the President should be used in the interest of the people and in order to do that the President must use whatever power the Constitution does not expressly deny him."[11]

Need for a Strong Domestic Presidency

Today, the presidency is an inherently strong office, made so by the federal government's increased policy responsibilities. Although individual presidents differ in their capacity for leadership, the office they hold requires active involvement in a broad range of policy areas.

The federal government of today consists of thousands of programs and hundreds of agencies. Congress is poorly suited to directing and coordinating them. Congress is a fragmented institution that acts through negotiation, bargaining, and compromise. It is not structured in a way that would enable it to routinely oversee government activity and develop comprehensive approaches to policy. It has 535 members, none of whom is authorized to speak for the whole Congress and all of whom to one degree or another are free to pursue their own agenda.

In contrast, the presidency is structured in a way that fosters unity and decisiveness. Final authority rests with a single individual, the president, who is thereby able to direct the actions of others and undertake large-scale planning.[12] As a result, major domestic policy initiatives since the New Deal era have usually come from the White House. When President Dwight D. Eisenhower took office in 1953 and didn't immediately put forth legislative initiatives, a House committee chair told him, "That's not the way we do things here—you draft the bills, and we work them over."[13]

Although policy leadership on major domestic issues has shifted toward the president, the Constitution grants legislative authority to Congress (see "How the U.S. Differs"). This separation of powers is a major constraint on the presidency, as will be discussed in a later section of the chapter.

HOW THE U.S. DIFFERS

CRITICAL THINKING THROUGH COMPARISONS

Systems of Executive Leadership

In writing the U.S. Constitution, the framers created the first of what today is called a presidential system. Executive authority rests with the president, while legislative authority is vested in Congress.

Later on, when democratic revolutions swept through European nations, they chose not to copy the American model. They adopted instead parliamentary systems where the prime minister is head of both the executive and legislative branches. In a presidential system, the voters separately chose the president and the legislative members. In a parliamentary system. the voters chose the legislative members who, in turn, select the prime minister.

Presidents depend on Congress to enact their legislative initiatives, and Congress's support is not guaranteed. In contrast, prime ministers, as the head of the legislative branch as well as of the executive branch, can usually count on legislative backing. Prime ministers are chosen by the majority party's members, who have the votes required to enact the prime minister's proposals.

Q: Which executive leadership would you prefer—a presidential system, in which the chief executive heads only the executive branch, or a parliamentary system, in which the chief executive heads both the executive and the legislative branches? Why?

Need for a Strong Foreign Policy President

The presidency has also been strengthened by the expanded scope of foreign policy. World War II fundamentally changed the nation's international role and the president's role in foreign policy. The United States emerged from the war as a global superpower, a giant in world trade, and the recognized leader of the non-communist world—a development that had a one-sided effect on America's institutions.[14] Because of the president's constitutional authority as the chief diplomat and military commander and the special demands of foreign policy leadership, the president, not Congress, assumed the dominant role.[15] Foreign policy requires singleness of purpose and, at times, fast action. The president, as the sole head of the executive branch, can act quickly and can speak authoritatively on behalf of the nation as a whole in its dealings with other nations. Congress—a large, divided, and often unwieldy institution—is poorly suited to such a response. The president's advantage was reluctantly admitted by Senator William Fulbright, a leading critic of the Vietnam War. Said Fulbright, "It has been circumstance rather than design which has given the executive its great predominance in foreign policy. The circumstance has been crisis, an entire era of crisis in which urgent decisions have been required again and again, decisions of a kind Congress is ill-equipped to make. . . . The President has the means at his disposal for prompt action; the Congress does not."[16]

Writing in the 1960s, political scientist Aaron Wildavsky also noted the president's preeminence in foreign policy, arguing that the nation has only one president but two presidencies: one domestic and one foreign.[17] Although

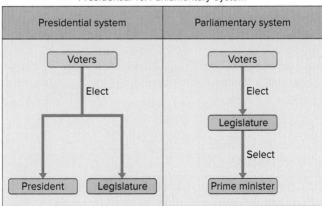

Presidential vs. Parliamentary System

Wildavsky's claim is now regarded as an overstatement stemming from the fact that he was writing in an era when Republican and Democratic lawmakers were united in their determination to contain Soviet communism (see Chapter 17), presidents still have an edge over Congress on foreign policy. Upholding America's credibility abroad can lead Congress, however reluctantly, to back the president on a foreign policy issue.[18] As a noted legal scholar observed, "The verdict of history, in short, is that the substantive content of American foreign policy is a divided power, with the lion's share falling usually, though by no means always, to the president."[19]

Congress has effectively handed decision-making power on some foreign policies to the president. For example, although the Constitution grants Congress the power to "regulate commerce with foreign nations," it has ceded much of that power to the president. Through the 1962 Trade Expansion Act, the 1974 Trade Act, and the 1977 International Emergency Economic Powers Act, the president was granted the authority to impose tariffs and economic sanctions on other countries. Every president since then has made use of the authorizations. President Trump, for instance, used them to start a trade war with China, placing tariffs on everything from Chinese-made steel to Chinese-made television sets. Some members of Congress spoke out against the tariffs, but Congress took no formal action and federal courts upheld the tariffs as a valid application of authority granted to the president by Congress.[20]

STAFFING THE PRESIDENCY

As the policy responsibilities of the presidency have expanded and as the executive bureaucracy has grown in size in response to heightened demands on the federal government (see Chapter 13), the staffing of the presidency has sharply increased. When Theodore Roosevelt was the president, he had a personal secretary and a handful of assistants. There was no White House Communication Office available to Roosevelt, or even a presidential press secretary.

All of that has changed. Today's presidents are assisted by a huge staff, one that is so large that it challenges presidents' ability to control what's done in their name.

The Executive Office of the President (EOP)

The key staff organization is the **Executive Office of the President (EOP)**, created by Congress in 1939 to provide the president with the staff necessary to coordinate the activities of the executive branch.[21] The EOP has since become the command center of the presidency. The EOP includes several units (see Figure 12-1), including the White House Office (WHO), which consists of the president's closest personal advisers; the Office of Management and Budget (OMB), which consists of experts who formulate and administer the federal budget (see Chapter 13); the National Security Council (NSC), which advises the president on foreign and military affairs; and the National Economic Council (NEC), which assists the president on economic policy.

Most EOP units are staffed by specialists, including economists, legal analysts, and policy experts. The National Security Council illustrates the policy support that a president gets from units within the EOP. Headed by the national security adviser, who is appointed by and has an office near the president, the NSC has a staff of roughly 400 people, many of whom are foreign or defense policy experts. The NSC gathers information and receives guidance from the State, Defense, and Intelligence Agencies to provide the president with precise assessments of national security threats and with plausible options when the need for policy action exists.

Council of Economic Advisers (CEA)

Council on Environmental Quality (CEQ)

Office of Science and Technology Policy

National Security Council (NSC)

Office of the U.S. Trade Representative

President

Office of Administration

Office of the Vice-President

Office of Management and Budget (OMB)

Office of National Drug Control Policy

White House Office

figure 12-1 THE EXECUTIVE OFFICE OF THE PRESIDENT

The Executive Office of the President (EOP) consists of the staff units that directly serve and report to the president. The EOP includes roughly 6,000 individuals, including top assistants who work closely with the president, such as National Security Adviser, the director of the Office of Management and Budget, and the press secretary. (*Source:* The White House)

A central EOP unit is the WHO. It includes the Communications Office, the Office of the Press Secretary, and the Office of Legislative Affairs. As these labels suggest, the WHO consists of the president's personal assistants, including top political advisers and press agents. These individuals tend to be skilled at developing political strategies and communicating with the public, the media, and other officials. Because of their close relationship with the president, they are among the most influential individuals in Washington.

The Vice President

Although the vice president holds a separate elective office from that of the president, the vice president is for all practical purposes part of the presidential team. Presidents, in fact, handpick their vice president. At the national conventions that nominate the parties' national ticket, the delegates defer to the presidential nominee's choice of a vice presidential candidate. In the 2020 election, Donald Trump stayed with Mike Pence, whom he had picked to run with him in 2016. Joe Biden selected California senator Kamala Harris as his running mate. Of black and South Asian descent, Harris was the first person of either descent to be nominated for the vice presidency by a major party.

The Constitution assigns legislative authority to the vice president. The vice president is the president of the Senate, which allows the vice president to preside over Senate proceedings. Vice presidents rarely do so, however. The job of the presiding officer is to recognize a senator who wants to speak on the bill under consideration. But because Senate rules allow every senator to speak on a pending bill if they choose to do so, the presiding officer does not have any real influence over what happens on the Senate floor. Accordingly, the vice president normally presides only when there's a possibility of a tie vote on a bill. Then, and only then, is the vice president allowed to vote on a bill. It's the key vote in that it decides the bill's fate. In 2021, for example, Vice President Kamala Harris cast the tie-breaking vote on the $1.9 trillion stimulus bill aimed at countering the economic downturn caused by the COVID-19 pandemic.

In contrast, although the vice president is part of the executive branch, the Constitution assigns no executive authority to the office. Accordingly, the vice president's role in the administration is determined by the president. At an earlier time, presidents largely ignored their vice presidents, who did not even have an office in the White House. The vice president was a safety valve, useful only if the president died (eight have died in office). Waiting around for the possibility that the president might die was unappealing to a politician who was seeking to influence policy. Daniel Webster and Henry Clay were among the prominent leaders who declined nomination as their party's vice-presidential candidate. Said Webster, "I do not propose to be buried until I am really dead."[22]

When Jimmy Carter assumed the presidency in 1977, he redefined the vice presidency by assigning important duties to his vice president and relocating him to an office in the White House, a practice followed by every president since then.[23] Trump, for instance, gave Vice President Pence the task, among others, of coordinating the administration's COVID-19 response, while Biden assigned Vice President Harris the task, among others, of overseeing immigration and voting rights. The most powerful of recent vice presidents is Dick Cheney, who served under President George W. Bush. Cheney played a key role in Bush's decision to invade Iraq in 2003 and devised the plan for handling enemy combatants detained in Iraq and Afghanistan, aspects of which were struck down by the Supreme Court as violations of U.S. law and the Geneva Conventions (see Chapter 4).[24] In contrast, although they met frequently, Trump didn't rely on Pence for advice, preferring his own counsel and that of a few trusted people, including talk-show host Sean Hannity.[25]

The Cabinet and Agency Appointees

The heads of the 15 executive departments, such as the Department of Defense and the Department of Agriculture, constitute the president's **cabinet**. They are appointed by the president, subject to confirmation by the Senate. Although the cabinet once served as the president's major advisory group, it has not played this role in nearly a century. As issues have grown in complexity, presidents have increasingly relied on presidential advisers for advice rather than seeking it from the cabinet as a whole. Nevertheless, cabinet members, as heads of major departments, are important figures in any administration. The president selects them for their prominence in politics, business, government, or the professions.[26] In every administration, a few of them, usually the attorney general or the secretary of state, defense, or treasury, become trusted advisers.

The responsibilities of the secretary of state provide an example of the key role played by cabinet officers. As head of the State Department, the secretary's duties include advising the president on foreign policy, overseeing the work of U.S. ambassadors, representing the United States in meetings with foreign leaders, participating as the U.S. representative in international conferences, and protecting U.S. citizens living abroad. During their tenure, recent secretaries of state have visited about 100 countries and traveled roughly a million miles in doing so.[27]

Although presidents rely on all of the cabinet departments, they work particularly closely with the departments of State and Defense (as well as the intelligence agencies). Other departments are sometimes more responsive to Congress than to the president. The Department of Agriculture, for example,

Shown here is Secretary of Defense Lloyd Austin. Although the Cabinet as a whole is less important today than in the past, key cabinet members are close advisers to the president. Austin's influence came into public view when he managed the Biden administration's efforts to provide Ukraine with military assistance in its war with Russia. (Chad J. McNeeley/RBM Vintage Images/Alamy Stock Photo)

relies more heavily on the support of farm-state senators and representatives than on the president's backing. The defense, diplomatic, and intelligence agencies are different. Their missions closely parallel the president's constitutional roles as commander in chief and chief diplomat. President Biden, for example, relied heavily on Secretary of State Antony Blinken and Defense Secretary Lloyd Austin to coordinate the administration's response to Russia's invasion of Ukraine.

In addition to cabinet secretaries, the president appoints the heads and top deputies of federal agencies and commissions, as well as the nearly 200 ambassadors. There are more than 2,000 full-time presidential appointees, a much larger number than are appointed by the chief executive of any other democracy.[28] About a third of these appointees (including ambassadors and agency heads, but not the president's personal advisers) are subject to Senate confirmation.

The Problem of Control

Although the president's appointees are a major asset, their large number poses a control problem for the president. President Truman kept a wall chart in the Oval Office that listed the more than 100 officials who reported directly to him.

He often told visitors, "I cannot even see all of these men, let alone actually study what they are doing."[29] Since Truman's time, the number of bureaucratic agencies has more than doubled, compounding the problem of presidential control over subordinates.[30]

The president's problem is most severe in the case of appointees who work in the departments and agencies. Their offices are located outside the White House, and their loyalty is sometimes split between their commitment to the president and their commitment to the agency they head. In 2018, President Trump discharged Attorney General Jeff Sessions, who had recused himself from overseeing the Justice Department's investigation into links between Russia and Trump's 2016 presidential campaign. When Trump pressured Sessions to reverse his recusal and halt the investigation, Sessions refused, citing Justice Department rules. Calling Sessions "disgraceful" and "very weak," Trump fired him.[31]

Lower-level appointees within the departments and agencies pose a different type of control problem. The president rarely, if ever, sees them, and many are political novices (most have less than two years of government or policy experience). They sometimes come to side with the agency in which they work because they depend on the agency's career bureaucrats for advice and information.

In short, the modern presidential office is a mixed benefit. Although presidential appointees enable presidents to extend their influence into every executive agency, these appointees do not always act in ways that serve the president's interest. (The subject of presidential control of the executive branch is discussed further in Chapter 13.)

BRIDGING THE POWER GAP

During his first months in office and in the midst of the Great Depression, Franklin D. Roosevelt accomplished the most sweeping changes in domestic policy in the nation's history. Congress moved quickly to pass nearly every New Deal initiative he proposed. In 1964 and 1965, Lyndon Johnson pushed landmark civil rights and social welfare legislation through Congress on the strength of the civil rights movement, the legacy of the assassinated President Kennedy, and large Democratic majorities in the House and Senate. When Ronald Reagan assumed the presidency in 1981, inflation and high unemployment had greatly weakened the national economy and created a mood for change, enabling Reagan to persuade Congress to enact some of the largest taxing and spending changes in history.

From presidencies such as these has come the popular impression that presidents have extraordinary control over national policy. However, each of these presidencies was marked by a special set of circumstances—a decisive election victory that gave added force to the president's leadership, a compelling national problem that convinced Congress and the public that bold presidential action was needed, and a president who was mindful of what was expected and pursued policies consistent with that expectation.[32]

When conditions are favorable, presidents can achieve great things. The problem for most presidents is that they serve at a time when conditions are not conducive to large achievements.[33] In 1994, reflecting on budget deficits and other constraints beyond his control, President Bill Clinton said he had no choice but "to play the hand that history had dealt."

There's another reality that presidents face. They operate in a system of divided power (see "How the U.S. Differs"). They have authority under the Constitution, but it's not sufficient to meet all the demands placed on them.[34] Although the president can propose legislation, for example, any such proposal is little more than words on paper if Congress, which has lawmaking authority, fails to agree.[35] Presidents can cajole members of Congress but cannot force them to act, which led political scientist Richard Neustadt to conclude that presidential power at root is "the power to persuade."[36] Noting that presidents lack the authority to boss Congress around, Neustadt said that their challenge is to persuade members of Congress that it's in their interest to back the president's agenda. President Truman expressed the same idea in more colorful terms: "The people can never understand why the President does not use his supposedly great power to make 'em behave. Well, all the President is, is a glorified public relations man who spends his time flattering, kissing and kicking people to do what they are supposed to do anyway."[37]

Nevertheless, presidents have ways to bridge the gap between the formal authority of their office and what's expected of them. The same two features of the presidency—a national constituency and singular authority—that have enabled them to claim national leadership also allow them to acquire the support they need.

Party Leader

America's system of separated powers has been a source of frustration for even the nation's more successful presidents. Theodore Roosevelt expressed the wish that he could "be the president and Congress too for just ten minutes." Roosevelt would then have had the power to enact as well as propose legislation.

For most presidents, the next best thing to being "Congress too" is having a Congress loaded with members of their party. As the party's highest elected official, the president is the party's acknowledged **party leader**. Party members in Congress expect the president to take the lead on major national issues and have a stake in helping the president succeed. Since World War II, the president's party has always lost seats, often a great many, when the president's approval rating is low. Democrats are the latest to learn that lesson. In the 2022 midterm elections with Biden's approval rating in the low 40 percent range, they lost House seats to the Republicans.

Party polarization has increased presidents' reliance on the party's members in Congress. In the bipartisan era after World War II, presidents could expect some support from members of the opposing party on legislative initiatives. Presidents can no longer take that for granted.[38] When Republicans took control of the House in Obama's third year in office, his legislative agenda came to a virtual standstill. Republican House Speaker John Boehner said of Obama's agenda "We're going to do everything—and I mean everything we can do—to kill it, stop it, slow it down, whatever we can."

Presidents are most successful when their party controls both houses of Congress, a situation known as *unified government* (see Figure 12-2). When the other party controls one or both houses, which is *divided government,* presidents have greater difficulty convincing Congress to follow their lead. During Trump's first two years in office, when Republicans controlled both the House and the Senate, 95 percent of the bills that he supported were enacted into law.[39] In 2019, with Democrats in control of the House, it dropped sharply.[40] Presidential historian Arthur Schlesinger noted the importance of having a congressional majority by saying, "In the end, arithmetic is decisive."[41] Seldom has that been clearer than with the $1.9 trillion COVID relief bill enacted early in Joe Biden's presidency. When it came up for a vote in Congress, not a single Republican backed it while every Democratic except one House member did so. In the Senate, the vote was a 50–50 tie, enabling Vice President Kamala Harris to cast the deciding vote.

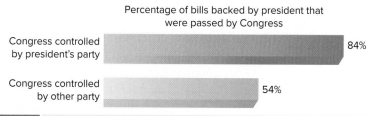

Percentage of bills backed by president that were passed by Congress

Congress controlled by president's party — 84%

Congress controlled by other party — 54%

figure 12-2 PRESIDENTS' LEGISLATIVE SUCCESS

Presidents can endorse legislation, but it takes Congress to enact it. Although presidents have had considerable success in getting congressional support for bills they have backed, they have fared much better when their party controlled Congress than when the other party controlled one or both chambers. (*Source:* Calculated by author from Congressional Quarterly reports from 1952 to 2020.)

The Bully Pulpit

President Theodore Roosevelt described the presidency as a **bully pulpit—** a platform from which to influence the nation's agenda. Presidents are the center of national attention, giving them an unrivaled opportunity to define what is at issue at any given moment and rally public support for their agenda. The president, in fact, gets more news coverage than all of the members of Congress combined.[42] Presidents' agenda-setting ability is a source of power. Dozens of policy problems exist at any given time, and only those that catch Congress's attention have a chance of making it into law. If a president can build public support for policy initiatives through the bully pulpit, the likelihood increases that Congress will take up the issue.[43]

Communication breakthroughs have strengthened the bully pulpit. Franklin Roosevelt used the new medium of radio for "fireside chats," in which he calmed Americans' fears of the Great Depression and told them what he was doing to put them back to work. Telegenic John F. Kennedy popularized the televised press conference as a way to speak directly to Americans about issues of the moment. Donald Trump turned tweeting into an instrument of everyday governing.[44]

Presidents' efforts to mobilize public support have blurred the line between campaigning and governing, resulting in what has come to be known as the **permanent campaign.**[45] Presidents now spend nearly half of their time preparing for and pitching their messages, a process that political scientist Samuel Kernell calls "going public."[46] Bill Clinton went so far as to have his pollster ask respondents where he should vacation. During his first three years in office, George W. Bush took more than 400 trips within the United States, primarily to states that were important to his reelection.[47] Donald Trump took the permanent campaign to its highest level yet with his daily tweets, frequent campaign-style rallies, and a social media advertising campaign that began during his first year in office.[48]

Presidents are not equally skilled in the use of the bully pulpit.[49] The most skilled have typically had a clear sense of what they wanted the country to be and an ability to communicate that vision effectively.[50] Ronald Reagan had it, which helped him alter the direction of domestic and foreign policy. Joe Biden proved to be less adroit. As his approval rating sank during his first year in office, despite notable legislative victories and a record high employment rate, critics cited his inability to effectively communicate his administration's achievements.[51]

With all presidents, there's a risk in the relentless pursuit of public support.[52] It can lead them to embrace policies that provide a short-term advantage rather than what would work best in the long run. As one observer put it, the danger is that a president will "never stop campaigning long enough to govern."[53] It's also the case that presidents are limited in their ability to control events. Adverse developments at home or abroad invariably cut away at a president's public support, and no amount of messaging from the White House can reverse it. George W. Bush's approval rating soared in the aftermath of the terrorist attacks of September 11, 2001, and then plummeted a few years later when the economy dipped and the war in Iraq floundered. More than half of post–World War II presidents including Bush have left office with a **presidential approval rating** of less than 50 percent (see Table 12-2).

Party polarization has limited presidents' ability to rally public support. From their first day in office, before they make even their first policy decision, recent presidents have faced overwhelming opposition from those who identify with the other party. And it's unwavering. No recent president has succeeded in getting opposing partisans to look favorably upon their handling of the presidency (see "Party Polarization").

table 12-2	PERCENTAGE OF PUBLIC EXPRESSING APPROVAL OF PRESIDENT'S PERFORMANCE			
President	Years in Office	Average During Presidency (%)	First-Year Average (%)	Final-Year Average (%)
Harry S Truman	1945–1952	41	63	35
Dwight D. Eisenhower	1953–1960	64	74	62
John F. Kennedy	1961–1963	70	76	62
Lyndon Johnson	1963–1968	55	78	40
Richard Nixon	1969–1974	49	63	24
Gerald Ford	1974–1976	46	75	48
Jimmy Carter	1977–1980	47	68	46
Ronald Reagan	1981–1988	53	58	57
George H. W. Bush	1989–1992	61	65	40
Bill Clinton	1993–2000	57	50	60
George W. Bush	2001–2008	51	68	33
Barack Obama	2009–2016	51	58	51
Donald Trump	2017–2020	39	38	44
Joe Biden			49	

Source: Averages compiled from Gallup polls.

P A R T Y
POLARIZATION

Conflicting Ideas

President of All the People, or Only Those of the Same Party?

Americans have been increasingly divided in their opinion of the president's performance. As would be expected, Democrats are more likely to approve of the performance of a Democratic president and disapprove of that of a Republican president, while the reverse is true of Republicans. However, as indicated by Gallup polls, the gap between Democrats' and Republicans' opinions has widened in recent years. During the three-decade period from the Truman presidency in the late 1940s to the Carter presidency in the late 1970s, the difference between the presidential approval levels of Republicans and Democrats averaged roughly 35 percent. The difference now is at the 80 percent level, as can be seen in the accompanying figure. As two *Washington Post* reporters noted, "We are simply living in an era in which Democrats dislike a Republican president (and Republicans dislike a Democratic one) even before he has taken a single official action."

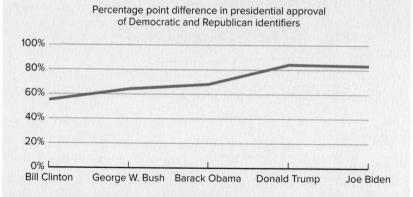

Percentage point difference in presidential approval of Democratic and Republican identifiers

Q: Why has the partisan approval gap widened?

A: The reasons are many, but one of them is that Democrats and Republicans are now further apart in their opinions on controversial policy issues. When it comes to these issues, presidents typically take positions in line with the prevailing opinion of their party. As a result, their positions please most of their party's followers while displeasing, even angering, most of those in the other party.

Going It Alone

Presidents have some authority to act on their own, where they would prefer but don't require the support of Congress, the courts, or the public. Only when they stretch this authority beyond reason are they likely to encounter strong opposition.

Executive Action   One way that presidents can act on their own is to exercise a **presidential veto**, which negates a law passed by Congress. The veto can be a formidable tool. Congress is seldom able to muster the two-thirds majority in each chamber required to override a veto, so the threat of a veto can sometimes get Congress to bend to the president's demands. However, as political scientist Richard Neustadt noted, the veto is also a sign of presidential weakness because it only arises when Congress is defying what the president wants.[54]

Presidents can also act on their own through **executive orders**, which are presidential directives that implement or interpret a law passed by Congress. Such orders are limited only by the requirement that they occur within the context of the law and do not violate a law. Recent presidents have issued about 75 such orders on average each year,[55] many of which have had a significant impact. Through a 2019 executive order, for example, Trump ordered millions of doses of COVID-19 vaccine in advance to ensure that Americans would have priority access when they became available. A limit on executive orders is that the next president can eliminate them with the stroke of a pen. On his first day in office, for example, Biden voided Trump's executive order banning travelers from several predominately Muslim countries.

Presidents also have the authority to act on their own in foreign policy through **executive agreements**—which are treaty-like agreements that presidents make on their own with foreign nations. In 1937, the Supreme Court ruled that executive agreements are legally binding as long as they do not conflict with the Constitution or laws enacted by Congress.[56] A treaty requires Senate approval and cannot normally be voided by the president, whereas an executive agreement becomes law simply based on the president's signature. Since World War II, presidents have negotiated over 17,000 executive agreements—more than 15 times the number of treaties ratified by the Senate during the same period (see Figure 12-3). These agreements span a wide range of policies, everything from military bases to cultural exchanges.[57]

Military Action   In no area, however, is the president's capacity for unilateral action clearer than in the use of military force. The United States has engaged in military action roughly 150 times since the end of World War II. Presidents have initiated military action solely on their authority in most of these instances (see Figure 12-4).[58] That was the case, for example, when President Trump

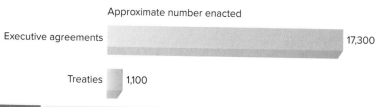

Approximate number enacted

figure 12-3 FORMAL AGREEMENTS WITH OTHER NATIONS

In the past eight decades, presidents have signed over 17,000 executive agreements with other countries—more than 15 times the number of treaties ratified by the Senate during the same period. Treaties require a two-thirds vote of the Senate for ratification. Executive agreements require only the signature of the president. (*Source:* U.S. Department of State. Figure based on the 1939–2013 period.)

launched a cruise missile attack on Syria, President Obama ordered a bombing campaign against Libya, President Clinton ordered an air attack on Serbia, and President George H. W. Bush ordered an invasion of Panama.

In some cases, presidents have hidden their plans even from top leaders in Congress until they were operational. When President Ronald Reagan ordered the invasion of Grenada in 1983, he waited until after the troops were on their way to inform congressional leaders. Speaker of the House Tip O'Neill was among those briefed by Reagan. "We weren't asked for advice," O'Neill said, "we were informed what was taking place."[59] Other members of Congress learned of the invasion when they woke in the morning to news reports saying that U.S. marines had landed in Grenada and were engaged in heavy fighting with the Cuban troops stationed there.

Going Too Far

Unilateral action can enable presidents to achieve their goals, but it comes at a cost if seen as an abuse of presidential power. On rare occasions, presidents have pursued their goals so zealously that Congress has taken steps to curb their use of power.

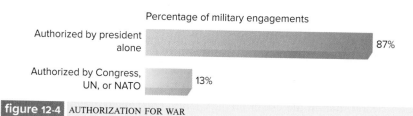

Percentage of military engagements

figure 12-4 AUTHORIZATION FOR WAR

Since World War II, the great majority of U.S. military engagements have been fought solely based on the president's authority as the commander in chief of the armed forces. (*Source:* Compiled by author from U.S. Department of Defense documents.)

President Joe Biden is shown here with Vice President Kamala Harris at a press briefing. Although the presidential office provides a bully pulpit from which to communicate with the American people, it is no guarantee that a president will be able to maintain a high level of public support. Biden's approval rating dropped after becoming president, contributing to his party's loss of the House in the 2022 midterm elections although it retained control of the Senate. (Geopix/Alamy Stock Photo)

Impeachment Congress's ultimate sanction is its authority under the Constitution to remove the president from office if found guilty of "Treason, Bribes, or other high Crimes and Misdemeanors." The House of Representatives decides by majority vote whether the president's actions are deserving of impeachment (placed on trial), and the Senate conducts the trial and then votes on the president's case, with a two-thirds vote required for removal from office. In 1868, Andrew Johnson came within one Senate vote of being removed from office for his opposition to Congress's Reconstruction policies after the Civil War. Bill Clinton was the second president to face Senate trial, having been impeached for lying under oath about a sexual relationship with Monica Lewinsky, a White House intern. The Senate acquitted Clinton by a 55–45 vote.

In 2020, the Senate also voted not to convict Donald Trump. The House had passed two articles of impeachment, one for abuse of power and one for obstruction of Congress in conjunction with Trump's withholding of military assistance to Ukraine in return for Ukraine initiating a corruption investigation against Joe Biden. The Senate vote split along party lines, with all of the Democratic senators voting for both articles of impeachment and all of the Republican senators voting against them, except for Utah's Mitt Romney, who voted to convict Trump on the charge of abuse of power. Romney and six other Republican senators voted to convict Trump in 2021 after he was impeached a second time for "incitement of insurrection" in conjunction with his role in the January 6 assault on the U.S. Capitol. The Senate tally was 10 votes short of what was needed for conviction, which would have disqualified Trump from holding federal office in the future.

Executive Overreach   The gravity of impeachment action and the difficulty of obtaining a Senate conviction make it an unlikely basis for curbing presidential power. Congress has had more success through legislation that limits a president's options. An example is the Budget and Impoundment Control Act of 1974, which prohibits a president from indefinitely withholding funds that have been appropriated by Congress. The legislation grew out of President Nixon's practice of withholding funds from programs he disliked.

Congress's most ambitious effort to curb presidential discretion is the War Powers Act. During the Vietnam War, Presidents Johnson and Nixon misled Congress, supplying it with intelligence estimates that painted a falsely optimistic picture of the military situation. Having been told the war was being won, Congress regularly voted to provide the money to keep it going. However, congressional support changed abruptly in 1971 after the publication in *The New York Times* of classified documents (the so-called Pentagon Papers) that revealed the White House had not been truthful about the war's progress.

In an attempt to limit future presidential wars, Congress in 1973 passed the War Powers Act. Nixon vetoed the measure, but Congress overrode his veto. The act does not prohibit the president from initiating combat but requires the president to consult with Congress, whenever feasible, before doing so and requires the president to inform Congress within 48 hours of the reasons for the military action. Unless Congress approves an extension, the War Powers Act requires hostilities to end within 60 days, although the president has an additional 30 days to safely withdraw the troops.

Each president since Nixon has claimed that the War Powers Act unlawfully infringes on their power as commander in chief, and the Supreme Court has not ruled on the issue, leaving open the question of its constitutionality. Nevertheless, Congress has made it clear that it wants more say in America's use of military force. After President Trump ordered the targeted assassination of Iran's top military general in early 2020, the House and Senate passed separate nonbinding resolutions that opposed war with Iran unless Congress authorized it.

Presidents also invite trouble when they push executive orders to the limits of the law or beyond. When Congress blocked one after another of his legislative initiatives, President Obama shifted to executive orders. "We can't wait for an increasingly dysfunctional Congress to do its job," Obama said. "Whenever they won't act, I will."[60] Obama proceeded to sign an executive order granting temporary deportation relief to roughly 4 million undocumented immigrants who had been in the United States for a substantial period and were leading productive lives. Obama's executive order had no clear basis in law and was invalidated by federal courts.

CASE STUDY

Politics in Action

Presidential Character

In 1966, William Bullitt, assisted by Sigmund Freud, published one of the first-ever psychological assessments of a president. Bullitt studied Woodrow Wilson's public statements and private correspondence to discover why Wilson was inclined to take unattainable policy positions. Bullitt concluded that Wilson had a psychological aversion to facts, preferring instead positions that aligned with his imagined view of the world. A case in point is when Wilson at the end of World War I tried to force his plan for new world order on European allies. They weren't interested, as was clear from their determination to forge a peace treaty that punished Germany for its role in plunging the world into war.[61]

Aude Guerrucci/Consolidated/Pool/dpa picture alliance/Alamy Stock Photo

Continued

A few years after Bullitt's publication, political scientist James David Barber proposed a general theory of "presidential character" based on psychological traits. Barber contended that presidents are psychologically predisposed to either be "active" (driven by a desire to lead) or "passive" (willing to defer to others). Barber further contended that presidents are psychologically predisposed to have either a "positive" view of politics (thriving on political give-and-take) or a "negative" view (resenting the criticism and compromise inherent in politics). Barber posited that "active-positive" presidents, of whom Franklin D. Roosevelt is an example, are the most likely to succeed in office. He proposed that "active-negative" presidents are potentially the most dangerous. Although such presidents are driven to succeed, their distaste for the routines of politics can result in aggressiveness, vengefulness, and deviousness. Barber placed Wilson in this category, where he also placed Richard Nixon, whose many accomplishments were tarnished when he was forced to resign his presidency for unlawful acts.[62]

Barber's thesis was widely accepted but also widely criticized as "armchair" psychoanalysis.[63] Although scholars continued to work on psychological theories of presidential action, it was not until Donald Trump's presidency that the issue received widespread public attention.[64] Trump's disregard for presidential norms and traditions, and his tendency to embrace those who agreed with him and to fire or publicly denigrate those who didn't, were among the reasons.[65]

Q: Using Barber's typology, where would you place Donald Trump? As president, was he active-positive, passive-positive, active-negative, or passive-negative? Do you find Barber's typology helpful as a way to think about Trump? What about Joe Biden? About presidents generally?

ASK YOURSELF: As president, was Trump determined to get his way on policy, or did he regularly defer to the policy goals of others? Did he relish the compromise that's inherent in politics, or did he insist on getting his way? Ask yourself the same questions about Biden. Are there lessons to be learned from evaluating a president through a psychological lens?

By acting too aggressively, presidents weaken their claim to national leadership. Every president at some point has had to deal with the harsh reality of the limits on their power. The fact is, they operate in a system where Congress and the courts have a say in what they can do.

THE ILLUSION OF PRESIDENTIAL GOVERNMENT

Presidents are the center of national attention. It's a key to their policy influence and ability to win the support of other leaders and the American people. However, by being constantly in the limelight, presidents contribute to the public's belief that they are in charge of the national government, a perception that political scientist Hugh Heclo calls "the illusion of presidential government."[66] If presidents are as powerful as they seem to be, they will be held responsible for policy failures as well as policy successes.

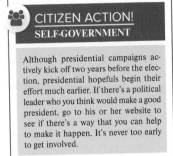

CITIZEN ACTION!
SELF-GOVERNMENT

Although presidential campaigns actively kick off two years before the election, presidential hopefuls begin their effort much earlier. If there's a political leader who you think would make a good president, go to his or her website to see if there's a way that you can help to make it happen. It's never too early to get involved.

Although the reality of presidential power is that it operates within the limits of a system of divided power, there are moments in every presidency when the illusion of presidential government seems real enough. Most newly elected presidents enjoy a **honeymoon period** during their first months in office. It is a time when Congress, the press, and the public are looking to the Oval Office's new occupant for ideas and leadership. But honeymoons don't last long. Political scientist Paul Light found that presidents are twice as likely to get bills through Congress in the first half of their first year in office than in the second half.[67]

As time passes, the momentum of a president's election fades, and opposition mounts.[68] Even successful presidents, like Johnson and Reagan, have had weak records in their final years. Franklin D. Roosevelt began his presidency with a remarkable period of achievement—the celebrated "Hundred Days"—that he was unable to duplicate at any point later in his four-term presidency.

Only rarely are presidents able to maintain a high level of public support throughout the full term of office. Few presidents have been able to do it through even the first year of their presidency. Their policy decisions invariably make enemies, and they are seen to be in charge of developments that they can only partially control, if at all. The economy is among them. When the economy is strong and growing, presidents' approval ratings are much higher on average than when the economy is weak or trending downward.[69] In fact, presidents do not have all that much control over the economy. If they did, they would make sure the economy was always strong. That situation says a lot about the American presidency. Although much of what happens during a president's watch is beyond the president's control, the illusion of presidential government leads many Americans to think the president is in control and must be performing poorly if things are going badly.

Therein rests an irony of the presidential office. More than from any constitutional grant, statute, or crisis, presidential power derives from the president's position as the sole official who can claim to represent the entire American public. However, because presidential power rests on a popular base, it erodes when public support declines. The irony is that the presidential office typically grows weaker as problems mount, which is the time when strong presidential leadership is most needed.[70]

SUMMARY

The presidency has become a much stronger office than the framers envisioned. The Constitution grants the president substantial military, diplomatic, legislative, and executive powers, and in each case the president's authority has increased measurably over the nation's history. Underlying this change is the president's position as the one leader chosen by the whole nation and as the sole head of the executive branch. These features of the office have enabled presidents to claim broad authority in response to the increased demands placed on the federal government by changing global and national conditions.

The responsibilities of the modern presidency require large numbers of advisers, policy experts, and managers. These staff members enable the president to extend control over the executive branch while providing the information necessary for policymaking. All recent presidents have discovered, however, that their control of staff resources is incomplete and that some things that others do on their behalf can work against what they are trying to accomplish.

Presidents operate in a system of divided powers, and their formal authority is not substantial enough to meet the demands placed on them. Nevertheless, they have ways to bridge the power gap. As the center of national attention, they have a "bully pulpit" from which to influence the nation's agenda. Their office also provides the basis for an ongoing effort (the permanent campaign) to generate public support for their initiatives. Then, too, members of Congress from the president's party look to the president for leadership, recognizing that the president's success can affect their reelection chances. Presidents also have some capacity "to go it alone." On their own authority, they can issue executive orders, forge executive agreements with other nations, and send troops into combat.

As sole chief executive and the nation's top elected leader, a president can always expect that his or her policy and leadership efforts will receive attention. However, other institutions, particularly Congress, have the authority to make presidential leadership effective. No president has come close to winning approval of all the programs he has placed before Congress, and presidents' records of success have varied considerably. The factors in a president's success include whether national conditions that require strong leadership from the White House are present, the stage of the president's term, and whether the president's party has a majority in Congress.

Presidential success ultimately rests on the backing of the American people. Recent presidents have made extensive use of the media to build public support for their programs, yet they have had difficulty maintaining that support throughout their terms of office. A major reason is that the public expects far more from its presidents than they can deliver.

CRITICAL THINKING ZONE

KEY TERMS

bully pulpit (*p. 346*)
cabinet (*p. 341*)
chief diplomat (*p. 330*)
chief executive (*p. 330*)
chief legislator (*p. 330*)
commander in chief (*p. 330*)
executive agreements (*p. 349*)
Executive Office of the President
 (EOP) (*p. 338*)
executive order (*p. 349*)

head of government (*p. 330*)
head of state (*p. 330*)
honeymoon period (*p. 355*)
limited presidency theory (*p. 334*)
party leader (*p. 344*)
permanent campaign (*p. 346*)
presidential approval rating (*p. 347*)
presidential veto (*p. 349*)
stewardship theory (*p. 334*)

APPLYING THE ELEMENTS OF CRITICAL THINKING

Conceptualizing: Define the *Whig theory* of the presidency and the *stewardship theory*. How did the increase in the federal government's policy responsibilities and the expanded role of the United States in world affairs contribute to the emergence of the powerful presidency suggested by the stewardship theory?

Synthesizing: Contrast the pre-1972 methods of selecting presidential nominees with the post-1972 method, noting particularly the public's increased role in the selection process.

Analyzing: Why is presidential power "conditional"—that is, why is it affected so substantially by circumstance, the nature of the issue, the makeup of Congress, and popular support? (The separation of powers should be part of your answer.)

OF POSSIBLE INTEREST

A Book Worth Reading: Richard E. Neustadt, *Presidential Power and the Modern Presidents* (New York: Free Press, 1990). A winner of multiple awards, this book is the classic analysis of presidential power. Although now somewhat dated in its arguments, it has had, as one leading political scientist put it, "a greater effect than any other book about a political institution."

A Website Worth Visiting: **www.ipl.org/div/potus** A site that profiles the nation's presidents, their cabinet officers, and key events during their time in office.

CHAPTER 13

THE FEDERAL BUREAUCRACY: ADMINISTERING THE GOVERNMENT

Robert Mills (American architect 1781–1855)/Ryan Rodrick Beiler/Shutterstock

> 66 From a purely technical point of view, a bureaucracy is capable of attaining the highest degree of efficiency, and is in this sense formally the most rational known means of exercising authority over human beings. 99
>
> Max Weber[1]

Seeking to extend the success of its popular 737 jet airliner, Boeing produced the 737 MAX. It had a new software system, the Maneuvering Characteristics Augmentation System (MCAS), which was intended to stabilize the aircraft while in flight. Barely a year after the jet entered service in 2017, 189 people died when a 737 MAX crashed after taking off in Indonesia. Five months later, a second 737 MAX went down after taking off in Ethiopia, killing all 157 people on board. The U.S. government blamed the crashes on Boeing, ordering the grounding of MAX 737s until the faulty new software system could be fixed. The system had repeatedly pushed down the nose of the fated aircraft even as the pilots tried desperately to bring it up.

The government itself had an indirect hand in the crashes. Oversight of commercial aircraft is entrusted to the Federal Aeronautics Administration (FAA), which had given Boeing wide latitude in determining whether the 737 MAX met minimum FAA standards before certifying that it was safe to fly. The FAA pursued the policy even though an internal watchdog warned that it could lead Boeing to cut corners on safety tests. The FAA was also slow in following up on the cause of the first crash, even though the MCAS software was among the possibilities cited by Indonesian investigators.[2]

As with the FAA, government agencies are seldom in the headlines unless something goes wrong. Nor do federal agencies rank high in public esteem. Even though most Americans respond favorably to personal encounters with the federal bureaucracy (as, for example, when a senior citizen applies for Social Security), they have a low opinion of the bureaucracy as a whole. One poll found, for example, that roughly two-thirds of Americans see the bureaucracy as "inefficient and wasteful."[3]

Studies have found that the U.S. federal bureaucracy compares favorably to government bureaucracies elsewhere. "Some international bureaucracies," Charles Goodsell writes, "may be roughly the same [as the U.S. bureaucracy] in quality of performance, but they are few in number."[4] The U.S. Postal Service, for example, has an on-time and low-cost record that few national postal services can match. On the other hand, high-level bureaucratic failures may be on the increase. Political scientist Paul Light documented a series of recent failures, including the government's failure to properly assess intelligence relating to the terrorist attacks of September 11, 2001, and its failure to react in ways that would have saved lives when Hurricane Katrina devastated New Orleans in 2005.[5] More recently, the government was slow to respond after the COVID-19 coronavirus surfaced in China. If it had acted sooner, thousands of lives would have been saved.[6]

Whatever its performance level, the federal bureaucracy is essential. Ambitious programs such as space exploration, Social Security, interstate highways, and the postal service would be impossible without the federal bureaucracy. The bureaucratic form of organization is found wherever there is a need to manage large numbers of people and tasks. Its usefulness is clear from the fact that virtually every large private organization is also a bureaucracy, although such organizations typically operate by a different standard than most public organizations. Efficiency is the chief goal of private bureaucracies but is only sometimes the goal of public bureaucracies. The most efficient way to administer government loans to college students, for instance, would be to give money to the first students who applied and then shut down the program when the money ran out. However, college loan programs, like many other government programs, operate on principles of fairness and need, which require that each application be judged on its merits.

In formal terms, **bureaucracy** is a system of organization and control that is based on three principles: hierarchical authority, job specialization, and formalized rules. These features are the reason bureaucracy, as a form of organization, is the most efficient means of getting people to work together on tasks of large magnitude. **Hierarchical authority** is a chain of command in which the officials and units at the top of a bureaucracy have authority over those in the middle, who in turn control those at the bottom. Hierarchy speeds up action by reducing conflict over the power to make decisions. **Job specialization** refers to explicitly defined duties for each job position and a precise division of labor within the organization. Specialization yields efficiency because each individual concentrates on a particular job and becomes proficient at it. **Formalized rules** are the established procedures and regulations by which a bureaucracy conducts its operations. Formalized rules enable workers to make quick and consistent judgments because decisions are based on preset rules rather than on a case-by-case basis.

Noted German sociologist Max Weber (1864–1920) was the first scholar to systematically analyze bureaucracies. Weber admired the bureaucratic form of organization for its efficiency but recognized that it carried a price. Bureaucrats'

America's armed services are prototypical bureaucracies. Service members have specialized roles and operate in rule-based and hierarchical ("chain of command") units. Shown here is U.S. military equipment being shipped to help Ukraine in its war with Russia. The bureaucratic form of organization enabled the shipment of thousands of tons of military hardware in a relatively short span of time.
(Conner Flecks/Alamy Stock Photo)

actions are dictated by position, specialty, and rule. In the process, they can become insensitive to circumstances. They stick to the rules even when bending them would produce a better outcome. "Specialists without spirit" was Weber's description of the bureaucratic mindset.[7]

This chapter examines both the need for bureaucracy and the problems associated with it. The chapter describes the bureaucracy's responsibilities, organizational structure, and management practices. The chapter also explains the "politics" of the bureaucracy. Although the three constitutional branches of government impose a degree of accountability on the bureaucracy, its sheer size confounds their efforts to control it fully. The chapter presents the following main points:

- *Bureaucracy is an inevitable consequence of complexity and scale.* Modern government could not function without a large bureaucracy. Through authority, specialization, and rules, bureaucracy provides a means of managing thousands of tasks and employees.

- *Bureaucrats naturally take an "agency point of view," seeking to promote their agency's programs and power.* They do this through their expert knowledge, support from clientele groups (those that benefit from the agency's programs), and backing from Congress or the president.

- *Although agencies are subject to oversight by the president, Congress, and the judiciary, bureaucrats exercise considerable power in their own right.*

ORIGIN AND STRUCTURE OF THE FEDERAL BUREAUCRACY

The federal bureaucracy was initially small (3,000 employees in 1800, for instance). The federal government's role was confined largely to defense and foreign affairs, currency and interstate commerce, and delivery of the mail. In the latter part of the 1800s, the bureaucracy began to grow rapidly in size, largely because economic growth was creating new demands on government. Farmers were among the groups clamoring for help, and in 1889 Congress created the Department of Agriculture. Business and labor interests also pressed their claims, and in 1903 Congress established the Department of Commerce and Labor. (A decade later, the department was split into separate commerce and labor departments.) The biggest spurt in the bureaucracy's growth, however, took place in the 1930s. Franklin D. Roosevelt's New Deal included the creation of the Securities and Exchange Commission (SEC), the Social Security Administration (SSA), the Federal Deposit Insurance Corporation (FDIC), the Tennessee Valley Authority (TVA), and numerous other

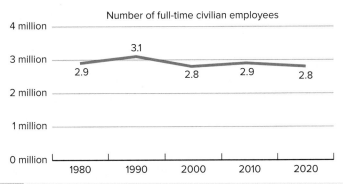

figure 13-1 NUMBER OF FULL-TIME FEDERAL EMPLOYEES

Despite the widespread view that the federal bureaucracy grows ever larger, the number of federal employees has been relatively stable since an expansion in the 1960s. One reason for the stability is improved technology. Many clerical tasks, for example, are now done with the help of computers. (*Source:* U.S. Bureau of the Census. Figure excludes federal grant and contract workers.)

federal agencies. Three decades later, Lyndon Johnson's Great Society initiatives, which thrust the federal government into policy areas traditionally dominated by the states, resulted in the creation of additional federal agencies, including the Department of Transportation and the Department of Housing and Urban Development.

Although the federal bureaucracy is sometimes portrayed as an entity that grows larger by the year, the facts say otherwise. Federal employment today is at roughly the same level that it was 40 years ago (see Figure 13-1), even though the U.S. population has increased greatly in size since then. Nevertheless, it is a large bureaucracy by any standard, particularly when the employment numbers include the several million workers who are hired through temporary federal grants and contracts, such as research scientists and highway construction workers.[8]

Types of Federal Agencies

At present, the U.S. federal bureaucracy has roughly 2.8 million full-time employees, who have responsibility for administering thousands of programs. The president and Congress get far more attention in the news, but the federal bureaucracy has a more direct impact on Americans' daily lives. It performs a wide range of functions; for example, it delivers the mail, oversees the national forests, administers Social Security, enforces environmental protection laws, maintains the country's defense systems, provides foodstuffs for school lunch programs, and regulates the stock markets.

The U.S. federal bureaucracy is organized along policy lines. One agency handles veterans' affairs, another specializes in education, a third is responsible for agriculture, and so on. No two units are exactly alike. Nevertheless, most of them take one of five forms: cabinet department, independent agency, regulatory agency, government corporation, or presidential commission.

The leading administrative units are the 15 **cabinet (executive) departments** (see Figure 13-2). Except for the Department of Justice, which is led by the attorney general, the head of each department is its secretary (for example, the secretary of defense), who also serves as a member of the president's cabinet. Cabinet departments vary greatly in size and budget. The smallest, with a mere 4,000 employees, is the Department of Education. The Department of Defense has the largest budget and workforce, with more than 700,000 civilian

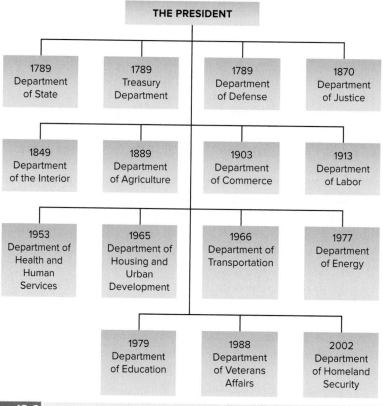

figure 13-2 CABINET (EXECUTIVE) DEPARTMENTS

Each cabinet department is responsible for a general policy area and is headed by a secretary or, in the case of Justice, the attorney general, who serves as a member of the president's cabinet. Shown is each department's year of origin.

employees (apart from the nearly 1.4 million uniformed active service members). The Department of Health and Human Services has the second largest budget, most of which goes for Medicaid and Medicare payments (but not Social Security payments, which are handled by the Social Security Administration, an independent agency).

The newest cabinet-level agency is the Department of Homeland Security (DHS), which was created in 2002 in response to the terrorist attacks on New York and Washington on September 11, 2001. DHS has responsibility for coordinating domestic antiterrorism efforts, including securing the nation's borders, enhancing defenses against biological attacks, preparing emergency personnel (police, firefighters, and rescue workers) for their roles in responding to terrorist attacks, and coordinating efforts to stop domestic terrorism.[9] The U.S. Immigration and Customs Enforcement (ICE) agency is located within DHS and is charged with stopping illegal immigration.

Each cabinet department has responsibility for a general policy area, such as defense or law enforcement. This responsibility is carried out within each department by operating units that typically carry the label "bureau," "agency," "division," or "service." Indeed, the cabinet departments are themselves bureaucracies in that most of the work is done by their units. The Department of Justice, for example, has 13 operating units, including the Federal Bureau of Investigation (FBI), the Civil Rights Division, the Tax Division, and the Drug Enforcement Administration (DEA).

Independent agencies resemble cabinet departments but typically have a narrower area of responsibility. They include organizations such as the Central Intelligence Agency (CIA) and the National Aeronautics and Space Administration (NASA). The heads of these agencies are appointed by and report to the president but are not members of the cabinet. Some independent agencies exist apart from cabinet departments because their placement within a department would pose symbolic or practical problems. NASA, for example, could be located in the Department of Defense, but such positioning would suggest that the space program exists for military purposes and not also for civilian purposes, such as space exploration and satellite communication.

The largest independent agency is the U.S. Postal Service. It has more than half a million career employees, which makes it larger than all of the cabinet departments except the Department of Defense. Established at the nation's founding, the postal service delivers the first-class letter for the same low price to any postal address in the United States, a policy made possible by its status as a government agency. If the postal service were a private firm, the price of a first-class stamp would vary by location, with remote areas of states such as Wyoming and the Dakotas paying extremely high rates.

Regulatory agencies have been created when Congress recognized a need for ongoing regulation of a particular economic activity. Examples of such agencies are the Securities and Exchange Commission (SEC), which oversees the stock and bond markets, and the Environmental Protection Agency (EPA), which regulates industrial pollution. In addition to their administrative function, regulatory agencies have a legislative function. They develop law-like regulations that regulated entities are required to follow. They also have a judicial function. They judge whether regulated entities are complying with legal requirements and can impose fines and other penalties on entities that aren't complying. In 2017, for example, Volkswagen paid a $2.8 billion fine for use of illegal software to cheat on emissions tests to avoid compliance with the Clean Air Act.

Government corporations are similar to private corporations in that they charge for their services and are governed by a board of directors. However, government corporations receive federal funding to pay for some of their operating expenses, and their directors are appointed by the president with Senate approval. Government corporations include the Federal Deposit Insurance Corporation (FDIC), which insures personal savings accounts against bank failures, and the National Railroad Passenger Corporation (Amtrak), which provides passenger rail service.

Presidential commissions provide advice to the president. Some of them are permanent bodies; examples include the Commission on Civil Rights and the Commission on Fine Arts. Other presidential commissions are temporary. An example is the Presidential Commission on Law Enforcement and the Administration of Justice, which was created by President Trump in 2020 to study ways to build community trust in law enforcement officers.

Federal Employment

The nearly 3 million full-time civilian employees of the federal government include professionals who bring their expertise to the problems involved in governing a large and complex society, service workers who perform such tasks as delivering the mail, and middle and top managers who supervise the work of the federal agencies. Most civil servants are hired through the government's **merit system**, whereby they have to score high on a competitive exam (as in the case of postal service, civil service, and foreign service employees) or have specialized training (as in the case of lawyers, engineers, and scientists).[10]

The merit system is an alternative to the **patronage system**, which governed federal employment during much of the 19th century. Patronage was the post-election practice of filling administrative offices with people who had supported the winning party. Critics labeled it a **spoils system**—a device for

HOW THE 50 STATES DIFFER

CRITICAL THINKING THROUGH COMPARISONS

The Size of State Bureaucracies

Although the federal bureaucracy is criticized as being "too big," it is smaller on a per-capita basis than every state bureaucracy. There is less than 1 federal employee for every 100 Americans. Illinois and Indiana, with roughly 1 state employee per 100 residents, have the smallest state bureaucracies. Hawaii, with more than 4 state employees per 100 residents, has the largest.

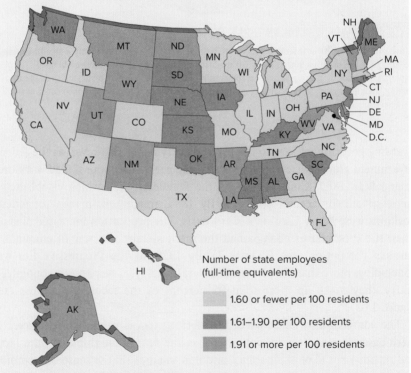

Number of state employees (full-time equivalents)

	1.60 or fewer per 100 residents
	1.61–1.90 per 100 residents
	1.91 or more per 100 residents

Source: U.S. Bureau of Labor Statistics, 2020.

Q: What typifies the states with larger per-capita bureaucracies?

A: In general, the less populous states, especially those that cover a large geographic area, have larger bureaucracies on a per-capita basis. This pattern reflects the fact that a state, whatever its population or area, must provide basic services such as highway maintenance and policing.

Percentage of federal employees

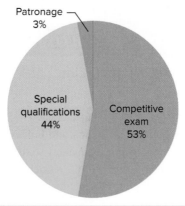

figure 13-3 HOW FEDERAL EMPLOYEES GOT THEIR JOBS

In the 19th century, most federal workers were patronage appointees. Today, only a small percentage get their jobs through that route. The great majority are merit appointees, having obtained federal employment either by placing high on a competitive civil service exam or by having specialized training, such as a medical or engineering degree. (*Source:* Estimated by the author from Office of Personnel Management data.)

awarding government jobs to friends and party hacks. However, as the federal government grew in size and complexity, the need for a more skilled workforce emerged. In 1883, Congress passed the Pendleton Act, which established a merit system for certain positions. By 1885, roughly 10 percent of federal positions were being filled on a merit basis. The proportion increased sharply when the Progressives championed the merit system as a way of eliminating partisan corruption (see Chapter 2). By 1920, as the Progressive Era was concluding, more than 70 percent of federal employees were merit appointees. Today, they make up more than 95 percent of the federal workforce (see Figure 13-3).[11]

The administrative objective of the merit system is **neutral competence**.[12] A merit-based bureaucracy is "competent" in the sense that employees are hired and retained based on their ability, and it is "neutral" in the sense that employees are not partisan appointees and are expected to be of service to everyone, not just those who support the incumbent president. Although the merit system contributes to impartial and proficient administration, it has its own biases and inefficiencies. Career bureaucrats tend to place their agency's interests ahead of those of other agencies and typically oppose efforts to trim their agency's programs. They are not partisans in a Democratic or Republican sense, but they are partisans in terms of protecting their agencies, as will be explained more fully later in the chapter.

The large majority of federal employees have a Graded Service (GS) job ranking. The regular civil service rankings range from GS-1 (the lowest rank) to GS-15 (the highest). College graduates who enter the federal service usually start at the GS-5 level, which provides an annual salary of roughly $31,000 for an entry-level employee. With a master's degree, employees begin at level GS-9 with a salary of roughly $46,000 a year. The master's degree held by many of them is an MPA (Master of Public Administration), a degree envisioned during the Progressive era by Woodrow Wilson, a political scientist at Princeton University and later a U.S. president. Wilson called upon universities to train technically proficient public administrators.[13] One of the first such programs was at the Maxwell School of Citizenship at Syracuse University, and today more than 500 colleges and universities offer the MPA.

CITIZEN ACTION!
SELF-GOVERNMENT

President John F. Kennedy called a career in public service "the highest calling." A study by Harvard University's Kennedy School of Government found that managers in the public sector derive more intrinsic satisfaction from their work than do those in the private sector. If you are considering a public-service career, consider first obtaining a master's degree in public administration or public policy. The entry-level salary is much higher than for those with a bachelor's degree and the responsibilities are greater, as are the prospects for promotion.

Federal employees' salaries increase with rank and length of service, reaching the $110,000 to $145,000 range for those who attain the highest level (GS-15). Although higher-level federal employees are underpaid in comparison with their counterparts in the private sector, while those in some lower-level jobs are comparatively overpaid, federal workers receive better fringe benefits— including full health insurance, secure retirement plans, and substantial vacation time and sick leave—than do most private-sector employees.

Federal employees can form labor unions, but their unions by law have limited scope; the government has full control of job assignments, compensation, and promotion. Moreover, the Taft-Hartley Act of 1947 prohibits strikes by federal employees and permits the firing of striking workers. When federal air traffic controllers went on strike anyway in 1981, President Reagan fired them. There are also limits on the partisan activities of civil servants. The Hatch Act of 1939 prohibited them from holding key jobs in election campaigns. Congress relaxed this prohibition in 1993, although some high-ranking administrators are still barred from holding such positions.

THE BUDGETARY PROCESS

Of special importance to executive agencies is the **budgetary process**—the process through which annual federal spending and revenue decisions are made. It is no exaggeration to say that agencies live and die by their budgets. No agency or program can exist without funding.

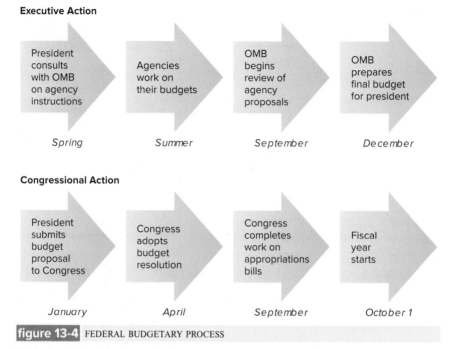

figure 13-4 FEDERAL BUDGETARY PROCESS

The budget begins with the president's instructions to the agencies and ends when Congress enacts the budget. The entire process spans about 18 months. (*Source:* See Schick, Allen, *The Federal Budget: Politics, Policy, Process,* 3d ed., Washington, D.C.: Brookings Institution, 2007.)

Agencies play an active role in the budgetary process, but the elected branches have final authority. The Constitution assigns Congress the power to tax and spend, but the president, as chief executive, also has a major role in determining the budget (see Chapter 12). The budgetary process involves give-and-take between Congress and the president as each tries to influence how federal funding will be distributed among various agencies and programs.[14] From beginning to end, the budgetary process lasts a year and a half (see Figure 13-4).

The President and Agency Budgets

The budgetary process begins in the executive branch when the president, in consultation with the Office of Management and Budget (OMB), establishes general budget guidelines. OMB is part of the Executive Office of the President (see Chapter 12) and takes its directives from the president. Hundreds of agencies are covered by the budget, and OMB uses the president's directives to issue guidelines for each agency's budget preparations. Each agency, for example, is assigned a budget ceiling that it cannot exceed in developing its budget proposal.

The agencies receive their guidelines in the spring and then work through the summer to create a detailed agency budget, taking into account their existing programs and new proposals. Agency budgets are then submitted to OMB in September for a full review, which invariably includes further consultation with each agency and the White House. OMB then finalizes the agency budgets and combines them into the president's budget proposal.

The agencies naturally seek additional funding for their programs, whereas OMB has the job of aligning the budget with the president's priorities. However, the president does not have any real say over most of the budget, about two-thirds of which involves mandatory spending. This spending is required by law and not subject to the president's authority, as in the case of Social Security payments to retirees. Accordingly, OMB focuses on the third of the budget that involves discretionary spending, which includes spending in areas such as defense, foreign aid, education, national parks, space exploration, and highways. In reality, even a large part of this spending is not truly discretionary. No president would slash defense spending to almost nothing or cut off all funding for the national parks. The president, then, works on the margins of the budget. In most policy areas, the president will propose a modest spending increase or decrease over the previous year.

Presidents occasionally take bolder action. In his first budget proposal, President Trump called for cutting funding for the State Department and the U.S. Agency for International Development by roughly 25 percent, a reflection of his belief that diplomacy was not the most effective way to advance America's global interests.

Congress and Agency Budgets

In January, the president's budget is submitted to Congress. During its work on the budget, the president's recommendations undergo varying degrees of change. Congress has constitutional authority over government spending, and its priorities are never the same as the president's, even when the congressional majority is of the same political party. When it is of the opposite party, its priorities differ substantially from those of the president.

On reaching Congress, the president's budget proposal goes to the House and Senate budget committees. Their job is to recommend overall spending and revenue levels. Once approved by the full House and Senate, the levels are a constraint on the rest of Congress's work on the budget.

The House and Senate appropriations committees take over at this point. As with the executive branch, these committees focus on discretionary spending programs, which are the only budget items subject to change. The House Appropriations Committee, through its 12 subcommittees, reviews the budget, which includes hearings with officials from each federal agency. Each subcommittee has responsibility for a particular substantive area, such as defense or agriculture. A subcommittee may cut an agency's budget if it concludes that the agency is overfunded or may increase the budget if it concludes that the agency is underfunded. The subcommittees' recommendations are then reviewed by the House Appropriations Committee as a whole. The budget is also reviewed by the Senate Appropriations Committee and its subcommittees. However, the Senate is a smaller body, and its review of agency requests is less exacting than that of the House. To a degree, the Senate Appropriations Committee serves as a "court of last resort" for agencies that have had their funding requests cut by OMB or by the House Appropriations Committee. The Senate, for example, restored most of the cuts to the State Department budget that President Trump had proposed. Senator Lindsey Graham (R-S.C.) had declared Trump's proposal "dead on arrival" when it was announced, and, indeed, Congress overrode Trump's plan during its budget negotiations.[15]

Throughout the budgetary process, members of the House and the Senate rely on the Congressional Budget Office (CBO), which is the congressional

Congress has the final authority over the budget, subject to a presidential veto. Shown here is a session of the House Appropriations Committee, which, through its 12 subcommittees, does most of Congress's work on the budget. (Chine Nouvelle/SIPA/Newscom)

equivalent of the OMB. If CBO believes that OMB or an agency has miscalculated the amount of money needed to carry out its mandated programs, it will alert Congress to the discrepancy.

After the House and Senate appropriations committees have completed their work, they submit their recommendations to the full chambers for a vote. If approved by a majority in the House and the Senate, differences in the Senate and House versions are then reconciled in a conference committee made up of select House and Senate members (see Chapter 11). Their reconciled version of the budget is then voted upon in the House and Senate and, if approved, is sent to the president to sign or veto. The threat of a presidential veto can be enough to persuade Congress to bend to some of the president's demands. In the end, the budget inevitably reflects both presidential and congressional priorities. Neither branch gets everything it wants, but each branch always gets some of what it seeks.

After the budget has been signed by the president, it takes effect on October 1, the starting date of the federal government's fiscal year. If agreement on the budget has not been reached by October 1, which has happened regularly in recent years, temporary funding legislation is required to maintain government operations until the final budget is enacted.

POLICY AND POWER IN THE BUREAUCRACY

The Constitution mentions executive agencies but does not grant them authority. Their authority derives from grants of power to the three constitutional branches: Congress, the president, and the courts. Administrative agencies' main task is **policy implementation**—that is, the carrying out of decisions made by Congress, the president, and the courts. When a directive is issued by Congress, the president, or the courts, the bureaucracy is charged with executing it. In implementing these decisions, the bureaucracy is constrained by the budget. It cannot spend money on an activity unless Congress has appropriated the necessary funds.

Some of what the bureaucracy does is fairly straightforward, as in the case of delivering the mail, processing government loan applications, and imprisoning those convicted of crimes. Yet the bureaucracy sometimes has discretion in implementing policy. Under federal law, for example, cannabis is illegal but, after several states legalized it for medical and recreational use, federal agents cut back on enforcing the law even though federal law, under the U.S. Constitution, supersedes conflicting state law.

Rule-making—determining how a law or executive order will be implemented—is the chief way administrative agencies exercise influence over policy.[16] Most of the provisions in the laws passed by Congress, for example, are expressed in general terms. It's left to the relevant agencies to define in detail how the law will work in practice. For instance, when Congress created the Consumer Financial Protection Bureau (CFPB) in 2010, the law contained a provision banning unfair, deceptive, and abusive lending practices. The provision did not spell out the practices in each of these categories. Bureaucrats in the CFPB determined which practices would be prohibited and what penalty lenders would pay if they failed to comply.

The rule-making process is subject to checks. After an agency develops the initial rules for an activity, they are published in the *Federal Register* and are then subject to comments and objections by interested parties. When the agency then publishes the final rules, it cannot implement them for 60 days, during which time Congress can change them. Mindful that their rules can be rejected, bureaucrats sometimes employ tactics aimed at reducing the possibility, such as publishing them when Congress is not in session and its members are out of town.[17]

In the course of their work, administrators generate policy ideas that get proposed to the White House or Congress. In 2019, for example, for the first time in more than two decades, Congress appropriated funds for gun violence research. Pressure to do so came from organizations that argued the funding was needed to study a problem that results in the death of more than 30,000 Americans annually. But pressure also came from agencies such as the National Institutes of Health, which are charged with protecting public health and recognize that gun violence is a public health problem as well as a criminal justice problem.

In sum, administrators initiate policy, develop it, evaluate it, apply it, and decide whether others are complying with it. The bureaucracy does not simply administer policy. It also *makes* policy.

The Agency Point of View

A key issue of bureaucratic policymaking is the perspective that bureaucrats bring to their decisions. Do they operate from the perspective of the president, or do they operate from the perspective of Congress? The answer is that, although bureaucrats are responsive to both of them, they are even more responsive to the needs of the agency in which they work, a perspective called the **agency point of view**. This outlook comes naturally to most high-ranking civil servants. More than 80 percent of top bureaucrats reach their high-level positions by rising through the ranks of the same agency.[18] Many of them become deeply committed to its work.[19] As one top administrator said when testifying before the House Appropriations Committee, "Mr. Chairman, you would not think it proper for me to be in charge of this work and not be enthusiastic about it . . . would you? I have been in it for thirty years, and I believe in it."[20] One study found, for example, that social welfare administrators

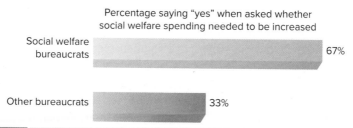

Percentage saying "yes" when asked whether
social welfare spending needed to be increased

Social welfare
bureaucrats — 67%

Other bureaucrats — 33%

figure 13-5 BUREAUCRATS' VIEW OF SOCIAL WELFARE SPENDING

Bureaucrats in social welfare agencies are far more likely than bureaucrats in other agencies to think increased spending on social welfare is necessary. An "agency point of view" is prevalent in the federal bureaucracy. (*Source:* Adapted from Aberbach, Joel D., and Rockman, Bert A., "Clashing Beliefs within the Executive Branch," *American Political Science Review,* vol. 70, 1970, 461.)

were twice as likely as other civil servants to believe that social welfare spending should be increased (see Figure 13-5).[21]

Professionalism also cements agency loyalties. High-level administrative positions have increasingly been filled by scientists, engineers, lawyers, educators, physicians, and other professionals. Most of them take a job in an agency whose mission they support, as in the case of the aeronautical engineers who work for NASA or the doctors who work for the National Institutes of Health (NIH).

Although the agency point of view distorts government priorities, bureaucrats have little choice but to look out for their agency's interests. The president and members of Congress differ in their constituencies and thus in the agencies to which they are most responsive. Republican and Democratic officials also differ in their priorities, a reality that is never more apparent than when party control of the presidency or Congress changes. Some agencies rise or fall in their level of political support for that reason alone. In sum, if an agency is to operate successfully in America's partisan system of divided power, it must seek support wherever it can find it. If the agency is a low priority for the president, it needs to find backing in Congress. If Republican lawmakers want to cut the agency's programs, it must turn to Democratic lawmakers for help. In other words, agencies are forced to play politics if they want to protect their programs.[22] An agency that sits on the sidelines while other agencies seek support from the White House and Congress is likely to lose out in budget negotiations.[23]

Sources of Bureaucratic Power

In promoting their agency's interests, bureaucrats rely on their specialized knowledge, the support of interest groups that benefit from their programs, and the backing of the president and Congress.

The Power of Expertise Most of the policy problems confronting the federal government are extraordinarily complex. Whether the problem relates to space travel or hunger in America, a solution requires deep knowledge of the problem. Much of this expertise is provided by bureaucrats. They spend their careers working in a particular policy area, and many of them have had scientific, technical, or other specialized training (see "How the U.S. Differs").[24] For their part, elected officials are generalists, none more so than the president, who must deal with dozens of issues. Members of Congress acquire some expertise through their committee work, but most of them lack the time, training, or inclination to become deeply knowledgeable of the issues they handle. It's not surprising that Congress and the president rely heavily on career administrators for policy advice.

All agencies acquire some influence over policy through their careerists' expertise. No matter how simple a policy issue may appear at first, it nearly always has layers of complexity. The recognition that the United States has a trade deficit with China, for example, can be the premise for policy change, but this recognition does not begin to address basic issues such as the form the new policy might take, its probable cost and effectiveness, and its links to other issues, such as America's standing in Asia. Among the officials most likely to understand these issues are the career bureaucrats in the Treasury Department, the State Department, the Commerce Department, and the Federal Trade Commission.

The Power of Clientele Groups Most federal agencies were created to promote, protect, or regulate an economic interest. Indeed, nearly every major interest in society—commerce, labor, agriculture, banking, and so on—has a corresponding federal agency. In most cases, these interests are **clientele groups** in the sense that they benefit directly from the agency's programs. As a result, clientele groups can be counted on to lobby Congress and the president on behalf of their agency when its programs and funding are being reviewed.[25] When President Trump, in his fiscal year 2021 budget, proposed to make deep cuts in affordable housing funds, food stamps, and Medicaid, the affected groups lobbied Congress to protect the programs, arguing that the federal government's safety net was what kept economically vulnerable people from succumbing to abject poverty and ill health.[26]

The relationship between an agency and its clientele group is a reciprocal one. Just as a clientele group can be expected to protect its agency, the agency will work to protect the group.[27] The Department of Agriculture, for instance, is a dependable ally of farm interests year after year. The same cannot be said of the president or Congress as a whole, which must balance farmers' demands against those of other groups.

HOW THE U.S. DIFFERS

CRITICAL THINKING THROUGH COMPARISONS

Educational Backgrounds of Bureaucrats

In staffing its bureaucracy, the U.S. government tends to hire persons with specialized education to hold specialized jobs. In contrast, Great Britain tends to recruit its top bureaucrats from the arts and humanities, on the assumption that a broad education is the best preparation. Germany takes a different approach, believing that training in law provides bureaucrats with an understanding of the intersection of law and administration. These tendencies (see figure) were documented by political scientist Guy Peters in his comparative study of the college majors of senior civil servants.[28]

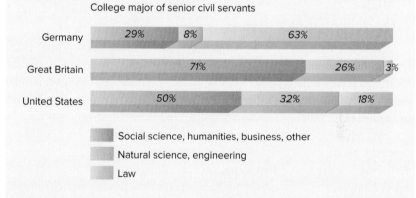

College major of senior civil servants

Germany — 29% | 8% | 63%
Great Britain — 71% | 26% | 3%
United States — 50% | 32% | 18%

Social science, humanities, business, other
Natural science, engineering
Law

Q: Why might the hiring pattern for the U.S. bureaucracy make it more likely that civil servants in the United States will develop an agency point of view than will civil servants in some democracies?

A: Compared with civil servants in Europe, those in the United States are more likely to have a specialized college degree. They tend to work in agencies aligned with their specialty, as in the case of the aeronautical engineers at NASA, the medical researchers at the National Institutes of Health, and the statisticians at the Bureau of Labor Statistics. Their training can strengthen their belief in the importance of their agency's mission, thereby increasing the likelihood they will develop an agency point of view.

The Power of Friends in High Places   Although the goals of the president or Congress can conflict with those of the bureaucracy, they need it as much as it needs them. An agency's resources—its programs, expertise, and group support—can help elected officials achieve their policy goals. When Barack Obama announced early in his presidency the goal of making the United States less dependent on foreign oil, he needed the help of the Department of Energy's experts to develop programs that would further that objective. At a time when other agencies were feeling the pinch of a tight federal budget, the Department of Energy's budget nearly doubled.

Agencies also have allies in Congress. Agencies with programs that benefit important key voting blocs are particularly likely to have congressional support. A prime example is the Department of Agriculture. Although the agricultural sector is just one of the president's many concerns, it is a primary concern of farm-state senators and representatives. They can typically be counted on to support Department of Agriculture funding and programs.

Democracy and Bureaucratic Accountability

The federal bureaucracy's policy influence is at odds with democratic principles. The bureaucratic form of governing is the antithesis of the democratic form. Bureaucracy entails hierarchy, command, permanence of office, appointment to office, and fixed rules, whereas self-government involves equality, consent, rotation of office, election to office, and open decision making. The president and members of Congress are accountable to the people through elections. Bureaucrats are not elected and yet exercise a degree of independent power. Studies have found that in the process of implementing the policy decisions of Congress and the president, bureaucrats sometimes deviate from what the policymakers intended, a phenomenon known as *bureaucratic drift.*[29]

Their influence raises the question of **bureaucratic accountability**—the degree to which bureaucrats can be held accountable for the power they exercise. To a small degree, they are accountable directly to the public. In some instances, for example, agencies are required to hold public hearings before issuing new regulations. For the most part, however, bureaucratic accountability occurs largely through the president, Congress, and the courts.[30]

Accountability Through the Presidency

Periodically, presidents have launched broad initiatives aimed at making the bureaucracy more responsive. The most recent was the National Performance Review, which Bill Clinton began when he became president in 1993. He had campaigned on the issue of "reinventing government" and assembled "reinventing teams," which produced 384 specific recommendations grouped into four broad imperatives: reducing red tape, putting customers first, empowering administrators, and eliminating wasteful spending.[31] Although different in its particulars, the National Performance Review was like earlier reform panels, including the Brownlow, Hoover, and Volcker Commissions,[32] which sought with some success to improve the bureaucracy's efficiency, responsiveness, and accountability.

Presidents can also intervene more directly through *executive orders* to force agencies to pursue particular administrative actions. In the closing days of his presidency, for example, Bill Clinton ordered federal agencies to take the steps necessary to ensure that eligible individuals with limited English proficiency obtained full access to federal assistance programs.

Nevertheless, presidents do not have the time or knowledge to exercise personal oversight of the federal bureaucracy. It is far too big and diverse. Presidents rely instead on management tools that include reorganization, presidential appointees, and the executive budget.[33]

Several presidents have created commissions aimed at making the bureaucracy more efficient, responsive, and accountable. The most recent such commission was the National Performance Review of the Clinton administration, which, among its nearly 400 recommendations, proposed cutting the number of regulations to reduce the paperwork ("red tape") required of those applying for government programs or contracts. Pictured here is Vice President Al Gore who was placed in charge of the review by President Bill Clinton. (REUTERS PHOTOGRAPHER/Alamy Stock Photo)

Reorganization   The bureaucracy's size—its hundreds of separate agencies—makes it difficult for presidents to coordinate its activities. Agencies pursue independent and even conflicting paths. For example, the United States spends more than $50 billion annually to gather intelligence on threats to the nation's security and does so through several agencies. Each of them has its own priorities and a desire to retain control of the intelligence information it has gathered. A lack of communication between the CIA and the FBI may have contributed to the failure to prevent the terrorist attacks on the World Trade Center and the Pentagon on September 11, 2001. Each agency had information that might have disrupted the attack if the information had been shared.

Presidents have sought to streamline the bureaucracy in an attempt to make it more accountable. After the intelligence breakdown in 2001, for example, President George W. Bush commissioned a study of the intelligence agencies, which resulted in creation of the Office of the Director of National Intelligence in 2004. Fifteen intelligence agencies, including the CIA and the FBI, now report directly to the director of national intelligence, who has responsibility for coordinating their activities. Like most reorganizations, this one improved agency performance, but not dramatically. Although the various intelligence agencies now share more information than previously, they have continued to operate somewhat independently of each other—an indication of the tendency of agencies to protect their sphere of operation.

Presidents have had more success in controlling the bureaucracy by moving activities out of the agencies and into the Executive Office of the President (EOP). As explained in Chapter 12, the EOP is directly under White House control and functions to a degree as the president's personal bureaucracy. The EOP now makes some policy decisions that, at an earlier time, would have been made in the agencies. For example, the National Security Council staff, which is part of the EOP, has assumed some of the policy responsibility that once belonged to State and Defense Department staffs.

Presidential Appointments   For day-to-day oversight of the bureaucracy, presidents rely on their political appointees. The president has roughly 2,000 full-time partisan appointees, 20 times the number appointed, for example, by the British prime minister.

The top positions in every agency are held by presidential appointees. They are appointed by the president and can be removed from office at the president's discretion. Their influence is greatest in agencies that have broad authority. Some agencies, like the Social Security Administration (SSA), operate within guidelines that limit what agency heads can do. Although the SSA has a huge budget and makes monthly payments to more than 40 million Americans, recipient eligibility is determined by fixed rules. The head of the SSA does not have the option, say, of granting a retiree an extra $100 a month because the retiree is facing financial hardship. At the other extreme are the regulatory agencies, which have considerable latitude in their decisions. President Trump's initial EPA director, Scott Pruitt, was an outspoken critic of the EPA and, during his first year in office, the EPA initiated 40 percent fewer cases for violation of pollution laws and imposed 65 percent fewer monetary penalties than the EPA did in the Obama administration's first year.[34]

Nevertheless, there are limits to what presidents can accomplish through their appointees. Many appointees lack detailed knowledge of the agencies they head, making them dependent on agency careerists. By the time they come to understand the agency's programs, they often leave. The typical presidential appointee stays on the job for only two years before moving on to other employment.[35]

Executive Budget and Rule-Making   As discussed earlier in the chapter, agencies' annual budgets in the first instance are developed within budget limits established by the president, which gives the president an opportunity to shape what agencies can do, and what they can't. In his first Executive Budget, President Trump proposed the largest cut ever in the budget of the Environmental Protection Agency (EPA), reflecting his belief that it had been too aggressive in interpreting and enforcing its mandate. In contrast, in his first Executive Budget, President Biden proposed the largest increase ever in the EPA's budget, believing it needed to aggressively protect the environment from environmental pollution, including the carbon dioxide emissions that are driving climate change.[36]

Of the management tools available to the president, none is more valuable than the Office of Management and Budget (OMB). As discussed earlier, OMB has substantial control over agency budgets. It also reviews agency regulations before they go into effect. Regulations established through rule-making established by the agencies affect everything from how business will be regulated to how student loans will be administered. In practice, OMB lacks the resources to review all such rules and closely examines fewer than a thousand out of the tens of thousands of rules proposed each year. OMB's rule-making oversight tends to be reactive—triggered in most cases when an affected firm or group complains about a proposed rule. "Reactive oversight," notes scholar William West, "allows the White House to focus its limited resources on agency initiatives that are problematic while ignoring the majority that are not."[37]

Accountability Through Congress

A common misconception is that the president, as the chief executive, has sole authority over executive agencies. In fact, Congress also claims ownership because it is the source of each agency's programs and funding. One presidential appointee asked a congressional committee whether it had a problem with his plans to reduce an agency's programs. The committee chair replied, "No, you have the problem, because if you touch that bureau I'll cut your job out of the budget."[38]

The most substantial control that Congress exerts over the bureaucracy is through its "power of the purse." Congress has constitutional authority over spending; it decides how much money will be appropriated for agency programs. Without funding, a program simply does not exist, regardless of the importance the agency assigns it.

Congressional control also works through the authorization process. No agency or program can exist unless authorized by an act of Congress. Congress can also exert control by taking authority away from an agency. In 1978, as a first step in what would become a decades-long wave of deregulation, Congress passed the Airline Deregulation Act, which took away the Civil Aeronautics Board's authority to set airfares and gave it to the airlines.

As well, Congress exercises control through its oversight function, which involves monitoring the bureaucracy's work to ensure its compliance with legislative intent.[39] If an agency steps out of line, Congress can call hearings to ask tough questions and, if necessary, take legislative action to correct the problem. Bureaucrats are required by law to appear before Congress when asked to do so, and the mere possibility of being grilled by a congressional panel can lead administrators to stay in line. The effect is not altogether positive. Bureaucrats are sometimes reluctant to innovate out of a fear that it will anger some members of Congress.[40]

Nevertheless, Congress lacks the time and expertise to define in detail how programs should be run.[41] Accordingly, Congress has delegated much of its oversight responsibility to the Government Accountability Office (GAO). At an earlier time, the GAO's role was limited largely to keeping track of agency spending. The GAO now also monitors whether agencies are implementing policies in the way that Congress intended. When the GAO finds a problem with an agency's handling of a program, it notifies the appropriate congressional committees, which can then take corrective action.

Oversight cannot correct mistakes or abuses after they happen. Recognizing this limit, Congress has devised ways to constrain the bureaucracy *before* it acts. The simplest method is to draft laws that contain specific instructions on how the bureaucracy is to implement them. In doing so, Congress limits administrators' options. *Sunset provisions* are another restrictive device. These provisions establish a specific date when all or part of a law will expire unless extended by Congress. Sunset provisions are a method of countering the bureaucracy's reluctance to give up outdated programs. However, because members of Congress usually want the programs they create to last, most bills do not have a sunset provision.

Accountability Through the Courts

The bureaucracy is also overseen by the judiciary. Legally, the bureaucracy derives its authority from acts of Congress, and an injured party can bring suit against an agency on the grounds that it has failed to carry out a law properly. If the court agrees, the agency must change its policy. In 1999, for example, a federal court approved a settlement in favor of African American farmers who had demonstrated that the Department of Agriculture had systematically favored white farmers in granting federal farm loans.[42]

Nevertheless, the courts tend to support administrators if their actions are generally consistent with the law they are administering. The Supreme Court has held that agencies can apply any reasonable interpretation of statutes unless Congress has stipulated something to the contrary.[43] This position reflects the Court's recognition that administrators must have discretionary authority if they are to operate effectively and that the federal courts would be overloaded with cases if petitioners could challenge every administrative rule they disliked.

The Court is less deferential when the *major question doctrine* is at issue. This doctrine applies when an ambiguous grant of power to a bureaucratic agency underpins regulatory action that could have a truly major impact. In a 6–3 ruling in 2022, for example, the Supreme Court invoked the doctrine to limit the authority of the Environmental Protection Agency (EPA) to regulate carbon emissions from power plants beyond the boundary of the plants themselves. At issue was whether existing legislation allowed the EPA to place state-level caps on carbon emissions, which could have the effect of requiring some power plants to close or alter their method of producing electricity (for example, by requiring a plant to shift from coal to cleaner-burning natural gas as its fuel source). The Court held that the EPA could take such action only if Congress were to pass legislation that explicitly authorized it.[44]

Accountability Within the Bureaucracy Itself

Recognition of the difficulty of ensuring adequate accountability of the bureaucracy through the presidency, Congress, and the courts has led to the development of mechanisms of accountability within the bureaucracy itself. Four of these mechanisms—the Senior Executive Service, administrative law judges, whistleblowing, and demographic representativeness—are particularly noteworthy.

Senior Executive Service   The agency point of view within the bureaucracy is partly a result of career patterns. Most civil servants work in the same agency throughout their time in government service. As they acquire the skills and knowledge associated with a particular agency, they rise through its ranks and derive job satisfaction and security from supporting its mission.

Detecting Misinformation

Is There a "Deep State"?

In recent years, the claim that the United States is run by a "deep state" has gained wide acceptance. The claim holds that high-ranking people in government agencies are able to control much of what government does, separate from the influence of the voters and elected officials. In a recent ABC News/*Washington Post* poll, respondents were asked whether they agreed that "military, intelligence, and government officials . . . secretly manipulate government policy." Half of the respondents agreed, while a third called the claim a "conspiracy theory," with the rest saying they were unsure. Republicans and Democrats were equally likely to believe in the deep state's existence, whereas young adults (ages 18–29) were the most likely (59 percent) to say the deep state is real, while senior citizens were the least likely (37 percent) to accept the claim.

Lightspring/Shutterstock

Is that claim fact, or is it fake?

Investigations by journalists and others have failed to uncover any evidence of the deep state's existence. The origins of the claim would also lead one to question its validity. The idea of a deep state was initially pushed on the Internet by conspiracy theorists. Although the deep state claim is unfounded, it is accurate to say that the interests of career government officials are sometimes at odds with those of elected officials and the voters. Career bureaucrats are committed to their agencies' programs, funding, and mission, and they try to protect them even when such action runs counter to what the people's representatives are seeking to do.

Recognizing that the bureaucracy's employment system encourages an agency point of view, in 1978 Congress established the **Senior Executive Service (SES)**. The SES represents a compromise between a president-led bureaucracy and an expert one.[45] The SES consists of roughly 7,000 top-level career civil servants who qualify through a competitive process to receive a higher salary than their peers but, in return, can be assigned by the president to any position within the bureaucracy. Unlike the president's regular appointees, SES bureaucrats cannot be fired; if the president relieves them of their job, they have "fallback rights" to their former rank in the regular civil service.

The SES has been less successful in practice than its proponents anticipated. A study found that SES employees are usually assigned to agencies that match their policy expertise, which is typically the same agency in which they have spent their career. Their value rests in significant part on their knowledge of its programs, and to locate them elsewhere would normally diminish their value. Said a former senior executive, "I got promoted because I became an expert in the policies in that area, not because I'm such a great executive who can go anywhere and do anything."[46]

Administrative Law Judges   Individuals will sometimes believe that they have been unfairly disadvantaged by a bureaucrat's decision and will contest it. Such disputes are usually handled by an **administrative law judge**. Administrative law judges are charged with protecting individuals from arbitrary, prejudicial, or incorrect decisions by an agency. These judges are empowered to administer oaths, seek evidence, take testimony, make factual and legal determinations, and render decisions. However, they operate through a less formal process than do regular federal judges. Administrative law hearings usually take place in an office or a meeting room rather than a courtroom, and administrative law judges do not wear a robe or sit on a high bench. The system is designed to provide a less formal, less expensive, and faster method of resolving administrative disputes than would be the case if they were handled through the regular federal courts. Under some circumstances, the decision of an administrative law judge can be appealed to such a court, although this seldom occurs.

Whistleblowing   Although the bureaucratic corruption that is commonplace in some countries is rare in the United States, a certain amount of fraud and abuse is inevitable in any large bureaucracy. One way to limit such practices is **whistleblowing**—encouraging employees to report misconduct by their superiors. The Whistleblower Protection Act protects them from retaliation by their superiors and gives them a financial reward when their information results in substantial savings to government.

Nevertheless, whistleblowing is not for the fainthearted. Many federal employees are reluctant to report instances of misbehavior because they fear

Employees who report misconduct by their superiors are known as whistleblowers. Many recent cases have centered on fraudulent Medicare and Medicaid billing by doctors and health services. In 2020, for example, Universal Health Services, Inc. was forced to pay more than $100 million for conspiring to give patients unnecessary treatments that were then billed to the federal government. (Kristoffer Tripplaar/Alamy Stock Photo)

retaliation. Their superiors might claim that they are malcontents or liars and seek ways to ruin their careers. A case in point is the whistleblower who alerted Congress that President Trump appeared to be withholding military assistance to Ukraine in an effort to solicit its investigation into Democratic presidential candidate Joe Biden. Trump tweeted that the whistleblower was "a liar" and said, "I want to know who's the [whistleblower], who's the person who gave the whistleblower the information? Because that's close to a spy." Although the Whistleblower Protection Act prohibits officials from publicly revealing the identity of a whistleblower, Trump continued to press for the information. Senator Rand Paul (R-Ky.) subsequently released the alleged whistleblower's name on the Senate floor.[47]

Demographic Representation   Although the bureaucracy is an unrepresentative institution in the sense that its officials are not elected, it can be representative in the demographic sense. This concept was endorsed in 1961 by the President's Commission on Equal Employment Opportunity, which was created by President John F. Kennedy. The commission concluded that, if civil servants were more demographically representative of

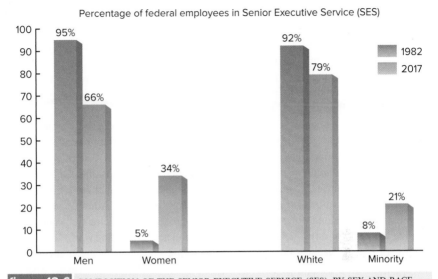

Percentage of federal employees in Senior Executive Service (SES)

figure 13-6 COMPOSITION OF THE SENIOR EXECUTIVE SERVICE (SES), BY SEX AND RACE IN 1982 AND 2017

Source: Office of Personnel Management, 2020.

the general public, they would treat the various groups and interests in society more fairly.[48]

The federal government has made progress in improving the employment status of women and, to a lesser extent, minorities. If all employees are taken into account, the federal bureaucracy comes reasonably close to being representative of the nation's population. Moreover, women and minorities are better represented among the top ranks of administrators than they are in Congress or the judiciary. Nevertheless, the bureaucracy is not demographically representative at the top level. The highest-ranking federal employees are those in the Senior Executive Service (SES). About two in every three such employees are male, and about four in every five are white (see Figure 13-6). However, the SES is far more representative today than four decades ago, when white males accounted for roughly 9 in 10 SES employees.

In any case, **demographic representativeness** is only a partial answer to the problem of bureaucratic accountability. Careerists in the defense and welfare agencies, for example, have similar demographic backgrounds but differ markedly in their policy views. Each group believes that the goals of its agency should be a top priority. In this sense, agency loyalty trumps demographics. Once in an agency, civil servants—regardless of demographic background—tend to become advocates for its programs.

SUMMARY

Bureaucracy is a method of organizing people and work, based on the principles of hierarchical authority, job specialization, and formalized rules. As a form of organization, bureaucracy is the most efficient means of getting people to work together on tasks of great magnitude and complexity. It is also a form of organization that is prone to waste and rigidity, which is why efforts are always being made to reform it.

The United States could not be governed without a large federal bureaucracy. The day-to-day work of the federal government, from mail delivery to the provision of Social Security to international diplomacy, is done by federal agencies. Federal employees work in roughly 400 major agencies, including cabinet departments, independent agencies, regulatory agencies, government corporations, and presidential commissions, yet the bureaucracy is more than simply an administrative giant. Administrators have discretion when making policy decisions. In the process of implementing policy and creating the rules for implementing policy, they influence how policy works in practice.

Administrative agencies operate within budgets established by the president and Congress, and they participate in the budgetary process. The process begins with the president's budget instructions, conveyed through OMB, to the agencies. They then develop their budgets, which are consolidated and sent by the president to Congress, where the House and Senate budget and appropriations committees do the bulk of the work, including holding hearings involving agency heads. Throughout, Congress, the president, and the agencies seek to promote their respective budgetary goals.

Administrators are actively engaged in politics and policymaking. The fragmentation of power and the pluralism of the American political system result in a contentious policy process, which leads government agencies to compete for power and resources. Accordingly, civil servants tend to have an agency point of view: They seek to advance their agency's programs and repel attempts by others to weaken them. In promoting their agencies, civil servants rely on their policy expertise, the backing of their clientele groups, and the support of the president and Congress.

Administrators are not elected by the people they serve, yet they wield substantial independent power. Because of this, the bureaucracy's accountability is a central issue. The major checks on the bureaucracy occur through the president, Congress, and the courts. The president has some power to reorganize the bureaucracy and the authority to appoint the political head of each agency. The president also has management tools (such as the executive budget), which can be used to limit administrators' discretion. Congress can influence bureaucratic agencies through its authorization and funding powers and through various devices (including enabling provisions, sunset provisions, and oversight hearings) that can increase administrators' accountability. The judiciary's role in ensuring the bureaucracy's accountability is smaller than that of the elected branches, but the courts have the authority to force agencies to act in accordance with legislative intent, established procedures, and constitutionally guaranteed rights. Internal checks on the bureaucracy—the Senior Executive Service, administrative law judges, whistleblowing, and demographic representativeness—are also mechanisms for holding the bureaucracy accountable.

CRITICAL THINKING ZONE

KEY TERMS

administrative law judge (*p. 385*)
agency point of view (*p. 374*)
budgetary process (*p. 369*)
bureaucracy (*p. 361*)
bureaucratic accountability (*p. 378*)
cabinet (executive) departments (*p. 364*)
clientele groups (*p. 376*)
demographic representativeness (*p. 387*)
formalized rules (*p. 361*)
government corporations (*p. 366*)
hierarchical authority (*p. 361*)
independent agencies (*p. 365*)

job specialization (*p. 361*)
merit system (*p. 366*)
neutral competence (*p. 368*)
patronage system (*p. 366*)
policy implementation (*p. 373*)
presidential commissions (*p. 366*)
regulatory agencies (*p. 366*)
rule-making (*p. 373*)
Senior Executive Service (SES)
(*p. 385*)
spoils system (*p. 366*)
whistleblowing (*p. 385*)

APPLYING THE ELEMENTS OF CRITICAL THINKING

Conceptualizing: Explain what is meant by *agency point of view.* Why do bureaucrats tend to have an agency point of view?

Synthesizing: Contrast the patronage system and the merit system as methods of hiring government employees.

Analyzing: What are the major sources of bureaucrats' power? What mechanisms for controlling that power are available to the president and Congress?

OF POSSIBLE INTEREST

A Book Worth Reading: Charles T. Goodsell, *The New Case for Bureaucracy* (Washington, D.C.: CQ Press, 2014). A well-written book by an eminent scholar that documents the importance and effectiveness of the U.S. federal bureaucracy.

A Website Worth Visiting: **www.whistleblower.org** The Government Accountability Project is a nonpartisan organization devoted to protecting and encouraging whistleblowers in the private sector as well as the public sector.

14
CHAPTER

THE FEDERAL JUDICIAL SYSTEM: INTERPRETING THE LAW

Photov.com/Pixtal/age fotostock

" It is emphatically the province and duty of the judicial department to say what the law is. Those who apply the rule to particular cases, must of necessity expound and interpret that rule. If two laws conflict with each other, the courts must decide on the operation of each. "

JOHN MARSHALL[1]

Through its ruling in *Dobbs v. Jackson Women's Health Organization* (2022), the Supreme Court by a 5-4 vote took away a woman's right to choose abortion, a precedent that had stood for a half-century. Brushing aside the long-standing legal principle of abortion access, the Court's majority argued that the 1973 Supreme Court decision that established a woman's right to choose was "egregiously wrong from the start." The Court's majority went on to say, "[The earlier Court's] reasoning was exceptionally weak, and the decision has had damaging consequences. And far from bringing about a national settlement of the abortion issue, [the decision has] enflamed debate and deepened division."[2]

The Court's abortion ruling illustrates three key points about court decisions. First, the judiciary is an important policymaking body. Some of its rulings are as consequential as a law of Congress or an executive order of the president. Second, the judiciary has considerable discretion in its rulings. The *Dobbs* decision was not based on a straightforward reading of the law, or else the justices would not have divided 5–4 on the ruling. Third, the judiciary is a political as well as a legal institution. The abortion ruling was decided by political appointees. All five justices who voted to disallow abortion were appointed to the Court by a Republican president. Of the other four justices, three were Democratic appointees.

This chapter describes the federal judiciary. Like the executive and legislative branches, the judiciary is an independent branch of the U.S. government, but, unlike the other two branches, its top officers are appointed rather than elected. The judiciary is not a democratic institution, and its role is different from and sometimes more controversial than those of the executive and legislative branches. This chapter explores this issue in the process of discussing the following main points:

- *The federal judiciary includes the Supreme Court of the United States, which functions almost exclusively as an appellate court; courts of appeals, which hear appeals; and the district courts, which hold trials.* Each state has a court system of its own, which for the most part is independent of supervision by the federal courts.

- *Judicial decisions are constrained by applicable constitutional law, statutory and administrative law, and precedent.* Nevertheless, political factors have a major influence on judicial appointments and decisions; judges are political officials as well as legal ones.

- *The judiciary has become an increasingly powerful policymaking body in recent decades, raising the question of the judiciary's proper role in a democracy.*

JUDICIAL POWER

The Constitution establishes the judiciary as a separate and independent branch of the federal government. The Constitution provides for the Supreme Court of the United States but gives Congress the power to determine the number and types of lower federal courts.

Federal judges are nominated and appointed to office by the president, subject to confirmation by a majority of the Senate. The Constitution places no age, residency, or citizenship requirements on federal judges, unlike the president, senators, or representatives. Nor does the Constitution require judges to have legal training, although by tradition they do have it. Once seated on the bench, as specified in the Constitution, they "hold their offices during good behavior," which in practical terms means that they serve until they die or retire. No Supreme Court justice and only a handful of lower-court judges have been removed through impeachment and conviction by Congress, the method of early removal specified by the Constitution.

In *Federalist* No. 78, Alexander Hamilton argued that life tenure for federal judges was required for the judiciary's independence and authority. Hamilton noted that the judicial branch is the weakest of the three branches. Whereas congressional power rests on spending authority ("the power of the purse") and presidential power rests on control of military force ("the power of the sword"), judicial power rests on what Hamilton called "judgment"—the reasonableness and fairness of its decisions. The best way to ensure that judicial decisions met this standard, Hamilton argued, is to grant life tenure to federal judges to free them from interference by the president or Congress (see "How the U.S. Differs").

Constitutional Authority

The federal judiciary's authority is provided by Article III of the Constitution which reads in part, "Judicial power shall extend to all cases, in law and equity, arising under this Constitution, the laws of the United States, and treaties."

The Constitution requires that all trials arising under federal law must be decided by a jury, rather than a judge acting alone. As further protection against an unjust verdict, the jury's decision must be unanimous. The writers of the Constitution also sought to protect individuals from the power of government by reserving judicial power to the courts. Legislative trials (bills of attainder), which were allowed in England and used against opponents of those in power, are prohibited by the Constitution.

From the first days of the Constitution, it was understood that the federal courts would have exclusive authority to decide federal cases arising under *criminal law* (acts that government deems illegal), *civil law* (disputes between parties as to which one is in the right), and *procedural law* (rules government must follow to act lawfully). What was unclear was whether the courts would have the authority to decide *constitutional disputes*. Whether unintentionally or by design, the Constitution did not entrust to any unit of government the power to determine whether a government official or institution had exceeded its constitutional authority.

Some leading Americans assumed that the federal judiciary would have this authority. At the ratifying conventions of 8 of the 13 states, it was claimed that the federal judges would have the power to nullify actions that violated

HOW THE U.S. DIFFERS

CRITICAL THINKING THROUGH COMPARISONS

Supreme Court Justices' Term of Office

Once appointed to office, Supreme Court justices effectively have lifetime tenure, which distinguishes them from the president, senators, and House members, each of whom serves a limited fixed term. Lifetime tenure also distinguishes Supreme Court justices from judges in the high courts of other Western democracies. There, they serve for a fixed term or until the designated retirement age.[3] In Germany, for example, federal judges serve a 12-year term and face mandatory retirement at age 68. In contrast, U.S. Supreme Court justices typically serve past 75 years of age and spend more than 20 years on the Court.

Q: What are the advantages and disadvantages of a system of lifetime tenure for Supreme Court justices versus a system where they would serve for a fixed term with a mandatory retirement age?

A: The main advantage of lifetime tenure, which Alexander Hamilton identified at the writing of the Constitution, is that it insulates justices from political pressure. Although the claim would be difficult to prove, it could also be argued that longstanding judges make better decisions during their later years on the bench as a result of the experiences they have accumulated. In contrast, an advantage of a fixed term is that it reduces the risk of having a judge on the high court with severe physical or mental health problems. Another advantage is that it reduces the incentive, which occurs with lifetime tenure, to appoint young individuals to the high court with the expectation that they will serve for decades. Finally, a fixed-term appointment system would increase the fairness of the process. In the U.S. system, Supreme Court seats come open when a justice retires or dies, which can be unpredictable. The Nixon and Carter administrations are an extreme example of how this situation can favor one political party or the other. Republican president Richard Nixon had five vacancies during his time in office while Democratic president Jimmy Carter had none.

the Constitution.[4] Some prominent Americans believed otherwise. In response to the Alien and Sedition Acts of 1798, Kentucky passed a resolution, authored by Thomas Jefferson, that declared a state could nullify a federal law that it believed was unconstitutional. The Kentucky Resolution declared that "the several states who formed that instrument [the Constitution], being sovereign and independent, have the unquestionable right to judge of its infraction."

An opportunity for the judiciary to claim the power to make constitutional judgments arose after the presidential election of 1800, in which John Adams, the Federalist Party nominee, lost his bid for a second term after a bitter campaign against Jefferson, the nominee of the Democratic-Republican Party (the forerunner of today's Democratic Party). Between November 1800, when Jefferson was elected, and March 1801, when he was inaugurated, the Federalist-controlled Congress created 59 additional lower-court judgeships, enabling Adams to appoint loyal Federalists to the positions before he left office. However, Adams's term expired before his secretary of state could give all the appointees their judicial commission. Recognizing that they could not take office without the commission, Jefferson told his secretary of state, James Madison, not to

John Marshall presided over the Supreme Court during the nation's formative years. A judicial activist, he worked through court rulings to strengthen the power of the national government and bolster the Court as an independent and co-equal branch of government. Marshall is the longest-serving chief justice in the nation's history. He was on the Court from 1801 to 1835, which spanned the administrations of six presidents. (Art Reserve/Alamy Stock Photo)

deliver them. William Marbury was one of those denied his commission, and he asked the Supreme Court to issue a writ of mandamus (a court order directing an official to perform a specific act) that would force Madison to deliver it.

Judicial Review

In *Marbury v. Madison* (1803), which many analysts regard as the most important constitutional ruling in the nation's history, the Supreme Court established the power of **judicial review**, which is the power of the judiciary to decide whether a government official or institution has acted within the limits of the Constitution and, if not, to declare its action null and void.

In the *Marbury* opinion, Chief Justice John Marshall wrote that Marbury had a legal right to his commission but then said that the Court did not have the authority to issue him a writ of mandamus. Congress in 1789 had passed a law that granted the Court the power to issue such writs, but Marshall said the law was invalid because it expanded the Court's authority beyond what the Constitution specified.[5]

Marshall's ruling was ingenious because it asserted the power of judicial review without allowing either the president or Congress to reject the claim. In saying that Marbury had a right to his commission, the Court in effect said that President Jefferson had violated the Constitution by failing to faithfully execute the law. However, because the Court did not order Jefferson to deliver the commission, he was deprived of the opportunity to disobey the Court's ruling. At the same time, the Court rebuked Congress for passing legislation that exceeded its authority under the Constitution. Congress also had no way to retaliate. It could not force the Court to accept the power to issue writs of mandamus if the Court itself refused to issue them.

Marbury v. Madison was of utmost significance in establishing the judiciary as a co-equal branch of government. It was vitally important in a second way as well. If each state had been allowed, as Jefferson argued, to decide for itself whether it would obey a national law, the nation as a nation would have dissolved at the time of the Civil War, perhaps earlier.

Federal Court System

Federal courts include district courts, courts of appeals, specialty courts (such as the U.S. Court of Federal Claims), and the Supreme Court (see Figure 14-1). The Supreme Court is by far the most prominent of these courts, which might give the impression that it's the only court that's truly relevant. It's a mistaken view. Judge Jerome Frank once wrote of the "upper-court myth," which is the view that lower courts blindly follow the rulings handed down by the courts above them.[6] The reality is that federal courts at all levels exercise judicial power.

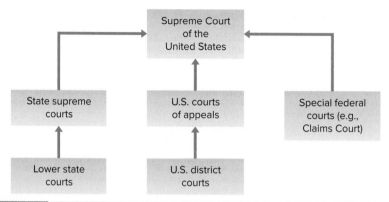

figure 14-1 THE FEDERAL JUDICIAL SYSTEM

This simplified diagram shows the relationships among the various levels of federal courts and between state and federal courts. The losing party in a case can appeal a lower-court decision to the court at the next highest level, as the arrows indicate. Decisions normally cannot be moved from state courts to federal courts unless they raise a U.S. constitutional issue, such as whether a defendant's right to a fair trial has been violated.

The federal court system includes courts of original jurisdiction as well as courts of appellate jurisdiction. A court's **jurisdiction** is its authority to hear cases of a particular type. Jurisdiction is important because it defines each court's role in the judicial system. **Original jurisdiction** is the authority to be the first court to hear a case. Such courts are where trials are held and where most cases end. However, in some instances, the losing party will appeal the decision, which brings appeals (or appellate) courts into the process. They have **appellate jurisdiction**, which is the authority to review cases that have already been tried. Appellate courts do not retry cases or seek new facts; instead, they review cases to determine whether a trial court correctly applied the facts and the law when hearing a case.

U.S. District Courts

The lowest federal courts are the district courts. There are 94 federal district courts altogether—at least 1 in every state and as many as 4 in the most populous states. Each district includes several judges, who number roughly 700 in all.

The federal district courts have original jurisdiction. They are trial courts. Nearly all criminal and civil cases arising under federal law are argued first in the district courts. In a district court case, the two sides present their case to a jury for a verdict. Nearly all cases at this level are presided over by a single judge. Most federal cases end with the district court's verdict. Typically, the losing party chooses not to appeal the decision to a higher court.

District court judges are expected to follow the established law. The Supreme Court stated this expectation in a 1982 case, *Hutto v. Davis*: "Unless we wish anarchy to prevail within the federal judicial system, a precedent of this Court must be followed by the lower federal courts no matter how misguided the judges of those courts may think it to be."[7] However, the idea that lower courts are rigidly bound to Supreme Court rulings is part of the upper-court myth. The facts of a case before a district court may not closely match those of a case settled by the Supreme Court. The lower-court judge then must decide whether a different legal judgment is appropriate. As well, ambiguities or unaddressed issues in Supreme Court rulings give lower courts some flexibility in deciding cases.

The power of district court judges is nowhere more evident than when they strike down a congressional or executive act as unconstitutional. In the U.S. judicial system, unlike that of some democracies, the power of judicial review is not reserved for the highest court. In 2022, for example, a federal district court judge in Florida struck down as unconstitutional the Biden administration's mandate requiring individuals to wear a mask when traveling by plane or train to limit the spread of COVID-19.

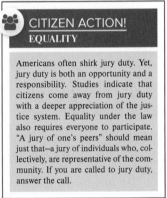

CITIZEN ACTION!
EQUALITY

Americans often shirk jury duty. Yet, jury duty is both an opportunity and a responsibility. Studies indicate that citizens come away from jury duty with a deeper appreciation of the justice system. Equality under the law also requires everyone to participate. "A jury of one's peers" should mean just that—a jury of individuals who, collectively, are representative of the community. If you are called to jury duty, answer the call.

U.S. Courts of Appeals

Cases appealed from district courts go to federal courts of appeals, which are the second level of the federal court system. Courts of appeals do not use juries. Ordinarily, no new evidence is submitted in an appealed case. Instead, appellate courts base their decision on a review of the lower-court record. Appellate judges act as overseers, reviewing trial court decisions and correcting what they consider to be legal errors.

The United States has 13 courts of appeals. Eleven of them have jurisdiction over a "circuit" made up of the district courts in anywhere from three to nine states (see Figure 14-2). Of the other two appeals courts, one has jurisdiction over the District of Columbia (the D.C. "circuit"), and the other (the U.S. Court of Appeals for the Federal Circuit) has jurisdiction over appeals involving patents and international trade, regardless of the circuit in which they arise. Between 6 and 26 judges sit on each court of appeals, but each case usually is heard by a panel of 3 judges. On rare occasions, all the judges of a court of appeals sit as a body (*en banc*) to resolve difficult controversies, typically those stemming from conflicting decisions within the same circuit. Each circuit is monitored by a Supreme Court justice, who typically takes the lead in reviewing appeals that originated with that circuit. Conflict or inconsistency in how the different circuits are applying a law can lead the Supreme Court to review such cases.

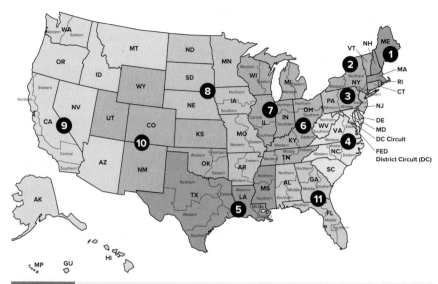

figure 14-2 GEOGRAPHIC BOUNDARIES OF U.S. COURTS OF APPEALS

The United States has 13 courts of appeals, each of which serves a "circuit" (geographical area). Eleven of these circuit courts serve anywhere from three to nine states, as the map shows. The other two are located in the District of Columbia: the Court of Appeals for the District of Columbia and the Court of Appeals for the Federal Circuit, which specializes in appeals involving patents and international trade. Within each circuit are federal district courts. Each state has at least one district court within its boundaries. Larger states, such as California (which has four district courts, as can be seen on the map), have more than one. (*Source:* Administrative Office of the U.S. Courts.)

Courts of appeals offer the only hope of reversal for most appellants because the Supreme Court hears so few cases. The Supreme Court reviews less than 1 percent of the cases heard by federal appeals courts.

Specialty Courts

The federal judiciary includes a few specialty courts, all of which were created by Congress under authority granted by the Constitution. Their jurisdiction is limited to cases of a specific type. Among these courts are the U.S. Court of Federal Claims, which hears cases in which the U.S. government is being sued for damages; the U.S. Court of International Trade, which handles cases involving appeals of U.S. Customs Office rulings; the U.S. Court of Military Appeals, which hears appeals of military courts-martial; and bankruptcy and immigration courts.

When it established these courts, Congress chose to have the judges on some of them serve a fixed term of 15 years in office rather than having lifetime appointments. Congress has also created Administration Law Judges, who serve for a fixed term and hear disputes involving federal regulations (see **Chapter 13**).

The Supreme Court of the United States

The Supreme Court of the United States is the nation's highest court. It has nine members—the chief justice and eight associate justices. The chief justice presides over the Court in meetings and when hearing cases but has the same voting power as each of the other justices.

Article III of the Constitution grants the Supreme Court both original and appellate jurisdiction. The Supreme Court's original jurisdiction includes legal disputes involving foreign diplomats and cases in which the opposing parties are state governments. The Court has convened as a court of original jurisdiction only a few hundred times in its history and has seldom done so in recent decades. One of the rarities was *South Carolina v. North Carolina* (2010), which involved a dispute over the distribution of water in the Catawba River, which flows through both states.[8]

The Supreme Court does its most important work as an appellate court. The Supreme Court's appellate jurisdiction extends to cases arising under the Constitution, federal law and regulations, and treaties. The Court also hears appeals involving legal controversies that cross state or national boundaries.

Although Article III of the Constitution prohibits Congress from altering the Supreme Court's original jurisdiction, it gives Congress the power to create

Shown here are the Supreme Court justices during the 2021–2022 term. Left to right in front are Samuel Alito, Clarence Thomas, John Roberts, Stephen Breyer, and Sonia Sotomayor. Left to right in the back are Brett Kavanaugh, Elena Kagan, Neil Gorsuch, and Amy Coney Barrett. Breyer retired at the end of the Court's term. The seat was filled by Ketanji Brown Jackson, the first African American woman to serve on the Court. (Fred Schilling/Collection of the Supreme Court of the United States/AC NewsPhoto/Alamy Stock Photo)

"exceptions" to the Supreme Court's appellate jurisdiction. Congress also has the power to change the size of the Supreme Court. It has had nine members since the Judiciary Act of 1869 but before that had varying numbers, as few as four and as many as 10.

Selecting and Deciding Cases   Nearly all cases that reach the Supreme Court do so after the losing party in a lower court asks the Court to hear its case. At this point, the **rule of four** comes into play. For a case to be accepted, at least four of the justices must agree to hear it. When that occurs, the Court issues a **writ of certiorari**, which is a request to the lower court to submit to the Court a record of the case. Each year, roughly 8,000 parties apply for certiorari, but the Court grants it in fewer than 100 cases.[9] When the Supreme Court does accept a case, chances are that most of the justices disagree with the lower court's ruling. About three-fourths of Supreme Court decisions reverse the lower court's decision.[10] When the Court declines to accept a case, it is effectively accepting the judgment of the lower court. Its decision stands as the final verdict in the case.

The Supreme Court seldom accepts a routine case, even if the justices believe that a lower court made a mistake. The Court's job is not to correct every error made by lower courts but to resolve major legal issues. The Court's own guidelines say that there must be "compelling reasons" for accepting a case, which include correcting serious departures from accepted legal standards, settling key questions of federal law, and reviewing lower-court rulings that conflict with a previous Supreme Court decision. In practice, the Court is guided by indicators of a case's significance (what judicial scholars call "Cue Theory"), including whether the U.S. government is a party to the case and whether lower courts are issuing conflicting rulings on an issue.[11]

The Court also weighs the features of a case in deciding whether to accept it. One feature is *ripeness*, which refers to whether the legal claim in a case is real and significant rather than based on future claims that might not occur. Another is *mootness*, which asks whether the circumstances that gave rise to the case still exist or have changed to such a degree that a decision is no longer relevant. A third is *standing*, which asks whether the party bringing the case is actually harmed by the action in question or is only marginally affected by it, if at all.[12] Finally, there's the *political question doctrine*, which holds that a challenge to the judgment of federal officials, as opposed to a challenge to their legal authority, is not within the jurisdiction of the courts.

During a Supreme Court hearing, the attorney for each side presents its oral argument, which typically is limited to 30 minutes.[13] Each side also provides the Court a written *brief,* which contains its fuller argument. The oral session is followed by the *judicial conference,* which is attended only by the nine justices and in which they discuss and vote on the case. The Chief Justice presides over both the public session and the private conference. The conference's proceedings are secret, which allows the justices to speak freely about a case and to change their minds as the discussion progresses.[14] In 2022, the Court's secretive process became public when a draft of its pending abortion ruling was leaked to a news outlet, which quickly published it. Within hours, a crowd in the thousands had gathered outside the Supreme Court building to protest its draft position.

Issuing Decisions and Opinions   After a case has been decided, the Supreme Court issues its ruling, which consists of a decision and one or more opinions. The **decision** indicates which party won the case. The most important part of the ruling, however, is the **opinion**, which provides the legal basis for the decision. Other courts are expected to use this basis in deciding on a similar case. In the landmark *Brown v. Board of Education* opinion, for instance, the Court held that government-sponsored school segregation is unconstitutional because it violates the Fourteenth Amendment guarantee of equal protection under the law to all citizens (see the discussion in Chapter 5). This opinion became the legal basis on which public schools throughout the South were ordered by lower courts to end their policy of racial segregation.

When a majority of the justices agree on the legal basis for a decision, the result is a **majority opinion**. In some cases, there is no majority opinion because, although a majority of the justices agree on the decision, they disagree on the legal basis for it. The result in such cases is a **plurality opinion**, which presents the view held by most of the justices who vote with the winning side. Another type of opinion is a **concurring opinion**, a separate view written by a justice (or justices) who votes with the majority but either disagrees with its reasoning or wants to expand on it. Another type is a **dissenting opinion**, where a justice (or justices) on the losing side explains the reasons for disagreeing with the majority's position. A final type is a ***per curiam* opinion**, which is an unsigned decision written for the Court as a whole. However, a justice who disagrees with a *per curiam* decision may choose to write a dissent and, if so, must sign it.

The Chief Justice, when among the justices in the majority, decides which justice will write the majority opinion. Otherwise, the senior justice in the majority picks the author. The justice who writes the Court's majority opinion has the responsibility to express accurately the majority's reasoning. The vote on a case is not considered final until the opinion is written and agreed upon, so give-and-take can occur during the writing stage. In rare instances, the writing stage has produced a change in the Court's decision. In *Lee v. Weisman* (1992), a case involving prayer at a public school graduation, Justice Anthony Kennedy originally sided with the four justices who said the prayer was permissible. While writing the 5–4 majority opinion, Kennedy found that he could not make a persuasive case for allowing it. He switched sides, resulting in a 5–4 majority the other way.

The Supreme Court also issues decisions through what's called the *shadow docket*. These decisions are made without oral presentations by the parties and typically are brief and rendered within days of when a case is filed.[15] Such decisions were rare until a few years ago but have become increasingly common and often involve controversial issues, which has made them a target of criticism. Such decisions are said to lack transparency and perhaps be a way for justices to exert their personal bias without the accountability of having to explain their decision in full. In 2021, for example, the Supreme Court issued a quick one-paragraph ruling that declined to block a Texas law that prohibited abortions after six weeks, which is earlier than some women discover that they're pregnant.[16] All of the justices who voted for the ruling had earlier expressed their opposition to abortion in one form or another. They were the same justices who, less than a year later, would overturn *Roe v. Wade*, ending a 50-year period in which women throughout the nation could choose abortion.

The State Courts

The American states are separate governments within the U.S. political system. The Tenth Amendment protects each state in its sovereignty, and each state has its own court system. Like the federal courts, state court systems have trial courts at the bottom level and appellate courts at the top.

Each state decides for itself the structure of its courts and the method of selecting judges. In some states, the governor appoints judges, but in most states judges are elected to office. The most common form involves competitive elections of either a partisan or a nonpartisan nature. Other states use a mixed system called the *retention election plan* (also called the *merit plan* or the *Missouri Plan* because Missouri was the first state to use it). In this system, the governor appoints a judge from a list of acceptable candidates provided by a judicial selection commission. At the first scheduled election after the judge has served for a year, the voters, by a simple "yes" or "no" vote, decide whether the judge should be retained in office (see "How the 50 States Differ").

Besides the upper-court myth, there exists a "federal court myth," which holds that the federal judiciary is the most significant part of the judicial system and that state courts play a subordinate role. This view is also inaccurate. More than 95 percent of the nation's legal cases are decided by state or local courts.

Moreover, nearly all cases that originate in state or local courts also end there. The federal courts do not come into the picture because the case does not involve a federal issue. The losing party in a divorce suit, for example, cannot appeal the decision to a federal court because no federal law is involved.

HOW THE 50 STATES DIFFER

CRITICAL THINKING THROUGH COMPARISONS

Principal Methods of Selecting State Judges

States vary in how they choose the judges on their highest court. The states with appointed judges give this power to the governor, except in Virginia, Connecticut, and South Carolina, where the legislature makes the choice. In the retention election system (also known as the merit or Missouri Plan), a seated judge is listed on the ballot, and voters decide whether the judge should be allowed to retain the position. In the competitive election system, candidates compete for the position, just as candidates do in elections for other offices.

■ Political appointment
■ Partisan/nonpartisan election
■ Retention election

Source: The Council of State Governments.

Q: What might explain why several states in the middle of the country use the retention election system of electing judges?

A: The retention election plan originated in the state of Missouri. Innovations in one state sometimes spread to adjacent states with similar political cultures.

In most state criminal cases, there is also no federal issue, unless state authorities are alleged to have violated a right protected by the U.S. Constitution, such as the right of the accused to remain silent (see Chapter 4). In such instances, an individual convicted in a state court, after exhausting appeals in the state system, can appeal to a federal court. If the federal court accepts the appeal, it ordinarily confines itself to the federal aspects of the case, such as whether the defendant's constitutional rights were violated.

Issues traditionally within the jurisdiction of the states sometimes become federal issues. Before the Supreme Court's *Obergefell v. Hodges* (2015) ruling, for example, states had the authority to deny a marriage license to same-sex couples. In deciding in *Obergefell* that the right to marry is protected by the due process and equal-protection clauses of the Fourteenth Amendment, the Supreme Court made it a federal issue.[17]

FEDERAL COURT APPOINTEES

Appointments to the federal courts are controlled by the president, who selects the nominees, and by the Senate, which confirms or rejects them. The quiet dignity of the courtroom gives the impression that the judiciary is as far removed from the world of politics as a governmental institution can be. In reality, federal judges and justices bring their political views with them to the courtroom and have opportunities to promote their beliefs through the cases they decide. Not surprisingly, the process by which federal judges are appointed is a partisan one.

Supreme Court Nominees

A Supreme Court appointment is a significant opportunity for a president.[18] Most justices retain their positions for many years, enabling presidents to influence judicial policy through their appointments long after they have left office. The careers of some Supreme Court justices provide dramatic testimony to the enduring nature of judicial appointments. For example, Franklin D. Roosevelt appointed William O. Douglas to the Supreme Court in 1939, and, for 30 years after Roosevelt's death in 1945, Douglas remained a strong liberal influence on the Court.

Presidents usually appoint jurists whose political backgrounds indicate that they will decide cases in the way that the president would want. Although Supreme Court justices are free to make their own decisions, their legal positions can usually be predicted from their background. A study by judicial scholar Robert Scigliano found that at least three of every four appointees have behaved on the Supreme Court as presidents could have expected.[19]

The importance of Supreme Court appointments has not been lost on the justices. They have sometimes timed their departure from the Court so that their replacement will be nominated by a like-minded president. Thurgood Marshall, the first Black justice, failed in his effort to do so. Marshall's health was in decline when Ronald Reagan was president, and he hated the idea of being replaced by a conservative justice. Marshall told his law clerk, "If I die when that man's president, I want you to just prop me up and keep me voting."[20] As it happened, Marshall outlived the Reagan presidency but resigned due to illness when Reagan's successor, George H. W. Bush, also a Republican, was in office. Bush chose Clarence Thomas, the second Black justice, to replace Marshall. Marshall was one of the most liberal justices ever to serve on the Court, while Thomas has been one of the Court's most conservative justices ever.

When a president picks a nominee to fill a vacancy on the Supreme Court, the nominee is appointed to the Court only if confirmed by a majority of the Senate. In 2016, following the death of Justice Antonin Scalia, the Senate's Republican majority refused to hold a vote on Democratic president Barack Obama's nominee, Merrick Garland. It was the first time in history such action

Shown here is Ketanji Brown Jackson testifying before the Senate Judiciary Committee during a hearing on her nomination to a seat on the Supreme Court. Like other recent confirmation hearings, Brown Jackson's hearing was marked by partisan rancor. She was confirmed by a 53–47 margin, receiving the votes of all Democratic and three Republican senators. (Christy Bowe/ZUMA Press Wire/ Alamy Stock Photo)

had been taken. It enabled Donald Trump to fill the seat with Neil Gorsuch when he became president in early 2017. However, in 2020, after the death of Justice Ruth Bader Ginsburg, Republicans were worried that they would lose the seat if Trump lost the upcoming election and rushed to confirm Amy Coney Barrett to fill it. Democrats denounced the move, noting that Republicans in 2016 had claimed that the only fair way to fill a vacancy in an election year was to let the winner of the presidential election make the choice. When Barrett's nomination came up for a vote in the Senate, she was confirmed without the vote of a single Democratic senator.

Nearly 20 percent of presidential nominees to the Supreme Court have been rejected by the Senate on grounds of judicial qualification, legal views, personal ethics, or partisanship. Most of these rejections occurred before 1900, and partisan politics was the usual reason. Garland was the first nominee to be denied confirmation in three decades. In 2017, Senate Republicans abolished the use of the filibuster to block Supreme Court nominees, decreasing the likelihood that future nominees will be rejected by the Senate.

None of the four most recent Supreme Court appointees would have been seated without the change. Each nominee was confirmed by a Senate vote of less than the 60–40 vote margin that would have been required if the filibuster had remained in place. Each nomination was bitterly contested with the vote dividing sharply along party lines—a sure sign that the polarization affecting other areas of political life has reached into the nation's judiciary. The confirmation vote on the most recent Supreme Court appointee—Ketanji Brown Jackson, who was nominated by President Biden and received a unanimous "well qualified" rating from the American Bar Association's Standing Committee on the Federal Judiciary—was 53–47 with only three Republican senators voting in her favor.

The partisan divide in the Senate over Supreme Court appointments has spilled over to the groups with a stake in influencing the process. Through televised ad campaigns and mobilizing their members to petition the White House and Senate, they try to sway the choice of a nominee. In *Electing Justices,* political scientist Richard Davis describes how Supreme Court appointments are now conducted more like political campaigns than by the dignified process envisioned by the writers of the Constitution.[21]

Lower-Court Nominees

The president typically delegates to the deputy attorney general the task of identifying nominees for lower-court positions, a process that includes seeking recommendations from U.S. senators of the president's party, and sometimes House members as well.

Nearly all recent district and appeals court nominees have come from the president's party.[22] A constraint on these appointments is the fact that nominees must be confirmed by the Senate. Senators from the opposing party will try to derail any nominee whom they perceive as holding extreme judicial views. They sometimes succeed, although their ability to do so has diminished. In 2014, Senate Democrats abolished the filibuster for lower-court nominations, a move that presaged its elimination for Supreme Court nominees in 2017 by Senate Republicans.

Although presidents are not as personally involved in selecting lower-court nominees as in naming potential Supreme Court justices, lower-court appointments are collectively significant. A president who serves two terms can shape the federal judiciary for years to come. By the time he left office, Democrat Barack Obama had appointed about a third of the seated federal judges. Republican George W. Bush appointed a similar number during his eight years in office.

Judges' partisan backgrounds affect their decisions. A study of the voting records of appellate court judges found, for example, that Democratic appointees were more likely than Republican appointees to side with defendants who claimed the government violated their civil liberties.[23] Such tendencies should not be interpreted to mean that federal judges engage in blatant partisanship on the bench. Most lower-court cases are clear-cut enough that judges have limited leeway in how they interpret the law. In addition, judges prize their judicial independence. They are officers of a separate branch of government and secure in their tenure, factors that give them independence in applying the law. Nevertheless, analysts worry that the judiciary is changing. Some recent judicial nominees have been chosen based more on partisan ideology than on their legal qualifications, raising the question of whether they will act impartially in deciding cases.[24]

Personal Backgrounds of Judicial Appointees

Women and minorities are underrepresented on the federal bench, just as they are underrepresented in Congress and at the top levels of the executive branch. Roughly 25 percent of federal judges are women and 20 percent are minorities. Women and minorities are key Democratic constituencies, and most of the minority group and female appointees were nominated by a Democratic president (see Figure 14-3).

In recent decades, the Supreme Court has become demographically more representative. Until Sandra Day O'Connor was appointed in 1981, no woman had served on the Supreme Court. Since then, five more women have been appointed. For more than 200 years, the Court always had a Protestant majority. Before the 20th century, only one Catholic (Roger Taney) had served

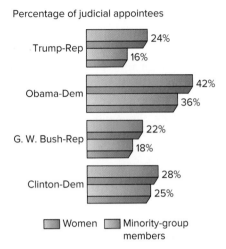

Percentage of judicial appointees

Trump-Rep 24% / 16%

Obama-Dem 42% / 36%

G. W. Bush-Rep 22% / 18%

Clinton-Dem 28% / 25%

Women   Minority-group members

figure 14-3 PRESIDENTS, POLITICAL PARTIES, AND THE APPOINTMENT OF WOMEN AND MINORITIES TO THE FEDERAL BENCH

Reflecting differences in their parties' coalitions, recent Republican and Democratic presidents have differed in the percentage of women and minority-group members that they appointed to the federal bench. (Pew Research Center, 2021.)

on the Court. Until the appointment of Louis D. Brandies in 1916, no Jewish justices had ever served. Today, two of the justices are Jewish, six are Catholic, and only one is Protestant. Thurgood Marshall in 1967 was the first Black justice. Antonin Scalia in 1986 was the Supreme Court's first justice of Italian descent. Sonia Sotomayor, who was appointed in 2009, is the first Hispanic justice. Greater demographic diversity, however, has not been accompanied by greater diversity in educational background. All of the current justices were trained at Harvard Law School or Yale Law School.

In one important respect, the Supreme Court is less diverse than in the past. Elective office (particularly a seat in the U.S. Senate) was once a common route to the Supreme Court, but recent appointees have come from the appellate courts (see Table 14-1). Presidents have increasingly sought nominees who will decide cases in the way the president would like, and appellate court judges have a track record of rulings that are predictive of how they're likely to respond to cases that come before the Supreme Court. Critics think the tendency to only appoint appellate judges has weakened the Court. They note that Supreme Court decisions have political as well as legal consequences and have concluded that the Court would be strengthened if some of the justices had high-level political experience. Many of the leading justices of the past, including John Marshall and Earl Warren, had political rather than judicial backgrounds.[25]

table 14-1 JUSTICES OF THE SUPREME COURT			
Justice	Year of Appointment	Nominating President	Position Before Appointment
Clarence Thomas	1991	G. H. W. Bush	Judge, D.C. Circuit Court of Appeals
John Roberts Jr.	2005	G. W. Bush	Judge, D.C. Circuit Court of Appeals
Samuel Alito Jr.	2006	G. W. Bush	Judge, 3rd Circuit Court of Appeals
Sonia Sotomayor	2009	Obama	Judge, 2nd Circuit Court of Appeals
Elena Kagan	2010	Obama	Solicitor general of the United States
Neil Gorsuch	2017	Trump	Judge, 10th Circuit Court of Appeals
Brett Kavanaugh	2018	Trump	Judge, D.C. Circuit Court of Appeals
Amy Coney Barrett	2020	Trump	Judge, 7th Circuit Court of Appeals
Ketanji Brown Jackson	2022	Biden	Judge, D.C. Circuit Court of Appeals

THE NATURE OF JUDICIAL DECISION MAKING

Unlike the president or members of Congress, federal judges make their decisions within the context of a legal system. Yet they are also political officials: They constitute one of three co-equal branches of the national government. As a result, their decisions are both legal and political.

Legal Influences on Judicial Decisions

Article III of the Constitution bars a federal court from issuing a decision except in response to a case presented to it. Unlike the situation in some countries, a U.S. court cannot issue an advisory opinion. Until they have an actual case to decide, judges cannot issue a ruling and then are bound by the facts of the case. A dispute over religious freedom cannot be used to issue a ruling on environmental regulation. As federal judge David Bazelon noted, a judge "can't wake up one morning and simply decide to give a helpful little push to a school system, a mental hospital, or the local housing agency."[26]

table 14-2	SOURCES OF LAW THAT CONSTRAIN THE DECISIONS OF THE FEDERAL JUDICIARY

U.S. Constitution: The federal courts are bound by the provisions of the U.S. Constitution. However, many of the provisions are expressed in general terms, giving judges a degree of discretion when interpreting their meaning in the context of a particular case.

Statutory law: The federal courts are constrained by statutes and by administrative regulations derived from statutes. Many laws, however, are somewhat vague in their provisions and often have unanticipated applications. As a result, judges have some freedom in deciding cases based on statutes.

Precedent: Federal courts tend to follow precedent (or *stare decisis*), which is a legal principle based on how courts decided previous cases on the same issue. Because times change and not all cases have a clear precedent, judges have some discretion in deciding whether the outcome of earlier cases applies to a current case.

The law is also a major constraint on the courts. Although a president or Congress can make almost any decision that is politically acceptable, the judiciary must work within the limits of the law. When asked by a friend to "do justice," Justice Oliver Wendell Holmes Jr. said that he was bound to follow the law rather than his sense of right and wrong.[27]

The judiciary works within the context of three main sources of law: the Constitution, legislative statutes, and legal precedents (see Table 14-2). The Constitution of the United States is the nation's highest law, and judges and justices are sworn to uphold it. When a case raises a constitutional issue, a court must apply relevant provisions of the Constitution to the case. For example, the Constitution prohibits the states from printing their own currency. If a state decided that it would do so, anyway, a federal judge would be obligated to rule against the practice.

The large majority of cases that arise in courts involve issues of statutory law rather than constitutional law. *Statutory law* is legislative (statute) law. Congress has enacted tens of thousands of laws in its history, many of which sooner or later became the subject of court action. In such cases, courts must apply the statute in question. A company that is charged with violating an air pollution law, for example, will be judged within the context of that statute— what it permits and what it prohibits, as well as what penalties apply if the company is found to have broken the law. In most cases involving statutory law, the law is clear enough that, when the facts of the case are determined, the decision is relatively straightforward. Statutory law also comes into play in judges' decisions in cases involving *administrative law,* which consists of the rules, regulations, and decisions that government agencies make in the process of implementing and enforcing statutory law.

The U.S. legal system was developed from the English common-law tradition, which includes the principle that court decisions should be consistent with **precedent** (or *stare decisis*), a term that refers to previous court rulings on similar cases. Deference to precedent is important to the judiciary's credibility. If it routinely changed its interpretation of the law, it would create the impression that the law is whatever judges on a given day decide it will be. Respect for precedent also lends clarity to the law. If courts routinely ignored how previous cases had been decided, they would create confusion and uncertainty about what is lawful and what is not. A business firm that is seeking to comply with environmental protection laws, for example, can develop company policies that will keep the company safely within the law if court decisions in this area are consistent. If courts routinely ignored precedent, a firm could unintentionally engage in an activity that a court might conclude was unlawful.

Although judges are required to follow the Constitution, statutes, administrative laws, and precedent, the law is not always a precise guide, with the result that judges can have leeway in their rulings.[28] The Constitution, for example, is a sparsely worded document and must be adapted to new and changing situations. The judiciary also has no choice at times but to assess the meaning of statutory law. Statutes are typically more detailed in their provisions than is the Constitution, but Congress cannot always anticipate the specific applications of a legislative act and often drafts broadly worded statutes. The judiciary is then required to determine what the language means in the context of a specific case. Precedent is an even less precise guide in that precedent is specific to particular cases. A new case may differ from its closest precedent or rest at the intersection of conflicting precedents. In such instances, a judge must determine which precedent, if any, applies to the case at hand.

When hearing a case involving statutory law or administrative regulation, judges often try to determine whether the meaning of the statute or regulation can be determined by common sense (the "plain meaning rule"). The question for the judge is the intent of the law or regulation. Courts will sometimes study the legislative record to determine what Congress had in mind when enacting a law. An example is a case that involved the question of whether employment protection for those with disabilities should be extended to include nearsighted people. In this instance, the court ruled that they were not protected by the legislation. If nearsighted people were to be classified as "disabled," then half of the American public would be considered disabled, which was not what Congress intended.

The Supreme Court's ruling in *Bostock v. Clayton County* (2020), involving LGBT discrimination in the workplace, illustrates the ambiguity that sometimes

In 1953, President Dwight Eisenhower (on the right) selected Earl Warren, governor of California, to be the Chief Justice of the Supreme Court. Both were Republicans, but Eisenhower became disenchanted when Warren regularly sided on court decisions with the Court's Democratic appointees. Eisenhower eventually said that he had made a "mistake" in picking Warren to head the Court. (MediaNews Group/Oakland Tribune/Getty Images)

exists in the law. The Court developed its ruling in the context of the 1964 Civil Rights Act, which prohibits workplace discrimination but makes no mention of discrimination based on sexual orientation. The Court concluded that this type of discrimination is among the types of job-related discrimination prohibited by the Civil Rights Act.[29] In this instance, the Court was "making" law. It was deciding how legislation enacted by Congress applied to behavior that Congress had not considered when it wrote the legislation.

Political Influences on Judicial Decisions

When judges have leeway in deciding a case, political influences can affect their decisions. These influences come from both inside and outside the judicial system.

Inside Influences: Judges' Political Beliefs   Although the judiciary sym-
bolizes John Adams's description of the U.S. political system as "a government
of laws, and not of men," court rulings are not simply an extension of the laws.
They are also influenced by the political beliefs of the men and women who
sit on the federal bench.[30] Changes in the Supreme Court's membership, for
example, can bring about a change in its position. Brett Kavanaugh's appointment to the Court in 2018 produced that kind of change. Although the justice
he replaced, Anthony Kennedy, usually voted with the Court's conservative
justices, he sometimes switched sides. He voted with the Court's liberal justices, for example, in a 2016 case that struck down a Texas law that sought to
reduce abortion access by increasing the requirements that abortion clinics
would have to meet to stay open.[31] In contrast, Kavanaugh was part of the 5-4
majority in *Dobbs v. Jackson Women's Health Organization* (2022) that took
away women's constitutional right to choose abortion.[32]

The possibility that judges' political beliefs will enter into their decisions is
higher for the Supreme Court than the lower courts because the disputes that
reach the Supreme Court are often difficult to resolve. If they were clear-cut, they
would have been resolved in the lower courts. A study by University of Chicago
law professor William Landes and Judge Richard Posner (appointed to the federal
bench by President Ronald Reagan) showed that justices' political backgrounds
have a pronounced influence on their decisions. Landes and Posner examined
the voting records of the 43 Supreme Court justices who had sat on the Court
between 1937 and 2008, assessing whether a justice's vote in a case favored the
liberal or the conservative side. For example, in cases alleging that the government
had violated a criminal defendant's constitutional rights, a vote in favor of the
government was considered conservative and a vote in favor of the defendant was
considered liberal. Landes and Posner then ranked the 43 justices on the frequency with which they voted on the liberal or conservative side of cases. All 10
of the most conservative justices were appointed by a Republican president, and
7 of the 10 most liberal justices were appointed by a Democratic president.[33]
Republican president Dwight Eisenhower appointed two of the most liberal
justices, William Brennan and Earl Warren. As he was leaving the presidency,
Eisenhower was asked whether he had made any mistakes as president. He
replied, "Yes, two, and they are both sitting on the Supreme Court."[34]

Political scientists Jeffrey Segal and Harold Spaeth examined thousands of
non-unanimous Supreme Court decisions, looking at the extent to which each
justice voted on the same or opposite side of each of the other justices. A
clear pattern emerged. Democratic appointees were more likely to vote with
other Democratic appointees, whereas Republican appointees tended to vote
with other Republican appointees. Segal and Spaeth conclude that the "[policy]
preferences of the justices go a long way toward explaining their decisions."[35]

Segal and Spaeth's study covered a period when the Republican and Democratic parties were less polarized. More recent studies have found that the gap in the votes of Republican and Democratic appointees on the Supreme Court has widened (see "Party Polarization: Has Polarization Reached into the Supreme Court?"). The finding is not surprising given recent presidents' determination to pick nominees who can be counted upon to support their party's position on legal disputes.

The impact of justices' personal beliefs on their decisions can be exaggerated. Justices operate within the confines of established laws and legal principles, which constrain their choices. Indeed, decisions that divide sharply along party lines account for only some Supreme Court decisions. In the past two decades, roughly half of the decisions have been decided by a 9-to-0, 8-to-1, or 7-to-2 margin. In *United States v. Jones* (2012), for instance, the Supreme Court unanimously held that law enforcement officials had exceeded their authority under the law by placing a GPS tracking device on a suspect's car without first obtaining a search warrant from a judge.[36]

The big picture, then, is that justices' decisions must be seen as a mix of law and politics.[37] The justices operate within a legal institution and the confines of the laws but are not fully removed from the politics that led to their appointment to the Court.

Outside Influences: The Public, Interest Groups, and Elected Officials

Federal judges are not elected and are not as responsive as elected officials to public opinion. Early in his tenure as chief justice, John Roberts said, "I think the most important thing for the public to understand is that we are not a political branch of government. They don't elect us. If they don't like what we're doing, it's more or less just too bad."[38]

Nevertheless, the Supreme Court has normally stayed close enough to public opinion to reduce the likelihood of outright defiance of its decisions.[39] In the long run, the legitimacy of the judiciary requires that the public see its decisions as fair and unbiased. The Supreme Court has sometimes tempered its rulings to get public support or reduce public resistance. In the 1954 *Brown v. Board of Education* case, for example, the justices, recognizing that school desegregation would be an explosive issue in the South, required only that desegregation take place "with all deliberate speed" rather than immediately or on a fixed timetable.

More so than they did in the past, Americans are now questioning the Supreme Court's impartiality. Their reaction is attributable in part to disagreement with specific Court decisions and in part to the perception that the Court is driven by a political agenda rather than by adherence to the law. The result has been a large decline in Americans' approval of the Court's performance

PARTY POLARIZATION

Conflicting Ideas

Has Polarization Reached the Supreme Court?

In response to the charge that the judiciary is ideologically biased, Chief Justice John Roberts said, "We do not have Obama judges or Trump judges, Bush judges or Clinton judges. What we have is an extraordinary group of dedicated judges doing their level best to do equal right to those appearing before them." Associate Justice Sonia Sotomayor has expressed doubts about whether judges are unbiased. "I think each judge on every court has to remember that we have an obligation to keep open minds that are willing to change with time and experience," she said. "If we don't show it, people will believe . . . that we are just political creatures and not independent judges."

Numerous studies support the claim that Supreme Court justices are both independent and political in their decisions. Legal provisions and principles guide their decisions, as is particularly evident in rulings that are unanimous or nearly so. In contrast, the influence of justices' political beliefs is particularly evident when the Court is sharply divided. In such instances, it is seldom the case that each side is comprised almost equally of Democratic and Republican appointees. The typical pattern has all or most Republican appointees on one side of the decision and all or most Democratic appointees on the other side.

This tendency has become more pronounced in recent years, suggesting that the party polarization affecting other aspects of the nation's politics has invaded the nation's highest court. Shown below is a graph indicating the frequency that Republican and Democratic appointees have backed the

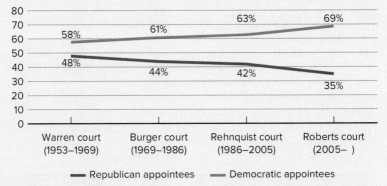

Estimated by the author from data in Herbert M. Kritzer, "Polarized Justice? Changing Patterns of Decisionmaking in the Federal Courts." *Kansas Journal of Law and Public Policy* 28 (2018): 332.

Continued

liberal side (for example, siding with labor rather than business in a labor dispute) on the thousands of non-unanimous court cases during the tenure of the four most recent chief justices (Earl Warren, Warren Berger, William Rehnquist, and John Roberts). As can be seen, the gap has widened over time with Democratic appointees increasingly on the liberal side of the decision and Republican appointees on the opposite side.

Q: Are there arguments for and against the rising level of partisanship in the Supreme Court?

A: On one side, it can be argued that Supreme Court rulings influenced by partisanship bring those rulings more closely into line with what most Americans want, not in every case but in many cases. On the other side, rulings derived from partisan beliefs contradict the principle of equal justice in that such rulings tip the scale toward the side with a majority on the Court.

(see **Figure 14-4**). Two decades ago, more than three in five Americans approved of the job that the Court was doing. Today, only two in five do so.

Because interest groups have more direct ways to influence their decisions, judges are often more responsive to groups than to the public. Groups can, for instance, submit *amicus curiae* ("friend of the court") briefs to make a

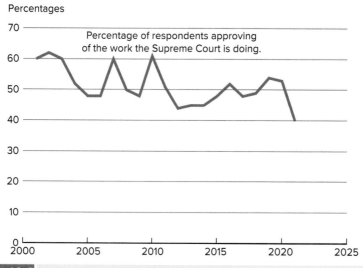

figure 14-4 PUBLIC APPROVAL OF THE SUPREME COURT

Public approval of the Supreme Court's performance has declined in recent years in part because of a growing perception that the justices have a political agenda. (*Source:* Gallup polls)

court aware of their position on a case being heard or under consideration for a hearing by an appellate court (see Chapter 9). They can also file lawsuits to get their way. Groups that do so pick their cases carefully, selecting those that offer the greatest chance of success. They are also careful in picking the courts in which they will file, knowing that some judges will be more sympathetic than others to their position. Some groups rely almost entirely on legal action, knowing they have a better chance of success in the courts than with Congress or the White House. The American Civil Liberties Union (ACLU) has filed hundreds of lawsuits over the years on issues of individual rights, including suits aimed at protecting the privacy of information stored on cell phones and computers.

Elected officials, especially those at the state level, are also frequent litigants. State officials are quick to contest federal actions that they believe infringe on their constitutional authority or are unwarranted assertions of federal power. Republican governors and state attorney generals have sued the Biden administration on several issues, including an order requiring employees of large firms to be vaccinated against COVID-19 or be tested regularly. During the Trump administration, Democratic state officials challenged a number of its actions in court, including Trump's executive order banning travelers from seven predominantly Muslim countries.

Although disputes between Congress and the president have less frequently spilled over into the courts than disputes between the federal and state governments, Congress and the presidency have substantial ways to influence the courts. Congress can, for example, rewrite legislation that it feels the judiciary has misinterpreted. Meanwhile, the president has some control over the cases that come before the courts. During President Trump's first year in office, for example, the Justice Department pursued only a third as many civil rights lawsuits as the Justice Department averaged each year during the Obama administration.[40] The president and Congress's chief opportunity to influence the courts is, of course, their power to decide who will sit on the federal bench. Democratic and Republican lawmakers have been determined to appoint judges whose policy views align with their own.

DEMOCRACY AND JUDICIAL POWER

Federal judges are unelected officials with lifetime appointments, which places them beyond the reach of the voters. A basic question in any democracy is how far judges should go in substituting their judgments for those of elected officials. This question is most compelling when courts apply their power of **judicial review** to declare that an executive or legislation action is unconstitutional. In such instances, they are placing their judgment above that of the people's representatives and in a way that is nearly always final. The difficulty of amending the Constitution, which requires approval by two-thirds majorities in the House and Senate and three-fourths of the state legislatures, makes it an impracticable means of reversing a constitutional ruling.

Judicial review is a particularly formidable source of judicial power in the American case. Few democracies divide power as thoroughly as does the United States, which splits it among three branches as well as between the national and state levels. Also, the U.S. system grants individuals a broad range of rights that are protected from infringement by the government. Each of these features of the American system is a potential source of constitutional dispute. What's the dividing line between legislative and executive power? Between national and state power? Between individual rights and the power of government? U.S. federal courts have the final say on these questions. As Chief Justice Charles Evans Hughes noted in 1907, "We live under a constitution, but the Constitution is what the judges say it is."

Theories of Judicial Decision-Making

Judicial power raises the question of how it should be exercised. What standard should judges apply when deciding difficult cases? Not surprisingly, competing theories have developed about how judges and justices should act. The theories are complex enough that a thoughtful discussion could fill an entire book. Nevertheless, it's instructive to briefly summarize four of the leading theories:

1. The doctrine of **judicial restraint** holds that judges should defer to precedent and to the policy decisions of elected lawmakers in nearly all situations. Advocates say that, when judges substitute their views for those of elected representatives, they undermine the fundamental principle of self-government— the right of the majority, through its elected representatives, to determine how it will be governed.[41]

2. The doctrine of **judicial activism** holds that, although judges should generally defer to elected officials, they should only do so when, from their perspective, they believe officials are acting within their constitutional authority. They also contend that precedent should be respected only if based on legal reasoning that is as sound today as it was when the precedent was established.[42]

3. **Originalism theory** holds that the meaning of constitutional provisions is fixed in the time of their writing and should be binding on judicial officers. Originalists hold to the idea that the writers of the Constitution or a constitutional amendment had a particular meaning in mind and that constitutional rulings should be consistent with that meaning.[43]

4. **Living constitution theory** holds that constitutional law should change to reflect changing values and conditions. Advocates of this theory see constitutional provisions as containing fundamental principles, such as liberty and self-government, that should be applied in the context of the needs of today's society as opposed to the needs of society when the provision was written.[44]

Over its history, the Supreme Court has had strong proponents of each doctrine. Chief Justice John Marshall was an avowed activist who used the Court to enlarge the judiciary's power and foster a strong federal government (see Chapters 2 and 3). Associate Justice Oliver Wendell Holmes Jr. was Marshall's philosophical opposite, claiming that the judiciary should defer to the elected branches unless they blatantly overstep their authority.[45] Among more recent justices, Antonin Scalia was the foremost advocate of originalism theory, whereas justices William Brennan and Stephen Breyer were leading proponents of living constitution theory. Critics have not contested the sincerity of these justices' beliefs but have noted that, in each case, the justice's judicial theory aligned with his political background and, in this sense, provided a basis for decisions the justice might have preferred anyway.

Pictured here is Supreme Court Justice Antonin Scalia. Until his death in 2015, he was the foremost proponent of originalism, the judicial doctrine that holds judges in applying a law should be guided by the meaning intended by those who wrote it. (SCOUS/Alamy Stock Photo)

Politicians have also been outspoken on how they think judges should act, none more loudly than those who complain about "activist judges" who "legislate from the bench." However, they complain only when an "activist" court decision doesn't go their way and are silent when it does. The truth is, activist judges—defined as those who don't readily defer to precedent and the decisions of elected officials—have existed on both the left and the right. In the period after World War II, for example, liberal justices had a majority on the Supreme Court and struck down a large number of state laws in the course of expanding fair-trial rights and civil rights (see Chapters 4 and 5). In recent years, the conservative majority on the Supreme Court has pursued an activist agenda, striking down more precedents and acts of Congress than were overturned in the previous half-century (see "Case Study: *Citizens United v. Federal Election Commission* (2010)").[46]

CASE STUDY   Politics in Action

Citizens United v. Federal Election Commission (2010)

In *Citizens United*, the Supreme Court concluded that Congress had overstepped its constitutional authority in banning campaign contributions by corporations and unions. The Court's majority held that the law banning such contributions infringed on their First Amendment right of free expression. Writing for the majority, Justice Anthony Kennedy said, "If the First Amendment has any force, it prohibits Congress from fining or jailing citizens, or associations of citizens, for simply engaging in political speech." The ruling also reversed precedent that stretched back to the early 1900s. In previous cases, the Supreme Court had upheld Congress's authority to regulate campaign spending by corporations. The Court's minority would have upheld that precedent. It argued that corporations and unions are not what the framers had in mind when referring to "the people" in the First Amendment and that unrestricted spending by corporations would allow their voice to drown out the voice of the people.

In deciding *Citizens United*, the Supreme Court's nine justices split 5-4, with all five justices in the majority (Roberts, Alito, DenisProduction/Shutterstock

Kennedy, Scalia, and Thomas) having been appointed to the Court by a Republican president. The four justices (Breyer, Ginsburg, Sotomayor, and Stevens) in the minority were Democratic appointees, except for Stevens, who was appointed to the Court three decades earlier by President Gerald Ford, a moderate Republican.

Q: If you had been on the Supreme Court, how would you have voted in the Citizens United case?

ASK YOURSELF: Would you, as a Supreme Court justice, have been inclined to defer to Congress and precedent in ruling on the case? Or would you have been willing to overturn the law passed by Congress and reverse the precedent established by previous Court rulings? (If the former, you would be classified as an advocate of judicial restraint. If the latter, you would be classified as a judicial activist.)

What Is the Judiciary's Proper Role?

The debate over the proper role of judges is a normative one, rooted in opposing values rather than factual evidence. There is no conclusive way of settling the issue because the Constitution does not define, nor even hint at, the method by which judges should reach their decisions.

Nevertheless, the debate is important. For one thing, judicial rulings can have a large impact on people's everyday lives. When the Supreme Court upholds the president's war-making power, strikes down a woman's right to abortion, orders a prison to reduce overcrowding, expands environmental regulation, limits collective bargaining, or makes other critical decisions, it affects not only the people and interests directly involved but those connected to them. Judicial decisions, even if fair, are not neutral. They help some people and interests and harm others.

In addition, the United States is a constitutional democracy that recognizes both the power of the majority to rule and the right of the minority to have its freedom and interests protected. Although the judiciary was not established as the nation's final authority on all things relating to the use of political power, it was established as a co-equal branch of government charged with responsibility for protecting individual rights and intervening when elected officials exceed their constitutional authority. The question of how far the courts should go in asserting their authority, and on what basis, is one that every student of government should consider.

SUMMARY

At the lowest level of the federal judicial system are the district courts, where most federal cases begin. Above them are the federal courts of appeals, which review cases appealed from the lower courts. The U.S. Supreme Court is the nation's highest court. Each state has its own court system, consisting of trial courts at the bottom and one or two appellate levels at the top. Cases originating in state courts ordinarily cannot be appealed to the federal courts unless a federal issue is involved, and then the federal courts can choose to rule only on the federal aspects of the case. Federal judges at all levels are nominated by the president, and, if confirmed by the Senate, they are appointed by the president to the office. Once on the federal bench, they serve until they die, retire, or are removed by impeachment and conviction.

The Supreme Court is unquestionably the most important court in the country. The legal principles it establishes are binding on lower courts, and its capacity to define the law is enhanced by the control it exercises over the cases it hears. However, it is inaccurate to assume that lower courts are inconsequential (the upper-court myth). Lower courts have considerable discretion, and the great majority of their decisions are not reviewed by a higher court. It is also inaccurate to assume that federal courts are far more significant than state courts (the federal court myth).

The courts have less discretionary authority than elected institutions do. The judiciary's positions are constrained by the facts of a case and by the laws as defined through the Constitution, legal precedent, and statutes (and government regulations derived from statutes). However, existing legal guidelines are seldom so precise that judges have no choice in their decisions. As a result, political influences have an impact on the judiciary. It responds to national conditions, public opinion, interest groups, and elected officials, particularly the president and members of Congress. Another political influence on the judiciary is the personal beliefs of judges, who have individual preferences that affect how they decide issues that come before the courts. It's not surprising that partisan politics plays a significant role in judicial appointments and decisions.

In recent decades, as the Supreme Court has crossed into areas traditionally left to lawmaking majorities, the issue of judicial power has become more pressing, which has prompted claims and counterclaims about the judiciary's proper role. Advocates of judicial restraint argue that the Constitution entrusts broad issues of the public good to elected institutions and that the courts should be exceptionally deferential to their judgment. Proponents of judicial activism counter that the courts should seek to protect and advance fundamental constitutional principles even when such rulings go against the wishes of elected officials. Adherents of originalism theory hold that the meaning of constitutional provisions is fixed at the time of their writing and should be binding on judicial officers. Living constitution theory advocates say that constitutional law should change to reflect changing values and conditions. Each theory about the judiciary's role is normative. The Constitution is silent on the proper method of interpreting it.

CRITICAL THINKING ZONE

KEY TERMS

appellate jurisdiction (*p. 396*)
concurring opinion (*p. 401*)
decision (*p. 401*)
dissenting opinion (*p. 401*)
judicial activism (*p. 418*)
judicial restraint (*p. 418*)
judicial review (*p. 395*)
jurisdiction (*p. 396*)
living constitution theory (*p. 419*)

majority opinion (*p. 401*)
opinion (*p. 401*)
original jurisdiction (*p. 396*)
originalism theory (*p. 418*)
plurality opinion (*p. 401*)
per curiam opinion (*p. 401*)
precedent (*p. 411*)
rule of four (*p. 400*)
writ of certiorari (*p. 400*)

APPLYING THE ELEMENTS OF CRITICAL THINKING

Conceptualizing: Define *majority opinion, concurring opinion,* and *dissenting opinion* in the context of Supreme Court decision making. What role is the majority opinion expected to play in decisions made by lower-court judges?

Synthesizing: Contrast the doctrines of judicial restraint and judicial activism.

Analyzing: Explain the influence of politics on the selection of Supreme Court justices and on the decisions the justices make. In comparison with lower-court judges, why would Supreme Court justices be expected to let their political beliefs play a greater role in their decisions? (Consider the nature of the cases heard by the Supreme Court.)

OF POSSIBLE INTEREST

A Book Worth Reading: Linda Greenhouse, *Justice on the Brink* (New York: Random House, 2021). This book by a long-time observer of the Supreme Court provides a riveting look at the inside workings of the current Court.

A Website Worth Visiting: www.oyez.org/ An easy-to-use website that includes the full versions of historic and recent Supreme Court decisions and information on cases currently being heard by the Court.

15
CHAPTER

ECONOMIC AND ENVIRONMENTAL POLICY: CONTRIBUTING TO PROSPERITY

CLOSED
We are temporarily quarantined due to COVID-19 virus

StockMediaSeller/Shutterstock

❝ We the People of the United States, in Order to . . . insure domestic Tranquility. ❞

PREAMBLE, U.S. CONSTITUTION

The economy was in turmoil in 2020. Restaurants, theaters, and small businesses by the tens of thousands were shuttered. Weekly unemployment applications were the highest on record. The stock market was tanking; it lost 10 percent of its value on one day alone, which was the biggest one-day drop ever. Streets in many of the country's cities were largely empty of traffic. Americans were sheltering in their homes, trying to avoid the threat of the COVID-19 coronavirus. Was the United States headed for an economic meltdown that would rival the Great Depression of the 1930s?

Few economists predicted as much, and for good reason. When the Great Depression struck in 1929, there were no government programs in place to stabilize and stimulate the economy. Panic set in, worsening the crisis. Businesses cut back on production, investors fled the stock market, depositors withdrew their bank savings, and consumers slowed their spending—all of which fueled the downward spiral. In 2020, however, the government stepped in to steady the economy through adjustments in interest rates and government spending. A key initiative was a $2 trillion stimulus bill, which included direct cash payments to individuals and families, an increase in unemployment benefits, financial assistance to hospitals, and loans to financially strapped companies.

This chapter examines economic and environmental policy. As was discussed in Chapter 1, public policy is a decision by the government to follow a course of action designed to produce a particular result. In this vein, economic policy aims to promote and regulate economic interests and foster economic growth and stability. This chapter presents the following main ideas:

- *Through regulation, the U.S. government imposes restraints on business activity for the purpose of promoting economic efficiency and equity.* Regulatory action includes protecting the environment from the harmful effects of business and consumer activity.

- *Through promotion, the U.S. government helps private interests achieve their economic goals.* Business, in particular, benefits from the government's promotional efforts, including tax breaks and loans.

- *Through its taxing and spending decisions (fiscal policy), the U.S. government seeks to generate a level of economic supply and demand that will maintain economic prosperity.* Fiscal policy can be conducted through the use of either demand-side or supply-side tools.

- *Through its money supply decisions (monetary policy), the U.S. government— through the Federal Reserve System ("the Fed")—seeks to stimulate economic growth at a level that's not inflationary.*

GOVERNMENT AS REGULATOR OF THE ECONOMY

An **economy** is a system of production and consumption of goods and services that are allocated through exchange. When a shopper selects an item at a store and pays for it with cash or a credit card, the transaction is one of the millions of exchanges that make up the economy.

In *The Wealth of Nations* (1776), Adam Smith advanced the doctrine of **laissez-faire economics**, which holds that private firms should be free to make their own production decisions. Smith reasoned that firms will produce a good when there is a demand for it (that is, when people are willing and able to buy it). Smith argued that the profit motive is the "invisible hand" that guides supply decisions in a capitalist system. He also acknowledged that laissez-faire capitalism has limits. Certain areas of the economy, such as roadways, are natural monopolies and are better handled by the government than by private firms. The government is also needed to impose order on private transactions by regulating banking, currency, and contracts. Otherwise, Smith argued, the economy should be left largely in private hands.

table 15-1	THE MAIN OBJECTIVES OF REGULATORY POLICY	
Objective	Definition	Representative Actions by Government
Efficiency	Fulfillment of society's needs with as few of its resources as possible; the greater the output for a given input, the greater the efficiency	Preventing restraint of trade; requiring producers to pay the costs of environmental damage; regulating business only when justified on a cost–benefit basis
Equity	Ensuring that the outcome of an economic transaction is fair to each party	Requiring firms to protect workers' safety; requiring them to inform consumers of risks or defects associated with their products

Although laissez-faire economics prevailed in the United States during the 19th century, the government was not sidelined completely. Through the Pacific Railways Act of 1862, for example, Congress authorized the issuance of government bonds and the use of public lands to build the transcontinental railroad, which, although operated by private firms, was subject to government regulation. Nevertheless, it was not until the 1930s Great Depression that the government assumed a large, ongoing role in the economy. The United States today has what is called a *mixed economy.* Although the economy operates mainly through private transactions, government plays a significant role. New prescription drugs, for example, cannot be marketed until they've been tested and the Food and Drug Administration (FDA) has certified them as safe and effective. The U.S. government even owns some industries (for example, the Tennessee Valley Authority, which produces electricity). Nevertheless, in comparison, say, to the Scandinavian countries, where the government provides health care to all citizens and controls several major industries, including the airlines, the United States relies more heavily on free-market mechanisms.

One way that the U.S. government participates in the economy is through the **regulation** of business activity.[1] U.S. firms are not free to do anything they please. They operate within the limits of government regulation, which is designed to promote economic *efficiency* and *equity* (see Table 15-1).

Efficiency Through Government Intervention

Economic efficiency occurs when the output of goods and services is the highest possible for the amount of input (such as labor and material) that went into producing it.[2] *Efficiency* peaks when there is no waste—society is getting as many goods and services as possible from the resources used to produce them.

Promoting Competition   Adam Smith and other classical economists argued that the free market is the optimal means of achieving efficiency. In producing goods and services, firms will try to use as few resources as possible to keep their prices low, which will make their products more attractive to consumers. To compete, less efficient producers will have to cut their production costs or face the loss of customers to lower-priced competitors.

Markets are not always competitive, however. If a producer can acquire a monopoly on a particular product or conspires with other producers to fix the price of the product at an artificially high level, the producer does not have to be concerned with efficiency. Consumers who need a product have no choice but to pay the seller's price. Price fixing was prevalent in the United

This 1914 cartoon shows railroad companies petitioning the Interstate Commerce Commission (depicted as Uncle Sam) for permission to raise their rates. The first federal regulatory agency, the ICC, was created by Congress in 1887 to regulate the railroads to stop them from gouging their customers on routes where they had a monopoly. The ghost in the background is that of William Henry Vanderbilt, the wealthiest of the railroad tycoons. (Library of Congress Prints & Photographs Division [LC-DIG-ppmsca-28030])

States in the late 19th century, when large trusts came to dominate many areas of the economy, including the oil, railroad, and sugar industries. Railroad companies, for example, had no competition on short routes and charged such high rates that many farmers went broke because of the cost of shipping their crops to markets. In 1887, Congress enacted the Interstate Commerce Act, which created the Interstate Commerce Commission (ICC) and assigned it responsibility for regulating railroad practices, including shipping rates.

The goal of such regulatory activity is to improve efficiency by restoring market competition or by placing a limit on what monopolies can charge for goods and services. Business competition today is overseen by a wide range of federal agencies, including the Federal Trade Commission (FTC). In 2016, for example, the FTC blocked for a second time an attempted merger of Office Depot and Staples, saying "it would lead to higher prices" for office supplies. On the other hand, the FTC has allowed concentrated ownership in industries such as oil and automobiles, where the capital costs are so high that small firms cannot hope to compete.[3] The policy also reflects the fact that market competition in many sectors is no longer simply an issue of domestic firms. For example, the major U.S. automakers—Chrysler, Ford, and General Motors—compete for customers not only with each other but also with Asian and European auto manufacturers, such as Honda and BMW.

Deregulation and Underregulation   Although government regulation is intended to increase economic efficiency, it can have the opposite effect if it unnecessarily increases the cost of doing business.[4] Firms have to devote work hours to monitoring and implementing government regulations. These costs are efficient to the degree that they produce corresponding benefits. However, if the government places excessive regulatory burdens on firms, they waste resources in the process of complying. The result of overregulation is higher-priced goods that are more expensive for consumers and less competitive in the domestic and global markets.

To curb overregulation, Congress in 1995 enacted legislation that prohibits administrators in some instances from issuing a regulation unless they can show that the benefits outweigh the costs. A more substantial response is **deregulation**—the rescinding of regulations already in force to improve efficiency. This process began in 1977 with the Airline Deregulation Act, which eliminated the requirement that airlines provide service to smaller cities and gave the airlines the authority to set ticket prices (before then, the prices were set by a government agency). The policy change worked as intended. Competition between airlines increased on routes between larger cities, resulting in cheaper airfares on these routes. Congress followed airline deregulation with the partial deregulation of the trucking, banking, energy, and communications industries, among others.

| C A S E | **Politics in Action** |
| S T U D Y | |

The Subprime Mortgage Crisis

"Moral hazard" is a justification for government regulation. Economist Paul Krugman describes moral hazard as the situation in which "one person makes the decision about how much risk to take, while someone else bears the cost if things go badly."

Few developments illustrate the problem more clearly than the subprime home mortgage crisis that triggered the near collapse of America's financial sector in 2008. Several years earlier, financial regulations on mortgage lending had been relaxed. By 2006, a third of mortgages were being given to

Tero Vesalainen/Shutterstock

people with a weak credit record. Banks had leveraged their assets at roughly 30 to 1–up from the previous level of 12 to 1–to grant ever more mortgages to make ever larger profits. This put the entire housing industry at risk if the economy turned bad and homeowners were unable to keep up with their mortgage payments, which is what happened in 2007-2008. Banks found themselves in possession of millions of houses that had been abandoned or were in default.

America's taxpayers were the ones who saved the banks from collapsing. Congress appropriated hundreds of billions of dollars in loans to keep Bank of America, Citibank, and other major banks from going bankrupt. They were considered "too big to fail." If they went down, the entire economy could have gone down with them, yet it was their risky investments that imperiled them. Another party–the taxpayers–bore the cost, which is the definition of a "moral hazard."

Q: Are there circumstances in which "too big to fail" is sensible public policy? What's the best way to prevent the problem from happening in the first place?

ASK YOURSELF: Would you bail out large banks if their collapse would have a domino effect, taking down other businesses with them? If you would bail out large banks in that situation, then they're "too big to fail." In terms of preventing the problem, do you trust banks to regulate themselves? Or is tight government regulation required?

Deregulation can be carried too far.[5] Freed of regulatory restrictions, firms can engage in reckless or unethical practices. Such was the case with the sub-prime mortgage crisis that struck in 2008 (see "Case Study: The Subprime Mortgage Crisis"). In 1999, Congress repealed the Great Depression-era Glass-Steagall Act, which had restricted retail banks from using depositors' funds to make risky investments. Banks jumped at the opportunity, luring marginally qualified home buyers by offering low-interest rates and small down payments. When the economy weakened, many homeowners defaulted on their mortgages, precipitating the 2008 financial crisis. In 2010, Congress responded by enacting the most substantial regulation of financial institutions since the New Deal era. Designed to curb the abuses that contributed to the financial crisis, the Dodd-Frank Wall Street Reform and Consumer Protection Act empowers the govern-ment to oversee financial activities more closely. It also created a new federal agency, the Consumer Financial Protection Bureau, to protect consumers from exploitation by credit card companies, lending institutions, and other creditors.

The crisis in America's financial system demonstrates that the issue of business regulation is not a simple question of whether or not to regulate. Too much regulation can burden firms with excessive implementation costs, whereas too little regulation can give firms the leeway to engage in risky or unethical practices. Either too little or too much regulation can result in economic inefficiency.

Equity Through Government Intervention

The government intervenes in the economy to bring equity as well as efficiency to the marketplace. **Economic equity** occurs when an economic transaction is fair to each party.[6] A transaction can be considered fair if each party enters into it freely and ethically. For example, if a seller knows that a product is defective or poses a health risk, equity requires that a potential buyer be informed of it.

The first wave of equity regulation came during the Progressive Era of the early 1900s when reformers sought to stop deceptive business practices. The creation of the Food and Drug Administration (FDA) in 1907 was part of the reform effort. Unsafe foods and drugs were being sold to unsuspecting customers, and the FDA was charged with keeping them off the market.

The second wave of equity regulation came during the 1930s Great Depression when New Deal reformers sought to broadly restrict unfair busi-ness practices. The Securities and Exchange Act of 1934, for example, sought to protect investors from dishonest or imprudent stock and bond brokers. The New Deal also provided greater equity for organized labor. The Fair Labor Standards Act of 1938, for example, required employers to pay workers a minimum wage.

In the 1960s, the federal government began requiring tobacco companies to put health warnings on cigarette packs. The warning labels and other efforts to get Americans to stop smoking have saved millions of lives. (DanBrandenburg/E+/Getty Images)

The third wave of regulatory reforms came in the 1960s and 1970s and sought to promote environmental protection, consumer protection, and worker safety. Ten federal agencies, including the Consumer Product Safety Commission and the Environmental Protection Agency, were established to prevent harmful business activity. Among the products declared to be unsafe in the 1960s and 1970s were cigarettes, leaded paint, and leaded gasoline.

This regulatory activity has had a remarkable effect. Consider cigarettes, for example. Beginning in the 1960s, the federal government required cigarette manufacturers to put warning labels about the dangers of smoking on cigarette packs. At the time, more than 40 percent of American adults were cigarette smokers. Today, that figure is 20 percent. As the number of smokers has declined, so has the incidence of lung cancer, emphysema, and other smoking-related ailments. A Yale University study estimated that 8 million lives have been saved in the United States through anti-tobacco regulation.[7] How many lives is that? That's twice the number of all the people currently living in Boston, San Francisco, Seattle, Dallas, Atlanta, and Minneapolis combined.

The FDA recently started to regulate e-cigarettes, banning the distribution of free samples on grounds that the practice was designed to lure young people into using them. Manufacturers challenged the ban, but a federal appeals court sided with the FDA, finding that the products are "indisputably highly addictive and pose health risks, especially to youth, that are not well understood."[8]

The Politics of Regulatory Policy

Although business firms fought the Progressive Era and New Deal reforms, their opposition diminished when they realized that they had some influence over the decisions of the regulatory agencies. Pharmaceutical firms, for example, cultivated a relationship with the FDA that, at times, has served their interest. In the 1990s, for instance, drug companies convinced the FDA to streamline its drug-safety reviews to hasten the marketing of new drugs.[9] One fast-tracked drug, Vioxx, had to be taken off the market in 2004 after it was found to cause strokes and heart attacks.

The third wave of regulatory reforms of the 1960s and 1970s differed from the Progressive and New Deal reforms in their structure. Most of the regulatory agencies established in the third wave were granted responsibility not for a single industry but firms of all types. The Environmental Protection Agency (EPA), for example, is charged with regulating environmental pollution of almost any kind by almost any firm. Because newer agencies such as the EPA deal with so many industries, no single industry can easily influence their decisions.

Most of the older agencies, including the Federal Communications Commission (FCC) and the Securities and Exchange Commission (SEC), are run by a commission whose members are nominated by the president and serve fixed terms but cannot be removed by the president during their term of office, which is a reason they sometimes get too friendly with the industries they regulate. Most of the newer agencies, including the EPA, are headed by a single director who can be removed from office at the president's discretion. As a result, the newer agencies tend to be more responsive to the president than to the firms they oversee.

As in other policy areas, Republican and Democratic lawmakers often disagree on regulatory issues. Although lawmakers of both parties see a need to regulate business, Republican lawmakers have closer ties to business and lean toward less regulation. When the Dodd-Frank Act came up for a vote in 2010, for example, nearly every congressional Democrat voted for it and nearly every congressional Republican voted against it. In 2017, with the Republicans in control of the presidency and Congress, Republican lawmakers weakened the Dodd-Frank Act by reducing restrictions on the lending practices of smaller banks.

GOVERNMENT AS PROTECTOR OF THE ENVIRONMENT

The full costs of business activity are not always borne by producers and consumers. Consider, for example, a company whose industrial wastes seep into a nearby river. The price that consumers pay for the company's products does not reflect the cost to society of the polluted water. **Externalities** is the term that economists use to describe such unpaid costs.

Before the 1960s, the federal government did not require firms to pay to reduce externalities. The publication in 1962 of Rachel Carson's *Silent Spring* helped launch the environmental movement. Written at a time when the author

Environmental laws and regulations have led to greatly reduced levels of air and water pollution. Shown on the left is a photo of Los Angeles from the time when yellowish-gray polluted air ("smog") regularly hung over the city. On the right is a photo of today's Los Angeles. ((smog): Daniel Stein/E+/ Getty Images; (clear): ekash/E+/Getty Images)

was dying of breast cancer, *Silent Spring* exposed the threat to birds and animals from pesticides such as DDT. Carson's appearance at a Senate hearing contributed to legislative action that produced the 1963 Clean Air Act and the 1965 Water Quality Act—the first major federal laws aimed at protecting the environment from human pollution. Firms would be required to install antipollution devices to reduce their harmful air and water emissions.

Environmental Protection

The Environmental Protection Agency was created in 1970. Proposed by Republican president Richard Nixon and enacted by the Democratic-controlled Congress, the EPA was given responsibility for enforcing the nation's environmental laws, including the levying of fines and sanctions on firms that violate them.

Environmental regulation has led to dramatic improvements in air and water quality. Pollution levels today are far below their levels in the 1960s, when yellowish-gray fog ("smog") enveloped cities like Los Angeles and New York and when some bodies of water, like the Potomac River and Lake Erie, were open sewers. In 1969, the Cuyahoga River, which flows through Cleveland, burned for a half-hour after sparks from a passing train ignited oil-slickened debris floating on it. Over the past five decades, as a result of regulatory policies, toxic waste emissions have been halved, hundreds of polluted lakes and rivers have been revitalized, energy efficiency

CITIZEN ACTION!
SELF-GOVERNMENT

Self-government includes responsible citizenship. Like governments, citizens have an obligation to protect our shared environment. If you have a car, accelerate more slowly and walk rather than drive short distances. In your residence, use lights sparingly, moderate the temperature, and use low-energy appliances and lighting. And drink tap water rather than bottled water. Nearly the entire cost of bottled water is due to the plastic container, which is a nonbiodegradable petroleum product.

has improved, food supplies have been made safer, and urban air pollution has declined by 60 percent.[10]

Climate Change and Energy Policy

No environmental issue receives more attention today than global warming. The earth's temperature level has been rising, and the rate of increase has accelerated since the mid-1970s (see Figure 15-1). The National Oceanic and Atmospheric Administration has tracked annual temperatures for nearly 150 years. Nine of the ten of the globe's warmest years on record have occurred in the past decade.[11] Scientists theorize that the temperature rise is attributable to emissions from oil, coal, and other carbon-based fuels, and they say that dire consequences—including water shortages, rising sea levels, and extreme heatwaves—will result unless carbon emissions are curbed.

Some U.S. policymakers favor an aggressive effort to reduce climate change. Others say that such an effort should wait until the consequences of climate change are better understood. And others challenge the scientific consensus, saying that the evidence for the climate change thesis is faulty or inconclusive.

The United States has lagged behind most Western countries, including Germany, France, and Great Britain, in reducing its greenhouse gas emissions. The reasons are several, including policy disagreement and the structure of the U.S. political system. The division of power among the president, the House,

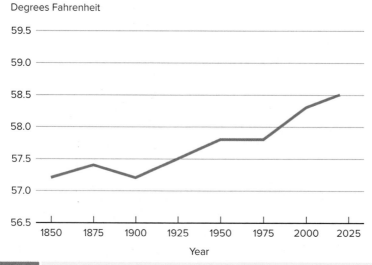

figure 15-1 AVERAGE TEMPERATURE OF THE EARTH'S SURFACE

The average surface temperature of the earth has risen substantially in the past century and has done so at an accelerating pace in the past four decades. (*Source:* National Aeronautics and Space Administration, 2022)

and the Senate makes it difficult to garner the support necessary to implement costly regulatory policies. In 2015, at the United Nations Climate Change Conference in Paris, the participating countries, including the United States, unanimously agreed to voluntarily "reduce their carbon emissions as soon as possible." On becoming president in 2017, Donald Trump, a skeptic of climate change, withdrew the United States from the Paris accord, making it one of only a handful of countries that were not part of the agreement. One of Joe

---

F	A	K	E	**Detecting Misinformation**
F	A	C	T	

Is Weather an Indicator of Climate Change?

After the usually warm winter of 2020, polls found an increase in the number of Americans who believed that climate change was occurring. Polls conducted during the winter of 2019, when a polar vortex settled in over a large part of the central United States, found an increase in the number of people who denied that climate change was occurring. Clearly, many Americans equate climate change and the weather.

Is that claim fact, or is it fake?

Climate change and weather are different. Weather is what's happening today. Climate change is what's been happening over a lengthy period. Nine of the warmest years on record have occurred in the past decade, which is a sign of climate change. However, on any given day or period during the past decade, it

Andrei Stepanov/Shutterstock

might have been unusually warm or cold—that's the weather. It's not shocking that many people conflate the two. We tend to rely on personal experience for many of our opinions, and a string of cold winter days can persuade us that global warming is fiction. During a severe ice storm, Donald Trump said climate change is a "total, and very expensive, hoax." Climate scientists draw their conclusions differently. They examine decades of temperature and other data from hundreds of locations across the globe, looking for patterns over time. A conclusion based on the weather we're experiencing today is a single data point. Climate scientists deduce what's happening from millions of data points stretching back more than a century.

Biden's first actions as president was to restore the United States as a party to the Paris accord.

In 2022, the Supreme Court in a 6–3 decision limited the federal government's ability to reduce carbon emissions. At issue was whether the Environmental Protection Agency (EPA) had the authority to regulate power plants beyond the boundary of the plants themselves by placing state-level caps on power plant emissions. If implemented, the policy could have the effect of forcing some power plants to change how they generate electricity by, for example, switching from coal to natural gas as the fuel source. The Court held that existing legislation did not clearly grant this authority to the EPA and that it could take such action only if Congress were to explicitly authorize it.[12]

The issue of climate change is confounded by the fact that no single nation can solve the problem on its own. When carbon emissions get into the atmosphere, they affect conditions elsewhere. The problem is also confounded by the rapid economic expansion of China, India, and other developing nations, which has increased the level of carbon emissions. Officials in these countries say they should not have to bear most of the costs of curbing global warming because the problem stems largely from decades of carbon emissions by the industrialized nations, including the United States. In turn, fully industrialized countries have argued that the recent spike in carbon emissions is caused by developing countries and that the problem cannot be solved unless they reduce their emissions (see "How the U.S. Differs").

HOW THE U.S. DIFFERS

CRITICAL THINKING THROUGH COMPARISONS

Carbon-Fuel Emissions and Global Warming

The United States is topped only by China as the world's largest source of carbon-fuel emissions. In fact, as World Population Review data indicate, the five leading countries account for more than half of the world's total with China alone contributing nearly a third. Developing nations say the global warming problem was caused largely by decades of pollution by the United States and other fully industrialized nations and that they should bear most of the burden of reducing carbon emissions. Industrialized nations say that China and other developing nations are today the biggest source of the problem and that carbon reduction cannot be achieved without curbing their emissions.

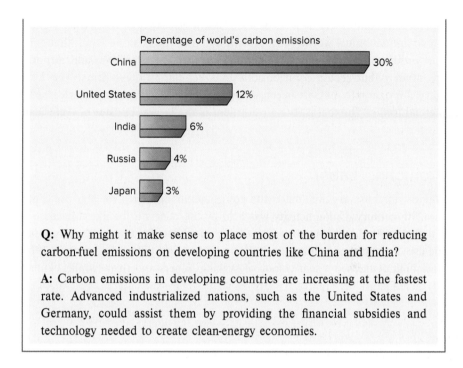

Percentage of world's carbon emissions

China — 30%

United States — 12%

India — 6%

Russia — 4%

Japan — 3%

Q: Why might it make sense to place most of the burden for reducing carbon-fuel emissions on developing countries like China and India?

A: Carbon emissions in developing countries are increasing at the fastest rate. Advanced industrialized nations, such as the United States and Germany, could assist them by providing the financial subsidies and technology needed to create clean-energy economies.

GOVERNMENT AS PROMOTER OF ECONOMIC INTERESTS

Congress in 1789 gave a boost to the nation's shipping industry by imposing a tariff on goods brought into the United States on foreign ships, which prompted importers to make greater use of American ships. Since that first beneficial policy, the U.S. government has provided thousands of direct and indirect benefits to economic interests. The following sections describe some of these benefits.

Promoting Business

Loans and tax breaks are among the ways that government promotes business interests. Firms receive loan guarantees, direct loans, tax credits for capital investments, and tax deductions for capital depreciation. The $2 trillion stimulus bill that Congress enacted in early 2020 in response to the COVID-19 coronavirus pandemic included $500 billion for financially strapped firms.

The most significant contribution that government makes to business is in the traditional services it provides, such as education, transportation, and defense. Colleges and universities, which receive substantial funding from

federal and state governments, provide businesses with most of their professional and technical workforce and with much of the basic research that goes
into product development. The nation's roadways, waterways, and airports
are other public-sector contributions that benefit business firms. The U.S.
Navy, for example, patrols ocean shipping lanes to keep them safe for commercial traffic. The fact is, the government is the largest booster of American
business.

Promoting Labor

Support for business dominated the government's approach to labor well into
the 20th century. Union activity was held by the courts to be illegal because it
interfered with the rights of business. Government hostility toward labor included
the use of police and soldiers to break up strikes. In Ludlow, Colorado in 1914,
state militia attacked a tent colony of striking miners and their families, killing
19, including 11 children.

A major contribution that government makes to economic interests—particularly business but also
labor and agriculture—is through public colleges and universities. Supported in significant part by
taxpayer dollars, they provide research and workforce training of benefit to economic interests,
which otherwise would have to pay the costs themselves. Shown here is a campus scene of the
University of California, Berkeley. (Yurim/Shutterstock)

The 1930s Great Depression brought about a change in labor policy. The National Labor Relations Act of 1935, for example, gave workers the right to bargain collectively and prohibited businesses from disrupting union activities or discriminating against union employees. Government support for labor now also includes minimum-wage and maximum-work-hour guarantees, unemployment benefits, safer and more healthful working conditions, and nondiscriminatory hiring practices.

Nevertheless, government policy is less friendly to labor than to business. Slightly more than half of the states, for example, have right-to-work laws that give workers in a unionized workplace the option of not joining the union. They get the benefit of union-negotiated contracts but don't contribute dues to the union. In 2018, the U.S. Supreme Court in a 5–4 decision broadened that limitation on unions by ruling that public-sector unions cannot collect mandatory dues. The ruling overturned a 1977 decision that held public-sector workers could be required to pay union dues because they benefit from collective bargaining agreements. In its 2018 ruling, the Court argued that a mandatory dues requirement violates members' First Amendment rights because dues can be used by unions to advocate for policy positions that some members oppose.[13]

Promoting Agriculture

Government support for agriculture has a long history. The Homestead Act of 1862, for example, opened government-owned lands to settlement. The federal government provided 160 acres of land free to any family that staked a claim, built a house, and farmed the land for five years.

Government programs today provide billions of dollars of assistance annually to farmers, small and large. Federal payments account for more than a fifth of net agricultural income, making America's farmers among the most heavily subsidized in the world. This assistance is intended, in part, to reduce the market risks associated with farming. Weather, global conditions, and other factors can radically affect crop and livestock prices from one year to the next, and federal subsidies lend stability to farmers' income.

FISCAL POLICY AS AN ECONOMIC TOOL

During the nation's early years, the United States periodically faced an economic downturn in the form of an **economic recession** or a more severe **economic depression**. The prevailing economic theory held that the best policy was to do nothing, that the economy was self-correcting and would recover on its own.

The greatest economic collapse in the nation's history—the Great Depression of the 1930s—shattered that belief. The economy did not rebound on its own but instead continued on its downward spiral. When President Franklin D. Roosevelt took office in 1933, he tossed aside the old idea about economic recovery in favor of massive government spending and job programs designed to stimulate the economy and put Americans back to work. The success of Roosevelt's New Deal changed policymakers' thinking. Ever since, when the economy goes into a downslide, the government has stepped in with policies designed to give it a boost.[14]

The government's efforts to maintain a healthy economy occur in part through Congress's taxing and spending decisions, which together are referred to as its **fiscal policy**.

Demand-Side Policy

The use of fiscal policy as a tool for managing the economy originated in the early 1900s with the theories of British economist John Maynard Keynes. Noting that firms tend to cut their production and workforce when the economy weakens, Keynes challenged the traditional notion that government should also cut back on its spending. Keynes argued that a downturn can be shortened only if government compensates for the slowdown in private spending by increasing its spending. In doing so, the government pumps money into the economy, which stimulates consumer spending, which in turn stimulates business production and creates jobs, thereby hastening the economic recovery.[15]

Keynes' theory is rooted in **demand-side economics**. It emphasizes the consumer "demand" component of the supply-demand relationship (see Figure 15-2). When the economy is sluggish, the government, by increasing its spending, places additional money in the hands of consumers. With more money in their pockets, they spend more, which boosts demand for products, prompting firms to hire the workers needed to produce the products. This line of reasoning

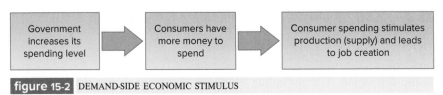

figure 15-2   DEMAND-SIDE ECONOMIC STIMULUS

When the economy is sluggish, demand-side economics holds that government should increase its spending to boost consumer spending (demand), which will create jobs and stimulate production (supply).

HOW THE 50 STATES DIFFER

CRITICAL THINKING THROUGH COMPARISONS

Federal Taxes and Benefits: Winners and Losers

Fiscal policy (the federal government's taxing and spending policies) varies in its impact on the states. *Business Insider* calculated how much firms and residents in each state send to the federal government in tax and other payments, and then how much firms and residents in each state receive from the federal government as a result of Social Security payments, contracts, and so on. The biggest loser is New Jersey, which sends $2,784 more per capita to Washington than it gets back. Massachusetts ($1,532) and Connecticut ($1,242) are the next two biggest losers. The biggest winner is New Mexico, which gains $9,624 per capita from federal spending and taxing. West Virginia ($7,981) and Mississippi ($7,902) are the next biggest winners.

Net federal payments per capita
- $4,000 or more
- $2000–3,999
- $1–1,999
- $0 or less

Q: Why are many of the "winners" in the southeastern part of the U.S.?

A: States in the southeastern area are not as wealthy as most states. Because of this, they pay fewer federal taxes while getting more federal assistance for programs designed to help low-income individuals. As well, a large number of the nation's military installations and defense contractors—a large source of federal money—are located in the southeastern area of the country.

prompted the $1.9 trillion stimulus bill that Congress passed in 2021 in response to the economic slowdown caused by the COVID-19 pandemic. It included cash payments directly to individuals and families, with the expectation that the resulting spending would create jobs and spark production.

Although demand-side policy is typically applied during an economic downturn, it can also be used to slow down the economy during an inflationary period (a time of rapidly rising prices). By cutting back on its spending, the government places less money in consumers' hands, thereby weakening the demand for products and bringing down prices in the process.

Democratic lawmakers have been particularly partial to demand-side policy. Lower-income Americans are a core Democratic constituency and are the people most likely to lose their job during an economic downturn. Accordingly, Democratic lawmakers have typically responded to a sluggish economy with increased government spending (demand-side fiscal policy), which offers direct help to the unemployed and stimulates consumption, which in turn produces job growth. The $1.9 trillion stimulus bill enacted by Congress in 2021 passed strictly along party lines. Democrats voted for it, whereas no Republican in either the House or Senate did so.

Supply-Side Policy

Republican Party leaders are more likely to see an economic downturn through the lens of business firms. Republicans have typically resisted large spending increases because the government has to borrow the money, which creates upward pressure on interest rates, including the rates that business firms have to pay for loans.

Rather than demand-side policy, Republicans have relied on **supply-side economics**, which emphasizes the production side of the supply-demand equation. Supply-side policies were a cornerstone of the Reagan and Bush administrations' response to slowing economic growth.[16] Instead of government spending programs to boost consumer spending, Republican presidents Reagan and Bush turned to large tax cuts for companies and upper-income taxpayers as a means of stimulating business activity. In the case of the Bush tax cuts, which had the overwhelming support of Republican lawmakers but only a few Democratic votes, the tax savings for Americans in the top 1 percent of income averaged $54,493 per year, compared with $611 for those in the middle 20 percent, and $67 for those in the bottom 20 percent.[17] Supply-side theory holds that if firms and wealthier individuals have more money to spend, they will invest it in production (supply), which will boost employment and consumer spending (see Figure 15-3). Supply-side policy has been called *trickle-down economics*—the notion that wealth at the top will trickle down to everyone below.

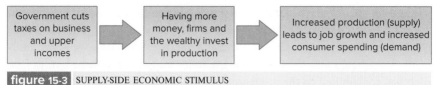

figure 15-3 SUPPLY-SIDE ECONOMIC STIMULUS

When the economy is sluggish, supply-side economics holds that government should cut taxes on businesses and wealthy taxpayers to boost investment in production (supply), which will create jobs and increase consumer spending (demand).

Fiscal Policy: Practical and Political Limits

Demand-side and supply-side policies are not without cost. They tend to result in a **budget deficit**, the situation where the government spends more in a year than it receives in taxes and other revenue. The shortfall increases the **national debt**, which is the total amount that the federal government owes to creditors from having to borrow money to cover its deficits. In recent years the federal government has heavily borrowed each year, which has resulted in a sharp rise in the national debt (see Figure 15-4). In turn, the interest payments owed on the national debt have increased each year and now

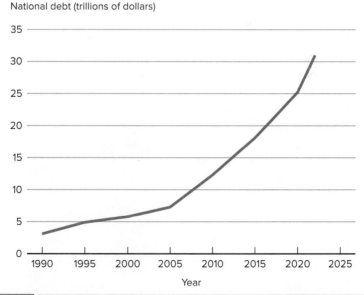

figure 15-4 NATIONAL DEBT, 1990–2025

The national debt, which is the total cumulative debt owed by the federal government, has risen sharply since 2000 owing to overly steep tax cuts, costly wars in the Middle East, and stimulus spending in response to the steep economic downturns that began in 2008 and 2020. (*Source:* Federal Reserve)

account for roughly 10 percent of total federal spending, reducing the amount available for government programs and making it harder for policymakers to justify either heavier spending or a steep tax cut to stimulate a weak economy

Each political party likes to blame the other for these problems but, in fact, each has contributed to them. Democrats' demand-side policies have added to the national debt, as have Republicans' supply-side policies. The national debt has increased every year since the late 1990s regardless of which party was in power at the time.

MONETARY POLICY AS AN ECONOMIC TOOL

Fiscal policy is one instrument of economic management available to the government. A second is **monetary policy**, which is based on adjustments in the amount of money in circulation. Monetarists (economists who emphasize monetary policy) contend that the money supply is the key to sustaining a healthy economy. Milton Friedman, the leading theorist, held that supply and demand are best controlled by manipulating the money supply.[18] Too much money in circulation contributes to inflation because too many dollars are chasing too few goods, which drives up prices. Too little money in circulation slows the economy because consumers lack the ready cash and easy credit required to maintain spending levels. Monetarists believe in increasing the money supply when the economy needs a boost and decreasing the supply when it needs to be slowed down.

Pictured here are the two most influential economists of the 20th century. On the left is Milton Friedman, who pioneered the theory of monetary policy. On the right is John Maynard Keynes, who developed fiscal policy theory. ((Left): Financial Times/ullstein bild/Getty Images; (right): Keystone-France/Gamma-Keystone/Getty Images)

The Fed

Control over the money supply rests not with the president or Congress but with the Federal Reserve System ("the Fed"). Created by the Federal Reserve Act of 1913, the Fed is directed by a board of governors whose seven members serve for 14 years, except for the chair and vice-chair, who serve 4-year terms. All members are appointed by the president with the approval of the Senate. The Fed does not have "customers" as do other banks. It is a "bankers' bank." It assists and regulates all national banks and those state banks that elect to become members of the Federal Reserve System—about 6,000 banks in all.

The Fed has several tools by which to add or subtract money from the economy, seeking a balance that will permit steady growth without causing an unacceptable level of inflation (see Table 15-2). One tool used by the Fed is to raise or lower the percentage of funds that member banks are required to hold in reserve—these are funds that they cannot loan or invest. When the Fed raises the reserve rate, member banks are required to keep more of their money out of circulation, thereby reducing the money supply. When it lowers the reserve rate, the banks have more money to lend to consumers and firms, which puts more money into circulation. During the 2008 subprime mortgage crisis, the Fed reduced the reserve rate several times so that member banks would have more money available to deal with the shortfall resulting from failed mortgages.

A second and more publicly visible way in which the Fed affects the money supply is by lowering or raising the interest rate that member banks pay when they borrow money from the Federal Reserve. When the Fed raises the interest rate, banks in turn raise the rate they charge their customers for new loans, which discourages borrowing, thereby reducing the amount of money entering the economy. Conversely, when the Fed lowers the interest rate on its loans, banks are able to lower the rate they charge customers for loans, which leads to additional borrowing, resulting in an increase in the money supply. As the economy slowed

table 15-2	MONETARY POLICY: A SUMMARY OF THE FED'S POLICY TOOLS
Reserve Rate	Amount of their assets that member banks must keep on hand: The rate can be lowered to increase the money supply or raised to decrease it.
Interest Rate	Interest rate charged to member banks when they borrow from the Fed: The rate can be lowered to increase the money supply or raised to decrease it.
Buying of Securities	By buying securities, the Fed gives money to the seller, which increases the money supply. By selling securities, the Fed receives money from the buyer, which decreases the money supply.

in 2020, for example, the Fed dropped the interest rate nearly to zero, enabling member banks to lower their rates, making loans more affordable.

The Fed also has a third mechanism—the buying and selling of government securities. When it sells government securities in exchange for cash, the Fed is taking buyers' money out of circulation, thereby reducing the money supply. By contrast, when it buys government securities, the Fed is putting money in the hands of the sellers, thereby adding to the money supply.

The severity of the 2008 economic downturn, which has been labeled the Great Recession, prompted the Fed to apply a controversial fourth mechanism. Known as *quantitative easing (QE)*, it came into use after the Fed had lowered interest rates almost to the point of zero and therefore could not lower them further as a means of injecting money into the economy. It then turned to QE, which began with the purchasing of assets held by member banks, such as their mortgage-backed securities. The Fed took risky securities off the banks' hands and gave them money they could loan to firms and consumers at historically low rates. Eventually, the Fed spent more than $3 trillion on QE, which is more money than is generated in a full year by the economy of every country except the United States, China, Japan, and Germany.

Where did the Fed come up with this vast sum of money? For all practical purposes, it was created out of thin air. The Fed is the nation's central bank and essentially has the power to print money and keep printing it. And that's what it did from 2009 until it stopped in 2014. The spending had the effect of strengthening financial institutions by relieving them of weak assets while giving them cash that they could lend out, thereby increasing the money supply.

QE is considered a tool of "last resort," to be used only when other tools have reached the point that they are no longer effective.[19] If too much money is pumped into the economy, it can eventually trigger an inflationary rise in the prices of goods and services.

The Fed and Control of Inflation

Although the meltdown of financial markets in 2008 placed the Fed in the role of trying to stimulate the economy, a sluggish economy is not the only problem the Fed is expected to address. Another is **inflation**—an increase in the prices of goods and services. Before the late 1960s, inflation was a minor problem, rising by less than 4 percent annually. However, inflation jumped during the last years of the Vietnam War and remained high throughout the 1970s, reaching a postwar high of 13 percent in 1979. The impact was substantial. Prices were rising but personal income was stagnant. Many Americans were forced to cut back on basics, such as food purchases and medical care. Borrowing rates skyrocketed. The interest rate on business loans and home mortgages topped 15 percent—up from 5 percent a few years earlier.

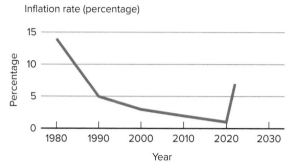

Inflation rate (percentage)

figure 15-5 U.S. INFLATION RATE, 1980–2025

After a period of high inflation in the early 1980s, inflation stayed low for decades only to rise dramatically as economic activity picked up with the easing of the COVID-19 pandemic. Heightened consumer demand and disrupted supplies of production material combined to send prices rapidly higher.

In 2021, for the first time in four decades, the economy was again disrupted by high inflation. The COVID-19 pandemic had led companies here and abroad to cut back on production. Then, when the pandemic began to ease, there was a shortage of the supplies that firms needed to restore their production level. That shortage led to a shortage of goods available to consumers, which contributed to a rise in the price of the goods that were available. The result of this and other developments was a rapid increase in the inflation rate (see Figure 15-5). It had been below 2 percent in 2020 and reached 7 percent in 2022 with no sign that it would quickly drop. The effect was felt particularly when shopping for food and at the gas station. The price of gasoline had been in the $3 a gallon range and jumped to $5 in several states and was more than $6 in parts of California.

At this point, the Fed took action. To fight inflation, the Fed applies policies the opposite of those used to fight an economic downturn. By increasing interest and reserve rates and by selling government securities, the Fed takes money out of the economy, which has the effect of reducing economic demand. As demand weakens, the prices of goods and services drop, thereby easing inflationary pressure. In 2021 and 2022, the Fed raised interest rates step-by-step and increased the selling of securities, all for the purposes of taking money out of the economy in an effort to bring down the rate of inflation.

The Politics of the Fed

Compared with fiscal policy, monetary policy can be implemented more quickly. The Fed can adjust interest and reserve rates on short notice, thus providing the economy with a psychological boost to go along with the actual effect of a change in the money supply. In contrast, changes in fiscal policy usually take months to implement. Congressional action is relatively slow, and new taxing and spending programs ordinarily require a preparation period before they can be put into effect. The greater flexibility of monetary policy is a reason the Fed has emerged as the institution with the primary responsibility for keeping the U.S. economy on a steady course.[20]

When the Fed was created in 1913, no one imagined that it would have a large policy role. Economists had not yet "invented" the theory of monetary policy. Much has changed since then. The Fed has become a powerful truly institution, which raises a basic issue. As an unelected body, should it be allowed to have so much power over people's lives?

Members of the Federal Reserve Board are appointed by the president and confirmed by the Senate but are not subject to removal. They serve for fixed terms and, once in office, are largely beyond the control of elected officials. And whose interests should the Fed represent—those of the public as a whole or those of the banking sector? The Fed is not an entirely impartial body. Although it relies on economic theory and data in making decisions, it is a "bankers' bank" and tends to protect its member banks, as it did during the economic downturn when through quantitative easing it purchased their risky securities. To be sure, the policy also helped ordinary Americans. Their economic problems would have increased if banks had struggled to operate. But did the Fed give banks too

Presented with a photo of the White House or U.S. Capitol, most Americans would be able to identify the building. Some might even recognize a photo of the Supreme Court's building, but fewer would be able to identify the building in this photo. It houses one of the most powerful institutions in Washington, the Federal Reserve ("The Fed"). (Glow Images)

much leeway in their use of the money? Should it have required the banks to use much of that money to make consumer and business loans at extraordinarily low rates? Should it have limited their ability to use the money for their own investments? The Fed did neither of these things, with the result that consumers benefitted less from the Fed's policy than they could have benefitted.

Regardless, the Fed is part of the new way of thinking about the federal government's role in the economy that emerged during the 1930s Great Depression. Through its economic management and regulatory activities, the government has assumed an ongoing role in managing the economy, and the overall result has been impressive. Although the American economy has suffered from economic downturns during the roughly three-quarters of a century in which the U.S. government has played a significant policy role, none of them has matched the severity of earlier depressions. The more recent downturns have been made shorter and less severe through government intervention. (The economic policies of the federal government in the areas of social welfare and national security are discussed in Chapters 16 and 17.)

Summary

Although private enterprise is the main force in the American economic system, the federal government plays a significant role through its policies to regulate, promote, and stimulate the economy.

Regulatory policy is designed to achieve efficiency and equity, which require the government to intervene, for example, to maintain competitive trade practices (an efficiency goal) and to protect vulnerable parties in economic transactions (an equity goal). Many of the regulatory decisions of the federal government, particularly those of older agencies (such as the Food and Drug Administration), are made largely in the context of group politics. Business lobbies have an especially strong influence on the regulatory policies that affect them. In general, newer regulatory agencies (such as the Environmental Protection Agency) have policy responsibilities that are broader in scope and apply to a larger number of firms than those of the older agencies. As a result, the policy decisions of the newer agencies are more often made in the context of party politics. Republican administrations are less vigorous in their regulation of business than are Democratic administrations.

Business is the major beneficiary of the federal government's efforts to promote economic interests. A large number of these programs, including those that provide loans and research grants, are designed to assist business firms, which are also protected from failure through measures such as tariffs and favorable tax laws. Labor, for its part, obtains government assistance through laws covering areas such as worker safety, the minimum wage, and collective bargaining. Yet America's individualistic culture tends to put labor at a disadvantage, keeping it less powerful than business in its dealings with the government. Agriculture is another economic sector that depends substantially on government's help, particularly in the form of income stabilization programs such as crop insurance subsidies.

The U.S. government pursues policies that are designed to protect and conserve the environment. Today, there are many environmental programs, including those aimed at preventing air and water pollution. The continuing challenge, exemplified by climate change, is to find a proper balance among the nation's natural environment, its economic growth, and its energy needs.

Through its fiscal and monetary policies, Washington attempts to maintain a strong and stable economy—one characterized by high productivity, high employment, and low inflation. Fiscal policy is based on government decisions in regard to spending and taxing, which are aimed at either stimulating a weak economy or dampening an overheated (inflationary) economy. Fiscal policy is worked out through Congress and the president and consequently is responsive to political influences. Democratic lawmakers typically prefer demand-side fiscal policy, which relies on increased government spending as a way to put more money in consumers' pockets. When they spend the money, it stimulates business production and job growth. Republican lawmakers typically prefer supply-side fiscal policy, which relies on tax cuts for business and high-income taxpayers. They are expected to invest much of their extra income in business activity, resulting in an increase in jobs and consumer spending.

Monetary policy is based on the money supply and works through the Federal Reserve System, which is headed by a board whose members hold office for fixed terms. The Fed, as the Federal Reserve is commonly called, has become the primary instrument for managing the economy. It can affect the amount of money circulating in the economy by raising or lowering the interest rate that banks are charged for borrowing from the Fed, by raising or lowering the percentage of the funds (reserve rate) that member banks are required to keep on hand, and by buying and selling securities.

CRITICAL THINKING ZONE

KEY TERMS

budget deficit (*p. 443*)
demand-side economics (*p. 440*)
deregulation (*p. 428*)
economic depression (*p. 439*)
economic efficiency (*p. 426*)
economic equity (*p. 430*)
economic recession (*p. 439*)
economy (*p. 425*)

externalities (*p. 432*)
fiscal policy (*p. 440*)
inflation (*p. 446*)
laissez-faire economics (*p. 425*)
monetary policy (*p. 444*)
national debt (*p. 443*)
regulation (*p. 426*)
supply-side economics (*p. 442*)

APPLYING THE ELEMENTS OF CRITICAL THINKING

Conceptualizing: Define *economic efficiency* and *economic equity.* Provide an example of a regulatory policy aimed at achieving economic efficiency. Also provide one that has economic equity as its goal.

Synthesizing: Contrast demand-side economics and supply-side economics in terms of theory, government policy, and partisan politics.

Analyzing: What are the tools of monetary policy? How are they applied to deal with an economic recession? How are they applied to deal with high inflation?

OF POSSIBLE INTEREST

A Book Worth Reading: Milton Friedman, *Capitalism and Freedom* (Chicago: University of Chicago Press, 2002). First published in 1962, this classic by the Nobel Prize–winning economist provides a defense of free markets that argues against Keynesian economics, which had been the prevailing approach to managing the economy.

A Website Worth Visiting: **www.ftc.gov** The website of the Federal Trade Commission, one of the older regulatory agencies, has information on pending disputes. The site gives the reader a sense of how the regulatory process works in practice.

16
CHAPTER

INCOME, WELFARE, AND EDUCATION POLICY: PROVIDING FOR PERSONAL SECURITY

CashGuy/Shutterstock

66 We the People of the United States, in Order to . . . promote the general Welfare. **99**

PREAMBLE, U.S. CONSTITUTION

At issue was the 2017 Tax Cuts and Jobs Act, the first major tax overhaul in nearly two decades. Republican Mitch McConnell, the Senate majority leader, said the legislation "tells middle class Americans 'we heard you.'" Republican senator Tim Scott of South Carolina exclaimed, "This is a monumental moment that marks a clear win for the American people." Republican congressman John Curtis of Utah said that the legislation would help "families by simplifying the tax code, making American businesses more competitive, and by generating hundreds of thousands of American jobs and producing real economic growth."

Congressional Democrats had a sharply different view. House minority whip Steny Hoyer of Texas said, "Today, 227 Republicans voted to raise taxes on 36 million middle-class households and to add at least $1.7 trillion to our national debt, all in order to provide massive tax breaks to the top one percent. This is not tax reform; it doesn't even merit being called a tax cut." Vermont senator Bernie Sanders called it a "farce." Oregon senator Ron Wyden called it "an unpopular, deficit exploding corporate giveaway . . . . This is the ultimate betrayal of the middle class."

At the writing of the Constitution, James Madison noted that no issue is more likely to provoke conflict than the question of how society's resources are distributed.[1] And, indeed, a host of government policies, including taxes, touch directly or indirectly on the distribution of resources and have rarely been resolved without a partisan fight. This chapter examines three such policy areas: income policy, which centers on the question of how taxes are distributed; welfare policy, which examines the programs aimed at helping the economically disadvantaged; and education policy, which includes the issue of how to prepare individuals for economically productive lives. The chapter covers the following main points:

- *Tax policy and market changes have contributed to America's widening income gap.* Democrats and Republicans differ sharply in their tax policies and philosophies.

- *Welfare policy has been a partisan issue, with Democrats taking the lead on government programs to alleviate economic insecurity and Republicans acting to slow down or limit these initiatives.* Social welfare programs are designed to reward and foster self-reliance or, when this is not possible, to provide benefits only to those individuals who are truly in need.

- *A prevailing principle in the United States is equality of opportunity, which in terms of public policy is most evident in the area of public education.* The United States invests heavily in its public schools and colleges.

INCOME POLITICS AND POLICIES

America's middle class was once the envy of the world. The nation's economic boom after World War II had launched an unprecedented era of shared prosperity—good-paying jobs, rising levels of home ownership, and growing numbers of college graduates.

The situation today is different. The American middle class has been shrinking (see Figure 16-1). A half-century ago, six in ten Americans lived in a middle-class household, defined as a household earning between two-thirds and two times the nation's median income. Today, five in ten live in such a household. The decline is even steeper in terms of income. A half-century ago, middle-class Americans were earning 61 percent of the nation's income. That's

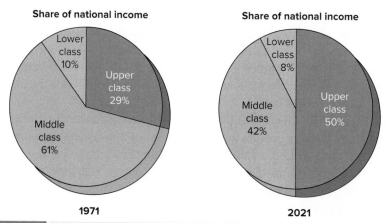

figure 16-1   INCOME SHARE OF AMERICA'S ECONOMIC CLASSES, 1971 AND 2021

In the half-century between 1971 and 2021, the nation's income shifted sharply to upper-income Americans, such that they now receive half of all income that Americans earn. (*Source:* Pew Research Center, 2022. Middle-class households are those whose annual household income is two-thirds to double the U.S. median household income after incomes have been adjusted for household size. Lower-class households have adjusted incomes below that level while upper-class households have an income above that level.)

down to 42 percent. The plight of lower-class Americans has been worse. Even though they make up substantially more of the population than a half-century ago (29 percent versus 21 percent), their share of the nation's income has dropped from 10 percent to 8 percent.

The "winners" in Americans' shifting fortunes are households whose income is more than twice the median income. They now account for about three in ten Americans and capture half the nation's income, up from less than 30 percent a half-century ago.

The Shifting Income Distribution

Until the 1930s Great Depression, the federal government openly sided with business firms and the wealthy. Efforts to organize unions and improve wages were blocked by government action. That approach changed with Franklin D. Roosevelt's New Deal. Congress enacted pro-labor legislation that included a minimum-wage law, collective bargaining rights, and social security for retirees. Congress also adopted a steeply **progressive income tax**, which is a tax where the marginal tax rate increases as income level increases. The top rate was set at 79 percent on incomes above $5 million, more than three times the 24 percent rate in place before the Depression.

Business firms claimed that the policies would wreck the nation's economy, but it grew rapidly after World War II. As the economy boomed, so did workers'

World War II destroyed much of Europe and Japan's manufacturing sector enabling U.S. firms to dominate world markets after the war, fueling an economic boom that lifted millions of American families into the middle class. (American Photo Archive/Alamy Stock Photo)

wages, spawning an ever-larger middle class. The boom was fueled by the strength of America's manufacturing sector. The United States had emerged from the war with its factories intact, whereas factories elsewhere were damaged by the war. The United States was far and away the world's leading manufacturer, which was a boon for America's factory workers.

The best-paying factory jobs were held by union workers. Armed with collective bargaining rights, they had achieved high wages and, in some cases, employer-paid health insurance and pensions. At its peak in the 1950s, a third of America's workers were unionized, and their income was a third higher than that of their nonunion counterparts. The minimum wage also contributed to the rising standard of living, particularly for unskilled workers. It put a floor on their income and helped push up the hourly pay of those just above them on the wage scale. Social Security was also making a difference. It provided retired workers a guaranteed source of monthly income.

Equally dramatic was the impact of the GI Bill, which Congress enacted near the end of World War II. It gave military veterans cash payments for college and vocational training and provided nearly interest-free loans for home purchases and small business ventures. Before the GI Bill, college and home ownership were out of the reach of most families. By the time the original GI Bill expired, nearly 8 million veterans had received education assistance, 2.5 million had acquired a home loan, and hundreds of thousands had received small business and farm loans.

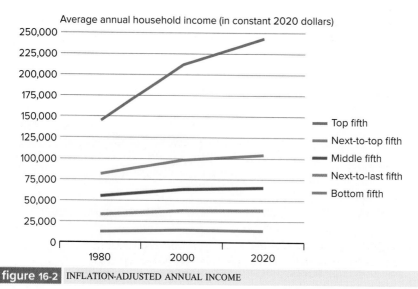

figure 16-2 INFLATION-ADJUSTED ANNUAL INCOME

Over the past four decades, the real income of the bottom 60 percent of households has not changed significantly, whereas those in the top 40 percent, and particularly those in the top 20 percent, have seen substantial increases in their real income. (*Source:* U.S. Census Bureau figures. Dollar amounts are expressed in 2020 dollars to control for the effect of inflation.)

Income nearly doubled in every income category during the postwar boom and, in the case of poorer families, more than doubled.[2] But the gain then came to an abrupt halt (see Figure 16-2). In terms of real income, which is the amount of income adjusted for inflation, families in the bottom 60 percent of income make close to the same amount today as they did in 1980, even though there are more families today in which two adults hold jobs than was true in 1980. On the other hand, the top two-fifths of American households have seen a rise in their income. Income in real dollars for the next-to-top fifth rose on average from about $82,000 in 1980 to roughly $105,000 today. The top fifth have done even better—their income rose over the four decades from about $148,000 a year on average to more than $240,000 today. The major winners by far, however, have been the top 1 percent. Their average income has increased more than threefold, going from more than $400,000 in 1980 to more than $1.3 million today.[3] Their share of national income is at the level it was in the 1920s, a time when income inequality was at its peak.

Policy and Economic Change

Politicians and pundits regularly link income gains among top earners with wage stagnation among middle earners, as if the first explains the second. In fact, the two developments are not closely related. The explanation for why top earners have done so well in recent decades owes substantially to changes in tax policy, whereas wage stagnation owes chiefly to changes in the nation's economy.

Tax Policy Change and Income Inequality   In the period after World War II, income inequality was kept in check by tax policy. The estate tax and a high marginal tax rate on upper incomes–through 1963, the top rate never dropped below 70 percent–made it difficult for people to accumulate a large fortune.[4] Tax policy, as economist Paul Krugman noted, had a "compression effect."[5] It put downward pressure on high incomes, which kept the gap between high earners and other Americans from widening.

The gap grew when Republican Ronald Reagan became the president in 1981 and implemented supply-side economics, which assumes that tax cuts for corporations and high-income individuals will stimulate economic growth (see Chapter 15). Under Reagan, the highest marginal tax rate dropped from 70 percent to 50 percent, and then to 28 percent. The rate was subsequently increased to 38.5 percent when Democrat Bill Clinton was the president. However, when Republican George W. Bush became the president in 2001, he, like Reagan, pursued a supply-side economic policy that brought the rate down to 35 percent. All tax brackets got a tax cut under Bush, but the big winners were those with high incomes. The middle fifth paid on average about $1,000 less in taxes a year as a result of the Bush-era tax cuts, whereas the average was about $6,000 for those in the top fifth. The largest tax savings went to those in the top 1 percent. Their average tax cut–nearly $55,000 a year–was more than 50 times that of middle-income taxpayers.

Even more advantageous for high earners was a cut in the **capital gains tax** (the tax individuals pay on gains in capital investments such as stocks and property) that was part of the Bush tax package. It dropped from 28 percent to 15 percent, far below the tax that Americans pay on their regular income. Although most Americans do not buy and sell stocks, a large majority of high earners do so.[6] For those in the top 1 percent, capital gains account for about a third of their pretax income.[7] That situation reflects the fact that *wealth* (the value of a person's assets, such as the property and stocks they own) is highly concentrated in the United States. The top 1 percent of households own 40 percent of all the nation's wealth, averaging more than $10 million per household. The bottom 80 percent of Americans have a mere 7 percent of the nation's wealth.[8] The top 1 percent received about 75 percent of the total tax savings from the cut in capital gains.[9] A Congressional Research Service study concluded that "changes in capital gains and dividends were the largest contributor to the increase in the overall income inequality."[10]

It should be noted, however, that the income gains of America's top earners from the Reagan and Bush tax cuts did not come at the direct expense of other taxpayers. Their tax savings were financed through government borrowing, which means the cost was shifted to future generations. The Congressional Budget Office (CBO) estimated that the Bush tax cuts added more than $1.5 trillion to the national debt, not including interest on the borrowed money.

The 2017 Tax Cuts and Jobs Act enacted when Republican Donald Trump was the president was similar to the Reagan and Bush tax cuts. All income categories received tax reductions, which were funded through government borrowing. The CBO estimates that the bill will add roughly $1.7 trillion to the budget deficit by 2027. Like the earlier tax cuts, the 2017 cuts were tilted in favor of higher-income taxpayers. Middle-income households received an average annual tax cut of $930, while those in the top 1 percent got an average of $51,140 (see Figure 16-3).

Economic Change and Wage Stagnation   Wage stagnation has different roots than the widening income gap. Rather than government policy, changes in the American economy have been the prime factor in holding down the income of the average American worker.

American goods and services after World War II accounted for roughly half of all goods being produced worldwide. U.S. products were in demand around the globe, which contributed to the creation of millions of well-paying factory jobs (see Chapter 17). That situation gradually gave way to a global market in which U.S. manufacturers compete with those of Japan, Germany, Korea, and other countries.

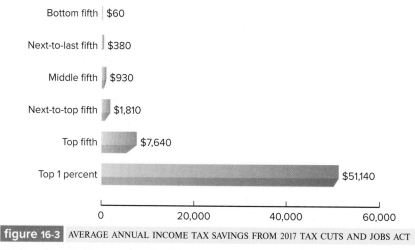

figure 16-3   AVERAGE ANNUAL INCOME TAX SAVINGS FROM 2017 TAX CUTS AND JOBS ACT

The tax cuts resulted in tax savings for all income groups, but high-income households had by far the biggest tax savings. (*Source:* Tax Policy Center, 2020.)

By 1970, the United States had become a net importer. It was buying more goods from abroad than it was selling overseas. Factory jobs were lost in the process. That loss was accompanied by a sharp decline in union membership. Today, only about one in eight workers is a union member, most of whom work in the public sector, including teachers, police, and civil servants, rather than in the private sector. Economist Lawrence Mishel estimates that as much as a third of the wage erosion among some types of workers owes to the decline in private-sector unions.[11]

Job growth in the United States since the 1970s has been in the service sector—areas such as banking, rental services, health care, entertainment, fast food, and housekeeping. Some service-sector employees are well paid, particularly those who work for tech and financial firms. But there's a much larger number of service-sector workers—such as food servers, store clerks, hotel staff, artists, lower-level administrators, and taxi drivers—who make less money than their factory counterparts.[12] In addition, service-sector jobs have a smaller multiplier than factory jobs. The typical manufacturing job generates three times as much economic activity as the typical retail trade job.[13] Autoworkers are a prime example. When new cars leave the factory, they generate a wide range of economic activity—they support car dealerships, gas stations, repair shops, auto parts makers, tire makers, and more. Service-sector jobs don't have anywhere near that kind of ripple effect.

In the 1970s, manufacturing-sector jobs began to disappear as Americans increasingly purchased goods made abroad. Most of the newer American jobs are in the service sector. Many of these jobs pay lower wages and provide fewer benefits than factory jobs. (Photodisc/Getty Images)

In his 2016 presidential campaign, Donald Trump promised to fix wage stagnation and sought to revitalize the nation's manufacturing sector upon taking office, largely through tax incentives, reduced regulation, and trade policy. He imposed tariffs on some products, including imported steel and aluminum, in an effort to protect U.S. manufacturers from lower-priced foreign competitors, particularly those in China (see Chapter 17). Some U.S. lawmakers criticized these policies on grounds that they would raise the prices that U.S. companies and consumers pay for products. But the policies, which were a sharp break from the past, also had substantial public support. What's uncertain is whether the nation's manufacturing sector can be resurrected in an era of globalized trade. The sector did not rebound during Trump's term as president despite his efforts to revitalize it.[14]

The Partisan Divide

The Democratic and Republican parties are far apart on income policy. Congressional Democrats have pressed for raising taxes on the wealthy, opposed at each turn by Republican lawmakers. Democrats have framed their argument in terms of fairness, while Republicans have framed their argument in terms of economic growth. Their positions mirror those of their party's voters. A Pew Research Center poll found that 75 percent of Democrats, compared with only 29 percent of Republicans, would support a tax increase on the wealthy and corporations to expand aid to the poor.

If the parties are split on the issue, business groups are not. They dominate Washington lobbying (see Chapter 9) and are attentive to tax issues. As the 2017 tax cut bill was being negotiated in Congress, business groups lobbied aggressively for its passage.[15] The U.S. Chamber of Commerce alone spent $17 million lobbying Congress during the three months that the bill was under debate.[16] The lobbying effort by business groups paid off. They gained a large tax cut. The legislation reduced the corporate tax rate from 35 percent to 21 percent.

WELFARE POLITICS AND POLICIES

Most Americans are able to meet their housing, food, clothing, and transportation needs. Some cannot. They are the nation's poor.

The U.S. government defines the **poverty line** as the annual cost of a thrifty food budget, multiplied by three to include the cost of housing, clothes, and other necessities. Families whose income falls below that line are officially considered poor. In 2023, the poverty line for a family of four was set at an annual income of roughly $28,000. That works out to $19 per person per day to cover all of a family's needs. By the government's formula, roughly one in seven American families lives in poverty.[17] If they could somehow join hands and form a line, it would stretch all the way from New York City to Los Angeles, then back again.

The United States has a higher poverty rate than other Western democracies. It is twice that of France and Germany and significantly higher than that of neighboring Canada. Compared with the United States, most Western democracies have more programs aimed at keeping families from falling into poverty, including universal government-provided health care, family and children cash allowances, and subsidized child care.[18]

America's poor include individuals of all ages, races, and regions, but they are concentrated among certain groups. Urban and rural dwellers have much higher poverty rates than suburbanites. Minority-group members have a poverty rate twice that of whites. Women have a poverty rate exceeding that of men. Children are one of America's most impoverished groups. One in every six American children—more than 10 million in total—lives in poverty (see "How the 50 States Differ"). Most poor children live in families with a single parent, usually the mother. Single-parent, female-headed families are roughly five times as likely as two-income families to fall below the poverty line, a situation referred to as "the feminization of poverty."[19]

Public Assistance Programs

Until the 1930s Great Depression, state governments had responsibility for the poor. Welfare was among the policy areas deemed reserved to the states by the Tenth Amendment and to be adequately addressed by them, even though they offered few welfare services. Individuals were expected to fend for themselves, and those unable to do so were usually supported by relatives and friends. That approach changed during the Great Depression—a period when one in four workers couldn't find a job and another one in four had only part-time work. Income fell sharply and, as it did, so did state tax revenues. Most states were too broke to help the poor. Federal tax revenues had also declined but, unlike the states, the federal government has unlimited power to print and borrow money.

Expanding the Federal Role   During the Depression, the federal government was in the hands of officials—President Franklin D. Roosevelt and a Democratic congressional majority—who were willing to use the federal government's spending power to help the poor.[20] Republican leaders opposed their initiatives but gradually accepted the idea that the federal government has a welfare role while arguing it should be kept as small as practicable.[21]

HOW THE 50 STATES DIFFER

CRITICAL THINKING THROUGH COMPARISONS

Child Poverty Rates

Based on the government-defined poverty line, about one in five American children lives in poverty. However, poverty is spread unevenly among the states. At one extreme are Louisiana and Mississippi, which have a child poverty rate above 25 percent. At the other extreme are New Hampshire and Utah, where less than 10 percent of children live in poverty.

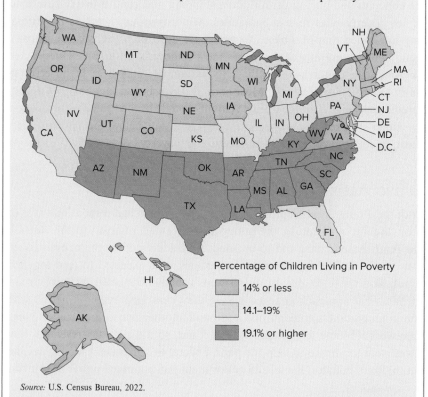

Percentage of Children Living in Poverty

14% or less

14.1–19%

19.1% or higher

Source: U.S. Census Bureau, 2022.

Q: What might explain the difference in child poverty levels between the states?

A: States differ considerably in their natural wealth, level and type of economic activity, level of education, number of newer immigrants, and percentage of minority-group members. Each of these factors is correlated with the level of child poverty.

Most Depression-era poverty programs were meant to be temporary, such as the Works Progress Administration, which put millions of Americans to work constructing roads, public hospitals, and the like. But a few programs were designed to last. One was Supplemental Security Income (SSI), which provides federal assistance to low-income elderly people and individuals with disabilities. Another was the Aid for Dependent Children program, later renamed the Aid for Families with Dependent Children (AFDC) program, which provided financial assistance to poor single mothers—those who had little or no income by reason of the father's death or desertion.

The second wave of antipoverty programs came in the 1960s when the federal government was again in the hands of a Democratic president, Lyndon Johnson, and a Democratic-controlled Congress. They enacted the largest set of antipoverty programs in the nation's history, including the food stamps program, subsidized housing, and Medicaid, which is government-paid health insurance for those of low income. The programs had broad public support. A Gallup poll found that two-thirds of Americans believed that the government had "a responsibility to try to do away with poverty in this country." Nevertheless, there was a clear partisan divide on the issue. When the Medicaid program came up for a vote, more than 70 percent of congressional Republicans voted

Scholar and activist Michael Harrington called the poor "the other America." One in seven Americans lives in poverty, some of whom are homeless. Shown here is a homeless teenager sleeping near a bridge. (Roman Bodnarchuk/Shutterstock)

against it, claiming that the federal government had no business getting involved in health care.

The 1960s were the high watermark of the government's antipoverty efforts. Since then, only a few major programs have been created. The largest is the 2010 Affordable Care Act, which, among its provisions, expanded Medicaid eligibility to those who are slightly above the poverty line and provides subsidies to help other lower-income families buy health insurance.[22] The legislation was enacted solely on Democratic votes. No Senate or House Republican voted for the bill.

There have also been cutbacks in welfare programs, most notably through the 1996 Welfare Reform Act (see Chapter 3). The 1996 legislation eliminated the AFDC program, which had placed no limit on how long a family could receive benefits, replacing it with the Temporary Assistance to Needy Families (TANF) program, which limits eligibility for most families to five years (see "Case Study: Welfare Reform Act of 1996"). In addition, TANF provides states with a block grant to be used to conduct training programs to teach job skills to able-bodied adults. Developed by Republican lawmakers as a way to cut welfare rolls and costs, the 1996 act had the overwhelming support of congressional Republicans, whereas a majority of congressional Democrats voted against it.

The 1996 legislation dramatically reduced the size of the welfare rolls. Within five years of its enactment, the number of people on welfare had dropped by 50 percent. The decline was not simply the result of TANF. The American economy was expanding at a rapid rate in the late 1990s, which created millions of new jobs.[23] Nevertheless, even as the economy weakened in 2000, the number of welfare recipients continued to decline. Although the downward trend was reversed somewhat during the economic recession that began in 2008, the number of American families receiving assistance payments has dropped sharply since TANF replaced AFDC (see Figure 16-4).

Eligibility for Public Assistance Programs such as TANF, Medicaid, and food stamps are **public assistance** programs. They are labeled as such because they're funded with general tax revenues and are available only to individuals in financial need. These programs are often referred to as "welfare" and the recipients as "welfare cases." Eligibility for these programs is established by a **means test**—applicants must prove that they lack the means to support themselves. Means-tested programs are typically based on an income threshold. Those with incomes below a specified level of income are eligible for the benefit, whereas those above it are not.

The requirement that individuals must prove that they're poor in order to receive a benefit adds to the expense of public assistance programs. In addition to payments to recipients, local caseworkers and supervisors are needed to determine whether applicants' incomes are below the designated amount and

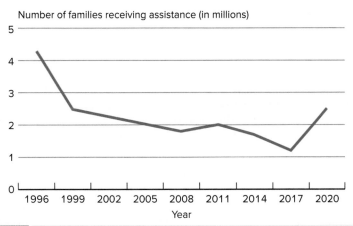

figure 16-4 NUMBER OF FAMILIES RECEIVING PUBLIC ASSISTANCE

After the 1996 Welfare Reform Act replaced the 1930s family assistance program that had no time limit or work requirement with the Temporary Assistance for Needy Families (TANF) program, which included both provisions, the number of families receiving public assistance declined sharply. The economic downturn accompanying the COVID-19 pandemic is the reason for the increase in the number of families on public assistance in 2020. (*Source:* U.S. Department of Health and Human Services, 2022.)

then to check on possible changes in a recipient's income level (see Figure 16-5). Administrative costs account for about 10 percent of federal spending on food stamps and about 5 percent of spending on Medicaid.

Means testing is consistent with America's culture of individualism—the belief supports the notion that public assistance should be available only to those who truly can't make it on their own. The distinctiveness of the American approach can be seen by comparing the U.S. health care system with that of European countries. They provide government-paid medical care to all citizens. If people become ill, they simply go to a clinic or hospital for treatment at

figure 16-5 THE WELFARE BUREAUCRACY

Because U.S. social welfare benefits are distributed on the basis of demonstrated need, a large bureaucracy is required to determine applicants' eligibility and monitor whether changes in recipients' circumstances make them ineligible for further assistance.

government expense, no questions asked. In contrast, Americans receive government-paid health care only if they meet the eligibility criteria. Even then, to be eligible, they must apply beforehand for the insurance and prove they are too poor to buy it on their own.[24]

Because of America's federal system, most public assistance programs, although funded primarily by the federal government, are administered by the states, which have some control over benefits and eligibility. There is a wide variation, for example, in the amount of family assistance that states provide. Some states provide more than $600 a month, while others provide less than $400.

Not all forms of public assistance involve direct cash payments to recipients. For instance, the food stamps program (formally called the Supplemental Nutrition Assistance Program, or SNAP) provides an **in-kind benefit**. Rather than cash, recipients receive cash-equivalent cards or coupons that can be used only for grocery items. On average, a food stamp recipient receives the cash equivalent of about $121 a month, which works out to about $1.40 per meal. Critics say that food stamps stigmatize their users by making it obvious to onlookers in the checkout line that they are "welfare cases." Other critics say that the program is too costly and that too many undeserving people get food stamps.

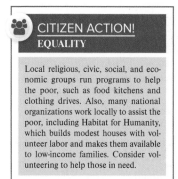

CITIZEN ACTION!
EQUALITY

Local religious, civic, social, and economic groups run programs to help the poor, such as food kitchens and clothing drives. Also, many national organizations work locally to assist the poor, including Habitat for Humanity, which builds modest houses with volunteer labor and makes them available to low-income families. Consider volunteering to help those in need.

Social Insurance Programs

Public assistance programs are not America's only social welfare policies. It also has **social insurance** programs, which are based on the same pay-to-be-eligible principle as insurance. Individuals have to pay a special payroll tax while working to be eligible for the benefit. Social Security is the best-known example. Established in the 1930s as part of Franklin D. Roosevelt's New Deal, it provides monthly Social Security benefits to retirees who paid Social Security taxes on their income during their working years. The current payroll tax rate on employees is 6.2 percent, with employers also being required to pay a 6.2 percent tax.

When Medicaid—health care for the poor—was enacted in 1965, Congress also enacted Medicare, which is health care for retirees. Unlike Medicaid, which is a public assistance program, Medicare is a social insurance program. As is the case with Social Security, it is financed by a special tax—currently 1.45 percent—on workers' wages, with employers also paying 1.45 percent.

Social Security and Medicare are **entitlement programs**, meaning that individuals who meet the eligibility criteria are entitled to the benefit. Government cannot deny it. In contrast, public assistance programs are not entitlement programs. The poor do not have an unqualified claim to benefits. Government can choose at will to cancel a public assistance program or change its eligibility criteria, as in the case of TANF, which reduced the length of time a family can receive assistance.

Social Security and Medicare are federal programs in their entirety. States do not administer them or have a say in eligibility or benefits. Recipients get the same benefit regardless of where they live. Social Security and Medicare are highly efficient programs. They do not require a large bureaucracy to check and recheck recipients' eligibility. When workers reach the prescribed age and conditions of eligibility, they automatically qualify for the benefits. Less than 1 percent of Social Security spending is taken up by administrative costs. Medicare is more administratively complex in that it involves payments to doctors and hospitals. Even so, according to a Kaiser Family Foundation study, only about 2 percent of Medicare spending is for expenses other than patient care. In contrast, some private insurance companies—which advertise heavily and seek to make a profit—spend up to 20 percent of their revenue on nonpatient care.[25]

Social Security and Medicare are not poverty programs. Recipients come from all income groups. Nevertheless, Social Security helps keep millions of Americans out of poverty. About one-fourth of America's seniors have no significant monthly income aside from Social Security. On the other hand, the higher one's income while working, the larger the Social Security payment on retirement. Such individuals pay more in Social Security taxes during their working years and get a larger benefit on retirement. The average monthly benefit is about $1,700, but some recipients get less than $1,000, whereas others get more than $3,000.

The Politics of Welfare Policy

Public assistance and social insurance programs differ markedly in their level of public support. Americans are more than twice as likely to oppose cuts in Social Security—a social insurance program—than to oppose cuts in antipoverty programs. The difference reflects America's cultural values. Social insurance programs are funded by special payroll taxes on workers and are widely seen as something that recipients have "earned." In contrast, public assistance programs are funded by the taxpayers as a whole and are widely seen as "handouts"—not earned and, in the minds of many, not deserved by many of the recipients.

Support for public assistance is weakened by the perception that people on welfare prefer welfare to work and gradually become dependent on it. Studies indicate the claim is true for some recipients but not for the large majority. Most recipients are only temporarily on welfare because, for instance, of job layoffs

Detecting Misinformation

Does Welfare Create Dependency?

Many Americans believe that public assistance programs, commonly known as welfare programs, create dependency, reducing recipients' interest in finding work. A Cato Institute poll found, for example, that nearly half of the respondents believed that welfare programs "make poor people dependent and encourage them to stay poor."[26]

Jonathan Weiss/Shutterstock

Is that claim fact, or is it fake?

There are people who make no effort to hold a job and for whom public assistance is nearly a way of life.[27] However, most poor Americans are on welfare by circumstance rather than personal choice. In an exhaustive poverty study, economists Signe-Mary McKernan and Caroline Ratcliffe found that most recipients are on welfare only for a while and for reasons largely beyond their control, such as a job layoff or desertion by the father.[28] When the COVID-19 coronavirus outbreak in early 2020 led to business closures, more than 10 million Americans lost their jobs in the first two weeks alone. Many of them received some form of public assistance before returning to work when businesses reopened.

during an economic recession.[29] Support for public assistance programs is also weakened by the widespread belief that the government spends far more on such programs than on social insurance programs. The opposite is true. Spending on Social Security and Medicare, which assist retirees regardless of income, is nearly double the amount spent on public assistance programs, which help only those in financial need. Families in the top fifth of the income population actually receive more in Social Security and Medicare benefits than the government spends in total on TANF, SSI, food stamps, and housing subsidies for the poor.[30]

Social Security has arguably been the most successful federal program in history, giving tens of millions of older Americans a level of economic security they would otherwise not have. The fact that Social Security is funded through a special payroll tax on employees during their working years has protected it from political criticism and budget cuts. Social Security is a benefit that is perceived as having been "earned," and therefore deserved, by its recipients. (Scott Olson/Getty Images)

Because they don't have strong public support, public assistance programs are a frequent political target (see "Party Polarization: Government's Social Welfare Role"). In 2014, for instance, congressional Republicans sought a $40 billion reduction in the food stamp program, settling for an $8 billion cut after a threatened veto by Democratic president Barack Obama. Social Security, by contrast, has withstood partisan challenges. In 2005, President George W. Bush proposed to partially privatize Social Security—workers would have had the option of putting a portion of their Social Security tax payments into a personal retirement account. Bush was forced to back down in the face of strong resistance from senior citizens, spearheaded by AARP—a seniors' group that is one of Washington's most powerful lobbies. In contrast, groups that lobby Congress on behalf of the poor lack the clout to pressure lawmakers into enacting policies benefitting the poor.[31]

Polls over the past 50 years have repeatedly found that Americans, consistent with their cultural values, see jobs rather than public assistance as the answer to poverty. That outlook is the basis for the Earned Income Tax Credit (EITC), which was enacted in 1975 under Republican President Gerald Ford and expanded during the presidencies of Republican Ronald Reagan and Democrat Bill Clinton. EITC provides a refundable tax credit to low-income wage earners. Workers with sufficiently low income receive an EITC payment on filing their taxes, with the amount varying with income level and the number of dependents. The maximum yearly payment for a family with two children, for instance, is roughly $6,000. EITC is now the federal government's largest means-tested cash assistance program. According to U.S. Census Bureau calculations, the EITC lifts about a third of low-income Americans above the poverty line. EITC is a reward for working—a program that's in line with America's cultural values.

EDUCATION POLITICS AND POLICIES

Nearly all Americans endorse the principle of **equality of opportunity**—the idea that people should have a reasonable chance to succeed if they make the effort. It is a form of equality shaped by personal freedom because personal success or failure depends on what people do with their opportunities. It has been said that equality of opportunity gives individuals an equal chance to become unequal.

Equality of opportunity is an ideal. Americans do not start life on an equal footing. It was said of one successful American politician, whose father was rich and successful in politics, that "he was born on third base and thought he hit a triple."[32] Some Americans are born into privilege, and others start life in such abject poverty that few of them escape it. Nonetheless, equality of opportunity

The Supreme Court has held that American children are entitled to an "adequate" education but do not have a right to an "equal" education. America's public schools differ greatly in quality primarily as a result of differences in the wealth of the communities they serve. Some public schools are over-crowded and have few facilities and little equipment. Others are very well equipped, have spacious facilities, and offer small class sizes. (FatCamera/E+/Getty Images)

is more than a catchphrase. It is the philosophical basis for a number of government programs, none more so than public education.

Public Education: Leveling Through the Schools

During the nation's first century, the question of a free education for all children was a contentious issue. Wealthy interests feared that an educated public would challenge their political and economic power. For their part, egalitarians saw free public education as a means of helping ordinary people get ahead in life. The egalitarians won out. Public schools quickly sprang up in nearly every community.[33]

Equality continues to be a guiding principle of American public education. Unlike countries that divide children, even at the grade school level, into different tracks that lead ultimately to different occupations, the curriculum in U.S. schools is relatively standardized. Of course, public education has never been a uniform experience for American children. During the first half of the 20th century, public schools for Black children in the South were designed to keep them down, not lift them up. Today, many children in poorer neighborhoods attend overcrowded, understaffed, and underfunded public schools. The quality of education depends significantly on the wealth of the community in which the child resides. The Supreme Court has upheld disparities in school funding, saying that the states are obliged to give all children an "adequate" education as opposed to one that is "equal" across communities.[34]

The uneven quality of America's public schools is a reason its students rank below Canadian and European students on standardized reading, math, and science tests (see "How the U.S. Differs"). Because U.S. neighborhoods are more segregated by income than European neighborhoods, America's poor children are more likely to go to schools where most of the other students are also poor. Moreover, because the wealth of a community affects the level of school funding, schools with a high proportion of poor students tend to have fewer resources, even though the need is greater. In fact, the best predictor of students' performance on standardized tests is the wealth of the community in which their school is located.[35] A Stanford University study found that children from low-income families are five years behind children from high-income families in average literacy skills by the time they reach high school.[36]

Nevertheless, through its public schools, the United States seeks to broadly educate its children. Public education was labeled "the great leveler" when it began in the early 19th century, and the tradition continues. Few countries make an equivalent spending effort. Per-pupil spending on public schools is substantially higher in the United States than in Europe. America's commitment to broad-based education extends to college. The United States has the

HOW THE U.S. DIFFERS

CRITICAL THINKING THROUGH COMPARISONS

Education Performance

Studies indicate that U.S. students score comparatively low on standardized tests. In the most recent Organization for Economic Cooperation and Development (OECD) assessment, based on 15-year-old student performance in math, the United States trailed nearly every Asian and Western European country. The accompanying chart shows the average math test scores for selected countries.

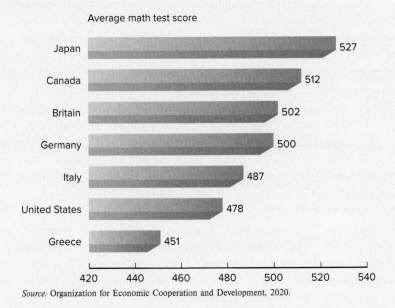

Average math test score

Japan	527
Canada	512
Britain	502
Germany	500
Italy	487
United States	478
Greece	451

Source: Organization for Economic Cooperation and Development, 2020.

Q: Why might the United States lag behind other advanced, industrialized democracies in student performance even though it spends more heavily on public education?

A: Compared with most democracies, the United States has a relatively high proportion of non-native-speaking children, who on average do less well in school than other students. The United States also has a high level of residential segregation. Children residing in poor neighborhoods tend to do less well in school.

world's largest system of higher education—it has roughly 4,000 two- and four-year colleges.[37] The nation's extensive education system preserves both the myth and the reality of an equal-opportunity society. The belief that success is within the reach of anyone who works for it could not be sustained if the public education system was reserved for the privileged few.

The Federal Government's Role in Education Policy

Education is largely the responsibility of state and local governments, and they continue to provide roughly 90 percent of school funding. They also decide most school policies, everything from the length of the academic year to teachers' qualifications.

At an earlier time, the federal government played almost no part in education policy. The situation began to change after World War II when economic and social change made the public more aware of defects in the nation's education system and looked to the federal government for help. Federal education programs are administered through the Department of Education, a cabinet-level agency that was created in 1979. The size of the Department

CITIZEN ACTION!
EQUALITY

Local schools, particularly those in poorer neighborhoods, often welcome the help of college students. Schools have a need for tutors who can help students with reading, math, science, and other subjects. Consider volunteering. You can put what you know to work while helping children get ahead.

of Education is an indicator of the degree to which education remains largely a state and local policy responsibility. The Department of Education is easily the smallest of the executive departments, with only 4,400 employees. The next smallest is the Department of Labor, which is four times the size.

Federal Grants-in-Aid for Education   As part of President Johnson's War on Poverty, the federal government began in the 1960s to provide financial assistance in the education area. The 1965 Elementary and Secondary Education Act became the cornerstone of the federal government's efforts to assist public schools. The legislation authorizes funds for items such as school construction, textbooks, special education, and teacher training. Although Johnson's goal was to help schools in poorer areas, members of Congress insisted that all states and districts be eligible for some funding. As a result, the formulas for allocating the grants favor poorer school districts, but not by a large margin.

Johnson's War on Poverty also included a targeted education program—Head Start. Aimed at helping poor children at an early age, Head Start provides free preschool education to low-income children to help them succeed when they reach kindergarten age. However, Head Start has never been funded at a level that would allow all eligible children to participate. Today, only about a third of eligible children are enrolled.[38]

The 1965 Higher Education Act, which President Johnson signed into law at his alma mater, Texas State University, is the basis for federal assistance to institutions of higher education. Among its components are Pell Grants, federal loans to college students, and federally subsidized college work-study programs. Pell Grants account for the largest share of federal spending. Millions of college students over the years have received Pell Grants, which are reserved for students from modest- and low-income families. The federal student loan program has also helped millions of students, although it is a relatively small spending item in that most of the money is returned through loan repayment. In 2010, as a cost-saving measure, the federal government took control of the loan program. Before then, some student loans were issued by banks, which had the safety of government-insured loans while receiving a fee for handling them.

Student loans have become increasingly burdensome. According to Federal Reserve Bank data, state governments in the 1970s provided nearly 75 percent of the funding for public colleges, which had the effect of holding down college costs. But states in the 1980s started to cut their funding and continued to do so, such that the states now provide less than 25 percent of college funding. As a result, college costs have been shifted to students, most of whom have no choice but to rely heavily on student loans. Student loan debt now exceeds credit card debt.

In 2022, President Joe Biden exercised his executive authority to cancel up to $20,000 in debt for Pell Grant recipients and up to $10,000 for non-Pell Grant recipients with eligibility limited to borrowers with an income of less than $125,000 ($250,000 for married couples). Many Republicans spoke out against the loan forgiveness, arguing that it added to the national debt and was unfair to taxpayers who hadn't gone to college and to former students who had paid off their college loans. A Morning Consult-Political poll found that Americans were divided on the policy with 48 percent in support and 43 percent opposed. Support divided sharply along party lines with 72 percent of Democrats favoring the policy compared with 26 percent of Republicans.

Partisan Conflict over Education Policy   Many of the partisan differences that affect federal welfare policy also affect federal education policy. Democrats are more inclined to find the answer to improved schools in increased federal spending on education, particularly in poorer communities, whereas Republicans tend to prefer market-like mechanisms such as achievement tests.

Partisan conflict over education has spilled into policy areas largely outside the scope of federal authority. School choice is one example. Charter schools, which are publicly funded but have wider latitude than other public schools in designing curricula and picking students, are strongly championed by many Republican lawmakers. Many Democratic lawmakers have criticized charter schools on the grounds they weaken the regular public schools by siphoning away funding and top students.

Federal involvement in public school education is inherently partisan and controversial, given America's tradition of state and local control over schools. Yet lawmakers at all levels have shown from time to time that they can come together. In 2015, with majority support from Democrats and Republicans, Congress passed the Every Student Succeeds Act (ESSA). It replaced the controversial 2001 No Child Left Behind Act (NCLB), which mandated standardized national testing and tied schools' federal funding to student test performance. ESSA includes mandatory testing and sanctions on schools that underachieve but eliminates NCLB's "one size fits all" approach, giving states flexibility in determining the form of student testing and what constitutes underachievement. ESSA is funded through $20 billion in annual federal assistance to the states.

The American Way of Promoting Economic Security

All democratic societies promote economic security, but they do so in different ways and at varying levels. Economic security has a higher priority in European democracies than in the United States. European democracies have instituted programs such as government-paid health care for all citizens, compensation for all unemployed workers, and retirement benefits for all elderly citizens. As this chapter shows, the United States provides these benefits only to some citizens in each category. By contrast, the American system of higher education dwarfs those in Europe.

The differences between the European and American approaches to welfare stem from historical and cultural differences. Democracy in Europe developed in reaction to centuries of aristocratic rule, which brought the issue of economic privilege to the forefront. European democracies initiated sweeping social welfare programs and high taxes on the wealthy as ways to create greater economic equality. Social inequality was harder to root out because it was thoroughly embedded in European society, shaping everything from social manners to education. Private schools and university training were reserved for the elite, a tradition that, although now in the past, has had a lingering effect on how Europeans think about educational opportunities.

The American experience was a different one. Democracy in America grew out of a tradition of limited government that emphasized personal liberty,

PARTY POLARIZATION

Conflicting Ideas

Government's Social Welfare Role

Economic benefits are distributed in America through the economic marketplace in the form of jobs, wages, dividends, and the like and through the government in the form of programs such as Social Security, Medicaid, and food stamps. In few areas have the differences between the Republican and Democratic parties been more consistent over the years than their opinions of public welfare programs. Although both parties see a need for some sort of safety net for the economically vulnerable, the Democratic Party has taken the lead on expanding it. Nearly every major U.S. social insurance and public assistance program was put into place by Democratic lawmakers, usually in the face of opposition from their Republican counterparts. As a recent Pew Research Center poll revealed, the policy opinions of Democratic and Republican voters coincide with the policy positions of their parties.

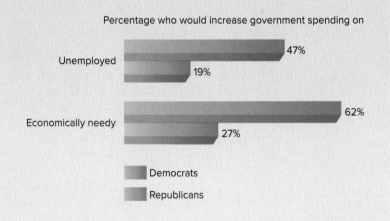

Percentage who would increase government spending on

Unemployed — Democrats 47%, Republicans 19%

Economically needy — Democrats 62%, Republicans 27%

Democrats
Republicans

Q: What's your opinion on how far government should go in providing economic assistance to those who are less well off?

which included a belief in self-reliance. This belief contributed to Americans' strong support for public education, their weak support for public assistance, and their preference for low taxes. Unlike political equality, the idea of economic equality has never captured Americans' imagination. Political scientists Stanley Feldman and John Zaller found that Americans' support for public assistance programs rests more on a feeling of compassion for the poor than on an ideological commitment to economic sharing.[39] Political scientist Robert Lane noted that Americans have a preference for market justice, meaning that they prefer that society's material benefits be allocated largely through the economic marketplace rather than through government policies.[40] It is not surprising that the United States has a higher level of income inequality and poverty than other Western democracies.

SUMMARY

The United States has several areas of policy that affect Americans' economic well-being. Tax policy is one of these policy areas. In recent decades, taxes on higher incomes and capital gains have been lowered substantially, which has contributed to a dramatic increase in income inequality. At an earlier time, a range of government policies, everything from a high tax rate on upper incomes to the GI Bill, had the opposite effect, reducing the gap between the wealthy and the rest of America.

Wage stagnation has been a persistent problem for a half century. In terms of real income, America's lower- and middle-income workers are getting roughly the same pay today as they did in 1970. Although government policy has played a part in this development, it is mainly a consequence of changes in the U.S. economy. In the period after World War II, the U.S. manufacturing sector was booming, providing millions of well-paying jobs, particularly for union workers. Since 1970, the manufacturing sector has shrunk dramatically, giving way to the service sector, where jobs on average pay less.

The United States has a complex social welfare system of multiple programs addressing specific welfare needs. Many social welfare problems are targeted for the poor. Roughly one in seven Americans falls below the government-defined poverty line, including a disproportionate number of children, female-headed families, minority-group members, and rural and inner-city dwellers. Public assistance programs, as anti-poverty programs are called, are available only to individuals who qualify for benefits by meeting the specific eligibility criteria.

Not all welfare programs are in the public assistance category. There are also social insurance programs, including Social Security and Medicare, which are funded by payroll taxes paid by potential recipients, who, in this sense, earn the benefits they later receive. Because of this arrangement, social insurance programs have broad public support. In contrast, public assistance programs are funded with general tax revenues and are targeted at individuals and families in financial need. Because of a widespread belief that many welfare recipients could get along without assistance if they tried, these programs do not have broad public support, receive only modest funding, and sharply divide the two parties. Democrats have taken the lead on government programs to alleviate economic insecurity, while Republicans have sought to cut back or decentralize these initiatives.

Compared to other democracies, the United States spends more heavily on public education, a policy consistent with its cultural emphasis on equality of opportunity. That policy is evident, for example, in standardized school curricula and the nation's extensive system of public colleges and universities. Like social welfare, however, education is a partisan issue involving disputes over such issues as charter schools and spending levels.

CRITICAL THINKING ZONE

KEY TERMS

capital gains tax (*p. 457*)
entitlement programs (*p. 466*)
equality of opportunity (*p. 470*)
in-kind benefit (*p. 466*)
means test (*p. 464*)

poverty line (*p. 460*)
progressive income tax (*p. 454*)
public assistance (*p. 464*)
social insurance (*p. 466*)

APPLYING THE ELEMENTS OF CRITICAL THINKING

Conceptualizing: The Supreme Court has held that American children are entitled to an "adequate education" but not an "equal education." Explain the difference.

Synthesizing: Contrast social insurance benefits and public assistance benefits. How do they differ in terms of how individuals qualify to get a benefit? How do they differ in terms of the level of public support they have?

Analyzing: How has U.S. social welfare policy been influenced by America's federal system of government and by Americans' belief in individualism?

OF POSSIBLE INTEREST

A Book Worth Reading: Thomas Piketty, *Capital in the Twenty First Century* (Cambridge, Mass.: Belknap Press, 2014). This award-winning bestseller explores the history of income inequality and its reemergence in extreme form in recent decades.

A Website Worth Visiting: www.journalistsresource.org Journalist's Resource, located at Harvard University's Kennedy School of Government, is dedicated to identifying the top policy-relevant research and connecting it to current issues. Many of its postings are in the areas of income, social welfare, and education policy.

17
CHAPTER

FOREIGN POLICY: PROTECTING THE NATIONAL INTEREST

lightfieldstudios/123RF

❝ We the People of the United States, in Order to . . . provide for the common defence. ❞

PREAMBLE, U.S. CONSTITUTION

After Russia invaded Ukraine in February of 2022, the full set of America's foreign policy tools was in play. U.S. diplomats met with their counterparts in Western Europe to ensure a united response to the invasion. The U.S. military launched an airlift to rush weapons and other military equipment to help Ukrainian forces. The U.S. intelligence community monitored Russia's military deployments, sharing that information with Ukrainian forces. U.S. economic agencies supplied Ukraine with humanitarian assistance while working to cripple the Russian economy through sanctions on its financial, commercial, and energy sectors.

Unlike other policy areas, foreign policy rests on relations with actors outside rather than within the country. As a result, the chief instruments of national security policy differ from those of domestic policy. One of these

Russia's invasion of Ukraine in 2022 provoked a strong response from the United States, including the shipment to Ukraine of military equipment. Pictured here are Russian armored vehicles destroyed by Ukrainian forces. (Drop of Light/Shutterstock)

instruments is *diplomacy*—the process of negotiation between countries. *Military power* is another instrument of foreign policy. *Intelligence gathering*—the process of monitoring other countries' activities—is yet another instrument. *Economic exchange,* the fourth instrument of foreign affairs, centers on international trade and global economic security.

Although the driving force behind every nation's foreign policy is its *national interest* (what's best for the nation in terms of its relationship with other nations), international relations scholars differ in their view of how a nation can best protect its national interest.[1] **Realism theory** holds that nation-states are intrinsically self-interested and that there is no effective authority above the state. Realists see the world as anarchic, where agreed-upon international rules are followed only when it's in a state's interest to do so. For realists, the survival of the state is the overriding goal of foreign policy. Preservation rather than morality guides state action. Policymakers are rational and therefore will not engage in actions that weaken the state and will take protective action when it is threatened. It's irrational for a nation to pursue idealistic foreign policy goals if they make the state vulnerable to outside threats. Realists do not dismiss the value of alliances but see them as appropriate only when they strengthen a state's security, as when a balance of power alliance deters possible aggressors.[2]

Liberalism theory acknowledges the risks of a dangerous world but focuses on individual liberty. It holds that state power must be restrained if individual rights are to be upheld. The best way to ensure restraint at the state level, according to liberalism theory, is free elections and constitutional protections of basic civil liberties, as well as civilian control of the military. Liberal theorists also emphasize the importance of international organizations like the United Nations to foster cooperation among states and punish states that violate international norms and agreements. Liberalism is a moral theory that sees democracy as the preferred form of government and looks unfavorably upon authoritarian nations because they tend to use military force to threaten neighboring states and repress their citizens.[3]

Each theory helps to explain aspects of international relations, including U.S. foreign policy. America's foreign relations include an extraordinary array of activities—so many that they could not be addressed adequately in an entire book, much less a single chapter. There are roughly 200 countries in the world, and the United States has relations of one kind or another with all of them. This chapter narrows the subject by concentrating on the four major instruments of foreign policy:

- *U.S. diplomacy aims to advance American interests through bilateral and multilateral negotiation and agreement, as well as through international institutions and organizations.*
- *The United States maintains a high degree of military preparedness, which requires a substantial level of defense spending and worldwide deployment of U.S. conventional and strategic forces.*
- *The United States invests heavily in intelligence gathering to protect against foreign threats, including international terrorism.*
- *Changes in the international marketplace have led to increases in trade and greater economic interdependence among nations, which has had a marked influence on the U.S. economy and America's foreign policy.*

DIPLOMACY

Diplomacy is the process of negotiation between countries. Nations typically prefer to settle their differences by talking rather than fighting. By definition, acts of diplomacy involve two (*bilateral*) or more (*multilateral*) nations.

The lead diplomatic agency of the United States is the Department of State, which is headed by the Secretary of State. The State Department is a relatively small organization. Only about 25,000 people—foreign service officers, policy analysts, administrators, and others—work at State. Nevertheless, it has the most presidential appointees of any agency. In addition to those at the department's top level, the president appoints the nearly 200 U.S. ambassadors who head the overseas embassies. At an earlier time, ambassadors made many of the State Department's key decisions affecting the host country. After communication became faster and more secure, those decisions increasingly were made by officials in Washington. The main purpose of the embassies today is to assist American citizens and promote U.S. interests in the host countries. When WNBA basketball star Brittney Griner was arrested in Russia in 2022, for example, the U.S. embassy in Russia worked to ensure that she was being treated properly.

The secretary of state is often described as second in importance only to the president within the executive branch. Whether the secretary actually has this status has varied. Donald Trump had a tense relationship with his first secretary of state, Rex Tillerson, and eventually fired him, in part because Tillerson after one cabinet meeting called Trump a "moron." In contrast, Barack Obama chose Hillary Clinton as his first secretary of state because he wanted her to play a leading foreign policy role.

The National Security Council (NSC) also has a key role in U.S. diplomatic policy. The NSC's job is to coordinate foreign policy so that what's being done in one area, such as diplomacy, aligns with what's being done in other areas, such as trade or defense. The NSC includes the vice president, secretary of state, secretary of defense, and a few others. The president's

Diplomacy is a key component of U.S. foreign policy, and the Department of State is the lead diplomatic agency. Among the presidential advisors pictured here is Secretary of State Antony Blinken (seated on the left, next to Vice President Kamala Harris). (dpa picture alliance/Alamy Stock Photo)

National Security Advisor is on the NSC and supervises its staff. The national security advisor is based at the White House and has sometimes had more influence over foreign policy than the secretary of state. President Richard Nixon's national security advisor, Henry Kissinger, is the prime example. He influenced Nixon's Vietnam policy, negotiated Nixon's historic trip to China to defuse hostilities with that country, and contributed to Nixon's decision to seek a nuclear-arms treaty with the Soviet Union.[4] Kissinger was subsequently named as Nixon's secretary of state and, for two years, held both positions.

U.S. diplomacy also works through international organizations, especially the United Nations (UN). Based in New York, the UN is the top international organization for ongoing diplomacy between nations. Recognizing the opportunities presented by the UN, Congress in 1947 created the U.S. Mission to the United Nations, headed by the U.S. Ambassador to the United Nations, who represents the United States in Security Council meetings and advises the president and secretary of state.

Soft Power

Some forms of diplomacy epitomize what is called **soft power**—the ability of a country through noncoercive means to convince other countries to do what it would like them to do. Soft power differs from **hard power**—the use of military force, coercion, or payments to get countries to comply. The term "soft power" was coined by Harvard political scientist Joseph Nye who served in national security positions during two presidencies. Nye identified a country's culture, values, and foreign policies as the keys to its soft power. If these are attractive to other countries, they might follow its lead.[5]

The Peace Corps exemplifies the application of soft power. Begun by President John F. Kennedy in the early 1960s, it has sent hundreds of thousands of Americans to countries around the world to live with local families and contribute to the local community. They have been called the nation's "goodwill ambassadors."

The World Trade Organization (WTO) is also an example of soft power. Although not formally established until 1995, it has its origins in GATT (General Agreement on Tariffs and Trade), an organization that the United States created nearly four decades earlier. The WTO, which today includes more than 150 nations, seeks to promote global free

CITIZEN ACTION!
SELF-GOVERNMENT

In his 1961 inaugural address, President John F. Kennedy said, "Ask not what your country can do for you. Ask what you can do for your country." His call was not just a call to military service. The Peace Corps provides Americans the opportunity to work for two years in a developing country. AmeriCorps is a second U.S. public service program. It includes Teach for America, where college grads teach for two years in high-need U.S. schools.

trade through reductions in tariffs, protections for intellectual property (copyrights and patents), and other market-based policies. The WTO aligns with the American preference for market-based economies and is also seen as a security safeguard given that war rarely breaks out between countries with strong trade relations. The International Monetary Fund (IMF) and the World Bank, which the United States created after World War II, also promote market-based economies. The IMF makes short-term loans to countries with balance-of-payments deficits. In return, the countries are required to adopt market-driven policies. For its part, the World Bank makes long-term development loans to countries for capital investment projects such as dams, highways, and factories.

Foreign assistance is also part of soft power diplomacy. Foreign aid was not a significant part of America's foreign policy strategy until after World War II when it initiated the Marshal Plan, named after its originator, Secretary of State George C. Marshall. It provided an unprecedented amount of aid (more than $100 billion in today's dollars) to help Western European countries rebuild from the war.

Since then economic and humanitarian assistance has been a key instrument of U.S. diplomatic policy. The lead agency for much of this effort is the United States Agency for International Development (USAID), which has operations in more than 75 countries. It's an independent federal agency but operates under the policy guidance of the secretary of state.

No country comes even close to matching the United States in terms of total foreign aid spending since World II. In terms of total annual spending, the United States is still the leader but has fallen behind Canada and several European countries in per capita annual foreign assistance.[6] America's fiscal problems, and its costly wars in Iraq and Afghanistan, have led to reductions in foreign aid. Public opinion is also an obstacle. Most Americans believe that the United States spends heavily on foreign aid. Some even believe that the elimination of foreign aid programs would save enough money to balance the federal budget.[7] In fact, foreign aid accounts for less than 1 percent of the budget. And much of this spending is not actual dollars but is instead in the form of foodstuffs and military hardware produced by American firms and sent overseas.

As the United States has cut back on foreign aid, China has stepped up its spending. Through loans and grants, China is investing in infrastructure and commercial projects in dozens of countries in Africa, South America, and Asia. It is also pursuing mining and drilling projects in many of these countries, seeking to secure the raw materials needed to sustain its economic growth. In a sense, China is following the path laid out by the United States after World War II when it used foreign aid to expand its influence.

Diplomatic Success

When Americans think about their nation's role in the world, many of them think about its wars. But several of the nation's major achievements have been triumphs of diplomacy, as a few post-World War II examples will illustrate. They are not meant to diminish the diplomatic failures, some of which involved "nation-building" in the aftermath of a U.S. invasion. That was the case in Afghanistan and Iraq, which are discussed later in the chapter.

The Marshal Plan is on every list of U.S. diplomatic triumphs. In addition to helping Western Europe recover from the devastation of World War II, it created friendly ties between the recipient countries and the United States. Two of the countries involved, Germany and Italy, had been enemies of the United States during the war. The Marshall Plan also laid the groundwork for the North Atlantic Treaty Organization (NATO), which is America's chief military alliance.

Another example of diplomatic success is the negotiations to prevent a nuclear war that spanned every administration from Dwight Eisenhower's in the 1950s to Gerald Ford's in the 1970s.[8] Nuclear bombs were dropped on Japan to end World War II but have not been used since. Diplomacy produced the International Atomic Energy Agency with responsibility for monitoring and restricting the development of nuclear technology; the Non-Proliferation Treaty aimed at controlling the spread of nuclear weapons; and the Strategic Arms Limitation Talks, which prompted the United States and the Soviet Union to reduce and cap their nuclear weapons.

President Richard Nixon's decision in the early 1970s to reach out to China to end their decades-long conflict is another diplomatic triumph. It paved the way for China's opening to the world, which included market reforms and eventual membership in the WTO. The policy also served to isolate the Soviet Union, which later on, prodded by President Ronald Reagan, abandoned its centralized economy and gave up its control of Eastern Europe.

The Paris Climate Agreement is a final example. In the two years leading up to the 2015 Paris conference, President Obama worked at getting China and India to join the agreement. The two countries depend heavily on coal and are among the top emitters of carbon dioxide. Without China and India, an agreement on reducing carbon emissions would have been feeble. To demonstrate America's commitment and in the face of intense opposition, Obama issued an executive order restricting America's use of coal. His efforts bore fruit when, in advance of the Paris summit, China for the first time specified a target date for its peak emissions. It did so in a statement issued jointly with the United States.[9]

What do these successful diplomatic efforts have in common? They were exercises in soft power. The United States was able to get what it wanted by

Shown here is President Barack Obama at the 2015 Paris conference on climate change. Obama's diplomatic overtures to China and India are regarded as a key reason for the adoption of the Paris Agreement, an international climate change treaty. (COP21/Alamy Stock Photo)

convincing other nations that it was something they should also want. The examples also show that soft power is not a tool limited to diplomatic negotiations with other democracies. In three of the examples, the United States was negotiating with autocratic regimes.[10]

MILITARY POWER

The Department of Defense (DOD), which has roughly 1,400,000 active-duty uniformed personnel and 750,000 civilian employees, is charged with the nation's military security. DOD includes the departments of the Army, Navy (which includes the Marines), Air Force, and Space Force and is headed by the secretary of defense, who represents the four services in their relations with Congress and the president. The secretary of defense is always an influential policymaker, but the influence of recent secretaries has varied considerably. The most powerful might be Donald Rumsfeld, who was President George W. Bush's first secretary of defense and a strong advocate of the U.S. invasion of Iraq in 2003.

Presidents also get advice from the Joint Chiefs of Staff, which includes the top-ranking officer from each of the uniformed services. The chair of the Joint Chiefs of Staff is the main military adviser to the President, secretary of defense, and the National Security Council (NSC).

Military Capabilities

The United States has a large nuclear arsenal based on the concept of **mutually assured destruction (MAD)**. The assumption is that any nation will be deterred from launching a full-scale nuclear attack on the United States by the knowledge that, even if it destroyed the United States, it also would be destroyed. America has a second-strike capability—that is, the ability to absorb a first-strike nuclear attack and survive with enough nuclear capacity for a massive retaliation (second strike). Russia has the same capacity, and the two nations have agreed to cap the size of their nuclear arsenals. However, they are not the world's only nuclear powers, and the major nuclear threat to the United States might be North Korea, a rogue nation that has recently expanded its nuclear arsenal and developed long-range missiles capable of reaching the United States.

Although equipped to fight a nuclear war, the U.S. military is organized primarily to fight a conventional war. The armed forces are currently structured to fight two medium-sized conventional wars simultaneously. It doesn't have the strength to fight an all-out conventional war of the type waged in World War II. Fighting that kind of war would require the reintroduction of the military draft (see "How the 50 States Differ").

America's national security is bolstered by alliances, the most important of which is the North Atlantic Treaty Organization (NATO). NATO has nearly 30 member nations, including the United States, Canada, and most European countries. NATO's charter requires each country, if another member is attacked, to come to its defense—"an attack on one, is an attack on all."

The strength of the U.S. armed forces rests on its exacting training and advanced weaponry. The U.S. military is second to none in its destructive power. Linked to sophisticated surveillance, targeting, and communication systems, the military's weaponry give it more firepower than its personnel level would suggest. An example is the U.S. Army's 155mm howitzer. Although its range is roughly the same as that of similar-sized howitzers, it's accompanied by a ballistic computation system that locates incoming artillery fire, allowing it to return fire with precise accuracy.

Although America's military firepower provides an advantage in conventional warfare, it is less decisive in unconventional wars of the type fought in Vietnam and Afghanistan. The insurgents employed guerrilla tactics, including hit-and-run attacks, and small-group operations, which are difficult to contest. Such wars require the United States to get the support of the people or, as it's called, "winning their hearts and minds." If insurgents are denied popular support, their military capability falls dramatically. Tactically, an unconventional war is fought with small and highly mobile combat units that can seek out

HOW THE 50 STATES DIFFER

CRITICAL THINKING THROUGH COMPARISONS

The All-Volunteer Military's Recruits

The United States had an active military draft until 1973, during which time each state, on a per-capita basis, contributed nearly the same number of U.S. military personnel. Today's military is an all-volunteer force, and the states' contributions on a per-capita basis vary widely, as the accompanying map indicates. Hawaii and Alaska have the largest number of military volunteers relative to the population, whereas Minnesota and Iowa have the lowest.

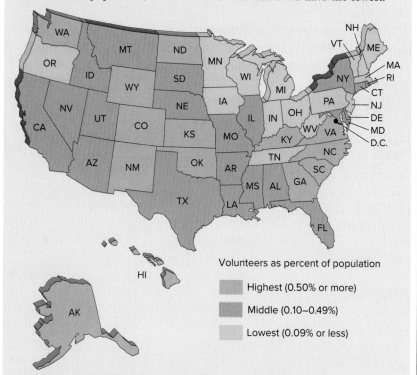

Volunteers as percent of population

Highest (0.50% or more)

Middle (0.10–0.49%)

Lowest (0.09% or less)

Source: Calculated from Department of Defense and U.S. Census Bureau data, 2020.

Q: What might explain why military recruits come disproportionately from states such as Alaska, Wyoming, and Oklahoma?

A: According to Department of Defense data, military recruits are more likely to come from rural areas, particularly those where hunting is prevalent and where there are fewer well-paying jobs for young adults.

insurgents and provide security to local populations while training indigenous military and police forces to assume responsibility for their nation's security.[11] The U.S. military has been gradually building its capacity in unconventional warfare. It has, for example, increased the number of special operations units, such as the Army Special Forces and the Navy SEALs.

America at War

The United States was a late entry into World War I and decommissioned most of its military forces after it ended, maintaining a tradition that with few exceptions had defined its foreign policy since the country's beginning. The United States had avoided European entanglements and didn't require a large standing army to defend its borders. A different America emerged after World War II. It had more land, sea, and air power than any other country and more than a hundred overseas military installations. Since then, the United States has been deeply involved in world affairs, including several costly wars.

The Cold War with the Soviet Union   Although the United States was victorious in its fight against Germany and Japan in World War II, it was not fully at peace. The United States found itself facing off against the communist government of the Soviet Union, which had extended its power after the war through communist takeovers in Poland, Hungary, Czechoslovakia, and other Eastern European nations. The United States and the Soviet Union became locked in what was called the **Cold War**, where the United States pursued a doctrine of **containment**—the notion that Soviet expansion could be stopped only by the determined use of American power.[12] Containment policy was extended to include China when communists took control of that country in 1949.

Containment policy led the United States to base troops in Europe and Asia and then into a war in Asia. When the Soviet-backed communist government of North Korea invaded South Korea in 1950, President Truman sent U.S. forces into the conflict. Nearly 35,000 U.S. troops lost their lives in the Korean War, which ended in a stalemate after Chinese troops entered the war on the side of the North Koreans. A decade later, the United States was again at war. Communists were making inroads in South Vietnam, and U.S. policymakers believed that, if it fell to the communists, so too would Laos, Cambodia, and the rest of Southeast Asia—the *domino theory*. Although U.S. forces had military superiority, Vietnam was a guerrilla war, with no front lines and few set battles.[13] U.S. public opinion, most visibly among the young, gradually turned against the war. U.S. combat troops left Vietnam in 1973, and two years later North Vietnamese forces completed their takeover of the country. Vietnam was the costliest and most painful application of containment doctrine: 58,000 Americans lost their lives in the fighting.

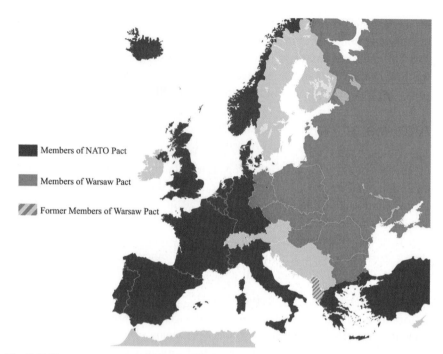

Members of NATO Pact

Members of Warsaw Pact

Former Members of Warsaw Pact

The Cold War pitted the United States against the Soviet Union, each with its sphere of influence and military alliance. Shown on the map are the countries that were part of NATO, the U.S.-led alliance, and the Warsaw Pact, the Soviet-led alliance. (vectorissimo/Shutterstock)

Wars in Afghanistan and the Middle East   After the Soviet Union pulled its troops out of Eastern Europe in 1989, marking the end of the Cold War, President George H.W. Bush called for a "new world order." Bush embraced liberalism theory and pursued a policy of **multilateralism**—the idea that major nations should act together in response to problems and crises. Included in Bush's plan was a stronger role for multinational organizations such as the United Nations and NATO.

Multilateralism defined America's response after Iraq invaded Kuwait in 1990. A half-million troops, mostly American but including contingents from nearly two dozen nations, drove Iraq out of Kuwait in four days, prompting Bush to declare that the United States had "kicked the Vietnam syndrome [the legacy of America's defeat in Vietnam] once and for all." But the Gulf War was not decisive. Believing that an overthrow of Saddam Hussein's regime would destabilize Iraq, Bush halted hostilities, allowing Hussein to stay in power. He was ordered by a UN resolution to dismantle his weapons programs but repeatedly interfered with attempts to verify their status, raising suspicions about his plans.

Although multilateralism also defined the Clinton administration's forceful response to Serb atrocities in Bosnia and Kosovo during the 1990s,[14] George W. Bush rejected his father's approach to international relations when he became the president in 2001. He announced plans to reduce America's overseas commitments, a position that changed abruptly when terrorists attacked the World Trade Center and the Pentagon on September 11, 2001. Barely a month after the attacks, the United States invaded Afghanistan, whose Taliban-led government had granted sanctuary and training sites to the al Qaeda terrorists who carried out the attacks. Supported by troops from other NATO countries, U.S. forces quickly toppled the Taliban government but failed to destroy the Taliban's fighting capacity.

Two years later, Bush claimed that Iraq's Saddam Hussein was stockpiling weapons of mass destruction (WMDs)—chemical and biological weapons, and possibly nuclear weapons—for use against U.S. interests. Surrounded by advisers who were adherents of realism theory, Bush ordered the invasion of Iraq, despite intense opposition from France, Germany, and Russia (see "Case Study: Invasion of Iraq"). British troops were also involved, but the U.S. attack was essentially an act of **unilateralism**—a situation in which a nation takes action on its own.[15] The Iraqi regime quickly collapsed, but the post-invasion phase, as in Afghanistan, was more challenging than Bush had anticipated. Age-old animosities among Sunni, Shiite, and Kurdish groups within Iraq frustrated efforts at political compromise and fueled internal violence. Moreover,

---

CASE STUDY

Politics in Action

Invasion of Iraq

Although the U.S. system is based on checks and balances, there is an area where one branch has the upper hand. Since World War II, the United States has engaged in military hostilities roughly 150 times, usually at the instigation of the president. A case in point is the 2003 invasion of Iraq. The signal that President George W. Bush was targeting Iraq came in his 2002 State of the Union Address when he grouped Iraq with Iran and North Korea in what he called an "axis of evil." Later, Bush asked Congress for authorization to attack Iraq if it refused to turn over its WMDs. Bush claimed Iraq had WMDs and was preparing to use them. Citing intelligence reports, Bush said, "The evidence indicates that Iraq is reconstituting its nuclear weapons program."

Continued

During the congressional debate, Senator Robert Byrd (D-W. Va.) repeatedly asked the administration to reveal its intelligence reports, but few were forthcoming. The vote in Congress, which occurred a year after the 9/11 terrorist attacks—a time when Americans were still worried about the possibility of another such attack—was one-sided. The House vote was 297-133 in Bush's favor, while the Senate vote was 77-23.

When Bush first indicated the possibility of an invasion, opinion polls indicated that less than half the public thought it was a good idea. But Bush, as the accompanying figure indicates, was able to use the news media to carry his message. Reporters were focused so intently on the White House that Bush administration sources were quoted roughly 10 times as often as were the war's congressional opponents. By the time of the invasion, 76 percent of respondents in a Gallup poll expressed approval—with four of every five of them expressing "strong approval."

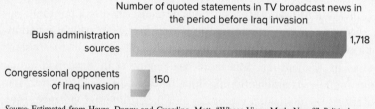

Number of quoted statements in TV broadcast news in the period before Iraq invasion

Bush administration sources — 1,718

Congressional opponents of Iraq invasion — 150

Source: Estimated from Hayes, Danny and Guardino, Matt, "Whose Views Made News?" *Political Communication* 27(2010):73. Based on ABC, CBS, and NBC coverage, August 1, 2002–March 19, 2003.

As it turned out, the Bush administration's claim that Iraq had WMDs was faulty. Although U.S. weapons inspectors searched high and low in Iraq for such weapons, they found none of consequence. However, having started a war, the United States was caught up in it and, for years thereafter, was still engaged in hostilities in the region.

Q: What checks are there on a president who is determined to take the nation to war? What are the conditions, if any, in which those checks might be powerful enough to dissuade the president from doing so?

ASK YOURSELF: What actions are available to Congress? When is Congress likely to invoke them? If the president were to order U.S. forces into combat in the face of congressional opposition, would Congress have any recourse? What about a situation where most Americans are opposed to the prospect of war? What costs would that impose on a president and the president's party? Are these costs significant enough to dissuade a president from acting?

weapons inspectors did not find the WMDs that the Bush administration had claimed were in Iraq's possession, which undermined public support for the war.[16]

The Iraq invasion destabilized the Middle East. A deadly civil war in Syria, Iran's entry into the conflict, anti-Americanism, and other factors spawned a radical Islamic group—ISIS (also known as the Islamic State and ISIL). From an initial base in Syria, it swept across the border into Iraq in 2014, seizing a large swath of territory and declaring its intent to establish a Caliphate—an Islamic state headed by a supreme religious and political leader. As the threat mounted, President Barack Obama ordered targeted airstrikes on ISIS forces, a policy that continued when President Donald Trump took office. The United States sided with the rebels in the Syrian civil war but did not provide it with air support. Russia also interceded in the Syrian civil war, but on the side of Syrian President Bashar Hafez al-Assad, providing airpower that tipped the war in his favor.

Most analysts regard the U.S. involvement in Afghanistan and the Middle East as a failure. Today, the Taliban are back in control of Afghanistan. Syria is controlled by its Russian-backed autocratic government. Al Qaeda and ISIS are operating in several Muslim countries, including Yemen and Libya. Iraq is intact but has a broken political system.[17]

Some analysts contend that the failure owes to America's unwillingness to unleash the full force of its military. Other analysts subscribe to the idea that the United States failed to recognize the difficulty of extracting itself from unwinnable conflicts. The easy part was toppling the Afghan and Iraqi regimes. The difficult part was "democracy building"—creating a stable constitutional government to replace the old one. Bush's secretary of state, Colin Powell, a former army general, had warned of the danger, invoking the Pottery Barn rule—"you break it, you own it."

Military intervention offers no guarantee of long-term success. Regional and internal conflicts typically stem from enduring ethnic, religious, factional, or national hatreds or chronic problems such as famine, overcrowding, or government corruption. Although these hatreds or problems can sometimes be suppressed momentarily, they are often too deep-seated to be contained. Even with the world's most powerful military, the United States has found it difficult to achieve success in the war against terrorism. Wars of this type do not lend themselves to quick and tidy battlefield solutions. It is one thing to defeat a conventional army in open warfare but quite another to prevail in a conflict in which the fight is not so much a battle for territory as it is a struggle for people's loyalties, especially when they harbor age-old distrust of each other, as in the case of the competing religious and ethnic groups in Afghanistan, Iraq, and Syria.

Shown here is a scene from America's hasty withdrawal of troops from Afghanistan in 2021. The withdrawal was quickly followed by a takeover of Afghanistan by the Taliban, who had been driven from power when the United States invaded in 2001. The war was the longest in U.S. history and has become a symbol of the futility of America's recent wars. (Afghanistan Archive/Alamy Stock Photo)

Renewed Conflict with Russia and China   Although terrorism and turmoil in the Middle East have dominated U.S. military policy for the past two decades, it is but one of America's foreign policy challenges. Containing the spread of nuclear weapons is another. The United States and other countries have worked together to block or retard nuclear weapon development by North Korea and Iran but with only some success.

Russia's actions are a more immediate concern. Russian President Vladimir Putin has sought to reestablish Russia as a world power, believing that "the collapse of the Soviet Union was the greatest catastrophe of the 20th century."[18] Realists warned that Putin would respond forcefully to NATO's expansion into Eastern Europe, which during the Cold War had been part of the Soviet bloc.[19] And that's precisely what he did. In 2014, Putin ordered the invasion and annexation of Ukraine's the Crimea Peninsula and helped Russian separatists to take over parts of eastern Ukraine, a strategy he had previously employed in Georgia and Moldova. Then in 2022, he ordered the invasion of Ukraine with the goal of taking over the whole of the country. When that failed, he sought to annex large parts of eastern and southern Ukraine.

The United States, backed by its NATO allies, responded by imposing stiff economic sanctions on Russia, seeking to weaken Russia and punish it for

Ukrainian President Volodymyr Zelensky has come to symbolize the West's hope of restoring what a U.S. official called the "global international security order." Zelensky's leadership has inspired resistance inside and outside Ukraine to Russia's invasion. (Dmytro Larin/Shutterstock)

launching the first large-scale war on European soil since World War II. The United States and NATO countries also acted to bolster the Ukrainian government, providing it with an unprecedented level of military equipment, including aircraft, tanks, long-range artillery, and devastatingly effective antitank and antiaircraft systems. Russia had expected the Ukrainian government to fall quickly but greatly underestimated the determination of Ukraine's people, the skill of its armed services, and the strength of its leadership, particularly that of its president, Volodymyr Zelensky. In the first days of the war, when many Western analysts believed that Russia would easily prevail, the U.S. embassy offered Zelensky safe passage out of the country to set up a government in exile. He replied, "The fight is here; I need ammunition, not a ride."

China is also pursuing an increasingly aggressive foreign policy.[20] It has enlarged its navy, which had been structured to protect China's territorial waters but is now being configured to operate throughout the Pacific. China launched its first aircraft carrier in 2012 and is in the process of building attack submarines and missile ships. China has also claimed huge coastal areas in the South China Sea as being within its territorial boundaries, even though by international law the areas belong to other countries, including Vietnam and the Philippines. When these countries contested China's claims, the Chinese navy responded forcibly. China has also said it might use force to take Taiwan, which it claims is part of China. Taiwan is the island where Chinese nationalist troops retreated after losing China's civil war to the communist side in 1949.

Concern with China's military buildup has been magnified by its embrace of Russia. China was the only country to side with Russia when the UN Security Council voted to censure Russia for the 2014 Crimean takeover, and China abstained on the vote to censure Russia for invading Ukraine in 2022. Barely two weeks before Russia invaded Ukraine and having been informed it would happen, China signed a pact with Russia declaring a "new era" in the global order. China endorsed Russia's rights in Ukraine while Russia declared its support for China's claim to Taiwan. In their joint communiqué, Putin and Chinese President Xi Jinping declared, "Friendship between the two States has no limits. There are no 'forbidden' areas of cooperation."[21]

U.S. policymakers had an optimistic view of the world following the collapse of the Soviet Union in 1991 and the opening of China's economy in the 1980s. They envisioned an era where liberalization through multilateralism, the spread of democracy, and global trade relations would redefine the international order. That optimism has turned to pessimism. Ambassador Nicholas Burns, one of America's most experienced diplomats, describes today's world as "the most challenging . . . for the United States since World War II."[22]

Politics of National Defense

Defense spending by the United States is far higher than that of any other nation. The United States accounts for more than one-third of all military spending worldwide (see **Figure 17-1**). The U.S. defense budget is nearly 3 times that of China and more than 10 times that of Russia. The spending by America's NATO allies is about half that of the United States but, in combination with U.S. spending, accounts for just over half of all military spending worldwide.[23]

The defense industry has a large voice in national security policy. In his 1961 farewell address, President Dwight D. Eisenhower, who commanded U.S. forces in Europe during World War II, warned Americans against "the unwarranted influence" and "misplaced power" of what he termed "the military-industrial complex." Eisenhower was referring to the fact that national defense is big business, involving the annual expenditure of hundreds of billions of dollars.[24] As Eisenhower described it, the **military–industrial complex** has three main components: the military establishment, the arms industry, and the members of Congress from states and districts that depend on the arms industry. All three benefit from a continuously high level of defense spending.

Defense spending levels are among the reasons that analysts argue that U.S. military policy is driven largely by the interests of policy elites, the military,

Percentage of worldwide military spending

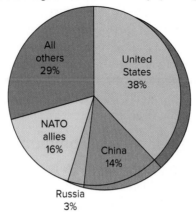

WORLDWIDE MILITARY SPENDING

The United States is easily the world's largest military spender. China is second, spending about a third as much as the United States. All other countries spend much less. (*Source:* Stockholm International Peace Research Institute, 2022.)

and weapons firms. A second reason is presidents' ability on their own authority to take the nation to war (see **Chapter 12**). While the claim of elite influence is generally true, the public can play a key role, particularly when a war is not going well with no decisive end in sight. At that point, public support for the war typically erodes, which raises the political costs to lawmakers if they seek to escalate U.S. involvement and pushes them toward de-escalation and a winding down of hostilities.[25] A swing in public opinion against the Vietnam War forced U.S. policymakers to withdraw American troops in 1973. Public opinion on the Iraq war soured even more quickly, partly because the stated reason for the war—the threat of Iraq's WMDs—proved faulty. A lack of public support for continuing the war in Afghanistan led President Trump to declare that U.S. involvement there would end and contributed to President Biden's decision to end it in 2021 despite the urging of some military leaders to keep troops in the country.

INTELLIGENCE GATHERING

The United States keeps a watchful eye on other nations to protect itself from actions harmful to its national interest. Much of the responsibility for gathering this information falls on federal intelligence agencies. Two are independent agencies—the Office of the Director of National Intelligence (ODNI), which oversees and coordinates the efforts of the intelligence agencies, and the

Central Intelligence Agency (CIA), which gathers and assesses information overseas. The other agencies are located within a larger department, such as the National Security Agency (NSA), which is part of the Department of Defense and specializes in electronic communication surveillance.

For a long period, the annual budget for U.S. intelligence agencies was classified information, but Congress in 2007 voted to make it public. The combined total annual budget for the intelligence agencies is roughly $90 billion.

Reshaping the Intelligence Community

Of the various intelligence agencies, the CIA is easily the best known. Established after World War II as the successor to the Office of Strategic Services (OSS), which was in charge of clandestine missions during the war, the CIA is the only intelligence agency that is allowed by law to carry out covert operations.

In the 1950s, acting under presidential orders, the CIA organized coups that led to the overthrow of popularly elected governments in Iran and Guatemala and the installation of autocrats friendly to the United States. Those actions resulted in criticism of the CIA that intensified in 1961 after a CIA-trained unit of Cuban Americans suffered a crushing defeat when they landed in Cuba to overthrow Fidel Castro's regime. Then, during the Vietnam War, despite a law prohibiting it from conducting surveillance within U.S. borders, it infiltrated the antiwar movement. When this and other abuses of its legal authority became known,[26] Congress created House and Senate committees to oversee CIA activities. The change was only somewhat successful. William Casey, the director of the CIA under President Reagan, lied to Congress in 1987 about illegal covert activities in Central America, which resulted in further congressional hearings and restraints on the CIA.

The CIA came under additional criticism in the aftermath of the 9/11 terrorist attacks on New York City and Washington. Both the CIA and the FBI, which is in charge of domestic surveillance, had information on the terrorists that, if pieced together, might have led to their arrest before they could carry out the attack.[27] To reduce the chances of a similar failure, Congress created ODNI to oversee and coordinate the nation's intelligence program. The Director of National Intelligence prepares the president's daily intelligence briefing, a classified document based on intelligence gathered by all the relevant agencies. The briefing was previously conducted by the Director of the CIA, who now reports to the Director of National Intelligence. The creation of ODNI has strengthened the nation's intelligence assessments but not as fully as hoped. Intelligence agencies are secretive by nature, including a reluctance to share everything they know with each other.

Some observers believe that if the nation's intelligence agencies had been more willing to share information, the terrorist attacks on New York City and Washington, D.C. on September 11, 2001, might have been prevented. Although these agencies now share their information more fully, they still operate somewhat independently. The tendency reflects each agency's determination to protect its role in intelligence gathering. (Central Intelligence Agency)

The War on Terrorism

Although the intelligence agencies engage in a wide range of activities, most of which are hidden from public view, none has been more important in the past two decades than their role in fighting terrorism. America's initial response to al Qaeda's 9/11 terrorist attacks was an invasion of Afghanistan but it was soon apparent that military force was insufficient. Intelligence agencies would be key in locating terrorists before they could strike.

The government only occasionally announces that a planned terrorist attack has been foiled, but reliable estimates suggest that numerous suspected terrorists have been identified, tracked, and detained through the work of the FBI and CIA.[28] Some of these efforts, however, have brought discredit to the United States. The CIA had created "black site" prisons where they held detainees captured in Afghanistan and Iraq. Some of them were subject to waterboarding and other forms of torture to force them to disclose information. When waterboarding was used against American soldiers captured during the Korean war, the United States called it a violation of the Geneva Conventions governing the treatment of prisoners of war. Upon becoming the president in 2009, Barack Obama outlawed waterboarding over the protests of the CIA, which claimed it had saved "thousands of lives."[29]

The 9/11 terrorist attacks were devised by al Qaeda's leader, Osama bin Laden. In 2011, acting on intelligence provided by the CIA, U.S. special operations forces raided a compound in Pakistan where Osama bin Laden was hiding. Bin Laden was killed during the clandestine raid. His killing has become the most visible symbol of the successful role of intelligence in fighting terrorism. The most visible failure was the intelligence estimates of Saddam Hussein's weapons systems, which contributed to the ill-fated invasion of Iraq in 2003. What's still debated, however, is whether the fault lies mostly with the intelligence agencies or with the Bush administration, which publicized only the intelligence reports that supported its contention that Hussein was a dangerous threat to the United States.[30]

Electronic surveillance has been a major component of the intelligence community's antiterrorism effort. The NSA has been collecting Americans' phone records as a means of detecting terrorist activity. When a pattern of calls or e-mails suggests the possibility of a terrorist plot, the NSA can apply for a warrant to listen in on a suspect's calls. Congressional authorization for the program ends in 2024, at which time it will expire unless Congress renews it. There's a good possibility that Congress will renew it, given that terrorist groups like al Qaeda and ISIS have expanded the range of countries in which they are operating. Brian Michael Jenkins, who served as an adviser to the National Commission on Terrorism, concluded that the United States will be at war with radical Islamic terrorists "for years to come."[31]

By law and tradition, intelligence agencies are prohibited from partisan activity but sometimes get caught up in partisan politics. During the 2016 presidential election, intelligence agencies received information indicating that the Russians had violated the law against foreign involvement in U.S. elections by hacking information detrimental to the campaign of Democratic nominee Hillary Clinton. After the election, the CIA issued a report detailing the nature of Russia's interference. Donald Trump responded angrily to the CIA's assessment, saying it was designed to cast doubts on the legitimacy of his election and calling it "politically motivated." The CIA's analysis matched that of the other intelligence agencies and the intelligence community fired back with a written statement that said that the findings were neither wrong nor politically driven but rather aimed at protecting U.S. institutions from Russian interference.[32]

America's intelligence agencies were back in the headlines in 2022 in an unaccustomed role, gathering classified intelligence so that it could be made public. As Russia elevated its troop presence on the Ukrainian border, intelligence agencies were providing President Biden with information about Russia's intentions, which Biden then used at televised press conferences to preempt Russia's disinformation efforts. Once the war started, the intelligence agencies returned to their clandestine role, gathering information on Russia's military movements to share with Ukraine. When news stories broke that the information had been used to target and kill Russian generals and sink Russia's naval command ship in the Black Sea, the U.S. officials characteristically denied all knowledge of the claims. Pentagon press secretary John Kirby said, "We do not provide intelligence on the location of senior military leaders on the battlefield or participate in targeting decisions of the Ukrainian military."

ECONOMIC EXCHANGE

National security is more than an issue of diplomacy, military might, or intelligence. It is also a question of maintaining a strong position in the global economy.

Numerous U.S. agencies contribute to protecting and enhancing U.S. economic interests abroad. They include the U.S. International Trade Commission, which, among other things, analyzes trade issues for the White House and Congress, maintains the U.S. tariff schedule, and safeguards U.S. intellectual property rights. Another specialized agency is the U.S. Trade and Development Agency, which assists U.S. firms in finding export markets for infrastructure projects. Yet another is the Export-Import Bank, which helps U.S. companies respond to export opportunities. A total of roughly two-dozen federal agencies are involved in strengthening America's position in global markets, including subunits within the departments of Commerce, Agriculture, Labor, Energy, State, and Treasury.

America's Position in the Global Economy

Geographically, the world has three major economic centers. One is the United States, which produces roughly a fifth of the world's goods and services. Another center, accounting for about a fourth of the world's economy, is the European Union (EU), which contains most European countries, including Germany and France. The third center is the Pacific Rim, anchored by the economies of Japan and China, which together account for roughly a fourth of the world's economy.

In some ways, the United States is easily the strongest of the three centers. According to the Switzerland-based World Economic Forum, the United States is economically more competitive than its major rivals. The United States owes this position to several factors, including its technological innovation, financial institutions, and extensive higher education system. The U.S. economy is also the most diversified of the three. In addition to its industrial base, the country's vast, fertile plains and advanced farming methods have made it the world's leading agricultural producer. The United States also has abundant natural resources and has recently surged to the top in terms of oil and natural gas production.[33] It is the only one of the three economic centers with the capacity to be "energy independent" in the sense that, if necessary, it could meet its energy needs from domestic resources alone.

Nevertheless, the United States does not have the option of "going it alone" to thrive economically. To meet Americans' production and consumption needs, the country depends on other countries' raw materials, finished goods, markets, and capital. The efforts of the United States in the world economy include foreign trade and global economic security.

Foreign Trade

World War II resulted in the destruction of much of the factory capacity of Europe and Asia, whereas U.S. industrial capacity was unscathed and had expanded to meet wartime needs. When the war ended, the United States was producing two-thirds of the world's manufacturing goods and, even a decade later, was still producing half. As other nations rebuilt from the war, they needed American goods, and the United States was easily the world's major exporter.[34]

The U.S. advantage was unsustainable. As Europe and Japan bounced back from the war, they increasingly sought to sell their goods in foreign markets. America now had competition in global trade and, by the early 1970s, the U.S. balance of trade had leveled off. Each year since then, the United States has had a negative balance of trade, consuming more goods from abroad than it has shipped overseas (see Figure 17-2).

As the United States was losing its competitive advantage, the global economy was changing. Business practices were evolving in response to heightened competition and advances in communication and transportation. Large U.S. firms had become *multinational corporations* (or *transnational corporations*)

figure 17-2   U.S. BALANCE OF TRADE

After World War II, the United States had a trade surplus. In recent years, as in every year since 1975, the United States has had a trade deficit, meaning that its imports have exceeded its exports. (*Source:* U.S. Bureau of Economic Analysis, 2022. Figures are constant 2010 U.S. dollars. Figure for 2022 based on projections.)

with operations in multiple countries. A firm could be headquartered in New York with its factories in Thailand, giving it the best of both worlds—access to management skills and finance in New York and access to low-wage workers in Thailand. **Economic globalization**—the situation where nations' economies are interdependent—was underway.

Free Trade Versus Protectionism   Although global trade was expanding, it was limited by **tariffs**—the taxes that countries levy on goods shipped in from another country. Even if a firm could manufacture a product more cheaply in one country, it would be prohibitively expensive in another country if that country levied a high tariff on the product. To rid themselves of the problem, firms began lobbying Congress for agreements with other countries based on the principle of **free trade**—trade based on greatly reduced or no tariffs. They quickly gained the backing of a traditional ally, Republican leaders in Washington. "The freer the flow of world trade," said President Ronald Reagan, "the stronger the tides of human progress."

Developments elsewhere added to the momentum behind free trade. European nations were on a path to economic integration—a passport-free Europe with few tariffs. Trade between European countries would increase, with American firms losing out unless tariffs were reduced on their products. Economists contributed to the free-trade momentum. Their economic models indicated that free trade would result in a net gain for the U.S. economy.[35] Free trade would lead to a loss of jobs, but that cost would be more than offset by the availability to American consumers of lower-priced goods, everything from clothing to television sets.

In 1993, Congress enacted the first major free-trade agreement, NAFTA (North American Free Trade Agreement), which established a largely free market between the United States, Canada, and Mexico. It passed with the support of more than 70 percent of Senate and House Republicans, whereas fewer than half of the Democrats in each chamber voted for it. The political divide on NAFTA surfaced again the next time Congress voted on free trade. At issue in 2011 were bilateral free-trade agreements with Panama, Colombia, and Korea. Each was voted on separately, and they won the support on average of 96 percent of congressional Republicans and only 32 percent of congressional Democrats.

To a member of Congress, free trade is often a question of its impact on his or her constituency. Although most members of Congress support free trade in principle, they don't always do so when voting on a specific trade agreement. If it will harm a major interest in their district or state, they might opt for **protectionism**—the use of tariffs or other trade barriers to protect domestic producers from foreign competitors. With their ties to labor, Democratic lawmakers have been more protectionist because of the threat that free trade poses to jobs while Republican lawmakers with their ties have been more inclined toward free trade.

Many once-thriving U.S. factory operations have relocated overseas, devastating the workers and localities that depended on them, making global trade a contentious political issue. (Viktor Fischer/ Alamy Stock Photo)

Donald Trump's "America First" Policy   Donald Trump's five immediate predecessors, starting with Ronald Reagan and running through Barack Obama, were advocates of free trade, in part out of their belief that it was a net benefit that contributed to economic growth. Trump was a foreign policy realist at heart and took a different stand. In his inaugural address, he said, "From this moment on, it's going to be America First. Every decision on trade . . . will be made to benefit American workers and American families. We must protect our borders from the ravages of other countries making our products, stealing our companies, and destroying our jobs. Protection will lead to great prosperity and strength."

On taking office, Trump withdrew the United States from the 12-nation Trans-Pacific Partnership (TPP) trade agreement that Obama had negotiated and was pending congressional approval. Trump then renegotiated NAFTA, unveiling the new agreement in 2018 under a new name, the United States-Mexico-Canada Agreement (USMCA). Trump also targeted China, claiming that it was stealing intellectual property, subsidizing its industries, and manipulating its currency, all for the purpose of gaining a trade advantage. He imposed tariffs on steel, aluminum, and other products imported from China, which responded by erecting barriers to the import of U.S. goods. Protectionism did not fully define Trump's "America First" policy. He negotiated a limited trade agreement with Japan in 2019 while seeking trade agreements with Great Britain and the European Union (EU). But he altered the progress toward free trade forged by Republican lawmakers and his presidential predecessors.[36]

When he took office in 2021, Joe Biden followed Trump's lead in part. He didn't seek to rejoin the Trans-Pacific Partnership and didn't end the trade war with China.[37] He had been critical of Trump's policies, but the politics of trade had changed. Although opinion polls indicated that most Americans favor free trade,[38] it rarely affects their vote choice. A consumer who pays a low price for a 4K television set doesn't stop to give "thanks" to free trade. But workers who lose their jobs to foreign competitors think about the issue when they vote, as do communities where a local factory has relocated overseas. Instead of pursuing free trade agreements, Biden has negotiated smaller arrangements with friendly governments, seeking through trade relations to tighten the link between the United States and its allies. Biden has also stressed domestic production as a way to create high-paying jobs and protect against disruptions in the global economy. As U.S. firms sought to increase production after the easing of the COVID-19 pandemic, they were often stymied because their products included parts supplied by overseas firms, many of which had cut back on production because of the pandemic or were unable to ship parts because of breakdowns in global transportation systems. In 2022, at Biden's urging, Congress authorized $200 billion in federal funding for domestic semi-conductor production to overcome America's dependence on foreign firms, including Chinese firms, for its supply of computer chips.

Protecting International Commerce

Although many Americans see the nation's armed forces as having a strictly military purpose, there is also an economic purpose—protecting international commerce. Trade depends on the free flow of goods, which requires open sea, air, and land routes. Since World War II, the United States has had the lead in this area, most visibly through its naval presence. The U.S. Navy patrols every major shipping lane, including the Persian Gulf, through which much of the world's oil flows, and the South China Sea, which is the shortest shipping route from Europe, the Middle East, and Africa to Pacific nations. An indicator of America's sea power is its fleet of aircraft carriers. The United States has 11 carriers, 1 in reserve, and 2 under construction. No other country has more than three.

The economic role of naval power has come into prominence in the past few years as China has flexed its power by laying claim to islands in the South China Sea off the coasts of Vietnam and the Philippines. The area has untapped oil reserves, which China claims belong to it while also claiming the right to keep foreign shipping out of the islands' territorial waters. The United States has refused to recognize China's claims and has sent ships through the disputed waters and conducted joint naval exercises with Southeast Asian countries, one of whom is its former adversary, Vietnam.

America's role in protecting international commerce goes beyond projecting military power, most notably in its effort to strengthen global financial markets. The need to do so became apparent in the global economic downturn of 2008 when financial institutions worldwide teetered on the edge of failure.[39] In response, U.S. policymakers subjected America's leading banks to a "stress test" to determine their ability to withstand defaults on the debt they are owed. Banks that failed the test were provided government loans to protect them from such defaults. U.S. policymakers have encouraged and helped other nations to do the same, recognizing that major financial institutions operate around the globe and that the collapse of even one of them could send the world economy into a downward spiral.

Cybersecurity is also a concern. Just as a critical hack of the U.S. electrical grid would plunge millions of Americans into darkness, a coordinated cyberattack on the financial sectors of the United States and other major economies would have far-reaching effects because today's financial infrastructures are global, interconnected, and digital. The United States has devoted enormous resources, including simulated attacks to detect vulnerable spots, to prevent such an occurrence.

The lesson is clear. Just as America's national interest requires effective diplomacy, appropriate uses of force, and collection of vital intelligence, it also rests on a thoughtful approach to the global economy. In a world where national economies are inextricably linked and mutually dependent, there is no alternative.

SUMMARY

The chief instruments of national security policy are diplomacy, military force, intelligence gathering, and economic exchange. These are exercised through specialized agencies of the U.S. government, which are largely responsive to presidential leadership, such as the Departments of State and Defense. National security policy has also relied on international organizations, such as the United Nations and the World Trade Organization, which are responsive to the global concerns of major nations.

Diplomacy has rested largely on soft power, which is the ability of a nation through noncoercive means to get other nations to do what it would like them to do. A major instrument of diplomacy is foreign assistance, an area in which the United States has been a world leader for three-fourths of a century. Diplomacy has been marked by large failures, particularly when the United States has tried to engage in "nation-building" in countries with cultures unlike that of the United States. But diplomacy has also brought about some of America's greatest foreign policy successes since World War II including, for example, efforts to limit the spread and use of nuclear weapons.

Military force has been a persistent tool of U.S. foreign policy since the end of World War II. Briefer wars in Korea, the Persian Gulf, the Balkans, and Syria are joined on the list of American wars by lengthy conflicts in Vietnam, Afghanistan, and Iraq, and even they do constitute the whole of the list. The initial period of post-World War II conflict was defined by the Cold War with the Soviet Union and, to a lesser degree, with China. The more recent period was been defined by the war on terrorism. These wars have been only somewhat successful in securing America's objectives, and have failed in some cases.

The nation's intelligence gathering is largely hidden from public view but is a vital part of foreign policy decision-making. Key military, diplomatic, and economic policies have rested on the quality of the information provided by intelligence agencies. A persistent issue is holding intelligence agencies accountable for their covert actions. Many of these agencies' biggest successes, and some of their most controversial acts, have occurred in the context of the war on terrorism.

The United States takes economic factors into account in its foreign policy. This has meant, for example, that trade has played a large part in defining relationships between the United States and other countries. The trading system that the United States helped erect after World War II has given way to one that is global in scale and more competitive. The movement toward free trade agreements in the 1990s has recently given way to an effort to strengthen America's domestic producers as a means of job creation and protection against disruptions in the global supply chain.

CRITICAL THINKING ZONE

KEY TERMS

Cold War (*p. 489*)
containment (*p. 489*)
economic globalization (*p. 503*)
free trade (*p. 503*)
hard power (*p. 483*)
liberalism theory (*p. 481*)
military–industrial
  complex (*p. 496*)

multilateralism (*p. 490*)
mutually assured destruction
  (MAD) (*p. 487*)
protectionism (*p. 503*)
realism theory (*p. 480*)
soft power (*p. 483*)
tariffs (*p. 503*)
unilateralism (*p. 491*)

APPLYING THE ELEMENTS OF CRITICAL THINKING

Conceptualizing: Explain the difference between realism theory and liberalism theory in international relations. Which one is more closely associated with soft power? With hard power?

Synthesizing: Contrast free trade and protectionism as approaches to global trade and competition. Identify policies associated with each approach.

Analyzing: Two objectives of U.S. foreign policy are defense security and economic security. What are the mechanisms for pursuing each of these objectives?

OF POSSIBLE INTEREST

A Book Worth Reading: Joseph Nye, *Presidential Leadership and the Creation of the American Era* (Princeton, N.J.: Princeton University Press, 2013). An insightful look at the role various U.S. presidents have played in shaping the nation's place in the world. The author's earlier award-winning book, *Soft Power,* helped change the way policymakers think about foreign policy.

A Website Worth Visiting: **www.cfr.org** The Council on Foreign Relations brings together foreign policy leaders, analysts, scholars, and others in order to promote a better understanding of international issues. Its website includes foreign policy reports, assessments, speeches, and other information.

APPENDICES

The Declaration of Independence
IN CONGRESS, JULY 4, 1776

The Unanimous Declaration of the Thirteen
United States of America

When, in the course of human events, it becomes necessary for one people to dissolve the political bands which have connected them with another, and to assume, among the powers of the earth, the separate and equal station to which the laws of nature and of natures God entitle them, a decent respect to the opinions of mankind requires that they should declare the causes which impel them to the separation.

We hold these truths to be self-evident, that all men are created equal; that they are endowed by their Creator with certain unalienable rights; that among these are life, liberty, and the pursuit of happiness. That, to secure these rights, governments are instituted among men, deriving their just powers from the consent of the governed; that, whenever any form of government becomes destructive of these ends, it is the right of the people to alter or to abolish it, and to institute a new government, laying its foundation on such principles, and organizing its powers in such form, as to them shall seem most likely to effect their safety and happiness. Prudence, indeed, will dictate that governments long established, should not be changed for light and transient causes; and, accordingly, all experience hath shown, that mankind are more disposed to suffer, while evils are sufferable, than to right themselves by abolishing the forms to which they are accustomed. But, when a long train of abuses and usurpations, pursuing invariably the same object, evinces a design to reduce them under absolute despotism, it is their right, it is their duty, to throw off such government and to provide new guards for their future security. Such has been the patient sufferance of these colonies, and such is now the necessity which constrains them to alter their former systems of government. The history of the present King of Great Britain is a history of repeated injuries and usurpations, all having, in direct object, the establishment of an absolute tyranny over these States. To prove this, let facts be submitted to a candid world:

He has refused his assent to laws the most wholesome and necessary for the public good.

He has forbidden his governors to pass laws of immediate and pressing importance, unless suspended in their operation till his assent should be obtained; and, when so suspended, he has utterly neglected to attend to them.

He has refused to pass other laws for the accommodation of large districts of people, unless those people would relinquish the right of representation in the legislature; a right inestimable to them, and formidable to tyrants only.

He has called together legislative bodies at places unusual, uncomfortable, and distant from the depository of their public records, for the sole purpose of fatiguing them into compliance with his measures.

He has dissolved representative houses repeatedly for opposing, with manly firmness, his invasions on the rights of the people.

He has refused, for a long time after such dissolutions, to cause others to be elected; whereby the legislative powers, incapable of annihilation, have returned to the people at large for their exercise; the state remaining, in the meantime, exposed to all the danger of invasion from without, and convulsions within.

He has endeavored to prevent the population of these States; for that purpose, obstructing the laws for naturalization of foreigners, refusing to pass others to encourage their migration hither, and raising the conditions of new appropriations of lands.

He has obstructed the administration of justice, by refusing his assent to laws for establishing judiciary powers.

He has made judges dependent on his will alone, for the tenure of their offices, and the amount and payment of their salaries.

He has erected a multitude of new offices, and sent hither swarms of officers to harass our people, and eat out their substance.

He has kept among us, in time of peace, standing armies, without the consent of our legislatures.

He has affected to render the military independent of, and superior to, the civil power.

He has combined, with others, to subject us to a jurisdiction foreign to our Constitution, and unacknowledged by our laws; giving his assent to their acts of pretended legislation:

For quartering large bodies of armed troops among us:

For protecting them by a mock trial, from punishment, for any murders which they should commit on the inhabitants of these States:

For cutting off our trade with all parts of the world:

For imposing taxes on us without our consent:

For depriving us, in many cases, of the benefit of trial by jury:

For transporting us beyond seas to be tried for pretended offences:

For abolishing the free system of English laws in a neighboring province, establishing therein an arbitrary government, and enlarging its boundaries, so as to render it at once an example and fit instrument for introducing the same absolute rule into these colonies:

For taking away our charters, abolishing our most valuable laws, and altering, fundamentally, the powers of our governments:

For suspending our own legislatures, and declaring themselves invested with power to legislate for us in all cases whatsoever.

He has abdicated government here, by declaring us out of his protection, and waging war against us.

He has plundered our seas, ravaged our coasts, burnt our towns, and destroyed the lives of our people.

He is, at this time, transporting large armies of foreign mercenaries to complete the works of death, desolation, and tyranny, already begun, with circumstances of cruelty and perfidy scarcely paralleled in the most barbarous ages, and totally unworthy of the head of a civilized nation.

He has constrained our fellow citizens, taken captive on the high seas, to bear arms against their country, to become the executioners of their friends, and brethren, or to fall themselves by their hands.

He has excited domestic insurrections amongst us, and has endeavored to bring on the inhabitants of our frontiers, the merciless Indian savages, whose known rule of warfare is an undistinguished destruction of all ages, sexes, and conditions.

In every stage of these oppressions, we have petitioned for redress, in the most humble terms; our repeated petitions have been answered only by repeated injury. A prince, whose character is thus marked by every act which may define a tyrant, is unfit to be the ruler of a free people.

Nor have we been wanting in attention to our British brethren. We have warned them, from time to time, of attempts made by their legislature to extend an unwarrantable jurisdiction over us. We have reminded them of the circumstances of our emigration and settlement here. We have appealed to their native justice and magnanimity, and we have conjured them, by the ties of our common kindred, to disavow these usurpations, which would inevitably interrupt our connections and correspondence. They, too, have been deaf to the voice of justice and of consanguinity. We must, therefore, acquiesce in the necessity which denounces our separation, and hold them as we hold the rest of mankind, enemies in war, in peace, friends.

We, therefore, the representatives of the United States of America, in general Congress assembled, appealing to the Supreme Judge of the world for the rectitude of our intentions, do, in the name, and by the authority of the good people of these colonies, solemnly publish and declare, that these united colonies are, and of right ought to be, free and independent states: that they are absolved from all allegiance to the British Crown, and that all political connection between them and the state of Great Britain is, and ought to be, totally dissolved; and that, as free and independent states, they have full power to levy war, conclude peace, contract alliances, establish commerce, and to do all other acts and things which independent states may of right do. And, for the support of this declaration, with a firm reliance on the protection of Divine Providence, we mutually pledge to each other our lives, our fortunes, and our sacred honor.

The foregoing Declaration was, by order of Congress, engrossed, and signed by the following members:

JOHN HANCOCK

New Hampshire
Josiah Bartlett
William Whipple
Matthew Thornton

Massachusetts Bay
Samuel Adams
John Adams
Robert Treat Paine
Elbridge Gerry

Rhode Island
Stephen Hopkins
William Ellery

Connecticut
Roger Sherman

Samuel Huntington
William Williams
Oliver Wolcott

New York
William Floyd
Philip Livingston
Francis Lewis
Lewis Morris

New Jersey
Richard Stockton
John Witherspoon
Francis Hopkinson
John Hart
Abraham Clark

Pennsylvania
Robert Morris
Benjamin Rush
Benjamin Franklin
John Morton
George Clymer
James Smith
George Taylor
James Wilson
George Ross

Delaware
Caesar Rodney
George Reed
Thomas McKean

Maryland
Samuel Chase
William Paca
Thomas Stone
Charles Carroll,
  of Carrollton

Virginia
George Wythe
Richard Henry Lee

Thomas Jefferson
Benjamin Harrison
Thomas Nelson, Jr.
Francis Lightfoot Lee
Carter Braxton

North Carolina
William Hooper
Joseph Hewes
John Penn

South Carolina
Edward Rutledge
Thomas Heyward, Jr.
Thomas Lynch, Jr.
Arthur Middleton

Georgia
Button Gwinnett
Lyman Hall
George Walton

Resolved, That copies of the Declaration be sent to the several assemblies, conventions, and committees, or councils of safety, and to the several commanding officers of the continental troops; that it be proclaimed in each of the United States, at the head of the army.

The Constitution of the United States of America[1]

We the People of the United States, in Order to form a more perfect Union, establish Justice, insure domestic Tranquility, provide for the common defence, promote the general Welfare, and secure the Blessings of Liberty to ourselves and our Posterity, do ordain and establish this CONSTITUTION for the United States of America.

ARTICLE I

Section 1

All legislative Powers herein granted shall be vested in a Congress of the United States, which shall consist of a Senate and House of Representatives.

Section 2

The House of Representatives shall be composed of Members chosen every second Year by the People of the several States, and the Electors in each State shall have the Qualifications requisite for Electors of the most numerous Branch of the State Legislature.

No Person shall be a Representative who shall not have attained to the Age of twenty-five Years, and been seven Years a Citizen of the United States, and who shall not, when elected, be an Inhabitant of that State in which he shall be chosen.

[Representatives and direct Taxes[2] shall be apportioned among the several States which may be included within this Union, according to their respective Numbers, which shall be determined by adding to the whole Number of free Persons, including those bound to Service for a Term of Years, and excluding Indians not taxed, three fifths of all other Persons.][3] The actual Enumeration shall be made within three Years after the first Meeting of the Congress of the United States, and within every subsequent Term of ten Years, in such Manner as they shall by Law direct. The Number of Representatives shall not exceed one for every thirty Thousand, but each State shall have at Least one Representative; and until such enumeration shall be made, the State of New Hampshire shall be entitled to chuse three, Massachusetts eight, Rhode-Island and Providence Plantations one, Connecticut five, New York six, New Jersey four, Pennsylvania eight, Delaware one, Maryland six, Virginia ten, North Carolina five, South Carolina five, and Georgia three.

When vacancies happen in the Representation from any State, the Executive Authority thereof shall issue Writs of Election to fill such Vacancies.

The House of Representatives shall chuse their Speaker and other Officers; and shall have the sole Power of Impeachment.

---

[1]This version, which follows the original Constitution in capitalization and spelling, was published by the United States Department of the Interior, Office of Education, in 1935.
[2]Altered by the Sixteenth Amendment.
[3]Negated by the Fourteenth Amendment.

Section 3

The Senate of the United States shall be composed of two Senators from each State, chosen by the Legislature thereof, for six Years; and each Senator shall have one Vote.

Immediately after they shall be assembled in Consequence of the first Election, they shall be divided as equally as may be into three Classes. The Seats of the Senators of the first Class shall be vacated at the Expiration of the second Year, of the second Class at the Expiration of the fourth Year, and of the third Class at the Expiration of the sixth Year, so that one-third may be chosen every second Year; and if Vacancies happen by Resignation, or otherwise, during the Recess of the Legislature of any State, the Executive thereof may make temporary Appointments until the next Meeting of the Legislature, which shall then fill such Vacancies.

No Person shall be a Senator who shall not have attained to the Age of thirty Years, and been nine Years a Citizen of the United States, and who shall not, when elected, be an Inhabitant of that State for which he shall be chosen.

The Vice President of the United States shall be President of the Senate, but shall have no vote, unless they be equally divided.

The Senate shall chuse their other Officers, and also a President pro tempore, in the absence of the Vice President, or when he shall exercise the Office of President of the United States.

The Senate shall have the sole Power to try all Impeachments. When sitting for that purpose they shall be on Oath or Affirmation. When the President of the United States is tried, the Chief Justice shall preside: And no person shall be convicted without the Concurrence of two thirds of the Members present.

Judgment in Cases of Impeachment shall not extend further than to removal from Office, and disqualification to hold and enjoy any Office of honor, Trust, or Profit under the United States: but the Party convicted shall nevertheless be liable and subject to Indictment, Trial, Judgment and Punishment, according to Law.

Section 4

The Times, Place and Manner of holding Elections for Senators and Representatives, shall be prescribed in each State by the Legislature thereof; but the Congress may at any time by Law make or alter such Regulations, except as to the Places of Chusing Senators.

The Congress shall assemble at least once in every Year, and such Meeting shall be on the first Monday in December, unless they shall by Law appoint a different Day.

Section 5

Each House shall be the Judge of the Elections, Returns and Qualifications of its own Members, and a Majority of each shall constitute a Quorum to do Business; but a smaller number may adjourn from day to day, and may be authorized to compel the Attendance of absent Members, in such Manner, and under such Penalties, as each House may provide.

Each House may determine the Rules of its Proceedings, punish its Members for disorderly Behaviour, and, with the Concurrence of two thirds, expel a Member.

Each House shall keep a Journal of its Proceedings, and from time to time publish the same, excepting such Parts as may in their Judgment require Secrecy; and the Yeas and Nays of the Members of either House on any question shall, at the Desire of one fifth of those Present, be entered on the Journal.

Neither House, during the Session of Congress, shall, without the Consent of the other, adjourn for more than three days, nor to any other Place than that in which the two Houses shall be sitting.

Section 6

The Senators and Representatives shall receive a Compensation for their Services, to be ascertained by Law, and paid out of the Treasury of the United States. They shall in all Cases, except Treason, Felony, and Breach of the Peace, be privileged from Arrest during their Attendance at the Session of their respective Houses, and in going to and returning from the same; and for any Speech or Debate in either House, they shall not be questioned in any other Place.

No Senator or Representative shall, during the Time for which he was elected, be appointed to any civil Office under the Authority of the United States, which shall have been created, or the Emoluments whereof shall have been increased, during such time; and no Person holding any Office under the United States shall be a Member of either House during his continuance in Office.

Section 7

All Bills for raising Revenue shall originate in the House of Representatives; but the Senate may propose or concur with Amendments as on other bills.

Every Bill which shall have passed the House of Representatives and the Senate, shall, before it becomes a Law, be presented to the President of the United States; if he approve he shall sign it, but if not he shall return it, with his Objections, to that House in which it shall have originated, who shall enter the Objections at large on their Journal, and proceed to reconsider it. If after such Reconsideration two thirds of that House shall agree to pass the bill, it shall be sent, together with the objections, to the other House, by which it shall likewise be reconsidered, and if approved by two thirds of that House, it shall become a Law. But in all such Cases the Votes of both Houses shall be determined by Yeas and Nays, and the Names of the Persons voting for and against the Bill shall be entered on the Journal of each House respectively. If any Bill shall not be returned by the President within ten Days (Sundays excepted) after it shall have been presented to him, the Same shall be a Law, in like Manner as if he had signed it, unless the Congress by their Adjournment prevent its Return, in which Case it shall not be a Law.

Every Order, Resolution, or Vote to which the Concurrence of the Senate and House of Representatives may be necessary (except on a question of Adjournment) shall be presented to the President of the United States; and before the Same shall take Effect, shall be approved by him, or being disapproved by him, shall be repassed by two thirds of the Senate and House of Representatives, according to the Rules and Limitations prescribed in the Case of a Bill.

Section 8

The Congress shall have Power To lay and collect Taxes, Duties, Imposts and Excises, to pay the Debts and provide for the common Defence and general Welfare of the United States; but all Duties, Imposts and Excises shall be uniform throughout the United States;

To borrow money on the credit of the United States;

To regulate Commerce with foreign Nations, and among the several States, and with the Indian Tribes;

To establish a uniform rule of Naturalization, and uniform Laws on the subject of Bankruptcies throughout the United States;

To coin Money, regulate the Value thereof, and of foreign Coin, and fix the Standard of Weights and Measures;

To provide for the Punishment of counterfeiting the Securities and current Coin of the United States;

To establish Post Offices and post Roads;

To promote the Progress of Science and useful Arts, by securing for limited Times to Authors and Inventors the exclusive Right to their respective Writings and Discoveries;

To constitute Tribunals inferior to the Supreme Court;

To define and punish Piracies and Felonies committed on the high Seas, and Offenses against the Law of Nations;

To declare War, grant Letters of Marque and Reprisal, and make Rules concerning Captures on Land and Water;

To raise and support Armies, but no Appropriation of Money to that Use shall be for a longer Term than two Years;

To provide and maintain a Navy;

To make Rules for the Government and Regulation of the land and naval forces;

To provide for calling forth the Militia to execute the Laws of the Union, suppress Insurrections and repel Invasions;

To provide for organizing, arming, and disciplining the Militia, and for governing such Part of them as may be employed in the Service of the United States, reserving to the States respectively, the Appointment of the Officers, and the Authority of training the Militia according to the discipline prescribed by Congress;

To exercise exclusive Legislation in all Cases whatsoever, over such District (not exceeding ten Miles square) as may, by Cession of particular States, and the acceptance of Congress, become the Seat of the Government of the United States, and to exercise like Authority over all Places purchased by the Consent of the Legislature of the State in which the Same shall be, for the Erection of Forts, Magazines, Arsenals, Dock-yards, and other needful Buildings;—And

To make all Laws which shall be necessary and proper for carrying into Execution the foregoing Powers, and all other Powers vested by this Constitution in the Government of the United States, or in any Department or Officer thereof.

Section 9

The Migration or Importation of such Persons as any of the States now existing shall think proper to admit, shall not be prohibited by the Congress prior to the Year one thousand eight hundred and eight, but a tax or duty may be imposed on such Importation, not exceeding ten dollars for each Person.

The privilege of the Writ of Habeas Corpus shall not be suspended, unless when in Cases of Rebellion or Invasion the public Safety may require it.

No bill of Attainder or ex post facto Law shall be passed.

No capitation, or other direct, Tax shall be laid unless in Proportion to the Census or Enumeration herein before directed to be taken.

No Tax or Duty shall be laid on Articles exported from any State.

No Preference shall be given by any Regulation of Commerce or Revenue to the Ports of one State over those of another: nor shall Vessels bound to, or from, one State, be obliged to enter, clear, or pay Duties in another.

No Money shall be drawn from the Treasury, but in Consequence of Appropriations made by Law; and a regular Statement and Account of the Receipts and Expenditures of all public Money shall be published from time to time.

No Title of Nobility shall be granted by the United States: And no Person holding any Office of Profit or Trust under them, shall, without the Consent of the Congress, accept of any present, Emolument, Office, or Title, of any kind whatever, from any King, Prince, or foreign State.

Section 10

No State shall enter into any Treaty, Alliance, or Confederation; grant Letters of Marque and Reprisal; coin Money; emit Bills of Credit; make any Thing but gold and silver Coin a Tender in Payment of Debts; pass any Bill of Attainder, ex post facto Law, or Law impairing the Obligation of Contracts, or grant any Title of Nobility.

No State shall, without the Consent of the Congress, lay any Imposts or Duties on Imports or Exports, except what may be absolutely necessary for executing its inspection Laws; and the net Produce of all Duties and Imposts, laid by any State on Imports or Exports, shall be for the use of the Treasury of the United States; and all such Laws shall be subject to the Revision and Control of the Congress.

No state shall, without the Consent of Congress, lay any duty of Tonnage, keep Troops, or Ships of War in time of Peace, enter into any Agreement or Compact with another State, or with a foreign Power, or engage in War, unless actually invaded, or in such imminent Danger as will not admit of delay.

ARTICLE II

Section 1

The executive Power shall be vested in a President of the United States of America. He shall hold his Office during the Term of four years, and, together with the Vice President, chosen for the same Term, be elected, as follows:

Each State shall appoint, in such Manner as the Legislature thereof may direct, a Number of Electors, equal to the whole Number of Senators and Representatives to which the State may be entitled in the Congress: but no Senator or Representative, or Person holding an Office of Trust or Profit under the United States, shall be appointed an Elector.

[The Electors shall meet in their respective States, and vote by Ballot for two persons, of whom one at least shall not be an Inhabitant of the same State with themselves. And they shall make a List of all the Persons voted for, and of the Number of Votes for each; which List they shall sign and certify, and transmit sealed to the Seat of the Government of the United States, directed to the President of the Senate. The President of the Senate shall, in the Presence of the Senate and House of Representatives, open all the Certificates, and the Votes shall then be counted. The Person having the greatest Number of Votes shall be the President, if such Number be a Majority of the whole Number of Electors appointed; and if there be more than one who have such Majority, and have an equal Number of Votes, then the House of Representatives shall immediately chuse by Ballot one of them for President; and if no Person have a Majority, then from the five highest on the List the said House shall in like Manner chuse the President.

But in chusing the President, the Votes shall be taken by States, the Representation from each State having one Vote; a quorum for this Purpose shall consist of a Member or Members from two-thirds of the States, and a Majority of all the States shall be necessary to a Choice. In every Case, after the Choice of the President, the Person having the greatest Number of Votes of the Electors shall be the Vice President. But if there should remain two or more who have equal votes, the Senate shall chuse from them by Ballot the Vice President.][4]

The Congress may determine the Time of chusing the Electors, and the Day on which they shall give their Votes; which Day shall be the same throughout the United States.

No person except a natural-born Citizen, or a Citizen of the United States, at the time of the Adoption of this Constitution, shall be eligible to the Office of President; neither shall any Person be eligible to that Office who shall not have attained to the Age of thirty-five years, and been fourteen Years a Resident within the United States.

In Case of the Removal of the President from Office, or of his Death, Resignation, or Inability to discharge the Powers and Duties of the said Office, the same shall devolve on the Vice President, and the Congress may by Law provide for the Case of Removal, Death, Resignation, or Inability, both of the President and Vice President, declaring what Officer shall then act as President, and such Officer shall act accordingly, until the disability be removed, or a President shall be elected.

The President shall, at stated Times, receive for his Services a Compensation, which shall neither be increased nor diminished during the Period for which he shall have been elected, and he shall not receive within that Period any other Emolument from the United States, or any of them.

Before he enter on the execution of his Office, he shall take the following Oath or Affirmation:—"I do solemnly swear (or affirm) that I will faithfully execute the Office of President of the United States, and will, to the best of my Ability, preserve, protect, and defend the Constitution of the United States."

Section 2

The President shall be Commander in Chief of the Army and Navy of the United States, and of the Militia of the several States, when called into the actual Service of the United States; he may require the Opinion, in writing, of the principal Officer in each of the executive Departments, upon any subject relating to the Duties of their respective Offices, and he shall have Power to Grant Reprieves and Pardons for Offenses against the United States, except in Cases of Impeachment.

He shall have Power, by and with the Advice and Consent of the Senate, to make Treaties, provided two-thirds of the Senators present concur; and he shall nominate, and by and with the Advice and Consent of the Senate, shall appoint Ambassadors, other public Ministers and Consuls, Judges of the supreme Court, and all other Officers of the United States, whose Appointments are not herein otherwise provided for, and which shall be established by Law: but the Congress may by Law vest the Appointment of such inferior Officers, as they think proper, in the President alone, in the Courts of Law, or in the Heads of Departments.

---

[4]Revised by the Twelfth Amendment.

The President shall have Power to fill up all Vacancies that may happen during the Recess of the Senate, by granting Commissions which shall expire at the End of their next Session.

Section 3

He shall from time to time give to the Congress Information of the State of the Union, and recommend to their Consideration such Measures as he shall judge necessary and expedient; he may, on extraordinary occasions, convene both Houses, or either of them, and in Case of Disagreement between them, with respect to the Time of Adjournment, he may adjourn them to such Time as he shall think proper; he shall receive Ambassadors and other public Ministers; he shall take care that the Laws be faithfully executed, and shall Commission all the Officers of the United States.

Section 4

The President, Vice President and all civil Officers of the United States, shall be removed from Office on Impeachment for, and Conviction of, Treason, Bribery, or other high Crimes and Misdemeanors.

ARTICLE III

Section 1

The judicial Power of the United States, shall be vested in one supreme Court, and in such inferior Courts as the Congress may from time to time ordain and establish. The Judges, both of the supreme and inferior Courts, shall hold their Offices during good Behaviour, and shall, at stated Times, receive for their Services, a Compensation, which shall not be diminished during their Continuance in Office.

Section 2

The judicial Power shall extend to all Cases, in Law and Equity, arising under this Constitution, the Laws of the United States, and Treaties made, or which shall be made, under their Authority;—to all Cases affecting ambassadors, other public ministers and consuls;—to all cases of admiralty and maritime Jurisdiction;—to Controversies to which the United States shall be a Party;—to Controversies between two or more states;—between a State and Citizens of another State;[5]—between Citizens of different States—between Citizens of the same State claiming Lands under Grants of different States, and between a State, or the Citizens thereof, and foreign States, Citizens, or Subjects.

In all Cases affecting Ambassadors, other public Ministers and Consuls, and those in which a State shall be Party, the supreme Court shall have original Jurisdiction. In all the other Cases before mentioned, the supreme Court shall have appellate Jurisdiction, both as to Law and Fact, with such Exceptions, and under such Regulations as the Congress shall make.

---

[5]Qualified by the Eleventh Amendment.

The trial of all Crimes, except in Cases of Impeachment, shall be by Jury; and such Trial shall be held in the State where the said Crimes shall have been committed; but when not committed within any State, the Trial shall be at such Place or Places as the Congress may by Law have directed.

Section 3

Treason against the United States, shall consist only in levying War against them, or in adhering to their Enemies, giving them Aid and Comfort. No Person shall be convicted of Treason unless on the Testimony of two Witnesses to the same overt Act, or on Confession in open Court.

The Congress shall have power to declare the Punishment of Treason, but no Attainder of Treason shall work Corruption of Blood, or Forfeiture except during the Life of the Person attainted.

ARTICLE IV

Section 1

Full Faith and Credit shall be given in each State to the public Acts, Records, and judicial Proceedings of every other State. And the Congress may by general Laws prescribe the Manner in which such Acts, Records and Proceedings shall be proved, and the Effect thereof.

Section 2

The Citizens of each State shall be entitled to all Privileges and Immunities of Citizens in the several States.

A Person charged in any State with Treason, Felony, or other Crime, who shall flee from Justice, and be found in another State, shall on demand of the executive Authority of the State from which he fled, be delivered up, to be removed to the State having Jurisdiction of the crime.

No Person held to Service or Labour in one State, under the Laws thereof, escaping into another, shall, in Consequence of any Law or Regulation therein, be discharged from such Service or Labour, but shall be delivered up on Claim of the Party to whom such Service or Labour may be due.

Section 3

New States may be admitted by the Congress into this Union; but no new State shall be formed or erected within the Jurisdiction of any other State; nor any State be formed by the Junction of two or more States, or parts of States, without the Consent of the Legislatures of the States concerned as well as of the Congress.

The Congress shall have Power to dispose of and make all needful Rules and Regulations respecting the Territory or other Property belonging to the United States; and nothing in this Constitution shall be so construed as to Prejudice any Claims of the United States, or of any particular State.

Section 4

The United States shall guarantee to every State in this Union a Republican Form of Government, and shall protect each of them against Invasion; and on Application of the Legislature, or of the Executive (when the Legislature cannot be convened) against domestic Violence.

ARTICLE V

The Congress, whenever two-thirds of both Houses shall deem it necessary, shall propose Amendments to this Constitution, or, on the Application of the Legislatures of two-thirds of the several States, shall call a Convention for proposing Amendments, which, in either Case, shall be valid to all Intents and Purposes, as part of this Constitution, when ratified by the Legislatures of three-fourths of the several States, or by Conventions in three-fourths thereof, as the one or the other Mode of Ratification may be proposed by the Congress; Provided that no Amendment which may be made prior to the Year One thousand eight hundred and eight shall in any Manner affect the first and fourth Clauses in the Ninth Section of the first Article; and that no State, without its Consent, shall be deprived of its equal Suffrage in the Senate.

ARTICLE VI

All Debts contracted and Engagements entered into, before the Adoption of this Constitution, shall be as valid against the United States under this Constitution, as under the Confederation.

This Constitution, and the Laws of the United States which shall be made in Pursuance thereof; and all Treaties made, or which shall be made, under the Authority of the United States, shall be the supreme Law of the Land; and the Judges in every State shall be bound thereby, any Thing in the Constitution or Laws of any State to the Contrary notwithstanding.

The Senators and Representatives before mentioned, and the Members of the several State Legislatures, and all executive and judicial Officers, both of the United States and of the several States, shall be bound by Oath or Affirmation to support this Constitution; but no religious Tests shall ever be required as a qualification to any Office or public Trust under the United States.

ARTICLE VII

The Ratification of the Conventions of nine States shall be sufficient for the Establishment of this Constitution between the States so ratifying the same.

Done in Convention by the Unanimous Consent of the States present the Seventeenth Day of September in the Year of our Lord one thousand seven hundred and Eighty seven, and of the Independence of the United States of America the Twelfth. In Witness whereof We have hereunto subscribed our Names.[6]

---

[6]These are the full names of the signers, which in some cases are not the signatures on the document.

George Washington
President and deputy from
  Virginia

New Hampshire
John Langdon
Nicholas Gilman

Massachusetts
Nathaniel Gorham
Rufus King

Connecticut
William Samuel Johnson
Roger Sherman

New York
Alexander Hamilton

New Jersey
William Livingston
David Brearley
William Paterson
Jonathan Dayton

Pennsylvania
Benjamin Franklin
Thomas Mifflin
Robert Morris
George Clymer
Thomas FitzSimmons
Jared Ingersoll
James Wilson
Gouverneur Morris

Delaware
George Read
Gunning Bedford, Jr.
John Dickinson
Richard Bassett
Jacob Broom

Maryland
James McHenry
Daniel of St. Thomas
  Jenifer
Daniel Carroll

Virginia
John Blair
James Madison, Jr.

North Carolina
William Blount
Richard Dobbs Spaight
Hugh Williamson

South Carolina
John Rutledge
Charles Cotesworth
  Pinckney
Charles Pinckney
Pierce Butler

Georgia
William Few
Abraham Baldwin

Articles in Addition to, and Amendment of, the Constitution of the United States of America, Proposed by Congress, and Ratified by the Legislatures of the Several States, Pursuant to the Fifth Article of the Original Constitution[7].

AMENDMENT I

Congress shall make no law respecting an establishment of religion, or prohibiting the free exercise thereof; or abridging the freedom of speech, or of the press; or the right of the people peaceably to assemble, and to petition the Government for a redress of grievances.

AMENDMENT II

A well regulated Militia, being necessary to the security of a free State, the right of the people to keep and bear Arms shall not be infringed.

AMENDMENT III

No Soldier shall, in time of peace, be quartered in any house, without the consent of the Owner, nor in time of war, but in a manner to be prescribed by law.

---

[7]This heading appears only in the joint resolution submitting the first ten amendments, which are collectively known as the Bill of Rights. They were ratified on December 15, 1791.

AMENDMENT IV

The right of the people to be secure in their persons, houses, papers, and effects, against unreasonable searches and seizures, shall not be violated, and no Warrants shall issue, but upon probable cause, supported by Oath or affirmation, and particularly describing the place to be searched, and the persons or things to be seized.

AMENDMENT V

No person shall be held to answer for a capital or otherwise infamous crime, unless on a presentment or indictment of a Grand Jury, except in cases arising in the land or naval forces, or in the Militia, when in actual service in time of War or public danger; nor shall any person be subject for the same offence to be twice put in jeopardy of life or limb; nor shall be compelled in any criminal case to be a witness against himself, nor be deprived of life, liberty, or property, without due process of law; nor shall private property be taken for public use, without just compensation.

AMENDMENT VI

In all criminal prosecutions, the accused shall enjoy the right to a speedy and public trial, by an impartial jury of the State and district wherein the crime shall have been committed, which district shall have been previously ascertained by law, and to be informed of the nature and cause of the accusation; to be confronted with the witnesses against him; to have compulsory process for obtaining witnesses in his favour, and to have the Assistance of Counsel for his defence.

AMENDMENT VII

In suits at common law, where the value in controversy shall exceed twenty dollars, the right of trial by jury shall be preserved, and no fact tried by a jury, shall be otherwise reexamined in any Court of the United States, than according to the rules of the common law.

AMENDMENT VIII

Excessive bail shall not be required, nor excessive fines imposed, nor cruel and unusual punishments inflicted.

AMENDMENT IX

The enumeration of the Constitution, of certain rights, shall not be construed to deny or disparage others retained by the people.

AMENDMENT X

The powers not delegated to the United States by the Constitution, nor prohibited by it to the States, are reserved to the States respectively, or to the people.

Amendment XI [1795]

The Judicial power of the United States shall not be construed to extend to any suit in law or equity, commenced or prosecuted against one of the United States by Citizens of another State, or by Citizens or Subjects of any Foreign State.

Amendment XII [1804]

The Electors shall meet in their respective States and vote by ballot for President and Vice-President, one of whom, at least, shall not be an inhabitant of the same State with themselves; they shall name in their ballots the person voted for as President, and in distinct ballots the person voted for as Vice-President, and they shall make distinct lists of all persons voted for as President, and of all persons voted for as Vice-President, and of the number of votes for each, which lists they shall sign and certify, and transmit sealed to the seat of the government of the United States, directed to the President of the Senate;—The President of the Senate shall, in the presence of the Senate and House of Representatives, open all the certificates and the votes shall then be counted;—The person having the greatest number of votes for President, shall be the President, if such number be a majority of the whole number of Electors appointed; and if no person have such majority, then from the persons having the highest numbers not exceeding three on the list of those voted for as President, the House of Representatives shall choose immediately, by ballot, the President. But in choosing the President, the votes shall be taken by states, the representation from each state having one vote; a quorum for this purpose shall consist of a member or members from two-thirds of the states, and a majority of all the states shall be necessary to a choice. And if the House of Representatives shall not choose a President whenever the right of choice shall devolve upon them, before the fourth day of March next following, then the Vice-President shall act as President, as in the case of the death or other constitutional disability of the President.—The person having the greatest number of votes as Vice-President, shall be the Vice-President, if such number be a majority of the whole number of Electors appointed, and if no person have a majority, then from the two highest numbers on the list, the Senate shall choose the Vice-President; a quorum for the purpose shall consist of two-thirds of the whole number of Senators, and majority of the whole number shall be necessary to a choice. But no person constitutionally ineligible to the office of President shall be eligible to that of Vice-President of the United States.

Amendment XIII [1865]

Section 1

Neither slavery nor involuntary servitude, except as a punishment for crime whereof the party shall have been duly convicted, shall exist within the United States, or any place subject to their jurisdiction.

Section 2

Congress shall have power to enforce this article by appropriate legislation.

Amendment XIV [1868]

Section 1

All persons born or naturalized in the United States, and subject to the jurisdiction thereof, are citizens of the United States and of the State wherein they reside. No State shall abridge the privileges or immunities of citizens of the United States; nor shall any State deprive any person of life, liberty, or property, without due process of law; nor deny to any person within its jurisdiction the equal protection of the laws.

Section 2

Representatives shall be apportioned among the several States according to their respective numbers, counting the whole number of persons in each State, excluding Indians not taxed. But when the right to vote at any election for the choice of electors for President and Vice-President of the United States, Representatives in Congress, the Executive and Judicial officers of a State, or the members of the Legislature thereof, is denied to any of the male inhabitants of such State, being twenty-one years of age, and citizens of the United States, or in any way abridged, except for participation in rebellion, or other crime, the basis of representation therein shall be reduced in the proportion which the number of such male citizens shall bear to the whole number of male citizens twenty-one years of age in such State.

Section 3

No person shall be a Senator or Representative in Congress, or elector of President and Vice-President, or hold any office, civil or military, under the United States, or under any State, who, having previously taken an oath, as a member of Congress, or as an officer of the United States, or as a member of any State legislature, or as an executive or judicial officer of any State, to support the Constitution of the United States, shall have engaged in insurrection or rebellion against the same, or given aid or comfort to the enemies thereof. But Congress may by a vote of two-thirds of each House, remove such disability.

Section 4

The validity of the public debt of the United States, authorized by law, including debts incurred for payment of pensions and bounties for services in suppressing insurrection or rebellion, shall not be questioned. But neither the United States nor any State shall assume or pay any debts or obligation incurred in aid of insurrection or rebellion against the United States, or any claim for the loss or emancipation of any slave; but all such debts, obligations, and claims shall be held illegal and void.

Section 5

The Congress shall have the power to enforce, by appropriate legislation, the provisions of this article.

AMENDMENT XV [1870]

Section 1

The right of citizens of the United States to vote shall not be denied or abridged by the United States or by any State on account of race, color, or previous condition of servitude.

Section 2

The Congress shall have power to enforce this article by appropriate legislation.

AMENDMENT XVI [1913]

The Congress shall have power to lay and collect taxes on incomes, from whatever source derived, without apportionment among the several States, and without regard to any census or enumeration.

AMENDMENT XVII [1913]

The Senate of the United States shall be composed of two Senators from each State, elected by the people thereof, for six years; and each Senator shall have one vote. The electors in each State shall have the qualifications requisite for electors of the most numerous branch of the State legislatures.

When vacancies happen in the representation of any State in the Senate, the executive authority of such State shall issue writs of election to fill such vacancies: Provided, That the legislature of any State may empower the executive thereof to make temporary appointments until the people fill the vacancies by election as the legislature may direct.

This Amendment shall not be so construed as to affect the election or term of any Senator chosen before it becomes valid as part of the Constitution.

AMENDMENT XVIII [1919]

Section 1

After one year from the ratification of this article the manufacture, sale, or transportation of intoxicating liquors within, the importation thereof into, or the exportation thereof from the United States and all territory subject to the jurisdiction thereof for beverage purposes is hereby prohibited.

Section 2

The Congress and the several States shall have concurrent power to enforce this article by appropriate legislation.

Section 3

This article shall be inoperative unless it shall have been ratified as an Amendment to the Constitution by the legislatures of the several States, as provided in the Constitution, within seven years from the date of the submission hereof to the States by the Congress.

AMENDMENT XIX [1920]

The right of citizens of the United States to vote shall not be denied or abridged by the United States or by any State on account of sex.

Congress shall have power to enforce this article by appropriate legislation.

AMENDMENT XX [1933]

Section 1

The terms of the President and Vice-President shall end at noon on the 20th day of January, and the terms of Senators and Representatives at noon on the 3d day of January, of the years in which such terms would have ended if this article had not been ratified; and the terms of their successors shall then begin.

Section 2

The Congress shall assemble at least once in every year, and such meeting shall begin at noon on the 3d day of January, unless they shall by law appoint a different day.

Section 3

If, at the time fixed for the beginning of the term of the President, the President elect shall have died, the Vice-President elect shall become President. If a President shall not have been chosen before the time fixed for the beginning of his term or if the President elect shall have failed to qualify, then the Vice-President elect shall act as President until a President shall have qualified; and the Congress may by law provide for the case wherein neither a President elect nor a Vice-President elect shall have qualified, declaring who shall then act as President, or the manner in which one who is to act shall be selected, and such person shall act accordingly until a President or Vice-President shall have qualified.

Section 4

The Congress may by law provide for the case of the death of any of the persons from whom the House of Representatives may choose a President whenever the right of choice shall have devolved upon them, and for the case of the death of any of the persons from whom the Senate may choose a Vice-President whenever the right of choice shall have devolved upon them.

Section 5

Sections 1 and 2 shall take effect on the 15th day of October following the ratification of this article.

Section 6

This article shall be inoperative unless it shall have been ratified as an amendment to the Constitution by the legislatures of three-fourths of the several States within seven years from the date of its submission.

AMENDMENT XXI [1933]

Section 1

The eighteenth article of amendment to the Constitution of the United States is hereby repealed.

Section 2

The transportation or importation into any State, Territory, or possession of the United States for delivery or use therein of intoxicating liquors, in violation of the laws thereof, is hereby prohibited.

Section 3

This article shall be inoperative unless it shall have been ratified as an amendment to the Constitution by conventions in the several States, as provided in the Constitution, within seven years from the date of the submission hereof to the States by the Congress.

AMENDMENT XXII [1951]

No person shall be elected to the office of the President more than twice, and no person who has held the office of President, or acted as President, for more than two years of a term to which some other person was elected President shall be elected to the office of the President more than once.

But this Article shall not apply to any person holding the office of President when this Article was proposed by the Congress, and shall not prevent any person who may be holding the office of President, or acting as President, during the term within which this Article becomes operative from holding the office of President or acting as President during the remainder of such term.

This article shall be inoperative unless it shall have been ratified as an amendment to the Constitution by the legislatures of three-fourths of the several states within seven years from the date of its submission to the states by the Congress.

AMENDMENT XXIII [1961]

Section 1

The District constituting the seat of Government of the United States shall appoint in such manner as the Congress may direct:

A number of electors of President and Vice-President equal to the whole number of Senators and Representatives in Congress to which the District would be entitled if it were a State, but in no event more than the least populous State; they shall be in addition to those appointed by the States, but they shall be considered, for the purposes of the election of President and Vice-President, to be electors appointed by a State; and they shall meet in the District and perform such duties as provided by the twelfth article of Amendment.

Section 2

The Congress shall have power to enforce this article by appropriate legislation.

AMENDMENT XXIV [1964]

Section 1

The right of citizens of the United States to vote in any primary or other election for President or Vice President, for electors for President or Vice President, or for Senator or Representative in Congress, shall not be denied or abridged by the United States or any state by reason of failure to pay any poll tax or other tax.

Section 2

The Congress shall have the power to enforce this article by appropriate legislation.

AMENDMENT XXV [1967]

Section 1

In case of the removal of the President from office or of his death or resignation, the Vice President shall become President.

Section 2

Whenever there is a vacancy in the office of the Vice President, the President shall nominate a Vice President who shall take office upon confirmation by a majority vote of both Houses of Congress.

Section 3

Whenever the President transmits to the President Pro Tempore of the Senate and the Speaker of the House of Representatives his written declaration that he is unable to discharge the powers and duties of his office, and until he transmits to them a written declaration to the contrary, such powers and duties shall be discharged by the Vice President as Acting President.

Section 4

Whenever the Vice President and a majority of either the principal officers of the executive departments or of such other body as Congress may by law provide, transmit to the President Pro Tempore of the Senate and the Speaker of the House of Representatives their written declaration that the President is unable to discharge the powers and duties of his office, the Vice President shall immediately assume the powers and duties of the office as Acting President.

Thereafter, when the President transmits to the President Pro Tempore of the Senate and the Speaker of the House of Representatives his written declaration that no inability exists, he shall resume the powers and duties of his office unless the Vice President and a majority of either the principal officers of the executive departments or of such other body as Congress may by law provide, transmit within four days to the President Pro Tempore of the Senate and the Speaker of the House of Representatives their written declaration that the President is unable to discharge the powers and duties of his office. Thereupon Congress shall decide the issue, assembling within forty-eight hours for that purpose if not in session. If the Congress, within twenty-one days after receipt of the latter written declaration, or, if Congress is not in session, within twenty-one days after Congress is required to assemble, determines by two-thirds vote of both Houses that the President is unable to discharge the powers and duties of his office, the Vice President shall continue to discharge the same as Acting President; otherwise, the President shall resume the powers and duties of his office.

AMENDMENT XXVI [1971]

Section 1

The right of citizens of the United States, who are eighteen years of age or older, to vote shall not be denied or abridged by the United States or by any State on account of age.

Section 2

The Congress shall have the power to enforce this article by appropriate legislation.

AMENDMENT XXVII [1992]

No law varying the compensation for the service of Senators and Representatives shall take effect until an election of Representatives shall have intervened.

GLOSSARY

administrative law judge An official who presides at a trial-like administrative hearing to settle a dispute between an agency and someone adversely affected by a decision of that agency.

affirmative action Programs designed to ensure that women, minorities, and other traditionally disadvantaged groups have full and equal opportunities in employment, education, and other areas of life.

agency point of view The tendency of bureaucrats to place the interests of their agency ahead of other interests and ahead of the priorities sought by the president or Congress.

agenda setting The power of the media through news coverage to focus the public's attention and concern on particular events, problems, issues, personalities, and so on.

agents of socialization Agents, such as the family and the media, that have significant impact on citizens' political socialization.

alienation A feeling of personal powerlessness that includes the notion that government does not care about the opinions of people like oneself.

Anti-Federalists Opponents of the Constitution during the debate over ratification.

apathy A feeling of personal disinterest in or lack of concern.

appellate jurisdiction The authority of a given court to review cases that have already been tried in lower courts and are appealed to it by the losing party; such a court is called an appeals court or appellate court. (See also **original jurisdiction**.)

authoritarian government A form of government in which those in power openly repress their opponents in order to stay in power.

authority The recognized right of officials to exercise power as a result of the positions they hold. (See also **power**.)

bicameral legislature A legislature that has two chambers (the House and the Senate, in the case of the United States).

bill A proposed law (legislative act) within Congress or another legislature. (See also **law**.)

Bill of Rights The first 10 amendments to the Constitution. They include rights such as freedom of speech and religion and due process protections (for example, the right to a jury trial) for persons accused of crimes.

block grants Federal grants-in-aid that permit state and local officials to decide how the money will be spent within a general area, such as education or health. (See also **categorical grants**.)

budgetary process The process through which annual federal spending and revenue determinations are made.

bully pulpit A term referring to the communication platform provided to the president as a result of being the center of national attention.

bureaucracy A system of organization and control based on the principles of hierarchical authority, job specialization, and formalized rules. (See also **formalized rules; hierarchical authority; job specialization**.)

bureaucratic accountability The degree to which bureaucrats are held accountable for the power they exercise.

cabinet A group consisting of the heads of the (cabinet) executive departments, who are appointed by the president, subject to confirmation by the Senate. The cabinet was once the main advisory body to the president but no longer plays this role.

cabinet (executive) departments The major administrative organizations within the federal executive bureaucracy, each of which is headed by a secretary or, in the case of Justice, the attorney general. Each department has responsibility for a major function of the federal government, such as defense, agriculture, or justice. (See also **independent agencies**.)

candidate-centered campaigns Election campaigns and other political processes in which candidates, not political parties, have most of the initiative and influence. (See also **party-centered campaigns**.)

capital gains tax The tax that individuals pay on money gained from the sale of a capital asset, such as property or stocks.

categorical grants Federal grants-in-aid to states and localities that can be used only for designated projects. (See also **block grants**.)

checks and balances The elaborate system of divided spheres of authority provided by the U.S. Constitution as a means of controlling the power of government. The separation of powers among the branches of the national government, federalism, and the different methods of selecting national officers is part of this system.

chief diplomat The constitutional role that assigns the president responsibility for relations with other countries.

chief executive The constitution role that assigns the president responsible for executing the laws and administering the executive branch.

chief legislator The constitutional role that give the president authority to recommend legislative measures to Congress and to assess the state of the Union.

citizens' groups Also called noneconomic groups, organized interests formed by individuals drawn together by opportunities to promote a cause in which they believe but that does not provide them significant individual economic benefits. (See also **economic groups; interest group**.)

civic duty The belief of an individual that civic and political participation is a responsibility of citizenship.

civil liberties The fundamental individual rights of a free society, such as freedom of speech and the right to a jury trial, which in the United States are protected by the Bill of Rights.

clear-and-present-danger test A test devised by the Supreme Court in 1919 to define the limits of free speech in the context of national security. According to the test, government cannot abridge political expression unless it presents a clear and present danger to the nation's security.

clientele groups Special interest groups that benefit directly from the activities of a particular bureaucratic agency and therefore are strong advocates of the agency.

cloture A parliamentary maneuver that, if a three-fifths majority votes for it, limits Senate debate to 30 hours and has the effect of defeating a filibuster. (See also **filibuster**.)

Cold War The lengthy period after World War II when the United States and the USSR were not engaged in actual combat (a "hot war") but were nonetheless locked in a state of deep-seated hostility.

collective (public) goods Benefits that are offered by groups (usually citizens' groups) as an incentive for membership but that are nondivisible (such as a clean environment) and therefore are available to nonmembers as well as members of the particular group. (See also **free-rider problem; private [individual] goods**.)

commander in chief The constitutional role that places the president in charge of the nation's armed services.

commerce clause The authority granted Congress in Article I, Section 8, of the Constitution "to regulate commerce" among the states.

common-carrier function The media's function as an open channel through which political leaders can communicate with the public. (See also **partisan function; signaling [signaler] function; watchdog function**.)

concurring opinion A separate opinion written by a Supreme Court justice who votes with the majority in the decision on a case but who disagrees with the reasoning. (See also **dissenting opinion; majority opinion; plurality opinion**.)

confederacy A governmental system in which sovereignty is vested entirely in subnational (state) governments. (See also **federalism; unitary system**.)

conference committee A temporary committee formed to bargain over the differences in the House and Senate versions of a bill. A conference committee's members are usually appointed from the House and Senate standing committees that originally worked on the bill.

constituency The people residing within the geographic area represented by an elected official.

constitution The fundamental law that defines how a government will legitimately operate.

constitutional democratic republic A government that is constitutional in its provisions for minority rights and rule by law; democratic in its provisions for majority influence through elections; and a republic in its mix of deliberative institutions, which check and balance each other.

constitutionalism The idea that there are lawful limits on the power of government.

containment A doctrine, developed after World War II, based on the assumptions that the Soviet Union was an aggressor nation and that only a determined United States could block Soviet territorial ambitions.

cooperative federalism The situation in which the national, state, and local levels work together to solve problems.

corporate power The power that corporations exercise in their effort to influence government and maintain control of the workplace.

Critical thinking Critical thinking involves deciding what can reasonably be believed and then using the information to reach a thoughtful conclusion.

cultural (social) conservatives Those who believe government power should be used to uphold traditional values. (See also **economic liberals; economic conservatives; cultural [social] liberals**.)

cultural (social) liberals Those who believe it is not government's role to buttress traditional values at the expense of unconventional or new values. (See also **economic liberals; economic conservatives; cultural [social] conservatives**.)

decision A vote of the Supreme Court in a particular case that indicates which party the justices side with and by how large a margin.

de facto discrimination Discrimination on the basis of race, sex, religion, ethnicity, and the like that results from social, economic, and cultural biases and conditions. (See also **de jure discrimination**.)

de jure discrimination Discrimination on the basis of race, sex, religion, ethnicity, and the like that results from a law. (See also **de facto discrimination**.)

delegate An elected representative whose obligation is to act in accordance with the expressed wishes of the people he or she represents. (See also **trustee**.)

demand-side economics A form of fiscal policy that emphasizes "demand" (consumer spending). Government can use increased spending or tax cuts to place more money

in consumers' hands and thereby increase demand. (See also **fiscal policy; supply-side economics**.)

demographic representativeness The idea that the bureaucracy will be more responsive to the public if its employees at all levels are demographically representative of the population as a whole.

denials of power A constitutional means of limiting governmental action by listing those powers that government is expressly prohibited from using.

deregulation The rescinding of excessive government regulations for the purpose of improving economic efficiency.

devolution The passing down of authority from the national government to the state and local governments.

direct democracy A form of government in which citizens meet and directly decide on issues of governing. The form is impractical except at the local level.

direction An opinion dimension; whether people have a pro or con opinion on an issue.

disinformation False information that is spread with the intent to deceive.

dissenting opinion The opinion of a justice in a Supreme Court case that explains his or her reasons for disagreeing with the majority's decision. (See also **concurring opinion; majority opinion; plurality opinion**.)

dual federalism A doctrine based on the idea that a precise separation of national power and state power is both possible and desirable.

due process clause The clause of the Constitution (included in the Fourteenth Amendment) that has been used by the judiciary to apply Bill of Rights protections to the actions of state governments.

echo chambers Refers to media outlets where audience members are exposed to messages that support what they already believe.

economic conservatives Those who believe government tries to do too many things that should be left to private interests and economic markets. (See also **economic liberals; cultural [social] liberals; cultural [social] conservatives**.)

economic depression A very severe and sustained economic downturn. Depressions are rare in the United States; the last one was in the 1930s.

economic efficiency An economic principle holding that firms should fulfill as many of society's needs as possible while using as few of its resources as possible. The greater the output (production) for a given input (for example, an hour of labor), the more efficient the process.

economic equity The situation in which the outcome of an economic transaction is fair to each party. An outcome can usually be considered fair if each party enters into a transaction freely and is not unknowingly at a disadvantage.

economic globalization The increased interdependence of nations' economies. The change is a result of technological, transportation, and communication advances that have enabled firms to deploy their resources across the globe.

economic groups Interest groups that are organized primarily for economic reasons but that engage in political activity in order to seek favorable policies from government. (See also **citizens' groups; interest group**.)

economic liberals Those who believe government should do more to assist people who have difficulty meeting their economic needs on their own. (See also **economic conservatives; cultural [social] liberals; cultural [social] conservatives**.)

economic recession A moderate but sustained downturn in the economy. Recessions are part of the economy's normal cycle of ups and downs.

economy A system for the exchange of goods and services between the producers of those goods and services and the consumers of them.

Electoral College An unofficial term that refers to the electors who cast the states' electoral votes.

electoral votes The method of voting used to choose the U.S. president. Each state has the same number of electoral votes as it has members in Congress (House and Senate combined). By tradition, electoral voting is tied to a state's popular voting. The candidate with the most popular votes in a state (or, in a few states, the most votes in a congressional district) receives its electoral votes.

elitism The notion that wealthy and well-connected individuals exercise power over certain areas of public policy.

entertainment function The efforts of media outlets to make their content pleasurable in order to attract the audience needed to make a profit and remain in business.

entitlement program An individual benefit program, such as Social Security, that requires government to provide a designated benefit to any person who meets the legally defined criteria for eligibility.

enumerated (expressed) powers The 17 powers granted to the national government under Article I, Section 8, of the Constitution. These powers include taxation and the regulation of commerce, as well as the authority to provide for the national defense.

equal-protection clause A clause of the Fourteenth Amendment that forbids any state to deny equal protection of the laws to any individual within its jurisdiction.

equality The notion that all individuals are equal in their moral worth and are thereby entitled to equal treatment under the law.

equality of opportunity The idea that all individuals should be given an equal chance to succeed on their own.

equal rights (civil rights) The right of every person to equal protection under the laws and equal access to society's opportunities and public facilities.

establishment clause The First Amendment provision stating that government may not favor one religion over another or favor religion over no religion and prohibiting Congress from passing laws respecting the establishment of religion.

exclusionary rule The legal principle that government is prohibited from using in trials evidence that was obtained by unconstitutional means (for example, illegal search and seizure).

executive agreement A formal agreement with a foreign nation made by a president on his or her own authority.

Executive Office of the President (EOP) The EOP includes a number of units, including the White House Office (WHO), Office of Management and Budget (OMB), National Security Council (NSC), National Economic Council (NEC), which are staffed by political and policy experts to assist the president on policy issues and management of the executive branch.

executive order A presidential directive on how a law is to interpreted or administered. An executive order must be based on an existing law and cannot violate any provision of the law.

externalities Burdens that society incurs when firms fail to pay the full costs of production. An example of an externality is the pollution that results when corporations dump industrial wastes into lakes and rivers.

federalism A governmental system in which authority is divided between two sovereign levels of government: national and regional. (See also **confederacy; unitary system**.)

Federalists Supporters of the Constitution during the debate over ratification.

filibuster A procedural tactic in the U.S. Senate whereby a minority of legislators prevent a bill from coming to a vote by holding the floor and talking until the majority gives in and the bill is withdrawn from consideration. (See also **cloture**.)

filter bubbles The situation where algorithms filter content such that a social-media user only encounters information that aligns with the user's beliefs, thus trapping them in a self-defined bubble.

fiscal federalism The expenditure of federal funds on programs run, in part, through states and localities.

fiscal policy A tool of economic management by which government can attempt to maintain a stable economy through its taxing and spending policies. (See also **demand-side economics; monetary policy; supply-side economics**.)

formalized rules A basic principle of bureaucracy; the standardized procedures and established regulations by which a bureaucracy conducts its operations. (See also **bureaucracy**.)

framing The process by which certain aspects of a situation are highlighted while other aspects are downplayed or ignored.

free-exercise clause A First Amendment provision that prohibits the government from interfering with the practice of religion.

free-market system An economic system based on the idea that government should interfere with economic transactions as little as possible. Free enterprise and self-reliance are the collective and individual principles that underpin free markets.

free-rider problem The situation in which the benefits offered by a group to its members are also available to nonmembers. The incentive to join the group and to promote its cause is reduced because nonmembers (free riders) receive the benefits (for example, a cleaner environment) without having to pay any of the group's costs. (See also **collective [public] goods**.)

freedom of expression Americans' freedom to communicate their views, the foundation of which is the First Amendment rights of freedom of conscience, speech, press, assembly, and petition.

free trade The condition in which tariffs and other barriers to trade between nations are kept to a minimum.

gender gap The tendency of women and men to differ in their political attitudes and voting preferences.

gerrymandering The process by which the party in power draws election district boundaries in a way that enhances the reelection prospects of its candidates.

government corporations Government bodies, such as the U.S. Postal Service and Amtrak, that are similar to private corporations in that they charge for their services but differ in that they receive federal funding to help defray expenses. Their directors are appointed by the president with Senate approval.

grants-in-aid Federal cash payments to states and localities for programs they administer.

grants of power The method of limiting the U.S. government by confining its scope of authority to those powers expressly granted in the Constitution.

grassroots party A political party organized at the level of the voters and dependent on their support for its strength.

Great Compromise The agreement of the constitutional convention to create a two-chamber Congress with the House apportioned by population and the Senate apportioned equally by state.

hard money Campaign funds given directly to candidates to spend as they choose.

hard news News stories about breaking events involving public figures, major issues, or significant disruptions to daily routines.

hard power The use of military force, coercion, or payments to get countries to comply with a nation's demands.

head of government Term used to describe a country's highest-ranking executive official.

head of state The largely ceremonial role whereby the president serves as a representative of the country (a role that in Great Britain, for example, is exercised by the monarch).

hierarchical authority A basic principle of bureaucracy; the chain of command within an organization whereby officials and units have control over those below them. (See also **bureaucracy**.)

honeymoon period The president's first months in office, a time when Congress, the press, and the public are more inclined than usual to support presidential initiatives.

identity politics The situation where people base their concerns on a group identity (such as race or religion) and align themselves with those who share that identity to the exclusion of other groups.

ideology A general belief about the role and purpose of government.

imminent lawless action A legal test that says government cannot lawfully suppress advocacy that promotes lawless action unless such advocacy is aimed at producing, and is likely to produce, imminent lawless action.

implied powers The federal government's constitutional authority (through the "necessary and proper" clause) to take action that is not expressly authorized by the Constitution but that supports actions that are so authorized. (See also **"necessary and proper" clause**.)

in-kind benefit A government benefit that is a cash equivalent, such as food stamps or rent vouchers. This form of benefit ensures that recipients will use public assistance in a specified way.

inalienable (natural) rights Those rights that persons theoretically possessed in the state of nature, prior to the formation of governments. These rights, including those of life, liberty, and property, are considered inherent and as such are inalienable. Since government is established by people, government has the responsibility to preserve these rights.

incumbent The current holder of a particular public office.

independent agencies Bureaucratic agencies that are similar to cabinet departments but usually have a narrower area of responsibility. Each such agency is headed by a presidential appointee who is not a cabinet member. An example is the National Aeronautics and Space Administration.

individualism The idea that people should take the initiative, be self-sufficient, and accumulate the material advantages necessary for their well-being.

inflation A general increase in the average level of prices of goods and services.

information commons Refers to the period when Americans throughout the country were exposed through the media to a more or less common portrayal of national politics.

inside lobbying Direct communication between organized interests and policymakers, which is based on the assumed value of close ("inside") contacts with policymakers.

intensity An opinion dimension; how strongly people feel about an issue.

interest groups Organizations that actively seek to influence public policy. (See also **citizens' [noneconomic] groups; economic groups**.)

iron triangle A small and informal but relatively stable group of well-positioned legislators, executives, and lobbyists who seek to promote policies beneficial to a particular interest. (See also **issue network**.)

issue network An informal and relatively open network of public officials and lobbyists who come together in response to a proposed policy in an area of interest to each of them. Unlike an iron triangle, an issue network disbands after the issue is resolved. (See also **iron triangle**.)

job specialization A basic principle of bureaucracy holding that the responsibilities of each job position should be defined explicitly and that a precise division of labor within the organization should be maintained. (See also **bureaucracy**.)

judicial activism The doctrine that the courts should develop new legal principles when judges see a compelling need, even if this action places them in conflict with precedent or the policy decisions of elected officials. (See also **judicial restraint**.)

judicial restraint The doctrine that the judiciary should broadly defer to precedent and the judgment of legislatures. The doctrine claims that the job of judges is to work within the confines of laws set down by tradition and lawmaking majorities. (See also **judicial activism**.)

judicial review The power of courts to decide whether a governmental institution has acted within its constitutional powers and, if not, to declare its action null and void.

jurisdiction (of a court) A given court's authority to hear cases of a particular type. (See also **appellate jurisdiction; original jurisdiction**.)

jurisdiction (of a congressional committee) The policy area in which a particular congressional committee is authorized to act.

laissez-faire economics A classic economic philosophy holding that owners of business should be allowed to make their own pro-duction and distribution decisions without government regulation or control.

law A legislative proposal, or bill, that is passed by both the House and the Senate and is not vetoed by the president. (See also **bill**.)

lawmaking function The authority (of a legisla-ture) to make the laws necessary to carry out the government's powers. (See also **oversight function; representation function**.)

Lemon test A three-part test to determine whether a law relating to religion is valid under the religious establishment clause. To be valid, a law must have a secure purpose, serve neither to advance nor inhibit religion, and avoid excessive government entanglement with religion.

libel The publication of false material that damages a person's reputation.

liberalism theory An international relations theory that emphasizes individual liberty, which can best be achieved when states have a democratic system and strong legal protections and when they work together to protect and promote these arrangements.

liberty The principle that individuals should be free from arbitrary and oppressive

government so that they can think and act as they choose.

limited government A government that is subject to strict limits on its lawful uses of power and, hence, on its ability to deprive people of their liberty.

limited presidency theory A theory that prevailed in the 19th century and held that the presidency was a limited or restrained office whose occupant was confined to expressly granted constitutional authority. (See also **stewardship theory**.)

linkage institutions Institutions that connect citizens with government. Linkage institu-tions include elections, political parties, interest groups, and the media.

Living constitution theory Holds that constitu-tional provisions should be applied in the context of the needs of today's society as opposed to the needs of society when the provision was written.

lobbying The process by which interest-group members and lobbyists attempt to influence public policy through contacts with public officials.

majoritarianism The idea that the majority prevails not only in elections but also in determining policy.

majority opinion A court opinion that results when a majority of the justices are in agreement on the legal basis of the decision. (See also **concurring opinion; dissenting opinion; plurality opinion**.)

means test The requirement that applicants for public assistance must demonstrate they are poor in order to be eligible for the assistance. (See also **public assistance**.)

median voter theorem The theory that parties in a two-party system can maximize their vote by locating themselves at the position of the median voter—the voter whose preferences are exactly in the middle.

merit system An approach to managing the bureaucracy whereby people are appointed to government positions on the basis of either competitive examinations or special qualifications, such as professional training. (See also **patronage system**.)

midterm election The congressional election that occurs midway through the president's term of office.

military–industrial complex The three compo-nents (the military establishment, the industries that manufacture weapons, and the members of Congress from states and districts that depend heavily on the arms industry) that mutually benefit from a high level of defense spending.

misinformation False information that is held or spread without regard for intent.

monetary policy A tool of economic management that is based on the manipulation of the amount of money in circulation. (See also **fiscal policy**.)

money chase The fact that U.S. campaigns are very expensive and candidates must spend a great amount of time raising funds in order to compete successfully.

multilateralism The situation in which nations act together in response to problems and crises.

multiparty system A system in which three or more political parties have the capacity to gain control of government, separately or in coalition.

mutually assured destruction (MAD) The assumption that any nation will be deterred from launching a full-scale nuclear attack on the United States by the knowledge that, even if it destroyed the United States, it, too, would be destroyed.

nationalization The process by which authority in the American federal system has shifted gradually from the states to the national government.

"necessary and proper" clause The authority granted Congress in Article I, Section 8, of the Constitution "to make all laws which shall be necessary and proper" for the implementation of its enumerated powers. (See also **implied powers**.)

neutral competence The administrative objective of a merit-based bureaucracy. Such a bureaucracy should be "competent" in the sense that its employees are hired and retained on the basis of their expertise and "neutral" in the sense that it operates by objective standards rather than partisan ones.

New Federalism Term used by Republican presidents Nixon and Reagan to express the idea that federal programs, regulations, and spending in policy areas traditionally reserved for the states should be reduced.

New Jersey (small-state) Plan A constitutional proposal for a strengthened Congress but one in which each state would have a single vote, thus granting a small state the same legislative power as a larger state.

news The news media's version of reality, usually with an emphasis on timely, dramatic, and compelling events and developments.

news media (press) Print, broadcast, cable, and Internet organizations that are in the news reporting business.

nomination The selection of a particular individual to run as a political party's candidate (its "nominee") in the general election.

objective journalism A model of news reporting that is based on the communication of "facts" rather than opinions and that is "fair" in that it presents all sides of partisan debate. (See also **partisan press**.)

opinion A court's written explanation of its decision, which informs others of the legal basis for the decision. Supreme Court opinions are expected to guide the decisions of lower courts. (See also **concurring opinion; dissenting opinion; majority opinion; plurality opinion**.)

Originalism theory Holds that the meaning of constitutional provisions is fixed in the time of their writing and that constitutional rulings should be consistent with that meaning.

original jurisdiction The authority of a given court to be the first court to hear a case. (See also **appellate jurisdiction**.)

outside lobbying A form of lobbying in which an interest group seeks to use public pressure as a means of influencing officials.

oversight function A supervisory activity of Congress that centers on its constitutional responsibility to see that the executive branch carries out the laws faithfully. (See also **lawmaking function; representation function**.)

packaging In modern campaigning, the process of recasting a candidate's record into an appealing image.

partisan function Efforts by media actors to influence public response to a particular party, leader, issue, or viewpoint.

party (partisan) polarization The condition in which opinions and actions in response to political issues and situations divide substantially along political party lines.

party-centered campaigns Election campaigns and other political processes in which political parties, not individual candidates, hold most of the initiative and influence. (See also **candidate-centered campaigns**.)

party caucus A group that consists of a party's members in the House or Senate and that serves to elect the party's leadership, set policy goals, and plan party strategy.

party coalition The groups and interests that support a political party.

party competition A process in which conflict over society's goals is transformed by political parties into electoral competition in which the winner gains the power to govern.

party identification The personal sense of loyalty that an individual may feel toward a particular political party. (See also **party realignment**.)

party leaders The members of the House and Senate who are chosen by the Democratic or Republican caucus in each chamber to represent the party's interests in that chamber and who give some central direction to the chamber's work.

party organizations The party organizational units at national, state, and local levels; their influence has decreased over time because of many factors. (See also **candidate-centered campaigns; party-centered campaigns; primary election**.)

party realignments Elections or sets of elections in which the electorate responds strongly to an extraordinarily powerful issue that has disrupted the established political order. A realignment has a lasting impact on public policy, popular support for the parties, and the composition of the party coalitions. (See also **party identification**.)

party unity The degree to which a party's House or Senate members act as a unified group to exert collective control over legislative action.

patronage system An approach to managing the bureaucracy whereby people are appointed to important government positions as a reward for political services they have rendered and because of their partisan loyalty. (See also **merit system; spoils system**.)

per curiam opinion An unsigned decision written for the court as a whole.

permanent campaign The use by recent presidents of campaign-style methods, such as polls and mass rallies, on an ongoing basis in an effort to bolster their public support.

pluralism A theory of American politics that holds that society's interests are substantially represented through the activities of groups and that, in most policy decisions, government is chiefly responsive to the interest group most directly affected by the policy.

plurality opinion A court opinion that results when a majority of justices agree on a decision in a case but do not agree on the legal basis for the decision. In this instance, the legal position held by most of the justices on the winning side is called a plurality opinion. (See also **concurring opinion; dissenting opinion; majority opinion**.)

policy implementation The primary function of the bureaucracy; the process of carrying out the authoritative decisions of Congress, the president, and the courts.

political action committee (PAC) The organization through which an interest group raises and distributes funds for election purposes. By law, the funds must be raised through voluntary contributions.

political culture The characteristic and deep-seated beliefs of a particular people.

political interest The level of interest that a citizen has in politics; political interest is a prime determinant of whether a citizen will pay attention to politics and participate through voting.

political movements Also called social movements, active and sustained efforts to achieve social and political change by groups of people who feel that government has not been properly responsive to their concerns.

political participation Involvement in activities intended to influence public policy and leadership, such as voting, joining political groups, contacting elected officials, demonstrating for political causes, and giving money to political candidates.

political party An ongoing coalition of interests joined together to try to get their candidates for public office elected under a common label.

political science The systematic study of government and politics.

political socialization The learning process by which people acquire their political opinions, beliefs, and values.

politics The process through which a society settles its conflicts.

population In a public opinion poll, the people (for example, the citizens of a nation) whose opinions are being estimated through interviews with a sample of these people.

pork Also called pork-barrel spending; spending whose tangible benefits are targeted at a particular legislator's constituency.

poverty line As defined by the federal government, the annual cost of a thrifty food budget for an urban family of four, multiplied by three to allow also for the cost of housing, clothes, and other expenses. Families below the poverty line are considered poor and are eligible for certain forms of public assistance.

power The ability of persons or institutions to control policy. (See also **authority**.)

precedent A judicial decision that serves as a rule for settling subsequent cases of a similar nature.

presidential approval rating A measure of the degree to which the public approves or disapproves of the president's performance in office.

presidential commissions Organizations within the bureaucracy that are headed by commissioners appointed by the president. An example is the Commission on Civil Rights.

presidential veto The power of the president to veto an act of Congress. A veto can only be overridden by a two-thirds vote of the House and Senate.

primary election Also called a direct primary, a form of election in which voters choose a party's nominees for public office. In most states, eligibility to vote in a primary election is limited to voters who designated themselves as party members when they registered to vote.

priming The process in which the media highlight certain aspects of an issue or event and not other aspects, thereby affecting how people respond to the issue or event.

prior restraint Government prohibition of speech or publication before the fact, which is presumed by the courts to be unconstitutional unless the justification for it is overwhelming.

private (individual) goods Benefits that a group (most often an economic group) can grant directly and exclusively to individual members of the group. (See also **collective [public] goods**.)

procedural due process The constitutional requirement that government must follow proper legal procedures before a person can be legitimately punished for an alleged offense.

progressive income tax A tax on personal income in which the tax rate increases as income increases; in other words, the tax rate is higher for higher income levels.

proportional representation system A form of representation in which seats in the legislature are allocated proportionally according to each political party's share of the popular vote. This system enables smaller parties to compete successfully for seats. (See also **single-member districts**.)

protectionism The placing of the immediate interests of domestic producers (through, for example, protective tariffs) above that of free trade between nations.

public assistance Social welfare programs funded through general tax revenues and available only to those in financial need. Eligibility for such a program is established by a means test. (See also **means test; social insurance**.)

public opinion The politically relevant opinions held by ordinary citizens that they express openly.

public opinion poll A device for measuring public opinion whereby a relatively small number of individuals (the sample) are interviewed for the purpose of estimating the opinions of a whole community (the population). (See also **sample**.)

public policies Decisions by government to pursue particular courses of action.

realism theory An international relations theory that says states are preoccupied with self-preservation, that they rationally take whatever action is necessary to protect themselves, and that it is irrational for them to assume that they can rely on the protection of states that don't have a direct stake in their preservation.

reapportionment The reallocation of House seats among states after each census as a result of population changes.

reasonable-basis test A test applied by courts to laws that treat individuals unequally. Such a law may be deemed constitutional if its purpose is held to be "reasonably" related to a legitimate government interest.

redistricting The process of altering election districts in order to make them as nearly equal in population as possible. Redistricting takes place every 10 years, after each population census.

registration The practice of placing citizens' names on an official list of voters before they are eligible to exercise their right to vote.

regulation Government restrictions on the economic practices of private firms.

regulatory agencies Administrative units, such as the Securities and Exchange Commission (SEC) and the Environmental Protection Agency (EPA), that have responsibility for monitoring and regulating ongoing economic activities and regulating industrial pollution, respectively.

representation function The responsibility of a legislature to represent various interests in society. (See also **lawmaking function; oversight function**.)

representative democracy A government in which a majority of citizens govern through the election of their representatives. Such governments differ in the amount of power granted to elected representatives, everything from nearly unlimited power to power that is substantially checked by institutional and constitutional restraints.

representative government A form of government in which the people govern through the election of their representatives.

republic A form of government in which the people's representatives decide policy through institutions structured in ways that foster deliberation, slow the progress of decision making, and operate within restraints that protect individual liberty. To the framers, the Constitution's separation of powers and other limits on power were defining features of a republican form of government, as opposed to a democratic form, which places no limits on the majority.

reserved powers The powers granted to the states under the Tenth Amendment to the Constitution.

right of privacy A right implied by the freedoms in the Bill of Rights that grants individuals a degree of personal privacy upon which government cannot lawfully intrude. The right gives individuals a level of free choice in areas such as reproduction and intimate relations.

rule-making The process by which bureaucratic agencies develop and make known the details on how legislation will be implemented. Rule-making is a main source of bureaucratic power.

rule of four A Supreme Court rule whereby, when a losing party appeals a lower-court ruling, the case is accepted by the Supreme only if at least four justices agree to hear it.

salience An opinion dimension; how highly people rank an issue relative to other issues.

sample In a public opinion poll, the relatively small number of individuals who are interviewed for the purpose of estimating the opinions of an entire population. (See also **public opinion poll**.)

sampling error A measure of the accuracy of a public opinion poll, mainly a function of sample size and usually expressed in percentage terms.

selective incorporation The process by which certain rights (for example, freedom of speech) contained in the Bill of Rights become applicable through the Fourteenth Amendment to actions by the state governments.

self-government The principle that the people are the ultimate source and proper beneficiary of governing authority; in practice, a government based on majority rule.

Senior Executive Service (SES) Top-level career civil servants who qualify through a competitive process to receive higher salaries than their peers but who can be assigned or transferred by order of the president.

seniority A member of Congress's consecutive years of service on a particular committee.

separated institutions sharing power The principle that, as a way to limit government, its powers should be divided among separate branches, each of which also shares in the power of the others as a means of checking and balancing them. The result is that no one branch can exercise power decisively without the support or acquiescence of the others.

separation of powers The division of the powers of government among separate institutions or branches.

service strategy The use of personal staff by members of Congress to perform services for constituents in order to gain their support in future elections.

signaling (signaler) function The responsibility of the media to alert the public to important developments as soon as possible after they happen or are discovered. (See also **common-carrier function; partisan function; watchdog function**.)

single-member districts The form of representation in which only the candidate who gets the most votes in a district wins office. (See also **proportional representation system**.)

single-member system Also called a winner-take-all system or a plurality, an electoral system in which the candidate who gets the most votes (the plurality) in an election district is elected to office from that district.

slander Spoken falsehoods that damage a person's reputation.

social capital The sum of the face-to-face interactions among citizens in a society.

social contract A voluntary agreement by individuals to form a government that is then obligated to work within the confines of that agreement.

social insurance Social welfare programs are based on the "insurance" concept, requiring that individuals pay into the program in order to be eligible to receive funds from it. An example is Social Security for retired people. (See also **public assistance**.)

soft news News stories with a sensational or entertaining element designed to attract consumers who might not otherwise pay attention to news.

soft power The use by a country of noncoercive means to convince other countries to do what it would like them to do.

sovereignty The supreme (or ultimate) authority to govern within a certain geographic area.

spoils system The practice of granting public office to individuals in return for political favors they have rendered. (See also **patronage system**.)

standing committees Permanent congressional committees with responsibility for a particular area of public policy. An example is the Senate Foreign Relations Committee.

stewardship theory A theory that argues for a strong, assertive presidential role, with presidential authority limited only at points specifically prohibited by law. (See also **Whig theory**.)

strict-scrutiny test A test applied by courts to laws that attempt a racial or ethnic classification. In effect, the strict-scrutiny test eliminates race or ethnicity as legal classification when it places minority-group members at a disadvantage. (See also **suspect classifications**.)

suffrage The right to vote.

super PACs Election committees that are unrestricted in their fundraising and spending as long as they do not coordinate their campaign efforts with that of a candidate.

supply-side economics A form of fiscal policy that emphasizes "supply" (production). An example of supply-side economics is a tax cut for business. (See also **demand-side economics; fiscal policy**.)

supremacy clause Article VI of the Constitution, which makes national law supreme over state law when the national government is acting within its constitutional limits.

suspect classifications Legal classifications, such as race and national origin, that have invidious discrimination as their purpose and therefore are unconstitutional. (See also **strict-scrutiny test**.)

symbolic speech Action (for example, the waving or burning of a flag) for the purpose of expressing a political opinion.

tariffs The taxes that a country levies on goods shipped into it from other countries.

Three-Fifths Compromise A compromise worked out at the 1787 convention between northern states and southern states. Each slave was to be counted as three-fifths of a person for purposes of federal taxation and congressional apportionment (number of seats in the House of Representatives).

trustee An elected representative whose obligation is to act in accordance with his or her own conscience as to what policies are in the best interests of the public. (See also **delegate**.)

two-party system A system in which only two political parties have a chance of acquiring control of the government.

tyranny of the majority The potential of a majority to monopolize power for its own gain and to the detriment of minority rights and interests.

unilateralism The situation in which one nation takes action against another state or states.

unitary system A governmental system in which the national government alone has sovereign (or ultimate) authority. (See also **confederacy; federalism**.)

unit rule The rule that grants all of a state's electoral votes to the candidate who receives most of the popular votes in the state.

veto The president's rejection of a bill, thereby keeping it from becoming law unless Congress overrides the veto.

Virginia (large-state) Plan A constitutional proposal for a strong Congress with two chambers, both of which would be based on numerical representation, thus granting more power to the larger states.

watchdog function The accepted responsibility of the media to protect the public from incompetent or corrupt officials by standing ready to expose any official who violates accepted legal, ethical, or performance standards. (See also **common-carrier function; partisan function; signaling [signaler] function**.)

whistleblowing An internal check on the bureaucracy whereby employees report instances of mismanagement that they observe.

writ of certiorari Permission granted by a higher court to allow a losing party in a legal case to bring the case before it for a ruling; when such a writ is requested of the U.S. Supreme Court, four of the Court's nine justices must agree to accept the case before it is granted certiorari.

NOTES

CHAPTER ONE

[1] Michael B. Mathias and Daniel Kolak, eds., *John Stuart Mill on Liberty* (New York: Pearson, 2006), 43.

[2] Zacc Ritter, "Amid Pandemic, News Attention Spikes; Media Favorability Flat," *Gallup News*, April 9, 2020, https://news.gallup.com/opinion/gallup/307934/amid-pandemic-news-attention-spikes-media-favorability-flat.aspx.

[3] Economist/YouGov poll, December 2019, https://today.yougov.com/topics/politics/articles-reports/2019/12/05/america-ukraine-russia-poll.

[4] Thomas E. Patterson, *How America Lost Its Mind* (Norman: University of Oklahoma Press, 2019), 5.

[5] James D. Agresti, "National Poll Shows Voters Are Widely Misinformed About Key Issues," *Just Facts*, November 15, 2017, https://www.justfacts.com/news_2017_poll_voter_knowledge.asp.

[6] Wendy Gross, Tobias H. Stark, Jon Krosnick, Josh Pasek, Gaurav Soods, Trevor Tompson, Jennifer Agiesta, and Dennis Junius, "Americans' Attitudes Toward the Affordable Care Act," Stanford University, 2012, p. 9. https://pprg.stanford.edu/wp-content/uploads/Health-Care-2012-Knowledge-and-Favorability.pdf.

[7] American Council of Trustees and Alumni, "A Crisis in Civic Education," 2016, https://www.goacta.org/images/download/A_Crisis_in_Civic_Education.pdf.

[8] Theodore Sorsensen when he was a Institute of Politics Fellow at Harvard Kennedy School in 2002.

[9] Bianca DiJulio, Jamie Firth, and Mollyann Brodie, "Data Note: Americans' Views On The U.S. Role In Global Health," *Kaiser Family Foundation*, Jan 23, 2015. http://www.kff.org/global-health-policy/poll-finding/data-note-americans-views-on-the-u-s-role-in-global-health/; "As Sequester Deadline Looms, Little Support for Cutting Most Programs," Pew Research Center, February 22, 2013, http://www.people-press.org/2013/02/22/as-sequester-deadline-looms-little-support-for-cutting-most-programs/.

[10] Mark Bauerlein, *The Dumbest Generation* (New York: Penguin, 2008), 28.

[11] Derek Thompson, "Where Did All the Workers Go? 60 Years of Economic Change in 1 Graph," *The Atlantic*, January 26, 2012, https://www.theatlantic.com/business/archive/2012/01/where-did-all-the-workers-go-60-years-of-economic-change-in-1-graph/252018/.

[12] Scott Althaus, "Free Falls, High Dives, and the Future of Democratic Accountability." In *The Politics of News/The News of Politics*, 2nd ed. Doris Graber, Denis McQuail, and Pippa Norris, eds. (Washington, D.C.: Congressional Quarterly Press, 2007), 185.

[13] Steven Kull, Clay Ramsay, and Evan Lewis, "Misperceptions, the Media, and the Iraq War," *Political Science Quarterly*, 118 (Winter 2003–2004): 569–98.

[14] Jeffrey M., Berry and Sarah Sobieraj, *The Outrage Industry* (New York: Oxford University Press, 2016).

[15] See, for example, Allyson Chiu, "Rush Limbaugh on Coronavirus: 'The Common Cold' That's Being 'Weaponized' Against Trump," *Washington Post*, February 25, 2020, https://www.washingtonpost.com/nation/2020/02/25/limbaugh-coronavirus-trump/; Aaron Rupar, "Hannity claims he's 'never called the virus a hoax' 9 days after decrying Democrats' 'new hoax,'" *Vox*, March 20, 2020, https://www.vox.com/2020/3/20/21186727/hannity-coronavirus-coverage-fox-news.

[16] See, for example, Norbert Schwarz, "Metacognitive Experiences in Consumer Judgment and Decision Making," *Journal of Consumer Psychology*, 14 (2004): 332–48, cited in Adam J. Berinsky, "Rumors and Health Care Reform: Experiments in Political Information," *British Journal of Political Science*, 47 (2017): 241–62.

[17] Daniel Kahneman, *Thinking Fast and Slow* (New York: Farrar, Straus and Giroux, 2011), 201.

[18] Gordon Pennycook and David G. Rand, "Lazy, Not Biased," *Cognition*, 188 (2018): 39–50.

[19] See Michael Foley, *American Credo: The Place of Ideas in American Politics* (New York: Oxford University Press, 2007).

[20]James Bryce, *The American Commonwealth,* vol. 2 (New York: Macmillan, 1960), 247–54. First published in 1900.

[21]Bryce, *The American Commonwealth,* 132.

[22]Quoted in "The Originality of the United States Constitution," *Yale Law Journal* 5 (1896): 239.

[23]Louis Hartz, *The Liberal Tradition in America* (New York: Harcourt, Brace, 1952), 12.

[24]Alexis de Tocqueville, *Democracy in America,* vol. 2 (New York: Vintage Classics, 1990), 89.

[25]Bryce, *The American Commonwealth,* 182.

[26]T. J. Mathews and Anne K. Driscoll, "Trends in Infant Mortality in the United States, 2005–2014," Centers for Disease Control and Prevention, March 2017, https://www.cdc.gov/nchs/products/databriefs/db279.htm.

[27]Quoted in Ralph Volney Harlow, *The Growth of the United States,* vol. 2 (New York: Henry Holt, 1943), 497.

[28]Pew Research Center poll, April 2015.

[29]Michelangelo Landgrave and Alex Nowrasteh, "Criminal Immigrants: Their Numbers, Demographics, and Countries of Origin," Cato Institute, March 15, 2017. https://www.cato.org/publications/immigration-reform-bulletin/criminal-immigrants-their-numbers-demographics-countries.

[30]*Tinker v. Colwell,* 193 U.S. 473 (1904).

[31]Martin Luther King Jr., speech at civil rights march on Washington, August 28, 1963.

[32]William Watts and Lloyd A. Free, eds., *The State of the Nation* (New York: University Books, Potomac Associates, 1967), 131.

[33]Harold D. Lasswell, *Politics: Who Gets What, When, How* (New York: McGraw Hill, 1936).

[34]Russell Hardin, *Liberalism, Constitutionalism, and Democracy* (New York: Oxford University Press, 1999).

[35]Foucault's phrasing was a deliberate inversion of von Clausewitz's famous line "War is politics by other means." Foucault is not the only writer who has applied this inversion.

[36]See, for example, Anton Troianovski, "Russia Takes Censorship to New Extremes, Stifling War Coverage," *New York Times,* March 4, 2022. https://www.nytimes.com/2022/03/04/world/europe/russia-censorship-media-crackdown.html

[37]Adam Przworski and José María Maravall, eds., *Democracy and the Rule of Law* (New York: Cambridge University Press, 2003).

[38]See Robert Dahl, *On Democracy* (New Haven, Conn.: Yale University Press, 2000).

[39]Figures are based on a 40-hour work week for 52 weeks using 2020 national minimum-wage amounts, which were $7.25 for the United States, $10.09 for Germany, and $10.82 for France.

[40]See William G. Domhoff, *Who Rules America? Challenges to Corporate and Class Dominance,* 7th ed. (New York: McGraw Hill, 2013).

[41]C. Wright Mills, *The Power Elite* (New York: Oxford University Press, 1965).

[42]See Joseph A. Schumpeter, *Capitalism, Socialism and Democracy* (New York: Harper, 1975).

[43]E. E. Schattschneider, *Two Hundred Million Americans in Search of a Government* (New York: Holt, Reinhart and Winston, 1969), 42.

CHAPTER TWO

[1]Quoted in Charles S. Hyneman, "Republican Government in America," in George J. Graham Jr. and Scarlett G. Graham, eds., *Founding Principles of American Government,* rev. ed. (Chatham, N.J.: Chatham House, 1984), 19.

[2]See John Harmon McElroy, *American Beliefs: What Keeps a Big Country and a Diverse People United* (Chicago: I. R. Dee, 1999).

[3]See Russell Hardin, *Liberalism, Constitutionalism, and Democracy* (New York: Oxford University Press, 1999); A. John Simmons, *The Lockean Theory of Rights* (Princeton, N.J.: Princeton University Press, 1994).

[4]Thomas Hobbes, *Leviathan* (1651).

[5]John Locke, *Second Treatise on Civil Government* (1690).

[6]It was not until the 1950s that Americans referred more often to themselves as "Americans" than they did as a resident of the state in which they lived. See, Daniel J. Hopkins, *The Increasingly United States: How and Why American Political Behavior Nationalized* (Chicago: University of Chicago Press, 2018).

[7]Quoted in "The Constitution and Slavery," Digital History website, December 1, 2003.

[8]Speech of Melancton Smith at the New York Constitutional Ratifying Convention, June 20, 1788. http://teachingamericanhistory.org/library/document/melancton-smith-new-york-ratifying-convention/.

[9]Gaillard Hunt, ed., *The Writings of James Madison* (New York: Putnam, 1904), 274.

[10]During the nation's history, every amendment has been proposed by Congress and only one amendment—the Twenty-First, which repealed the prohibition on alcohol—was ratified by state

conventions. The others were ratified by state legislatures.

[11]See Vincent Ostrom, *The Political Theory of a Compound Republic: Designing the American Experiment* (Lanham, Md.: Lexington Books, 2007).

[12]See *Federalist* Nos. 47 and 48.

[13]Richard Neustadt, *Presidential Power* (New York: Macmillan, 1986), 33.

[14]Martin Diamond, *The Founding of the Democratic Republic* (Itasca, Ill.: Peacock, 1981), 62–71.

[15]George Thomas, "'America Is a Republic, Not a Democracy' Is a Dangerous—And Wrong—Argument," *The Atlantic,* November 2, 2020, https://www.theatlantic.com/ideas/archive/2020/11/yes-constitution-democracy/616949/.

[16]Leslie F. Goldstein, "Judicial Review and Democratic Theory: Guardian Democracy vs. Representative Democracy," *Western Political Quarterly,* 40 (1987): 391–412.

[17]See Douglas Bradburn, *The Citizenship Revolution: Politics and the Creation of the American Union 1774-1804* (Charlottesville: University of Virginia Press, 2009).

[18]Benjamin Ginsberg, *The Consequences of Consent* (New York: Random House, 1982), 22.

[19]Robert Dahl, *Pluralist Democracy in the United States* (Chicago: Rand McNally, 1967), 92.

[20]This interpretation is taken from Walter Lippmann, *Public Opinion* (New York: Free Press, 1965), 178–79.

[21]Michael McGeer, *A Fierce Discontent: The Rise and Fall of the Progressive Movement in America, 1870-1920* (New York: Free Press, 2005).

[22]Charles S. Beard, *An Economic Interpretation of the Constitution* (New York: Macmillan, 1941). First published in 1913.

[23]John M. Scheb and John M. Scheb II, *Introduction to the American Legal System* (Clifton Park, N.Y.: Delmar Cengage Learning System, 2001), 6.

[24]See Randall G. Holcombe, *From Liberty to Democracy* (Ann Arbor: University of Michigan Press, 2002).

CHAPTER THREE

[1]Woodrow Wilson, *Constitutional Government in the United States* (New York: Columbia University Press, 1908), 173.

[2]David A. Lieb, Geoff Mulvihill, and Andrew DeMillo, "At least 27 states file lawsuits over Biden's vaccine mandate for businesses."

Associated Press wire story, November 5, 2021, https://www.11alive.com/article/news/nation-world/biden-vaccine-mandate-for-businesses-lawsuit/507-a15c24eb-a0eb-4f96-bed3-9823c79d1aa0.

[3]Ibid.

[4]Ohio, et al. v Occupational Safety and Health Administration (2022).

[5]See Samuel Beer, *To Make a Nation* (Cambridge, Mass.: The Belknap Press of Harvard, 1984).

[6]Daniel J. Hopkins, *The Increasingly United States: How and Why American Political Behavior Nationalized* (Chicago: University of Chicago Press, 2018).

[7]Antifederalist No. 9. This essay appeared in the *Independent Gazetteer* on October 17, 1787, under the pen name "Montezuma."

[8]Alison L. LaCroix, *The Ideological Origins of American Federalism* (Cambridge, Mass.: Harvard University Press, 2010).

[9]William M. Lunch, *The Nationalization Of American Politics* (Berkeley, CA: University of California Press, 1987).

[10]*McCulloch v. Maryland,* 4 Wheaton 316 (1819).

[11]*Gibbons v. Ogden,* 22 Wheaton 1 (1824). [22 U.S. 1 (1824)].

[12]Oliver Wendell Holmes Jr., *Collected Legal Papers* (New York: Harcourt, Brace, 1920), 295–96.

[13]See John C. Calhoun, *The Works of John C. Calhoun* (New York: Russell & Russell, 1968).

[14]*Dred Scott v. Sanford,* 19 Howard 393 (1857).

[15]*U.S. v. Cruikshank,* 92 U.S. 452 (1876).

[16]*Slaughter-House Cases,* 16 Wallace 36 (1873); *Civil Rights Cases,* 109 U.S. 3 (1883).

[17]*Plessy v. Ferguson,* 163 U.S. 537 (1896).

[18]See, for example, Douglas A. Blackmon, *Slavery by Another Name: The Re-Enslavement of Black America from the Civil War to World War II* (New York: Anchor Books, 2009).

[19]*Santa Clara County v. Southern Pacific Railroad Co.,* 118 U.S. 394 (1886).

[20]*U.S. v. E. C. Knight Co.,* 156 U.S. 1 (1895).

[21]*Hammer v. Dagenhart,* 247 U.S. 251 (1918).

[22]*Lochner v. New York,* 198 U.S. 25 (1905).

[23]Alfred H. Kelly, Winifred A. Harbison, and Herman Belz, *The American Constitution,* 7th ed. (New York: Norton, 1991), 529; but also see Kimberley Johnson, *Governing the American State: Congress and the New Federalism, 1877-1929* (Princeton, N.J.: Princeton University Press, 2006).

[24]James E. Anderson, *The Emergence of the Modern Regulatory State* (Washington, D.C.: Public Affairs Press, 1962), 2–3.

[25]*Schechter Poultry Corp. v. United States,* 295 U.S. 495 (1935).

[26]*NLRB v. Jones and Laughlin Steel,* 301 U.S. 1 (1937).

[27]*American Power and Light v. Securities and Exchange Commission,* 329 U.S. 90 (1946).

[28]Louis Fisher, *American Constitutional Law,* 6th ed. (Durham, N.C.: Carolina Academic Press, 2005), 390.

[29]*United States v. Butler,* 297 U.S. 1 (1936).

[30]As will be discussed in Chapter 5, the Supreme Court also altered the constitutional doctrine of federalism in the area of civil rights. The two-race system upheld in the *Plessy* decision was struck down in 1954 as a violation of the Fourteenth Amendment's equal protection clause.

[31]See Thomas Anton, *American Federalism and Public Policy* (Philadelphia: Temple University Press, 1989).

[32]Morton Grodzins, *The American System: A New View of Government in the United States* (Chicago: Rand McNally, 1966).

[33]John D. Nugent, *Safeguarding Federalism: How States Protect Their Interests in National Policymaking* (Norman: University of Oklahoma Press, 2009).

[34]Rosella Levaggi, *Fiscal Federalism and Grants-in-Aid* (Brookfield, Vt.: Avebury, 1991).

[35]Beth Fouhy, "GOP Governors Press Congress to Pass Stimulus Bill," *Associated Press wire story,* January 31, 2009.

[36]Paul R. Dommel, *The Politics of Revenue Sharing* (Bloomington: Indiana University Press, 1974).

[37]Timothy J. Conlan, *From New Federalism to Devolution* (Washington, D.C.: Brookings Institution, 1998).

[38]The Supreme Court played a role in devolution by retreating somewhat from its New Deal-era ruling that Congress's commerce power is "as broad as the needs of the nation." In *United States v. Lopez* (1995), the Court cited the Tenth Amendment in striking down a federal law banning the possession of guns within a thousand feet of a school. The Court ruled that the ban had "nothing to do with commerce, or any sort of economic activity." The Court then applied the Eleventh Amendment (which protects a state from being sued in federal court by a private citizen without its consent) to limit Congress's authority. In *Kimmel v. Board of Regents* (2000), the Court held that state government employees cannot sue their state for violating federal age-discrimination policies. The Court ruled that states have the authority to decide the retirement age of their own employees.

[39]*National Federation of Independent Business v. Sebelius,* 567 U.S. 519 (2012).

[40]*National Federation of Independent Business v. Sebelius,* 567 U.S. 519 (2012).

[41]*California v. Texas,* 141 S. Ct. 2104 (2021).

[42]Andrew W. Dobelstein, *Politics, Economics, and Public Welfare* (Englewood Cliffs, N.J.: Prentice-Hall, 1980), 5.

[43]Lloyd A. Free and Hadley Cantril, *The Political Beliefs of Americans* (New York: Simon & Schuster, 1968), 21.

[44]Survey for the Times Mirror Center for the People and the Press by Princeton Survey Research Associates, July 12–27, 1994.

CHAPTER FOUR

[1]Julian P. Boyd, ed., *The Papers of Thomas Jefferson,* vol. 12 (Princeton, N.J.: Princeton University Press, 1955), 440.

[2]*United States v. Jones,* No. 10-1250 (2012).

[3]*Barron v. Baltimore,* 32 U.S. (7 Pet.) 243 (1833).

[4]*Gitlow v. New York,* 268 U.S. 652, 1925.

[5]*Fiske v. Kansas,* 274 U.S. 30 (1927); *Near v. Minnesota,* 283 U.S. 697 (1931); *Hamilton v. Regents, U. of California,* 293 U.S. 245 (1934); *DeJonge v. Oregon,* 299 U.S. 253 (1937).

[6]*Near v. Minnesota,* 283 U.S. 697 (1931).

[7]*Mapp v. Ohio,* 367 U.S. 643 (1961).

[8]*Weeks v. United States,* 232 U.S. 383 (1914).

[9]*Gideon v. Wainright,* 372 U.S. 335 (1963).

[10]*Malloy v. Hogan,* 378 U.S. 1 (1964).

[11]*Miranda v. Arizona,* 384 U.S. 436 (1966); see also *Escobedo v. Illinois,* 378 U.S. 478 (1964).

[12]*Pointer v. Texas,* 380 U.S. 400 (1965).

[13]*Klopfer v. North Carolina,* 386 U.S. 213 (1967).

[14]*Duncan v. Louisiana,* 391 U.S. 145 (1968).

[15]*Benton v. Maryland,* 395 U.S. 784 (1969).

[16]Although the Supreme Court has categorically excluded child pornography from First Amendment protection, it has struggled otherwise to develop a legal test for determining whether sexual material is obscene. It has said that such material must be of a "particularly offensive type" and must be perceived as such by a "reasonable person," but in practice the Court

has had trouble applying that standard, or any other, in determining the sexually explicit material that adults are not allowed to produce, see, or possess.

[17]*Schenck v. United States,* 249 U.S. 47 (1919).

[18]*Dennis v. United States,* 341 U.S. 494, 1951.

[19]See, for example, *Yates v. United States,* 354 U.S. 298 (1957); *Noto v. United States,* 367 U.S. 290 (1961); *Scales v. United States,* 367 U.S. 203 (1961).

[20]*Brandenburg v. Ohio,* 395 U.S. 444 (1969).

[21]*R.A.V. v. St. Paul,* No. 90-7675 (1992).

[22]*Wisconsin v. Mitchell,* No. 92-515 (1993).

[23]*Snyder v. Phelps,* No. 09-7571 (2011).

[24]*United States v. O'Brien,* 391 US 367 (1968).

[25]*Texas v. Johnson,* 109 S. Ct. 2544, (1989).

[26]*National Socialist Party v. Skokie,* 432 U.S. 43 (1977).

[27]*Forsyth County v. Nationalist Movement,* No. 91-538 (1992).

[28]*New York Times Co. v. United States,* 403 U.S. 713 (1971).

[29]*Nebraska Press Assn. v. Stuart,* 427 U.S. 539 (1976).

[30]*Milkovich v. Lorain Journal,* 497 U.S. 1 (1990); see also *Masson v. The New Yorker,* No. 89-1799 (1991).

[31]*New York Times Co. v. Sullivan,* 376 U.S. 254 (1964).

[32]*Engel v. Vitale,* 370 U.S. 421 (1962).

[33]*Abington School District v. Schempp,* 374 U.S. 203 (1963).

[34]*Wallace v. Jaffree,* 472 U.S. 38 (1985).

[35]*Kennedy v. Bremerton School District,* No. 21-418 (2022).

[36]*Van Orden v. Perry,* No. 03-1500 (2005).

[37]*Van Orden v. Perry,* No. 03-1500 (2005).

[38]*Lemon v. Kurtzman,* 403 U.S. 602 (1971).

[39]*Board of Regents v. Allen,* 392 U.S. 236 (1968).

[40]*Oregon v. Smith,* 494 U.S. 872 (1990).

[41]*Burwell v. Hobby Lobby Stores,* No. 13-354 (2014); see also, *Little Sisters of the Poor Saints Peter and Paul Home v. Pennsylvania,* No. 19-431 (2020).

[42]*Carson v Makin,* No. 20-1088 (2022).

[43]*Edwards v. Aguillard,* 487 U.S. 578 (1987).

[44]*United States v. Miller,* 307 U.S. 174 (1939),

[45]*District of Columbia v. Heller,* 554 U.S. 570 (2008).

[46]*McDonald v. Chicago,* 561 U.S. 3025 (2010).

[47]*New York State Rifle & Pistol Association Inc. v. Bruen,* No. 20-843 (2022).

[48]*Griswold v. Connecticut,* 381 U.S. 479 (1965).

[49]*Bowers v. Hardwick,* 478 U.S. 186 (1986).

[50]*Lawrence v. Texas,* 539 U.S. 558 (2003).

[51]*Roe v. Wade,* 401 U.S. 113 (1973).

[52]*Webster v. Reproductive Health Services,* 492 U.S. 490 (1989); see also *Rust v. Sullivan,* No. 89-1391 (1991).

[53]*Planned Parenthood v. Casey,* No. 91-744 (1992).

[54]Ibid.

[55]*June Medical Services v. Russo,* No. 18-1323 (2020); see also *Whole Woman's Health v. Hellerstedt,* No. 15-274 (2016).

[56]*Dobbs v. Jackson Women's Health Organization,* No. 19-1392 (2022).

[57]*McNabb v. United States,* 318 U.S. 332 (1943).

[58]The structure and content of the discussion that follows on arrest, search, interrogation, formal charge, trial, appeal, and punishment are informed by Walter F. Murphy and Michael N. Danielson, *Robert K. Carr and Marver H. Bernstein's American Democracy* (Hinsdale, Ill.: Dryden Press, 1977), 465–74.

[59]David Fellman, *The Defendant's Rights Today* (Madison: University of Wisconsin Press, 1979), 256.

[60]*Riley v. California,* No. 13-132 (2014); see also, *Carpenter v. United States,* No. 16-402 (2018).

[61]*Board of Education of Independent School District No. 92 of Pottawatomie County v. Earls,* No. 01-332 (2002).

[62]*Michigan v. Sitz,* No. 88-1897 (1990).

[63]*Indianapolis v. Edmund,* No. 99-1030 (2001).

[64]*Missouri v. Siebert,* 542 U.S. 600 (2004).

[65]*Miranda v. Arizona,* 384 U.S. 436 (1966).

[66]*Johnson v. Zerbst,* 304 U.S. 458 (1938).

[67]*Gideon v. Wainwright,* 372 U.S. 335 (1963).

[68]*Witherspoon v. Illinois,* 391 U.S. 510 (1968).

[69]*Flowers v. Mississippi,* No. 17-9572 (2019); the precedent was set in *Batson v. Kentucky,* 476 U.S. 79 (1986).

[70]*Ramos v. Louisiana,* 139 S. Ct. 1647 (2020).

[71]*Weeks v. United States,* 232 U.S. 383 (1914).

[72]*United States v. Leon,* 468 U.S. 897 (1984).

[73]*Nix v. Williams,* 467 U.S. 431 (1984).

[74]*Horton v. California,* 496 U.S. 128 (1990).

[75]*Atkins v. Virginia,* No. 01-8452 (2002); see also *Montgomery v. Louisiana,* No. 14-280 (2016); *Jones v. Mississippi,* No. 18-1259 (2021).

[76]*Lockyer v. Andrade,* No. 01-1127 (2003); see also *Ewing v. California,* No. 01-6978 (2003).

[77]*Pennsylvania v. Finley,* 481 U.S. 551 (1987).

[78]*Townsend v. Sain,* 372 U.S. 293 (1963).

[79]*Williams v. Taylor,* No. 99-6615 (2000); *Shinn v. Ramirez,* No. 20-1009 (2022).

[80]See, for example, National Institute of Justice, "Racial Profiling and Traffic Stops," January 10, 2013, www.nij.gov/topics/law-enforcement/legitimacy/pages/traffic-stops.aspx.

[81]*Jacobson v. Massachusetts,* 197 U.S. 11 (1905).

[82]*Zucht v. King,* 260 U.S. 174 (1922).

[83]Scott Bomboy, "Current constitutional issues related to vaccine mandates," *Constitution Daily,* August 6, 2021. https://constitutioncenter.org/blog/current-constitutional-issues-related-to-vaccine-mandates

[84]Adam Liptak, "Supreme Court Blocks Biden's Virus Mandate for Large Employers," *New York Times,* January 13, 2022. https://www.nytimes.com/2022/01/13/us/politics/supreme-court-biden-vaccine-mandate.html

[85]Charles Lane, "In Terror War, 2nd Track for Suspects," *The Washington Post,* December 1, 2001, A1.

[86]*Korematsu v. United States,* 323 U.S. 214 (1944).

[87]*Rasul v. Bush,* No. 03-334 (2004); *al-Odah v. United States,* No. 03-343 (2004).

[88]*Hamdi v. Rumsfeld,* No. 03-6696 (2004).

[89]*Hamdan v. Rumsfeld,* No. 05-184 (2006).

[90]CNN poll, 2008.

[91]See Alpheus T. Mason, *The Supreme Court: Palladium of Freedom* (Ann Arbor: University of Michigan Press, 1962); see also Jeffrey Rosen, *The Most Democratic Branch: How the Courts Serve America* (New York: Oxford University Press, 2006).

CHAPTER FIVE

[1]Abraham Lincoln, "Speech on the Dred Scott Decision," Springfield, Illinois, June 26, 1857.

[2]*The Washington Post* wire story, May 14, 1991.

[3]Robert Nisbet, "Public Opinion versus Popular Opinion," *Public Interest* 41 (1975): 171.

[4]*Plessy v. Ferguson,* 163 U.S. 537 (1896).

[5]Ada Lois Sipuel Fisher, Danney Gable, and Robert Henry, *A Matter of Black and White: The Autobiography of Ada Lois Sipuel Fisher* (Norman: University of Oklahoma Press, 1996).

[6]*Brown v. Board of Education of Topeka,* 347 U.S. 483 (1954).

[7]*Swann v. Charlotte-Mecklenburg County Board of Education,* 402 U.S. 1 (1971).

[8]Christopher Jencks and Meredith Phillips, eds., *The Black-White Test Score Gap* (Washington, D.C.: Brookings Institution, 1998).

[9]*Milliken v. Bradley,* 418 U.S. 717 (1974).

[10]*Parents Involved in Community Schools v. Seattle,* No. 05-908551 U.S. 701 (2007); *Meredith, Custodial Parent and Next Friend of McDonald v. Jefferson County Board of Education,* No. 05-915548 U.S. 938 (2007).

[11]Grover J. "Russ" Whitehurst, Richard V. Reeves, and Edward Rodrigues, "Segregation, Race, and Charter Schools," Center on Children and Families, Brookings Institution, October 2016, pp. 23–26.

[12]*Loving v. Virginia,* 388 U.S. 1 (1967).

[13]*Craig v. Boren,* 429 U.S. 190 (1976).

[14]*Rostker v. Goldberg,* 453 U.S. 57 (1980).

[15]*United States v. Virginia,* 518 U.S. 515 (1996), No. 94-1941 (1996).

[16]Michael J. Klarman, *From Jim Crow to Civil Rights: The Supreme Court and the Struggle for Racial Equality* (New York: Oxford University Press, 2004), 236.

[17]*Smith v. Allwright,* 321 U.S. 649 (1944).

[18]*Oregon v. Mitchell,* 400 U.S. 112 (1970).

[19]*Shelby County v. Holder,* No. 12-96 (2013).

[20]*Brnovich v. Democratic National Committee,* No. 19-1257 (2021).

[21]*Cooper v. Harris,* 136 S. Ct. 2512 (2017); Adam Liptak, "Supreme Court Restores Alabama Voting Map That a Court Said Hurt Black Voters," *New York Times,* February 7, 2022, https://www.nytimes.com/2022/02/07/us/politics/supreme-court-alabama-redistricting-congressional-map.html.

[22]See Manny Fernandez, "Study Finds Disparities in Mortgages by Race," *The New York Times,* October 15, 2007; see also U.S. Conference of Mayors report, 1998; Survey by Federal Financial Institutions Examination Council, 1998.

[23]Debra Kamin, "Black Homeowners Face Discrimination in Appraisals," *New York Times,* October 25, 2020. https://www.nytimes.com/2020/08/25/realestate/blacks-minorities-appraisals-discrimination.html

[24]"Public Backs Affirmative Action, but Not Minority Preferences," Pew Research Center report, June 2, 2009, web release.

[25]*University of California Regents v. Bakke,* 438 U.S. 265 (1978).

[26]*Adarand v. Peña,* 515 U.S. 200 (1995). This decision reversed an earlier ruling, *Fullilove v. Klutnick,* 448 U.S. 448 (1980).

[27]*Grutter v. Bollinger,* 539 U.S. 306 (2003).

[28]*Fisher v. University of Texas,* No. 14-981 (2016).

[29]Nicholas Lemann, "Can Affirmative Action Survive?" *The New Yorker,* July 26, 2021. https://www.newyorker.com/magazine/2021/08/02/can-affirmative-action-survive

[30]See, for example, Gloria J. Browne-Marshall, *Race, Law, and American Society: 1607 to Present* (New York: Routledge, 2007).

[31]Douglas A. Blackmon, *Slavery by Another Name: The Re-enslavement of Black America from the Civil War to World War II* (New York: Anchor Books, 2009).

[32]Eric J. Sundquist, *King's Dream: The Legacy of Martin Luther King's "I Have a Dream" Speech* (New Haven, Conn.: Yale University Press, 2009).

[33]See, for example, Alejandro Del Carmen, *Racial Profiling in America* (Upper Saddle River, N.J.: Prentice-Hall, 2007).

[34]Sentencing Project, "Report of The Sentencing Project to the United Nations Human Rights Committee Regarding Racial Disparities in the United States Criminal Justice System," August 2013. http://sentencingproject.org/wp-content/uploads/2015/12/Race-and-Justice-Shadow-Report-ICCPR.pdf.

[35]See Keith Reeves, *Voting Hopes or Fears?* (New York: Oxford University Press, 1997); Tali Mendelberg, *The Race Card* (Princeton, N.J.: Princeton University Press, 2001); Juliet Eilperin, "What's Changed for African Americans since 1963, by the Numbers," *The Washington Post,* August 22, 2013.

[36]NBC/Marist poll, December 2014.

[37]"Findings," Stanford Open Policing Project, 2018. https://openpolicing.stanford.edu/findings/.

[38]National Office of Drug Control Policy, U.S. Department of Justice, 1997; see also, "Criminal Justice Facts," Sentencing Project, 2018. https://www.sentencingproject.org/criminal-justice-facts/.

[39]Sarah DeGue, Katherine A. Fowler, and Cynthia Calkins, "Deaths Due to Use of Lethal Force by Law Enforcement," *American Journal of Preventive Medicine* 51 (2016): S173–S187.

[40]Ram Subramanian and Leily Arzy, "State Policing Reforms Since George Floyd's Murder," Brennan Center for Justice, New York University, May 21, 2021. https://www.brennancenter.org/our-work/research-reports/state-policing-reforms-george-floyds-murder

[41]See Kathleen S. Sullivan, *Women and Rights Discourse in Nineteenth-Century America* (Baltimore, Md.: Johns Hopkins University Press, 2007).

[42]*Tinker v. Colwell,* 193 U.S. 473 (1904).

[43]See Jane Mansbridge, *Why We Lost the ERA* (Chicago: University of Chicago Press, 1986).

[44]Congress set a time deadline (1982) on ratification of the ERA. Three additional states have since ratified the ERA, most recently by Virginia in 2020. Advocates have challenged in court Congress's ability to put a time limit on ratification. A complicating factor is that four states that had ratified the ERA have since rescinded it. Neither of these issues has been fully addressed by the Supreme Court, which leaves open the question of the ERA's ratification.

[45]U.S. Department of Education, National Center for Education Statistics, 2017.

[46]"Women are increasingly becoming the primary breadwinners," *The Californian,* April 24, 2020. https://eccalifornian.com/women-are-increasingly-becoming-the-primary-breadwinners/#:~:text=In%202018%2C%20Prudential%20surveyed%20more,half%20of%20their%20household%20income.

[47]See Sara M. Evans and Barbara Nelson, *Wage Justice* (Chicago: University of Chicago Press, 1989).

[48]Jennifer L. Lawless and Richard L. Fox, *It Takes a Candidate: Why Women Don't Run for Office* (New York: Cambridge University Press, 2005).

[49]Marshall Ganz, *Why David Sometimes Wins: Leadership, Organization and Strategy in the California Farm Worker Movement* (New York: Oxford University Press, 2009).

[50]Fox News poll, September 2017.

[51]*Department of Homeland Security v. Regents of the University of California,* No. 18-1587 (2020).

[52]See David E. Wilkins, *American Indian Politics and the American Political System* (Lanham, Md.: Rowman & Littlefield, 2006); Eric C. Henson et al., *The State of the Native Nations: Conditions under U.S. Policies of Self-Determination* (New York: Oxford University Press, 2007).

[53]William Evans and Julie Topoleski, *The Social and Economic Impact of Native American Casinos,* NBER Working Paper No. 9198 (Cambridge, Mass.: National Bureau of Economic Research, September 2002).

[54]W. Dale Mason, "Tribes and States: A New Era in Intergovernmental Affairs," *Publius,* 28 (1998): 129.

[55]Data from U.S. Census Bureau, 2018, and Office of Minority Health, U.S. Department of Health and Human Services, 2018.

[56]*Lau v. Nichols,* 414 U.S. 563 (1974).

[57]See Timothy P. Fong, *Contemporary Asian American Experience: Beyond the Model Minority* (Upper Saddle River, N.J.: Prentice-Hall, 2009).

[58]Scott Jaschik, "The Numbers and the Arguments on Asian Admissions," *Inside Higher Ed,* August 7, 2017. https://www.insidehighered.com/admissions/article/2017/08/07/look-data-and-arguments-about-asian-americans-and-admissions-elite.

[59]Abby Budiman and Neil Ruiz, "Key facts about Asian Americans, a diverse and growing population," Pew Research Center, April 29, 2021.

[60]Stefanie K. Johnson and Thomas Sy, "Why Aren't There More Asian Americans in Leadership Positions?," *Harvard Business Review,* December 19, 2016. https://hbr.org/2016/12/why-arent-there-more-asian-americans-in-leadership-positions.

[61]See Gordon Chang, ed., *Asian Americans and Politics* (Stanford, Calif.: Stanford University Press, 2001).

[62]*Kimel v. Florida Board of Regents,* No. 98-791528 U.S. 62 (2000); but see *CBOCS West, Inc. v. Humphries,* No. 06-1431553 U.S. 442 (2008).

[63]*Board of Trustees of the University of Alabama v. Garrett,* No. 99-1240 (2002); *Tennessee v. Lane,* No. 02-1667541 U.S. 509 (2004).

[64]*Obergefell v. Hodges,* 576 U.S. No. 14-556 (2015).

[65]*Bostock v. Clayton County,* No. 17-1618 (2020).

[66]*Fulton vs. City of Philadelphia,* No. 19-123 (2021).

[67]Gunnar Myrdal, *An American Dilemma: The Negro Problem and Modern Democracy* (New York: Harper, 1944).

[68]Latoya Hill, "COVID-19 Cases and Deaths by Race/Ethnicity: Current Data and Changes Over Time," Kaiser Family Foundation, February 22, 2022. https://www.kff.org/coronavirus-covid-19/issue-brief/covid-19-cases-and-deaths-by-race-ethnicity-current-data-and-changes-over-time/

CHAPTER SIX

[1]James Bryce, *The American Commonwealth,* vol. 2 (Indianapolis, Ind.: Liberty Fund, 1995), 225. First published in 1888.

[2]Elisabeth Noelle-Neumann, *The Spiral of Silence,* 2nd ed., ch. 1 (Chicago: University of Chicago Press, 1993).

[3]See, for example, Dean R. Hoge and Teresa L. Ankney, "Occupations and Attitudes of Student Activists Ten Years Later," *Journal of Youth and Adolescence,* 11 (1982): 365.

[4]See Herbert Asher, *Polling and the Public,* 7th ed. (Washington, D.C.: CQ Press, 2007).

[5]Peverill Squire, "Why the 1936 Literary Digest Poll Failed," *Public Opinion Quarterly* 53 (1988): 125-133.

[6]Gallup poll, November 2021.

[7]See, for example, Benjamin G. Bishin, *Tyranny of the Minority* (Philadelphia: Temple University Press, 2009).

[8]"If Polls Say People Want Gun Control, Why Doesn't Congress Just Pass It?" *Associated Press,* March 7, 2018, https://wtop.com/national/2018/03/if-polls-say-people-want-gun-control-why-doesnt-congress-just-pass-it/.

[9]See, for example, Emily Ekins, "Why Did Republicans Outperform The Polls Again?" FiveThirtyEight, March 2, 2021. https://fivethirtyeight.com/features/why-did-republicans-outperform-the-polls-again-two-theories/

[10]Seth Stevens-Davidowitz, *Everybody Lies: Big Data, New Data, and What the Internet Can Tell Us About Who We Really Are* (New York: Dey St., 2017), 7-9.

[11]Thomas E. Patterson, *How America Lost Its Mind* (Norman: University of Oklahoma Press, 2019), 33.

[12]Herbert Hyman, *Political Socialization* (Glencoe, Ill.: Free Press, 1959), 51.

[13]M. Kent Jennings and Richard G. Niemi, *Generations and Politics* (Princeton, N.J.: Princeton University Press, 1981).

[14]See Orit Ichilov, *Political Socialization, Citizenship Education, and Democracy* (New York: Teachers College Press, 1990).

[15]See, however, Dietram A. Scheufele, Matthew C. Nisbet, and Dominique Brossard, "Pathways to Political Participation: Religion, Communication Contexts, and Mass Media," *International Journal of Public Opinion Research,* 15 (Autumn 2003): 300-24; Michele F. Margolis, *From Politics to the Pews* (Chicago: University of Chicago Press, 2018).

[16]Noelle-Neumann, *Spiral of Silence.*

[17]Walter Lippmann, *Public Opinion* (New York: Free Press, 1965), p. 3.

[18]See, for example, David Broockman and Joshua Kalla, "The Manifold Effects of Partisan Media on Viewers' Beliefs and Attitudes: A Field Experiment with Fox News Viewers."

OSF Preprints. April 1, 2022. doi:10.31219/osf.io/jrw26.

[19]Christopher Adolph, Kenya Amano, Bree Bang-Jensen, Nancy Fullman, and John Wilkerson, "Pandemic Politics: Timing State-Level Social Distancing Responses to COVID-19," *Journal of Health Politics, Policy and Law,* August 2020, pp. 1-17. https://doi.org/10.1215/03616878-8802162

[20]See, for example, Kristi Andersen, *The Creation of a Democratic Majority, 1928-1936* (Chicago: University of Chicago Press, 1979).

[21]See Angus Campbell, Philip Converse, Warren Miller, and Donald Stokes, *The American Voter* (New York: Wiley, 1960), chs. 3 and 4.

[22]Martin P. Wattenberg, *Where Have All the Voters Gone?* (Cambridge, Mass.: Harvard University Press, 2002).

[23]YouGov poll, December, 2021, https://www.washingtonpost.com/politics/2022/01/07/republicans-big-lie-trump/.

[24]Some scholars define ideology in a stricter way, arguing that it can be said to exist only when an individual has a consistent pattern of opinions across a broad range of specific issues. By this definition, most Americans don't have an ideology. This conception is analytically useful in some situations, but it blunts the discussion of general belief tendencies in the public as a whole, which is the purpose here.

[25]There is no logical reason, of course, why an economic liberal also has to be a cultural liberal. Although most economic liberals are also cultural liberals, some are not. The term *populist* (although some analysts prefer the term communitarian) is used to describe an individual who is an economic liberal and a cultural conservative. Similarly, some economic conservatives are cultural liberals. They believe government should refrain from undue intervention in the economic marketplace and in people's private lives. The term *libertarian* is used to characterize someone with this set of beliefs.

[26]"Ku Klux Klan," *History,* undated. Downloaded January 2, 2018, http://www.history.com/topics/ku-klux-klan.

[27]Kenneth D. Wald, *Religion and Politics in the United States* (Lanham, Md.: Rowman & Littlefield, 2003); Robert D. Putnam and David E. Campbell, *American Grace: How Religion Divides and Unites Us* (New York: Simon & Schuster, 2012).

[28]"Religious composition of 18-29 year olds," Pew Research Center Religious Landscape Study, downloaded on April 21, 2022. https://www.pewresearch.org/religion/religious-landscape-study/age-distribution/18-29/

[29]Arlie Russell Hochschild, *Strangers in Their Own Land* (New York: The New Press, 2016).

[30]Arlie Russell Hochschild, *Strangers in Their Own Land* (New York: The New Press, 2016).

[31]See, for example, Daniel J. Hopkins, *The Increasingly United States: How and Why American Political Behavior Nationalized* (Chicago: University of Chicago Press, 2018); Perry Bacon, Jr., "The U.S. has four political parties stuffed into a two-party system," *Washington Post,* March 8, 2022. https://www.washingtonpost.com/opinions/2022/03/08/americas-four-party-system/

[32]Lois Duke Whitaker, ed., *Voting the Gender Gap* (Urbana: University of Illinois Press, 2008).

[33]Yuval Feinstein, "The Rise and Decline of 'Gender Gaps' in Support for Military Action: United States, 1986-2011," *Gender & Society* 13 (2017): 618-655.

[34]Liz Hamel, Lunna Lopes, Cailey Munana, and Mollyann Brodie, "The Kaiser Family Foundation/Washington Post Climate Change Survey," *KFF,* November 27, 2019, https://www.kff.org/report-section/the-kaiser-family-foundation-washington-post-climate-change-survey-main-findings/.

[35]Andrew Sullivan, "America Wasn't Built for Humans," *New York Magazine,* September 19, 2017, http://nymag.com/daily/intelligencer/2017/09/can-democracy-survive-tribalism.html.

[36]Christopher Achen and Larry Bartels, *Democracy for Realists: Why Elections Do Not Produce Responsive Government* (Princeton, N.J.: Princeton University Press, 2016).

[37]See, for example, Amy Chua, *Political Tribes: Group Instincts and the Fate of Nations* (New York: Penguin Press, 2018). American politics has been trending in that direction, which has deepened the divide between America's groups and has contributed to political polarization (see "Party Polarization" boxes throughout the book).

[38]George Gallup, "Polls and the Political Process—Past, Present, and Future," *Public Opinion Quarterly,* 40 (1965): 547-48.

[39]Clinton Rossiter and James Lare, *The Essential Lippmann: A Political Philosophy for Liberal Democracy* (Cambridge, Mass.: Harvard University Press, 1982), 99.

[40]Robert J. Samuelson, "What If We're to Blame? Public Opinion and Muddled Policies," *The Washington Post,* November 1, 2006.

[41]See Bruce Ackerman and James Fishkin, *Deliberation Day* (New Haven, Conn.: Yale University Press, 2004), 5; Christopher Achen and Larry Bartels, *Democracy for Realists: Why Elections Do Not Produce Responsive Government* (Princeton, N.J.: Princeton University Press, 2016).

[42]Zacc Ritter, "Amid Pandemic, News Attention Spikes; Media Favorability Flat," *Gallup News,* April 9, 2020, https://news.gallup.com/opinion/gallup/307934/amid-pandemic-news-attention-spikes-media-favorability-flat.aspx.

[43]See R. Michael Alvarez and John Brehm, *Hard Choices, Easy Answers* (Princeton, N.J.: Princeton University Press, 2002); see also Samuel L. Popkin, *The Reasoning Voter* (Chicago: University of Chicago Press, 1991).

[44]Robert S. Erikson, Michael B. MacKuen, and James A. Stimson, *The Macro Polity* (New York: Cambridge University Press, 2008), xxi.

[45]Vincent Hutchings, *Public Opinion and Democratic Accountability: How Citizens Learn About Politics* (Princeton, N.J.: Princeton University Press, 2005).

[46]See, for example, Sidney Verba and Norman H. Nie, *Participation in America: Political Democracy and Social Equality* (New York: Harper & Row, 1972), 332.

[47]Martin Gilens and Benjamin I. Page, "Testing Theories of American Politics: Elites, Interest Groups, and Average Citizens," *Perspectives on Politics,* 12 (2014): 564–81.

[48]Noam Chomsky and Edward S. Herman, *Manufacturing Consent: The Political Economy of the Mass Media* (New York: Pantheon, 2002); see also William Domhoff, *Who Rules America?* 5th ed. (New York: McGraw Hill, 2005).

[49]James Druckman and Lawrence Jacobs, *Who Governs? Presidents, Public Opinion, and Manipulation* (Chicago: University of Chicago Press, 2015).

[50]Scott McClellan, *What Happened: Inside the Bush White House and Washington's Culture of Deception* (New York: Public Affairs, 2008).

[51]See, for example, Daniel Kahneman, Amos Tversky, and Paul Slovic, *Judgment Under Uncertainty: Heuristics & Biases* (Cambridge, UK: Cambridge University Press, 1982); Daniel Kahneman, *Thinking Fast and Slow* (New York: Farrar, Straus and Giroux, 2013).

[52]Pew Research Center polls, July 2015 and August 2016.

[53]Bradley Jones, "Support for Free Trade Agreements Rebounds Modestly, but Wide Partisan Differences Remain," Pew Research Center, April 25, 2017, http://www.pewresearch.org/fact-tank/2017/04/25/support-for-free-trade-agreements-rebounds-modestly-but-wide-partisan-differences-remain/.

[54]The leading case on schools and free speech rights is *Tinker v. Des Moines Independent Community School District,* 393 U.S. 503 (1969).

[55]V. O. Key Jr., *Public Opinion and American Democracy* (New York: Knopf, 1964).

[56]"Notes from the Editors," *Monthly Review,* 50 (1999), https://monthlyreview.org/1999/03/01/mr-050-10-1999-03_0/.

[57]Quoted in Anthony King, "Running Scared," *The Atlantic,* January 1997.

[58]Christopher Wlezien, "The Public as 'Thermostat,'" *American Journal of Political Science* 39 (1995): 981–1000.

[59]David Mayhew, *Congress: The Electoral Connection* (New Haven, Conn.: Yale University Press, 2004), 5.

[60]Anthony King, *Running Scared* (New York: Free Press, 1999).

[61]David A. Fahrenthold, Rosalind S. Helderman, and Jenna Portnoy, "What Went Wrong for Eric Cantor," *The Washington Post,* June 11, 2014, https://www.washingtonpost.com/politics/what-went-wrong-for-eric-cantor/2014/06/11/0be7c02c-f180-11e3-914c-1fbd0614e2d4_story.html.

[62]See, for example, Benjamin I. Page and Robert Y. Shapiro, "Effects of Public Opinion on Policy," *American Political Science Review,* 77 (March 1983): 178; Richard Sobel, *The Impact of Public Opinion on U.S. Foreign Policy* (New York: Oxford University Press, 2001); James Stimson, *Tides of Consent: How Public Opinion Shapes American Politics* (New York: Cambridge University Press, 2004); Jeff Manza and Fay Lomax Cook, "A Democratic Polity: Three Views of Policy Responsiveness to Public Opinion in the United States," *American Politics Research,* 30 (2002): 630–67; John W. Kingdon, *Agendas, Alternatives, and Public Policies,* 2d ed. (New York: Longman, 2003), 148–49.

CHAPTER SEVEN

[1]Walter Lippmann, *Public Opinion* (New York: Free Press, 1965), 36.

[2]U.S. Commission on Civil Rights data, accessed in 2022.

[3]Quoted in Ralph Volney Harlow, *The Growth of the United States* (New York: Henry Holt, 1943), 312.

[4]Russell Dalton, "The Myth of the Disengaged American," Web publication of the Comparative Study of Electoral Systems, October 2005, 2.

[5]See, for example, Craig Leonard Brians and Bernard Grofman, "Election Day Registration's Effect on U.S. Voter Turnout," *Social Science Quarterly* 82 (2001): 170–183.

[6]Keesha Gaskins and Sundeep Iyer, "The Challenge of Obtaining Voter Identification," Brennan Center for Justice, July 18, 2012, www.brennancenter.org/publication/challenge-obtaining-voter-identification.

[7]*Crawford et al. v. Marion County Election Board et al.,* No. 07-21 (2008).

[8]Sam Corbett-Davies, Tobias Konitzer, and David Rothschild, "Poll: 60% of Republicans Believe Illegal Immigrants Vote; 43% Believe People Vote Using Dead People's Names," *The Washington Post,* October 24, 2016, https://www.washingtonpost.com/news/monkey-cage/wp/2016/10/24/poll-60-of-republicans-believe-illegal-immigrants-vote-43-believe-people-vote-using-dead-peoples-names/.

[9]See, Benjamin Highton, "Voter Identification Laws and Turnout," *Annual Review of Political Science* 20 (2017): 149–67, https://www.annualreviews.org/doi/abs/10.1146/annurev-polisci-051215-022822.

[10]Justin Levitt, "The Truth About Voter Fraud," Brennan Center for Justice, November 9, 2007, https://www.brennancenter.org/publication/truth-about-voter-fraud.

[11]Justin Levitt, "The Truth About Voter Fraud," Brennan Center for Justice, November 9, 2007, https://www.brennancenter.org/publication/truth-about-voter-fraud.

[12]Emily Bazelon, "A Crusader Against Voter Fraud Fails to Prove His Case," *New York Times,* June 19, 2018, https://www.nytimes.com/2018/06/19/opinion/a-crusader-against-voter-fraud-fails-to-prove-his-case.html.

[13]Ivor Crewe, "Electoral Participation," in David Butler, Howard R. Penniman, and Austin Ranney, eds., *Democracy at the Polls* (Washington, D.C.: American Enterprise Institute, 1981), 251–53.

[14]Richard Boyd, "Decline of U.S. Voter Turnout," *American Politics Quarterly,* 9 (April 1981): 142.

[15]Patterson, *The Vanishing Voter,* 135.

[16]Markus Prior, *Hooked: How Politics Captures People's Interest* (New York: Cambridge University Press, 2019).

[17]Dominik Schraff, "Politically Alienated Through Low-Wage Work? Evidence from Panel Data," *SPSR* 25 (2019): 19–39. https://onlinelibrary.wiley.com/doi/full/10.1111/spsr.12342

[18]Russell J. Dalton, "The Myth of the Disengaged American," *CSES Report,* October 25, 2005.

[19]Open Secrets, "PAC Profile: Moveon." https://www.opensecrets.org/political-action-committees-pacs/moveon-org/C00341396/summary/2022

[20]Robert Putnam, *Bowling Alone: The Collapse and Revival of American Community* (New York: Simon & Schuster, 2000).

[21]Dalton, "Myth of the Disengaged American," 2.

[22]U.S. Department of Labor statistics, 2016.

[23]See Benjamin Ginsberg, *The Consequences of Consent* (New York: Random House, 1982), ch. 2.

[24]See, for example, Charles J. Stewart, Craig Allen Smith, and Robert E. Denton Jr., *Persuasion and Social Movements,* 5th ed. (Long Grove, Ill.: Waveland Press, 2007).

[25]Sidney Tarrow, *Power in Movement* (New York: Cambridge University Press, 1998).

[26]Joan Donovan, "MAGA Isn't a Typical Protest Movement," *The Atlantic,* January 15, 2021. https://www.theatlantic.com/ideas/archive/2021/01/maga-isnt-a-normal-protest-movement/617685/

[27]Kim Eckart, "New nationwide survey shows MAGA supporters' beliefs about the pandemic, the election and the insurrection," *UW News,* February 5, 2021. https://www.washington.edu/news/2021/02/05/new-nationwide-survey-shows-maga-supporters-beliefs-about-the-pandemic-the-election-and-the-insurrection/

[28]Bryan T. Gervais and Irwin L. Morris, *Reactionary Republicanism: How the Tea Party in the House Paved the Way for Trump's Victory* (New York: Oxford University Press, 2018).

[29]Elizabeth A. Harris and Alexandra Alter, "Book Ban Efforts Spread Across the U.S.," *New York Times,* February 8, 2022, https://www.nytimes.com/2022/01/30/books/book-ban-us-schools.html

[30]Michael Levitin, "Occupy Wall Street Did More Than You Think," *The Atlantic,* September 14, 2021. https://www.theatlantic.com/ideas/archive/2021/09/how-occupy-wall-street-reshaped-america/620064/ By Michael Levitin

[31]See, for example, Endre Borbáth and Swen Hutter, "Protesting Parties in Europe," *Party Politics,* May 8, 2020. https://journals.sagepub.com/doi/10.1177/1354068820908023

[32]Michael Schnell, "Poll finds only 18 percent support 'defund the police,'" *The Hill,* March 8, 2021. https://thehill.com/homenews/news/542108-poll-finds-only-18-percent-support-defund-the-police/

[33]Brittany Shepherd, "Majority of Americans think Jan. 6 attack threatened democracy: POLL," ABC News, January 2, 2022. https://abcnews.go.com/Politics/majority-americans-jan-attack-threatened-democracy-poll/story?id=81990555&cid=social_twitter_abcn

[34]William Watts and Lloyd A. Free, eds., *The State of the Nation* (New York: University Books, Potomac Associates, 1967), 97.

[35]Sidney Verba and Norman Nie, *Participation in America* (New York: Harper & Row, 1972), 131.

[36]Jan E. Leighley and Jonathan Nagler, *Who Votes Now?: Demographics, Issues, Inequality, and Turnout in the United States* (Princeton, N.J.: Princeton University Press, 2014).

[37]Larry M. Bartels, *Unequal Democracy,* 2nd ed. (Princeton, N.J.: Princeton University Press, 2016).

CHAPTER EIGHT

[1]E. E. Schattschneider, *Party Government* (New York: Rinehart, 1942), 1.

[2]See John Aldrich, *Why Parties? The Origin and Transformation of Political Parties in America* (Chicago: University of Chicago Press, 1995); L. Sandy Maisel, *American Political Parties and Elections* (New York: Oxford University Press, 2007).

[3]E. E. Schattschneider, *The Semisovereign People: A Realist's View of Democracy in America* (New York: Holt, Rinehart & Winston, 1961), 140.

[4]Thomas E. Patterson, *The Vanishing Voter* (New York: Knopf, 2002), ch. 2.

[5]See Richard P. McCormick, *The Second American Party System: Party Formation in the Jacksonian Era* (Chapel Hill: University of North Carolina Press, 1966).

[6]Aldrich, *Why Parties?* 151.

[7]Before the New Deal era, the term "progressive" rather than "liberal" was used to describe people who advocated business regulation and economic assistance through government action.

[8]Kristi Andersen, *The Creation of a Democratic Majority, 1928–1936* (Chicago: University of Chicago Press, 1979).

[9]See Kevin Phillips, *The Emerging Republican Majority* (New Rochelle, N.Y.: Arlington House, 1969).

[10]See Arthur C. Paulson, *Electoral Realignment and the Outlook for American Democracy* (Boston: Northeastern University Press, 2006).

[11]Richard M. Scammon and Ben J. Wattenberg, *The Real Majority* (New York: Coward-McCann, 1970).

[12]John Green, Mark Rozell, and William Clyde Wilcox, eds., *The Christian Right in American Politics* (Washington, D.C.: Georgetown University Press, 2003).

[13]Jacob S. Hacker and Paul Pierson, *Off Center: The Republican Revolution and the Erosion of American Democracy* (New Haven, Conn.: Yale University Press, 2006); James E. Campbell, *Polarized: Making Sense of a Divided America* (Princeton, N.J.: Princeton University Press, 2016).

[14]Gary Miller and Norman Schofield, "The Transformation of the Republican and Democratic Party Coalitions in the U.S.," *Perspectives on Politics,* 6 (2008): 433–50; Thomas E. Patterson, *Is the Republican Party Destroying Itself?* (Seattle, Wash.: KDP, 2020).

[15]Pew Research Center polls, 1987 for the 1980s figures and various dates for the more recent figures.

[16]See, James Davison Hunter, *Culture Wars: The Struggle to Define America* (New York: Basic Books, 1991).

[17]See Duncan Black, "On the Rationale of Group Decision-Making," *Journal of Political Economy,* 56 (1948): 23–24; Anthony Downs, *An Economic Theory of Democracy* (New York: HarperCollins, 1957).

[18]Jocelyn Kiley, "In Polarized Era, Fewer Americans Hold a Mix of Conservative and Liberal Views," Pew Research Center, October 27, 2017, http://www.pewresearch.org/fact-tank/2017/10/23/in-polarized-era-fewer-americans-hold-a-mix-of-conservative-and-liberal-views/?utm_source=Pew+Research+Center&utm_campaign=0abc6f17c9-EMAIL_CAMPAIGN_2017_10_26&utm_medium=email&utm_term=0_3e953b9b70-0abc6f17c9-400267813.

[19]Bill Bishop, *The Big Sort: Why the Clustering of Like-Minded America Is Tearing Us Apart* (New

York: Houghton Mifflin, 2008); Alan A. Abramowitz, "U.S. Senate Elections in a Polarized Era," in Burdett A. Loomis, ed., *The U.S. Senate: From Deliberation to Dysfunction* (Washington, D.C.: CQ Press, 2011), 27–48.

[20]2020 election exit polls.

[21]Ruy Teixeira and Alan Abramowitz, "The Decline of the White Working Class and the Rise of a Mass Upper Middle Class," Brookings Institution, Washington, D.C., 2008, chrome-extension://efaidnbmnnnibpcajpcglclefindmkaj/https://www.brookings.edu/wp-content/uploads/2016/06/04_demographics_teixeira.pdf.

[22]American National Election Studies (ANES) surveys, 2000–2016 elections.

[23]Presidential election exit polls, 1980–2020; see also Lois Duke Whitaker, ed., *Voting the Gender Gap* (Urbana: University of Illinois Press, 2008); Karen M. Kaufmann, "The Gender Gap," *PS: Political Science & Politics,* July 2006, 447–53.

[24]See John B. Judis and Ruy Teixeira, *The Emerging Democratic Majority* (New York: Scribner, 2002).

[25]James G. Gimpel, "Latinos and the 2002 Election: Republicans Do Well When Latinos Stay Home," Center for Immigration Studies, University of Maryland, January 2003, https://cis.org/Latinos-and-2002-Election; see also Jorge Ramos, *The Latino Wave: How Hispanics Are Transforming Politics in America* (New York: Harper Paperbacks, 2005); F. Chris Garcia and Gabriel Sanchez, *Hispanics and the U.S. Political System: Moving into the Mainstream* (Upper Saddle River, N.J.: Prentice-Hall, 2007).

[26]Douglas E. Schoen and Zoe Young, "Democrats Must Face the Reality of Their Latino Voter Problem," *The Hill,* December 26, 2021. https://thehill.com/opinion/campaign/587231-democrats-must-face-the-reality-of-their-latino-voter-problem

[27]Thomas E. Patterson, *Is the Republican Party Destroying Itself?* (Seattle, Wash.: KDP, 2020).

[28]Micah L. Sifrey, *Spoiling for a Fight: Third-Party Politics in America* (New York: Routledge, 2003).

[29]Daniel A. Mazmanian, *Third Parties in Presidential Elections* (Washington, D.C.: Brookings Institution, 1984), 143–44.

[30]Lewis L. Gould, *Four Hats in the Ring: The 1912 Election and the Birth of Modern American Politics* (Lawrence: University Press of Kansas, 2008).

[31]See Lawrence Goodwyn, *The Populist Movement* (New York: Oxford University Press, 1978).

[32]See, for example, Eli Watkins, "How Gary Johnson and Jill Stein Helped Elect Donald Trump," *CNN,* November 25, 2016, https://www.cnn.com/2016/11/10/politics/gary-johnson-jill-stein-spoiler/index.html.

[33]See Anthony King, *Running Scared* (New York: Free Press, 1997); but also see James E. Campbell, *The American Campaign: U.S. Presidential Campaigns and the National Vote* (College Station: Texas A&M Press, 2008).

[34]See Paul S. Herrnson and John C. Green, eds., *Responsible Partisanship* (Lawrence: University Press of Kansas, 2003).

[35]See Paul S. Herrnson, "The Roles of Party Organizations, Party-Connected Committees, and Party Allies in Elections," *The Journal of Politics,* 71 (2009): 1207–24.

[36]See Marjorie Randon Hershey, *Party Politics in America,* 17th ed. (New York: Routledge, 2017).

[37]Kathleen Hall Jamieson, *Packaging the Presidency: A History and Criticism of Presidential Campaign Advertising,* 3rd ed. (New York: Oxford University Press, 1996).

[38]Darrell M. West, *Air Wars: Television Advertising in Election Campaigns, 1952–2004,* 6th ed. (Washington, D.C.: CQ Press, 2013).

[39]Brad Adgate, "The 2020 Elections Will Set (Another) Ad Spending Record," *Forbes,* September 3, 2019, https://www.forbes.com/sites/bradadgate/2019/09/03/the-2020-elections-will-set-another-ad-spending-record/#3d75bc101836.

[40]See R. Douglas Arnold, *Congress, the Press, and Political Accountability* (Princeton, N.J.: Princeton University Press, 2013).

[41]Andrew Prokopandrew, "Do Presidential Debates Matter? Here's the Political Science Evidence," *Vox,* September 26, 2016, https://www.vox.com/2016/9/12/12847632/debates-trump-clinton-polls-political-science.

[42]Quoted by Nancy Gibbs in her Theodore H. White Lecture, Harvard Kennedy School, November 15, 2017.

[43]Quoted in Andrew Gripp, "Is Television Ruining Our Political Discourse?" *IVN,* September 26, 2015, https://andrewgripp.wordpress.com/2015/09/26/is-television-ruining-our-politicaldiscourse/.

[44]Federal Election Commission projection, 2020.

[45]Federal Election Commission, 2018.

[46]David B. Magelby, J. Quin Monson, and Kelly D. Patterson, eds., *Dancing Without Partners:*

How Candidates, Parties and Interest Groups Interact in the New Campaign Finance Environment (Provo, Utah: Brigham Young University Press, 2005).

[47]Bill Allison, "The 2020 Presidential Race Might Be Remembered As When the Dam Broke on Money in U.S. Politics," *Fortune,* February 13, 2020, https://fortune.com/2020/02/13/2020-election-campaign-spending-money/.

[48]Emmett H. Buell Jr. and Lee Sigelman, *Attack Politics: Negativity in Presidential Campaigns Since 1960* (Lawrence: University Press of Kansas, 2008). For opposing views on the effect of negative advertising, see Stephen Ansolabehere and Shanto Iyengar, *Going Negative* (New York: Free Press, 1995); and John Geer, *In Defense of Negativity* (Chicago: University of Chicago Press, 2006).

[49]Darrell M. West, *Air Wars: Television Advertising in Election Campaigns, 1952–2004,* 6th ed. (Washington, D.C.: CQ Press, 2013), 140–46.

[50]See, for example, Robert Farley, "Romney's Solar Flareout," *FactCheck.org,* June 1, 2012, http://factcheck.org/2012/06/romneys-solar-flareout/.

[51]John Sides and Lynn Vavreck, "What Really Decided the 2012 Election, in 10 Graphs," *The Washington Post,* October 14, 2013.

[52]Brad Lockerbie, *Do Voters Look to the Future?* (Albany: State University of New York Press, 2009).

[53]"The Perception Gap," More in Common, poll conducted in 2019, https://perceptiongap.us/.

Chapter Nine

[1]E. E. Schattschneider, *The Semisovereign People: A Realist's View of Democracy in America* (New York: Holt, Rinehart & Winston, 1960), 35.

[2]Megan R. Wilson, "Analysis: More Than 6,000 Lobbyists Have Worked on Taxes in 2017," *The Hill,* December 1, 2017, http://thehill.com/business-a-lobbying/business-a-lobbying/362796-analysis-more-than-6000-lobbyists-have-worked-on.

[3]Anthony J. Nownes, *Total Lobbying: What Lobbyists Want (and How They Try to Get It)* (New York: Cambridge University Press, 2006).

[4]See Matthew J. Burbank, Ronald J. Hrebenar, and Robert C. Benedict, *Parties, Interest Groups, and Political Campaigns* (Boulder, Colo.: Paradigm, 2008).

[5]James M. Strickland, "A Quiet Revolution in State Lobbying: Government Growth and Interest Populations," *Political Research Quarterly* 74 (2021): 1181–1196, https://journals.sagepub.com/doi/abs/10.1177/1065912920975490.

[6]E. Pendleton Herring, *Group Representation Before Congress,* (Washington, D.C.: Brookings Institution, 1929), 78.

[7]U.S. Bureau of Labor Statistics, 2020.

[8]See Jack L. Walker, *Mobilizing Interest Groups in America* (Ann Arbor: University of Michigan Press, 1991).

[9]See Nownes, *Total Lobbying.* The author is indebted to Professor Anthony Nownes of the University of Tennessee for the observations contained in this paragraph.

[10]Christopher J. Bosso, "The Color of Money: Environmental Groups and the Pathologies of Fund Raising," in Allan J. Cigler and Burdett Loomis, eds., *Interest Group Politics,* 4th ed. (Washington, D.C.: CQ Press, 1995), 101–3.

[11]Arbitron Radio Research and Corporation for Public Broadcasting Financial Reports, 2015.

[12]Mancur Olson, *The Logic of Collective Action,* rev. ed. (Cambridge, Mass.: Harvard University Press, 1971), 64.

[13]Theda Skocpol, *Diminished Democracy* (Norman: University of Oklahoma Press, 2003).

[14]Olson, *The Logic of Collective Action,* 147.

[15]Tyler O'Neil, "What the Left Doesn't Want You to Know About Trump's Tax Cuts," *PJMedia,* April 15, 2019, https://pjmedia.com/trending/what-the-left-doesnt-want-you-to-know-about-trumps-tax-cuts/; Dylan Matthews and Alexia Fernandez Campbell, "The Numbers Are in, and the House Republican Tax Bill Raises Taxes on Over a Quarter of Americans," *Vox,* November 8, 2017. https://www.vox.com/policy-and-politics/2017/11/6/16614540/house-republican-tax-plan-paul-ryan-tax-policy-center.

[16]Tyler O'Neil, "What the Left Doesn't Want You to Know About Trump's Tax Cuts," *PJMedia,* April 15, 2019, https://pjmedia.com/trending/what-the-left-doesnt-want-you-to-know-about-trumps-tax-cuts/; Dylan Matthews and Alexia Fernandez Campbell, "The Numbers Are in, and the House Republican Tax Bill Raises Taxes on Over a Quarter of Americans," *Vox,* November 8, 2017. https://www.vox.com/policy-and-politics/2017/11/6/16614540/house-republican-tax-plan-paul-ryan-tax-policy-center.

[17]Jeffrey N. Birnbaum, "Washington's Power 25: Which Pressure Groups Are Best at Manipulating the Laws We Live By?" *Fortune,* December 8, 1997.

[18]Frank R. Baumgartner, Jeffrey M. Berry, Marie Hojnacki, David C. Kimball, and Beth L. Leech, *Lobbying and Policy Change: Who Wins, Who Loses, and Why* (Chicago: University of Chicago Press, 2009).

[19]Norman J. Ornstein and Shirley Elder, *Interest Groups, Lobbying, and Policymaking* (Washington, D.C.: CQ Press, 1978), 82–86.

[20]See Paul S. Herrnson, Ronald G. Shaiko, and Clyde Wilcox, *The Interest Group Connection: Electioneering, Lobbying, and Policymaking in Washington,* 2nd ed. (Washington, D.C.: CQ Press, 2004).

[21]Quoted in a *National Journal* excerpt in Thomas E. Patterson, *The American Democracy,* 9th ed. (New York: McGraw Hill, 2009), 245b.

[22]See John Mark Hansen, *Gaining Access* (Chicago: Chicago University Press, 1991); Bruce Wolpe and Bertram Levine, *Lobbying Congress* (Washington, D.C.: CQ Press, 1996).

[23]Center for Responsive Politics data, 2020, https://www.opensecrets.org/lobby/.

[24]Bara Vaida, "K-Street Paradox: $1.3 Million per Hour," *National Journal,* March 13, 2010.

[25]Quoted in Ornstein and Elder, *Interest Groups, Lobbying, and Policymaking,* 77.

[26]Matej Mikulic, "Pfizer's Revenue from 1st Quarter 2010 to 4th Quarter 2021," *Statista,* March 2, 2022. https://www.statista.com/statistics/254351/quarterly-revenue-of-pfizer-since-2006/

[27]Steve Reinberg, "Debate Builds over Drug Companies' Fees to FDA," *Washington Post,* April 13, 2007.

[28]"Wall Street spends record $2bn on US election lobbying". *Financial Times.* March 8, 2017.

[29]Lee Epstein and C. K. Rowland, "Interest Groups in the Courts," *American Political Science Review,* 85 (1991): 205–17.

[30]Richard Davis, *Electing Justice: Fixing the Supreme Court Nomination Process* (New York: Oxford University Press, 2005).

[31]OpenSecrets.org, 2020, https://www.opensecrets.org/industries/indus.php?Ind=D.

[32]Hugh Heclo, "Issue Networks and the Executive Establishment," in Anthony King, ed., *The New American Political System* (Washington, D.C.: American Enterprise Institute, 1978), 87–124.

[33]Norman J. Ornstein and Shirley Elder, *Interest Groups, Lobbying, and Policymaking* (Washington, D.C.: CQ Press, 1978), 88–93.

[34]See, for example, Gallup poll of January 2018.

[35]Christopher Ingraham, "Nobody Knows How Many Members the NRA Has, but Its Tax Returns Offer Some Clues," *The Washington Post,* February 26, 2016, https://www.washingtonpost.com/news/wonk/wp/2018/02/26/nobody-knows-how-many-members-the-nra-has-but-its-tax-returns-offer-some-clues/.

[36]Quoted in Mark Green, "Political PAC-Man," *The New Republic,* December 13, 1982, 20; see also Richard Skinner, *More Than Money: Interest Group Action in Congressional Elections* (Lanham, Md.: Rowman & Littlefield, 2006); Mark J. Rozell, Clyde Wilcox, and David Madland, *Interest Groups in American Campaigns,* 2nd ed. (Washington, D.C.: CQ Press, 2005).

[37]Jacob Pramuk, "AARP Warns Republicans It Has 'Strong Opposition' to Obamacare Replacement Bill," CNBC, May 25, 2017, https://www.cnbc.com/2017/05/25/aarp-has-strong-opposition-on-a-health-bill-that-slams-seniors.html.

[38]Federal Election Commission data, 2020.

[39]Federal Election Commission data, 2020.

[40]Jennifer Babson and Kelly St. John, "Momentum Helps GOP Collect Record Amounts from PACs," *Congressional Quarterly Weekly Report,* December 3, 1994, 3456.

[41]*Citizens United v. Federal Election Commission,* 558 U.S. 50 (2010).

[42]Karl Evers-Hillstrom, "Super PACs Outmaneuver Outdated Rules to Leave Voters in the Dark," OpenSecrets.org, March 18, 2020, https://www.opensecrets.org/news/2020/03/sunshine-week-2020-super-pacs-loophole/.

[43]Bernie Sanders, "Overturn Citizens United," *U.S. News & World Report,* January 13, 2012, www.usnews.com/debate-club/are-super-pacs-harming-us-politics/overturn-citizens-united.

[44]Bradley Smith, "Super PACs Level the Playing Field," *U.S. News & World Report,* January 13, 2012, www.usnews.com/debate-club/are-super-pacs-harming-us-politics/super-pacs-level-the-playing-field.

[45]Jack L. Walker, *Mobilizing Interest Groups in America* (Ann Arbor: University of Michigan Press, 1991), 112.

[46]Theodore J. Lowi, *The End of Liberalism: The Second Republic of the United States* (New York: Norton, 1979).

[47]Larry Bartels, *Unequal Democracy: The Political Economy of the New Gilded Age* (Princeton, N.J.: Princeton University Press, 2008).

[48]Martin Gilens and Benjamin I. Page, "Testing Theories of American Politics: Elites, Interest Groups, and Average Citizens," *Perspectives on Politics,* 12 (2104): 564–81, http://citeseerx.ist.psu.edu/viewdoc/download;jsessionid=37EDA24D1D5DA87AEB950CEFE63883FF?doi=10.1.1.668.8647&rep=rep1&type=pdf.

[49]See, for example, James A. Stimson, *Tides of Consent: How Public Opinion Shapes American Politics* (New York: Cambridge University Press, 2004).

CHAPTER TEN

[1]Theodore H. White, *The Making of the President, 1972* (New York: Bantam Books, 1973), 327.

[2]See Bill Kovach and Tom Rosenstiel, *The Elements of Journalism* (New York: Three Rivers Press, 2001).

[3]Nancy Kranich, "The Information Commons," Brennan Center for Justice, New York University School of Law, 2004, https://www.aaup.org/sites/default/files/files/InformationCommons.pdf.

[4]Marcus Prior, *Post-Broadcast Democracy* (New York: Cambridge University Press, 2007).

[5]Frank Luther Mott, *American Journalism, a History: 1690-1960* (New York: Macmillan, 1962), 114–15; see also Si Sheppard, *The Partisan Press: A History of Media Bias in the United States* (Jefferson, N.C.: McFarland, 2007).

[6]Edwin Emery, *The Press and America: An Interpretive History of the Mass Media* (Englewood Cliffs, N.J.: Prentice-Hall, 1977), 350.

[7]Quoted in Mott, *American Journalism,* 529.

[8]Quoted in David Halberstam, *The Powers That Be* (New York: Knopf, 1979), 208–9.

[9]Martin J. Wattenberg, *Is Voting for Young People?* (New York: Pearson Longman, 2008), 32.

[10]Editor and Publisher Yearbook data for 1975.

[11]See David T. Z. Mindich, *Tuned Out: Why Americans under 40 Don't Follow the News* (New York: Oxford University Press, 2005).

[12]See, for example, Thomas E. Patterson and Robert D. McClure, *The Unseeing Eye* (New York: Putnam, 1976).

[13]Marcus Prior, *Post-Broadcast Democracy* (New York: Cambridge University Press, 2007).

[14]Filipe R. Campante and Daniel Hojman, "Media and Polarization," Faculty Research Working Paper Series, Harvard Kennedy School, December 2009, https://projects.iq.harvard.edu/files/wcfia/files/rcampante_media_polarization.pdf.

[15]See, for example, Seth Flaxman, Sharad Goel, and Justin M. Rao, "Filter Bubbles, Echo Chambers, and Online News Consumption," *Public Opinion Quarterly* 80 (2016): 298–320, chrome-extension://efaidnbmnnnibpcajpcglclefindmkaj/https://5harad.com/papers/bubbles.pdf.

[16]Ezra Klein, "Unpopular Mandate," *The New Yorker,* June 25, 2012, 33.

[17]David Weaver, Lars Willnat, and Cleve Wilhoit, "The American Journalist in the Digital Age," *Journalism & Mass Communication Quarterly* 96 (2019): 101–130, doi:10.1177/1077699018778242.

[18]Edmund L. Andrews, "Media Consolidation Means Less Local News, More Right Wing Slant," Insights, Stanford Graduate School of Business, July 30, 2019, https://www.gsb.stanford.edu/insights/media-consolidation-means-less-local-news-more-right-wing-slant.

[19]For reasons that are not fully understood, conservatives have a much stronger preference for partisan talk show. According to both polling and ratings data, conservative talk show hosts dominate the partisan talk show sector. They attract roughly 90 percent of the partisan talk show audience.

[20]Ibid.

[21]Elizabeth Grieco, "Americans' main sources for political news vary by party and age," Pew Research Center, April 1, 2020, https://www.pewresearch.org/fact-tank/2020/04/01/americans-main-sources-for-political-news-vary-by-party-and-age/.

[22]Jeffrey Gottfried, Michael Barthel, and Amy Mitchell, "Trump, Clinton Voters Divided in Their Main Source for Election News," Pew Research Center, January 18, 2017, http://www.journalism.org/2017/01/18/trump-clinton-voters-divided-in-their-main-source-for-election-news/.

[23]Kathleen Hall Jamieson and Joseph N. Cappella, *Echo Chamber* (New York: Oxford University Press, 2008), 232; various Pew Research Center surveys.

[24]See, for example, J. Sonia Huang and Wei-Ching Wang, "Application of the Long Tail Economy to the Online News Market," *Journal of Media Economics,* 27 (2014): 158–76.

[25]Matthew Hindman, *The Myth of Digital Democracy* (Princeton, N.J.: Princeton University Press, 2009), 90–91.

[26]Douglas A. McIntyre, "Breitbart Audience Steady at 83 Million," *24/7 Wall Street,* September 30, 2017, https://247wallst.com/media/2017/09/30/breitbart-audience-steady-at-83-million/.

[27]Zach Exley, "Black Pigeon Speaks: The Anatomy of the Worldview of an Alt-Right YouTuber," Shorenstein Center on Media, Politics, and Public Policy, Harvard Kennedy School, Harvard University, June 28, 2017, https://shorensteincenter.org/anatomy-of-alt-right-youtuber/.

[28]"Top 50 Blogs," Personal Democracy, undated, downloaded May 13, 2022, https://personaldemocracy.com/blogs/top.

[29]"Social media usage in the United States," Statista, February 23, 2022, https://www.statista.com/topics/3196/social-media-usage-in-the-united-states/#:~:text=Facebook%20is%20the%20most%20popular,share%20of%20nearly%2072%20percent.

[30]"Partisanship and Political Animosity in 2016," Pew Research Center, June 2016, http://www.people-press.org/2016/06/22/partisanship-and-political-animosity-in-2016/.

[31]Eli Pariser, *The Filter Bubble* (New York: Penguin Books, 2011).

[32]See, for example, Matthew Levendusky, *How Partisan Media Polarize America* (Chicago: University of Chicago Press, 2013).

[33]Kathleen Hall Jamieson and Joseph N. Cappella, *Echo Chamber* (New York: Oxford University Press, 2010), 195–98.

[34]Carmen Stavrositu, "Selective Exposure," in Kerric Harvey, ed., *Encyclopedia of Social Media and Politics* (Thousand Oaks, Calif.: Sage, 2014): 1117–19.

[35]McKay Coppins, "How the Left Lost Its Mind," *The Atlantic,* July 2, 2017, https://www.theatlantic.com/politics/archive/2017/07/liberal-fever-swamps/530736/.

[36]Diana Mutz, *In-Your-Face Politics* (Princeton, N.J.: Princeton University Press, 2015).

[37]Paul Starr, "Governing in the Age of Fox News," *The Atlantic,* January/February 2010, https://www.theatlantic.com/magazine/archive/2010/01/governing-in-the-age-of-fox-news/307838/; Natalie Jomini Stroud, "Media Use and Political Predispositions: Revisiting the Concept of Selective Exposure," *Political Behavior,* 30 (2008): 341–66.

[38]Linley Sanders, "Trust in Media 2022: Where Americans get their news and who they trust for information," YouGov, April 5, 2022, https://today.yougov.com/topics/politics/articles-reports/2022/04/05/trust-media-2022-where-americans-get-news-poll.

[39]See, for example, Jonathan M. Ladd, *Why Americans Hate the Media and How It Matters* (Princeton, NJ: Princeton University Press, 2012).

[40]See Rodger Streitmatter, *Mightier Than the Sword: How the News Media Have Shaped American History* (Westport, Conn.: Praeger, 2008).

[41]Kathleen Hall Jamieson and Karlyn Kohrs Campbell, *The Interplay of Influence,* rev. ed. (Boston: Wadsworth, 2005), 4.

[42]Donald Shaw and Maxwell McCombs, *The Emergence of American Political Issues: The Agenda-Setting Function of the Press* (St. Paul, Minn.: West, 1977).

[43]Bernard C. Cohen, *The Press and Foreign Policy* (Princeton, N.J.: Princeton University Press, 1963), 13.

[44]See Kathleen Hall Jamieson, *Eloquence in an Electronic Age* (New York: Oxford University Press, 1988), 42.

[45]David Bauder, "Hero or villain, Ocasio-Cortez remains a media fixation," AP wire story, March 11, 2019, https://apnews.com/article/bill-nye-donald-trump-ap-top-news-alexandria-ocasio-cortez-politics-025984ff1f6c42afb0de60c9baf72e60; Elahe Izadi, "The media can't ignore Marjorie Taylor Greene. Can they figure out how to cover her?" *Washington Post,* February 5, 2021, https://www.washingtonpost.com/lifestyle/media/marjorie-taylor-greene-media/2021/02/05/6a619830-64d3-11eb-886d-5264d4ceb46d_story.html.

[46]Stephen J. Farnsworth and S. Robert Lichter, *The Mediated Presidency: Television News and Presidential Governance* (Lanham, Md.: Rowman & Littlefield, 2006).

[47]One of the classic studies of this tendency is Kiku Adatto, "Sound Bite Democracy, Joan Shorenstein Center on the Press," Politics, and Public Policy, Research Paper R-2, Harvard University, June 1990.

[48]Thomas E. Patterson, *Out of Order* (New York: Knopf, 1992).

[49]Robert Entman, "Framing: Towards Clarification of a Fractured Paradigm," in Denis McQuail, ed., *McQuail's Reader in Mass Communication Theory* (London: Sage, 2002), 391–92.

[50]The classic study of priming is Shanto Iyengar, Mark Peters, and Donald Kinder, "Experimental Demonstrations of the 'Not-So-Minimal' Consequences of Television News Programs," *The American Political Science Review,* 76 (1982): 848–58.

[51]The classic study of priming is Shanto Iyengar, Mark Peters, and Donald Kinder, "Experimental Demonstrations of the 'Not-So-Minimal' Consequences of Television News Programs," *The American Political Science Review,* 76 (1982): 848–58.

[52]See, for example, Steve Scalise, "Biden's agenda raised prices on everything for everyone," Fox News, April 19, 2022, https://www.foxnews.com/opinion/biden-democrats-inflation-prices-steve-scalise; "Inflation, supply chain problems, and labor shortages are driving up wages and costs," MSNBC, April 16, 2022, https://www.msn.com/en-us/news/other/inflation-supply-chain-problems-and-labor-shortages-are-driving-up-wages-and-costs/vi-AAR6cXQ?%2525252525252525253Bocid=hmlogout.

[53]Greg Prince, "Trump's Tweets Are Seen by Less Than One Percent of His Followers, Social Media Expert Claims," *Newsweek,* January 3, 2018, http://www.newsweek.com/trump-tweets-one-percent-mainstream-media-769207.

[54]See, for example, Joseph N. Cappella and Kathleen Hall Jamieson, *Spiral of Cynicism* (New York: Oxford University Press, 1997), 159.

[55]Craig Silverman, "Lies, Damn Lies, and Viral Content," Tow Center for Digital Journalism, Columbia University, February 10, 2015, https://www.cjr.org/tow_center_reports/craig_silverman_lies_damn_lies_viral_content.php.

[56]Thomas E. Patterson, *Out of Order* (New York: Knopf, 1993).

[57]Based on numerous studies, especially those conducted by Center for Media and Public Affairs.

[58]See, for example, Mark Rozell, "Press Coverage of Congress," in Thomas Mann and Norman Ornstein, eds., *Congress, the Press, and the Public* (Washington, D.C.: American Enterprise Institute and Brookings Institution, 1994), 109.

[59]Jay Rosen, *What Are Journalists For?* (New Haven, Conn.: Yale University Press, 1999), 295; Thomas E. Patterson, *How America Lost Its Mind* (Norman: Oklahoma University Press, 2019), 61–62.

[60]Eric Alterman, *What Liberal Media?* (New York: Basic Books, 2008),

[61]See, for example, Hayes Brown, "It's about time the House Jan. 6 Committee flexed on Kevin McCarthy," MSNBC, May 12, 2022, https://www.msnbc.com/opinion/msnbc-opinion/jan-6-committee-adds-needed-pressure-kevin-mccarthy-trump-allies-n1295399; Julia Musto, "Mark Meadows: Jan. 6 House panel sought to publicly 'vilify' him," Fox News, April 30, 2022, https://www.foxnews.com/politics/mark-meadows-jan-6-house-panel-sought-to-publicly-vilify-him.

[62]See, for example, Thomas E. Patterson, *The Mass Media Election* (New York: Praeger, 1980), 159–65.

[63]See, Kevin Arcenaux and Martin Johnson, *Changing Minds of Changing Channels: Partisan News in an Age of Choice* (Chicago: University of Chicago Press, 2013); Thomas E. Patterson, "Young People and News," report of the Joan Shorenstein Center on the Press, Politics, and Public Policy, Kennedy School of Government, Harvard University, July 2007, http://www.hks.harvard.edu/presspol/research/carnegie-knight/young_people_and_news_2007.pdf.

[64]Martin P. Wattenberg, *Is Voting for Young People,* 4th ed. (New York: Routledge, 2016), ch. 8.

[65]Sarah Sobieraj and Jeffrey M. Berry, "From Incivility to Outrage: Political Discourse in Blogs, Talk Radio, and Cable News," *Political Communication,* 28 (2011): 27.

[66]Sarah Sobieraj and Jeffrey M. Berry, "From Incivility to Outrage: Political Discourse in Blogs, Talk Radio, and Cable News," *Political Communication,* 28 (2011): 27–28.

[67]Sarah Sobieraj and Jeffrey M. Berry, "From Incivility to Outrage: Political Discourse in Blogs, Talk Radio, and Cable News," *Political Communication,* 28 (2011): 30.

[68]See, for example, Rachel Maddow, "Inequality meets corporate greed," MSNBC, November 22, 2011, https://www.msnbc.com/rachel-maddow-show/income-inequality-meets-corporate-greed-msna33920.

[69]Yochai Benkler, Robert Faris, and Hal Roberts, *Network Propaganda: Manipulation, Disinformation, and Radicalization in American Politics* (New York: Oxford University Press, 2018), 13.

[70]Bernard Goldberg, *Bias: A CBS Insider Exposes How the Media Distort News* (New York: Harper Paperbacks, 2003).

[71]David D'Alessio and Mike Allen, "Media Bias in Presidential Elections: A Meta-Analysis," *Journal of Communication,* 50 (2000): 133–56.

[72]Matthew Gentzkow and Jesse M. Shapiro, "What Drives Media Slant?" *Econometrica* 78 (2010): 35–71, https://www.jstor.org/stable/25621396.

[73]Thomas E. Patterson, "A Tale of Two Elections," Shorenstein Center on Media, Politics, and Public Policy, Harvard University, December 17, 2020, https://shorensteincenter.org/patterson-2020-election-coverage/.

[74]Based on data provided author by Center for Media and Public Affairs.

[75]Meg Kelly and Elyse Samuels, "How Russia Weaponized Social Media, Got Caught, and Escaped Consequences," *The Washington Post,* November 18, 2019, https://www.washingtonpost.com/politics/2019/11/18/how-russia-weaponized-social-media-got-caught-escaped-consequences/.

[76]Nicholas Confessore and Daisuke Wakabayashi, "Russians Spun American Rage Into a Weapon," *The New York Times*, October 10, 2017.

[77]See, for example, "Fact vs. Fiction: Russian Disinformation on Ukraine," U.S. Department of State, January 20, 2022, https://www.state.gov/fact-vs-fiction-russian-disinformation-on-ukraine/.

[78]W. Lance Bennett and Steven Livingston, "The Disinformation Order: Disruptive Communication and the Decline of Democratic Institutions," *European Journal of Communication* 33 (2018); 122–139.

[79]Quoted in Stephen Bates, *Realigning Journalism with Democracy: The Hutchins Commission, Its Times, and Ours* (Washington, D.C.: The Annenberg Washington Program of Northwestern University, 1995), 11.

[80]Thomas E. Patterson, "Doing Well and Doing Good," Joan Shorenstein Center on the Press, Politics, and Public Policy, Kennedy School of Government, Harvard University, December 2000, http://www.hks.harvard.edu/presspol/publications/reports/soft_news_and_critical_journalism_2000.pdf.

[81]Patterson, "Doing Well and Doing Good," 3–5; see also Michele Weldon, *Everyman News: The Changing American Front Page* (Columbus: University of Missouri Press, 2007), 37; Walter C. Dean and Atiba Pertilla, "I-Teams and 'Eye Candy': The Reality of Local TV News," in Tom Rosensteil, Marion Just, Todd L. Belt, Atiba Pertilla, Walter Dean, and Dante Chinni, eds., *We Interrupt This Newscast* (New York: Cambridge University Press, 2007), 31–35; Matthew Robert Kerbel, *If It Bleeds It Leads* (New York: Basic Books, 2000).

[82]Mark Thompson, *Enough Said: What's Gone Wrong with the Language of Politics* (New York: St. Martin's Press, 2016), 106.

[83]Foer, *World Without Mind,* 139.

[84]Franklin Foer, *World Without Mind: The Existential Threat of Big Tech* (New York: Penguin Press, 2017), 147. Reference to the number of users is from CrowdTangle's website.

[85]See, for example, Deborah Serani, "If It Bleeds, It Leads," *Psychoanalysis and Psychotherapy* 24 (2008): 240–250, https://www.researchgate.net/publication/247898920_If_It_Bleeds_It_Leads_The_Clinical_Implications_of_Fear-Based_Programming_in_News_Media.

[86]"Ebola Worries Rise, But Most Are 'Fairly' Confident in Government, Hospitals to Deal With Disease," Pew Research Center, October 21, 2014, https://www.pewresearch.org/politics/2014/10/21/ebola-worries-rise-but-most-are-fairly-confident-in-government-hospitals-to-deal-with-disease/.

[87]Neil Postman, *Amusing Ourselves to Death: Public Discourse in the Age of Show Business* (New York: Viking, 1985), 106.

[88]Wattenberg, *Is Voting for Young People?*, 75–80.

[89]Nielsen Company audience report, 2017.

[90]Herbert A. Simon, "Designing Organizations for an Information-Rich World," in Martin Greenberger, ed., *Computers, Communication, and the Public Interest* (Baltimore, Md.: Johns Hopkins University Press, 1971), 40–41.

[91]Kevin McSpadden, "You Now Have a Shorter Attention Span Than a Goldfish," *Time,* May 14, 2015, http://time.com/3858309/attention-spans-goldfish/.

[92]"U.S. Texting Statistics," The Local Project, undated, downloaded on May 12, 2022, https://www.localproject.net/docs/texting-stats/.

[93]"Daily time spent reading newspapers per capita in the United States from 2010 to 2018 (in minutes)," Statista. Downloaded October 24, 2017: https://www.statista.com/statistics/186934/us-newspaper-reading-habits-since-2002/

[94]Ryan Chittum, "Print Newspapers Still Dominate Readers' Attention: Another Look at How Much Time Is Spent Reading Newspapers Online and in Print," *Columbia Journalism Review,* October 31, 2017, http://archives.cjr.org/the_audit/newspapers_time_spent.php.

[95]Letter of Thomas Jefferson to Richard Price, January 8, 1789.

[96]Thomas E. Patterson, *How America Lost Its Mind* (Norman, OK: University of Oklahoma Press, 2019), 31.

CHAPTER ELEVEN

[1]Roger H. Davidson and Walter J. Oleszek, *Congress and Its Members,* 10th ed. (Washington, D.C.: CQ Press, 2008), 4.

[2]See Paul S. Herrnson, *Congressional Elections: Campaigning at Home and in Washington,* 7th ed. (Washington, D.C.: CQ Press, 2012).

[3]See Gary C. Jacobson, *The Politics of Congressional Elections,* 8th ed. (New York: Longman, 2012).

[4]David Mayhew, *Congress: The Electoral Connection* (New Haven, Conn.: Yale University Press, 2004), 5.

[5]Bruce Cain, John Ferejohn, and Morris P. Fiorina, *The Personal Vote* (Cambridge, Mass.: Harvard University Press, 1987).

[6]Information provided by Clerk of the House.

[7]Lara E. Chausow, R. Eric Peterson, and Amber Hope Wilhelm, "Senate Staff Levels in Member, Committee, Leadership, and Other Offices, 1977–2014," Congressional Research Service, March 19, 2015, https://www.scribd.com/doc/315590129/Senate-Staff-Levels-in-Member-Committee-Leadership-And-Other-Offices-1977-2014.

[8]"Total Number of MPs, Peers and Staff," House of Commons Library, October 3, 2016. House of Commons members who hold leadership positions have larger staffs than the three people of the typical member.

[9]Edward Sidlow, *Challenging the Incumbent: An Underdog's Undertaking* (Washington, D.C.: CQ Press, 2003); David C. W. Parker, *The Power of Money in Congressional Campaigns, 1880–2006* (Norman: University of Oklahoma Press, 2008). See also Marian Currinder, *Money in the House: Campaign Funds and Congressional Party Politics* (Boulder, Colo.: Westview Press, 2008).

[10]Federal Election Commission data.

[11]OpenSecrets.org data, 2018.

[12]A race without an incumbent—called an open-seat election—typically brings out a strong, well-funded candidate from each party when the parties are closely matched in a state or district.

[13]Federal Election Commission data, 2020.

[14]*Rucho v. Common Cause,* No. 18-422 (2019).

[15]Bill Bishop, *The Big Sort: Why the Clustering of Like-Minded America Is Tearing Us Apart* (New York: Houghton Mifflin, 2008).

[16]Jesse Sussell and James A. Thomson, "Are Changing Constituencies Driving Rising Polarization in the U.S. House of Representatives," Rand Corporation, 2015, https://www.rand.org/pubs/research_reports/RR896.html. See also Thomas E. Mann, "Polarizing the House of Representatives: How Much Does Gerrymandering Matter?" in Pietro S. Nivola and David W. Brady, eds., *Red and Blue Nation? Characteristics and Causes of America's Polarized Politics,* Vol. 1 (Washington, D.C.: Brookings Institution Press, 2006).

[17]Quoted in "A Tale of Myths and Measures: Who Is Truly Vulnerable?" *Congressional Quarterly Weekly Report,* December 4, 1993, 7; see also Dennis F. Thompson, *Ethics in Congress* (Washington, D.C.: Brookings Institution, 1995).

[18]The classic formulation of this theory is Angus Campbell, "Surge and decline: A study of electoral change," *Public Opinion Quarterly,* 24 (1960): 397–418. https://doi.org/10.1086/266960

[19]James E. Campbell, *The Presidential Pulse of Congressional Elections* (Lexington: University Press of Kentucky, 1993).

[20]Robert Erikson, "The Puzzle of Midterm Losses," *Journal of Politics,* 50 (November 1988): 1011–29.

[21]Exit polls, 2022.

[22]See Eric D. Lawrence, Forrest Maltzman, and Steven S. Smith, "Who Wins? Party Effects in Legislative Voting," *Legislative Studies Quarterly,* 31 (2006): 33–69; Elaine C. Kamarck, "Increasing Turnout in Congressional Primaries," Brookings Institution, July 2014, 10, https://www.brookings.edu/wp-content/uploads/2016/06/KamarckIncreasing-Turnout-in-Congressional-Primaries72614.pdf.

[23]Elaine C. Kamarck and James Wallner, "Anticipating Trouble: Congressional Primaries and Incumbent Behavior," Brookings Institution, October 2018, https://www.brookings.edu/wpcontent/ uploads/2018/10/GS_10292018_Primaries-and-Incumbent-Behavior.pdf; Sean M. Theriault, *Party Polarization in Congress* (New York: Cambridge University Press, 2008); Barry C. Burden, "Candidate Positions in U.S. Congressional Elections," *British Journal of Political Science,* 34 (2004): 211–27.

[24]Eliana Johnson, "Ingraham's Insurrection," *National Review,* June 12, 2014, www.

nationalreview.com/2014/06/ ingrahamsinsurrection-eliana-johnson.

[25]Linda L. Fowler and Robert D. McClure, *Political Ambition* (New Haven, Conn.: Yale University Press, 1989).

[26]Jo Mannies, "Outside money played outsized role in McCaskill-Hawley Senate race," St. Louis Public Radio, December 4, 2018, https://news. stlpublicradio.org/post/outside-money-played-outsized-role-mccaskill-hawley-senate-race# stream/0.

[27]*Congressional Quarterly Weekly Report,* various dates.

[28]Kenneth Lowande, Melinda Ritchie and Erinn Lauterbach, "Descriptive and Substantive Representation in Congress: Evidence from 80,000 Congressional Inquiries," *American Journal of Political Science* 63 (2019): 644–659. https://www.jstor.org/stable/45132502

[29]Cited in Ryan Lizza, "The Obama Memos," *The New Yorker,* January 30, 2012, 36.

[30]Steven Smith, *Party Influence in Congress* (New York: Cambridge University Press, 2007); Barbara Sinclair, *Party Wars: Polarization and the Politics of National Policy Making* (Norman: University of Oklahoma Press, 2006).

[31]Danielle Thomsen, *Opting Out of Congress* (New York: Cambridge University Press, 2017).

[32]Frances E. Lee, *Insecure Majorities: Congress and the Perpetual Campaign* (Chicago: University of Chicago Press, 2016), 200–3.

[33]Frances E. Lee, *Insecure Majorities: Congress and the Perpetual Campaign* (Chicago: University of Chicago Press, 2016), 200–3, 139.

[34]Quoted in Jonathan Rauch, "How American Politics Went Insane," *The Atlantic,* July/August 2016, https://www.theatlantic.com/magazine/ archive/2016/07/how-american-politics-went-insane/485570/.

[35]Elaina Plott, "Paul Ryan Pledges: No Immigration Reform Under Obama," *National Review,* October 27, 2015, https://www. nationalreview.com/2015/10/paul-ryan-promises-no-immigration-reform-obama-administration/.

[36]Unlike the Speaker of the House, the Senate majority leader is not the chamber's presiding officer. The Constitution assigns this position to the vice president of the United States. But because the vice president is allowed to vote only in case of a tie, the vice president rarely attends Senate sessions. In the absence of the vice president, the president pro tempore (temporary president) has the right to preside over the Senate. By tradition, the president pro tempore is the majority party's most senior member, but the position is largely honorary. The Senate's presiding officer has no real power because any senator who wants to speak on a bill has the right to do so.

[37]Quoted in Stephen E. Frantzich and Claude Berube, *Congress: Games and Strategies* (Lanham, Md.: Rowman & Littlefield, 2009), 159.

[38]Jane Mayer, "How Mitch McConnell Became Trump's Enabler-in-Chief," *The New Yorker,* April 12, 2020. https://www.newyorker.com/ magazine/2020/04/20/how-mitch-mcconnell-became-trumps-enabler-in-chief

[39]Randall Strahan, *Leading Representatives: The Agency of Leaders in the Politics of the U.S. House* (Baltimore, Md.: Johns Hopkins University Press, 2007); David King, *Turf Wars* (Chicago: University of Chicago Press, 1997).

[40]See Stephen E. Frantzich and Steven E. Schier, *Congress: Games and Strategies* (Dubuque, Iowa: Brown & Benchmark, 1995), 127.

[41]See Gerald S. Strom, *The Logic of Lawmaking* (Baltimore, Md.: Johns Hopkins University Press, 1990).

[42]Pew Research Center, "Beyond Distrust: How Americans View Their Government," November 23, 2015, http://www.people-press. org/2015/11/23/beyond-distrust-how-americans-view-their-government/.

[43]John R. Hibbing and Elizabeth Theiss-Morse, *Stealth Democracy: Americans' Belief About How Government Should Work* (New York: Cambridge University Press, 2002).

[44]See Barbara Sinclair, *Unorthodox Lawmaking: New Legislative Processes in the U.S. Congress,* 3rd ed. (Washington, D.C.: CQ Press, 2007).

[45]See Gary Orfield, *Congressional Power: Congress and Social Change* (New York: Harcourt Brace Jovanovich, 1975).

[46]James L. Sundquist, "Congress and the President: Enemies or Partners?" in Lawrence C. Dodd and Bruce I. Oppenheimer, eds., *Congress Reconsidered* (New York: Praeger, 1977), 240.

[47]Kelly Dittmar, Kira Sanbonmatsu, Susan J. Carroll, Debbie Walsh, and Catherine Wineinger, "Representation Matters: Women in the U.S. Congress," Center for American Women and Politics, Eagleton Institute of Politics, Rutgers University, 2017,

https://cawp.rutgers.edu/sites/default/files/resources/representationmatters.pdf.

[48]Sarah F. Anzia and Christopher R. Berry, "The Jackie (and Jill) Robinson Effect: Why Do Congresswomen Outperform Congressmen?" *American Journal of Political Science,* 55 (2011): 478-93, https://onlinelibrary.wiley.com/doi/abs/10.1111/j.1540-5907.2011.00512.x.

[49]Craig Volden, Alan E. Wiseman, and Dana E. Wittmer, "Women's Issues and Their Fates in the US Congress," *Political Science Research & Methods,* 40 (2018): 679-96, https://www.cambridge.org/core/journals/political-science-research-and-methods/article/womens-issues-and-their-fates-in-the-us-congress/817B6C136C6CC03F4A13514A93E4AAEA.

[50]Brian Frederick, "Are Female House Member Still More Liberal in a Polarized Era," *Congress & the Presidency,* 36 (2009): 181-202, https://www.tandfonline.com/doi/abs/10.1080/07343460902948097.

[51]Judith Warner, "104 Women in Congress. Does It Matter?," *Politico Magazine,* January/February 2015, https://www.politico.com/magazine/story/2015/01/104-women-in-congress-does-it-matter-113903.

[52]Barry C. Burden, *Personal Roots of Representation* (Princeton, N.J.: Princeton University Press, 2007).

[53]Keith Krehbiel, "Are Congressional Committees Composed of Preference Outliers?" *American Political Science Review,* 84 (1990): 149-64; Richard L. Hall and Bernard Grofman, "The Committee Assignment Process and the Conditional Nature of Committee Bias," *American Political Science Review,* 84 (1990): 1149-66.

[54]See, for example, Alan Abramowitz, *The Disappearing Center: Engaged Citizens, Polarization and American Democracy* (New Haven, Conn.: Yale University Press, 2011).

[55]Joel A. Aberbach and Mark A. Peterson, eds., *The Executive Branch* (New York: Oxford University Press, 2005), 534-35.

[56]Joel Aberbach, *Keeping a Watchful Eye* (Washington, D.C.: Brookings Institution, 1990); David Rosenbloom, *Building a Congress Centered Public Administration* (Tuscaloosa: University of Alabama Press, 2001).

[57]Lauren Carroll, *PolitiFact,* July 6, 2017, http://www.politifact.com/truth-o-meter/article/2017/jul/06/17-intelligence-organizations-or-four-either-way-r/.

CHAPTER TWELVE

[1]Jeffrey Goldberg, "James Mattis Denounces President Trump, Describes Him as a Threat to the Constitution," *The Atlantic,* June 3, 2020, https://www.theatlantic.com/politics/archive/2020/06/james-mattis-denounces-trump-protests-militarization/612640/.

[2]James W. Davis, *The American Presidency* (New York: Harper & Row, 1987), 13; Sidney Milkis and Michael Nelson, *The American Presidency: Origins and Development, 1790-2007,* 7th ed. (Washington, D.C.: CQ Press, 2015); see also Bruce Ackerman, *The Failure of the Founding Fathers* (Cambridge, Mass.: Belknap Press of Harvard University Press, 2005).

[3]Jeffrey E. Cohen, *The President's Legislative Policy Agenda* (New York: Cambridge University Press, 2012), pp. 13-15.

[4]See James W. Ceaser, *Presidential Election: Theory and Development* (Princeton, N.J.: Princeton University Press, 1969).

[5]"It's the Media, Stupid, Not Advertising," Media Tenor, March 1, 2020, data provided to author by Media Tenor.

[6]James Bryce, *The American Commonwealth* (New York: Commonwealth Edition, 1908), 230.

[7]Quoted in Wilfred E. Binkley, *President and Congress,* 3rd ed. (New York: Vintage, 1962), 142.

[8]Peri E. Arnold, *Remaking the Presidency* (Lawrence: University Press of Kansas, 2009).

[9]Theodore Roosevelt, *An Autobiography* (New York: Scribner, 1931), 383.

[10]See Richard M. Pious, *The American Presidency* (New York: Basic Books, 1979), 83.

[11]Harry S. Truman, *Years of Trial and Hope* (New York: Signet, 1956), 535.

[12]Erwin C. Hargrove, *The Effective Presidency: Lessons on Leadership from John F. Kennedy to George W. Bush* (Boulder, Colo.: Paradigm, 2007).

[13]Quoted in Richard J. Ellis, *The Development of the American Presidency* (New York: Routledge, 2015), 194.

[14]See Thomas S. Langston, *The Cold War Presidency: A Documentary History* (Washington, D.C.: CQ Press, 2006).

[15]See Garry Wills, *Bomb Power: The Modern Presidency and the National Security State* (New York: Penguin Press, 2010).

[16]Quoted in Duncan Watts, *The American Presidency* (Edinburgh, Scotland: University of Edinburgh Press, 2009), 104.

[17]Aaron Wildavsky, "The Two Presidencies," *Trans-Action,* December 1966, 7.

[18]Pfiffner, *Modern Presidency,* ch. 6.

[19]Quoted in Jonathan Masters, "U.S. Foreign Policy Powers: Congress and the President," Council on Foreign Relations, March 2, 2017, https://www.cfr.org/backgrounder/us-foreign-policy-powers-congress-and-president.

[20]Susan Decker, "Trump's 25% Steel Import Tariffs Upheld by U.S. Appeals Court," *Bloomberg News,* February 28, 2020, https://www.bloomberg.com/news/articles/2020-02-28/trump-s-25-steel-import-tariffs-upheld-by-u-s-appeals-court.

[21]John P. Burke, *The Institutionalized Presidency* (Baltimore, Md.: Johns Hopkins University Press, 1992); Charles E. Walcott and Karen M. Hult, *Governing the White House* (Lawrence: University Press of Kansas, 1995).

[22]Quoted in Stephen J. Wayne, *Road to the White House* (New York: St. Martin's Press, 1992), 143; but see Jody C. Baumgartner, *The American Vice Presidency Reconsidered* (Westport, Conn.: Praeger, 2006).

[23]James E. Hite, *Second Best: The Rise of the American Vice Presidency* (San Diego, CA: Cognella Academic Publishing, 2013).

[24]Barton Gellman, *Angler: The Cheney Vice Presidency* (New York: Anchor Books, 2008).

[25]Matthew Rozsa, "Trump depends on Sean Hannity's help every night," Salon, May 14, 2018. https://www.salon.com/2018/05/14/trump-depends-on-sean-hannitys-help-every-night-report/

[26]See Jeffrey E. Cohen, *The Politics of the United States Cabinet* (Pittsburgh, Pa.: University of Pittsburgh Press, 1988); Shirley Anne Warshaw, *Powersharing: White House–Cabinet Relations in the Modern Presidency* (Albany: State University of New York Press, 1995).

[27]State Department data as of 2020.

[28]James Pfiffner, *The Modern Presidency* (New York: St. Martin's Press, 1994), 123; James Pfiffner, "Recruiting Executive Branch Leaders: The Office of Presidential Personnel," Brookings Institution, Spring 2001, www.brookings.edu/research/articles/2001/03/spring-governance-pfiffner.

[29]Quoted in James MacGregor Burns, "Our Super-Government—Can We Control It?" *The New York Times,* April 24, 1949, 32.

[30]See Paul C. Light, *Thickening Government: Federal Hierarchy and the Diffusion of Accountability* (Washington, D.C.: Brookings Institution, 1995).

[31]Peter Baker, Katie Benner, and Michael D. Shear, "Jeff Sessions Is Forced Out as Attorney General as Trump Installs Loyalist," *The New York Times,* November 7, 2018, https://www.nytimes.com/2018/11/07/us/politics/sessions-resigns.html.

[32]Stephen Skowronek, *The Politics Presidents Make* (Cambridge, Mass.: Belknap Press of Harvard University, 1997).

[33]Erwin Hargrove, *The Power of the Modern Presidency* (New York: Knopf, 1974); see also John H. Kessel, *Presidents, the Presidency, and the Political Environment* (Washington, D.C.: CQ Press, 2001); Skowronek, *Presidential Leadership in Political Time.*

[34]John P. Burke, *Presidential Power: Theories and Dilemmas* (Boulder, Colo.: Westview Press, 2016).

[35]Charles O. Jones, *The Presidency in a Separated System* (Washington, D.C.: Brookings Institution, 2005).

[36]Thomas P. (Tip) O'Neill, with William Novak, *Man of the House: The Life and Political Memoirs of Speaker Tip O'Neill* (New York: Random House, 1987), 297, 33.

[37]Quoted in Ryan Lizza, "The Obama Memos," *The New Yorker,* January 30, 2012, 44.

[38]Sanford Levinson and Jack M. Balkin, *Democracy and Dysfunction* (Chicago, IL: University of Chicago Press, 2019).

[39]John T. Bennett, "Trump's Winning Pattern with Legislation Might Become a Thing of the Past: CQ Vote Studies," *Roll Call,* February 28, 2019, https://www.rollcall.com/2019/02/28/trumps-winning-pattern-with-legislation-might-become-a-thing-of-the-past-cq-vote-studies/.

[40]"Tracking Congress in the Age of Trump," *FiveThirtyEight,* https://projects.fivethirtyeight.com/congress-trump-score/votes/.

[41]Quoted in Lizza, "The Obama Memos," 49.

[42]Matthew Eshbaugh-Soha, *Breaking Through the Noise: Presidential Leadership, Public Opinion, and the News Media* (Palo Alto, CA: Stanford University Press, 2011), p. 16; Jeffrey E. Cohen, "The Presidency and the Mass Media," *The Oxford Handbook of the American Presidency* (New York: Oxford University Press, 2009).

[43]Brandice Canes-Wrone and Scott de Marchi, "Presidential Approval and Legislative Success," *The Journal of Politics* 64 (2002): 491–509.

[44]Michael D. Shear, Maggie Haberman, Nicholas Confessore, Karen Yourish, Larry Buchanan, and Keith Collins, "How Trump Reshaped the Presidency in Over 11,000 Tweets," *The New York Times*, November 2, 2019, https://www.nytimes.com/interactive/2019/11/02/us/politics/trump-twitter-presidency.html.

[45]Sidney Blumenthal, *The Permanent Campaign* (Boston: Beacon Press, 1980); Brendan J. Doherty, *The Rise of the President's Permanent Campaign* (Lawrence, KS: University of Kansas Press, 2012).

[46]Samuel Kernell, *Going Public: New Strategies of Presidential Leadership*, 3rd ed. (Washington, D.C.: CQ Press, 1997), 1; see also Robert M. Eisinger, *The Evolution of Presidential Polling* (New York: Cambridge University Press, 2003); Stephen J. Farnsworth and S. Robert Lichter, *Mediated Presidency: Television News & Presidential Governance* (Lanham, Md.: Rowman & Littlefield, 2005).

[47]Anthony Corrado and Kathryn Dunn Tenpas, "Permanent Campaign Brushes Aside Tradition," Brookings Institution, March 30, 2004, https://www.brookings.edu/opinions/permanent-campaign-brushes-aside-tradition/.

[48]Thomas E. Patterson, "News Coverage of Donald Trump's First 100 Days," Shorenstein Center on Media, Politics and Public Policy, Harvard Kennedy School, Harvard University, Cambridge, MA, May 18, 2017, https://shorensteincenter.org/news-coverage-donald-trumps-first-100-days/; Michael Wolff, *Fire and Fury: Inside the Trump White House* (New York: Henry Holt, 2018); Julia Carrie Wong, "'Way Ahead of the Field': Inside Trump's Unprecedented Social Media Campaign," *The Guardian*, July 3, 2019, https://www.theguardian.com/us-news/2019/jul/02/way-ahead-of-the-field-inside-the-trump-campaigns-unprecedented-social-media-campaign.

[49]David Goetsch, *Effective Leadership* (Upper Saddle River, N.J.: Prentice-Hall, 2004).

[50]Stephen Skowronek, *Presidential Leadership in Political Time* (Lawrence: University of Kansas Press, 2008).

[51]Brian Karem, "Joe Biden Has a Problem," The Washington Diplomat, August 24, 2021. https://washdiplomat.com/op-ed-joe-biden-has-a-problem/

[52]Joe Klein, "The Perils of the Permanent Campaign," *Time*, October 5, 2005, http://content.time.com/time/magazine/article/0,9171,1124332,00.html.

[53]David A. Graham, "Trump Never Stopped Campaigning Long Enough to Govern," *The Atlantic*, June 18, 2019, https://www.theatlantic.com/ideas/archive/2019/06/trump-cant-relaunch-a-campaign-that-never-stopped/591949/.

[54]Richard E. Neustadt, *Presidential Power and the Modern Presidents* (New York: Free Press, 1990), 71–72.

[55]This figure includes formal presidential memorandums, which have the same legal status as executive orders but take a somewhat different form.

[56]*United States v. Belmont*, 57 U.S. 758 (1937).

[57]Robert DiClerico, *The American President*, 6th ed. (Englewood Cliffs, N.J.: Prentice-Hall, 1999), 47.

[58]See, for example, Barry M. Blechman and Stephen S. Kaplan, *Force Without War* (Washington, D.C.: Brookings Institution, 1978); Arthur M. Schlesinger Jr., *War and the American Presidency* (New York: Norton, 2004).

[59]Quoted in Antonio Thompson and Christos Frentzos, *The Routledge Handbook of American Military and Diplomatic History* (New York: Routledge, 2013), 301.

[60]Matt Compton, "We Can't Wait: President Obama in Nevada," The White House, October 24, 2011, https://obamawhitehouse.archives.gov/blog/2011/10/24/we-cant-wait-president-obama-nevada.

[61]William Bullitt, *Thomas Woodrow Wilson: A Psychological Study* (Boston: Houghton Mifflin, 1966).

[62]James David Barber, *The Presidential Character: Predicting Performance in the White House* (Englewood Cliffs, NJ: Prentice-Hall, 1972).

[63]See, for example, Walter Shapiro, "Essay: The Character Issue: Enough Already," *Time*, December 7, 1987, http://content.time.com/time/subscriber/article/0,33009,966148-2,00.html.

[64]See, for example, Aubrey Immelman and Anne Marie Griebie, "The personality profile and leadership style of U.S. president Donald J. Trump in office," paper presented at the 43rd Annual Scientific Meeting of the International Society of Political Psychology, Berlin, Germany, July 14–16, 2020. http://digitalcommons.csbsju.edu/psychology_pubs/129/

[65]See, Stephen G. Walker, "The Psychology of Presidential Decision Making," in George C. Edwards III and William G. Howell, eds., *The Oxford Handbook of the American Presidency* (New York: Oxford University Press, 2010).

[66]Glenn Kessler and Meg Kelly, "President Trump Made 2,140 False or Misleading Claims in His First Year," *The Washington Post,* January 20, 2018, https://www.washingtonpost.com/news/fact-checker/wp/2018/01/20/president-trump-made-2140-false-or-misleading-claims-in-his-first-year/?utm_term=.c2f5bab7d97f.

[67]Paul Light, *Presidents' Agenda* (Baltimore, Md.: Johns Hopkins University Press, 1999).

[68]James P. Pfiffner, *The Strategic Presidency: Hitting the Ground Running,* 2nd ed. (Chicago: Dorsey Press, 1996).

[69]John E. Mueller, "Presidential Popularity from Truman to Johnson," *American Political Science Review,* 64 (March 1970): 18–34; Kathleen Frankovic, "Public Opinion in the 1992 Campaign," in Gerald M. Pomper, ed., *The Election of 1992* (Chatham, N.J.: Chatham House, 1993); Chris J. Dolan, *The Presidency and Economic Policy* (Lanham, Md.: Rowman & Littlefield, 2007).

[70]Hugh Heclo, "Introduction: The Presidential Illusion," in Hugh Heclo and Lester M. Salamon, eds., *The Illusion of Presidential Government* (Boulder, Colo.: Westview Press, 1981), 2.

Chapter Thirteen

[1]Max Weber, *Economy and Society* (New York: Bedminster Press, 1968), 223. Translated and edited by Guenther Roth and Claus Wittich. Originally published in 1921.

[2]Michael Laris, Ian Duncan, and Lori Aratani, "FAA's Lax Oversight Played Part in Boeing 737 Max Crashes, but Agency Is Pushing to Become More Industry-Friendly," *The Washington Post,* October 28, 2019, https://www.washingtonpost.com/local/trafficandcommuting/faas-lax-oversight-played-part-in-boeing-737-max-crashes-but-agency-is-pushing-to-become-more-industry-friendly/2019/10/27/bc0bf184-f4e1-11e9-ad8b-85e2aa00b5ce_story.html.

[3]Reason-Rupe poll, July 2014.

[4]Charles T. Goodsell, *The Case for Bureaucracy,* 2d ed. (Chatham, N.J.: Chatham House, 1985), 55-60.

[5]Paul C. Light, "Cascade of Failures: Why Government Fails, and How to Stop It," Brookings Institution, July 2014, https://www.brookings.edu/wp-content/uploads/2016/06/Light_Cascade-of-Failures_Why-Govt-Fails.pdf.

[6]Ed Pilkington and Tom McCarthy, "The Missing Six Weeks," *The Guardian,* March 28, 2020, https://www.theguardian.com/us-news/2020/mar/28/trump-coronavirus-politics-us-health-disaster

[7]Weber, *Economy and Society,* 23.

[8]Paul Light, *A Government Ill-Executed* (Cambridge, Mass.: Harvard University Press, 2009); "The True Size of Government," Volker Alliance, September 29, 2017, https://www.volckeralliance.org/true-size-government.

[9]See Mark Sauter and James Carafano, *Homeland Security* (New York: McGraw Hill, 2005).

[10]The merit system is overseen by two independent agencies. The Office of Personnel Management supervises the hiring and job classification of federal employees. The Merit Service Protection Board hears appeals from career civil servants who have been fired or face other disciplinary action.

[11]Office of Personnel Management data, 2016.

[12]Gregory A. Huber, *The Craft of Bureaucratic Neutrality: Interests and Influence in Governmental Regulation of Occupational Safety* (New York: Cambridge University Press, 2007); Herbert Kaufman, "Emerging Conflicts in the Doctrine of Public Administration," *American Political Science Review* 50 (December 1956): 1060.

[13]Woodrow Wilson, "The Study of Administration," *Political Science Quarterly* 2 (1887): 197-222.

[14]See Allen Schick, *The Federal Budget: Politics, Policy, Process,* 3rd ed. (Washington, D.C.: Brookings Institution, 2007).

[15]Zeeshan Aleem, "Trump Wants to Gut the State Department by 25 Percent," *Vox,* February 12, 2018, https://www.vox.com/policy-and-politics/2018/2/12/17004372/trump-budget-state-department-defense-cuts.

[16]See Cornelius M. Kerwin, *Rulemaking,* 3rd ed. (Washington, D.C.: CQ Press, 2003); Daniel E. Hall, *Administrative Law: Bureaucracy in a Democracy* (Upper Saddle River, N.J.: Prentice-Hall, 2005).

[17]Rachel Augustine Potter, *Bending the Rules: Procedural Politicking in the Bureaucracy* (Chicago: University of Chicago Press, 2019).

[18]See Hugh Heclo, *A Government of Strangers* (Washington, D.C.: Brookings Institution, 1977), 117-18.

[19]The classic study of how the work of an agency can become a vocation for its employees is Herbert Kaufman, *The Forest Ranger: A Study in Administrative Behavior* (Baltimore, MD: Johns Hopkins University Press, 1967).

[20]Quoted in Aaron Wildavsky, *The Politics of the Budgetary Process,* 4th ed. (Boston: Little, Brown, 1984), 19; see also Dennis D. Riley, *Bureaucracy and the Policy Process: Keeping the Promises* (Lanham, Md.: Rowman & Littlefield, 2005).

[21]Joel D. Aberbach and Bert A. Rockman, "Clashing Beliefs Within the Executive Branch," *American Political Science Review,* 70 (June 1976): 461.

[22]Norton E. Long, "Power and Administration," *Public Administration Review,* 10 (Autumn 1949): 269; Joel D. Aberbach and Bert A. Rockman, *In the Web of Politics* (Washington, D.C.: Brookings Institution, 2000).

[23]William Niskanen, "Nonmarket Decision Making," *American Economic Review* 58 (1968): 293–305.

[24]See B. Guy Peters, *The Politics of Bureaucracy,* 5th ed. (New York: Routledge, 2001).

[25]See, for example, Ed Blazina, "Transit Leaders Lobby Congress to Restore Federal Grants for New Projects," *Pittsburgh Post-Gazette,* March 19, 2018, http://www.post-gazette.com/news/transportation/2018/03/19/American-Public-Transportation-Association-federal-grants-cut-by-Trump-lobby-Congress-bus-rapid-transit/stories/201803190141.

[26]Long, "Power and Administration," 269; see also John Mark Hansen, *Gaining Access* (Chicago: University of Chicago Press, 1991).

[27]Long, "Power and Administration," 269; see also John Mark Hansen, *Gaining Access* (Chicago: University of Chicago Press, 1991), 118.

[28]See B. Dan Wood and Richard W. Waterman, *Bureaucratic Dynamics* (Boulder, Colo.: Westview Press, 1994); Edward C. Page and Bill Jenkins, *Policy Bureaucracy: Government with a Cast of Thousands* (New York: Oxford University Press, 2005).

[29]Mathew McCubbins, Roger Noll, and Barry Weingast, "Administrative Procedures as Instruments of Political Control," *Journal of Law, Economics, and Organization,* 3 (1987): 243–277.

[30]William T. Gormley Jr. and Steven J. Balla, *Bureaucracy and Democracy* (Washington, D.C.: CQ Press, 2003); Kevin B. Smith, *Public Administration: Power and Politics in the Fourth Branch of Government* (New York: Oxford University Press, 2006).

[31]James P. Pfiffner, "The National Performance Review in Perspective," working paper 94-4, Institute of Public Policy, George Mason University, 1994, 2.

[32]*Seila Law LLC v. Consumer Financial Protection Bureau,* No. 19-7 (2020).

[33]*Seila Law LLC v. Consumer Financial Protection Bureau,* No. 19-7 (2020).

[34]Environmental Integrity Project data, February 2018, http://www.environmentalintegrity.org/news/civil-penalties-decline-under-trump-administration/.

[35]Heclo, *Government of Strangers,* 104.

[36]"EPA Would See Highest Funding Ever Under Biden Budget Plan," Bloomberg Law, March 28, 2022. https://news.bloomberglaw.com/environment-and-energy/epa-would-see-highest-funding-level-ever-under-biden-budget-plan

[37]William F. West, "The Administrative Presidency as Reactive Oversight: Implications for Positive and Normative Theory," *Public Administration Review,* 75 (2015): 523–33.

[38]William F. West, "The Administrative Presidency as Reactive Oversight: Implications for Positive and Normative Theory," *Public Administration Review,* 75 (2015): 225.

[39]See Joel D. Aberbach, *Keeping a Watchful Eye* (Washington, D.C.: Brookings Institution, 1990).

[40]Douglas A. Van Belle and Kenneth M. Mash, *A Novel Approach to Politics* (Washington, D.C.: CQ Press, 2006).

[41]See Donald Kettl, *Deficit Politics* (New York: Macmillan, 1992).

[42]*Pigeford v. Veneman,* U.S. District Court for the District of Columbia, Civil Action No. 97-1978 (1999).

[43]See *Vermont Yankee Nuclear Power Corp. v. National Resources Defense Council, Inc.,* 435 U.S. 519 (1978); *Chevron v. National Resources Defense Council,* 467 U.S. 837 (1984); *Heckler v. Chaney,* 470 U.S. 821 (1985); but see *FDA v. Brown & Williamson Tobacco Co.,* 529 U.S. 120 (2000).

[44]*West Virginia v. Environmental Protection Agency,* No. 20-1530 (2022).

[45]See Mark W. Huddleston, "The Carter Civil Service Reforms," *Political Science Quarterly,* (Winter 1981–82): 607–22.

[46]Ed O'Keefe, "Senior Executive Service Needs Overhaul, Outside Study Finds," *The Washington Post,* August 20, 2009.

[47]Jordain Carney, "Rand Paul Reads Alleged Whistleblower's Name on Senate Floor," *The Hill,* February 4, 2020, https://thehill.com/homenews/senate/481417-rand-paul-reads-alleged-whistleblowers-name-on-senate-floor.

[48]See Brian J. Cook, *Bureaucracy and Self-Government* (Baltimore, Md.: Johns Hopkins University Press, 1996).

CHAPTER FOURTEEN

[1]*Marbury v. Madison,* 5 U.S. 137 (1803).

[2]*Obergefell v. Hodges,* No 14–556 (2015).

[3]Steven G. Calabresi and James Lindgren, "Term Limits for the Supreme Court: Life Tenure Reconsidered," in Roger C. Cramton and Paul D. Carrington, eds., *Reforming the Court: Term Limits for Supreme Court Justices* (Durham, N.C.: Carolina Academic Press, 2006).

[4]Henry J. Abraham, *The Judicial Process,* 6th ed. (New York: Oxford University Press, 1993), 320–22.

[5]*Marbury v. Madison,* 1 Cranch 137 (1803).

[6]From a letter to the author by Frank Schwartz of Beaver College; this section reflects substantially Professor Schwartz's recommendations to the author, as does the later section that addresses the federal court myth.

[7]*Hutto v. Davis,* 370 U.S. 256 (1982).

[8]*South Carolina v. North Carolina* 558 U.S. 256 (2010).

[9]Supreme Court of the United States data. https://www.supremecourt.gov/about/justicecaseload.aspx.

[10]Henry Glick, *Courts, Politics, and Justice,* 3rd ed. (New York: McGraw Hill, 1993), 120.

[11]See, for example, Stuart H. Teger and Douglas Kosinski, "The Cue Theory of Supreme Court Certiorari Jurisdiction: A Reconsideration," *The Journal of Politics,* 42 (1980): 834–846; Rebecca Salokar, *The Solicitor General: The Politics of Law* (Philadelphia, PA: Temple University Press, 1994); Sam Gersten, "Supreme Court Decision-Making," *Penn Journal of Philosophy, Politics & Economics* 10 (2015): 67–98. https://repository.upenn.edu/spice/vol10/iss1/4

[12]For the content of this paragraph, the author is indebted to Professor Tony Wiley of Dodge City Community College.

[13]Timothy R. Johnson, Paul Wahlbeck, and James Spriggs, "The Influence of Oral Arguments on the U.S. Supreme Court," *American Political Science Review,* 100 (2006): 99–113.

[14]Lawrence Baum, *The Supreme Court,* 8th ed. (Washington, D.C.: CQ Press, 2003), 120.

[15]Stephen I. Vladeck, "The Solicitor General and the Shadow Docket," *Harvard Law Review* 132 (2019): 123–163. chrome-extension://efaidnbmnnnibpcajpcglclefindmkaj/https://harvardlawreview.org/wp-content/uploads/2019/11/123-163_Online.pdf

[16]John Fritze, "Senate battles over Supreme Court 'shadow docket' in the wake of Texas abortion law," *USA Today,* September 29, 2021. https://www.usatoday.com/story/news/politics/2021/09/29/senate-battles-over-supreme-court-shadow-docket-after-abortion-ruling/5895306001/

[17]*Obergefell v. Hodges,* No 14–556 (2015).

[18]See Richard Davis, *Electing Justices* (New York: Oxford University Press, 2005).

[19]Robert Scigliano, *The Supreme Court and the Presidency* (New York: Free Press, 1971), 146; see also Lee Epstein and Jack Knight, *The Choices Justices Make* (Washington, D.C.: CQ Press, 1998); Stefanie A. Lundquist, David A. Yalof, and John A. Clark, "The Impact of Presidential Appointments to the Supreme Court: Cohesive and Divisive Voting Within Presidential Blocs," *Political Research Quarterly,* 53 (2000): 795–814.

[20]Quoted in Kermit L. Hall and Kevin T. McGuire, *The Judicial Branch* (New York: Oxford University Press, 2005), 77.

[21]Richard Davis, *Electing Justices* (New York: Oxford University Press, 2005).

[22]See Virginia A. Hettinger et al., *Judging on a Collegial Court: Influences on Federal Appellate Decision Making* (Charlottesville: University of Virginia Press, 2006).

[23]John Gottschall, "Reagan's Appointments to the U.S. Courts of Appeals," *Judicature,* 48 (1986): 54.

[24]See, for example, "Politicization in the Federal Judiciary and Its Effect on the Federal Judicial Function," *New York University Journal of Legislation & Public Policy,* 19 (2017), https://papers.ssrn.com/sol3/papers.cfm?abstract_id=2995008.

[25]Benjamin H. Barton, *The Credentialed Court: Inside the Cloistered, Elite World of American Justice* (New York: Encounter Books, 2022).

[26]Quoted in Louis Fisher, *American Constitutional Law* (New York: McGraw Hill, 1990), 5.

[27]Quoted in Charles P. Curtis, *Law and Large as Life* (New York: Simon & Schuster, 1959), 156–57.

[28]See Lee Epstein and Jack Knight, *The Choices Justices Make* (New York: Longman, 1995); Thomas G. Hansford and James F. Spriggs II, *The Politics of Precedent on the Supreme Court* (Princeton, N.J.: Princeton University Press, 2006).

[29]*Bostock v. Clayton County,* No. 16-1817 (2020).

[30]John Schmidhauser, *The Supreme Court* (New York: Holt, Rinehart & Winston, 1964), 6.

[31]*Whole Woman's Health v. Hellerstedt,* 579 U.S. 582 (2016).

[32]*Dobbs v. Jackson Women's Health Organization,* No.19-1392 (2022).

[33]William M. Landes and Richard A. Posner, "Rational Judicial Behavior: A Statistical Study," *The Journal of Legal Analysis* 1 (2009): 775–831. https://papers.ssrn.com/sol3/papers.cfm?abstract_id=1126403

[34]Quoted in Baum, *Supreme Court,* 37.

[35]Jeffrey A. Segal and Harold J. Spaeth, *The Supreme Court and the Attitudinal Model Revisited* (New York: Cambridge University Press, 2002), 404.

[36]*United States v. Jones,* 565 U.S. 400 (2012).

[37]Devins and Baum, *The Company They Keep.*

[38]Brian Lamb, Susan Swain, and Mark Farkas, *The Supreme Court* (New York: Public Affairs, 2010), 6.

[39]Stephen L. Wasby, *The Supreme Court in the Federal Judicial System,* 4th ed. (Chicago: Nelson-Hall, 1993), 53.

[40]Rob Arthur, "Trump's Justice Department Isn't Enforcing Civil Rights," *Vice News,* February 23, 2018, https://news.vice.com/en_us/article/wj44y4/trumps-justice-department-isnt-enforcing-civil-rights.

[41]See, for example, Evan Tsen Lee, *Judicial Restraint in America* (New York: Oxford University Press, 2011).

[42]See, for example, James R. Rogers and Georg Vanberg, "Resurrecting Lochner: A Defense of Unprincipled Judicial Activism," *Journal of Law, Economics, & Organization* 23 (2007): 442–468.

[43]Antonin Scalia, *A Matter of Interpretation: Federal Courts and the Law* (Princeton, NJ: Princeton University Press, 1998).

[44]Stephen Breyer, "Our Democratic Constitution," James Madison Lecture, New York University Law School, New York, October 22, 2001.

[45]Henry J. Abraham, "The Judicial Function Under the Constitution," *News for Teachers of Political Science,* 41 (Spring 1984): 14.

[46]Frank H. Easterbrook, "Do Liberals and Conservatives Differ in Judicial Activism," *University of Colorado Law Review,* 73 (2002): 1401.

Chapter Fifteen

[1]Marc Allen Eisner, Jeffrey Worsham, and Evan J. Rinquist, *Contemporary Regulatory Policy* (Boulder, Colo.: Lynne Rienner, 2006).

[2]This section relies substantially on Alan Stone, *Regulation and Its Alternatives* (Washington, D.C.: CQ Press, 1982).

[3]See Marc Allen Eisner, *Regulatory Politics in Transition,* 2nd ed. (Baltimore, Md.: Johns Hopkins University Press, 2000).

[4]See Richard A. Harris and Sidney M. Milkis, *The Politics of Regulatory Change* (New York: Oxford University Press, 1996).

[5]Lawrence E. Mitchell, *Corporate Irresponsibility* (New Haven, Conn.: Yale University Press, 2003).

[6]H. Peyton Young, *Equity: In Theory and Practice* (Princeton, N.J.: Princeton University Press, 1995).

[7]Michael Greenwood, "8 Million Lives Saved Since Surgeon General's Tobacco Warning 50 Years Ago," *YaleNews,* January 7, 2014, http://news.yale.edu/2014/01/07/8-million-lives-saved-surgeon-general-s-tobacco-warning-50-years-ago.

[8]Ann E. Marimow, "FDA Can Regulate E-cigarettes Just Like Conventional Cigarettes, Appeals Court Says," *The Washington Post,* December 10, 2019, https://www.washingtonpost.com/local/legal-issues/fda-can-regulate-e-cigarettes-just-like-conventional-cigarettes-appeals-court-says/2019/12/10/e4c28836-cffc-11e9-b29b-a528dc82154a_story.html.

[9]Board on Population Health and Public Health Practice, *The Future of Drug Safety: Promoting and Protecting the Health of the Public* (Washington, D.C.: National Academies Press, 2007).

[10]See Walter A. Rosenbaum, *Environmental Politics and Policy,* 10th ed. (Washington, D.C.: CQ Press, 2016); Norman J. Vig and Michael E. Kraft, eds., *Environmental Policy: New Directions for the Twenty-First Century* (Washington, D.C.: CQ Press, 2003).

[11]Earthobservatory data, 2022. https://earthobservatory.nasa.gov/world-of-change/global-temperatures

[12]*West Virginia v. Environmental Protection Agency,* No. 20-1530 (2022).

[13] *Janus v. American Federation of State, County and Municipal Employees,* No. 16-1466 (2018).

[14] Elliot A. Rosen, *Roosevelt, the Great Depression, and the Economics of Recovery* (Charlottesville: University of Virginia Press, 2007).

[15] See Robert Lekachman, *The Age of Keynes* (New York: Random House, 1966).

[16] See Bruce Bartlett, *Reaganomics: Supply-Side Economics* (Westport, Conn.: Arlington House, 1981).

[17] Paul Krugman, "Hey, Lucky Duckies," *The New York Times,* December 3, 2002, A31.

[18] Alan O. Ebenstein, *Milton Friedman: A Biography* (New York: Palgrave Macmillan, 2007).

[19] Edward Hadas and Hugh Dixon, "Quantitative Easing: A Therapy of Last Resort," *The New York Times,* January 1, 2009, www.nytimes.com/2009/01/11/business/worldbusiness/11iht-views12.1.19248009.html.

[20] Martin Mayer, *FED: The Inside Story of How the World's Most Powerful Financial Institution Drives the Markets* (New York: Free Press, 2001).

CHAPTER SIXTEEN

[1] *Federalist* No. 10.

[2] Chad Stone, Danilo Trisi, Arloc Sherman, and Roderick Taylor, "A Guide to Statistical Trends in Income Inequality," Center on Budget & Policy Priorities, August 29, 2018, https://www.cbpp.org/research/poverty-and-inequality/a-guide-to-statistics-on-historicaltrends-in-income-inequality.

[3] U.S. Census Bureau, 2020.

[4] Emmanuel Saez and Thomas Piketty, "Income Inequality in the United States: 1913-1998," *Quarterly Journal of Economics,* 118 (2003): 1-39.

[5] Paul Krugman, *The Conscience of a Liberal* (New York: Norton, 2007), 7-8.

[6] David Kocieniewski, "Since 1980s, the Kindest of Tax Cuts for the Rich," *The New York Times,* January 18, 2012.

[7] Andrew Flowers, "The Top 1 Percent Earns a Lot from Cashing In on Investments," *FiveThirtyEight,* January 20, 2015, http://fivethirtyeight.com/datalab/the-top-1-percent-earns-a-lot-from-cashing-in-on-investments/.

[8] Kathleen Elkins, "80% of Americans Own an Unbelievably Small Portion of the Country's Wealth," *Business Insider,* June 15, 2015, www.businessinsider.com/inequality-in-the-us-is-much-more-extreme-than-you-think-2015-6.

[9] Adam Looney and Kevin B. Moore, "Changes in the Distribution of After-Tax Wealth: Has Income Tax Policy Increased Wealth Inequality?" Federal Reserve Board, Washington, D.C., 2015.

[10] Thomas L. Hungerford, "Changes in the Distribution of Income Among Tax Filers Between 1996 and 2006: The Role of Labor Income, Capital Income, and Tax Policy," Congressional Research Service, December 29, 2011, Washington, D.C.

[11] Lawrence Mishel, "Unions, Inequality, and Faltering Middle-Class Wages," Economic Policy Institute, August 29, 2012, www.epi.org/publication/ib342-unions-inequality-faltering-middle-class/.

[12] Katie Sanders, "Rattner: Manufacturing Wages Today in America Lower Than Average Wages in the Economy as a Whole,'" *Punditfact,* March 30, 2014, www.politifact.com/punditfact/statements/2014/mar/30/steven-rattner/rattner-manufacturing-wages-today-america-lower-av/.

[13] Stephen Gold, "The Competitive Edge: Manufacturing's Multiplier Effect—It's Bigger Than You Think," *Industry Week,* September 2, 2014, www.industryweek.com/global-economy/competitive-edge-manufacturings-multiplier-effect-its-bigger-you-think.

[14] Economic Policy Institute, "Trump's trade policies have cost thousands of U.S. manufacturing jobs," August 10, 2020. https://www.epi.org/press/trumps-trade-policies-have-cost-thousands-of-u-s-manufacturing-jobs-action-is-urgently-needed-to-rebuild-the-manufacturing-sector-after-the-coronavirus-pandemic/

[15] Kenneth P. Vogel and Jim Tankersley, "With Billions at Stake in Tax Debate, Lobbyists Played Hardball," *The New York Times,* December 15, 2017, https://www.nytimes.com/2017/12/15/us/politics/lobbyists-tax-overhaul-congress.html?mtrref=www.google.com&auth=login-email.

[16] Ben Brody, "Business Groups Spent Big on Lobbying During the Tax Overhaul," *Bloomberg News,* January 23, 2018, https://www.bloomberg.com/news/articles/2018-01-23/tax-bill-prompts-business-to-pay-heavily-for-lobbying-campaigns.

[17] Center on Poverty & Social Policy, Columbia University, March 23, 2022, https://www.povertycenter.columbia.edu/news-internal/monthly-poverty-february-2022.

[18] Phil Harvey and Lisa Conyers, *The Human Cost of Welfare* (Westport, Conn.: Praeger, 2016).

[19] See Felicia Ann Kornbluh, *The Battle for Welfare Rights: Politics and Poverty in Modern*

America (Philadelphia: University of Pennsylvania Press, 2007).

[20]V. O. Key Jr., *The Responsible Electorate* (Cambridge, Mass.: Belknap Press of Harvard University, 1966), 43.

[21]Everett Carll Ladd, *American Political Parties* (New York: Norton, 1970), 205.

[22]The Affordable Care Act was not strictly an antipoverty program, though it had provisions aimed at helping low-income people. The legislation's larger goal was to increase health insurance coverage primarily through mandates on companies and individuals. Most companies with more than 200 employees are now required to provide their employees with health insurance, and most companies with 50 to 200 employees must provide insurance or pay a tax penalty. Individual Americans initially faced a tax penalty if they didn't have health insurance. In 2017, the Republican-controlled Congress eliminated that requirement.

[23]See Jason DeParle, *American Dream: Three Women, Ten Kids, and a Nation's Drive to End Welfare* (New York: Penguin, 2005).

[24]Alberto Alesina and Edward Glaeser, *Fighting Poverty in the U.S. and Europe* (New York: Oxford University Press, 2006).

[25]Kaiser Family Foundation, "A Primer on Medicare Financing," January 31, 2011, http://kff.org/health-reform/issue-brief/a-primer-on-medicare-financing/.

[26]Emily Ekins, "Poll: 77% Say Government Efforts to Fight Poverty Have Been 'Ineffective,'" Cato Institute, September 26, 2019, https://www.cato.org/blog/poll-77-say-government-efforts-fight-poverty-have-been-ineffective;

[27]Charles Murray, *Losing Ground: American Social Policy, 1950-1980* (New York: Basic Books, 1984).

[28]Signe-Mary McKernan and Caroline Ratcliffe, "Events That Trigger Poverty Entries and Exits," *Social Science Quarterly,* 86 (2005): 1146-69.

[29]Signe-Mary McKernan and Caroline Ratcliffe, "Events That Trigger Poverty Entries and Exits," *Social Science Quarterly,* 86 (2005): 1146-69.

[30]See Christopher Howard, *The Welfare State Nobody Knows* (Princeton, N.J.: Princeton University Press, 2006).

[31]Mark Byrnes, "U.S. Spending on Social Welfare Programs Is Way Up, but Far Less of It Goes to the Poorest," *CityLab,* May 19, 2014, https://www.citylab.com/equity/2014/05/us-spending-on-social-welfare-programs-is-way-up-but-far-less-of-it-goes-to-the-poorest/371124/.

[32]Said of George H. W. Bush at the 1988 Democratic Convention. The quote is variously attributed to Ann Richards or Jim Hightower.

[33]For a history of public education, see Joel H. Spring, *The American School 1642-2004* (New York: McGraw Hill, 2008).

[34]*San Antonio Independent School District v Rodriguez,* 411 U.S. 1 (1973).

[35]*The 2012 Kids Count Data Book: State Trends in Child Well-Being,* a report of the Annie E. Casey Foundation, July 25, 2012, www.aecf.org/resources/the-2012-kids-count-data-book/.

[36]Sean F. Reardon, Rachel A. Valentino, Demetra Kalogrides, Kenneth A. Shores, and Erica H. Greenberg, "Patterns and Trends in Racial Academic Achievement Gaps Among States, 1999-2011," Stanford University Graduate School of Education, August, 2013, https://cepa.stanford.edu/sites/default/files/reardon%20et%20al%20state%20achievement%20gaps%20aug2013.pdf.

[37]Based on Organization for Economic Cooperation and Development (OECD) data, 2006; see Douglas S. Reed, *On Equal Terms: The Constitutional Politics of Educational Opportunity* (Princeton, N.J.: Princeton University Press, 2003).

[38]U.S. Department of Education data, 2022.

[39]Stanley Feldman and John Zaller, "The Political Culture of Ambivalence: Ideological Responses to the Welfare State," *American Journal of Political Science,* 36 (1992): 268-307.

[40]Robert E. Lane, "Market Justice, Political Justice," *American Political Science Review,* 80 (June 1986): 383-402.

Chapter Seventeen

[1]See, for example, Peter Trubowitz, *Defining the National Interest* (Chicago: University of Chicago Press, 1997).

[2]Hans J. Morgenthau, *Politics among Nations: The Struggle for Power and Peace* (New York: Knopf, 1948); Kenneth Waltz, *Theory of International Politics* (New York: McGraw-Hill, 1979); John J. Mearsheimer, *The Great Delusion: Liberal Dreams and International Realities* (New Haven, CT: Yale University Press, 2019).

[3]Daniel Deudney and G. John Ikenberry, "The Nature and Sources of Liberal International Order," *Review of International Studies* 25 (1999): 179-196; Andrew Altman and Christopher Heath Wellman, *A Liberal Theory*

of International Justice (New York: Oxford University Press, 2011).

[4]See, for example, Thomas A. Schwartz, *Henry Kissinger and American Power: A Political Biography* (New York: Hill and Wang, 2020).

[5]Joseph Nye, *Bound to Lead: The Changing Nature of American Power* (New York, Basic Books, 1990); Joseph Nye, *Soft Power* (New York: Public Affairs, 2004); Joseph Nye, *The Future of Power* (New York: Public Affairs, 2012).

[6]Joe Myers, "Foreign aid: These countries are the most generous," World Economic Forum, August 19, 2016, https://www.weforum.org/agenda/2016/08/foreign-aid-these-countries-are-the-most-generous/.

[7]Bianca DiJulio, Jamie Firth, and Mollyann Brodie, "Data Note: Americans' Views on the U.S. Role in Global Health," *Kaiser Family Foundation,* January 23, 2015, http://www.kff.org/global-health-policy/poll-finding/data-note-americans-views-on-the-u-s-role-in-global-health/; "As Sequester Deadline Looms, Little Support for Cutting Most Programs," Pew Research Center, February 22, 2013, http://www.people-press.org/2013/02/22/as-sequester-deadline-looms-little-support-for-cutting-most-programs/.

[8]This example and the next one were derived in modified form from "America's top foreign policy successes? Diplomacy, not war," Politics and Current Affairs, June 29, 2018, https://bigthink.com/politics-current-affairs/americas-greatest-foreign-policy-successes-are-from-diplomacy-not-war/.

[9]Megan Darby, "Obama's climate legacy: China, India and the Paris pact," Climate Change News, January 17, 2017, https://www.climatechangenews.com/2017/01/17/obamas-climate-legacy-china-india-and-the-paris-pact/.

[10]"America's top foreign policy successes? Diplomacy, not war," Politics and Current Affairs, June 29, 2018, https://bigthink.com/politics-current-affairs/americas-greatest-foreign-policy-successes-are-from-diplomacy-not-war/.

[11]Thomas Rid and Thomas A. Keaney, eds., *Understanding Counterinsurgency Warfare* (New York: Routledge, 2010).

[12]See Mr. X. (George Kennan), "The Sources of Soviet Conduct," *Foreign Affairs,* 25 (July 1947): 566–82.

[13]David M. Barrett, *Uncertain Warriors: Lyndon Johnson and His Vietnam Advisors* (Lawrence: University Press of Kansas, 1993); see also

Stanley Karnow, *Vietnam: A History* (New York: Penguin, 1983).

[14]See Dag Henriksen, *NATO's Gamble* (Annapolis, MD.: Naval Institute Press, 2007).

[15]Nick Ritchie, *The Political Road to War with Iraq: Bush, 9/11 and the Drive to Overthrow Saddam* (New York: Routledge, 2007).

[16]Pew Research Center for the People and the Press, "Public Attitudes Toward the War in Iraq: 2003–2008," March 19, 2008, http://pewresearch.org/pubs/770/iraq-war-five-year-anniversary.

[17]Abbas Kadhim, "Iraq is forming a new government," Atlantic Council, February 3, 2022, https://www.atlanticcouncil.org/blogs/menasource/iraq-is-forming-a-new-government-but-getting-there-will-be-complicated/.

[18]Quoted in Jeffrey A. Engel, "Putin Wants to Make Russia Great Again," *DallasNews,* October 5, 2017, https://www.dallasnews.com/opinion/commentary/2017/10/05/putin-wants-make-russia-great.

[19]John Mearsheimer, "Why the West is principally responsible for the Ukrainian crisis," *The Economist,* March 19, 2022, https://www.economist.com/by-invitation/2022/03/11/john-mearsheimer-on-why-the-west-is-principally-responsible-for-the-ukrainian-crisis.

[20]Eliot Pence, "To Understand China's Aggressive Foreign Policy, Look at Its Domestic Politics," Council on Foreign Relations, October 8, 2020, https://www.cfr.org/blog/understand-chinas-aggressive-foreign-policy-look-its-domestic-politics.

[21]Andrew Osborn and Mark Trevelyan, "'No forbidden areas' in Russia-China friendship when it comes to defying U.S.," Reuters, February 4, 2022, https://globalnews.ca/news/8594859/russia-china-friendship-against-u-s/.

[22]Remarks of Nicholas Burns, World Affairs Council, Washington, D.C., June 23, 2011.

[23]"Military Expenditures," Stockholm International Peace Research Institute, 2020, https://www.sipri.org/research/armament-and-disarmament/arms-and-military-expenditure/military-expenditure.

[24]George C. Wilson, *This War Really Matters: Inside the Fight for Defense Dollars* (Washington, D.C.: CQ Press, 2000).

[25]John Mueller, "Trends in Popular Support for the Wars in Korea and Vietnam," *American Political Science Review,* 65 (June 1971): 358–75; see also John Mueller, "The Iraq Syndrome," *Foreign Affairs* (November/December 2005).

[26]See, Loch K. Johnson, *America's Secret Power: The CIA in a Democratic Society* (New York: Oxford University Press, 1989).

[27]"The 9/11 Commission Report," National Commission on Terrorist Attacks Upon the United States, undated, downloaded on May 20, 2022, https://govinfo.library.unt.edu/911/report/911Report_Exec.htm.

[28]Erik J. Dahl, "The Plots that Failed," *Studies in Conflict & Terrorism,* 34 (2011): 621–648, DOI: 10.1080/1057610X.2011.582628.

[29]Louise Boyle, "When we make mistakes, we admit them," Daily Mail, December 9, 2014, https://www.dailymail.co.uk/news/article-2867111/CIA-torture-report-reveals-waterboarding-sleep-deprivation.html.

[30]Glenn Kessler, "The Iraq War and WMDs: An intelligence failure or White House spin?" *Washington Post,* March 22, 2019, https://www.washingtonpost.com/politics/2019/03/22/iraq-war-wmds-an-intelligence-failure-or-white-house-spin/.

[31]Brian Michael Jenkins, "Fifteen Years On, Where Are We in the 'War on Terror'?" *Counter Terrorism Center Sentinel,* 9 (2016), https://ctc.usma.edu/fifteen-years-on-where-are-we-in-the-war-on-terror/.

[32]Mallory Shelbourne, "CIA: Director 'stands by' Russian interference assessment," The Hill, November 11, 2017, https://thehill.com/homenews/administration/359913-cia-director-stands-by-russian-interference-assessment/.

[33]U.S. government data, various agencies, 2022.

[34]William H. Branson, *Trends in U.S. International Trade and Investment Since World War II,* NBER Working Paper No. 469 (Cambridge, MA: National Bureau of Economic Research, April 1980).

[35]Robert Whaples, "Do Economists Agree on Anything? Yes!," *The Economists' Voice,* 3 (2006): 1–6.

[36]David Steven Jacoby, *Trump, Trade, and the End of Globalization* (Westport, CT: Praeger, 2018).

[37]Anne Krueger, "Biden's Frozen Trade Policy," Project Syndicate, February 28, 2022, https://www.project-syndicate.org/commentary/trump-trade-policy-frozen-in-place-under-biden-by-anne-o-krueger-2022-02.

[38]Gallup poll, February 2021.

[39]Paola Subacchi and Stephen Pickford, *Legitimacy vs. Effectiveness for the G20: A Dynamic Approach to Global Economic Governance* (London, UK: Royal Institute of International Affairs, October 2011), 2.

INDEX